T0418435

THE BAROQUE IN ARCHITECTURAL CULTURE, 1880–1980

The Baroque in
Architectural Culture, 1880–1980

Edited by

ANDREW LEACH
Griffith University, Australia

JOHN MACARTHUR
University of Queensland, Australia

MAARTEN DELBEKE
Ghent University, Belgium

ASHGATE

Published by
Ashgate Publishing Limited
Wey Court East
Union Road
Farnham
Surrey, GU9 7PT
England

Ashgate Publishing Company
110 Cherry Street
Suite 3-1
Burlington, VT 05401-3818
USA

www.ashgate.com

British Library Cataloguing in Publication Data
A catalogue record for this book is available from the British Library.

Library of Congress Cataloging-in-Publication Data
The baroque in architectural culture, 1880-1980 / [edited] by Andrew Leach, John Macarthur and Maarten Delbeke.
     pages cm
  Includes bibliographical references and index.
   ISBN 978-1-4724-5991-6 (hardcover) -- ISBN 978-1-4724-5992-3 (ebook) -- ISBN 978-1-4724-5993-0 (epub) 1. Architecture, Modern--20th century--Historiography. 2. Architecture, Baroque--Historiography. 3. Art, Baroque--Historiography. I. Leach, Andrew, 1976- editor. II. Macarthur, John, 1958- editor. III. Delbeke, Maarten, editor.
  NA680.B33 2015
  724'.16--dc23
                                                                                                2015011048

ISBN 9781472459916 (hbk)
ISBN 9781472459923 (ebk – PDF)
ISBN 9781472459930 (ebk – ePUB)

Research documented in this volume was supported by the Australian Research Council as Discovery Project DP0985834.

Australian Government

Australian Research Council

MIX
Paper from
responsible sources
FSC® C013985

Printed in the United Kingdom by Henry Ling Limited, at the Dorset Press, Dorchester, DT1 1HD

Contents

List of Figures

List of Contributors

Mathew Aitchison is an associate professor in the Faculty of Architecture, Design and Planning at the University of Sydney.

Denise R. Costanzo is an assistant professor in the Department of Architecture in the H. Campbell and Eleanor R. Stuckeman School of Architecture and Landscape Architecture at Penn State University.

Maarten Delbeke is Professor of Architectural History and Theory in the Department of Architecture and Urban Planning at Ghent University and an adjunct professor in the Urban Research Program at Griffith University.

Roberto Dulio is a researcher in the history of architecture in the Faculty of Architecture and Society at the Politecnico di Milano.

Ute Engel lectures in the Art History Department of the Ludwig-Maximilians University (LMU) in Munich and is presently preparing a new Corpus of Baroque Ceiling Paintings in Germany as a research project of the German Academies of Sciences and the Humanities.

Michael Hill is Head of Art History and Theory at the National Art School in Sydney, Australia.

Andrew Hopkins is an associate professor in the Department of Human Sciences at the University of L'Aquila.

Gro Lauvland is an associate professor in the Department of Architectural Design, History and Technology at the Norwegian University of Science and Technology (NTNU) in Trondheim.

Andrew Leach is Professor of Architectural History at Griffith University, where he holds an Australian Research Council Future Fellowship.

Evonne Levy is a professor in the Graduate Department of the History of Art at the University of Toronto.

John Macarthur is a professor in the School of Architecture at the University of Queensland, where he directs the Research Centre ATCH.

Silvia Micheli is a UQ postdoctoral research fellow at the University of Queensland.

Albert Narath is an assistant professor in Modern Architecture and Design at the University of California, Santa Cruz.

Eeva-Liisa Pelkonen is an associate professor at the Yale School of Architecture.

Marco Pogacnik is a research professor in the Department of Architecture, Construction and Conservation at the University of Venice IUAV.

Anthony Raynsford is an assistant professor in the Department of Art and Art History at San José State University.

Luka Skansi is a professor in the Faculty of Humanities and Social Sciences at the University of Rijeka, Croatia.

Francesca Torello is an adjunct associate professor in the School of Architecture at Carnegie Mellon University.

Acknowledgements

This volume is one outcome of a three-year project to study the significance of the historiography of the baroque for architectural culture in the twentieth-century. It was funded by the Australian Research Council (Discovery Project DP0985834) in conjunction with the University of Queensland, Griffith University, Ghent University and the Belgian Academy in Rome. Various papers in this volume were developed through sessions staged at the 28th Annual Conference of the Society of Architectural Historians, Australia and New Zealand (Brisbane, Qld., 2011), the 64th Annual Meeting of the Society of Architectural Historians (New Orleans, Louis., 2011, chaired by Evonne Levy) and the 2nd International Conference of the European Architectural History Network (Brussels, 2012). For their assistance in the preparation of this book and support for the various discussions that led to its compilation, the editors wish to particularly thank Alexandra Brown, Amy Clarke, Janina Gosseye, Dianne Michiels and Andrew Steen. We wish further to thank Valerie Rose, Caroline Spender and their colleagues at Ashgate for their encouragement and expertise in seeing this book into press.

Chapter 1
Defining a Problem:
Modern Architecture and the Baroque

Maarten Delbeke, Andrew Leach and John Macarthur

The Persistence of the Baroque in Modern Architecture

The idea that the writing and teaching of art and architectural historians has lent values and ambitions to the development of twentieth-century architecture is now widely accepted by its scholars. The studies that have considered this coincidence, and especially those written since the turn of the twenty-first century, have demonstrated the clear intellectual debt of modern architecture to modernist historians who were ostensibly preoccupied with the art and architecture of earlier epochs.[1] This volume extends this work by contributing to the dual projects of writing both the intellectual history of modern architecture and the modern history of architectural historiography. It considers the many and varied ways that historians of art and architecture have historicized modern architecture through its interaction, in particular, with the baroque: a term of contested historical and conceptual significance that has often seemed to shadow a greater contest over the historicity of modernism.

As the following chapters attest, whether this traffic of ideas was driven by the historian or fostered by the architect, the century leading up to the various postmodern declarations for the new historicism that emerged around 1980 evidences a long process of sifting through historical research and distilling from it moments – be they forms, concepts or models of the architect's practice and its scope – against which to calibrate the ambitions of architecture across the modern era. By considering the many examples presented here and the sometimes surprising extent of their inter-referentiality and their shared dependence on certain sources – even when put to drastically different uses – this book interrogates an historiographical phenomenon that is widely appreciated but rarely called to account.

In his landmark teleological history of modern architecture (*Space, Time and Architecture*, 1941), Sigfried Giedion gave this theme its most potent expression in his pairing together of images of two iconic spirals: on one hand, Vladimir Tatlin's Monument to the Third International (1919–20, Figure 1.1); and on the other, Francesco Borromini's dome for Sant'Ivo alla Sapienza (1642–60, Figure 1.2). The values shared between the baroque age and the modern were thus encapsulated on a single-page spread. As Giedion put it, writing of Sant'Ivo, Borromini accomplished "the movement of the whole pattern made up by its design flows without interruption from the ground to the lantern, without entirely ending even there." And yet he merely "groped" towards that which could "be completed effected" in modern architecture – achieving "the transition between inner and outer space."[2] We appreciate the instrumentality of Giedion's history better than his readers did in the 1940s, 1950s and 1960s, just as we now better understand how his analyses of these two projects absorbed and advanced the scholarship and criticism of such intellectual forebears as Jacob Burckhardt, Heinrich Wölfflin and, especially, August Schmarsow. This pairing of architectural works nonetheless emerges from the history of modern architecture as a moment of clarity in which history was rendered as a repertoire of ideas and examples that could be placed into conversation with the present and its recent past. This moment expressed a multivalent relationship that had been explored for several decades up to the time in which Giedion wrote and which would continue to fuel history's stake (and therefore that of the baroque) in modern architecture in the post-war years.

The century-long modernist trajectory this book follows tracks the parallel path taken by historiography itself. Indeed, if Wölfflin's *Renaissance und Barock* (1888; *Renaissance and Baroque*, 1964) is one kind of founding document for the modern historiography of architecture, then the baroque quickly figures in that field's core problems.[3] These, namely, are the questions of how architecture changes its appearance, function and meaning over time; and of how to present realized works of architecture as moments within processes of change.

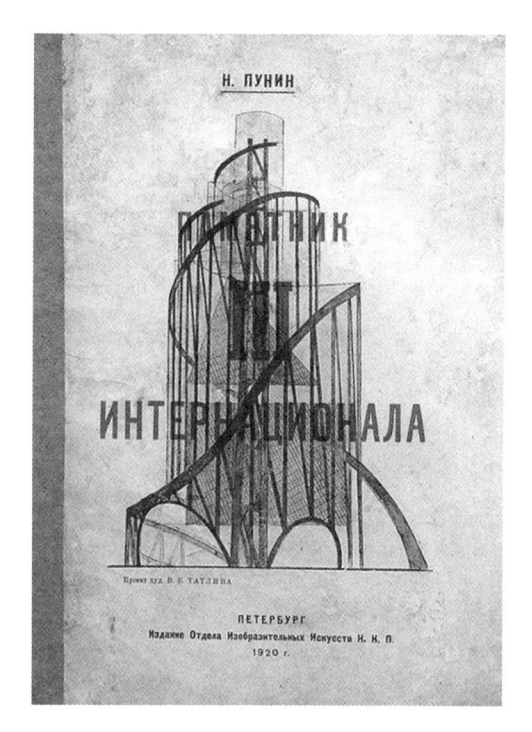 

Figure 1.1   Monument to the Third International, by Vladimir Tatlin
Source: Cover of Nikolai Punin, *Pamiatnik III Internatsionala* (St Petersburg: NKP, 1920).
Figure 1.2   Sant'Ivo alla Sapienza, by Francesco Borromini, Rome, 1642–60
Source: Photograph by Andrew Leach.

Wölfflin enacted a conceptually crucial divorce between architecture and its historical causes, demonstrating that one could refuse to regard the building as a symptom of the pathologies that give rise to it and treat historical problems that were not merely circumstantial in nature. In 1888 and in Wölfflin's hands one could, consequently, consider the visual experience of the façade of Il Gesù without giving thought to the Jesuit Order. That this would have been impossible a century later speaks to the historical contingencies of Wölfflin's positions, which nonetheless – and as the following chapters demonstrate again and again – informed the way baroque architecture was conceived and apprehended in the intervening decades.[4]

If *Renaissance und Barock* and *Space, Time and Architecture* describe two fundamental moments in the figuring of the baroque into the intersecting paths of modern architecture and modern architectural historiography, they have also become obvious starting points for considering the modern traffic of ideas between the historian and the architect. While the baroque continued to figure in the way that critics, theoreticians and historians thought through the parameters and problems of modern architecture, the debt these owe to thinking done by historians around the baroque in particular is not always (if at all) obvious to present-day discourse. (Vidler, in particular, has done much to clarify the means by which historical scholarship of such figures as Emil Kaufmann and Rudolf Wittkower belied its contemporaneity.[5]) As several of the following chapters demonstrate, through Sigfried Giedion (Costanzo, Pelkonen), Steen-Eiler Rasmussen (Raynsford), Bruno Zevi (Dulio), Christian Norberg-Schulz (Lauvland) and other key figures in this relationship, the problems of the baroque were seen to persist in the domains of modern architecture and the city: space versus monumentality, regional versus universal style, universalism versus cultural specificity, tradition versus renewal.[6]

Of greater import in the conceptualization of modern architecture, though, are those abstractions drawn from scholarship on the baroque that leave aside the baroque itself – those abstractions that proved mutually constructive in the concurrent development of modern architecture and modern historiography. From the

1870s and 1880s onwards, space, experience, visuality, form, context, function, rhetoricity, composition all in their turn emerged as values against which the canon was known and figured in modern architecture and which then informed the historicity of the present. Considering this theme and its interaction in light of a raft of historically determined abstractions shows how historical and architectural (or artistic) knowledge interacted across the modernist century. If the presence (or recurrence) of the baroque in twentieth-century architectural culture has often been casually admitted,[7] the following pages show that by considering the modern historicity of the baroque one can better appreciate a structural relationship between history and architecture that goes beyond the sheer persistence of certain concepts and precedents.

While architecture had long registered the significance of the ancient world and its enduring authority, as well as the discourse on origins that was central to architecture's positioning of itself in history and tradition across the eighteenth and nineteenth centuries, the modern construction of the baroque as an historical subject offered a privileged view on the artifice of history itself. It is only with late-nineteenth-century writing on the baroque, named as such, that an historicist view of architecture – but now historicist in the modern sense – emerges along with a capacity for prognostication that combined judgement of the past with prescriptions for actions in the present that were, themselves, seemingly authorized by history. Early in the nineteenth century, Hegel had already ensured that a notion of artistic progress had become inseparable from the concept of art.[8] This left the nineteenth century with the question of whether thresholds in that process could be identified and judged as progressive or deleterious. Such terms as baroque, *Spätrenaissance*, mannerism and rococo became, then, part of a general mechanism to determine and debate architectural values on historiographical grounds, describing breakpoints and continuities, which in their reception into the field of ideas shaping modern architecture constitutes something of its image – and one that shimmers differently in 1880, 1945 and 1980.

Of course, the term "baroque" is famously ambiguous, balanced as it is between naming an historical epoch, a period style and its development, and an attitude or artistic comportment that has been asserted by some to be a potentiality in every age and culture.[9] The baroque's precariousness as a conceptual and historical category has remained prone to the vicissitudes of the architect's approach and attitude to history and its activation in the present has been played out in debates around periodization, definitions of style, meaning, and historiographical agency in architecture. This has served to determine the availability and the contingency of the baroque and, more generally, a broader historical authority over modern architecture that consideration of the baroque helped to secure. The chapters of this book, however, show another and more fundamental precariousness: the overlapping stakes of the historian and the architect in the history of architecture.

The significance of the baroque is not only that it was once a style in need of a name and periodization but also that its perpetual re-evaluation implies participation in more complex historical structures of broader significance for modern architectural culture. Is the baroque, as Giedion suggests, already a pair to modernism because their respective experiments with form and space contrast so markedly with the dry academic classicism of the intervening period? Or is the baroque a first point of true historical difference from the present as we look back through a long modern era shaped by industrialization and reason?[10] Did architecture advance from this moment, as the modernist apologist Emil Kaufmann suggested in the 1930s?[11] Or did the end of the baroque age see it decline into instrumentalism, as such critics of modernism as Dalibor Vesely argued in the 1980s?[12] The possibility of the baroque figuring in a simple use of the past as a repository of admirable buildings becomes more remote when the architect's access to it, as a field shaped in history, is loaded with these intricacies. And since that past is subject to re-evaluation, as it surely is, the historian can be understood to offer new challenges to modern values that draw authority from historical narrative just as that same narrative is shaped through the historian's work.

Baroque into Service

Over the course of the displaced century addressed in this volume, the baroque was used both to clarify and to critique the concepts, relationships and ambitions of modern architecture through its interactions with history. That these themes might over time have cast off their anchorage to the baroque in a shift from the general to the particular suggests its innate utility to modern thought rather than its importance for modern architecture *per se*. These concepts were by no means either predominantly historical (found in history) or historiological (concerning history), but rather demonstrate the work that historians, too, were undertaking to distil concepts drawn from all manner of (modern) disciplines in order to address a broad range of questions posed across the arts and humanities.[13] Within architecture, one of the most important translations undertaken from the end of the nineteenth century around the concept and content of the baroque, concerns the historiographical accommodation of space, which more than any other historically legitimated value served to ground modern architecture conceptually. The idea that space is a quality of the senses is, though, at base psychological, arising from the work of Adolf Hildebrand and, later, Theodor Lipps.[14] It may have been a subject of architectural theory as early as the eighteenth century in the thinking of Etienne-Louis Boullée, but it took a fresh centrality in the writing of Gottfried Semper, August Schmarsow, Alois Riegl and, most famously, Sigfried Giedion, in whose hands space came to be treated as a medium proper to architecture as an art.[15]

   The baroque figured productively in the coincident disciplinary rise of psychology from philosophy of mind and of the history of art and architecture, framing both a subject of study and an historical repository of modern problems. Thinking around the relation of sight to bodily extension shaped, for instance, Schmarsow's understanding of the spatial experience of the walking subject and ultimately found its most profound modern expression in Le Corbusier's *promenade architecturale*. In the positioning of the subject and the directing of its view, and through illusions dissociating vision from bodily extension, the baroque and its theatricality provided a wealth of examples of spaces that could not be explained as volumes, but which instead required a notion of subjective experience. Such figures as Rasmussen and Norberg-Schulz eventually developed accounts of experience that set aside Giedion's technological determinism – as Raynsford and Lauvland explain later in this book. But for the clarifications these and other individuals offered the concept of space, by the later decades of the twentieth century architectural theory had returned to space and its experience in terms much closer to those proposed by Schmarsow at the end of the prior century.

   Riegl's examination of *bas-relief* sculpture led to different conclusions: a theory that spatial perception is not a fundamental mental faculty, but an acuity that developed historically from late Roman times to the seventeenth century.[16] In her contribution to this volume, Levy shows that the interaction of Riegl's thought with Wölfflin's produced modern art history's concept of period mentalities from what began as an essentialist account of perception. For Riegl (and later Wölfflin) space was not a property of architecture and its experience, but something that determined differences and commonalities among all the arts and the nature of the change historians registered in them over time. As a bastion of architectural modernism, the Bauhaus understood the concordance of the arts of architecture, painting and sculpture in the seventeenth century as evidence that the historic division between artistic disciplines was artificial and unnecessary. Conversely, for those from Norberg-Schulz to Karsten Harries for whom modernist functionalism emerged from neo-classical instrumentalism, the baroque is the most recent moment in western history wherein the arts could still interact on a common foundation.[17]

   In his essay on Geoffrey Scott's *The Architecture of Humanism* (1914), John Macarthur shows how Scott drew on concepts common to Wölfflin and his own nineteenth-century sources in aesthetics and psychology to conceptualize space and empathy. In the generation separating this book from Giedion's delivery of the lectures published as *Space, Time and Architecture* – mediated by such intellectual developments as Skansi describes – space became normalized as the preeminent quality of modern architecture. By the end of the 1940s, as Dulio shows, Zevi (for one) could treat space (rather than form) as architecture's self-evident natural basis.[18] If the advent of the modern concept of "space" coincided with its recognition in the baroque, then it was clearly less pure and decidedly more uneven in its first iterations than in the normative quality it would become by the middle of the twentieth century. Although such writers as Giedion and Scott claimed the authority of Wölfflin in its development – a claim that continues to resonate with our habitual knowledge of this chapter in architecture's intellectual history – the sensibility that Wölfflin predicated (and Schmarsow defined) continued to be the subject of intense discussion in the hands of Riegl, Brinckmann and others leading up to Giedion's presentation of the theme to a mass Anglophone audience. We find the baroque at each stage of this history, even if its presence reinforces little more than its conceptual elasticity and mobility.

Figure 1.3   Berlin Philharmonic, by Hans Scharoun, Berlin, 1960–63
Source: Wikimedia Commons.

The baroque was thus made to supply a pair of concepts that held modernism to be a spatial affair understood in dimensions and scale relations without social or historical context; and as an acuity in perceiving space in which individuals might be trained at any time or, conversely, which might be the mark of a particular historically formed subjectivity. The concurrence of these "modernisms" – themselves inconsistent even in their complementarity – is key to Giedion's book: the exceptional souls of the seventeenth century were able to perceive a quality that only became visible to the masses and had its apotheosis in modern industrial societies. Read in these terms the baroque makes a fine pedigree for Ludwig Mies van der Rohe's Barcelona Pavilion (1929) on account of its spatial composition, just as it predicated Hans Scharoun's Berlin Philharmonic (1960–63) for its empathetic power to hold the forming in the form (Figure 1.3).[19] The matrix of possible lineages drawn from the seventeenth century by the twentieth is extensive, as Anthony Raynsford shows in comparing Rasmussen's ahistorical and performative understanding of the lessons of baroque space with Giedion's teleology of architectural concepts. And if these descriptions of the effects of the historiography of the baroque fall on the side of its instrumental uses, it is, we argue, a result of the same flexibility that allowed scholars like Wölfflin's student Paul Frankl to take the model of the baroque as an historical case of abstract qualities and to use this to develop his history of the gothic, or Henri Focillon or Eugenio d'Ors to reflect on the formal patterns they argued as operating (albeit on different bases) throughout the history of art.[20]

As a basis for the claim that architecture and the arts were integral to the workings of a society, the baroque furthermore proved a fertile testing ground for opposing views on the subject that were given voice from the middle of the nineteenth century. In the wake of the antiquarian tradition – which read artefacts and their stylistic features as signifiers of the state of a culture – and under the impulse of contemporary political and religious concerns, art historians cast the baroque as a symptom of cultural decay. Baroque architecture and art functioned for Jacob Burckhardt, Benedetto Croce and many others as an index of the moral fibre of society menaced by such actors as the Jesuits and the papacy.[21] Even Richard Krautheimer, despite his groundbreaking scholarship on baroque Rome, understood that city's restitution in the Counter-Reformation as the visual representation of papal authority as a symptom of the papacy's decline in real political and economic power.[22] The theatricality of the baroque was an ephemeral instrument of make-believe, and its pretensions intrinsically false. From this point of view, the baroque is a monument to the fall of an architecture instrumentalized in a cultural politics, and thus an object lesson for modern architecture.

The baroque, though, could also be understood as the moment in history when the new institutions and building programmes of the centralist state emerged, providing prototypes that would eventually become truly modern after the French Revolution saw them cleansed of their absolutist aura. This view of the baroque as intrinsic to the birth of the modern state is articulated perhaps most clearly in Giulio Carlo Argan's *L'Europa delle capitali* (1964, *The Europe of the Capitals*). In Italy, France and throughout Europe, then, this same moment witnessed a concomitant transformation in market mechanisms and processes of upward social ability, which as Francis Haskell's *Patrons and Painters* (1963) famously argues, made new and indeed modern demands on architecture and the arts.

It is hardly accidental that in *Space, Time and Architecture* the historical emergence of Rome as a capital served as a foil for modernism's own universalist aspirations. Baroque Rome is therein cast as "a hope for a still intangible future," when it will "become indispensable" to "create a new form of central administration inspired by spiritual principles."[23] In Giedion's view, papal Rome delicately balanced urban planning and the disruption brought about by a multitude of actors laying claim to that same territory, a process enabled by the temporal weakness but spiritual authority of the papacy. In the pages of his book, the complexity of the capital of Christendom embodies modernist internationalism. The processes through which modern architecture's universalist principles became articulated in local realities reflected the seventeenth-century process of global evangelization that had necessitated the very materialization of a spiritual capital – and the problems of these parallel projects did not go unnoticed. As several contributions to this volume attest (like those of Levy, Engel, Aitchison, Pogacnik and Delbeke), the historiography of the baroque is deeply intertwined with various nationalist strains in art history, which either made claims on the historical origins of the baroque or on a local variety of the style generated by the transformation of Roman models.[24] Focillon, for instance, demonstrates how the perceived geographical universalism of the baroque was closely connected to the question of its very historicity. This was especially true for those who considered the baroque not as an historical style but as a stage in the cyclical "life of forms" that manifested itself at various times and places in accordance with local conditions. In this view, the universalism of the baroque did not reside in its overpowering appeal to humanity's moral and spiritual faculties, but in its presence as an ineluctable element of the very processes that bring art into being.

These competing conceptualizations of the baroque helped the discourse surrounding modernist architecture and its history to recognize that modernism, like the baroque, emerged in a society undergoing profound and not necessarily benign transformations that shaped the conditions in which architecture was produced and interpreted. The French architectural critic and historian Pierre Charpentrat argued that if architecture was deemed to assume a central (if fragile) place in such processes of transformation as these, the analogy between the baroque and modernism posed the question of the precise architectural programmes or strategies that could sustain those same ambitions. This pertained not only to the matter of how the art of architecture or the profession of the architect should find a place in the processes that constitute a society, but also to architecture's ability to give material and visual form to society's ambitions without succumbing to sheer instrumentality. Historians of the baroque tended to exemplify this precarious balance by opposing the figure of Bernini the court artist to that of Borromini the innovator – a pairing that remains a cornerstone of our baroque imaginary.[25]

Where architecture had long been defined and defended according to its relationship with the classical tradition, the baroque allowed modern architecture to open the dual themes of invention within and beyond tradition – a theme that by the 1920s assumed the more precise cast of invention within history. For the Bauhaus, the constructivists and those later schools that valorized historical rupture and true novelty, the work of Borromini, Bernini and Guarini sat in stark contrast to the high Renaissance and its apparent insistence on the ideal. But in the hands of a post-war generation of architects and critics, seventeenth-century architecture was an inventive appropriation of the classical tradition that could help to define a path out of the end game of an extreme modernist rationalism and ahistorical expressionism that Adorno and Horkheimer had so persuasively thrown into doubt.[26] Indeed, this moral dimension to the relationship of invention to tradition (history) was picked up explicitly in the art historical discourse of the post-war years, to the extent that Panofsky (as Leach here shows) positioned the baroque as a model of invention out of crisis within traditions that themselves inexorably tended toward a crisis state.[27] The increased attention to Borromini as one who took hold of the classical tradition and extended it beyond its own apparent limits resonated particularly strongly with the writers of the 1950s and 1960s who made significant advances into historical research on that figure while figuring him explicitly (as did Zevi, Moretti, Portoghesi and Panofsky) into the critical fortunes of architectural modernism.[28]

Modes and Modalities of the Baroque in Twentieth-century Architecture

That modern architecture sought an authority from history on an array of bases as it addressed these problems is only surprising in that history was not an explicit aspect of architectural debate in the early part of the twentieth century – except, among the avant-garde, in being positioned as something to overcome. That the baroque, in particular, has functioned as a vehicle for this authority raises more complex issues that shift according to the various contexts in which the baroque is "received," which in turn adds fuel to our claim, here, that the baroque provides a compelling historiological cross-section of architecture's modern movement. When we test the baroque against the most basic uses of history as a field of precedents for forms, strategies and ideas, the lenses through which its lessons are refracted quickly tell us a great deal more about the modern present than the seventeenth-century past. The baroque offered architects of the late-nineteenth century a language (never neutral, as Torello and Narath demonstrate in their chapters) disarticulating a particularly urban style from decidedly modern programmes. When Albert Ilg or Gustav Ebe invoked the baroque in the 1880s, it sustained abstractions that at once rendered it decidedly new and allowed for an independent intellectual path into the functionalist, organic and decorative traditions of the twentieth century.

As Ute Engel demonstrates in these pages, this same mechanism extended to encompass the historical scaffolding of modernist expressionism in the work of Erich Mendelsohn, for instance, or Rudolf Steiner, even as they offered a more explicit support for the early experiments in parametricism enacted by Pier Luigi Nervi and Luigi Moretti to which Roberto Dulio directs our attention. Moretti shows that the mechanisms by which precedents surpass the historicity of their sources had shifted from being entirely implicit to being entirely explicit, going so far as to explain the ways in which such architects as Michelangelo, Borromini and Guarini could inform architectural composition in his own time. This is hardly so straightforward as a question of quotation, and as Silvia Micheli shows, Paolo Portoghesi subjected the buildings and reconstructed compositional techniques of Borromini to a high degree of process in postmodernism's early phases as he sought to recover for his present the traditions to which they belonged. This mode of "mediation" allowed for a complex if staged exchange between baroque architecture and the modern, but the instrument would become blunt with time – a problem to which Delbeke and Leach return in their final contribution to this book.

Rooted in the Renaissance interpretation of classical forms yet willfully different (or so it appeared), the baroque seemed to test the limits of academic theory in the name of artistic freedom while pointing to such fundamentally different repertories and traditions as late antiquity and the gothic. Could the same be said of the modern? In its critique of institutionalized modernism, Robert Venturi's *Complexity and Contradiction in Architecture* (1966) recognized how the anti-academicist rhetoric of the modernist manifestos was counterbalanced by a form of practice deeply imbued by academic compositional principles. This duality allowed Venturi to equate the best of modernism with mannerist, baroque or rococo architecture precisely because, like its historical antecedents, it had appropriated a design code that it transformed and subverted at will.[29] It allowed, too, such critics as Leo Steinberg (as Michael Hill explains) to address the compositional principles of a building like San Carlo alle Quattro Fontane in terms that raised fundamentally modern problems. In Venturi's argument lingers the notion that the baroque capacity for subversion within tradition retrieved an original purity of purpose and principles that academicism itself was bound to forfeit for attempting to institutionalize that which worked against institutionalization. It is no coincidence, then, that in *Complexity and Contradiction* Venturi drew his baroque examples from the excessively innovative oeuvres of Borromini or Guarini rather than from the flamboyantly reasonable Bernini. According to historiographical commonplace the former "reinvented" architecture, while the latter extended the principles of such Renaissance predecessors as Andrea Palladio into the service of an ostentatious apparatus. The pioneers of modernism, suggests Venturi, chose reinvention over instrumentalization.[30]

Whether the attitude towards academicism actually generated "two baroques" is a matter of debate in post-war France. This separation not only made for two distinct genealogies of modern architecture, but it also raised questions about modernism's complicity with the modern state. According to Charpentrat France was unable to embrace modernism because of the deep entrenchment of academicism in French cultural politics. In his view, the rejection of Bernini's Louvre in favour of a solution designed by a committee reflecting the agenda of Louis XIV prefigures the limited reception of Le Corbusier in a social-democratic society bent on standardizing and professionalizing architectural production. The lesson modernism should learn from the baroque, Charpentrat argues, is architecture's potential to be its own agent – a quality he sees not in the formal repertory of academicism, but in the architect's insistence on the principle of creativity in the face of architecture's general tendency toward institutionalization.[31]

After all, one major development in the modern historiography of the baroque was the attempt to divorce it from its over-determined association with papal or Jesuit propaganda, followed by a newly historicized view of that association from a set of far more nuanced and multi-faceted positions. Bearing this narrative in mind, Giedion's unconditional embrace of baroque Rome as a prototype for the modern capital (reiterated on different terms in Colin Rowe and Fred Koetter's *Collage City*, 1978) might appear as a naïve and uninformed appropriation. Still, in the wake of Benedetto Croce and others, art historians, too, attempted to redefine the possible relations between the works of art and the functions they were assigned to perform in society. In his essay "Retorica e barocco" (1955, Rhetoric and Baroque), Argan cast the rhetoricality of the Roman baroque as a feature of a historical culture to which the arts belonged rather than as a regime imposed upon the arts by patrons and other external actors.

As Andrew Hopkins demonstrates later in this book, Rudolf Wittkower's landmark *Art and Architecture in Italy 1600–1750* (1958) leaned heavily on the premises of Argan's essay. Argan's redefined rhetoricality, then, became incorporated in perhaps the most influential attempt to dissociate the baroque from the many negative associations it had accrued over its century-long existence and to treat it as a period in the history of art and architecture essentially like any other. Reacting to Focillon's interpretation of the baroque, Pierre Francastel likewise argued that architecture, as an art form, could never be entirely understood as an instrument of external agendas.[32] Design emerges from an inevitable and insolvable friction between the agency of architecture and of the different parties that lay claim to it. He consequently regarded the demands made of architecture by religious or political patrons in the seventeenth and eighteenth centuries as entirely legitimate from an historical perspective, a reality of architectural production that positioned the patron as a sparring partner for the architect's desire to make material forms.[33] In this interaction, Charpentrat argued, lay architecture's true functionalism; because baroque patrons made such exorbitant demands on their architects, the baroque is the first truly functionalist architecture and, as such, a model for modernism.

The idea that it is the office of architecture to give shape to a society – albeit cast in different terms – extends to that other key sphere of modern architectural debate: the city. Therein, the baroque offered modern theoreticians of urban architecture and town planning a model of monumentality within urban space – and hence within a continuum of spatial scales extending from the interior to the public square in which theatricality occupies a conceptual pride of place. When Wittkower wrote in *Art and Architecture* of the relationship of Pietro da Cortona's new façade for Santa Maria della Pace (1656–57) to the square, he speaks of Cortona's application of "the experience of the theatre to town-planning." And later: "By projecting too far into the small piazza and absorbing any space there, a powerful plastic and at the same time chromatically effective motif is created that mediates between outside and inside."[34] Observations on the baroque like these, Lauvland argues, inspired Norberg-Schulz's attempt to incorporate phenomenology into a theory of the city with "place-making" at its centre. Baroque space is not just a matter of sensory or even psychological experience, but embodies a recoverable modality of being that modernity had left behind.

The humanist modernism propagated by Rasmussen and Norberg-Schulz took up a theme that was predicated in debate on the Vienna Ringstrasse and further explored in the relationship of monument to public space in the functionalist city schemes of Le Corbusier and his contemporaries: the public role of architecture in the modern city. Analysis of the transformation of Rome's urban fabric under the Borghese, Barberini, Pamphilj and Chigi popes was a crucial catalyst in post-war reflection in this problem. Baroque Rome not only involved a magnitude of public space that resonated with the scale of modern architecture and its discourse, but it also served to legitimize the activism of the architect in the city fabric – modern or historical. As Costanzo describes later in this book, those American architects whose reading of Giedion had seen them set their eyes on a spell in Rome to better design the public plazas of modern America. For Zevi, Argan and those of their contemporaries who appreciated the rhetoricality and theatricality of Rome, the baroque city offered lessons in both political and urban registers. When Zevi invited the audience at the commemorations of the 1967 tercentenary of Borromini's death to join him not at Sant'Ivo but at an artistic installation literally projecting Frank Lloyd Wright's spiralling Guggenheim upon Rome, he succinctly placed the modern era into a continuum that had been fed by Borromini's work, but to which it could not make an unmediated return.[35]

Zevi's provocative substitution of the ornate Temple of Divine Wisdom – a three-dimensional emblem saturated with religious meanings – with the slick, if convoluted, contour of a modern museum also points to remarkable lacunae in the way modernism received the baroque. Art history struggled to calibrate the relationship of the baroque to Catholic religiosity, yet architects – often acting as historians – cast this relationship almost without blinking as a question of architecture's inherent spirituality, expressed in terms of "spatiality," or of its political (but explicitly not religious) missions. The Catholic charge of the historical baroque seemed little more than a contingent instance of architecture's collaborations with the powers that exemplified its advanced modes of production or its psychological and sensory effectiveness. Perhaps the only exception to this attitude towards the religiosity of the baroque was the debate around the reform of religious art and architecture that took place from the nineteenth century onwards and which intensified in the decades preceding the Second Vatican Council.

The privileged place of "space" in the architectural discourse surrounding modernism also obfuscated another bone of contention in the art historical reception of the baroque: ornament. Arguably on the tail of *Complexity and Contradiction*'s subversion of modernism's stance towards ornament, ornamentality accounts for much discourse in the postmodernist uptake of the baroque and the emergence of the "neo-baroque." But in the period this volume takes into consideration ornament remains a metonymy for that which the baroque helped to theatricalize and render illusionistic. The embargo on historical motifs in modernism effectively framed the outlook of twentieth-century architects on the baroque, from Frank Lloyd Wright's invective against the cornice to Adolf Loos's idea of modern ornament as a folkish recursion.[36] The absence of both religiosity and ornamentation in the modernist digestions of the baroque defines the baroque precisely as a *modern* problem rather than as a problem of the seventeenth or, indeed, the nineteenth century. As a modern problem, the baroque emerges as a polyvalent historical construct, where each modality of its uptake has equal legitimacy when read as an instance of the problematic of history within the architectural discourse of the twentieth century.

Baroque into History

These themes describe something of the scope of the problems that the baroque was invoked to solve, as well as those themes that the baroque exposed as absent in the historical continuity of architectural discourse. The baroque served as a cypher for history, and those problems that once accrued to the baroque as a subject and which were left open by the advent of architectural postmodernism are very much those of history and its relationship with architecture as a whole. With what problems does the baroque leave us when we regard it as a presence in the history of modern architecture? What is the critical and intellectual legacy of this century-long moment in the way architectural history functions within architectural culture? These are questions to which Delbeke and Leach will return in the concluding chapter, but the intervening contributions track the changing conditions and shifting status of historical knowledge for architecture between the time in which Ilg posed the question of the future of the baroque (for Vienna) to the moment in which Portoghesi celebrated (in Venice) the presence of the past. They offer a view on the nature of architecture's historical consciousness in the century spanning from 1880 to 1980 that doubtless raises the question of history's stake in the present moment – or, indeed, vice versa.

If the decades this book treats can be read in terms of history's presence in modern architectural culture, it is clear that the mechanisms by which this presence is felt are far more diverse and (oftentimes) subtle than being the formal consequences of a constant review of architecture's historical canon in light of art historical research. This peculiar way of figuring history into architecture nonetheless long served as a form of historical consciousness, neither systematic, reflective nor consistent in its application or uptake. It allowed for what Manfredo Tafuri would identify in *Teorie e storia dell'architettura* (1968; *Theories and History of Architecture*, 1980) as architecture's own form of historical consciousness, which failed to account for the manifold ways in which historical knowledge and the engagement of architects with all manner of historical continuities informing what he would later recast after Foucault and *L'archéologie du savoir* (1969; *The Archaeology of Knowledge*, 1972) as the limits of architecture as an institution. Prior to this moment, architectural culture tended not to recognize the historicity of either the problems it regarded as entirely modern or the modernity in which its points of historical reference were held. In both directions, as we have seen above, this implicates the baroque: at once an effort, as Giedion had it, towards that which would be possible only after the Eiffel Tower; and as a concrete test case for the most abstract of modernist concepts. Tafuri pointed to the problem of architecture being (largely unwittingly) structured by an historiographically-informed historicism throughout the modern movement, even as it enacted a rhetorical rejection of history's measure. How, he asked, should history convey the past to the present as it attends to the task of making sense of it on its own terms?

These matters lead us to the problem of the place of architectural history within architectural culture and to the bases on which we might then draw distinctions between architectural history (and its tools and tasks) and such fields as the history of art, cultural history, conservation and restoration as well as architecture itself. As we can see in the watershed event of Borromini's 1967 tercentenary – about which Dulio, Micheli and Hill write below – the baroque remained a fertile ground whereupon problems in which it had long been implicated were addressed in a debate wherein history's traffic with architecture remained a live (if not unproblematic) matter.[37] The poles around which historians gathered in the wake of an overly modernist experience of architectural history – operative or instrumental on one hand, scientific or critical on the other – described a debate that would become a generational schism, and which would go on to inform the various ways in which history would figure in architectural culture from that moment to our present day. Where the academic research of pioneering art historians once distilled into architectural theory to problematize such matters as form, space and experience, its increased volume, specificity and specialization rendered those mechanisms difficult to maintain – and introduced new kinds of problems for the relationship of historical knowledge to architectural culture in the decades after the 1960s.

A history of writings on baroque architecture undoubtedly risks a charge of scholarly pedantry. If studying the historiography of the baroque would merely add further specialized conditions to understanding already obsolete myths of the historical necessity of modernism, then our book would deserve this charge. Read in one way, this volume instead presents a series of instances of the baroque's neutralization, and through this addresses relationships that are fundamental to the authority that architecture claims for itself as a body of knowledge and as a practice. The essays are ordered according to a rough chronology. In this the book reflects less a line through the history of the historiography of the baroque than a lack of any ordering structure by which these ideas were considered, taken up, set aside and normalized as architectural values. There may be a cumulative dimension to this debate, but it is haphazard, often failing to account for thinking and interpretations that had been undertaken out of sight (or mind) of the historian or architect in question.

To look at the baroque is to interrogate moments in the history of these relationships. It has been used to name just about every concern of twentieth-century architects, and in drawing a line between seventeenth-century exemplars and modern issues historians have had recourse to most models of historical interpretation. Considered as a test bed of the value of historical knowledge to architects, the essays in this volume observe occasions when the baroque was sheered of its cultural content to provide abstract formal principles, and how, in reaction, other historians have reloaded this baggage, savouring the pastness of the past and resisting its easy assimilation. Our primary concern has been the status of historical knowledge in the twentieth century, the work that it does in supplying and shaping precedents, but also in using the past as a basis from which to critique architecture's self-evidence in the critical present. That the baroque has at so many crucial points constituted that past is at least partly fortuitous. As the following essays demonstrate, however, the historical density of the baroque – its formal novelties and cultural over-determination – seems to offer a particularly poignant moment of reflection and clarity and to continue, therefore, to demand the attention of architecture and its historians.

Endnotes

1 Three recent books of this kind, treating overlapping topics, are Tournikiotis, *The Historiography of Modern Architecture* (1999); Vidler, *Histories of the Immediate Present* (2008); and Otero-Pailos, *Architecture's Historical Turn* (2010).

2 Giedion, *Space, Time and Architecture* (5th edn), 115.

3 Compare Leach, *What is Architectural History?*, 1–2.

4 The question of the "Jesuitness" of the architecture built for or by the Jesuits, often encapsulated in the notion of "Jesuit style," is closely bound-up with the historiography of the baroque. See the landmark essay by Wittkower, "Problems of the Theme," and the more recent discussion in Levy, *Propaganda and the Jesuit Baroque*, 15–41.

5 Vidler, *Histories of the Immediate Present*. Compare, too, Payne, *Rudolf Wittkower and Architectural Principles in the Age of Modernism*.

6 Consider the way these themes figured in a discourse bringing the new Brazilian capital into play with the baroque as a supreme moment of those modernist themes to which the baroque (in its reception) gave critical expression across the course of the twentieth century, to the point of becoming entirely commonplace. See, for instance, Castedo, *The Baroque Prevalence in Brazilian Art*.

7 Consider the recent treatment of Moretti in Reichlin and Tedeschi (eds), *Luigi Moretti*; and of the instances of twentieth-century "recurrence" documented in de Bruijn, Delbeke, Floris, et al. (eds), "Barok" = "Baroque."

8 Volumes 13, 14 and 15 of Hegel's *Werke in zwanzig Bänden* contain the materials of lectures on art and aesthetics delivered in the 1820s, which have also been published as *Aesthetics*. Bungay describes Hegel claims on the progress of art in *Beauty and Truth*, 74–89.

9 See, for instance, Panofsky, *What is Baroque?*; Blunt, *Some Uses and Misuses of the Terms Baroque and Rococo as Applied to Architecture*; Arangio-Ruiz (ed.), *Manierismo, barocco, rococo*; Lyttelton, *Baroque Architecture in Classical Antiquity*; Lambert, *The Return of the Baroque in Modern Culture*; Snyder, *L'estetica del barocco*; Ndalianis, *Neobaroque Aesthetics and Contemporary Entertainment*.

10 Compare Collins, *Changing Ideals in Modern Architecture, 1750–1950*.

11 Compare Kaufmann, *Von Ledoux bis Le Corbusier* and *Architecture in the Age of Reason*.

12 Veseley, *Architecture in the Age of Divided Representation*. Consider, also, Perez-Gomez, *Architecture and the Crisis of Modern Science*; and Harbison, *Reflections on Baroque*.

13 Consider Stamm, *Die Kunstformen des Barockzeitalters* or Rousset, *La littérature de l'âge baroque en France*, as well the issues of the *Journal of Aesthetics and Art Criticism* discussed by Leach later in this volume, on baroque in the arts.

14 See the chapters by Skansi and Macarthur in this volume.

15 See Mallgrave, *Modern Architectural Theory*, esp. 195–203; and Kruft, *A History of Architectural Theory*, 290–322.

16 Riegl, *Die spätrömische Kunstindustrie*.

17 Norberg-Schulz, *Intentions in Architecture*; Harries, *The Bavarian Rococo Church*; and *The Ethical Function of Architecture*.

18 Zevi, *Saper vedere l'architettura*.

19 Compare Hans Scharoun's preface to Charpentrat, *L'Art baroque*.

20 Frankl, *The Gothic*; Focillon, *Vie des forms*; D'Ors, *Lo barroco*.

21 On Burckhardt, see Levy, *Propaganda*, 29–30; and Croce, *Storia dell'età barocca in Italia*, 65–77.

22 Krautheimer, *The Rome of Alexander VII*, 140–56.

23 Giedion, *Space, Time and Architecture* (5th edn), 77.

24 Kaufmann, *Toward a Geography of Art*; Kubler and Soria, *Art and Architecture in Spain and Portugal and their American Dominions 1500 to 1800*; Hempel, *Baroque Art and Architecture in Central Europe*.

25 See, for instance, the portrayal of both artists in episode two of Simon Schama's BBC series *Power of Art*.

26 Adorno and Horkheimer, *Dialectic of Enlightenment*. On this point compare Marc Bloch's *Apologie pour l'histoire*.

27 This is the "lesson" of baroque art for modern culture in Panofsky, "What is Baroque?" Compare the report on Panofsky's lecture in *Vassar Miscellany News*, May 8, 1935, in which the headlines read thus: "Prof. Panofsky Lectures Here about Baroque," "Comparison with Mannerism Made; Explains Parallel in Drama and Literature" and "Baroque Period is the Second Great Climax of the High Renaissance."

28 See, for example, Zevi, *The Modern Language of Architecture*, 187–215; and Moretti, "The Series of Generalized Structures in Borromini's Work," 48–55.

29 Delbeke, "Mannerism and Meaning."

30 Venturi, *Complexity and Contradiction*, 23–7.

31 See Charpentrat, "À propos de l'architecture des années 60," as discussed in Delbeke's contribution below.

32 Francastel (ed.), *Les architectes célèbres*, "Introduction."

33 On this point, compare the later work of Joseph Connors, and especially *Borromini and the Roman Oratory*.

34 Wittkower, *Art and Architecture in Italy*, 2nd revised edition (1965), 159, 160.

35 Zevi, *Attualità del Borromini*, 530. See Dulio's chapter below for further consideration of this episode.

36 Loos, *Ornament and Crime*, 19–24; Wright, "The Passing of the Cornice," chapter 3 of *Modern Architecture*; compare Masheck, *Adolf Loos*, 139.

37 De Angelis d'Ossat (ed.), *Studi sul Borromini*.

Chapter 2
Engaging the Past:
Albert Ilg's *Die Zukunft des Barockstils*

Francesca Torello

Die Zukunft des Barockstils, eine Kunstepistel von Bernini dem Jüngern (The Future of the Baroque Style, a letter on art by Bernini the Younger) is a short pamphlet, published in Vienna in 1880. Its author, Albert Ilg, was an art historian, as well as a museum curator, prolific publicist and conservative art critic – an important if controversial figure in the Viennese cultural debate of the late nineteenth century.[1] In *Die Zukunft des Barockstils* Ilg constructs a polemical defence of the baroque, "rediscovering" its role as the dynastically characterized, unifying language of the multinational Habsburg Empire. For these reasons the pamphlet has been seen as a significant moment in the adoption of the neo-baroque as the official language of the Habsburg court and an influential vehicle of its "reinvention" as the Austrian national style in the last 20 years of the nineteenth century.[2]

The pamphlet was published at a time when the debate, at least in Vienna, was still dominated by discussion on gothic and Renaissance models, and precedes other, more famous texts that prompted the "re-discovery" of the baroque. It was directed to the general public, not to specialists; it is political rather than scholarly in essence, programmatic rather than reflective. Still, even the most resolute of Ilg's critics recognized both its importance and the necessity of offering a response. This essay reconsiders the positions expressed in the pamphlet, situates the text in its Viennese cultural context and focuses on its most immediate impact on the architectural debate.

The Pamphlet: Intent and Strategy

The pamphlet's opening sentence dispels any doubt as to its political aims: "The small world of artistic activity has a certain similarity with the large world of politics, certainly, at least, in its present development."[3] Its publication was situated in a time of intense debate over style, which, having monopolized the debate in architecture for many decades, was informing a fierce competition in the applied arts and the industrial craft production among the major European nations – especially since the advent of the international exhibition. While in the strictly academic field of art theory Germany had obtained a hard-won dominance, its contribution to the *Kunstindustrie* was not considered competitive on an international level. Ilg's pamphlet offers to the Habsburg Empire an alternative to its sufferance of the German hegemony in the style debate, not only by orienting Austria towards the choice of a new style, but also by pointing towards an alternative international model, France, and a different goal for its artistic endeavours, namely the progress of the applied arts as a counterpoint to a more speculative approach.

The political context is also important. The Habsburg Empire had recently experienced at the hands of Prussia both military defeat and the loss of its claim to a leading role among the German states. Austria was forced to accept the primacy of the newly created German Reich on the international scene and a concomitant influence over its internal affairs. These were major reasons for levelling criticism of the actions of the Viennese government, even for the German-speaking elites of the Empire. Ilg's positions reflect this attitude while at the same time trying to address another major political concern of his moment: the peculiar situation of the Habsburg Empire as a multinational entity.[4] To meet these aims Ilg re-casts the baroque in a new light, undermining the premises on which its negative status had been based and thereby activating it as an ideological force.

At the time of the pamphlet's publication, both the classicist and gothic traditions, which had dominated the artistic debate in the preceding years, had been heavily exploited by German cultural discourse. A strongly German-nationalistic rhetoric had even encroached upon the shared European tradition of the Renaissance through the popularization of the *Deutsche Renaissance*. The choice of the baroque as a new source for contemporary architecture and industrial arts was justified by the fact that this artistic language remained an unexploited reservoir in the frame of the style debate and – perhaps surprisingly for us today – then had a distinctly non-German connotation. In his controversial lecture of 1876, "Deutsche Kunst in Prag," the German art historian Alfred Woltmann admitted that the baroque was of Italian and Austrian origin, while at the same time insisting upon the interpretation of almost all other phases of Bohemian artistic culture as being dependent upon German influence.[5]

The first part of Ilg's pamphlet is not only a strong rejection of what he calls "cold classicism" – "Here [in Austria] the cold classicism of Schinkel and Bötticher would have been impossible"[6] – and a derision of the excesses of the *Deutsche Renaissance* revival. Ilg criticizes the "method" itself: depicting scientific precision and obsessive perfectionism in the study and application of styles from the past as a habit of German provenance, and stigmatizing it as an historical nonsense.[7] With a certain disregard for what he calls "academic purism,"[8] Ilg describes how the Austrian "spirit" and "blood" embrace life with its impure, changing forms. In this way it surpasses the mere copying of the styles of the past, making space for both artistic invention and adherence to the needs of contemporary society.

The rediscovery of the Renaissance, which Ilg describes as a first moment of respite from the strict and dry rule of classicism, like a fine rain that brings an arid steppe back to life,[9] serves to introduce the baroque as a matter of succession in a natural development[10] and to address its "impurity" as the result of a mix of influences of different national origins.[11] Indeed, even before naming the baroque as such Ilg defines the characteristics of an "ideal" style for Austria: lively, witty and more related to life than to arid theoretical studies. Variable and not strictly adherent to rule, this style would also be well-adapted to an Alpine landscape – more so than to a southern Mediterranean environment, as was the case with Greek classicism.[12] Deliberately using the history of the baroque – highlighting, reinterpreting, selectively forgetting – Ilg transforms the historical baroque into this "ideal," thereby finally reaching his goal: to enhance the appeal of the baroque to his contemporaries.

Editing History

Deliberately selecting only parts of the historical background of the baroque and leaving out other, less acceptable aspects, allows Ilg to open the very definition of the baroque for discussion, polishing its image and disarticulating it from its most burdensome heritage, and especially from its more problematic political and religious patrimony. The first step in this move is to distance the baroque from Rome and its religious references, acknowledging their importance to its history while at the same time situating them in a remote past. Both this past and its critics are cast, consequently, in a rather ironic light. Ilg deals, in particular, with the long-standing contempt and dread with which the secular components of Austrian society had regarded the Societas Jesu and its interference in Austrian culture:

> I regret it, but cannot do otherwise than to leave the honor to the truth, I must express it: baroque art is in part the Jesuits' doing. I admit, this origin is not suitable to arouse general sympathy for her, and my poor client has obviously to thank this circumstance in particular for the fact that she has until now remained the Cinderella of German art theory.[13]

The many different categories of the baroque, Ilg continues, "Barocke, Rokoko, Jesuitenstil und Zopfstil," had all been thrown chaotically into the one pot and used indiscriminately – but until that moment it was not good etiquette even to discuss the matter.[14] The boundaries of these individual categories nonetheless still remain blurred in Ilg's own text.[15]

"Everything savage or hideous, tasteless or absurd would be negatively defined as *zopfig*."[16] To recast the negative reputation of the baroque in a positive light, Ilg applies a lesson learned through the history of the "rediscovery" of the art of the Middle Ages. Before the gothic could be appreciated, the best examples had to be isolated from a mass of "unpleasant, monstrous artifacts" that were likewise considered gothic – Ilg quotes the authority of Goethe confronted by the Strasburg Cathedral. In the same way, Italians of past centuries considered that style as the quintessence of the barbaric.[17] The judgement of style, Ilg appreciates, is historically subject to change; the proliferation of artifacts can, at times, be confusing; and, as Ilg seems to imply with the reference to the gothic, each style must be evaluated on its own terms and not for its proximity to the rules of classicism.

Ilg therefore situates the most clearly negative examples of baroque art in a rather recent past and in the context of a repressive era of Habsburg rule.[18] He refers to a new fashion in interior decoration, inspired by French models and aptly named the *Blondel'schen Styl* by the newspapers, which around 1830 substituted the simpler taste that characterized the early decades of the nineteenth century.[19] Succeeding to the throne in 1835, Ferdinand I took possession of the former apartments of Maria Theresia and Joseph II at the Hofburg. To contain the refurbishment costs, it was decided to match the style of the new furniture to the original eighteenth-century decorations. The original rococo furniture was substituted with new furniture in *Blondel'schen Styl*, which was at this time also christened the "second rococo." This choice would be repeated in all the representative spaces of the dynasty, from the Hofburg to Schönbrünn to Hetzendorf, and naturally held sway over a generation of subsequent residential projects. The decorative scheme adopted in the Hofburg between 1839 and 1842 indeed became a standard for official use and came to represent the Habsburg dynasty through each phase of its decline.[20]

A Shared and Glorious Past, Reborn

Ilg's construction of a positive image for the baroque stems, in contrast, from its universality. He plays on two different "universalities," one artistic, the other political: on one hand, the ability to involve and integrate all the arts, techniques and crafts in the production of a work of art[21] and, on the other, the capacity to "overcome precedents and dissolve the individualities of each people to embrace the whole globe in a single rule."[22] Ilg is clear. The baroque to which he refers is not that of the Jesuits, nor "the ugly *Zopf* of the Restauration," but rather "der Stil des 18. Jahrhunderts!" – the golden age of the Habsburg Empire.[23] "Would it be a misfortune if the artistic blossoming of the days of Leopold, Carl VI or of the great Theresia would be renewed for us?"[24] Offering to the Viennese middle classes of the nineteenth century the image of living "as [the great eighteenth-century general and patron of the arts] Prinz Eugen, in palaces by Fischer von Erlach," he refers, *en passant*, to the only baroque building explicitly mentioned in the entire pamphlet.[25]

Die Zukunft des Barockstils participates in a cultural policy that had been defined quite clearly from the early days of neo-absolutism, after the revolution of 1848. The Habsburg Empire had been reorganized and centralized. Most of its cultural institutions had been tasked to highlight and emphasize the moments of cohesion in the complex culture of the multinational empire, a goal that had oriented the intellectual elite towards the rediscovery of the dynastic history of the House of Habsburg.[26] This included the strategic manipulation of the public image of the imperial family and involved, at times, the re-invention of historical events, monuments and characters – a process coming rather close, on many occasions, to the creation of historical myths.[27]

The reference to France as a positive cultural model reinforces this same abstraction – the glorious figures of the past, as well as their artistic artifacts, are divorced from their social and political settings to become transformed into timeless models. The baroque era, in Ilg's view, marks the creation of the power of France as a nation, but also the moment of greatest splendour of its art. The nineteenth-century citizens of France might have demonstrated great pride in their new Republic, but the French "are way too practical to refuse for a second time the endless advantages, the style of their Louis offers them, [just] because it smells of monarchy and tyranny."[28] With the revival of a "French baroque style" approaching official policy for Habsburg palace interiors, Ilg places the Austrian claim upon the baroque just after that of the French:

> After [them] no other population has had so great an advantage in accepting the inheritance of this great artistic
> era as the Austrian. The evidence is in its art history, of course, in those of its chapters which until now, out

of sheer enthusiasm for insignificant emanations of the art of our home country from earlier eras, and in part, also, as foreign voices are concerned, because of resentment and even for a little envy, were almost completely hushed up.[29]

Having separated the concept of the baroque from the more difficult aspects of its history, Ilg recreates it as an abstract ideal, describing the birth of a new generation of the baroque. The baroque is reborn, with roots in history, but not as a thing of the past – it has new force driving towards the future.[30] There is no descriptive or normative attachment to this declaration. Ilg does not provide the instruments with which to judge which artifacts, buildings or works of art are in fact part of this "Dritte Rokoko," or to distinguish them from "the ugly *Zopf* of the Restauration," or to instruct artists to reach this new ideal. He creates, in effect, a fictitious category, a stratagem that rendered the baroque more palatable for his contemporaries and which was readily adopted to collect under one name the plethora of "neo-baroque" experiences to appear at the end of the century.

The re-appearance of the baroque – which in Ilg's view was providentially situated at the end of a long chain of stylistic failures – satisfies the needs of contemporary life in every respect.[31] His baroque is popular, not elitist, and comfortable (there is a lot of emphasis on the word *bequem*). Finally, it is rentable: the distributive and constructive model of the baroque *palais*, transformed in a *Mietskaserne*, serves decorum as it attends also to the economic goals of the apartment owner – a member of that upper-middle class to whom Ilg's pamphlet would seem particularly directed.

A Visual Primer

Ilg did not write of specific buildings beyond the aforementioned reference to "Fischer von Erlach's palaces for Prinz Eugen." His pamphlet did not contain drawings, or any other form of illustration, which helped to preserve a degree of indeterminacy that served well Ilg's "political" purposes. In 1879 and 1880 though – at the moment in which *Die Zukunft des Barockstils* was published – a series of articles appeared in the *Allgemeine Bauzeitung* on the baroque heritage of Vienna, replete with lavish photographs and illustrations, under the name of a colleague of Ilg's at the Altertumsverein, Carl (Karl) Lind.[32] Imagining a well-constructed plot is tempting. Certainly, this was no coincidence, and it is indeed quite probable that the two were at least informed of each other's work. In fact, writing on the Portal of Palais Lichtenstein am Minoritenplatz in an article published in 1879, the art historian and preservation advocate Lind remarks:

> These grand Palais-buildings and the smaller constructions of this era, which were conserved for us, are still inadequately appreciated. The indifference with which these buildings were unfortunately regarded for too long will finally give way to their correct understanding and admiration, thanks to the efforts of a few art historians, who in this field have already achieved so much. But before that is accomplished, much still has to happen.[33]

The correspondence between Ilg's words and Lind's examples and images is rather striking. Ilg writes of "the style of the eighteenth century" and "the days of Leopold, Carl VI or of the great Theresia."[34] And during the course of 1879 Lind publishes the Johannes-Kapelle near the Karlssteg, the Brunnen am Hoher Markt, the Zeughaus and the aforementioned Portal of Palais Lichtenstein am Minoritenplatz.[35] In 1880 Lind's articles confront the masterpieces of the Viennese baroque, first the Karlskirche, then the Alte Aula of the Akademie des Wissenschaften, before finally turning to the Belvedere.[36]

The series seems to conclude in 1881, but a new installment on the Schwarzenberg summer residence appears in 1882.[37]

Lind's articles serve as a supplement to Ilg's text with their clearly defined historical background and powerful illustrations. His examples conjure up in their tangible materiality the "construction tradition of Vienna since the second Turkish siege" of which Ilg writes in the abstract. At the same time they serve as visual references and, furthermore, as models, offered to the avid eyes of the *Allgemeine Bauzeitung*'s readers, who we can justifiably imagine as professional architects in search of inspiration.

Figure 2.1 **Portal des Fürstlich Liechtenstein'schen Palais in Wien**

Source: Allgemeine Bauzeitung, 1879, Bl. 63 – ANNO/Österreichiesche Nationalbibliothek.

Figure 2.2   Kapelle nächst dem Karlsstege am Franz-Josefs Quai in Wien
Source: Allgemeine Bauzeitung, 1879, Bl. 39 – ANNO/Österreichische Nationalbibliothek.

DAS BÜRGERLICHE ZEUGHAUS IN WIEN.

Figure 2.3   Das Bürgerliche Zeughaus in Wien
Source: Allgemeine Bauzeitung, 1879, Bl. 62 – ANNO/Österreichische Nationalbibliothek.

Figure 2.4   Das K.K. Schloss Belvedere in Wien, Halle des Erdgeschosses
Source: Allgemeine Bauzeitung, 1880, Bl. 75 – ANNO/Österreichische Nationalbibliothek.

The photographs Lind publishes of the various buildings he discusses, together with plans and sections, provided clear examples of what Ilg had discussed in theory – but without yet proposing what would have been controversial designs in the neo-baroque manner. On the contrary, these buildings were treated as part of the shared heritage of Vienna's citizens. They seemed even worthier of publication and attention for being under threat: towards the end of the century both Ilg and Lind would come to participate in the collective creation of the myth of "Alt-Wien," lamenting the loss of the baroque fabric of historic Vienna through the transformation of the Ringstrasse.[38]

A Model Building

The association of Ilg's text with a neo-baroque design was made in the pages of this same *Allgemeine Bauzeitung*, but only in 1885. In that year its editor-in-chief, August Köstlin, published his second article therein with the title "Das neue Wien."[39] His first contribution, published in 1883, had been written to celebrate the expansion of the Ringstrasse and the advancement of Vienna's architectural culture, which in the eyes of Köstlin, an engineer, was a corollary to the great increase of construction activity in the capital.

Der „Ziererhof" in Wien; erbaut von Architekt C. König, k. k. Professor am Polytechnikum daselbst.

Architektonische Rundschau 1885. 1.

Verlag von J. Engelhorn in Stuttgart.

Figure 2.5   Der "Ziererhof" in Wien, erbaut von Architekt C. König, k.k. Professor am Polytechnikum daselbst

Source: Architektonische Rundshau, 1885, Tafel I – ANNO/Österreichische Nationalbibliothek.

In his second essay, Köstlin had to substantially reconsider his earlier and more positive assessment of contemporary Viennese architecture. For this, he blamed on one side the death of Heinrich von Ferstel, an influential professional figure in Viennese architectural culture and, on the other, the spreading of a "Nationalbarock – Bacillus." Köstlin never explicitly mentions Ilg, but refers instead to the activity of an "Agitator" behind this tendency.

In a long footnote to this text, Köstlin associates the Agitator's proposals with the design by Karl König for the Ziehrer-hof (1882–84).[40] This building, later known as Philipp-hof and now destroyed, was located at the crossing of important central thoroughfares between the old city and the Ringstrasse expansion, in proximity to the Albertina. The multi-storey building – at the time the Viennese venue of the Jockey Club – was characterized by a bold corner treatment with a rounded profile and a dome in explicit reference to the *Reitschultrakt* of the Hofburg, at the same time satisfying the requirements of the developers and adopting the *Nationalbarock* taste.

In his comments on the project, in the first issue of the *Architektonische Rundschau*, 1885, König seems to explicitly echo Ilg's pamphlet: "As examples I have used principally the palaces of the time of Leopold I and Carl VI. … An attempt to emulate the architectural character of that time is not completely far from my intention."[41]

Within a few years, the Ziehrer-hof became the *icon par excellence* of the real estate aggression towards the old city and of the decadent taste of *fin-de-siècle* architecture. Indeed, Ludwig Hevesi in 1899 writes of newly realized buildings on the Neuer Markt as "pure speculator's baroque with two corner domes," while in 1910 Hans Tietze laments that "every house has become a corner house."[42]

Figure 2.6   Fountain erected by Francis Joseph in 1889, Vienna
Source: Boston Public Library, Tupper Scrapbooks Collection, Volume 45, Vienna, p. 16, Courtesy of the Trustees of the Boston Public Library.

Köstlin's article of 1885 adopts a comparatively benign attitude towards this building, while being vehemently critical of the "Agitator," Ilg. Köstlin's restraint might be explained in light of König's positive reputation as a professor of the Technische Hochschule Wien, but the issue seems to transcend this isolated instance. The criticism he obliquely directs at Ilg's pamphlet was directed less towards the baroque style itself, or to its contemporary neo-baroque architectural manifestation, than towards the partisan cultural policy that had thrown its support behind it. Köstlin resented the derogatory stance that Ilg's pamphlet presupposed. In describing the baroque as the only patriotic style, Ilg insinuates that all the other styles – and their supporters – should be regarded as non-patriotic. For this same reason Jakob von Falke commented that the baroque is "a flag, under which a faction is gathering."[43] Köstlin rebuts one by one the elements of Ilg's argument in favour of the baroque, but his attention is primarily directed towards its political dimensions. The baroque style, he argues, is international, and to claim it as a quintessentially Viennese style is a fraud.[44] Ilg's ideas, he persists, also presuppose an unwelcome limitation of the creative freedom of the architect. In Köstlin's view, it is especially important to firmly reject Ilg's identification of the contemporary Viennese lifestyle with the baroque era, since this would imply the acceptance of an undemocratic "grand-seigneurliches" society.[45]

Patriotisch versus *wissenschaftlich*

The political focus of Köstlin's critique echoes two earlier articles by Camillo Sitte, who responded to Ilg's pamphlet in the immediate wake of its publication.[46] Sitte recognizes, albeit ironically, the pamphlet's rhetoric power and calls Ilg's rehabilitation of the baroque "a masterpiece of the finest sort." The "restoration" of the baroque – the politically loaded word is carefully chosen – is but a final digression from a path towards the future. Once this chapter is finally closed "it will not be possible to stay still."[47] Sitte appears to make ambiguous reference to hidden political plots behind the more explicit artistic implications of the neo-baroque: "Those who do it know very well why – and because they are doing it with flagrantly egotistical intention, it does neither them nor their goal any honour."[48] Sitte laments how the debate, focusing on style, has become sterile and ridiculous: "We always speak of style, just as the sick who always speak of health." His attention is focused especially on the *Wiener Styl*, which affords him the opportunity to deride Ilg for his biased, ludicrous praise of Hasenauer's work and his criticism of Semper: "In all this it is discussed gladly – it has become so fashionable – the new 'Viennese Style', of a specific Viennese Art."[49] Ilg's praise for Hasenauer is merely based on politics, as is the adoption of the *Nationalbarock*.

Sitte recalls the strength of an earlier response to Ilg's pamphlet by Rudolf Redtenbacher, published as a series of articles in the *Allgemeine Bauzeitung*.[50] By invoking Redtenbacher, a Swiss architect and a student of Semper, Sitte situates Ilg's pamphlet's not only in the frame of the debate on style, but in the specific discussion of the role of architectural history – or the *Geschichtschreibung der Baukunst*, as Redtenbacher has it.[51] In the polarized debate of the 1880s in Vienna, Redtenbacher represented the group of scholars and architects who hoped through Semper's theory and studies to reach a solution to the question of style – the same *Vertreter der Renaissance* of which Ilg himself writes.[52] Politically pro-German, or at least considered as such by their adversaries, the "Semperianer" recognized that the solution to the issue of style would come from being "more scientific." *Wissenschaftlich* is a motto that appears in the articles of both Redtenbacher and Koestlin.[53] When Ilg describes scientific precision as a dry and boring habit of German scholarship, as he does at the outset of his pamphlet, not only does he advocate for an "Austrian way" of writing art history, but furthermore chooses a side *within* the contemporary Viennese debate. Expressing his views against the Semperianer, Ilg creates a counter-motto that would come to appear regularly in his later work: *patriotisch*.

From Baroque to Modern

In *Die Zukunft des Barockstils* Ilg affirms that the architecture of the Ringstrasse "has been baroque for a long time," later adding the expression *konstruktiv genommen*.[54] Recognizing how, in the rehabilitation of the gothic, a fresh admiration for the technical aspects of construction had led the way to the promotion and appreciation of the artistic results, Ilg sought to present the baroque as separated from its decorative language, arguing instead that its distributive, spatial and constructive characteristics were most well-suited to the needs and habits of contemporary society. Redtenbacher had similarly invoked the separation of tectonic and compositional aspects from decorative considerations in his analysis of gothic and Renaissance architecture. His goal was to reconsider each era in the history of architecture for its response to tectonic problems in particular and in this task he defined the specific role of architectural history.[55] His popular articles were published in the *Allgemeine Bauzeitung* during the same years as the debates recalled above. Ilg might well have had these matters in mind when he effectively extended them to address the baroque.

The correlation between Ilg's ideas and those of König is even more important under this rubric. Teaching in those same years at the Technische Hochschule, König applied a method that would seem to translate Ilg's ideas into pedagogy. While his own style of choice was the neo-baroque, he primarily emphasized aspects of composition and structure in his teaching. The result was that many of his students, known in the city as *Barockschüler*, were able "to abstract" from the details and ornamentation of the baroque, as they "embrace[d] modernism later in their careers."[56] Admitting other influences in the professional trajectories of König's students, the list of their names remains impressive, including such Viennese architects as Max Fabiani, Oskar Strnad and Oskar Wlach, as well as renowned international figures like Frederick Kiesler, Rudolph Schindler, Richard Neutra and Josef Frank.

Ilg sanctioned the separation of structure from decoration as a stratagem to make the baroque more acceptable to his contemporaries. His strictly *patriotisch* agenda, together with König's adherence to the stylistic choice of the *Nationalbarock*, produced in the short term the success they desired – the adoption of the neo-baroque as an official language for the Habsburg Empire and its propagation at the end of the century. These very same strategies, though, also played a part in its rapid fall. Consider these words of the Viennese philosopher Josef Bayer, in which he echoes Ilg's sentiments, but now with regard to the search for a modern style: "In the end, gradually and imperceptibly, the new architectural problems are also leading to new formal ideas; and even the *changed rhythm of old forms*, ordered after a new principle of living, has already won a more essential and greater victory." The manner of looking at the buildings of the past had definitively changed. Bayer continues:

> I even dare to assert that the kernel-formation of a modern style is already here, *although we will not perceive its sign if we look at our buildings from the perspective of well-known historical styles*. Then only what is different becomes apparent, not what is common to them. What is now evident is the total attitude that we bring to the design of a building – the organization of its floor plan and our age's particular compositional tasks as such.[57]

Ilg's endorsement, as an historian, of the idea of giving separate consideration to construction and decorative aspects in the baroque had indeed given rise to unintended consequences for the critical fortunes of the neo-baroque and, with the rise of modern architecture, came to take on a life of its own.

Author's Note

An early version of this essay was presented at the 64th Conference of the Society of Architectural Historians in New Orleans in April 2011. I wish to thank the chair as well as the other members of the panel for their insightful comments and advice.

Endnotes

1   See Springer, "Biographische Skizze zu Albert Ilg," 319–45.
2   On these themes see Stachel, "Albert Ilg und die 'Erfindung' des Barocks als Österreischischer 'Nationalstil'," 100–152; and Ottlinger, "Von *Blondel'schen Styl* zum *Maria Theresien Stil*," 345–69. The adjective "Austrian" is the translation of the term *österreichisch* used in Ilg's pamphlet and by most of its commentators. The term refers at this time not only to Austria, but more generally to the Habsburg Empire.
3   Ilg, *Die Zukunft des Barockstils*, 1.
4   At this time the Empire was struggling to meet the growing demands of its numerous minorities without giving in to the most destructive of their nationalistic claims. These had become more numerous and more pressing since the recognition of Hungarian sovereignty with the *Ausgleich* or Compromise of 1867, which established the Dual Monarchy of Austria-Hungary. Requests of a cultural nature were part of this centrifugal tendency as much as the more strictly political ones.
5   In 1889 Cornelius Gurlitt would already reverse this judgement, describing Prague's baroque as "Deutsche Kunst." See Janatková, *Barockrezeption zwischen Historismus und Moderne*, 20–21.
6   Ilg, *Die Zukunft des Barockstils*, 7.
7   He writes: "Die komplette Wiederholung eines schon gewesenen Zustandes ist übrigens ja ein *Nonsens* in der Geschichte. Aber die erneute Durchbringung und Bestimmung unseres Kunsthandwerkes durch dieselben geistigen Principien und die Belebung einer der damaligen ähnlichen, auf gleichen künstlerischen Grundlagen basirenden Formenwelt scheint uns der Strömung der Zeit nach wahrscheinlich." Ilg, *Die Zukunft des Barockstils*, 30.
8   In this regard Margaret Olin notes: "Although the term 'Spätantike' adorned the Empire in the mantle of classic Greek art, keeping Roman art Greek also had the effect of combating purist ideas. Although, like others, Riegl often traced tendencies to different 'races' or nationalities, he thought that stylistic purity would spell the death of art. His writings persistently sought to show how only culture contact caused stylistic advances." In "Alois Riegl," 112.

9   "Die alte Tradition und die Nachbarschaft brachten Italien hier rasch an's Ruder und so hat die Wiener Richtung sich alsbald rückhaltlos der Renaissance dieses Landes und zwar seiner feinen früheren Renaissance in die Arme geworfen. Man athmete unter diesem Blüthenregen von Zierlichkeit und Grazie auf, der da mit Einemmale auf die dürre Steppe deutscher Kunstindustrie herniederrieselte …" Ilg, *Die Zukunft des Barockstils*, 7.

10 "Man schalt ihn nun einen Auswuchs der braven Renaissance, gewissermassen einen Wechselbalg, den dieser schönen Mutter eine böse Fee in die Wiege gelegt hatte, Verfall, Verwilderung u.s.f. Als ob in der natur – wozu der Mensch und sein ganzes Wesen sammt seiner Kunst ja ebenso gehört wie Pflanze und Gas, Thier und Mineral, von etwas Andere als von Weiterentwicklungen die Rede sein könnte!" Ilg, *Die Zukunft des Barockstils*, 16.

11 "Geschwungene, also unnatürliche, also unglückliche Mischung." Ilg, *Die Zukunft des Barockstils*, 13.

12 The idea that baroque and Roman art were "more closely related to our own art" than that of ancient Greece pervades Riegl's thinking. See Olin, "Alois Riegl," 113; and Riegl, *The Origins of Baroque Art in Rome*.

13 Ilg, *Die Zukunft des Barockstils*, 14. Part of Ilg's intent to rehabilitate the Baroque certainly stems from its characterization as a Catholic style. At the same time, he dismisses criticism based on its connection with the Jesuit Order as a complaint that does not apply to the contemporary baroque, that "baroque reborn" he calls "Dritte Rokoko." Compare Levy, *Propaganda and the Jesuit Baroque*.

14 He writes: "Lange dauerte es, bis einzelne Gelehrte sich herabließen, die Geschichte und Naturgeschichte jener etwas dunklen Gebiete in der Kunst der letzten Saecula zu studiren, die man als Barocke, Rokoko, Jesuitenstil und Zopfstil chaotisch in einem Topf zu werfen beliebt hatte, aber es gehörte gar nicht zum guten Ton, von der Sache nur zu reden …" Ilg, *Die Zukunft des Barockstils*, 15.

15 As Peter Stachel has demonstrated, this ambiguity persists in later writings by Ilg on this topic.

16 Ilg, *Die Zukunft des Barockstils*, 15.

17 He writes: "… schier in der Weise beinahe, wie Göthe [sic] erzählt, dass er früher alles Krausborstige und Ungeheuerliche für Gothisch angesehen habe, bevor ihn der Anblick des Straßburger Münsters eines Bessern belehrt hatte, oder wie die alten Italiener denselben Baustil für den Inbegriff von Barbarei erachteten." Ilg, *Die Zukunft des Barockstils*, 15.

18 He writes: "Das Bedürfnis bahnte sich aus dem Volke selbst dem Weg. Was auf diese Weise entstanden ist, kann trotz vieler Mängel, die ihm noch anhaften, nur als eine gesunde Reaction angesehen werden, nicht etwa als Rückfall in die Alte schlechte Barocke des Vormärzes – unserer Bewegung, denn seine Technik, Zeichnung und Formbildung legt von den seitdem gemachten Erfahrungen deutliche Proben ab." Ilg, *Die Zukunft des Barockstils*, 22.

19 Some important commissions of these years, which influenced the taste of the upper classes, include the Palais Lichtenstein and Palais Fries Pallavicini (Peter Hubert Desvignes) and, later the refurbishment "nach französicher Art" of the interiors of the Palais Coburg-Gotha, Palais Harrach and Palais Schey (all by Franz Schönthaler, who trained in France).

20 Ottlinger, "Von *Blondel'schen Styl* zum *Maria Theresien Stil*," 345–69; Nierhaus, "Höfisch und Österreichisch," 79–100.

21 He writes: "Kein anderer Stil umfaßt in gleicher Universalität alle Künste, Techniken und Handwerke, keine hat so viele von ihnen, die bis dahin nur in Anfängen vorhanden gewesen, zur Entfaltung gezeitigt oder so viele neue geschaffen … im harmonischsten Einklang mit der Architektur …" Ilg, *Die Zukunft des Barockstils*, 17.

22 Ilg, *Die Zukunft des Barockstils*, 34.

23 Ilg, *Die Zukunft des Barockstils*, 19.

24 Ilg, *Die Zukunft des Barockstils*, 42. On Maria Teresia, Johnston notes: "Although [she] has been eulogised by many post-1918 writers her forty-year reign ended in unpopularity. Only later did she come to be regarded as Mother of her Country. Having combined gentleness with vision, she seemed a kind of Queen of Heaven enthroned." Johnston, *The Austrian Mind*, 16.

25 This passage reads in full: "Für unsere Behausung taugt uns weder das pompeianische Atrium noch die gothische Ritterburg, noch die deutsche Renaissance-Wohnung mit ihren tiefen Sälen und hohen Treppengiebeln, vollständig aber das Modell aus jener Zeit, ob wir nun wie Prinz Eugen in Palästen Fischer's von Erlach wohnen wollen oder in jenen närrischen, behaglichen Bürgerhäuschen, wie sie auf den Märkten alter Städte noch zu finden sind." Ilg, *Die Zukunft des Barockstils*, 22.

26 Compare Olin, *The Cult of Monuments as a State Religion in Late 19th Century Austria*, 177–218.

27 The statues of Prinz Eugen and Erzherzog Karl on the Heldenplatz or *die Grosse Theresia* "mother of the country" embodied the golden eras of the Empire in a rather accessible popular representation, in the most prominent new public spaces along the Ringstrasse. Stripped of their historical substance and context, these figures serve, in Ilg's pamphlet as in those public spaces, as icons of glorious historical moments, sufficiently remote in time to constitute a benign heritage accommodating the Empire's many nationalities. See Nierhaus, "Schauplatz und Handlungsraum," 46–60; and Stachel, *Mythos Heldenplatz*.

28 Ilg, *Die Zukunft des Barockstils*, 33. Preceding this thought he also asks: "Zu welcher Zeit wären sie denn französischer gewesen diese Franzosen als in den Tagen der herrschaft genannter Stile?"

29 Ilg, *Die Zukunft des Barockstils*, 40.

30 He writes: "Unterbrochen, geschwächt, aber nicht ausgelöscht, flammte nach der Herrschaft des Empire's der Lebensfunke unseres Stils wieder empor. Aber er war nicht mehr der Alte, ein entnervter Greis, der Schatten seines einstigen Wesens. Was ihn vordem ausgezeichnet hatte, war ihm abhanden gekommen: die Fülle der Kräfte und Techniken, die Gelegenheit zu größeren Unternehmungen, die Allgemeinheit und die Popularität. All' dies hat ihm die theoretische Reform wieder geschaffen ... und nun hat eine dritte Geburtstunde geschlagen." Ilg, *Die Zukunft des Barockstils*, 20.

31 Ilg, *Die Zukunft des Barockstils*, 19, 21, 22.

32 Jäger-Sunstenau, *Lind, Karl (1831–1901)*, 217–18.

33 Lind, *Das Zeughaus der Stadt Wien*, 79.

34 "Wiens Baugeschichte seit der zweiten Türkenbelagerung, ... Wiens Barockarchitektur!" Ilg, *Die Zukunft des Barockstils*, 20.

35 Lind, "Die Johannes-Kapelle nächst dem Karlssteg in Wien," 47, plate 39; "Der Brunnen auf dem Hoher Markte zu Wien," 63–4, plate 50;,"Das Zeughaus der Stadt Wien," 79, plate 62; "Portal des fürstlich Liechtenstein'schen Palais am Minoritenplatz in Wien," 79–80, plate 63. For further reading on these buildings, see Czeike, *Historisches Lexikon Wien*, 1992–97.

36 Lind, "Die Karlskirche in Wien," 9–11, plates 4–6; "Die Alte Aula in Wien (Gebäude der k. Akademie des Wissenschaften)," 72–3, plates 50–51; "*Das k.und k. Schloss Belvedere, als Bauwerk besprochen*," 103–4, plates 71–5. Ilg's pupil and stalwart supporter of the neo-baroque within the Habsburg imperial family, Erzherzog Franz Ferdinand, later chose the Belvedere as his residence.

37 Lind, "Der fürstlich Schwarzenberg'sche Sommer-Palast in Wien," 104–5, plates 74–6.

38 Lind, "*Erinnerungen eines alten Wieners an Wiener Stadtbilder*," 105–11. See also Kassal-Mikula, "Alt-Wien unter die demolierungskrampen," 46–61, esp. note 22; and Ilg, *Alt-Wien in Wort und Bild*.

39 On Köstlin see Hoyer, "Köstlin, August," 342–3.

40 He writes: "Auffallenderweise genügte ihm nicht einmal der von Professor König erbaute 'Ziehrerhof' der, vornehmlich für Zwecke des Jockey-Klub bestimmt, in opulenter, grossartiger Weise geplant und durchgeführt, sich unseres vollen Beifalles erfreut. Alles Beweis genug, dass die Agitation gewiss auf fester, ehrlicher Überzeugung beruht hatte. Alles unterliegt, auch das menschliche Denken und Empfinden, in gewissem Grade der Mode oder der Zeitströmung. Diese aber begünstigt eben jetzt in hervorragendem Maasse (sic.) den Nationalitäts-Kultus." Köstlin, "Das Neue Wien," 1, note 1. On König, see Wagner-Rieger, "König, Karl," 36–7; Brandstetter, "Karl König."

41 "Als Vorbilder dienten mir hauptsächlich die Palastbauten aus der Zeit Leopold I und Carl VI, die sich einer Reihe von Beispielen in Wien und dessen Nähe erhalten haben, und die, so lange sie unversehrt bestehen, ihrer Zeit zum Ruhme und der Stadt zum Schmucke gereichen werden. Ein Versuch, den architektonischen Charakter jener Zeit nachzuahmen, lag nicht in entferntesten im meiner Absicht." *Architektonische Rundschau* 1885, no. 1, 1.

42 Hevesi, "Kunst auf der Strasse," 171; Tietze, "Der Kampf um Alt-Wien," 48. Both are quoted, but with no reference to the Ziehrer-hof, in Kassal-Mikula, "Alt-Wien unter dem Demolierungskrampen," 46–61, notes 25 and 7 resp.

43 Cited in Stachel, "Vollkommen passende gefässe ...," 288 and note 88.

44 He writes: "Der Wiener wurde also, wie schon gesagt, mit erfolg haranquirt, sich nicht von 'fremdgeborenen', 'eingewanderten' Architekten 'fremden' Architekturstyl aufpfropfen zu lassen ..." Köstlin, "Das Neue Wien," 1.

45 He writes: "Er hatte im Eifer der Agitation und Bekämpfung der 'fremden' Kunst übersehen, worin die bezaubernde Wirkung der Barocke-Schöpfungen unser Fischer von Erlach Periode vornehmlich besteht, ... was heutigen Tages in der volkreich gewordenen Grossstadt, in der demokratisch umgestalteten menschlichen Gesellschaft, auf den vertheuerten Grundparzellen einfach nicht mehr zu haben ist; er hatte übersehen, ... dass unsere Zeit, in Wien so gut wie anderwärts, nach anderem Ausdruck ringt als nach dem grand-seigneurlichen Barockstyls, der zumal für unser bürgerliches Wohnhaus absolut nicht passt." Köstlin, "Das Neue Wien," 2.

46 Sitte, "Offenes Schreiben an Dr. Ilg," and "Wiener Styl." Both articles appear in the recent volume Semsroth, Mönninger and Collins (eds), *Camillo Sitte*, 185–7 and 188–99, resp.

47 Sitte, "*Offenes Schreiben an Dr. Ilg*," in *Schriften*, 187.

48 Sitte, "Wiener Styl," in *Schriften*, 188.

49 Sitte, "Wiener Styl," 188. Sitte derides Ilg's positions in support of Hasenauer and against Semper well before Ilg's own famous critique of the Burgtheater ("Das neue Hofburgtheater" [1888], 1–2) and depiction of Hasenauer as a new Fischer von Erlach. Sitte straightforwardly comments: "Visitkarte: Gottfried Semper, Zeichner im Atelier Hasenauer. Ungefähr so, als wie Michelangelo, Bildhauergehilfe bei Maestro Baccio Bandinelli, oder A.W. Mozart, Notenhabschreiber der Firma Schikaneder." Sitte "Das Neue Wiener Styl," 191.

50 Redtenbacher, "Die Baubestrebungen der Gegenwart," 61–3 and 77–80; "Die Baukunst der Vergangenheit," 1–4 and 17–20. Redtenbacher was author of a tectonic theory advanced in two books in the early 1880s, especially *Die Architektonik der modernen Baukunst* (1883). A few introductory notes on Redtenbacher can be found in Mallgrave, *Modern Architectural Theory*, 195–204; and some of his writings appear in translation in Oechslin, *Otto Wagner, Adolf Loos and the Road to Modern Architecture*.

51 He elaborates: "Wenn es nun die Aufgabe der Architektur unser Zeit ist, sich zu klären und zu konsolidiren, an Tiefe zu gewinnen und von Vorurteilen sich zu läutern, so möchte man auch der *Geschichtschreibung der Baukunst* einen ähnlichen Läuterungsprozess wünschen. Auch sie, die wärend der Zeit der modernen Baubestrebungen aufgetaucht ist und sich ausgebildet hat, leidet noch an bedenklichen Mängeln, welche zu überwinden, ihr Ziel sein muss. Sie muss *wissenschaftlicher* werden, aus der Kinderschuhen der Dilettantismus herauszukommen, von Tendenzen aller Art sich zu befreien suchen." Redtenbacher, "Die Baubestrebungen der Gegenwart," 80. Italics mine.

52 Redtenbacher ("Die Baukunst der Vergangenheit") focuses on a re-reading of architectural history grounded in this debate, re-stating the values of the Renaissance: "Unsere heutige Baukunst kann sich nicht auf einen willkürlichen Standpunkt stellen, wir gehören immer doch der Neuzeit an, die mit der *Renaissance der Kunst*, mit der *Reformation des Glaubens*, mit der *Freiheit des Denkens*, mit der Erfindung der Buchdruckerkunst und der Entdeckung der Welt und des Menschen begann. Wir stehen immer doch auf dem Standpunkte, den wir ganz allgemein als Renaissance bezeichnen dürfen und wir können die Geschichte nicht ungeschehen machen, nicht zum Mittelalter zurückkehren." In "Die Baukunst der Vergangenheit," 19. Italics mine.

53 Of course the word *wissenschaftlich* is not politically charged *per se*. The term already appears as the last "stage" of art history in the thinking of Karl Otfried Müller (1797–1840). On the term *wissenschaftlich* in Eitelberger see Rampley, "The Idea of a Scientific Discipline," 54–79. On Semper's status in the debate see Franz and Nierhaus (eds), *Gottfried Semper und Wien*.

54 Ilg writes: "Schon sahen wir mehrere große Neubauten dieses Characters entstehen, außerdem neigen besonders zwei handwerke demselben zu, die Tischlerei und die Schlosserei – eben weil diese beiden von der Baukunst am meisten abhängen. Auch das Tapeten- und Möbelstoff nähert sich teilweise dem Stile und die mit der Toilette zusammenhängenden Gewerbe dürften bald nachfolgen. *In unserer Ringstrassenarchitektur sind wir eigentlich schon lange barock,* obgleich es die Wenigsten merken und zwar unter denen, die sich darüber täuschen, am allerwenigsten *die Vertreter der Renaissance* selber. In einem fort schwätzen sie vom fälschen Cinquecentopalast, dem sie die Zinskaserne nachgeformt haben – was aber besitzt der kolossale Kasten in Wahrheit von seinem Vorbild, das nicht blöß äußerlich daraufgekleckst, darangegypst und schablonirt wäre? Der alte Palazzo, nur eine Familie dienend, hatte ein Noblegeschoß mit breiten und hohen Fenstern; dazwischen aber mächtige Pfeiler   [Das] Ganze ist einfach im Großen, groß im Einfachen – was Alles aber der Ringstrassenhausherr nicht brauchen könnte, um auf seine Interessen zu kommen. Die stolzen Cornichenfenster mußten daher zusammenschrumpfen und eng an einander rücken, ferner vier bis fünfmal über einander aussteigen, damit die Mietskaserne ihrem zweck genüge – kurz, konstruktiv genommen geht daraus jenes himmelhohe Wohngebäu mit seinen vielen Fensterreihen hervor, wie es eben Wiens Baugeschichte seit der zweiten Türkenbelagerung so vielfach aufzuweisen hat, Wiens Barockarchitektur!" *Die Zukunft des Barockstils*, 23. Italics mine.

55 Redtenbacher, "Programm eine allgemeine Tektonik" and "Programm einer Architektonik." Mallgrave observes: "in short [Redtenbacher] proposes to mine the tectonic history of the field for lessons on how to reinvigorate underdeveloped formal systems using contemporary building methods." Mallgrave, *Modern Architectural Theory*, 200.

56 Long, "An Alternative Path to Modernism," 25 and note 41. Long discusses König's teaching methods, while also pointing out that other important mentors, such as Wagner and Loos, were often in contact with the same students.

57 Bayer, "Stilkrisen unser Zeit," 295. The translation is by Mallgrave, italics are mine. Mallgrave, *Modern Architectural Theory*, 201. Bayer (1827–1910), a philosopher educated in Prague, taught esthetics and architectural history at the Technische Hochschule Wien. See *Österreichisches Biographisches Lexicon*, vol. 1, 58–9. A few important excerpts from Bayer's writings are translated in Oechslin, *Otto Wagner, Adolf Loos and the Road to Modern Architecture*, 225–36. Also see Oechslin, "The Evolutionary Way to Modern Architecture," 363–410.

Chapter 3
Großstadt as *Barockstadt*:
Art History, Advertising and the
Surface of the Neo-Baroque

Albert Narath

Here capitalism and landlordism "their children have gathered, their city have built," and built it, apparently, with Rococo, Baroque, and Co. for their architects and decorators.

Grant Allen, 1890

In the middle of her 1911 novel *W.A.G.M.U.S.*, one of the earliest German-language works of fiction to take place within a modern department store, the author Margarete Böhme described a scene in the store's recently established furniture department. The character Karen Nickelson, an assistant in the department, discusses a pair of old wooden carved chests that had just arrived at the store. She explains to her manager that the pieces had to belong to the "German Renaissance," while the store's owner insisted that they belonged to the "Danzig Baroque." "The line is too simple and fine," she observes, "for *Baroque*; see, this is a purely architectonic movement, not in the least allied to *Baroque* or Rococo; I am sure it is rustic work of 1650 or even earlier."[1] Karen's astute visual argument reflected two decades of pioneering art historical analyses of the baroque by scholars from Cornelius Gurlitt to Heinrich Wölfflin.[2] Translated, however, from the realm of aesthetic contemplation to the idiom of shopping, the scene unfolds within a setting that might seem far removed from the hushed environment of the university lecture hall. Like the art galleries and grand carpet halls that emerged within Berlin department stores at the end of the nineteenth century, Böhme's description of the furniture department might be taken as a symbol for the uncanny conflation during this period of aesthetic cultivation with the fleeting and fickle gaze of the modern consumer. The finely tuned mechanisms of art historical analysis had become a vehicle for consumption.

Scholars have cast an important light on the connections between art history and the forces of capitalist modernity in Germany.[3] What interests us here is the previously unstudied role of the baroque in this process. In this essay, I argue that the carefully staged control of perception explored within baroque research in the 1880s and 1890s was closely related to the contemporaneous rise of another key area of visual research – modern advertising. As art historians described baroque façades with the language of the newspaper advertisement and as commentators, in turn, related the appearance of the advertisement to the persuasive effects of the baroque, architects themselves utilized both in their creation of a metropolitan neo-baroque dedicated to the attention-drawing play of surface effects. In its attempt to shed light on the intersection between the *Reklamewesen* of the baroque and the development of the neo-baroque in Berlin, this essay revolves around two case studies. The first is Gustav Ebe's design for a palatial residence for the advertising agent and publisher Rudolf Mosse, and the second is the architect Berhnhard Sehring's design for the main headquarters of the Tietz department store. Ultimately, this essay attempts to show that the specific mode of aesthetic attentiveness outlined by German art historians in their attempts to account for the formal effects of the baroque provided a flashpoint for important architectural debates concerning the experience of the modern metropolitan subject.

The Surface of the Baroque: Art History and Advertising

The connection between modern advertising and the baroque lies at the very heart of the historiography of the baroque, starting with a series of foundational art historical analyses of Giacomo da Vignola and Giacomo della Porta's plans for the façade of Il Gesù in Rome.

Figures 3.1 and 3.2   Plans for the façade of Il Gesù
Source: Heinrich Wölfflin, *Renaissance und Barock*, 1888.

By comparing engravings of Vignola's unbuilt composition and della Porta's scheme, art historians from Gurlitt to Wölfflin derived the basic formal characteristics of the baroque. Whereas Vignola's composition, still rooted in the artistic strategies of the Renaissance, aimed at the impression of lightness, calmness, crystalline clarity, and the direct interplay between interior and exterior, della Porta's façade had become, as Alois Riegl memorably put it, an "enormous wall in which everything has been set in motion vertically, horizontally and into depth."[4] On the surface of this wall, contradictions between verticality and horizontality and between upward motion and oppressive weight played themselves out in a display of nascent baroque dynamism.

In his foundational 1887 book *Geschichte des Barockstiles in Italien*, the architect, critic, and art historian Cornelius Gurlitt directly related the novelty of della Porta's wall to the visual strategies of the advertisement. Baroque architecture was, for him, a kind of *Reklamefläche* – an architectural billboard. After describing the façade's large repeating pedimental forms and its exaggeration of the central portal through the focused accretion of pediments, pilasters, columns and frames, Gurlitt argued, "The door attains an ever-greater importance, since the façade ceases to be the expression of the inner structure." Through its autonomous position, it becomes "a resplendent advertisement [*Reklame*] for the building, a showpiece [*Schaustück*]."[5]

Similar to Gurlitt's analysis of della Porta's earlier design for the façade of San Luigi dei Francesi, in which the effects of the building's "powerful wall" are likened to what he called a "patterned curtain" with only minimal relation to its interior, the "increasing richness of forms" deployed on the Gesù façade results in an almost a-tectonic effect.[6] "Architecture," he suggested, had to develop more and more according to the model of the designer or the painter from the school of Caravaggio, not for the sake of the expression of particular ideas, but rather in order to create new principles with light and shadow and with line-play and overlapping decorative forms that break away from the demands of a stubborn material and of structural truth.[7]

In this way, architecture sought out a new catalogue of formal effects that appealed directly to the eye.

Architecture became, in other words, *malerisch*. As has often been noted, the aesthetic category of the "painterly" played a central role in late-nineteenth-century accounts of the baroque.[8] The idea of the *malerisch* provided architectural historians with an overarching rubric for parsing the powerful formal effects of the baroque, as well as the underlying principles of style change. Art historians argued that painterly effects were generated by baroque architects through an illusion of movement, where the interplay of light and shadow, the dissolution of regular forms, and the overlapping of architectural elements creates a feeling of dynamism and restlessness. The eye is led "to and fro," as Wölfflin famously put it, across the blurred contours, superimpositions, and dislocations of the building's surface. This highly calibrated control of perception was generally considered crucial to the baroque's function as a tool for persuasion.

It is here that contemporary accounts of the nascent field of professional advertising went hand in hand with the art historical baroque. Gurlitt, Riegl, and Wölfflin's descriptions of the formal toolkit of the baroque architect – contrast, repetition, duplication, distortion, exaggeration, overlapping, flipping, framing, layering, and disruption – resonated deeply with the graphic strategies of the advertiser. In a discussion of the evolution of the modern advertisement, for example, the art historian and aesthetician Konrad Lange noted that in order to fulfil its function of "standing out from its neighbours," the printed ad "must be original, either through its baroque exaggeration or its baroque simplicity."[9] Whether affixed to a building or set into the pages of a newspaper, the advertisement, like the baroque façade, created a sensorium of the surface. Echoing art historical theories that connected the baroque's *malerisch* character to the primacy of vision, the senses of hearing, taste, smell, and touch which once mediated the customer's first-hand purchasing experience at the market stall were rendered obsolete. They gave way to the predominance of the faculty of vision.

In their manipulations of the surface, architecture and advertising shared a common preoccupation with the idea of attentiveness.[10] With the rediscovery of the baroque in the 1880s, the term *Aufmerksamkeit* was connected to a specific mode of visual experience in the writings of scholars such as Gurlitt, Wölfflin, and Riegl. This connection between heightened, yet vulnerable, states of attention and the *malerisch* quality of the style was, however, perhaps most clearly articulated by Geoffrey Scott in 1914:

> Since architecture itself does not move, and the movement is in our attention, drawn here and there by the design, held and liberated by its stress and accent, everything must depend upon the kind of attention the design invites. An attention that is restrained, however worthily, at the several points of the design; an attention at close focus and supplied by what it sees with a satisfying interest; an attention which is not led on, would yield no paramount sense of movement. … For this reason there exists in baroque architecture rhythm and direction and stress, but no repose – discord, even – till the eye comes to rest in the broad unity of the scheme, and the movements of the attention are resolved in controlling lines.[11]

This sense of directed movement, of controlled attention, connects the *malerisch* quality of the baroque to the notion of advertising put forward in the analyses of the Gesù façade. For art historians, della Porta's façade was a study in the close interplay of attention (*Aufmerksamkeit*) and distraction (*Ablenkung*) as they relate to the experience of architecture. To take one example, Wölfflin noted that the rectangular shape of the church's main doorway, with its segmental pediment, pilasters, base, and entablature, has the same proportions as the entire central section of the façade as a whole. This ratio is obscured, however, through the disruptive insertion of another pediment with half-columns into the area of the segmental pediment with pilasters. According to Wölfflin, in this concentration and amplification of form, "the insertion of another pediment and half-columns … detracts [or diverts attention, *Aufmerksamkeit*] from the authority of the pilaster order through its columns and sets itself up as the more important of the two orders presented as more important than the pilasters, thereby from them." He compared the building's effect on attention to "certain effects [or stimulants, *Reizmitteln*] in advanced musical composition."[12] Just like the *fortissimo* of a score, the formal effects of the baroque intensify the perceptual relationship between the viewer and the façade.

The conception of an architectural history of the baroque inflected through the concepts of attention and distraction was closely related to efforts by physiologists and psychologists to subject *Aufmerksamkeit* itself to observation, classification, and measurement. This can be seen in the work of the pioneering psychologist Wilhelm Wundt. In 1879, Wundt established what many historians of psychology consider as the first laboratory for experimental psychology. In his career-long effort to elucidate the mechanisms lying behind consciousness and experience, he championed a rigorous research method devoted to the observation and quantification of sensations. In a series of famous experiments, Wundt and his students recorded the time lapse between the registration of an external stimulus on a sense organ and the resulting movement of some member of the body. This was called the "reaction-time." The aim of these experiments was directed at recording as closely as possible the reaction time between a preliminary impression and a resulting motion.

Visuality was a privileged locus for the laboratory's enquiries into the transformation of a sensory stimulus into a psycho-physical impulse. The quantitative understanding of visual perception made it possible not only to measure attention, but also to guide and control it. Wundt's experiments therefore easily lent themselves to the purposes of advertising. One of the most direct applications of Wundt's ideas appeared in the experimental programme of the psychologist Harlow Stearns Gale. Gale was one of several North American students who travelled to Germany in the final decades of the nineteenth century to study under Wundt at his laboratory in Leipzig. After his time in Germany, Gale returned to the United States in 1895 as a professor of physiological psychology and director of the experimental psychology laboratory at the University of Minnesota. With the help of students in his seminars, he initiated multiple experiments into the psychological effects of advertising, including what he called "aesthetic experiments on proportions" and a series of investigations into attention.[13]

As reported in his self-published book *On the Psychology of Advertising*, based on a seminar from the academic year 1896–97, Gale and his students sought to measure and analyse the "attention value" of basic advertising motifs. They attempted to reproduce a subject's experience of rapidly turning the leaves of a magazine or newspaper.[14] In over 6,000 individual trials, subjects were positioned in a dark room furnished with a table, chair, and a small electric light rigged up to flash almost instantaneously. Complete pages taken from the advertising sections of three monthly magazines were fastened onto a vertical frame located two feet from the viewer. This distance was meant to approximate the conditions of reading. After a quick flash of light temporarily revealed a single magazine page, subjects were asked which part of the sheet first caught their attention. The length of the flash was deliberately conceived as the amount of time necessary to stimulate attention while disallowing the kind of comprehension gained from a more sustained encounter with the page.

The kind of perception staged in Gale's experiments was kindred in nature to the attentiveness stimulated by the formal composition of the baroque. This can be illustrated by comparing Gale's continually distracted subject with a famous portrait photograph of Wölfflin seated in his private study. The image depicts Wölfflin in the midst of contemplating a work of art. Like the participants in the advertising experiments, Wölfflin takes in the image at arm's length. Unlike Gale's experiments, however, he assumes a pose of sustained and contemplative engagement with the work of art.[15] The viewing conditions simulated in the Gale's laboratory contrasted sharply with the qualities of harmony, beauty, stasis, and balance that constituted the primary goals of "traditional" aesthetic contemplation. In several articles on art historical and pedagogical topics, Wölfflin contrasted this mode of cultivated and disciplined viewing with what he called the "savaged eye of today's man." This contrast followed the same logic as his distinction between Renaissance and baroque composition. Unlike the clarity and linearity of the Renaissance, Wölfflin linked this "straying of the eye without discipline," a characteristic attribute of spectatorship under the pressures of mass culture, to the *malerisch* effects of the baroque.[16] This, of course, was also the realm of the modern newspaper reader. The reader's fleeting attention continuously shifted from one stimulus to another, guided by a state of formal intoxication.

Surface Architecture

The architectural implications of this relationship between the aesthetic strategies of the baroque and the modern advertisement can be approached through the work of the Berlin-based architect and art historian Gustav Ebe. In 1886, Ebe published a monumental two-volume study entitled *Die Spät-Renaissance*. The book surveyed the evolution of architecture from Michelangelo to the emergence of neo-classicism. Its merit as an art historical source was soon questioned, and in time almost entirely forgotten, with the publication a year later of Cornelius Gurlitt's more thoroughly researched *Geschichte des Barockstiles in Italien*. Nevertheless, Ebe's book constituted one of the first attempts at a comprehensive history of art, architecture, and the decorative arts during the baroque era.

The book also sought to provide a theoretical and historical support for the renewed relevance of the baroque in contemporary architectural design. Reflecting the more general emergence of the baroque as a favoured historical model at the end of the nineteenth century, Ebe made clear at the beginning of the book that his own activity as an architect was the direct source of his "predilection for the study of the late-Renaissance." He boldly claimed: "Everything that has developed in architecture since [the late-Renaissance and baroque periods] is based consciously or unconsciously on the spatial combinations, as well as the constructions developed for them, devised in these disdained centuries."[17]

In addition to highlighting the style's political and cultural resonances, Ebe's conception of the baroque was closely tied to his critique of the legacy of "tectonic" theories of architecture. In his discussion of the Berlin work of Andreas Schlüter, for example, he contended: "If there is a transformation of antiquity which is also in accordance with northern fantasy, then the classical baroque of Schlüter corresponds with this more than the later Hellenistic Renaissance, whose primary objective – to dissolve the dichotomy between *Konstruktion* and *Kunstform* – could be just as little maintained as all earlier repetitions of the antique."[18] By distinguishing Schlüter's formal experimentation from the "Hellenistic Renaissance" in Berlin, Ebe raised a challenge to the tectonic school of the Bauakademie, which found its architectural expression in the buildings of Karl Friedrich Schinkel and its ultimate theoretical codification in Karl Bötticher's 1852 book *Die Tektonik der Hellenen*. In Bötticher's elaborate conception of tectonic expression, classical Greek architecture, reduced to its most basic elements, illustrated a perfect correspondence between a building's constructional system – its *Kernform* – and its exterior decorative scheme – its *Kunstform*. Ebe's conception of the baroque challenged the very notion of a union between construction and *Kunstform*.

Ebe's historical argument for the independence of the *Kunstform* in baroque architecture unfolded alongside his own resuscitation of the style in his practice. Starting in 1884, Ebe and his partner Julius Benda designed an urban palace for the powerful newspaper and advertising entrepreneur Rudolf Mosse.

Alongside other urban elites, Mosse represented the remarkable ascendancy of a wealthy and influential *Großbürgertum* in Berlin after the formation of the German Empire. In 1867, following a series of apprenticeships and jobs in bookstores and publishing offices, Mosse became convinced that Berlin was on the verge of transforming itself into an industrial and economic powerhouse: the *Metropole Deutschlands*, as he would call it. He opened his own newspaper advertising business in a building located at Friedrichstrasse 60, in the commercial heart of the Prussian capital.

The general spatial layout of the Mosse Palais consciously recalled the fluorescence of the *Palais* type in Berlin during the time of Friedrich I.[19] Ebe and Benda located the building's most important formal rooms in a block behind the Leipziger Platz façade. Completed in the first phase of construction, from 1883–84, this part of the project was described by commentators as drawing on Schlüter's language for the facade of the Royal Palace in Berlin. At one level, Ebe and Benda's appropriation of the German baroque at the Mosse Palais sought to reconcile the prevailing aristocratic and courtly connotations of the style with the recent emergence of a powerful and wealthy urban elite. At the same time, the project was an affirmation of the autonomy of the architectural surface. As can be seen in the widely published transverse section of the building, which shows that the main façade rises independently of the building's structural system, the Mosse Palais relied on an independent articulation of the surface. Through the contrasting textures and patterns created by the manipulation of elements such as the attic frieze, window frames, columns, pilasters, atlantes, rustication, and sculptural elements, the building operated as a kind of *Reklamefläche*, an architectural billboard that broadcasted Mosse's place in society.

Façade am Leipziger Platz.

Figure 3.3   Mosse Palais façade, Berlin, by Ebe and Benda, 1884–88

Ebe's manipulation of the *Kunstform* at the Mosse Palais resonated strongly with the graphic strategies that had been a subject of innovation in the Mosse office itself since its founding in the 1860s. Mosse's success was derived to a great degree from his carefully honed expertise in capturing the eye of the newspaper reader with optimal effect. Despite the seemingly chaotic and heterogeneous appearance of the typical advertising section in newspapers and magazines of the period, the format, order, and relative position of its individual components were carefully conceived. In the early 1880s, Mosse established an *Atelier für Inseratgestaltung* (Atelier for Advertisement Design) inside his Berlin office. The studio functioned as a kind of commercial laboratory devoted to the study and implementation of visual effects. Well before the founding of the first press research institute at the University of Leipzig in 1916, Mosse's atelier was concerned with optimizing the connection between newspaper advertising and perception. This was achieved through an examination of the relative effects of elements such as text content, typeface, framing, image, and the overall position of an advertisement on the page. One of the most significant results of this commercial research programme was the publication of a monumental *Klischee-Katalog* filled with over 1800 examples of fonts, signets, images, and borders. In addition to providing an extensive menu of motifs for the purpose of customized ordering, the catalogue was a record of the office's observation, categorization, and, ultimately, instrumentalization of perception.

Through its employment of these techniques, the newspaper was conceived of as an architectural facade. This is the subject of a rarely-discussed essay by the architect Hermann Muthesius published in the *Festschrift* produced by the Mosse company on the occasion of its fiftieth anniversary.[20] Muthesius argued that at its most basic level, the function of the newspaper advertisement is to attract attention ("die Aufmerksamkeit auf sich zu ziehen"). In this way, the extensive catalogue of formal operations developed over the years by Mosse followed at its most basic level the compositional principles of architecture. Returning to a theme that he often employed in his writings, Muthesius argued that the fundamental product of all human work was the creation of "rhythmic form." According to Muthesius, the areas of human activity that are most directly occupied with rhythm are music, as it relates to the ear, and architecture, as it relates to the eye. This essential connection to visuality means that the rules governing the composition of an architectural façade are the same ones underlying the newspaper advertisement's attempt to direct the gaze of the reader. If, as Muthesius suggested, "the entire domain of type and print falls under this concept of the architectural," then it is through the language of architecture that the basis for successful advertising is most effectively ascertained.[21]

In his analysis, Muthesius related the advertisement's triggering of sensation to the separation of beauty (*Schönheit*) from function (*Zweckmäßigkeit*) in a building. "In and of themselves," he claimed, "beauty and function have no inner connection to each other." Whereas architecture's functional obligations related to its fulfillment of practical needs, the beautiful was, as he put it, "an issue of sensation alone."[22] Arising from the shared principles of rhythm, proportion, colour, framing, and contrast, the visual effects of both the architectural facade and the advertisement are made possible by the manipulation of the *Kunstform*. Letters, borders, and images were to the *Inserat* what pilasters, friezes, and portals were to the exterior façade of the neo-baroque building.

Style Change and the City

This visual field also characterized the larger sensory environment of the modern metropolis. In his investigation of reading culture in Berlin during the Wilhelmine era, Peter Fritzsche has argued that the newspaper "was inseparable from the modern city and served as a perfect metonym for the city itself."[23] Contemporary observers of Berlin frequently employed the image of the newspaper to describe the distinct visual character of the metropolis. As a condensation of the city at large, the advertising section of the newspaper reflected the bewildering accretion of signs, posters, lettering, and electrically lit commercial displays in the streetscape. In the introduction to his popular 1895 book *Thinking, Feeling, Doing*, the experimental psychologist Edward Wheeler Scripture aligned the experience of the newspaper advertisement with the viewer's perception of the modern metropolis. Both presented examples of the negotiation between "a focus (or burning-point) of experience" and a wider "field of experience" that presents itself to a viewer when faced with a stimulus.[24]

As each new building in Berlin's developing commercial and residential districts sought to outdo its neighbor, the architecture of the city, like the advertising section of the newspaper, achieved what Cornelius Gurlitt described as a sustained state of "*fortissimo*." The traditionally sober architecture of Berlin had become "the most opulent, indeed the wildest in the world."[25] A cartoon published in an 1884 issue of *Fliegende Blätter* reflects the link between the accretion of architectural ornamentation and the logic of advertising.

The image depicts a group of city-dwellers hopelessly sucked into the entryway of a department store. A thick assemblage of advertisements frames the building's portal. As hats fly into the air and pedestrians grip for their lives onto the sides of buildings, architecture fulfils its function of "pulling in the public." In its manipulation of the *Kunstform* as a way of directing the attention of the onlooker, the building's commercial adornments function in an analogous way to the pediments, pilasters, and entablatures of the baroque façade.

The relation of this urban environment to attention was an important theme in the architect Adolf Göller's contemporaneous writings on the baroque.[26] Göller built an entire psychological theory of the baroque around the interconnection between attention and built form. In the first part of his book *Das ästhetische Gefühl*, Göller used Wundt's conception of the *Blickpunkt* to discuss the effect of exterior stimuli on attention.[27] He noted that each time we look, the surface of the retina is able to focus directly only on a single point in a field of vision. Peripheral objects appear vaguely defined and incomplete. This does not mean, however, that the eye must remain fixed to a single image in the *Blickpunkt*. A flash of light, sudden movement, or any other change to the field of vision is capable of shifting our attention to a previously outlying point of concentration.

As was the case in Gale's experiments on advertising, the stronger the image that enters the *Blickpunkt*, the more clearly and completely it captures our attention. Moreover, the strength of a sensorial impression increases the strength of our memory of it. Göller calls this power to recall an image our *Gedächtniskraft*. Stemming from the research of Wundt and, by extension, the work of the philosopher Johann Friedrich Herbart, Göller's treatment of perception revolved around the notion of a "memory image" (*Gedächtnisbild*). In several writings, he defined this term as the psychological residue of previously encountered forms. The mental work required in incorporating new sensorial impressions into the memory image becomes the basis for feelings of aesthetic enjoyment.

When mental work is no longer required in processing an impression, nothing more can be added to the memory image. This leads to the phenomenon of *Ermüdung* (jading), wherein forms lose their power to attract our attention. It is at this point that the architect or artist must devise new *Reizmittel* (stimulants) in an attempt to heighten visual effect. For Göller, the phenomenon of jading becomes a driving force in the change from one historical style to another.[28]

Figure 3.4   Cartoon of the "Riesen-Patent-Ventilator"
Source: Fliegende Blätter, 1884.

This concept was fundamental to Göller's psychological account of baroque architecture. For Göller, the baroque was both a specific point in the historical chronology of architecture and a more general state of form arising from the principles of hybridity, amplification, and increased stimulation. As architects in a baroque era heightened the impact of a building by arranging masses in new ways, by using new combinations of artistic forms within the plane of the façade, and by intensifying borrowed forms, the memory image of the observer was intensified. This occurs until the onset of a state of ultimate formal fatigue. "Like a conflagration," Göller suggested, "[the baroque] consumed all imaginable combinations of its own elements of form before it was extinguished." Ultimately, the baroque left "the sense of form utterly devastated."[29]

Göller's most thorough assessment of the baroque came in his 1888 book *Die Entstehung der architektonischen Stilformen*. The publication was devoted to a historical account of the development of architectural styles from the perspective of the aesthetic experience. In the book, Göller provided a basic definition of the baroque:

> With the term Baroque style, one signifies the transformation of architecture following the Renaissance, in which the existing elements of established structural forms [*Werkformen*], decorative ingredients, or the natural connection between both are discarded in order to heighten the formal appearance through abnormality and richness.[30]

Once again, the baroque's effects are achieved through the manipulation of the *Kunstform* at the expense of the expression of structural truth.[31] Göller noted: "No wonder that construction was now a hidden aspect of the building. One could no longer make an impression with it – that was now only possible with the exterior form! As a result, form only, but form *en masse*!"[32]

In this system, there is no such thing as an unchanging, ideal, and eternally beautiful style. Multiple times in his analyses of the baroque, Göller declared, "*Es ist keines bleibens!*"[33] In this way, the historical baroque resonated strongly with the situation of contemporary architects. Not only did architects at the end of the nineteenth century mine all past styles without compunction, but they also drove rapid changes in style. Göller saw no escape from architecture's increasing demands on attention. "The new style," he claimed, "would only have the choice between selecting from the forms of existing architectural styles or, developing a baroque style from the very beginning."[34]

The state of intoxication that Göller associated with the unbridled development of the *Kunstform* mirrors the constant search for novelty that commentators at the end of the nineteenth century attributed to the influence of fashion. He argued: "Only in recent architectural history does the fact occur that in the span of a few decades or years, one architectural style is lost and another is borrowed, just like one new costume [*Kleidertracht*] can replace another overnight."[35] Buildings and dresses evolved according to the same rules. In this way, Göller's theory of the baroque constituted a broader interrogation of the fate of architectural form under the forces of capitalism. Just as in Werner Sombart's contemporaneous interrogation of the production of continuous novelty in women's fashion, the amplified ornamentation of the neo-baroque was applied and perceived in the terms of exchange value. As Karl Scheffler put it in his 1913 book *Die Architektur der Großstadt*, the urban façade had become a *Handelsobjeckt*, an object of commerce. Unleashed from its functional and moral connection to structural motives, the façade now existed exclusively "for the external display of the commodity."[36]

The Tietz Department Store

Advertising and the aesthetic principles of the baroque found their most complete synthesis in Berlin through the development of the modern department store. Evident in common nicknames such as "glass palace," "palace of goods," or "palace of consumption," the department store had, in many ways, become the new baroque *Schloss*. In his 1908 book *Berliner Warenhäuser*, the author Leo Colze suggested:

> There are four rulers in Berlin, uncrowned emperors, whose strict regimes are everywhere acknowledged and whose governing decrees and proclamations give rise to much laudatory discussion. These uncrowned lords are the department stores, [they] are Wertheim, Tietz, Jandorf, and Kaufhaus des Westens. The transformation of Berlin into a major metropolis, a *Weltstadt*, is closely tied to the arrival of these shopping palaces.[37]

Echoing Mosse's nickname as the *Zeitungskönig*, a 1906 article in the journal *Soziale Revue* likened the names Tietz, Jandorf, and Wertheim to "German department store kings" and suggested that one could even speak of a "Tietz dynasty."[38] This new status was directly expressed on the exterior surfaces of Berlin's new department store buildings, where the neo-baroque was utilized as both a reminiscence of baroque palace architecture and a monumental advertisement.

Starting with Alfred Messel's famous design for the *Leipzigerstrasse* elevation of Wertheim Department Store, the façade emerged as a literal display of commodities. The glass façade reached its ultimate development at the Tietz Department Store, located as a pendent to Wertheim on the eastern end of *Leipzigerstrasse*. The architect Bernhard Sehring designed the building's grand interior staircase, lighting system, and exterior façades. The main attraction at Tietz was the building's expansive glass surface. Sehring's façade was dominated by two enormous fields of glass that stretched between a monumental sandstone projection marking the building's main entrance and a pair of side projections that provided secondary entries. Each glazed area measured 85 feet wide by 57 feet high. The surface's large panes of glass were divided almost imperceptibly through a matrix of extremely thin iron mullions. Extending through all of the store's floors, this was made possible by a series of load-bearing supports that stood almost seven feet behind the building's front surface. Architects celebrated the façade as the first curtain wall in Berlin. The building's front elevation was terminated vertically by an almost 10-foot-high sandstone cornice. Thanks to an innovative iron support system, the full weight of the cornice appeared to sit directly on top of the glass windows. Sehring's development of these neo-baroque architectural elements was rooted in both practical criteria and artistic motivations. Because of fire concerns, the city's *Baupolizei* limited the amount of glass that could be used on an elevation.

In the opinion of one visitor, Sehring's façade constituted "the apotheosis of the shop window."[39] It was repeatedly described as the *Endglied*, or termination point, of a development that led from the simple display window to "a single, imposing *Glashausschauseite*." By driving the logic of the shop window to its most extreme conclusion, the design represented an apotheosis of the *Kunstform*. While the neo-baroque language of the building's stone projections recalled the autonomous manipulation of the surface in the historical baroque, the project's glass curtain wall illustrated the further separation of surface from structure made possible by modern building materials and construction technologies.

Figure 3.5   Postcard of the Tietz Department Store
Source: Bernhard Sehring, 1899–1900.

In an essay on the department store, the writer Heinrich Pudor likened the Leipzigerstrasse façade of Tietz to the structure of the human body. Just as bones are situated on the inside of the body, covered over by an expressive surface of flesh, the idea of the curtain wall made it possible to displace a building's structural supports to the interior.[40]

In a review of Tietz for the journal *Berliner Architekturwelt*, the critic Hans Schliepmann noted that this structural system enabled Sehring to "build a gigantic and striking poster [*ein grosses und wirkungsvolles Plakat*] in front of the actual construction."[41] In this way, Tietz also constituted a culminating moment in the development of the modern advertisement. In addition to its extensive use as an image in ambitious (and to some, highly irritating) propaganda campaigns as a logo on signs, flyers, sandwich men, specially-decorated automobiles, and a battery of newspaper advertisements in the city's most popular dailies, the façade itself embodied the compositional principles of the advertisement. A memorial essay in honour of Sehring's 60th birthday noted that the building's façade constituted an "extraordinary escalation" of the advertisement.[42] Similarly, Schliepmann noted, "In the construction of department stores … the composition of the façade has essentially become a matter of an advertising display at is greatest scale."[43] Tietz was, in this way, a *Haus der Reklame*.[44]

Sehring's composition was especially effective at night. Over 10,000 electric bulbs illuminated the entire surface of the structure from within. Schliepmann noted, "In a dimension never before seen in Berlin, electric lighting – especially effective on the interior – is also drawn upon for the purposes of advertising, and here too Tietz trumps its predecessor Wertheim."[45] The glass portion of the façade allowed viewers on the building's exterior to see the dresses, textiles, and other products put on display inside. In addition, spectators could take in the even greater spectacle of shoppers browsing and purchasing items. According to one reviewer, this created a

> living advertisement that would be impossible in traditionally-conceived storefronts. … Those standing outside see the surging masses in the different departments of the store; they see the mass of merchandise from top to bottom and feel tempted to step inside. In a highly sophisticated way, the public itself therefore is used as a means for advertising.[46]

Like the *malerisch* decorations of the baroque façade brought to life, the "surging masses" of shoppers became an integral part of the store's decorational scheme. Dora Feigenbaum described this union of architecture and the commodity as an *Endglied* in the development of modern advertising."[47]

Feigenbaum also connected the Tietz façade to the aesthetic principles of the *malerisch*. "The pinnacle of economic-technological development," she argued, "corresponds to the union of painting and architecture."[48] From its sandstone neo-baroque ornamentation to its advanced glass skin, the architectural language at Tietz embodied the link between modern advertising and the visual strategies of the baroque. This becomes clear in contemporary accounts of the building's exterior effects. According to Schliepmann, "In the two glass surfaces, the eye searches in vain for a vertical construction form, and the stone entablature weighs down on the immense stretches of glass in a completely unmediated way."[49] As several commentators observed, the a-tectonic effects of the Tietz façade induced a sensation of restlessness. Caught between the continuous surface of the windows and the apparent weight of the entablature, the viewer's eye was not allowed the satisfaction of harmony and rest. Similar in its effect to art historical descriptions of the Gesù façade, Sehring's design could also be taken as a mature expression of the *Reklamewesen* of the neo-baroque.

Endnotes

1   Böhme, *The Department Store*, 300.

2   It is illuminating to note, in this regard, that Gurlitt's niece reportedly told Gurlitt that when he became a doctor, "Uncle Cornelius was not a medical doctor but a doctor of Rococo *Schraenken*." This story was reported in correspondence with Evonne Levy.

3   For example, see Schwartz, "Cathedrals and Shoes," *Blind Spots* and *The Werkbund*.

4   Riegl, *The Origins of Baroque Art in Rome*, 179.

5   Gurlitt, *Geschichte des Barockstiles in Italien*, 72.

6   Gurlitt, *Geschichte des Barockstiles in Italien*, 70.

7   Gurlitt, *Geschichte des Barockstiles in Italien*, 74.

8   See, for example, Payne, "Architecture, Ornament and Pictorialism" and Adler, "Painterly Politics."

9   Lange, "Der japanische Farbenholzschnitt," 90.

10 Jonathan Crary has shown that the category of attention became an important topos in debates about the nature of modernity within late-nineteenth-century visual culture. The most probing English-language account of the importance of attention during this time period remains his *Suspensions of Perception*. Crary has also engaged with this theme in "Attention, Spectacle, Counter-Memory," "Attention and Modernity in the Nineteenth Century," and "Unbinding Vision." For accounts of attention as it relates to early-twentieth-century Berlin, see Klonk, "Patterns of Attention" and Koepnick, *Framing Attention*.

11 Scott, *The Architecture of Humanism*, 116.

12 Wölfflin, *Renaissance and Barock*, 68; *Renaissance und Barock*, 56.

13 Documents related to the experiments on proportion are held among the Harlow Sterns Gale papers, vol. 1, box 2, University of Minnesota Archives, Minneapolis.

14 Gale, "On the Psychology of Advertising," 39–69.

15 For extended discussions of this photograph, see Koss, *Modernism after Wagner*, 77–83 and Celik, "Kinaesthetic Impulses," 211–12.

16 Wölfflin, "Wie man Skulpturen Aufnehmen Soll," 224–8. For an extended discussion of this article, see Celik, "Kinaesthetic Impulses," 201–12.

17 Ebe, *Die Spät-Renaissance*, 1–2.

18 Ebe, *Die Spät-Renaissance*, 626.

19 The design included a *cour d'honneur* based on the model of the *Hôtel particulier* outlined in Charles Augustin d'Aviler's 1691 *Cours d'architecture* (translated into German by the Berlin architect and theoretician Leonhard Christoph Sturm in 1699).

20 Muthesius, "Die künstlerische Zeitungsreklame." Although Muthesius's interest in the newspaper advertisement stemmed from his involvement in debates about advertising and design reform that unfolded within the intellectual orbit of the *Werkbund* after the turn of the twentieth century, his particular conception of the *Inserat* was rooted in the innovations of the Mosse office.

21 Muthesius, "Die künstlerische Zeitungsreklame," 82.

22 Muthesius, "Die künstlerische Zeitungsreklame," 82.

23 Fritzsche. *Reading Berlin 1900*, 23. The important role of the newspaper in the cultivation of a metropolitan reading culture, as well as in the subjective perception of the modern city itself, has been the subject of several recent studies. See, for example, Reuveni, *Reading Germany*; Ross, *Media and the Making of Modern Germany*. For an early study on the nature of the modern newspaper, see Wehle, *Die Zeitung*.

24 Scripture, *Thinking, Feeling, Doing*, 90.

25 Gurlitt, "Berliner Architektur," 30.

26 Although Göller was trained as an architect and taught classes on the technical aspects of building starting in the early 1880's at the Stuttgart *Polytechnikum*, he is best remembered for his lectures and publications dealing with architectural aesthetics. Göller's most important books were his 1887 *Zur Aesthetik der Architektur* and his posthumous manuscript *Das ästhetische Gefühl*, published in 1905.

27 Göller traces this concept back to the seventeenth-century philosopher Gottfried Wilhelm Leibniz's idea of "apperception."

28 Göller, "What is the Cause of Perpetual Style Change in Architecture?," 193–226.

29 Göller, "What is the Cause of Perpetual Style Change in Architecture?," 224.

30 Göller, *Die Entstehung der architektonischen Stilformen*, 359.

31 Göller noted, "In the wildest works of the Baroque style, the expression of the constructive or spatial performance of the building members are often lost or faked." *Die Entstehung der architektonischen Stilformen*, 359.

32 Göller, *Die Entstehung der architektonischen Stilformen*, 383.

33 Göller, *Die Entstehung der architektonischen Stilformen*, 453.

34 Göller, *Die Entstehung der architektonischen Stilformen*, 453.

35 Göller, *Die Entstehung der architektonischen Stilformen*, 439.

36 Scheffler, *Die Architektur der Großstadt*, 33.

37 Colze, *Berliner Warenhäuser*, 9.

38 Gladbach and Engel, "Beitrag zur Warenhausfrage," 274.

39 Bie, "Das Waarenhaus," 96.

40 Pudor, "Warenhäuser-Architektur," 25.

41 Schliepmann, "Zur Unseren Bildern," 319.

42 "Gedenkblatt zu seinem 60."

43 Schliepmann, "Zur Unseren Bildern," 318. Schliepmann also expressed this idea in "Das Geschäftshaus als Architekturproblem," 10–12.

44 Schliepmann, "Zur Unseren Bildern," 318.

45 Schliepmann, "Zur Unseren Bildern," 319.

46 Jaretzki, "Reklame und Architektur," 131.

47 Feigenbaum, "Die Reklame: Ihre Entwickelung und Bedeutung," 593.

48 Feigenbaum, "Die Reklame: Ihre Entwickelung und Bedeutung," 602.

49 Schliepmann, "Zur Unseren Bildern," 319.

Chapter 4

The "Restless Allure" of (Architectural) Form: Space and Perception between Germany, Russia and the Soviet Union

Luka Skansi

Space, Perception and City

The German sculptor and renowned art theorist Adolf Hildebrand witnessed the aftermath of radical transformations undergone by two important Italian historical squares: the Piazza Duomo in Florence and the Piazza San Marco in Venice. For different reasons, both had suffered a reconfiguration of their traditional spatial arrangements in the first decade of the twentieth century, the Florentine piazza having changed its ancient dimensions following the demolition of the episcopal palace, to the rear of the Baptistery, while the Venetian piazza had been brutally disfigured after the collapse of its bell-tower in 1902.

Hildebrand documented his experience in a curious article that appeared in 1908 in the German magazine *Raumkunst*. His emotional reactions to the new conditions of these two *piazze* are highly symptomatic, as are his reflections on the consequences of these urban transformations. In his eyes, the changes sustained by the Florentine square had permanently transformed the architectural sense of the Baptistery. Although the Baptistery was not, itself, directly implicated by the demolition of the episcopal palace, the erasure of its architectural background completely altered its significance. It had definitively lost its "rootedness" in relation to other monuments. It no longer served the task of defining the square between itself and the Duomo, while many of its details – the German sculptor focuses in particular on the reliefs of the bronze doors – no longer performed their original function of determining the character of those small spaces that had once existed between the Baptistery and its architectural setting. According to Hildebrand, the sculptural decoration of the lateral doors defined these small moments around the monument, and it had been composed to be observed from a space of that specific size: the reliefs defined the space, which were, at the same time, defined by it. In other words, for Hildebrand, form and space are indivisible: the form does not exist independent of the space in which it sits, and space can be defined only by means of an adequate volumetric and ornamental frame.

The astonishment of the German sculptor in front of the Piazza San Marco, orphaned of its monumental vertical element, is particularly significant. The complex is, for Hildebrand, now fundamentally altered, it is "stretched and glued to the ground," the basilica has become "small," "twisted" in relation to the square, "pushed into a corner;" the ornamentation of the Procuratie seems now to have assumed an unprecedented and disproportionate importance, behaving as "mice, when the cat is out of the house."[1]

In this case, too, the disappearance of an architectural element altered, in Hildebrand's eyes, not only the spatial configuration of the piazza, but the entire equilibrium of its parts. The tower, first of all, was the focal point of the square, "the strongest possible contrast to the disorder" represented by other buildings, which in turn comprised a rather horizontal complex of different architectures, each with its own language and structural rhythm. Secondly, the massive emergency of its collapse also undermined the scale of the ornamentation adorning the surrounding architecture because, following Hildebrand, the tower "influenced all further design on the square … without the tower, the spiritual relationship disappeared."[2]

"There is an intimate relationship" – Hildebrand continues – "between the character of the buildings and their spatial context."[3] This relationship is fundamental in defining the concept of form in general.

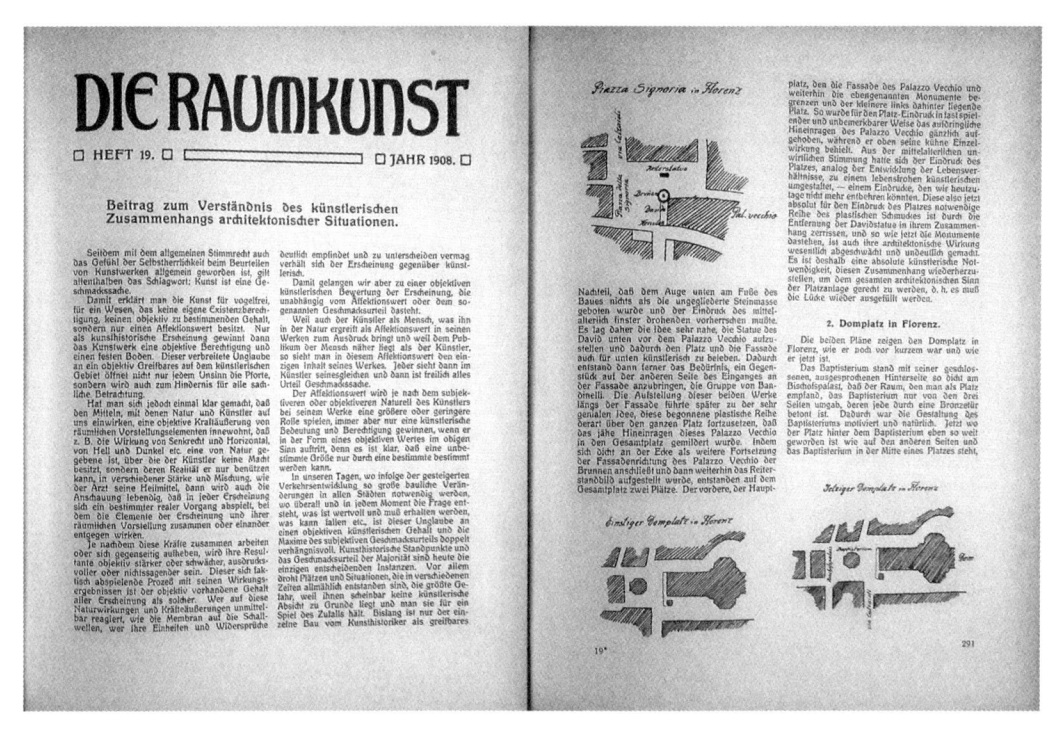

Figure 4.1   The transformation of the historical Italian square

Source: Adolf Hildebrand, "Beitrag zum Verständnis des künstlerischen Zusammenhangs architektonischer Situationen," *Die Raumkunst* 19 (1908).

An architectural or artistic work should be measured not only according to the "quality" of the form in and of itself, but more so according to its relationship with the space that defines it; mass and void are two indissoluble components, equally important for understanding the value of the artwork, its aesthetic significance. The spatiality of the form is, for Hildebrand, a "sensibility" that has been lost "with the development of museums and the conventions of considering works of art out of their original context, as individual, isolated." And the most difficult task of his present moment is to

> open people's eyes to the general law of all art, namely that the work of art is always conceived as a part of something larger, as part of a situation. … An artistic building is not valid solely in its own terms, but as part of an environment. The stronger this double life is, the wider the *field of action of the single image* [*Lebensraum des Einzelgebildes*] will be, and the greater, in turn, its artistic value will be.[4]

The sensibility shown by Hildebrand is far from unique. His words and his thoughts are not distant from those expressed by Albert Erich Brinckmann in his contemporaneous *Platz und Monument* (1908), which addressed, through the examination of a long series of European cities, the complex relationships that arise in the monumental spaces between architecture and sculptural elements. Using sketches, plans and photographs, Brinckmann structured a sort of handbook of urban composition in which he explored the different tools used in the history of urban planning: the juxtaposition of volumes and façades in relation to the articulation urban space, the positioning of statues as key elements for the articulation of the squares, the disposal of monumental fountains as optically corrective elements, the design of paving and the creation of differences in level in order to obtain effects of scale in specific public spaces.

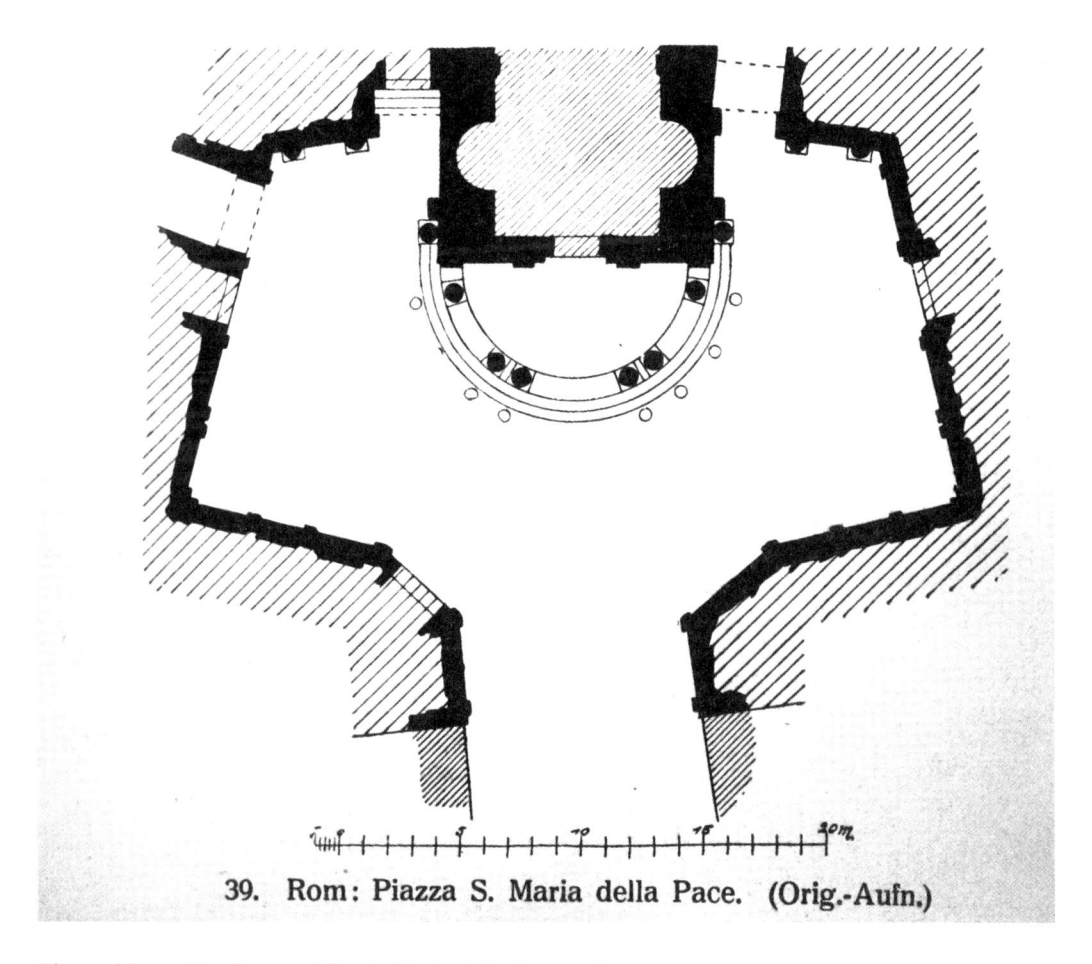

39. Rom: Piazza S. Maria della Pace. (Orig.-Aufn.)

Figure 4.2   The Piazza of Santa Maria della Pace in Rome
Source: Albert Erich Brinckmann, *Platz und Monument: Untersuchungen zur Geschichte und Ästhetik der Stadtbaukunst in neuerer Zeit* (Berlin, 1908).

Both of these authors, however, are indebted to a tradition defined at that time by the "artistic" viewing of the city that was well established in the German-speaking countries. On one hand is the famous *Der Städtebau nach seinen Künstlerischen Grundsätzen* (1889) by Camillo Sitte, where the concept of space becomes the leitmotif of urban analysis. Sitte's book is entirely focused on the study of the relationship between spatial contexts and architecture, between the size and characteristics of urban voids and the perception of the buildings, façades and objects that define them. On the other hand, the pioneering work of Hermann Maertens and, in particular, his *Das optische Masstab* (1877), defined a set of criteria for city planning entirely based on the viewpoints of the buildings. On the basis of his analyses, Maertens defined the physical and optical modes by which an observer perceives a work of architecture or a sculpture in urban space. He introduced an "optical scale" – only partially correlating with the "real" scale of the city – to structure the relationship between eye and object, based on factors of distance and the angle of observation. The different kinds of "information" on a building, or in Hildebrand's words, *single images* – the relationship of building to environment, the complete view of the building, the role of ornamental elements, and so forth – cannot be perceived simultaneously, but rather only in a temporal sequence following the movement of the observer in space.

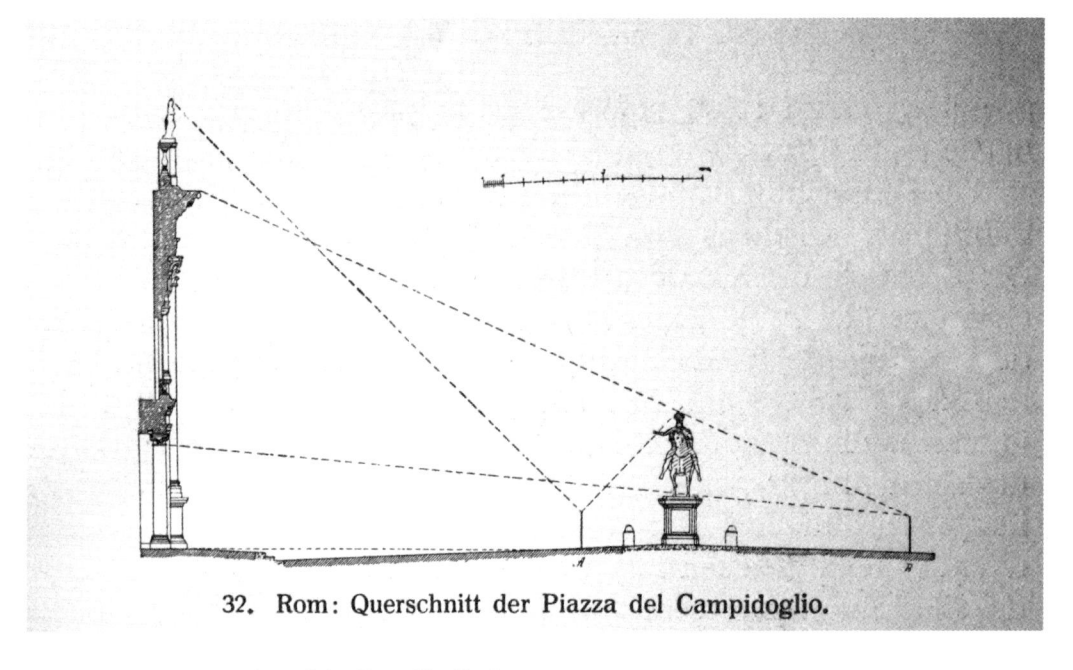

32. Rom: Querschnitt der Piazza del Campidoglio.

Figure 4.3 **The section of the Campidoglio Square**
Source: Albert Erich Brinckmann, *Platz und Monument: Untersuchungen zur Geschichte und Ästhetik der Stadtbaukunst in neuerer Zeit* (Berlin, 1908).

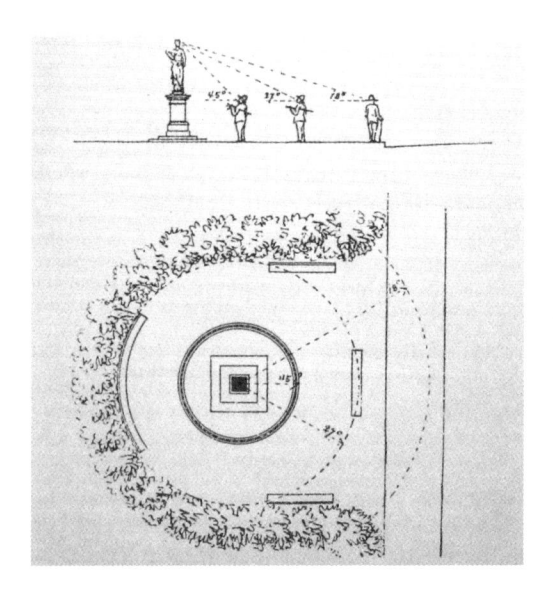

Figure 4.4 **The perception of monuments from different angles and distances**
Source: Hermann Maertens, *Das optische Masstab* (Bonn, 1877).

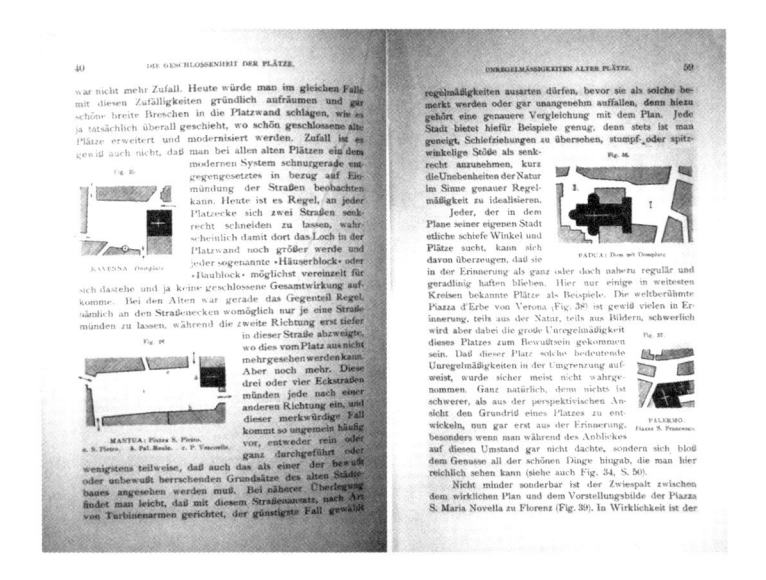

Figure 4.5 Camillo Sitte, *Der Städtebau nach seinen künstlerischen Grundsätzen*
Source: Vienna, 1889.

Indeed, the journal *Raumkunst* in which Hildebrand's essay first appeared expressed in a series of contributions its broader intentions to contribute to the education of a visual culture, towards a general artistic vision (*Künstlerische Sehen*) at all scales and in different disciplines of art and design, from wall painting, sculpture, interior design and architecture through to urban design.[5]

Although we can identify profound differences in the work of the various authors whose contributions to *Raumkunst* defined this programme,[6] it remains important to emphasize in this context their common view – one might call it an epistemological view – on the notion of form. These scholars each regard architecture as a complex phenomenon that does not end with those formal or linguistic aspects that are given by its volume and the set of architectural elements of which it is composed. It is delineated by relationships between its mass and the space it defines (or by which is defined): architecture is part of a broader spatial context and at the same time is itself a composite object that must be encountered and experienced in space and time.

There is, however, another crucial feature that connects the work of these authors. They together recognize in the relationship between object (the artwork) and subject (the observer) the centrality of the *process of perception*: the architectural or artistic object does not exist without a witness. The perceptual apparatus of man, his senses of vision or touch, indeed "measure" the work, value it and define its aesthetic criteria. This point is so fundamental that it became, for some of these authors, as will be seen later, the almost exclusive arbiter of architectural or artistic work.

Space, Perception and the Baroque

The revaluation of the "baroque" that took place in Germany between the last decades of the nineteenth century and the First World War is closely linked to this sensitivity to spatial aspects of form and to a growing emphasis on the process of perception. As is widely known, one of the main merits of Heinrich Wölfflin's historiography is his identification in the seventeenth-century arts of style with a specific idea of form: the baroque is, for Wölfflin, not a continuation or a "barbarization" of the Renaissance but an autonomous style, which insofar as its artistic value is concerned is absolutely equivalent in status to previous historical styles. "Baroque" – writes Wölfflin – "(or, let us say, modern art) is neither a rise nor a decline from classic, but a totally different art."[7] And later: "it is not a difference of quality if the baroque departed from the ideals of the age of Dürer and Raphael, but, as we have said, a different attitude to the world."[8]

His statements are supported by academic criteria that the Swiss art historian refined over the years spanning from *Renaissance und Barock* (1888) to the *Grundbegriffe* (1915) in order to support an art historical analysis operating on a large historiographical scale. His criteria are comparative in nature, defining the differences that characterize different epochs within an evolutionary view of history.[9] And among the so-called Renaissance and baroque periods[10] Wölfflin draws neat oppositions that essentially revolve, in fact, around the problem of the spatiality of form and its perception. In what he calls Renaissance and baroque a change occurs in the conception of form, and we witness therein a series of transformations: (1) from a linear to a *painterly* style, (2) from an epoch characterized by representation in planes to an epoch characterized by representation in depth, (3) from an epoch characterized by closed forms (*tectonic*) to one of open forms (*a-tectonic*), (4) from artworks made by parts of equal value, to artworks in which the individual elements are subordinated to a whole, (5) from a style in which objects are represented with absolute clarity to one in which they are depicted in a style of relative clarity.[11]

The baroque is therefore a *visual* art, or according to Wölfflin's famous definition, "malerisch" (painterly). Most of his analytical categories are based on visual effects because the art and architectural works he considers are composed of three-dimensional contrasts (rather than two-dimensional) and because the observer is an integral and constitutive part of their representation. He explains:

> Painterly architecture is particularly interested in making its basic form appear in as many and as various pictures as possible. While in the classic style the permanent form is emphasized and the variation of the appearance has beside it no independent value, the composition in the other case is from the outset laid out in "pictures." The more manifold they are, the more they diverge from the objective form, the more painterly the building is considered to be.[12]

Renaissance spaces are seen as absolute and intelligible, while in baroque artworks, spaces become complex to the point that they can be grasped only in a temporal succession. In other words, the mental reconstruction of Renaissance space is simultaneous and immediate, while the baroque is perceived through sequences and in the accumulation of images.

This *accumulation of images* is one of the fundamental thematics in the thought of Paul Frankl, one of Wölfflin's most brilliant students. In fact, he wrote a history of modern architecture on the basis of his teacher's comparative methods: *Die Entwicklungsphasen der neueren Baukunst* (1914). Frankl distinguished baroque architecture from that of the 1500s on the basis that the frontal image in baroque architecture was no longer necessarily the most important image, but rather one of what was potentially many: "It exists together with the other separate images as a partial representation."[13] But of what are the different *single images* comprised? Which of the architect's tools achieve this visual richness? Frankl lists a large array of factors – light and shade, distortions, convexity and concavity, elements that merge with others to confuse their legibility – that makes forms unclear: "This extreme lack of clarity gives to the whole composition a quality of *restless allure*."[14] And this is why, for Frankl, baroque architects give priority to the diagonal visualization of the building, since "the diagonal view now becomes a principal point of reference, because the dull lateral façade is a foil for the main façade. The view of any separate elevation does not satisfy us, since the others cannot be deduced from it."[15] This diagonal comprehension allows us to correlate the main façade with the rest of the building, or a sculptural detail with the whole artwork. And since, as explained above, there is no linearity or transitivity of meaning between the single, individual images, or parts – as in the case for either Frankl or Wölfflin in Renaissance buildings – the aesthetic value of baroque works lies in the relationship *between* different elements, the "tension" between systems. The observer is therefore called upon to continuously question the building in order to grasp the various nuances of the architecture by moving around and through: a process of perception that leads him, in a certain sense, to recomprise the fragments – the many images – into an overall, mental image of the building.

"Optical appearance" – continues Frankl – "is now primary not only for the impression (receptively) but also genetically. *The corporeal forms exist only to carry the visible phenomena. They serve light, not the reverse as in the first phase* [the Renaissance]."[16] According to Frankl, the baroque style comprises a *genetic* change in respect of the architecture of the first, Renaissance phase. It discards tectonic clarity since the new subject is the eye and the artwork maintains an ambiguous relationship with its own perception.[17] Its architects work with *a-tectonic* forms, with contrasts between light and shade; they curve masses, twist bodies, they build optical illusions: in this sense, the relationship with light becomes crucial. Light is sought out; it is key to achieving the desired effect. Rather than being "merely" illuminated baroque architecture seeks out an interdependent relationship with light, to incorporate it in the architecture itself and to render it as one of its own expressive elements.

Christof Thoenes recalls that the baroque and, in particular, the architecture of Borromini, was seen – up to the moment in which were written the German texts we are discussing – as heretical and impure, and was judged largely through "moral" criteria.[18] The credit of the historiographical work of authors like Schmarsow and Wölfflin, defined by Thoenes as "psychological," is that they renewed a sixteenth-century vision of architectural from: a permanent fact, firmly "anchored," something that should not move. Thoenes recognizes that by introducing into aesthetic criticism the categories of space and movement, they radically changed the entire historiographical problem of architecture. The reinterpretation of the baroque results, therefore, from a renewed definition of the status of form (space, movement) and, on the other, from a new critical lexicon, a new body of terms arising from a psychological, psychophysiological and empathetic reading of architecture and art. Thanks to the work of Wölfflin – starting from *Prolegomena zu einer Psychologie der Architektur* (1886) – movement becomes synonymous with emotional expression and psychology assumes responsibility for the explanation of how the observer perceives and understands the feelings expressed in art. With necessary distinctions, these theses were also the basis of August Schmarsow's historiographical work; for him architecture is *Raumgestalterin*, the creatress of space, and it can be experienced only through movement. According to Schmarsow, Borromini was motivated by a genuine "thirst for motion," introducing a "true rippling into the built mass" and making "a bursting, swelling and inhalation, a concerted conflation and constriction."[19] This is why, argues Thoenes, "for Schmarsow the aspect of architecture most readily perceived is *rhythm,* a fact which holds for the architecture of all epochs."[20] Thoenes states, however, that this vision of the baroque, described through concepts of dynamism and movement, was not entirely justified from the historiographical point of view because "if we return to Borromini's era, we find no traces of these concepts. ... [Dynamism] is in fact a retrospective projection of Modern expectations and tendencies onto the so called Baroque."[21]

Perception, Germany and Russia

> The perfect creations of the sunset of the Italian Renaissance, with the richness and fullness of their forms, with the strength and impetuosity of their pathos, reminiscent of a ripe and juicy fruit that overloads the branches that made them grow, remained for a long time misunderstood, both by admirers of beauty and art historians. Their shapes seemed only rude, abundance appeared annoying, their impetus violated offensively the cold beauty of the classic. Only after the works of Gurlitt, Schmarsow and Wölfflin and others, who have revealed, you may say, the perfection of these works and who defined baroque style as an independent phenomenon, it was possible to build a new compositional principle, the *principle of the painterly*, with its laws and its consequences.[22]

Reading this excerpt from one of the founding texts of the Soviet architect Moisej Ginzburg in the light of the proceeding discussion, it is revelatory to track its relationship with the German theoretical culture of the early twentieth century. His *Ritm v arhitekture* (1923) reads as though it was written in the first decade of the twentieth century by a German art historian – perhaps even by a pupil of Wölfflin – rather than by one of the principal figures of the constructivist avant-garde movement in the Soviet Union.[23] There are two reasons for this.

Firstly, the book had obviously appropriated topics from the German "formalist" debate. Ginzburg traces the essence of architecture – its aesthetic dimension – primarily in its formal characteristics, and specifically through rhythm, which is to say in the disposition of load-bearing elements in space. The load-bearing elements are defined by Ginzburg as elements of "driving forces" – similar, that is, to Wölfflin's metaphor of "vital forces." Yet the "laws of rhythm" are, for Ginzburg, architecture's "artistic laws:" definitions that are, in fact, quite anomalous when read in the context of the theoretical milieu that characterized the Soviet avant-garde movements of these years, with their insistence on utility, and on sociological and ideological issues in the architectural project.

Secondly, Ginzburg's debt to Germany is found in his vision of architecture as a multifaceted object that has to be read through a multiplicity of images. In this sense, his comparative reading of the Parthenon and the Erechtheion and his analysis of the different spatial displacement of the two Greek monuments serves to make this point. His reading recalls the interpretation of the relationship between monuments, city configuration and the movement of the observer, previously emphasized in the German text: for Ginzburg the Parthenon has an "elementary rhythm," the vision of its façade gives us "an extremely comprehensive view of its composition," and the movement confirms for us "the regularity of the monument." The Erechtheion, on the other hand, is "completely different," since it is composed of several entities, different arcade elements and projected volumes: "There is no stillness here," he writes, but rather a "liberation of movement, spontaneity of the built masses and a charming sense of surprise in the composition overall."[24] The general optical equilibrium is not given by symmetry and regularity, as it is in the Parthenon, but rather by a "set of pictorial effects" – those same effects that Wölfflin called *malerisch*.

Following this observation, we can find a third topic that Ginzburg's treatise clearly borrows from the German historiographical culture, both in its tenor and in its contents. Even for the Soviet architect the architecture of the baroque demands re-evaluation for its highly advanced use of light, its composition in depth, and for the optical illusions it creates:

> [The baroque] *tends toward indeterminacy, the vagueness of the overall.* … To achieve this, the architect recurs to the *elimination of boundaries and the exact limits of the monument. The play of light and shadow, the illumination of the architectural monument* becomes a new weapon *in solving compositional problems, the most important, changing and vibrant.*[25]

As noted above, the charm in which architects of this moment held baroque architecture lay with its loss of tectonic clarity and in the creation of ambiguities and complex images that should be perceived and experienced. Ginzburg concludes his reading of baroque devices with adjectives directly invoking the expressions used by Frankl and Wölfflin: "And, in fact, a genuinely *pictorial* architecture primarily models the mass and the details, with light and shadow, in whose contrast all its *restless essence* is manifest."[26]

Ginzburg's appreciation of baroque architecture follows the same principles as had informed the German theories. It should not be confused with an appreciation of its style or with a search for yet another linguistic motif to exhume in service of contemporary neo-historical operations. The subject of his discussion is not the "picturesque" language of the baroque, its style, but rather in the set of design tools that emerged from the work of baroque architects. The use of light, the denial of tectonics, the sculptural modelling of volumes, the complex design of space and the complex relationships between form and space: devices that are closely linked to the increased sensitivity to spatial aspects of form and that, after all, cannot be ascribed to a particular historical style. They represent tools pertinent to the entire history of architecture, used in different ways across the various epochs, and belong to what Wölfflin called an "art history without names." Ginzburg is completely aware of the nature of these tools, which is why they were available for him to consider as appropriate, too, for contemporary architecture.

A further point of contact between Ginzburg and Germany is represented by the recognition of the process of perception as a foundation for the entire theoretical discourse. In the introduction to his *Ritm v Arhitekture*, while defining the stages of mankind's psychophysical reactions to the vision of an object, Ginzburg claims that art's tendency is to emphasize an increasing difficulty of perception: the more vibrant the perception, the more complex the assimilation of a given object is likely to be. The *a-rhythmic* and non-regular forms, from the perspective of geometry and parataxis, prolong the perception: "the artist wants to force us to spend the maximum energy in perception; he wants to force us to find the law of rhythm in this apparent a-rhythmicity."[27] In the case of the Erechtheion the discourse becomes even clearer. Ginsburg sees this monument as a result of a kind of empathic composition that can be compared "with the songs and the dances of the primitive savages, that had moments of rhythmic acceleration and deceleration, a crescendo of dynamic action linked to the *growing intensity of perceptions*."[28]

The relationship between the Soviet architectural context and the theoretical construction of the Munich "formalist" school does not end with Ginzburg. Germany is an attractive pole for the young Russian students of the history and theory of art and architecture. The leading Russian historians of the first half of the twentieth century share a formative experience in Germany, and particularly in Munich, in which their ideas were shaped before the university chairs of art history, aesthetics and philosophy and the thinking of Konrad Fiedler, Theodor Lipps, August Schmarsow and Heinrich Wölfflin.

One figure who should be mentioned in this context is Aleksandr Gabričevskij, an art historian, theorist and colleague of Ginzburg at two major educational institutions in Moscow – Vchutemas and Rahn[29] – during these years. Gabričevskij experienced a formative period in Munich at Paul Frankl's chair during the years of the production and publication of his *Entwicklungsphasen*. Almost unknown to Western historiography, Gabričevskij's production was extraordinarily rich and concerned many varied theoretical aspects of artistic creation, music, philosophy and architecture, reflecting a range of interests and expertise extending from classical to contemporary subjects.[30] He is considered one of the founders of the modern historiography of art in the Soviet Union and, between 1923 and 1926, he taught three courses at the Vchutemas: "Renaissance," "History of Modern Painting" and "Theory of Spatial Arts." Gabričevskij's essays synthesize the German theoretical research on empathy and the theory of spatiality in the second half of the nineteenth century, but his knowledge of the German aesthetic literature becomes even more evident in the list of encyclopaedic entries he wrote for the dictionary of the Russian Bibliographic Institute.[31] Besides the monographic entries on "Tietze," "Schmarsow," "Riegl," "Schnaase" and "Worringer," he edited the entry "Formalnyj metod" (The Formal Method). He here identifies the main historiographical contribution of German-speaking scholars, not so much to the generally formalist approach to the study of art, but more so in their having institutionalized the contemporary *iskusstvovedenie* (art history) as an autonomous scientific discipline.[32]

It is not only art historians who kept an eye on these developments in Germany. In his essay "Teorija 'formal'nogo Metoda'" (1927), Boris Ejchenbaum attempted a first appraisal of the activity of the Soviet formalist literary school, emphasizing the important foundation that Wölfflin and Karl Voll[33] had served for their analytical work:

> In Germany, in fact, the theory and history of the figurative arts, the richest in experience and traditions, has taken a leading position in the study of the arts and begun to exert influence on both the general theory of art and on individual sciences, in particular, for example, on the study of literature.[34]

Ejchenbaum identifies in the work of German art historians new methods of interpretation that are strictly based on the materials of the same art, in other words, that are purely formal. This is precisely the effort of the Soviet literary formalists: to work primarily on the material of literature, to investigate laws that determine its linguistic and acoustic features. Contrasting the idea that form is an object containing other meanings (that of artistic value being found outside of form), they argued that form itself comprises an *inclusive* set, comprehensive and dynamic, independent from external correlations. If, for example, for symbolists poetry was a way of thinking with images, for formalists the poetic language is not *only* a language of images, but a utilitarian language, that serves to convey and communicate. Formalists perceive a complex system of languages, the practical purpose of which is secondary and the linguistic representations of which acquire an independent value.

Hence their interest in folk tales – constructed as they are with an ironic and allusive language – for poetry in general and for its lyrical digressions, for the paradox, for the way children communicate with one another and, finally, for the Futurist's *zaumnyj jazyk* (trans-mental language). As, perhaps, the most extreme stage of the autonomy of language, the trans-mental language, the arbitrary combination of sounds, is used as a technique to increase the difficulty of direct and automatic perception; artistic value is recognized in *perception* itself, which becomes the main object of the artwork. These features were also analysed in classic Russian literature in passages where subjects, actions or feelings were not named as such, but rather described, as they were seen, felt or understood to have happened for the first time – their becoming, in the course of the narrative, represented the artistic process identified by the formalists in the gradual perception of the object, action or meaning.

For the "formalist" culture, then, the problem of perception becomes the basis for a new reading of the art form. "Art" – writes Sklovskij – "is a way of 'feeling' the becoming of the object, while the 'already made' has no significance in art."[35] In this sense, art is defined *as a procedure*, with its own technique of *estrangement* (ostranenie), rendering perception more difficult and thereby obliging the mind to think of that which lies beneath the text (or, in the case of a work of art, a form). The similarities between this discourse and that of Wölfflin on the baroque are not casual:

> The baroque uses the same system of forms [as in Renaissance], but in place of the perfect, the completed, gives the restless, the *becoming*, in place of the limited, the conceivable, gives the limitless, the colossal. The ideal of beautiful proportion vanishes, interest concentrates not on being, but on happening. The masses, heavy and thickset, come into movement.[36]

Perception, Space and Vchutemas

If we search for concrete architectural consequences to the Soviet reception of German theories we encounter the theoretical and pedagogical work of Nikolaj Ladovskij. A figure active in various Moscow institutions and committees in the years immediately following the Revolution, Ladovskij was the founder and leader, along with Vladimir Krinskij and Nikolai Dokuchaev, of the movement of so-called "rationalist" architects.[37] His work, like that of other architects who gravitated to the group, was rarely understood in all its complexity, and was instead primarily seen in terms of its purportedly antagonistic opposition to the largest and most celebrated movement of constructivist architects – with the exception of a brilliant essay by Anatole Senkevitch, Jr., wherein the role of Ladovskij and his circle in the post-revolutionary context was properly valorized in all its complexity.[38]

Ladovskij promoted the most interesting didactic experiments conducted within the Vchutemas and based both his teaching and his research on analysis of the perception of architectural form and on the survey of its spatial dimensions. His research, followed by his students of the propaedeutic course "Space," represented a pioneering investigation on the plastic potentiality of architecture and had a major influence on Soviet architectural experiments of the 1920s. Along with courses on "Volume" and "Colour," his course on "Space" structured the famous Osnovnoe otdelenie (the foundation department) at the Vchutemas. This department comprised of an initial two-year-long training course that maintained some affinities with the Bauhaus *Vorkurs*.[39] After its completion, students were directed towards more advanced faculties and into various practical, specialist laboratories concerning metals, painting, poligraphics, and so forth. This introductory course was seen as the last "bastion" for the education of students in the general problems of art, a moment of resistance against immediate disciplinary specialization, and its task was to give students "the basic skills and the means of *artistic expression*." The analysis of space, as taught by Ladovskij, comprised a first step on the path towards a more specialized education in architecture in which students were taught how to "organize three-dimensional forms arranged in space" and how to model "forms of organic space."[40]

Ladovskij's educational process drew on the *psiho-analiticheskij metod* (psycho-analytic method), a teaching technique based on the exploration of students' psycho-physiological and perceptive abilities. Students were educated in what Hildebrand called *Kunstlerische sehen*, namely the refining of their sensitivity to (1) the vision of spatial forms, (2) the relationship between form and its context, and (3) the relationship between form and its viewpoints. "These three conditions" – explains Dokuchaev in the widely read pamphlet *Arkhitektura Vchutemasa* – "are the basic factors determining the main compositional tasks in each building."[41]

During this basic apprenticeship, students were asked to complete four exercises, each one directed to a different issue concerning the expressiveness of form. Each exercise composed, one might say, a *single image* of the future architecture; each solution represented a step towards the creation of a complex three-dimensional shape. In fact, students' responses to the four exercises were subsequently combined into a final model, made of clay or cardboard in a scale determined by the teacher.

Figure 4.6   **Photograph of a student model on the topic "Deep Frontal Composition" for the "Space" course at the Vkhutemas (Higher State Artistic Technical Studios), Moscow, between 1920 and 1926**

Source: Collection Centre Canadien d'Architecture/Canadian Centre for Architecture, Montréal; Gift of Howard Schickler and David Lafaille.

In the first exercise students were to give expressiveness to a two-dimensional plane. Without considering any wider spatial context and concentrating only on the frontal view of the surface, students were asked to work by cutting into the paper or modelling or digging the clay. The most frequent strategies they employed were the rhythmic play of voids, the manipulation and combination of papers of differing thicknesses. The second exercise saw students study the expression of a volume, thereby developing in a three-dimensional context the same devices that had been explored in the first stage. Cuts and excavations, vertical and horizontal rhythms were tested on an object "perceived by the observer through the movement around the vertical axis of the volume and through the dynamic-sensory perception of its form."[42] The third exercise, then, consisted of exploring the tectonic characterization of a three-dimensional object. Students were to express the massiveness of the volume by demonstrating the effects of weight. Mass, in Dokuchaev's words, "gives life to weight," and mouldings, cuts, contrasts between light and shadow, were used as design tools for expressing charge or release and to confer character upon the volume. The fourth and final exercise revisited the results of the previous three processes – the expression of plan, volume, mass – by placing a three-dimensional form in new conditions and a broader spatial context. The formal laws tested in earlier exercises were brought to bear upon new relationships, substituting other volumes into the same space and considering new points of view.

Figure 4.7   **Photograph of a student model on the topic "Finding and Constructing a Voluminous Form Based on Contrast and Rhythmical Combinations of Elements: Turn of the Form" for the "Space" course at the Vkhutemas (Higher State Artistic Technical Studios), Moscow, between 1920 and 1926**

Source: Collection Centre Canadien d'Architecture/Canadian Centre for Architecture, Montréal; Gift of Howard Schickler and David Lafaille.

On one hand, training in the expression of form; on the other, its constant re-evaluation according to ever-changing relations with space: from surface to volume, from the isolated object to the object in space. The psycho-analytic method sought to instil in students a sensitivity to the problems of formal expression, to teach design techniques that were, in fact, focused on "contrasting" the same form by throwing it into critical relief. In other words, Ladovskij's method trained students to define form by designing its negative – space. The tools of this technique were the rhythmic repetition of voids, contrasts between light and shadow, weight and lightness, linearity and materiality of the surface. These are all essentially of a visual and psychophysiological nature, which Ladovskij defined as scientific in an article in *Izvestija ASNOVA*.[43] In this sense, his approach differs from that implied by German aesthetic theory of the late nineteenth and early twentieth centuries for being, above all, a "de-empathized" vision of the process of perception. For Ladovskij, the psychophysical laws of perception led to a *rational architecture*: the capacity to build a platform of scientific, intelligible tools, serving an architecture of space. To transform, essentially, what were the sensibilities towards space expressed in German historiographical and analytical treatises into disciplinary tools of the architectural project.

Consider these aphorisms: "Architecture is the art that operates with space," writes Ladovskij, already in 1919. "Sculpture is the art which operates with form." "Space is present in every artistic discipline, but only architecture offers the possibility for a correct reading of space."[44] "*Space is the material of architecture, and not stone*. Space must assist the sculptural form in architecture."[45]

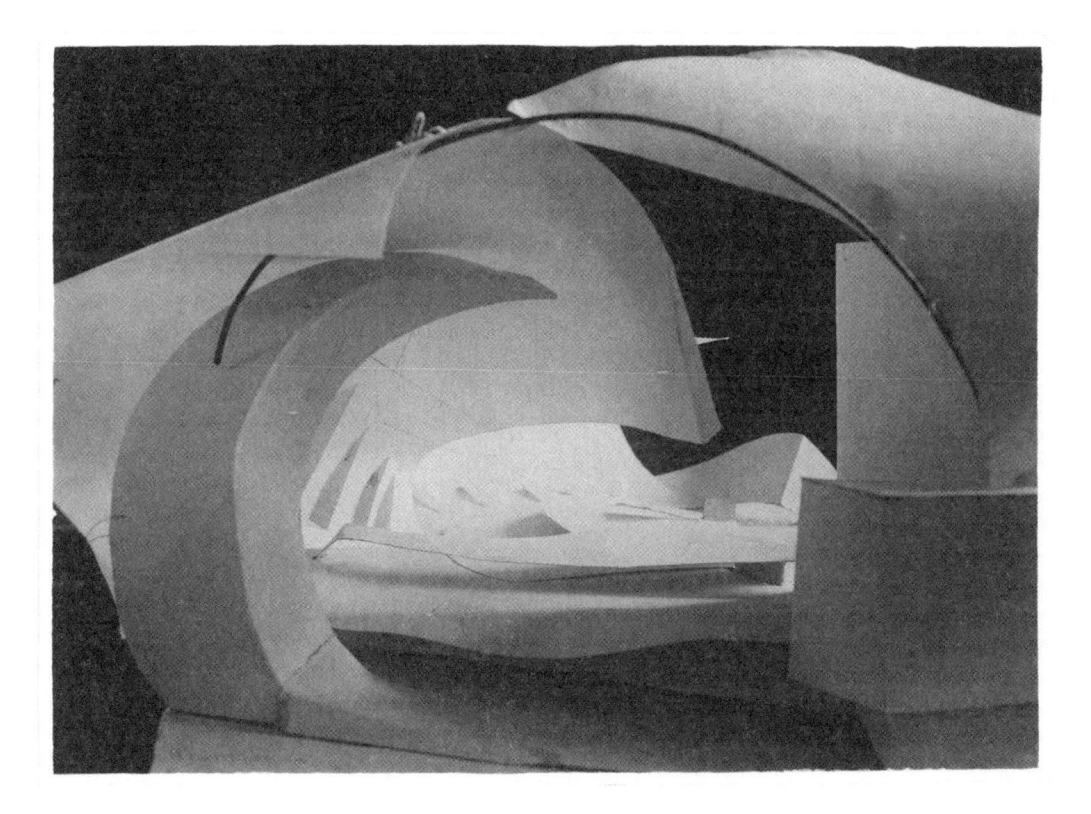

Figure 4.8   **Photograph of a student model on the topic "Deep Space with Strongly Emphasized Foreground" for the "Space" course at the Vkhutemas (Higher State Artistic Technical Studios), Moscow, between 1920 and 1926**

Source: Collection Centre Canadien d'Architecture/Canadian Centre for Architecture, Montréal; Gift of Howard Schickler and David Lafaille.

Rather than going deeper into Ladovskij's spatial sensitivity, it is important to emphasize, here, the nature of the uptake of German theories on spatiality within the Soviet context and its relationship, in turn, with the German setting. Although Ladovskij's words seem clearly derived from the fortunate definition that Schmarsow gave, in 1893, of architecture as *Raumgestalterin*, the art that creates space, it is rather difficult to demonstrate a direct relationship between these two authors.[46] It is possible, however, to contextualize Ladovskij's words in the Soviet cultural milieu of these years. Gabričevskij, for instance, wrote two major essays on spatial themes in 1923: "Arhitektura" and "Prostranstvo i massa v arhitekture" (Space and Mass in Architecture). Both pieces present an overview of the aesthetic and historical discussion on the notion of *Raumkunst* in German theory, from Georg Hegel to Theodor Lipps and down to Schmarsow. At the same time, behind Ginzburg's thoughts on the role of architecture's rhythmic component lies a strikingly similar vision. In his *Stil' i epoha* the architect of the Narkomfin states that "the fundamental problem of architecture is the delineation of space by means of material forms."[47] Both Ginzburg and Gabričevskij are active in the research programme of the Sekcija prostranstvennih iskustv (spatial arts section) of the Rahn – an institution that takes space as an object of multidisciplinary scientific discussion and investigation. Beyond the Rahn, an entire artistic milieu likewise took up the spatial problem of form as central to its research: Alexander Rodchenko, El Lissitzkij, Mikhail Matyushin, Naum Gabo (a former student of Wölfflin), to name just a few.

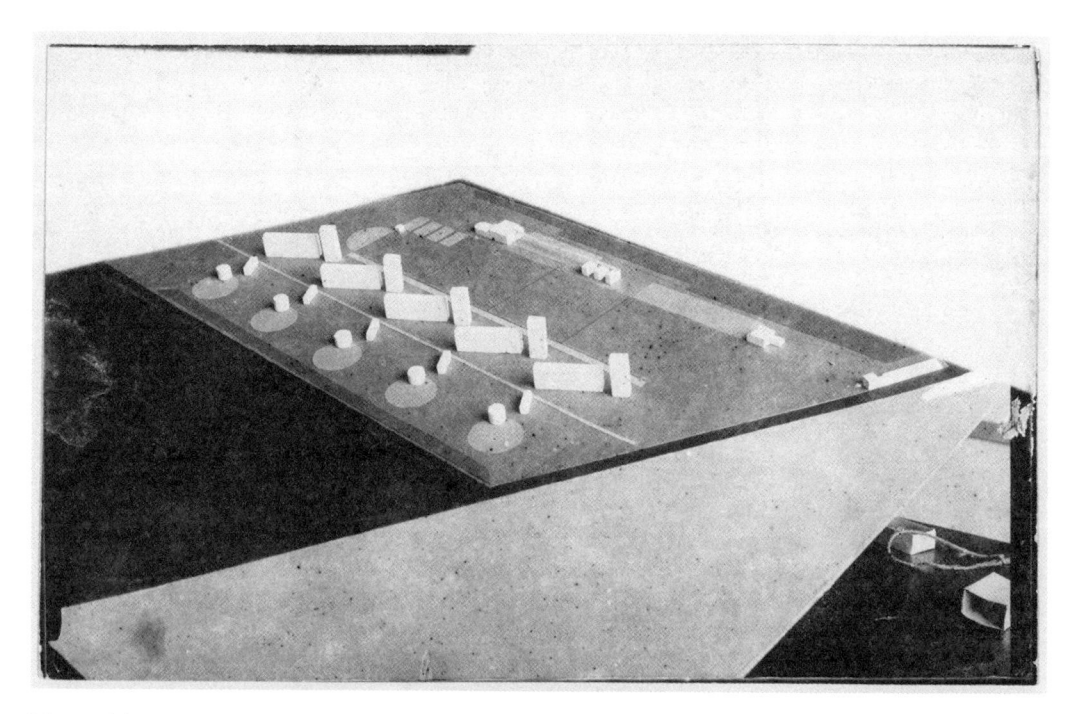

Figure 4.9   Photograph of a student model on the topic "Exercise on Creating the Expressive Spatial Design Composition out of the Architectural Volumes" for the "Space" course at the Vkhutein (Moscow Higher Technical Institute), Moscow, between 1929 and 1930

Source: Collection Centre Canadien d'Architecture/Canadian Centre for Architecture, Montréal; Gift of Howard Schickler and David Lafaille.

Finally, a number of art historians and theorists, some with very strong ties to Germany, base their formalist theory on the widely-read treatises introduced above: Pavel Florensky, for example, on the philosophical and epistemological notion of space; or Vladimir Favorskij on the evolution of techniques of spatial representation in art history.[48]

Favorskij, in fact, represents an additional – and perhaps even a definitive – link between the great era of German aesthetic thought and the educational processes to which the most renowned architecture school in the Soviet Union was subject in the years following the Revolution. He was a graphic and typographic designer, an engraver, painter, and teacher, but above all was an art theorist – a combination of expertise that made him a unique figure in Russia at that moment. An active artist dealing with the aesthetic problems of art and architecture in a theoretically structured way, while at the same time being engaged in the education of art and the organization of its institutions: between 1923 and 1926 he was rector of Vchutemas and was directly responsible for the appointments of Gabrichevskij and Florensky to strengthen the theoretical disciplines within that school.

As early as 1905 Favorskij had the crucial formative experience of studying painting at the private school of Simon Hollóssy and attending, until 1907, the art historical lectures of Karl Voll and Adolf Furtwängler. His major achievement of these years was his translation into Russian of Hildebrand's *Das Problem der Form der bildenden Kunst*, published in 1914 along with translations of nine other essays that the German sculptor had written in the first decade of the twentieth century – including the essay with which we began, namely "Beitrag zum Verständnis des künstlerischen Zusammenhangs."[49] The Favorskij edition of Hildebrand's work followed other important, roughly contemporary, translations of Wölfflin's *Die Klassische Kunst* (1912), *Renaissance und Barock* (1913) and *Kunstgeschichtliche Grundbegriffe* (1922) and, a little later, Brinckmann's *Raum und Plastik* (1935). So, too, were translated in these years the books and essays of Munich-based historians Wilhelm Hausenstein and Oskar Wulff, to give two more names from a long list of authors whose works were important to Russian readers. Beyond the history of art, too, many books by Oswald Spengler were already translated before the First World War, while seminal studies by Hermann Helmholtz, Ernst Mach and Wilhelm Wundt on physiology and optics, extremely important for the psycho-physiological dimensions of the formalist reading of art and architecture, were at the centre of the important epistemological debate concerning the relationships between science, politics and art – a debate with decisive impact on Marxist culture between the two revolutions of 1905 and 1917.[50]

In his brief introduction to the *Problema formy*, Favorskij defines Hildebrand as one of the most important intellectual authorities on contemporary art, while his works "should be regarded as monuments of the highest aesthetic culture of our time."[51] For Favorskij, the principles of *Problema formy* are based, on one hand, upon a "vital protest against the naturalistic art of the nineteenth century in which the *functional* aspect prevails often at the expense of visual integrity."[52] On the other, they underpin a renewed study of art history that is not merely limited to an historiographical process, but instead responds to an attempt to extrapolate from history its general principles and to produce meanings "for all, even for contemporary art, which can be countered by efforts *to build on an aesthetic that is exclusively based on the psychological foundations of perception.*"[53]

Hildebrand and the Soviet Union

Das Problem der Form der bildenden Kunst exercised an enormous influence on generations of German artists, from the final decade of the nineteenth century through to the First World War. Written while Hildebrand was residing in Italy, documenting a lively dialogue with Fiedler and Marees and drawing upon the physiological research of Hermann Helmholtz, his book casts the notion of *space* as holding a crucial, if not exclusively so, role in the figurative arts. His analysis of the perception of artworks brings Hildebrand – in the chapters regarding the techniques of representation – to a redefinition of the role of the artist.[54] Rather than attempting the true representation of objects, the artist should think about the way his work will be seen, felt, experienced. The artist, according to Hildebrand, must establish a vocabulary of effects to establish the illusion of the object, providing instructions for its perception based on differing viewpoints. Hildebrand called *existential* that form that depends exclusively on the object and which is not subject to deformation. In contrast to this, however, is *effectual* form, the product of expressing such effects as lighting, contrast, and relationships with context and background. The first is fixed. The second is active, establishing relationships and contrasts. "The artist enriches our intercourse with Nature so far as his individual talent enables him to bring the actual form into situations which lend it new but normal accents of effectiveness."[55]

The work thus exists in a constant relationship between form and its effects, between the isolated object and its ever-changing settings, between the depiction of an image and the isolation of its appearance. Thus, for Hildebrand, the artistic value of the artwork is measured by the quality of these relationships:

> … all the instructions in proportion which have been formulated for Art have arisen out of a fundamental misconception. The requisite proportions must be worked out each time anew with respect to the work as a whole. No work of art can result from a simple addition of invariable proportions in details. Only in such works of art as constantly repeat their parts in the total arrangement.[56]

In the absence of universal laws governing the representation of pictorial or sculptural elements, the "instructions" pertaining to these relationships must be periodically redefined according to internal and exterior changes in the nature of art and its perception. These laws are independent from the laws of a realistic or naturalistic representation because they are established according to the processes by which the observer perceives – and which demand of the artist that he inspires the observer using all the pictorial effects available to him. In this sense, for Hildebrand any realistic, mimetic attitude is totally superfluous, since it is the depiction of space, and not the depiction of the object, that is most problematic for the artist. Since the only effect that enlivens an object for its viewer is its spatial field, we might say that Hildebrand regards the legitimacy of any realistic or naturalistic attitude in artistic representation as having been definitively demolished by the modern theory of art. Art is an artifice, a summation of effects and techniques employed without ambitions toward reality. Space, however, is a tool for building plasticity and the appearance the artwork. It is the exclusive tool of artifice. And the artistic talent of a painter lay, for Hildebrand, in his discovery of an object's spatial values – in his expression of the *Kunstlerische sehen* (in Russian, *hudozhestvenno vedenie*). In this sense, space serves as a manifesto in relation to reality. From the intuitive sensorium of the body according to the Kantian conception of the problem it first becomes an aesthetic criteria, and then an artistic tool. From intuition, experience becomes illusion:

> Our relation to the world of vision consists chiefly in our perception of its spatial attributes. Without this, orientation in the outer world is absolutely impossible. We must, therefore, consider our general spatial ideas and the perception of spatial form as the most important facts in our conception of the reality of things.[57]

The influence of Hildebrand's text on Ladovskij and the whole rationalist environment cannot be underestimated. *Das Problem der Form* was written, however, as a manual for sculptural education, and besides a few short paragraphs and the aforementioned essay on the transformation of the squares of Florence and Venice, Hildebrand never really confronted architectural themes. The reflections of Ladovskij clearly rest upon far more heterogeneous body of sources than Hildebrand alone.

As this essay has attempted to show, different German-language sources are already present in the late-imperial cultural environment of Russia; at the same time, many figures act as channels of transmission between the two countries. And one should not think only of isolated channels: the issues of the spatiality of form, the centrality of the process of perception, the reception of the baroque – all themes that are deeply interconnected – are subjects of discussion across the entire academic community in Russia. In this sense, the panorama of cultural institutions in Moscow after the revolution appears increasingly rich and entwined. The more we look at the structure of the faculty of the leading Soviet school of art and architecture – the *Vchutemas* – the more the historiographical mystification, and narrowness, in which it had been confined is made evident. Besides the extraordinary graphic, volumetric and planning experiments of this school, the rejuvenation of its theoretical education after 1921 – tracking the contributions of Favorskij and Ginzburg, and then Gabričevskij and Florenskij – constituted a real critical counterpart to the well-known values of productivism, constructivism, appeals for the organization of production and for the activism of architects as the producers of a new socialist reality.

This counterpart had, however, a difficult existence, and performed a significant task for which there was little gratitude. Difficult because many of the cultural operations described in this essay would be immediately labelled as "formalism" and dismissed according to the criticism that cast this word in trivial and essentially speculative terms, emptying its meaning from its original complexity. Difficult, too, because the intellectuals who gave this body of ideas shape and purpose would be fought not only on academic grounds, but also and later, as experienced by Florenskij and Gabrichevskij, on an ideological terrain. It was also a thankless task, however, because in an epoch orientated towards the idolatry of technology, the exasperation of the role of function in architecture, the ideological ambitions of the architect to assume a central role in the process of revolutionary social change, to speak of space, form, light and shadow was to speak, essentially, of architecture's *autonomy*.

Author's Note

This essay documents research undertaken on the Vkhutemas Fonds in the collection of the Canadian Center for Architecture in Montreal, where I was a Visiting Scholar in 2012. To this institution, and its Study Centre in particular, I wish to express my sincerest thanks for their warm welcome and support.

Endnotes

1 Hildebrand, "Beitrag zum Verständnis des künstlerischen Zusammenhangs architektonischer Situationen," 292.

2 Hildebrand, "Beitrag zum Verständnis des künstlerischen Zusammenhangs architektonischer Situationen," 293.

3 Hildebrand, "Beitrag zum Verständnis des künstlerischen Zusammenhangs architektonischer Situationen," 289.

4 Hildebrand, "Beitrag zum Verständnis des künstlerischen Zusammenhangs architektonischer Situationen," 296.

5 The journal, which was subtitled *Halbmonatshefte fur Kritik und Gestaltung in der Baukunst un Verwandten Gebieten*, was based in Munich between 1908 and 1909. In its editorial board we find Theodor Fischer, Max Läuger and Richard Riemerschmid.

6 The differences characterize in particular Sitte and Maertens. These two architect-theoreticians often found themselves occupying diametrically opposite positions in their various debates. See, for example, the debate on the Cologne Cathedral and the discussion about the demolition project of the surrounding architecture, considered in Ladd, *Urban Planning and Civic Order in Germany*, 118–20.

7 Wölfflin, *Principles of Art History*, 14.

8 Wölfflin, *Principles of Art History*, 16.

9 On the relationship between German historiography and studies in cultural history, see Hassold, "The Baroque as a Basic Concept of Art," 3–28.

10 The chronological classifications are quite different from what was later recognized as the baroque style, as for example by Wittkower. Wölfflin considers Michelangelo the father of the baroque and accordingly set the beginning of the "baroque phase" in 1580. See introduction of Wölfflin's *Renaissance and Baroque*. His student Frankl, conversely, commenced it in 1550.

11 These concepts are expressed in Wölfflin's *Kunstgeschichtliche Grundbegriffe*.

12 Wölfflin, *Principles of Art History*, 64.

13 Frankl, *Principles of Architectural History*, 149.

14 Frankl, *Principles of Architectural History*, 148. Italics mine.

15 Frankl, *Principles of Architectural History*, 148. Frankl goes on (149) to use both architectural examples (Borromini's *S. Carlo alle Quattro Fontane*) and sculptural groups (as Bernini's *L'estasi di Santa Teresa*).

16 Frankl, *Principles of Architectural History*, 149. Italics mine.

17 The relation between the human eye and baroque was, of course, already pointed out by Wölfflin: "But for the baroque, new possibilities are given precisely by the fact that, beside the reality for the body, there exists a reality for the eye." Wölfflin, *Principles of Art History*, 72.

18 Thoenes, "Die Formen sind in Bewegung geraten" ("Form has been set in motion"), 63–73.

19 These phrases are taken from Thoenes's quotation of Schmarsow's *Barock und Rokoko*, where the latter describes the lantern of St. Ivo alla Sapienza. Thoenes, "Form has been set in motion," 67.

20 Thoenes, "Form has been set in motion," 67.

21 Thoenes states that the term "movement" appears in seventeenth-century documents only in reference to the precarious conditions of a structure ("the cupola is moving"). It is never used, however, as a metaphor to account for the relationship between the architectural work and a living organism. Thoenes quotes one exception from Borromini's *Opus architectonicum*: "In order to lend the façade its form, I imagined a person with outstretched arms wanting to embrace everyone who entered," but he defines it as "semantic, of rhetorical tradition." Thoenes, "Form has been set in motion," 68.

22 Italics mine. Ginzburg, *Saggi sull'architettura costruttivista*, 45.

23 For historical contextualization of Ginzburg's first work see Senkevitch, "Introduction" to Ginzburg, *Style and Epoch*; and Skansi, "Form, Style, History, Autonomy," 26–49.

24 Ginzburg, *Saggi sull'architettura costruttivista*, 47.

25 Ginzburg, *Saggi sull'architettura costruttivista*, 49. Italics mine.

26 Ginzburg, *Saggi sull'architettura costruttivista*, 50. Italics mine.

27 Ginzburg, *Saggi sull'architettura costruttivista*, 16.

28 Ginzburg, *Saggi sull'architettura costruttivista*, 47.

29 The *Rossijska akademija hudožestvennih nauk* (Russian Academy of Artistic Sciences). On Rahn see Bowlt (ed.), *Russian Art of the Avant-garde*; Perceva, "Poiski form vsaimosvjazi nauki i iskusstva (po materijalom Gahna);" and Skansi, "What is Artistic Form?"

30   See Markuzon, "Aleksandr G. Gabričevskij (1981–1968)"; Ol'ga Severzeva, "Breve profilo di un intelettuale negli anni di Stalin"; and Pogodin, *A. G. Gabričevskij*. Gabričevskij's books include *Sbornik Materialov*, *Teorija i istorija arhitekturi* and *Morfologija iskusstva*.

31   Gabričevskij, *Arhitektura* (1923), *Prostranstvo i massa v arhitekturi* (1923, Space and Mass in Architecture) and *Problema arhitekturnogo sinteza kak vzaimnoj organizacii massi i prostranstva* (1924, The Problem of Architectural Synthesis as a Mutual Organization of Mass and Space), all in *Teorija i istorija arhitekturi*. See this collection also for entries in the *Enciklopedičeskij slovar Russkogo bibliografičeskogo instituta Granat* (Moscow, 1926–27).

32   This theme is developed in Skansi, "What is Artistic Form?"

33   Voll (1867–1917) was a German scholar of the Renaissance and baroque, known for his comparative study of the paintings, *Vergleichende Gemäldestudien* (1908).

34   Ejchenbaum, "La teoria del 'metodo formale'," 33.

35   Sklovskij, "L'arte come procedimento," 86.

36   Wölfflin, *Principles of Art History*, 10.

37   This association is initially composed by Ladovskij, Efimov, Krinskij, Petrov, Dokuchaev and Mapu. See *Mastera sovjetskoj arhitekturi ob arhitekture*, 338.

38   Senkevitch, "Aspects of Spatial Form and Perceptual Psychology in the Doctrine of the Rationalist Movement in Soviet Architecture in the 1920s," 78–115. This fundamental essay is the result of Senkevitch's PhD dissertation, "Trends in Soviet Architectural Thought, 1917–1932" (1974).

39   Contact between the two schools is documented by Scheidig in *Crafts of the Weimar Bauhaus*.

40   Dokuchaev, *Arhitektura Vchutemasa*, vii.

41   Dokuchaev, *Arhitektura Vchutemasa*, viii.

42   Dokuchaev, *Arhitektura Vchutemasa*, ix.

43   Ladovskij retained the necessity of providing the architect of a basic psychology and physiology knowledge. Ladovskij, "Psiho-tehnicheskaja laboratorija arhitekturi," 7. Ladovskij named Hugo Munstenberg and his colleagues at the Harvard Psychological Laboratory as the main scientific source of his psychoanalytical method. See Senkevitch, "Aspects of Spatial Form."

44   Ladovskij, "Iz protokolov zasedanija komissii zhivopisno-skulpturno-arhitekturnogo sinteza," 343–4.

45   Ladovskij, "O roli prostrannstva v arhitekture i o haraktere sinteza arhitekturi, skulpturi i zhivopisi," 344. Italics mine.

46   "Psychologically, the intuited form of three dimensional space arises through the experiences of our sense of sight, whether or not assisted by other physiological factors. All our visual perceptions and ideas are arranged, are ordered, and unfold in accordance with this intuited form; and this fact is the mother lode of art whose origin we seek. … Our sense of space [*Raumgefühl*] and spatial imagination [*Raumphantasie*] press toward spatial creation [*Raumgestaltung*]; they seek their satisfaction in art. We call this art architecture; in plain words, it is the creatress of space [*Raumgestalterin*]." Schmarsow, *The Essence of Architectural Creation*, 286–7.

47   Ginzburg, *Stile ed epoca*, 77.

48   See Florenskij, *Lekcii vo Vchutemase 1923–24 gg*; and Favorskij, *Literarno-Teoretičeskoe nasledje*.

49   Favorskij initiated a translation of Voll's *Vergleichende Gemäldestudien* in 1916, but this was never completed.

50   On this topic see Skansi, "Form, Style, History, Autonomy."

51   Favorskij, *Problema formy*, 12.

52   Favorskij, *Problema formy*, 14. Italics mine.

53   Favorskij, *Problema formy*, 14. Italics mine.

54   This thesis is meticulously described by Hildebrand in "Visual and Kinesthetic Ideas," 229–32.

55   Hildebrand, *The Problem of Form*, 41.

56   Hildebrand, *The Problem of Form*, 45–6.

57   Hildebrand, *The Problem of Form*, 17.

Chapter 5
Geoffrey Scott, the Baroque, and the Picturesque

John Macarthur

Geoffrey Scott's *The Architecture of Humanism* of 1914 is known for its well-argued critique of nineteenth-century British architectural theory, but Scott also offers a new theory of architecture explained as "space," which draws upon German empathy theory of the previous decades. Scott's is the first account in English of space in the modern sense, as a perceptible quality of architecture, and indeed its medium. It is generally agreed that Scott's attack on nineteenth-century theory, what he called "the Fallacies," cleared the way for new thinking in the twentieth century. Whether the "humanist values" that the book proposed were that new thinking or a clever defence of tradition remains unclear, though, as his examples are almost exclusively drawn from the Italian baroque, and the humanist values draw as much on the picturesque as they do on empathy theory.

It is difficult to fix and analyse Scott's argument because his sources are not thoroughly acknowledged and are sometimes misleading. In part, this resulted from the form of Scott's book, which he intended as a model of fine writing without scholarly pedantry. Another problem is that he released a second edition of the book in 1924. This revised the latter chapters of the book and improved its rhetorical structure; but it also shifted Scott's argument. In particular it removed a long chapter, entitled "Art and Mind," which argued that future developments in architectural aesthetics would result from advances in empirical psychology.

The 1914 edition is now quite rare, but the second edition has been regularly reprinted. Much changed in architecture across that decade, and thinking of *The Architecture of Humanism* as a book of 1924 tends to confuse Scott's historical position. His discussion of the baroque can, and perhaps should, be conflated with the relation that Sigfried Giedion later made between the spatiality of the baroque and modernism by extending the thought of Heinrich Wölfflin, who was also one of Scott's sources. While it mostly reads as a defence of the Edwardian baroque, the new Epilogue of 1924 seems to support a modernist reading when Scott writes: "I would like to add a word on the subject of the baroque. I find this book frequently referred to as though its main purpose were the defence of that style. But that is to take the part for the whole, and to confuse my thesis with my illustrations."[1]

This essay analyses Scott's book and its revisions in order to unpick the theoretical sources for his "humanist values." The Preface acknowledges the influence of Burckhardt, Scott's employer, Bernard Berenson, and Heinrich Wölfflin's *Renaissance und Barock*.[2] In a crucial chapter on humanist values, which appears in both editions, there is a long footnote in which Scott cites his theoretical sources as Berenson and Theodor Lipps, while criticizing the leading English theorist of the day, Reginald Blomfield, for his dismissal of empathy theory.[3] The footnote ends by referring the reader seeking a more detailed understanding of empathy theory to the English theorist Vernon Lee. My approach here will be to put these scant references up against what we know of Scott's life and intellectual milieu, which is a good deal thanks to Richard Dunn.[4]

The Architecture of Humanism was written largely at the Villa I Tatti in Fiesole, where Scott was employed by Bernard and Mary Berenson as secretary, librarian and architect. Vernon Lee lived nearby in the Villa Il Palmerino, and is likely to have been a source of Scott's understanding of concepts from German art history and psychology. Scott was more a protégé of Mary Berenson than of Bernard, and it is from their extensive correspondence that we know so much about Scott. Through Mary Berenson and her remarkable family Scott knew the English intellectuals and writers known as the Bloomsbury group. On the basis of textual references in *The Architecture of Humanism*, I will argue that the work of two members of that group, Karin Stephen and Roger Fry, can, alongside that of Lee and Blomfield, provide a useful context for understanding Scott's book and how its argument changed in the space of a decade.

***

For Scott, "humanism" means both the perceptual psychology of empathy, or *Einfühlung* and, more familiarly, the revival of classical values in the Renaissance. Peter Reyner Banham thought this an appalling "double entendre," and certainly this double meaning given to "humanism" is a usage that risks confusion.[5] It is, however, important to Scott to recognize the historicity of ways of seeing, as signalled by the book's sub-title, *A Study in the History of Taste*. It is the question of how "taste" can mean an empirical account of immediate aesthetic pleasure, and also be a form of trained cultural acuities historically located: of how a present day experience of the baroque is, at a bodily level, the same as for people of the seventeenth century whose culture we understand from across an historical distance.

Scott writes that the values of humanism are lines, spaces, masses, and coherence.[6] The first three of these are aesthetic in the sense that they concern embodied perceptual experience and reflection on that experience. We experience these three values through movement. The eye follows lines. We understand what Scott called two-dimensional space on a building façade as being crowded, or open, with elements compressed in a bounded space or released. In three-dimensional space, the human body moves, sensing space by a combination of sight and bodily extension. Mass is understood as the force that opposes movement, and the sense that we have of great masses thrown into movement is what distinguished the Italian baroque. Scott's fourth humanist value, "coherence," is a capacity to conceptualize the purely aesthetic experience of the other values and to design buildings using that understanding. For Scott, as for Wölfflin, this capacity to conceptualize aesthetic experience is how it becomes historical. Thus far, Scott might seem to owe a great deal to *Renaissance und Barock*, as he suggests in his Preface. But a closer reading suggests a greater complexity of influences and ideas.

Scott diverges significantly from Wölfflin in the description of bodily locomotion in three-dimensional space. This has no source in Wölfflin, and instead seems close to the ideas of August Schmarsow, Wölfflin's rival. In the crucial footnote that I have already described, Scott does not refer to Wölfflin, from whom he most certainly got his formal categories of mass and movement, but instead to Lipps's theory of empathy and *Raumaesthetik*, and on Lipps we are referred to Lee. At the time he wrote the book Scott did not read German with any ease.[7] Scott's neighbour, Lee, on the other hand, was brought up speaking German, she published on Lipps in academic journals, considered Schmarsow's theories and corresponded with Wölfflin.

In "Beauty and Ugliness" of 1897, Lee and her partner in life and aesthetics, Clementina ("Kit") Anstruther-Thomson, developed their own independent concept of kinaesthetic empathy based on William James's theories and their mutual experiments with aesthetic sensitivity in the Uffizi. Lee and Thomson's publication came to the attention of Lipps, who corrected them soundly.[8] Lee went on to develop aspects of Lipps's theories, combining them with Karl Groos's concept of "inner mimicry" and insights of her own. She took Lipps to task for what she saw as the metaphysics that he falsely attached to an empirical psychology. It is significant that Lee continued to develop these ideas in her "Aesthetic Empathy and its Organic Accompaniments," and that this was published shortly before Scott commenced the later chapters of *The Architecture of Humanism* that dealt with empathy theory.[9] Some biographical context is necessary to understand Scott's relation with Lee and her ideas.

Vernon Lee was the *nom de plume* of Violet Paget (1856–1935): aesthetician, novelist, critic of music and the visual arts, feminist and one of the leading intellectuals of Florence in the late nineteenth and early twentieth centuries. Lee befriended Bernard Berenson when he first settled in Florence in 1892, praising his insights on their visits to galleries while offering to correct his inadequacies in literary style and his lack of psychological training. This relationship was unlikely to be sustained, and in 1897 Berenson, in a fit of pique, accused Lee and Thomson of plagiarizing ideas that they had gained from his conversation with them.[10] Lee wrote a well-considered rebuttal of the charges, but she and Bernard Berenson did not speak to one another again until 1920. Mary Berenson negotiated between the parties and by 1913 she had persuaded Lee to put aside her animus. When Scott first arrived at I Tatti in 1906 the argument must have been something of a legend, but being close to Mary Berenson he knew Lee and Thomson well. He spent Christmas Eve of 1912 at Il Palmerino[11] when he had finished what he called the "destructive" chapters of the *Architecture of Humanism* and was considering how to write the "constructive" remainder of the book based on his understanding of empathetic theories of space, theories on which Lee was writing at the time.[12]

In October 1913 Scott wrote to Mary Berenson of his difficulties in completing the book and alluding to his debts to Lee and his problems with her approach. Scott wrote that his "Humanist Values" chapter needed to go into "the ideated sensation theories of the Lipps-BB-Hildebrand-and (alas) Vernon-Lee-nexus," and that he had to go further than Bernard Berenson, who "sails too lightly over really grave philosophical difficulties ... and scandalizes the logical minded beyond measure." He also aimed to avoid the situation of the "ladies of San Gervasio" (the area of Il Palmerino) who risk being "wholly ridiculous by running the theory to death." He finds their reporting of their aesthetic experiences risible, mocking their exhibition of "'arrested' breathings and ... gaspings." At the same time, Scott writes that it is "sad that the truth should lie in that direction."[13]

Scott is writing about the amusement and disquiet that Lee and Thomson's exhibitions of aesthetic affects afforded Florentine society. Il Palmerino, as the couple were called, "experimented" with aesthetics in the Uffizi and in galleries across Italy, Lee observing and analysing Kit Thompson's putative aesthetic sensitivity. A sceptical friend, Dame Ethyl Smyth, described their confrontation with an antique bust in the Vatican Galleries:

> Vernon suddenly said: "Kit! Show us that bust!" Kit's proceedings were remarkable; in dead silence she advanced, then retreated, shaded her eyes, and finally ejaculated: "Look at that Johnny! How he sings ... how he sings!" Various technical details were then pointed out as proving their contention, though Vernon considered these as less important than the 'singing' quality discovered by her friend.[14]

However much Scott was on Berenson's side in the dispute with Lee, and indeed because of it, he clearly read Lee and her original and sophisticated concept of aesthetic experience. However much he felt distaste for Il Palmerino's exhibitionism, he thought Lee's ideas closer to the truth of aesthetic experience than the "scandalous" lack of logic in Berenson.

In "Humanist Values" Scott states that aesthetic experience is of "appearances" not facts, and here he is in accord with Lee where she writes that aesthetics concern "aspects not things."[15] They both follow Kant's dictum that the pleasure we have in representations is indifferent to the existence of the thing represented. For Lee and Scott, however, the aspect or relative spatial relation is irreducible in the representation. The point of view and atmospheric effects are the cause of one's view as much as the mountain itself, and we are as equally indifferent to these contingencies as we are to the mountain when we consider it aesthetically.

Scott's discussion of appearances precedes his explanation of empathy. He asks us to imagine a top-heavy façade, "the sight of a granite building raised (apparently) on a glass shopfront."[16] Our discomfort, Scott claims, has nothing to do with fears for the stability of the building, or analysis of its construction; rather, this is a bodily sensation. The first principle of humanism is thus that: "We have looked at the building and identified ourselves with its apparent state. *We have transcribed ourselves into terms of architecture*," He then goes on to list common metaphors of buildings "rising" and being "calm" or "restless," before stating: "The whole of architecture is, in fact, unconsciously invested by us with human movement and human mood. Here, then, is a principle complementary to the one just stated. *We transcribe architecture in terms of ourselves.*"[17]

Of Scott's two principles Lippsian *Einfühlung* accounts for only the latter. The other is what Lee, following Groos, calls "inner mimicry."[18] In "Aesthetic Empathy and its Organic Accompaniments," Lee argues strenuously that Lipps had taken a wrong turn by thinking of empathy as a symptom of a fuller projection of the visualizing ego onto objects, and thus, in her opinion, lapsing into metaphysics. Lee argued the continued significance of organic sensations and "motor images," that is, a process where the aesthetic image causes bodily effects in breathing, posture and the like, and where these in turn cause emotions, and in Scott's terms "transcribe ourselves in terms of architecture." Lee and Thomson developed this anthropopathy in their earlier work from the James-Lange hypothesis. These ideas are also the basis for Wölfflin's psychology in *Renaissance und Barock*, albeit a psychology based on different sources.

Mark Jarzombek calls this branch of the psychology of aesthetics "subject-objectification" and claims that without it empathy would not have had the success it did in art and architectural education.[19] If empathy were only projective anthropomorphism, the experience of art and nature could not be differentiated. However, subject-objectification supposes that the body is responding to aspects that are designed into the object by an artist with the aim to affect an observer. The art works enable objective responses in the body such as those

Lee observed affecting the highly sensitive Kit Thomson. It is this hypothesis that led Lee to write to Wölfflin about a passage in *Die klassische Kunst* concerning the experience of Michelangelo's sculpture. She asked him to clarify if the aesthetic experience that he described was psychical, as Lipps would have supposed, or physical. She was pleased that his reply was that it was a physical response, which agreed with her theories.[20]

After Scott's description of the aesthetic humanist values comes the conceptual value of order or coherence. This is the familiar classical "ordo" of symmetry, proportion, balance and the like, expressed through the orders of columns, but as Scott says these should be understood as we understand the symmetry and directionality of our bodies, not mathematically or geometrically. Interestingly, coherence is what nature lacks: "the groups that the eye, at any one glance, discovers in Nature, are not intelligible. They are understood only by successive acts of attention and elimination."[21]

Scott's claim of the lack of aesthetic order in nature is an attempt to resolve a problem in empathy theory, or, rather, subject-objectification. If aesthetic feeling is not conceptual, how is it that art causes the organic sensations of kinesthesis, and subsequently affects us in a way that is different to the effects of trees, rocks and mountains? Scott's answer is that the coherence put into the building by an architect is available to mental analysis simultaneously with its mass and movement. While the latter qualities are affecting in natural and artistic objects, coherence is a value of art alone. Architecture orders the lines, spaces and masses into a coordinated effect and, in response, our mind attends differently to its sense perceptions: "The eye and the mind must travel together; thought and vision move at one pace and in step. … Style, through coherence, subordinates beauty to the pattern of the mind, and so selects what it presents that all, at one sole act of thought."[22]

Scott's is thus not an account of sequential spatial experience but rather an experience of undifferentiated aesthetic experience. Thus while mundane sensory experience might be of successive spaces, one after another, architecture through "coherence" opens onto an undifferentiated duration of experience in "one sole act of thought."

Movement is the key term for three of Scott's purely aesthetic humanist values. The movement or implied direction of the line is simple enough, but Scott becomes more interesting in discussing space, which he first does as two-dimensional then as three-dimensional. His descriptions of building façades as two-dimensional spaces names and paraphrases Wölfflin. The baroque is not only a clear example of the role of movement in the creation of "space-values." Movement explains what people lacking sensitivity see as the distortions of baroque architecture. As Scott writes:

> the equipoise of Bramante's classicism aimed to "cancel all suggested movement." … But the baroque architects rejected this arrangement. They employed space adjustments which, *taken in isolation*, would be inharmonious. In their church facades, as Wölfflin has pointed out, they quite deliberately congested their forms. … Here, therefore, a movement, which in the midst of a Bramantesque design would be destructive and repugnant, is turned to account and made the basis of a more dramatic, but not less satisfying treatment, the motive of which is not peace, but energy.[23]

When Scott turns to three-dimensional space, however, he is much closer to Schmarsow and proposes a concept of space as bodily extension and locomotive potential. It is questionable that Scott knew Schmarsow's works directly, but Lee certainly did. In "Aesthetic Empathy" she quotes with approval Schmarsow's ideas of empathy as imagined and actual locomotion in space.[24] Scott, most likely drawing on Schmarsow's ideas, via Lee, writes: "Space, in fact, is liberty of movement. That is its value to us, and as such it enters our physical consciousness. We adapt ourselves instinctively to the spaces in which we stand, project ourselves into them, fill them ideally with our movements."[25]

His first example of this is a colonnade, the rhythm of which "compels" a forward movement, the eye making an imagined extension of the body before locomotive movement. Were the colonnade to end in a blank wall, Scott proposes that the experience would be merely aesthetic. It requires the coherence of a window or an altar, because "movement without motive and without climax contradicts our physical instincts: it is not humanised."[26] His next example is of a centralized space in which we do not change location. Although we do not walk about, the eye is drawn in all directions, and we have a physical image of that imagined movement because of breathing. The body fixed in position feels the expansion of air in the chest, which gives feelings of equipoise and control.[27]

Scott's synthesis of his various sources and his own experience seem to have reconciled the competing aesthetic theories of form and space that are associated with Wölfflin and Schmarsow: empathy as a relation of the body to forms, and empathy as a relation to space through bodily extension. Most likely his position results from his literary values of brevity and directness, as much as his prowess in synthesizing arguments. Nevertheless, he reaches a position much the same as Paul Frankl's better detailed, argued and evidenced combination of Schmarsow and Wölfflin in his *Die Entwicklungsphasen der neuren Baukunst* (*Principles of Architectural History*), which was, like Scott's book, first published in 1914. One can imagine that the projected but never realized second volume of *The Architecture of Humanism*, illustrated and replete with concrete examples as Scott planned it to be, would have been quite like Frankl's study.

***

What then is the relation of the baroque to Scott's humanism, and what did it mean to English readers of his time? Scott's book is ostensibly about the Italian Renaissance, but in fact Scott has little to say about the *quattrocento*. Bramante receives faint praise and Palladio is considered a pedant who weakened the cause. The period style that is now called baroque was more commonly named Late Renaissance in English usage at the time – corresponding to the German term *Spät-Renaissance* used as a book title by Ebe in 1886 – as baroque and had pejorative overtones of distortion and licentiousness. John Summerson quipped that nineteenth-century British architects looked at Borromini "much as a good schoolboy regards a prostitute."[28] But by the turn of the century, Late Renaissance was the dominant style of British architecture across the Empire and "baroque" was beginning to be used in the modern sense, most notably by Martin Briggs, whose *Baroque Architecture* of 1913 drew on Cornelius Gurlitt and critiqued the earlier prejudice.[29]

The British baroque revival was nationalistic, as elsewhere in Europe, but it had a particular relation to the dominant ideology of the Arts and Crafts. Imperial Britain required new corporate offices for government and business and a sense of grandeur was required. While the picturesque irregularity of the Art and Crafts, with its vernacular and rural associations, was increasingly out of step, the baroque revival allowed for the ongoing commitment to craft values and the opportunities for applied ornamentation – preferably drawing upon British sources from the seventeenth century. The portfolios of English examples that were the basis of architectural practice and education turned increasingly to classical details. John Belcher and Mervyn MacCartney's *English Architecture of the Late Renaissance* (published in six folio volumes from 1897) is the largest of the publications of the so-called "Wrenaissance:" the recovery of the architecture of Wren, Vanburgh, Hawksmoor and Archer as stylistic sources. Belcher's Institute of Chartered Accountants in Moorgate London, is an early and influential example of what Edwardian architecture was to become. Belcher wrote a book of theory, relatively simple precepts for architectural practice with which Scott's book has some commonalities. The closer model for Scott though must be Reginald Blomfield, whose book *The Mistress Art* (1908) was a key text of the period – and to it Scott refers in the crucial footnote cited above.

Scott decided to become an architect after receiving a disappointing upper second degree from New College, Oxford, in 1907. He had, however, won a prize, the annual Chancellor's Essay for *The National Character of English Architecture* (1908) and become a protégé of the Berensons, spending part of 1906 with Mary and her daughters touring Italy. Mary introduced him to the architect Cecil Pinsent and Scott enrolled at the Architectural Association School in London where he spent two terms in the 1907–8 academic year, ultimately finding that it lacked intellectual challenge.[30] In 1910, Scott and Pinsent set up practice in Florence based around work that Pinsent had been commissioned to undertake on I Tatti.

Scott and his fellow AA students must surely have attended the Royal Academy lectures of Blomfield, the newly appointed Professor of Architecture.[31] For four years (commencing in 1906) Blomfield lectured from material that was published as *The Mistress Art* in 1908.[32] It seems likely that Scott was irritated by Blomfield's boisterous and clubby prose and pretentions to scholarship. None of this was likely to impress the Oxford aesthete, a pupil of Gilbert Murray, who was dining at the time with Robbie Ross (the friend and literary executor of Oscar Wilde).[33] The chapter "Art and Mind," which appears in the first edition of Scott's book, begins with a satire on the concept of a "mistress art" in which the passion among the arts leads to ennui and then divorce. This was dropped from the 1924 edition. In the footnote on his sources Scott points out that Blomfield had given empathy theory a "frigid reception" in *The Mistress Art*.

Scott is closest to Blomfield on mass, order and the orders. Blomfield's design principle was the subordination of detail to the mass and general composition of the building volume. No one at the time, or since, has doubted the ability of architects of sensibility (such as Richard Norman Shaw) to invent compositions in a collage of balanced elements, each with their own integrity. But for Blomfield and his generation this purely picturesque understanding of building form had too many quaint associations, and lacked the three-dimensional coherence needed to project the grandeur of Imperial Britain. The skill of visually composing eclectic historical elements was also difficult to teach during the years in which the British were beginning to realize the necessity of schools of architecture such as those of the French and Americans. It is for this reason that Blomfield encouraged the study of the orders, even though he was almost a modernist in his formalism; he thought that architecture required a metric that had substantial cultural meaning. It is clear that Scott agrees with all of this, which, in his terms, describes the relationship between the three aesthetic humanist values and the coherence that the mind is to bring to them.

Scott's book is typical of Edwardian thought on architecture by proposing that style must be founded on taste rather than applied as a rule or code. Here taste is not an individual attribute but a community of feeling at an historical moment. Architects, such as Belcher and McCartney, typically sought this in identification with the nation. Blomfield's views are more complex (he was an expert on French architecture) but nevertheless nationalist. Responding to the need for an authentic style of 1914 Scott argued for a baroque classicism, as his peers had, but instead of following the nationalist path to explain how taste could be shared and a firm basis for stylistic choices, he makes a more fundamental argument. The psychology of perception could show how art could have common effects on all observers, directly and without associations, national or otherwise.[34] It makes a certain amount of sense to see *The Architecture of Humanism* as a piece of one-up-manship, with Scott's superior training in rhetoric and dialectic and his workable knowledge of psychological aesthetics showing Blomfield and the architectural establishment that they were more right than they knew, limited as they were by parochialism.

In Scott's destruction of the "Fallacies" of received architectural theory one is considered redeemable: the picturesque.[35] While nineteenth-century romanticism that insisted on a literary understanding of spatio-visual experience is damned, the picturesque, being a theory of painting, is shown to be deleterious only due to its abuse in romanticism. In an argument close to Blomfield's, Scott appreciates the "inoffensive charm" of English domestic architecture while claiming that to make an ideal of this picturesqueness leads to the misunderstanding of classical architecture as merely formal.[36] The picturesque as Scott describes it in this early chapter encompasses what he will go on to define as the first three aesthetic humanist values. It also gives him a novel definition of the baroque:

> To give the picturesque its grandest scope and yet to subdue it to architectural law – this was the baroque experiment and it is achieved. … It enlarged the classical formula by developing within it the principle of movement. But the movement is always logical. … It insists on coherent purpose, and its greatest extravagances of design where neither unconsidered nor inconsistent. *It intellectualised the picturesque.*[37]

Scott's contemporaries would have thought of the picturesque as it had been exemplified by Shaw, Aston Webb, or the more superficial popular taste for the Queen Anne style. This is what Scott means, and his view of contemporary architecture, like Blomfield's, is that it is overly directed to visual incident and lacking in classical order. But the apparent anachronism in placing the picturesque before the baroque in historical sequence emphasizes that Scott is also using picturesque as a term of aesthetics and art history just as Wölfflin does with the equivalent German term *malerisch*. Much of what Scott has to say about movement in his later chapters comes directly from Wölfflin's discussion of the *malerisch* qualities sought by baroque painters, and of how their uptake in architecture opens the question of how to understand these culture-wide changes in style. Scott states that the picturesque develops from the Italian *pittoresco* where it applied to the landscape backgrounds of figurative paintings.[38] Scott's causal relations are the reverse of those of Wölfflin, who argued that a taste for movement developed after the classical phase of the Renaissance. For Scott the aspect of movement already existed in the Renaissance in an innate perceptual interest in the "fantastic, unexpected, varied and grotesque" that the baroque disciplines and develops into a properly aesthetic order.[39]

If Scott had read Wölfflin this would have been Walter Armstrong's 1903 translation of *Die klassische Kunst*, in which *malerisch* is translated as picturesque. This is the typical translation in ordinary usage, but one that has been (generally) replaced in art historical discourse by "painterly." M.D. Hottinger in her 1932 translation of *Kunstgeschichtliche Grundbegriffe* invented the word "painterly" to offer a more lexically correct translation of *malerisch* as describing the qualities belonging to the painter, or *maler*. The neologism has the putative advantage of clarifying Wölfflin's distinction of the abstract quality of *malerisch* from things merely picturesque. He uses *das Malerische* as a pejorative, describing the misapprehension that *malerisch* qualities belong to the low genres of painting or their subjects. "Picturesque" is used in English with this same range of meaning, most notably by John Ruskin who contrasts a "lower" and a "noble" picturesque. There was scepticism among some art historians about Hottinger's translation, not least from Erwin Panofsky.[40] Frankl's translators, presumably with his knowledge, use picturesque for *malerisch* throughout his study of the reception of the gothic. Scott inflects picturesque to be pejorative or not, just as Wölfflin does with *malerisch*.

There are wider issues here concerning both the history of the picturesque and Wölfflin's reception in English. My point here, however, is that Scott's use of picturesque is neither clumsy nor idiosyncratic, but rather a near perfect point of contact between his two audiences: the English architectural debate and the German-influenced art-historical discourse of his friends in Florence. Scott furthermore offers something of a mild correction to Wölfflin by drawing on the longer history of pictorial form.

***

If Scott had read Wölfflin early in the century he might well have done so on the recommendation of Roger Fry who published an admiring account of the Armstrong translation of *Die klassische Kunst* in 1903. Fry was perhaps the most interesting English reader of Wölfflin, and Scott had been introduced to him and another key figure in the Bloomsbury group, Lady Ottoline Morrell in 1906 by Mary Berenson.[41]

Mary Berenson, formerly Mary Costelloe, née Pearsall Smith of Philadelphia, was a formidable intellectual in her own right. Mary's sister Alys, whose husband was the philosopher Bertrand Russell, had introduced Scott to Mary as a suitable companion for Mary's daughters of her first marriage, Ray and Karin Costelloe, on a motoring tour of Italy in 1906. Alys and Mary's brother, the essayist Logan Pearsall Smith, was a close friend of Fry's. Travelling to Florence with Scott were two members of what became known as "Bloomsbury:" John Maynard Keynes, with whom Scott was having an affair, and Lytton Strachey. Keynes and Strachey had been at Cambridge with Leonard Wolfe and Clive Bell, all of them members of the secretive Apostles discussion group, of which Fry had been a member.[42] They were taught by former apostle G.E. Moore, a colleague of Russell's, whose argument that beauty was a moral good was a foundation of Bloomsbury's culture. Before turning to Fry, it is useful to consider another member of the group: Karin Stephen née Costelloe, Mary's daughter who in 1914 married Adrian Stephen, brother of Vanessa Bell and Virginia Woolf.

Karin Costelloe disliked Scott on their 1906 motor tour referring to him as the "trembling debauchee."[43] But when Costelloe and Scott were staying at I Tatti in 1911 and 1912 they had a flirtation during which Scott considered proposing marriage to her. After some encouragement on her part, and then contrary advice from her mother, Karin rejected him.[44] Costelloe studied at Newham College Cambridge, tutored in philosophy by Russell, her uncle. She published the article "What Bergson means by Interpenetration," which would have been in press in 1912 during her romance with Scott. In those months at I Tatti Costelloe is also likely to have been working on another essay in which she takes her uncle to task for his misunderstandings of Bergson. This appeared in 1914, and her book *The Misuse of Mind*, with a Prefatory Note by Bergson himself was published in 1922.

"Art and Thought," the chapter Scott edited out of the second edition of *The Architecture of Humanism*, contains a reference to "Creative Evolution" that alludes both to Bergson's book of that title and to his ideas.[45] I argue, however, that it more directly refers to the conversations that Scott had with Costelloe in 1912, during the same months in which he was meeting Lee and which immediately precede his writing of the "positive" chapters of his book's first edition. While I think that there is some value in seeing parts of Scott's text through Bergson, the larger issue is why this chapter was dropped from the second edition, and the answer to this is the changing relationship between psychology and art theory.

What Scott might have taken from Costelloe's discussion of Bergson would have supported the concept of motor-images as a cause of affects, which he already knew from Lee, Lipps and Wölfflin. It would also have been relevant to the split between the first three humanist values of sensory perception and "coherence," which required conceptualization. This pairing of perception and cognition, body and mind is not an unfamiliar one, but in Scott's exposition it has some of the character of Bergson's insistence of the undifferentiatedness of the *durée* and the differentiating character of thought. Scott is quite rigorous in his insistence on the non-logical and non-conceptual nature of aesthetic experience. He writes: "the 'theories' of the art have blunted sensitive perception without achieving intellectual force."[46] In the earlier part of the book, Scott enjoys himself by launching witty and devastatingly blunt arguments against common theories of architecture. But in "Humanist Values" it becomes clear that the problem is not the fault of specific theories of architecture but of theory itself: past thinkers failing to understand that aesthetic experience is a whole of body state which exceeds conceptualization and indeed consciousness. As Scott writes: "Our theory does not say that the physical states enter largely into the spectator's consciousness. ... Their absence from consciousness is indeed a point of real importance."[47]

Scott suffered depression and writer's block as he attempted a second volume of *The Architecture of Humanism*. Costelloe's later contributions to psychoanalysis as Karin Stephen have led Mark Campbell to connect their conversations in 1912 and Scott's break down and psychiatric treatment in 1919.[48] He sees a wider pattern linking Scott's personal problems to a crisis in the development of architectural aesthetics, where the psychology that underpinned it in the late nineteenth century was being swept away by Freud, and with it the comportment of the connoisseur Scott undoubtedly was. Campbell's argument is supported by the elision of "psychology" in the second edition. Whether Freud or Bergson is the authority in question, dropping the claims to the truth of psychology is significant in understanding how and why the emphasis shifted toward a more formalist account of art in Scott's second edition. But Scott's acquaintance with the modernist writers and painters of the Bloomsbury group, particularly Roger Fry, is also relevant in interpreting the shift between the two editions.

The painter, art historian and critic Roger Fry met and befriended Bernard and Mary Berenson in Florence in 1898 and acknowledged Bernard's rather simplistic version of empathy theory, "tactile values," in his book on Bellini of 1899. Fry's reading of aesthetics along with his own observations of contemporary painting in Paris, from around 1906, lead to his curating an exhibition, in 1910, of Cezanne, Matisse, Picasso, Van Gogh and Gauguin, for which he coined the term Post-Impressionism. Scott had been introduced to Fry and other members of Bloomsbury by Mary Berenson in 1906 and had extensive discussions with him about a potential book of biographies of famous painters around 1908.[49] Although largely remembered as a writer on art, Fry was very interested in architecture and design. While discussing Scott's book project he would have been designing his precociously modern house, Durbins, for which construction began in 1909.[50] In 1912 Fry wrote to the *The Times* protesting the demolition of John Nash's Regent Street Quadrant and its replacement with Richard Norman Shaw's neo-baroque Piccadilly Hotel. Fry recommended John Burnet's presciently modern Kodak House of 1911 as what British architects should be aspiring to. In 1913, he began the Omega Workshops, producing modernist furniture and décor. As Virginia Woolf quipped, partly in reference to Fry's exhibition, "on or about 1910 human character changed"[51] and Scott was closely involved with those who observed this. Woolf's brother Adrian Stephen had married Karin Costelloe, and in the early 1920s Scott began an affair with Vita Sackville-West that continued until 1925 despite her increasing affection for Woolf.[52] Scott was the kind of Edwardian connoisseur that Bloomsbury was reacting against and what he made of this while preparing the second edition is intriguing. Certainly Berenson's well-known low opinion of modern art would have made it difficult for Scott to shift the patronage of the book sufficiently to acknowledge what had become apparent to him.[53] And this is the more so because he would have been aware that Fry's ideas on the direction of contemporary painting also grew out of his reading of Wölfflin on the baroque. In 1921 Fry wrote an article length review of Wölfflin's *Kunstgeschichtliche Grundbegriffe*, entitled "The Baroque," and published a polemic against the profession of architecture: *Architectural Heresies of a Painter*.

In "The Baroque," Fry gives an astute summary of Wölfflin's book, which he praises, and assimilates to his own ideas about artistic development. Fry identifies the post-impressionists with a reaction against the *malerisch* (he translates this as painter-like) character of impressionism, and a return to linearity and form. The post-impressionists are, according to Fry, like the neo-classical reaction to the baroque because they emphasize "the decorative unity of the picture surface [and attempt] to express volume and plastic relief in almost flat tones."[54] Fry feels that Wölfflin is biased in favouring the baroque, but sees the importance of Wölfflin's idea of a dialectical development of formal values in art. Thus Poussin, according to Fry, had learned the visuality of the baroque but properly subordinated this to values of design. This is entirely compatible with the relation to Scott's idea of baroque architecture as classicism asserting intellectual discipline over its picturesque values.

What then was the corollary of post-impressionism in the sibling art of architecture? Fry addressed the RIBA in 1921 with a polemic of 10 "architectural heresies" – elaborating on his 1912 letter about the Regent Street Quadrant. He decried historicism and complained that the art of architecture had been substituted with merely dressing buildings. Like Scott, he thought architects had mistaken "historico-social ideas" for aesthetic values. He writes, "Modern conditions and modern science have put into the hands of architects the greatest opportunity in the history of the world. They have missed it completely."[55] Like Wren and Perrault he claims that beauty in architecture is of two kinds, natural, which in Fry's case is functional, and secondly, in accord with Scott, is the expression of aesthetic ideas. Scott makes an oblique reference to Fry in the Epilogue to the second edition where he writes of the destruction of Nash's Regent Street Quadrant, and the hope that he has in the outrage that this caused.

***

How, or whether, Scott reconciled his knowledge of contemporary art and literature with *The Architecture of Humanism* and how it affected the second edition is difficult to judge. If we consider the 1914 edition of *The Architecture of Humanism*, then it sits with Berenson and Blomfield as a defence of traditional classical values, as commentators from David Watkin to Branco Mitrović have insisted. Others, such as Robert MacLeod, and Banham to a degree, see it as sitting on the cusp of modernism on account of its attack on nineteenth-century theory and its positive theorization of space. This latter interpretation of the book is supported by the Epilogue to the 1924 edition where Scott insists against unnamed commentators that he is not a proponent of the baroque, which was, he writes, an illustration and not the topic of the book.

> The baroque is in the highest degree interesting because, of its purely psychological approach to the problem of design. … But my argument goes essentially beyond that particular question, and if I have come back so frequently to the subject of the baroque, it is because it furnished a kind of acid test to the views I was considering.[56]

Equally telling is the demotion of psychology in the second edition where the perceptual theory chapter of the first edition is dropped and psychology is merely a proof that we need to be immersed in good architectural experiences. Scott summarizes the point of the book thus: "Where then, practically speaking, are we led? Simply to the necessity of a more habitual, a more saturated familiarity with the tradition of humanist architecture."[57]

By 1924 mechanical anthropopathic accounts of aesthetics such as Lee's were obsolete and Karin Stephen had turned from Bergson's perceptual motor functions to Freud's sub-conscious. At the same time Fry had shown that these turn of the century ideas from psychological aesthetics made sense in an independent, formalist art history. Like Wölfflin's journey from art-psychology in *Renaissance und Barock* to the simpler formalism of *Kunstgeschichtliche Grundbegriffe*, Scott sought the second edition of *The Architecture of Humanism* to be understood as cultural history rather than psychology.

Banham describes Scott's introduction of *Einfühlung* as interesting but not influential because it was merely an attempt to "give a show of objectivity to the extremely solipsistic attitude he is taking up."[58] Perhaps there is a degree of truth in this as Scott was more committed to the form and expression of his argument than to where it might lead. Whatever his intentions, though, Scott's aim to perfect the rhetorical form of his book and his complex intellectual and personal context made for a brilliant synthesis of architectural history and aesthetic theory, which has something to tell us about what baroque meant for English readers in 1914 and how it shifted register 10 years later.

Endnotes

1   Scott, *The Architecture of Humanism*, 263. All quotations from this book are taken from the 2nd edition of 1924.

2   Scott, *The Architecture of Humanism*, ix.

3   Scott, *The Architecture of Humanism*, 213–14.

4   Dunn has collected Scott's correspondence in researching his biographies of Scott. Scott's correspondence with Mary Berenson is held at the Villa I Tatti and referenced as Bernard and Mary Berenson, Papers, 1880–2002, Biblioteca Berenson, Villa I Tatti – The Harvard University Center for Italian Renaissance Studies. Mark Campbell has included biographical information in his more sophisticated accounts of Scott's architectural thought: "Geoffrey Scott and the Dream-Life of Architecture" and "Aspects Not Things."

5   Banham, *Theory and Design in the First Machine Age*, 67.

6   Scott, *The Architecture of Humanism*, 210–39.

7   Scott asks Mary Berenson to bring him a German dictionary in July 1917 as he wanted to read a German book he had on Bernini. He complains of lack of time to attend to learning German in August. Dunn, *The Letters of Geoffrey Scott*, 122; Scott to Berenson (18 July 1917), 238 and (6 August 1917), 241.

8   Lee describes Lipps's criticism in Lee and Anstruther-Thomson, *Beauty and Ugliness*, 88–92. She cites from Theodor Lipps in the *Archiv für systematische Philosophie* (1900).

9   Lee, "Aesthetic Empathy and Its Organic Accompaniments" and "The Central Problem of Aestethics," *Beauty and Ugliness*, 45–76 and 77–154, respectively.

10 Lee met Berenson sometime in the early 1890s in England with Kit. They were then friends of a kind in Florence through that decade, although Lee reviewed Berenson's publications harshly, until their plagiarism quarrel in August 1897. See Gunn, *Vernon Lee*, 149, 152–8 and Gagel, "1897, A Discussion of Plagiarism," passim.

11 Dunn, *The Letters of Geoffrey Scott*, Scott to Berenson (12 December 1912), 157–8.

12 Lee, *The Beautiful*.

13 Dunn, *The Letters of Geoffrey Scott*, Scott to Berenson (18 October 1913), 179–80.

14 Ethel Smyth, *What Happened Next*. Quoted Gunn, *Vernon Lee,* 157. Bernard Berenson, who admired Lee's intellect but found her impossible, had a very low opinion of Thomson and her and Lee's experiments, writing to Mary in 1892: "After lunch I met Vernon-Thomson in the Tribuna. They were there already and we pitched in at once, Vernon Lee talking like a steam engine, and neither of them looking at anything, … with Vernon at any rate could see what you mean, if she could stop to [do] it, but Thomson is profoundly stupid. She makes an overwhelmingly bovine impression." Quoted by Gagel, "1897, A Discussion of Plagiarism," 157.

15 Lee, *The Beautiful*, 8–11.

16 Scott, *The Architecture of Humanism*, 212.

17 Scott, *The Architecture of Humanism*, 221.

18 Lee, "Anthropomorphic Aesthetics," in Lee and Anstruther-Thomson, *Beauty and Ugliness*, 1–44, section IV, 23–5; and Lee, "The Central Problem of Aesthetics," 91–7.

19 Jarzombek, *The Psychologizing of Modernity*, 66–72.

20 Lee, "The Central Problem of Aestethics," 113–14.

21 Scott, *The Architecture of Humanism*, 237.

22 Scott, *The Architecture of Humanism*, 238.

23 Scott, *The Architecture of Humanism*, 225.

24 Lee, "Aesthetic Empathy," 74–5. She goes on to complain of Van de Velde's simplistic reduction of the ideas to the moving line of Jugend Styl.

25 Scott, *The Architecture of Humanism*, 227.

26 Scott, *The Architecture of Humanism*, 228.

27 These ideas have a source in Wölfflin although Scott could not have known them directly. See his *Renaissance and Baroque*; and "Prolegomena to a Pyschology of Architecture," 155.

28 Summerson, *Architecture in Britain*, 176.

29 Briggs also made favourable mention of Scott's book in "The Genius of Bernini."

30 Before the War the AA School was something of a gentlemen's club, distinguishing itself from the traditional apprenticeship in practice with a full-time education and devotion to sports. In 1906, shortly before Scott arrived, the AA founded its Revolver Club, and Blomfield fired the first shot. Cunningham, "A Case of Cultural Schizophrenia," note 35.

31 On Blomfield I rely on Macleod, *Style and Society*; and Fellows, *Sir Reginald Blomfield*.

32 Fellows, *Sir Reginald Blomfield*, 77.

33 Dunn, *Geoffrey Scott*, 146.

34 In a letter to Mary Berenson (4 March 1908) Scott completely disavows the nationalism of his prize essay which he makes clear was a ploy. Dunn, *The Letters of Geoffrey Scott*, 42.

35 This essay presents research that follows on from my use of Scott's insight in *The Picturesque*, 246–7.

36 Scott, *The Architecture of Humanism*, 68–9.

37 Scott, *The Architecture of Humanism*, 86–7, Scott's emphasis.

38 Scott, *The Architecture of Humanism*, 68–9.

39 Here Scott's ideas are close to Ruskin, to whom he owes more than his antipathy would suggest. See especially the essay "Grotesque Renaissance," in "The Stones of Venice," Ruskin, *The Library Edition*, vol. 6.

40 Waley, "The Swing of the Pendulum," 247. Panofsky showed how *malerisch* could be rendered, "in seven or eight different ways." Panofsky, *Meaning in the Visual Arts*, 329. Thanks to Erik Ghenoiu and Mathew Aitchison for this reference.

41 Dunn, *Geoffrey Scott*, 146.

42 They were greatly influenced by the philosopher G.E. Moore, Russell's colleague, on the idea that beauty and love were ethical virtues.

43 Dunn, *Geoffrey Scott*, 34.

44 Dunn, *Geoffrey Scott*, 102.

45 "A metaphysic of 'Creative Evolution' courts the despaired-of mysteries of Time and Space with new analogies from art." Scott, *The Architecture of Humanism*, 254.

46 Scott, *The Architecture of Humanism*, 239.

47 Scott, *The Architecture of Humanism*, 218.

48 Campbell, "Geoffrey Scott and the Dream-Life of Architecture," passim.

49 Dunn, *Geoffrey Scott*, 34, 65; *The Letters of Geoffrey Scott*, 47.

50 See Roger Fry, *Vision and Design*, 179–83. On this house also see Reed, *Roger Fry's Durbins*.

51 Woolf, *Mr Bennett and Mrs Brown*, 4; and *Roger Fry*, 153–162. See also Stansky, *On or About December 1910*, 2–4 and 237–51.

52 Woolf, a close friend of Roger Fry, didn't take to Scott and later wrote of the deficiencies of his character which brought to her mind "brilliant young men who remain 'brilliant' and young well into the 40ies and never do anything to prove it." Quoted in Dunn, *Geoffrey Scott*, ix.

53 See Shapiro, "Mr Berenson's Values," 209–26.

54 Fry, "The Baroque," 148.

55 Fry, *Architectural Heresies of a Painter*, 9.

56 Scott, *The Architecture of Humanism*, 261.

57 Scott, *The Architecture of Humanism*, 261–2.

58 Banham, *Theory and Design in the First Machine Age*, 67.

Chapter 6

Against Formalism:
Aspects of the Historiography of the Baroque in Weimar Germany, 1918–33

Ute Engel

Enthusiasm

A new wave of enthusiasm for the baroque passed through Germany in the 1920s, reversing the rejection of this period of art and architectural history as disgraceful, exuberant and grotesque.[1] Georg Dehio, one of Germany's most senior art historians, in 1926 reported the heightened admiration with which his contemporaries regarded the artistic mastery of the baroque; his critic Carl Neumann observed a modish turn towards, and even a fanaticism for, the baroque;[2] and Hugo Schnell, an emerging scholar at the time of the Weimar Republic, later remembered a "secret congeniality" between that period and the baroque era.[3] The increased popularity of the baroque in Weimar Germany is clearly evidenced by an increase in the number of publications on seventeenth- and eighteenth-century art, architecture and culture, ranging from scholarly productions to popular booklets and coffee-table books.[4] This body of scholarship was compounded by the renewed attraction, in the 1920s, to baroque monuments and architectural sites as a kind of modern mass tourism phenomenon, in which tens of thousands of visitors were purported to have been transported to such Bavarian baroque churches as the Wieskirche or Balthasar Neumann's Vierzehnheiligen by the developing coach trip business.[5]

It is worth noting the explanations offered for this fresh enthusiasm for the baroque by the art-historians of Weimar Germany. Dehio, for instance, hinted at a "fascination with the irrational and inexplicable."[6] More tellingly, though, Hugo Schnell invoked a new, vitalistic approach to life that had taken hold of Germany's youth (*Jugendbewegung*) after 1918. It uttered itself in an intensified, sensuous experience (*Erleben*) of body and space, a striving for flowing forms and rhythms and an indulgence in pathos and metaphysics. This "wave of life" (*Lebenswelle*), Schnell suggests, expressed itself as much in modern dance – he hints at Rudolf von Laban and Mary Wigman – as in a new lively comprehension of baroque art as essential (*wesenhaft*), spiritual, mystical and unlimited. Schnell finally observed that this new interpretation of the baroque established it as a parallel to the expressionism of the 1910s and 1920s.[7]

Viewed in this light, the special attention directed to the baroque at this moment formed part of the creative uprising and avant-garde experimentation that served to define Germany artistically and culturally in the Weimar period. Historically and politically, the Weimar Republic was almost constantly in a state of turmoil. The republican parliamentary system that had supplanted the Wilhelmine Empire in the Revolution of November 1918 – following the devastating losses of the First World War – was far from accepted by the majority of Germans. The young democracy was economically weakened by inflation in 1922–23 and would be further undermined by the international financial crisis of 1929. It was under immense and ever-growing political pressure from parties on the extremes of the right and the left alike. At the same time, concentrated in a few years of prosperity spanning from 1924 to 1928, Germany experienced a burst of modernization and sustained both the advent of a modern mass culture and technological progress to an unprecedented degree.[8]

What was the role played by the art historiography of baroque architecture in this historical and cultural situation? Generally speaking, signs of a highly creative potential also marked the writing of art historians of this moment. A plurality of new methods emerged to specifically attend to the problems raised by the baroque. Baroque and rococo art and architecture were contextualized into the cultural history of their time:

literature and music, religious beliefs and philosophical theories became major points of reference in the works of Max Dvořák in Vienna or Erwin Panofsky at the Hamburg school of art history.[9] Art historians like Hans Tietze in Vienna or Werner Weisbach in Berlin conceived of an iconography of the baroque as early as 1915 (in Tietze's case) or 1921 (for Weisbach).[10] This line of the historiography of art underwent a general reorientation towards *Geistesgeschichte* (the history of the human spirit).[11] Within this debate, the relationship between the baroque and the Counter-Reformation loomed large: whether it was the art of the baroque in general, as Weisbach argued, which represented the Roman Catholic church as reinforced in its struggle against the Protestant Reformation, or rather the art of mannerism, a new stylistic unit between Renaissance and baroque introduced by Alois Riegl and Max Dvořák[12] and emphatically supported by the younger scholars Nikolaus Pevsner and Walter Friedlaender, which specifically marked the period of approximately 1520–90.[13]

Hans Rose considered the late baroque as a collectivistic period related to absolutism, a view he conveyed in 1922 in a book on the secular architecture of seventeenth and eighteenth-century France. Rose reframed the notion of the *Gesamtkunstwerk*, a core concept in the German historiography of the baroque that had been developed since the mid-nineteenth century. He argued that the total work of art, in parallel to the total state of absolutism, acted to subordinate the individual – irrespective of whether the "individual" was a formal feature or the human subject.[14] In a further distinction within this debate, Heinrich Lützeler outlined a religious sociology of the baroque in 1931, which focused on the liturgical functions of its architecture.[15] Wilhelm Pinder likewise responded to the philosophical discussions on *Geistesgeschichte* with the development of his biologistical generation theory, organized by three-dimensionally conceived spaces of styles existing in time. In 1926, Pinder outlined the complex notion of a *Zeitwürfel*, a multi-perspectival space or "time cube" in which mannerism and baroque, for instance, could simultaneously co-exist and relate to one another in polar fluctuation.[16]

In considering the general tendencies within these multi-facetted methodological approaches to the historiography of the baroque in Weimar Germany, it becomes useful to consult one of the first critical evaluations of this body of scholarship. In 1946, René Wellek, a German immigrant to the United States, contributed an illuminating analysis of "The Concept of the Baroque in Literary Scholarship" to a special issue of the American *Journal of Aesthetics and Art Criticism* "on the Baroque Style in Various Arts." Wellek wrote as a literary historian, yet his testimony is equally pertinent to the discipline of art history. As he himself stressed, even though the histories of literature and art developed side by side, the categories for the evaluation of the baroque in literary history had nonetheless rested firmly on such groundbreaking art historical studies as Heinrich Wölfflin's *Kunstgeschichtliche Grundbegriffe* (1915, *Principles of Art History*).[17] Wellek identified two main reasons to explain the enthusiasm found in Weimar Germany for the baroque. The first of these concerns was a perceived affinity with the experience of expressionism, maintained, as observed above, by such authors as Hugo Schnell – although Wellek regarded the affinity less a "secret congeniality" than a "misunderstanding." Nonetheless, Wellek concedes that following the First World War historians of letters and art alike believed in the qualities shared between German expressionism and the baroque: "its turbulent, tense, torn diction and tragic view of the world."[18]

Secondly, Wellek discerned a general trend in the humanities of the 1920s away from positivism and formalism. Being "tired of the minutiae of research," historians had become "eager for sweeping generalizations." They sought to reveal the inner essence (*Wesen*) and the spirit (*Geist*) underlying the exterior appearance of form and material. Typological condensations were advanced as a method by which the "complexity of the historical process" could be condensed. The baroque, therefore, as outlined by Wellek, assumed a place within a basic typological pairing: the antithesis between classicism and anti-classicism. Based on this pairing the antithesis was applied to the poles of classical antiquity; Renaissance and neo-classicism on one side, opposing the gothic, baroque, romanticism and, finally, expressionism on the other. Wellek's position is overtly critical, and of this tendency he ironically remarked: "The method is pushed to absurd extremes: half the world's history and creations are baroque, all which are not purely classical, not flooded by the dry light of the intellect."[19]

Taking Wellek's astute analysis as a guide, we thus can identify two key concepts characterizing the art historiography of baroque architecture, and indeed the "baroque" in general, in Germany during the era of the Weimar Republic: expressionism and typology. We shall now consider them each in turn to better understand their impact upon the art historical and architectural culture of Weimar Germany.

Figure 6.1   Munich, Amalienburg in the park of Nymphenburg chateau, by François Cuvilliés, Hall of Mirrors

Source: Feulner, *Bayerisches Rokoko*, 1923 (ill. 24).

Expressionism

We begin with a consideration of the baroque in the light of expressionism, the German avant-garde movement in literature, art and architecture of the 1910s and 1920s.[20] It is evident that a large number of art historians of the Weimar period were engaged with this modern movement and that they began in this time to view the art and architecture of past periods – of the gothic and the baroque especially – with a focus on modes of ecstatic pathos and expressivity. Albert Erich Brinckmann, for instance, celebrated the "confluence of the spiritual and the sensual" in his works on baroque architecture and sculpture.[21] Adolf Feulner, though, was one of the most enthusiastic promoters of the Bavarian baroque and rococo. He declared himself, in 1923, to be primarily interested in the "expressive capacity" (*Ausdrucksgehalt*) of the baroque, in the rendering of the supernatural into the sensual (*Versinnlichung des Übersinnlichen*), in the "expression of the transcendent," and in the irrational and the "mysticism of light" (*Mystik des Lichts*).[22] Feulner dwelt extensively on the "dynamic of the interior form, … the ecstatic pathos, which is enlivened in the wildest raptures, which passes through every stage of affect."[23] He interpreted such Bavarian baroque churches as the Asamkirche at Munich as organic bodies consisting of animated, living, even liquid material, a fantastic "pathos of forms" (*Formenpathetik*) surrounding an enlivened, pulsing space.[24] Rococo buildings like the Amalienburg in the park of Munich's Nymphenburg Chateau (Figure 6.1) or the pilgrimage church of the Wies, where mirrors and window openings break up the tectonic structure, seemed to be transformed or even deformed by the superiority of the encroaching rocaille ornament. In Feulner's view these buildings dematerialized and dissolved into the unlimited, the illusive, and the infinite.[25]

This focus on the animation, organicism, spiritualization and expressivity of form in the historiography of the baroque to a certain degree responded to the architectural theory of the early years of the Weimar Republic. Architects like Bruno Taut, Hans Poelzig, Erich Mendelsohn, Hans Scharoun, Hugo Häring and even the young Walter Gropius placed architectural planning in the service of a "spiritual revolution," developing an architecture that was based less on rational, geometrical principles than on fantasy, dynamism and emotional appeal – "ecstatic dream" (*Rauschtraum*), as Scharoun called it.[26] This trend in modern architecture soon came to be called "expressionistic"[27] or "organic"[28] and critics established a relationship between this approach to building and the historical reference of the baroque. Paul Westheim, for example, compared Poelzig's buildings to the Zwinger at Dresden and to Sanssouci;[29] he also explained Poelzig's project of the Festspielhaus at Salzburg in terms of a supposed "spirit of the Rococo."[30]

In the history of art, the turn towards the sensuality, spirituality and creative energy of the baroque seems to have developed as a deliberate reaction to the concentration on formal and methodological questions dominating German art history from the 1880s to around 1915. In this time, such prominent art historians as Heinrich Wölfflin, Alois Riegl, August Schmarsow and Paul Frankl competed with one another in forging the history of art as a discipline based on scientific, objective principles – initially through a preoccupation with producing systems of classification of forms, styles and modes of reception.[31] The most famous of these schemes was Wölfflin's *Kunstgeschichtliche Grundbegriffe* of 1915.[32] The rigidity of his approach, which deliberately focused not on the creativity of the artist but on abstract formal principles, soon provoked the criticism of younger scholars, including many of his own students.[33]

As early as 1915 Brinckmann criticized Wölfflin's approach as too passive and receptive. In his *Die Baukunst des 17. und 18. Jahrhunderts in den romanischen Ländern*, Brinckmann instead proposed a theory of artistic development based upon the active, productive imagination of forms (*Vorstellungsformen*) by the artist or architect.[34] He argued for an understanding of form through an imaginative recreation of its design process from its ideation by the artist to its material realization. He also extended his deliberations on the new notions of building (*Baugedanken*), which had evolved from the mid-sixteenth century onwards, to the imagination of space (*Raumvorstellung*). By exploring the concept of space that Schmarsow had articulated in the 1890s and on which Frankl had recently expanded, Brinckmann established a set of terms and instruments to analyse the complexity of baroque space in particular: the grouping of spaces (*Raumgruppe*), the interlocking of spaces (*Verklammerung oder Verschränkung*), the penetration of spaces (*Raumdurchdringung*), and the melting of spaces (*Raumverschmelzung, Raumvermischung*).[35]

Other art historians had, even before the First World War, more radically abandoned formalistic analysis. The most influential of these was Wilhelm Worringer who, in his *Formprobleme der Gotik* (1911), proclaimed his ambitious goal of initiating a completely new mode of "intuitive historiography" (*intuitive Geschichtsforschung*), based not on rational objectivity but on the intuition of the historian, on his "divine capacities," as Worringer put it.[36] Building upon the aesthetic subjectivism of his "psychology of style" (*Stilpsychologie*), formulated in his first and most famous book *Abstraktion und Einfühlung* (1908),[37] Worringer postulated that the historian should be guided by intuitive speculation. Only in this way could he arrive at an "animated interpretation" (*lebendige Interpretation*) of works of art.[38] Worringer combined this claim with a transformation in his art historical language: away from rational analysis towards metaphors of emotional association and expressivity, aiming at an immediate, imaginative response on the part of the reader. This rendered Worringer an especially compelling point of reference for the artistic and literary avant-garde of his day. The first expressionists eagerly took up Worringer's concept of "expressive abstraction,"[39] just as Worringer himself was clearly influenced by the circle around the poet Stefan George.[40]

It was Worringer, too, who first aligned the history of art with the concept of a new hermeneutics affected by the general turn of the humanities in Germany towards *Geisteswissenschaft* as formulated especially by the philosopher Wilhelm Dilthey. These new hermeneutics, defined as a theory of understanding (*Verstehen*) – as opposed to explanation (*Erklären*) as the basic concept of the sciences – were conceived as an imaginative, spiritual process by which the interpreter enacts a congenial, sympathetic recreation of the work of art. This approach sought to surpass an empirical, formalistic analysis by recognizing the essential principles, as expressed in art, guiding the relationship of the human subject to the material and immaterial world in history.[41]

GEBRÜDER ASAM.
JOHANNESKIRCHE IN MÜNCHEN. INNERES. 1733.

Figure 6.2 **Munich, St. John's (so-called Asam-church), by Cosmas Damian and Egid Quirin Asam**

Source: Pinder, *Deutscher Barock*, 1912 (pl. 59).

The first art historian to transpose this new notion of art history to the baroque was Pinder, in his book *Deutscher Barock. Die großen Baumeister des 18. Jahrhunderts* – published in 1912 in the popular series of the *Blauen Bücher* (Blue Books).[42] Like Worringer, Pinder experimented with the evocation of baroque art and architecture by the means of an expressive literary style operating with metaphors full of pathos and imagination. He envisaged Baroque architecture as a spatial, mystical, ecstatic dream[43] and combined visual, textual and even associative aural effects into a multi-sensorial, synthetic experience. Consider, for example, his description of the Asam-church at Munich (Figure 6.2): "… The walls glow in the dark, the upper cornice falls over like a foaming wave and diffuses itself into the sky. … Everything solid slips away, reality drowns. You can hear a kind of spiritual buzzing as if expressed sometimes by the highest form of incorporeal music."[44]

After the First World War this kind of expressive, intuitive, mystifying art history immediately took hold. The brutality of the war had shattered ethical, social and aesthetic beliefs and the language of expressionism seemed to offer a way to come to terms with a broken reality. Art history accommodated a new awareness of chaos, destruction, deformation, and the explosion of form: corresponding to the experience of the trenches and the battlefields. It was sought and found especially in the baroque, the interpretation of which as an expressive force had already been prepared before the war. Thus Wilhelm Hausenstein described the baroque – in his highly suggestive book *Vom Geist des Barock* (1920)[45] – in such vibrantly expressive terms as "raging nature," "suddenness of an explosion,"[46] and as a "maximum of expression, tension of nerves,"[47] which "blasts itself into formlessness, therefore the suggestion of the infinite."[48] Hausenstein's metaphorical language descended, however, into drastic and bewildering imagery, as when he wrote of a baroque altar as "the interior of an ardently ripped up corpse. The ecstatic makes Harakiri."[49]

In his two volumes on baroque sculpture (1919), Brinckmann defines Renaissance, baroque and rococo as a staggering trilogy of "cheerfulness, pathos, ecstasy."[50] He dwells extensively on the baroque desire for expression (*Ausdrucksverlangen*) that leads, finally, to the explosion of form, tearing it into shreds.[51] Once the form is wrecked – the state Brinckmann calls "the destruction of form" (*Formzertrümmerung*) – pure spirituality is laid bare.[52] Brinckmann shares with many art historians of the Weimar Republic this interest in what he called the energetic enervation of form (*Innervationsformen*),[53] the tearing up of form into formlessness, into the indefinite, and from there to the infinitude of the cosmos – "the convergence of the spiritual and the sensual" as achieved, particularly, in the period of the baroque.[54]

Even the architecture of the baroque was now transformed into mystical, metaphysical visions – and transmitted to the reader in a language that was similarly spiritualized. Following the path prepared by Pinder in 1912, the process of writing architectural history was treated as proceeding from description to the analysis of forms, functions and spaces, through to an understanding of the overarching spiritual essence and the expression of spirituality in buildings. This stepwise methodology is made especially explicit in Max Hauttmann's formative book *Geschichte der kirchlichen Baukunst in Bayern, Schwaben und Franken, 1550–1780* (1921), where the ascent from analysis to what could be called architectural hermeneutics is even mirrored in the structure of the text.[55] In his final chapter on "expression" Hauttmann mused about the metaphysical atmosphere created in German mid-eighteenth-century churches like Johann Michael Fischer's Berg am Laim near Munich (Figure 6.3): "Architecture itself has become the bearer of an atmosphere, of a spiritual expression. A spirituality stirs up the most suspended … vibrates through these rooms. It rises ever more to the transcendental … when it can confine its visions in absolute space."[56]

This striving for the recognition of spiritual expression and an absolute, infinite space is, moreover, evaluated as the final climax not only of the hermeneutical process, but also of the historical development of the baroque as it had been achieved by mid-eighteenth-century Germany: "it corresponds to the German way of growing that with this last lies the emphasis, the climax," to again recall Hauttmann's words.[57] Feulner turned this purportedly German destination for the latest, the final, into a much more blatant pretention: "The final phase of a development coming from afar, the accomplishment of the baroque could only find its fulfilment in Germany."[58]

Figure 6.3   Munich, Berg am Laim, Collegiate Church, by Johann Michael Fischer
Source: Hauttmann, *Geschichte des kirchlichen Baukunst*, 1921 (pl. 21).

The eager search for the expressivity of the baroque thereby induced leading scholars of the Weimar Republic to turn the rational analysis of complex forms and spaces into an intuitive mystification of baroque and rococo art and architecture. These art historians seemingly perceived this mystification as the culmination of their work and had no sense of any inherent danger in the irrational and ahistorical tendencies their methods allowed.[59] Feulner, in fact, explicitly demanded that historians bring a "faithful sense" (*gläubiger Sinn*)[60] when dealing with a baroque church like Weltenburg (Figure 6.4):

> The space is inaccessible to the calculating intellect, because the experience of light and color, atmosphere and expression, is more powerful. You may set the lever wherever you want, but the intellect will soon fail because it is emotion to which is appealed to unilaterally. A systematic description of the building does not mean anything.[61]

Figure 6.4   Weltenburg, Abbey Church, by Cosmas Damian and Egid Quirin Asam
Source: Feulner 1923 (ill. 6).

Brinckmann likewise frankly declared that art historical analysis must and shall "capitulate in front of the inextricable mesh" of baroque art.[62] Indeed, it was Brinckmann's teacher Wölfflin who first conceded in 1913 that the eye – and with it the ratio – capitulated (both authors used the same verb with its militaristic origins) when trying to conceive of the glittering movement of a rococo room like the residence theatre at Munich: "and the moment is arriving when the eye capitulates and beholds only the torrent of the ensemble. … The artistic intention aims in the first place for the fascinating rhythm of a glimmering total movement."[63]

Typology

Wölfflin, whom the younger generation of Weimar scholars both admired and sought to surpass, had coined the major concepts of the historiography of the baroque as early as 1888 in his *Habilitationsschrift*, *Renaissance und Barock*.[64] Therein Wölfflin introduced a typological method for the study of the baroque – the second basic historiographical trend of the 1920s as noted by Wellek. In *Renaissance und Barock* Wölfflin characterized the baroque as an art of dissolution into the infinite, an art of pathos, delimination and ecstasy, deliberately contrasting it to the Renaissance:

> Renaissance art is the art of calm and beauty. … Baroque aims at a different effect. It wants to carry us away with the force of its impact, immediate and over-whelming. It gives us not a generally enhanced vitality, but excitement, ecstasy, intoxication. … We have no sense of release, but rather of having been drawn into the tension of an emotional condition.[65]

Wölfflin admitted that this interpretation of the baroque was influenced by his present-day experiences. He was, indeed, the first to propose a congeniality between his own time and the baroque, just as Schnell and others later mused on a "secret congeniality" between that period and their own 1920s. Wölfflin's point of reference was Richard Wagner, and he even quoted the last words of Isolde from *Tristan und Isolde*, which was first performed in 1865 in Munich: "One can hardly fail to recognize the affinity that our own age in particular bears to the Italian baroque. A *Richard Wagner* appeals to the same emotions: 'Ertrinken – versinken – unbewusst – hoechste Lust!' His conception of art shows a complete correspondence with those of the baroque."[66] At the same time, Wölfflin clearly drew on the tradition of artistic theory of the seventeenth and eighteenth centuries in which the semantic field of the term baroque was developed as anti-rational, extravagance, folly and decline – in short, the anti-classical principle.[67] Francesco Milizia in 1785 spoke, for example, of the works of Borromini as "delirio maggiore."[68] So Milizia's delirium became Wölfflin's ecstasy – opposed, as it was, to the clarity and rationalism of Renaissance and (neo-)classicism.

In this way, Wölfflin furthered the concept of the baroque as the anti-classical style and prepared the ground for a typological approach to history of art, which he condensed into opposing stylistic principles. Constructing basic oppositions between *Renaissance und Barock* (as his title describes), he outlined the principles of "linear and massive," "flat and spatial (substantial)," regular and irregular, or "the dissolution of the regular (a free style or one of painterly disorder)," "definition," and "elusiveness."[69] Between this book and his *Kunstgeschichtliche Grundbegriffe*, published in 1915, these concepts had become his famous set of five antithetic or bipolar terms: linear and painterly, plane and recession, closed and open form, multiplicity and unity, absolute and relative clarity.[70] Especially in light of the rigid yet persuasive argumentational clarity into which Wölfflin had distilled it by 1915, a typological approach to the baroque had become attractive to many scholars of the humanities in the Weimar Republic, in the history of art as well as in its neighbouring disciplines.[71] As Wellek had already noted by 1946, the baroque was, therein, assigned its place in the basic pairing of classicism and anti-classicism, in which the baroque was firmly fixed to the side of the gothic and romanticism.

The kinship between the baroque and the gothic – especially the late gothic – was, moreover, consolidated by German art historians preoccupied around 1900 with another dichotomy: the difference between Southern, Latinate (*romanisch*), Italian art on one side and, on the other, a Northern, Germanic art. Riegl, Wölfflin and Dehio variously promoted the concept of constant – as opposed to historically variable – stylistic principles of Nordic-Germanic art and architecture. Riegl differentiated between Northern-Germanic and Southern-Latinate art, especially in his posthumously published lectures *Die Entstehung der Barockkunst in Rom* (*The Origins of Baroque Art in Rome*, 1908).[72] Heinrich Wölfflin extended his *Kunstgeschichtliche Grundbegriffe* to a typology of Nordic versus Southern-Italian art in sections on "historical and national characteristics" ("Historisches und Nationales"), which he included into each of his main chapters,[73] and this focus became the major topic of his final book, *Italien und das deutsche Formgefühl* (*Italy and the German Sense of Form*), published in 1931. Georg Dehio finally recognized an "original and fundamentally German disposition of mind" ("deutsche Ur- und Grundstimmung," a term which can hardly be translated) in the third volume of his *Geschichte der deutschen Kunst* of 1926:[74] "a general principle that can be defined in short as the contrary to the classic,"[75] and which is defined by Dehio as the "sense for the immeasurable and secrecy of life," a love of dissonance, "the dusky, the suspending, the unlimited," the instinctive and irrational. As Dehio concluded, "gothic, romantic, baroque – they are all merely different names for the same thing."[76]

This a-historical typology became an obsession with German art historians in the first third of the twentieth century. It is evident, how easily this "secret gothic" (*geheime Gotik*) – as Worringer famously coined it in 1911[77] and which variously described an art of affectivity, subjectivity, spirituality and movement – could be extended to expressionism. Being conceived as representing an "original trait of the German spirit,"[78] the baroque was, moreover, integrated into the political concept of the Germanic, which had dominated the discourse on German national identity throughout the nineteenth century.[79] This Germanic myth was built up especially during the Wilhelmine Empire, when the newly unified German nation fenced itself off more and more from its European neighbours as a nation based upon the values of an organically grown community of people (*Volksgemeinschaft*), culture (*Kultur*) and education (*Bildung*) – as opposed to the supposedly mechanical, mercantile and rationally based collectivism of western societies and civilization.[80]

At the outbreak of the First World War in 1914 this antithetic typology, the Nordic-Germanic versus the Southern or Western-Latinate, was so forceful that it was immediately deployed by German war propaganda, coined as the German "Ideas of 1914" against the "Ideas of 1789," the ideas of the French Revolution.[81] Even the intellectual and academic elite supported, without hesitation, the German Imperial pathos on these grounds.[82] The war was soon transported into the heart of art history when the German military bombed the cathedral of Reims from October 1914 onwards, and the eminent French art historian Emil Mâle blatantly accused the Germans and their art as derivative, uncreative, only capable of imitation and mimicry. German art historians answered Mâle by taking recourse to the Germanic myth with even greater intensity:[83] Germanic art, they insisted, was generally different from the art of the West: not formal, not rational, but emotional, expressive, spiritual.

Shaped by the typological trend in German historiography and merged with the expressionistic strains of modernism, the baroque could thus be charged with political semantics. In this way it became especially attractive for German historians after 1918. Together with the late gothic, the baroque seemed to embody the best of the history of the German nation, the identity of which had been severely shaken and humiliated by the loss of the war, the breakdown of the Empire, international isolation, and the political, financial and social turmoil of the unbeloved Weimar Republic that ensued. The preoccupation with the baroque offered a contrast to the insecurities of the present. It promised to lead to the essence of a German spirit, the search of which emerged as a national task. Oskar Hagen, for example, suggested in his *Deutsches Sehen* of 1920 that the history of art could contribute to the spiritual reconstruction (*geistiger Wiederaufbau*) of the suffering Fatherland.[84] Weisbach also pleaded in his *Der Barock als Kunst der Gegenreformation* of 1921 for a turn away from the formalism of the pre-war era towards the realm of the spirit, because only there might Germans find consolation in their presently harsh fate:

> Under the pressure of years of war and revolution and being produced during heavy afflictions, this book aspires towards the realm of the spirit and the universal, which alone may serve to free from paralysing chains and break open confining limits and arbitrary barriers. It may be a consolation and a satisfaction for the German in his present fate to maintain this immortal realm in his hands.[85]

So art historians were quite prepared to play their part in the reconstruction of the shattered German identity after 1918, and many began to occupy themselves with German topics.[86] The period of the baroque offered an especially attractive model in history for the new national narratives:[87] The Thirty Years War had once devastated the country as had the recent World War; just as Germans had coped with rebuilding the nation after 1648, so too would they again recover after 1918. Consequently, not only was the baroque generally the subject of widespread attention, but the German baroque in particular drew the focus of the enthusiasm noted at the outset. The discursive models for the notion of a Germanized baroque, a specifically Nordic baroque, had already been formed in the Wilhelmine Empire and were only to be expanded after the war.[88] Germany, as told by the ubiquitous master-narrative, had absorbed both Italian baroque and French rococo and created an ingenious synthesis that surpassed and crowned the achievements of all the other nations in the eighteenth century. Brinckmann, in particular, propagated this notion in his volumes of the *Handbuch der Kunstwissenschaft* of 1919 and in his still well-known lecture *Von Guarino Guarini bis Balthasar Neumann* of 1932. He revelled in a German "special rococo" (*Sonderrokoko*), in parallel to a German "special gothic" (*Sondergotik*) – the synthesis of all former antitheses, the harmonization of form and content, the final triumph, the "fantastic cartouche of a global Baroque."[89] Baroque, as imagined in Brinckmann's words, is the dome of art history's edifice, and German rococo the golden lantern on its pinnacle, the apotheosis of art:

German rococo as the crown and the keystone of the entire baroque swallows up the achievements of single nations into an insoluble texture, it delivers everything in thesis and antithesis, it offers fulfillment of the baroque surpassing itself. German rococo is the totality and exhaustion of Christian-occidental art, apotheosis and end.[90]

Facing this kind of nationalistic over-estimation, which Brinckmann even enhanced with militaristic overtones in 1932 by writing of the "final victory of the spatial intention of the Baroque, which is won in Germany,"[91] it becomes clear how effectively certain German art historians offered ideological patterns with which Nazism would readily connect.

Conclusion

In this way the historiography of the baroque played a role in the semantic transformation of the humanities in the "Third Reich,"[92] and it was those art historians who were especially active in the Germanization of the baroque, like Brinckmann, Feulner or Pinder, who came into considerable proximity to National Socialism.[93] With the advent of Nazi Germany in 1933, competing strains the historiography of the baroque that had enjoyed a forum in the era of the Weimar Republic, like those based on *Geistesgeschichte* and iconography, were soon put to an end.

Theodor W. Adorno was among the first to point to the dangers of an over-stretching of the concept of the baroque to a cliché, although not in the context of the history of art, in his famous 1966 lecture on the "misused baroque."[94] Yet even during the Weimar Republic could be found voices critical of the distortion of the baroque in the service of typology and Germanization. In a critical review of Dehio's third volume of the *Geschichte der deutschen Kunst* Carl Neuman, writing in 1928, countered the "equation gothic = baroque = German," which in his view had been produced by the boundless confusion of his contemporaries. Neumann branded the recent "fanaticism of the baroque" (*Barocktaumel*) as the fashionable habit of "superior art snobs," which, notwithstanding its position in the field of art history, had been long since "supplanted by cubes and the flat roof."[95] Thus Neumann, himself not disinclined to a national characterization of art, proved to be far-sighted enough to realize the limitations of the dominating strands in the historiography of baroque art and architecture in Weimar Germany when confronted with modernity.

Endnotes

1 This chapter draws on my book *Stil und Nation*.

2 Dehio, *Geschichte der deutschen Kunst*, 301–2; see also Betthausen, *Georg Dehio*; and Neumann, "Ist wirklich Barock und Deutsch das Nämliche?" 546–7, which is a review of the third volume of Dehios *Geschichte der deutschen Kunst*.

3 Schnell, "Zur Bewertung des baierischen Barock im 19. und 20. Jahrhundert," 187–8, 192. Schnell was not alone in using the term congeniality (*Wahlverwandtschaft*, after the famous novel of Goethe) in the historiography of the baroque. Compare Müller, *Barockforschung*, 9–10; Voßkamp, "Deutsche Barockforschung in den zwanziger und dreißiger Jahren," 695–7. Schnell finished his PhD on the Bavarian baroque in 1931 at the University of Munich, later published in 1936 as *Der baierische Barock*. See also Hofstädter, "Hugo Karl Maria Schnell, 1904–1981."

4 Such as the highly successful and wide-spread series of *Die Blauen Bücher*. Compare Schnell, "Zur Bewertung des baierischen Barock im 19. und 20. Jahrhundert," 194.

5 Schnell, "Zur Bewertung des baierischen Barock im 19. und 20. Jahrhundert," 194.

6 Dehio, *Geschichte der deutschen Kunst*, 302–3.

7 Schnell, "Zur Bewertung des baierischen Barock im 19. und 20. Jahrhundert," 187–8, 192.

8 The historical literature on the Weimar Republic is vast. A good recent survey in English is Lee, *The Weimar Republic*.

9 On these figures see Aurenhammer, "Max Dvořák, (1874–1921)," 214–27; and Bredekamp, "Erwin Panofsy (1892–1968)," 61–75.

10 Tietze, "Neue Literatur über den deutschen Barock," 310; Weisbach, *Der Barock als Kunst der Gegenreformation*, preface.

11   On the history of art as *Geistesgeschichte* see Prange, *Die Geburt der Kunstgeschichte*, 210–15.

12   Riegl, *Die Entstehung der Barockkunst in Rom*; Dvořák, "Über Greco und den Manierismus," 259–76.

13   The main publications of this debate are Weisbach, *Der Barock als Kunst der Gegenreformation*; and "Gegenreformation – Manierismus – Barock," 16–28; Friedlaender, "Die Entstehung des antiklassischen Stiles in der italienischen Malerei um 1520," 49–86; Pevsner, "Gegenreformation und Manierismus," 243–62; and "Beiträge zur Stilgeschichte des Früh- und Hochbarock," 225–46.

14   Rose, *Spätbarock*, 8. On the concept of the *Gesamtkunstwerk*, see Garberson, "Historiography of the *Gesamtkunstwerk*," 1, 53–72; Junod, "Gesamtkunstwerk," 72–6.

15   Lützeler, "Zur Religionssoziologie deutscher Barockarchitektur," 557–84.

16   Pinder, *Das Problem der Generation in der Kunstgeschichte Europas*; on Pinder's generation theory, see Halbertsma, *Wilhelm Pinder und die deutsche Kunstgeschichte*, 61–81; Schwartz, *Blind Spots*, 103–20; Kanz, "Kunstgeschichte als 'geisteswissenschaftliche Biologie'," 325–34.

17   Wellek, "The Concept of the Baroque in Literary Scholarship," 77–9. The interchange between the historiography of baroque art and baroque literature – and especially the role of Wölfflin's *Kunstgeschichtliche Grundbegriffe* – has been regularly considered. See Müller, "Die Übertragung des Barockbegriffs," 95–112; König and Lämmert, *Literaturwissenschaft und Geistesgeschichte, 1910–1925*; Lepper, "Typologie, Stilpsychologie, Kunstwollen," 23–5.

18   Wellek, "The Concept of the Baroque in Literary Scholarship," 79.

19   Wellek, "The Concept of the Baroque in Literary Scholarship," 85–6.

20   See the important study by Bushart, *Der Geist der Gotik und die expressionistische Kunst*, and, more recently, the exhibition catalogue Beil and Dillmann (eds), *Gesamtkunstwerk Expressionismus*.

21   Brinckmann, *Barockskulptur*, vol. 2, 242.

22   Feulner, *Bayerisches Rokoko*, 14, 21–2.

23   Feulner, *Bayerisches Rokoko*, 115.

24   Feulner *Bayerisches Rokoko*, 24.

25   Feulner *Bayerisches Rokoko*, 39, 65–6.

26   Hans Scharoun in an undated letter of about 1920, quoted after Oswald Maria Ungers (ed.), *Die gläserne Kette*, 24–5. See Durth, "Die Neuerfindung der Welt als gute Wohnung im All," 342.

27   Miller Lane, *Architecture and Politics in Germany*, 51–64; Pehnt, *Expressionistic Architecture*; Pehnt, *Deutsche Architektur seit 1900*, 99–109. The term "expressionistic" was first applied to architecture by the critic Adolf Behne in a review of Bruno Taut's work of 1913. See Pehnt, *Expressionistic Architecture*, 99–100.

28   The formative author for a theory of organic architecture in Germany in the 1920s was Hugo Häring, especially in his essay "Wege zur form," first published in *Die Form* in 1925. On Häring see Brinitzer, *Organische Architekturkonzepte zwischen 1900 und 1960 in Deutschland*, 171–248.

29   Westheim, "Architektur," 100–101, quoted in Brinitzer, *Organische Architekturkonzepte zwischen 1900 und 1960 in Deutschland*, 96.

30   Westheim, "Festspielhaus in Salzburg," 245–7, quoted in Brinitzer, *Organische Architekturkonzepte zwischen 1900 und 1960 in Deutschland*, 98.

31   See Locher, *Kunstgeschichte als historische Theorie der Kunst*, 378–97; Prange, *Die Geburt der Kunstgeschichte*, 195–210; Adler and Frank, *German Art History and Scientific Thought*; on the competing concepts of Wölfflin, Riegl, Schmarsow and Frankl see in detail Engel, *Stil und Nation*.

32   On this famous book see recently Summers, "Art History Reviewed: Heinrich Wölfflin's *Kunstgeschichtliche Grundbegriffe*, 1915," 476–9.

33   Schnell still notes: "The narrow formal studies, for which Wölfflin had striven with great success, were now blown up." ("Die engen Formstudien, um die sich *Wölfflin* mit größtem Erfolg bemüht hatte, waren nun gesprengt.") – "Zur Bewertung des baierischen Barock im 19. und 20. Jahrhundert," 92.

34   Brinckmann, *Die Baukunst des 17. und 18. Jahrhunderts*, esp. 216–17. Brinckmann's book belonged to the influential series "Handbuch der Kunstwissenschaft." It was published in the same year as Wölfflin's *Grundbegriffe* (1915), but Wölfflin's concepts were obviously already well known through his university lectures and articles. Compare the testimony of Frankl, *Die Entwicklungsphasen der neueren Baukunst*, v, 139. On Brinckmann see Arend, "Albert Erich Brinckmann (1881–1958)," 123–43; "'Einen neuen Geist einführen?'," 179–98; and Levy, "The German Art Historians of World War I," esp. 393–9.

35   Brinckmann, *Die Baukunst des 17. und 18. Jahrhunderts*, esp. 76–89.

36 Worringer, *Formprobleme der Gotik*, 1–11; on Worringer see Öhlschläger, *Abstraktionsdrang*; Söntgen, "Wilhelm Worringer."

37 Worringer, *Abstraktion und Einfühlung*, esp. 2–3; see Bushart, "'Form' und 'Gestalt'," esp. 172–4.

38 Worringer, *Formprobleme der Gotik*, 1–4.

39 Worringer, *Abstraktion und Einfühlung*, 127. On the relationship between Worringer and Expressionism see esp. Bushart, *Der Geist der Gotik*, 18–52; Öhlschläger, *Abstraktionsdrang*.

40 Grebing, *Die Worringers*, 24.

41 On the hermeneutic concept of *Geistesgeschichte* see, for example, König and Lämmert (eds), *Literaturwissenschaft und Geistesgeschichte*; Barberowski, *Der Sinn der Geschichte*, 99–125; on the relationship to history of art see Bushart, "'Form' und 'Gestalt'," 168–74.

42 On Pinder see Halbertsma, *Wilhelm Pinder und die deutsche Kunstgeschichte*; Stöppel, "Wilhelm Pinder."

43 For example Pinder, *Deutscher Barock*, iv ("im architektonischen Traume"), xiii ("architektonischen Rausch"), xix ("zum mystischen Traume").

44 Pinder, *Deutscher Barock*, xx: "Die Wände glühen dunkel auf, die große Hohlkehle kippt wie eine schäumende Meereswoge über und verliert sich tief gegen den Himmel. … Alles Feste entschwebt, alle Realität ertrinkt. Man kann eine Art von geistigem Ohrensausen fühlen, wie es zuweilen von der höchsten körperlosen Musik erzeugt wird." Pinder does not paraphrase the Communist Manifesto of Karl Marx and Friedrich Engels of 1848, as might be inferred from its English translation, as quoted in Berman, *All that is Solid Melts into Air*, 21. The relevant passage of the Manifesto reads in its German original text: "Alles Ständische und Stehende verdampft," Lieber (ed.), *Karl-Marx-Ausgabe*, vol. 2, 821.

45 On Hausenstein see Imorde, "Barock und Moderne," 179–212; Imorde, "Selbstberauschung," 299–350.

46 Hausenstein, *Vom Geist des Barock*, 9–10.

47 Hausenstein, *Vom Geist des Barock*, 64.

48 Hausenstein, *Vom Geist des Barock*, 67.

49 Hausenstein *Vom Geist des Barock*, 13.

50 Brinckmann, *Barockskulptur*, vol. 1, 346.

51 Brinckmann, *Barockskulptur*, vol. 1, 205–6.

52 Brinckmann, *Barockskulptur*, vol. 1, 206; see also 183.

53 Brinckmann, *Barockskulptur*, vol. 1, 43–4.

54 Brinckmann, *Barockskulptur*, vol. 2, 242; compare 276.

55 See the sequence of the main chapters of Hauttmann, *Geschichte der kirchlichen Baukunst*, on "Tasks and Intentions of Building" ("Bauaufgaben und Baugesinnung"), "Types of Spaces" ("Die Raumarten"), "Mantle Forms" ("Die Mantelformen") and "Expression" ("Der Ausdruck").

56 Hauttmann, *Geschichte der kirchlichen Baukunst*, 256.

57 Hauttmann, *Geschichte der kirchlichen Baukunst*, 9.

58 Feulner, *Bayerisches Rokoko*, 24. Compare Pinder, *Deutscher Barock*, xii and his emphasis on the "process of the Germanisation" (*Verdeutschung*) of the baroque in Germany

59 This anti-rational tendency in German art history has been commented on in Müller, *Barockforschung*; Larsson, "Nationalstil und Nationalismus in der Kunstgeschichte der zwanziger und dreißiger Jahre," 177–80; and Halbertsma, *Wilhelm Pinder und die deutsche Kunstgeschichte*, 57–9. Jutta Held appropriately speaks of an "intuitionistic phenomenology" ("intuitionistische Wesensschau") and outlines its dangers at the transition into National Socialism – see "Kunstgeschichte im 'Dritten Reich'," esp. 40–41.

60 Feulner, *Bayerisches Rokoko*, 14.

61 Feulner, *Bayerisches Rokoko*, 16–17.

62 Brinckmann, *Barockskulptur*, vol. 1, 199.

63 Wölfflin, "Ueber den Begriff des Malerischen," 6–7.

64 The importance of this book for the historiography of the baroque has long since been accepted, see Tintelnot, "Zur Gewinnung unserer Barockbegriffe," 48–51; Müller, *Barockforschung*, 36–9; Holly, "Wölfflin and the Imagining of the Baroque," vol. 2, 1255–64; Imorde, "Barock und Moderne," 198–204. The literature on Wölfflin is vast, see for instance, Lurz, *Heinrich Wölfflin*; Wimböck, "Heinrich Wölfflin," 124–40.

65 Wölfflin, *Renaissance and Baroque*, 38.

66 Wölfflin, *Renaissance and Baroque*, 87. The italics are Wölfflin's.

67   On the conceptual history of the term "baroque" see most recently Oechslin, "'Barock'," vol. 2, 1225–54; Moser, "Barock," vol. 1, 578–618.

68   Milizia, *Memorie degli Architetti antichi e moderni*, vol. 2, 158.

69   Wölfflin, *Renaissance and Baroque*, 31–3. The German terms are: "linear und massig," "flächenhaft und räumlich (körperlich)," "Auflösung des Regelmäßigen (Freier Stil, malerische Unordnung)," "Unfassbarkeit ... (Das Unbegrenzte)," *Renaissance und Barock* (1986), 30–33.

70   Quoted after Fernie, *Art History and its Methods*, 127–51. On Wölfflin´s antithetic methodology see, for example, Holly, "Wölfflin and the Imagining of the Baroque," 1256; Locher, *Kunstgeschichte als historische Theorie der Kunst*, 383.

71   On typology as a core method of the humanities (*Geisteswissenschaft)* in the first half of the twentieth century in Germany, see Lepper, "Typologie, Stilpsychologie, Kunstwollen," 18–25.

72   See also Engel, "Riegl on the Baroque."

73   See also the characterization of Nordic-Germanic art in his final chapter, Wölfflin, *Kunstgeschichtliche Grundbegriffe*, 254–7.

74   Dehio, *Geschichte der deutschen Kunst*, vol. 3, 176–7. See also Garberson, "Historiography of the *Gesamtkunstwerk*," 176.

75   Dehio, *Geschichte der deutschen Kunst*, vol. 3, 285.

76   Dehio, *Geschichte der deutschen Kunst*, vol. 3, 177.

77   Worringer, *Formprobleme der Gotik*, 27; see Bushart, *Der Geist der Gotik*, 32–3.

78   Dehio, *Geschichte der deutschen Kunst*, vol. 3, 303.

79   The concept of the Germanic and Barbaric in fact can be traced back at least to the German humanism of the sixteenth century. See, *Barbar, Germane, Arier*; *Freiheit und Gemeinschaft*.

80   Nipperdey, *Deutsche Geschichte*, vol. 1, 593–4, 814–19; Bollenbeck, *Bildung und Kultur*.

81   Breuer, *Grundpositionen der deutschen Rechten*, 57–9, 90–102; See, *Freiheit und Gemeinschaft*, 170–72.

82   Nipperdey, *Deutsche Geschichte*, vol. 1, 596, 606–9, 778–9; Mommsen, *Bürgerliche Kultur und politische Ordnung*, 133–57, 178–215.

83   Mâle's text was translated into German and published as *Studien über die deutsche Kunst* with a series of replies by German art historians. See Levy, "The German Art Historians of World War I," 379–89.

84   Hagen, *Deutsches Sehen*, 1–2.

85   Weisbach, *Der Barock als Kunst der Gegenreformation*, preface, dated August 1920.

86   Larsson, "Nationalstil und Nationalismus in der Kunstgeschichte der zwanziger und dreissiger Jahre," 169–84. This focus on the achievements of German history was a general phenomenon of the humanities in the Weimar Republic. See Eckel, *Geist der Zeit*, 38–9.

87   On the writing of national histories in general see Berger, Donovan and Passmore (eds), *Writing National Histories*.

88   See Warnke, "Die Entstehung des Barockbegriffs in der Kunstgeschichte," vol. 2, 1201–23; Garberson, "Baroque Architecture and German National Identity in Art Historical Texts, ca. 1900," 165–79.

89   Brinckmann, *Barockskulptur*, vol. 2, 394.

90   Brinckmann, *Barockskulptur*, vol. 2, 404.

91   Brinckmann, *Von Guarino Guarini bis Balthasar Neumann*, 1.

92   See in general Müller, *Barockforschung*, 169–76; Oexle, "'Zusammenarbeit mit Baal'," 1–27; Bollenbeck and Knobloch (eds), *Semantischer Umbau der Geisteswissenschaften nach 1933 und 1945*. German art history in the "Third Reich" has been intensely researched of late. See the surveys Kahsnitz, "Der Deutsche Verein für Kunstwissenschaft im Nationalsozialismus;" and Hausmann, *Die Geisteswissenschaften im "Dritten Reich."*

93   On Brinckmann and National Socialism see Arend, "Albert Erich Brinckmann," 123–43; Arend, "'Einen neuen Geist einführen?'," vol. 2, 179–98; on Pinder see Halbertsma, *Wilhelm Pinder und die deutsche Kunstgeschichte*; "Kunstgeschichte im 'Dritten Reich'," 17–60. The role of Adolf Feulner is not yet clarified, yet see his book *Kunst und Geschichte* of 1942, which his heavily charged with Nazi ideology.

94   Adorno, "Der mißbrauchte Barock," 133–57; see Reijen, "Adorno und das Barock," vol. 1, 155–68.

95   Neumann, "Ist wirklich Barock und Deutsch das Nämliche?" 547.

Chapter 7
Riegl and Wölfflin in Dialogue on the Baroque

Evonne Levy

In spite of the pervasive influence of Alois Riegl's and Heinrich Wölfflin's writings on the study of Italian baroque architecture throughout the twentieth century, a fine-grained analysis of their deeply interrelated texts has not been undertaken.[1] Wölfflin first came to the subject in *Renaissance und Barock* of 1888 and Riegl responded fully to this text and to sections on the baroque in Wölfflin's *Die klassische Kunst* (1899; *Classic Art*, 1980) in the second and the third versions of his lecture course on the baroque on which the posthumous publication of 1908, *Die Enstehung der Barockkunst in Rom* (*The Origins of Baroque Art in Rome*, 2010), was based.[2] It is primarily in these lectures that we see that within their largely shared language for the baroque there are significant differences in their points of view: of how the baroque relates to modernity, of its political significance, of the role of artists versus patrons, amongst others. When Wölfflin returned to the baroque in the *Kunstgeschichtliche Grundbegriffe* (1915; *Principles of Art History*, 2015) he did so with full knowledge of Riegl's writings on the subject, including the latter's book-length essay *Das holländische Gruppenporträt* (1902; *The Group Portraiture of Holland*, 1999) and the lectures on Italian baroque art, which he reviewed in 1908.[3] Over a quarter of a century later, and influenced by *Lebensphilosophie*, Wölfflin's attitude towards the baroque became more positive, and we find numerous points of engagement and sympathy with Riegl's analyses.[4] Here their responses to each other's work will be analysed with an eye to how their principal conceptual and political differences belie their formal analyses, and the consequences for the role assigned to architecture.

Wölfflin's point of departure in studying the architecture of the still-maligned baroque was the connection made visible between the ancient Hellenistic and early modern baroques by the "Pergamania" that raged in Berlin in the mid-1880s.[5] Riegl's point of departure, by contrast, was most certainly the interest the baroque held as the awakening of a problematic modern subjectivity, driven by a crisis of subjectivity in the art of his day. Matthew Rampley correctly pointed out that Wölfflin acknowledged the kinship of the baroque to his times already in *Renaissance und Barock*,[6] but he only arrived at this position fully later, in the *Grundbegriffe*. In the latter – a Hildebrandian account replacing bodily empathy with a disembodied optical observer – Wölfflin rethought the baroque through the optical basis of impressionist painting. He already recognized painting in 1888 as the leading medium of his day but only touched upon it in an account of the baroque that instead focused on architecture.[7] Between 1888 and Riegl's lectures, painting had been placed at the centre of the question of the baroque in August Schmarsow's *Barock und Rokoko* which treated all media but which nonetheless made Antonio da Correggio its central protagonist.[8]

Riegl's baroque lectures accorded an important place to architecture, but since his history of art was organized around a Hegelian teleology, a succession in world history from objectivity to subjectivity, Riegl saw in all of the arts the same phenomena.[9] Nonetheless, Riegl acknowledged the difficulty of using architecture given the psychological terms of his analysis: "as architecture creates lifeless works, which is to say works without a will that are insensitive and motionless, and which do not recreate living work (human figures), there is no possibility of directly expressing psychological values. We can thus consider only the composition."[10] The projection of feelings onto forms in empathy theory – the basis for Wölfflin's *Prolegomena* and his *Renaissance und Barock* – is acknowledged by Riegl as one solution: "Notwithstanding this, buildings have a psychological effect on us: they are heavy, light, dark, bright, calm, restless and so forth."[11] Riegl nonetheless presses for formal manifestations in architecture of his concept of subjectivity and its related psychological qualities (emotion, mood):

> There is also a parallel between composition and concept. Is this true with Michelangelo's architecture? In his compositions, Michelangelo strives for the emancipation of deep space (*Tiefraum*), and as a concept he searches for the emancipation of feeling. Deep space and emotion are thus parallel ... two sides of the same coin, the psychological and the physical.[12]

In his lectures on the baroque Riegl contended with all media, but his *Das holländische Gruppenporträt* depends entirely on the psychological relations between depicted figures and beholder, and thus privileges figuration in painting. There is certainly a strong echo of Riegl's universality of the arts in Wölfflin's *Grundbegriffe*, alongside a strong emergence of painting and graphic media as the leading examples. Sculpture and architecture become secondary.

While it is often said that Wölfflin's 1888 *Renaissance und Barock* was the first to recuperate the baroque this is only true if you consider his attention to the period a recuperation. For, as Riegl noted in his review of the literature that formed part of the introduction to his lectures, Wölfflin is almost as judgmental as Burckhardt ("and offers nothing fundamentally new").[13] In this respect Cornelius Gurlitt's three-volume history of baroque architecture in Europe (1887–89) – because it was written by an architect and for modern architects seeking to understand the present in the past – was the first truly recuperative study, even though in Riegl's opinion Gurlitt had failed to *explain* the baroque.[14] Wölfflin's 1888 view of the origins of the baroque, limited to Rome and revolving around Michelangelo's work, was that of a repressive architecture, violently suppressing and subordinating individual forms. Wölfflin's highly idealized Renaissance, by contrast, was a period in which individual forms were coordinated, all life, all "Wille" (the near unique use of the word, central to Riegl's baroque, in the book). A book short on definitive statements about the historical motives for the change in style (in spite of the dedication of the second part to the reasons for the change in style), nonetheless reads as an anti-clerical view of the baroque. The behemoth Catholic Church modelled, for Wölfflin, the newly unified German *Großstadt*, which had found its genealogy in the imperial guise of Hellenistic Greece and its stylistic model in the Pergamon reliefs, newly installed in Berlin.[15]

In addition to finding that Wölfflin had made little advancement on Burckhardt, Riegl's most searing criticism of Wölfflin is that his criteria of "massiveness" and "movement" were "not deep enough" ("nicht tief genug").[16] I want to take his choice of the word *tief* seriously, for it offers a key to Riegl's baroque. *Tiefe* (depth or deep space) was a pillar in the sculptor Adolf von Hildebrand's *Das Problem der Form* (1893; *The Problem of Form*, 1907), where it was paired with "Fläche" (plane). Wölfflin took both terms over for his third pair of principles. But in *Renaissance und Barock* he contrasted "Fläche" (plane) and "Raum" (space), or, the "Flächenhaft" (planar) to the "räumlich" (*körperlich*).[17] Wölfflin sees the baroque working more in depth than the Renaissance, but this point is not of particular importance to him as he writes in 1888, for Wölfflin sees conflict between horizontal and vertical elements in elevation more than between elements in plan and in elevation.[18] Riegl makes *Tiefe*, and hence space itself, a pillar of his baroque.[19] Both Wölfflin and Riegl were influenced by Hildebrand and both understood his "one imaginary movement into space" necessary to create a sense of spatial unity as a quality of the baroque.[20] But in contrast to Wölfflin, Riegl sees "depth" as key: *Tiefe* is the formal index of subjectivity, which is in turn the *Wollen* of the baroque and of modernity.

As an important moment in the march towards modern subjectivity Riegl's baroque marked a transition in the relationships between will, emotion, and attentiveness. Will (the urge to power, rather than volition) is isolating, emotion is binding, and attentiveness (the ideal condition) allows for the individual to be connected (to others, to his environment) but to retain his individuality.[21] As the expression of will (in Renaissance art) gives way in the baroque to emotion (feelings), and then to a psychologically alert state of attentiveness, man passes from an objective relation to the world around him to a subjective one. In this scheme space is the medium of relationality, the formal substance of a subjective worldview. So when Riegl says that Wölfflin is not deep enough, two things are meant: that Wölfflin's baroque is neither spatially deep, nor subjective, and this is because Wölfflin's cyclical art history is not governed by a philosophy of history.

In his baroque lectures Riegl tracked the rise of subjectivity in formal qualities and historical typologies. For example, the rejection of the central plan favoured in antiquity and in the Renaissance signalled a new subjectivity, for the longitudinal church was a "deep" space. But unlike the earlier longitudinal churches the baroque was a truly spatial art because it demanded a "coherent spatial impression."[22] This newly unified space presupposed a view from afar or "distant vision" (*Fernsicht*); it created unrest, tension, uncertainty, movement and struggle. The Gesù, for example, is the church in which depth triumphs over a previously maintained balance between height and depth. There is much in Riegl's account that lines up with Wölfflin's immediately classic comparison of Giacomo della Porta's and Jacopo Barozzi da Vignola's designs: the crucial role of the Gesù in terms of invention and subsequently as a model, the quality of tension, the spatially unifying effect of the barrel vault, and even the characterization of the relative unimportance of the exterior with respect to the interior. But for Riegl the true importance of the shift to the longitudinal plan is in the introduction of depth, and hence interiority, or subjectivity.

The major conceptual differences between Wölfflin and Riegl are all the more important given how very closely they follow each other's analyses of key works. For example, Michelangelo's Medici Chapel played an exemplary role in Riegl's lectures, following closely on Wölfflin's analysis in *Die klassische Kunst* (1899). Both begin noting that architecture and sculpture were conceived together by the artist and both use as a foil Andrea Sansovino's tombs in Santa Maria del Popolo. Wölfflin's principal observation about the Medici chapel concerns the subordination of architecture to the figure, this being a characteristic of the baroque fully developed in his *Renaissance und Barock*. In spite of Wölfflin's shifting of some of the burden of the degeneration of the Renaissance to mannerism in *Die klassische Kunst*, intense feeling around the ill effects of the baroque tendency toward subordination burst through in his discussion of the Medici Chapel:

> There is no other room in the whole world where sculpture speaks with such force. The whole architectural setting … is entirely subordinated to the effect made by the figures. It seems almost as if the figures were intended to appear too big for the room … how difficult it is to get far enough away to see them properly, how one feels hemmed in; what then are we to say on learning that four more figures of river-gods lying on the floor, were to be included as well? The effect *would have been oppressive* and it would have been an emotional effect which had *nothing in common with the liberating beauty* of the Renaissance.[23]

Wölfflin observes further that the ducal tombs are not independent of the architecture:

> Only the sarcophagus and crowning figures are free of the wall while the hero himself is actually seated in the wall. Thus two elements usually spatially disparate are brought to a unified effect with the seated figure who is brought so low down that he comes between heads of lying ones.[24]

The allegorical figures are "immensely stimulating because of the variety of planes and the major contrasts of axial direction, yet they remain at rest in spite of all this enrichment."[25]

Riegl agreed with Wölfflin's view of the relation of sculpture to the wall behind it:

> Previously, one avoided seeing the wall if at all possible. So there is greater optical perception and the tactile limits are blurred more and more. In the Medici ensemble, the homogeneousness of tomb and wall expresses itself in two ways: 1. The statue of the deceased is placed in a niche and so is related closely to the wall (while the sarcophagus is situated in front of it); 2. on consideration, the wall decoration reveals a paltriness as it is divided into compartments; in itself it should count for little, but to act as a foil to the tomb figures in order to make them seem larger.[26]

And, he adopts Wölfflin's politically-inflected view of the pre-Renaissance composition as "coordinated," the Renaissance as "measured subordination," and the wall in Michelangelo's Medici chapel as "subordinated."

Though Riegl does not share Wölfflin's claustrophobic reaction to the oppressive arrangement of Michelangelo's figures, Wölfflin's casual observation that one must step back to see the tomb properly is integral to Riegl's historical scheme. He agrees that "the definite shift to the perspective view is a pre-requisite for the correct perception of the intended effect" but interprets the need for the distant view (*Fernsicht*) as "a deliberate intention to create optical effects," because it points to a subjective worldview.[27] Riegl also echoes Wölfflin's analysis of the allegorical figures:

Night seems to project forward, while Day seems to be moving backward. This gives the impression of rotation, characterized by all elements being in movement while the whole remains in the same spot: there is a strong sense of repose about the whole, but also extreme movement of individual elements being increasingly contradictory.[28]

In this and other passages Riegl sees antitheses or conflict between two states (tactile versus optical, movement versus repose, will versus emotion[29]) where Wölfflin saw only movement and only one sensation of subordination. And whereas Wölfflin's claims for the Medici Chapel remained allusive and somewhat Rieglian. ("A change of feeling is perceptible in all these figures. The atmosphere is no longer one of freedom and joy as it had been in the Sistine Chapel, and all movement is heavier and slower; the bodies seem mountainously ponderous, animated only by fits and starts of the will."[30]) Riegl identifies no particular mood but an emancipation of feeling, now in combat with the will. Michelangelo's *terribiltá* is an expression of the tremendous force of will counteracting vehement feelings.

Insofar as Wölfflin had (in 1888) evoked baroque architecture as organized by a kind of nebulous superstructure suppressing the individual, in *Die klassische Kunst* he symptomatically focused on the Medici allegories rather than the portraits, which he dismisses as such. Riegl by contrast sees in the Italian baroque the individual in an internal battle of will versus emotion, with emotion seeking liberation. Keeping the individual at the centre, Riegl, in contrast to Wölfflin, therefore sees in Giuliano's portrait the conflict between will (typical of Italian art) and emotion (an inner psychological impulse typical of northern art). In the more tranquil tomb of Lorenzo de'Medici where will retreats as emotions get the upper hand, the baroque sets in with emotions winning out over will, as in the work of Correggio and Bernini.[31] In the portrait of Giuliano this tension manifests in a conflict between his limbs (directed by his will), his turned head, and in the almost angry face (directed by his emotions). Because "emotions are in conflict with the will," the formal relations they entail are also in conflict: will is isolating (and tactile), emotions are connecting (and optical), they lead to the "disintegration of the self."[32] Hence for Riegl, the chapel with its layers of reliefs, with its strong planes and its increase in depth (with shadow) needs to be viewed from both near (*Nahsicht*) and from a unifying distance (*Fernsicht*).

In putting together Riegl's lectures, excluding the lectures on non-Italian subjects and entitling them *Die Entstehung der Barockkunst in Rom*, Arthur Burda and Max Dvořák implicitly related Riegl's work to Wölfflin's. For in *Renaissance und Barock* Wölfflin saw Rome as the place of origin and he did not entertain a baroque outside of Italy. Wölfflin retracted this position in the *Grundbegriffe* when he came around to the view of scholars who drew a line between the German gothic and the baroque as inherently northern in sensibility. But at this early moment the young Swiss Protestant scholar had a deeply-rooted anti-clerical view of the counter-reformatory baroque which he expressed in his formal analyses, such as Michelangelo's changes to Bramante's design of the cupola of St. Peter's:

Bramante's St. Peter's is not baroque. One finds here a cupola of the greatest scale, but around it Bramante arranged four neighboring domes which do not cramp it but which form a counterbalance. They maintain their own and their independence and curb the impression of the overpowering. Michelangelo by contrast counted precisely on this impression; he pushed the neighboring spaces so far in their scale that compared to the main space they can no longer maintain themselves and so he produced an absolutely dominating center, which makes everything else around it appear unfree and [there] against its own will.[33]

Wölfflin pits Church hierarchy against an entrapped individual here, a bald association of the late nineteenth-century view of the mass persuasion by which the counter-reformatory Catholic Church won people to the faith.

If Wölfflin's first (negative) baroque was counter-reformatory, Riegl's baroque lectures treated both North and South (Protestant and Catholic), showing how in the run up to the baroque the arts of these different regions had different relations to the three ways of being: the South is objective, an art in which will is expressed through hierarchical compositions to which individuals are subordinated; the North by contrast tends towards subjective relations expressed in coordinated compositions; individuality is retained amidst a general attentiveness and consciousness of the world. While the Protestant North is not in view in the published lectures, we can turn to Riegl's *Das holländische Gruppenporträt* for the northern side. In that text Riegl's reading of attentiveness through the psychological relations between figures and beholder is explicitly linked to the Dutch democracy: of individuals bound to the world out of pure selfless interest in it, without desire, without wishing to subdue it. This reading is implicitly critical of Wölfflin's *Renaissance und Barock* with its exclusive focus on (hierarchical) Rome. For Riegl, rather, North and South converged in the baroque when Italian art adopted northern subjectivity, its psychological character, though the two forms of *Wollen* are in tension. For instance, the intensification of psychology in Italian baroque works brings about not a northern form of introspection typically expressed as calmness, but a surplus of unmotivated action.[34]

How then does Catholic Riegl, sympathetic to Dutch democracy and northern *Aufmerksamkeit* and *Innerlichkeit* contend with Protestant Wölfflin's anti-clerical description of subordination in St. Peter's? While following Wölfflin's analysis rather closely Riegl makes subtle adjustments. He characterizes Bramante's plan as having elements which are "not rigorously subordinated" to the dome, and a cupola which "dominates but does not overwhelm."[35] Michelangelo's radical alteration of Bramante's plan for St. Peter's reveals him as father of the baroque, for he took Renaissance subordination much farther.[36] Although Wölfflin gave agency to Michelangelo in the change of style from Renaissance to baroque he remained (throughout his life) unable to answer the question "why does style change?" the answer to which always implicated larger forces. Riegl's attribution of the change in plan to Michelangelo makes an important point that may be responding to Wölfflin's inability to answer the question. Riegl focuses on Michelangelo's reassertion of the central plan (noting that most would have preferred return to a longitudinal plan) as a pursuit of his own *Kunstauffassung* in using his preferred form ("a rotating cone, that is a centralized building with severe subordination and the dimensions increased to the point of conflict"[37]). For Riegl it is quite definite that it was the artist's *Kunstwollen* against tradition, his patrons, and a broad consensus, that determined the form of the building. There is something enigmatic about Riegl's emphasis on Michelangelo's agency on the one hand and on the strongest form of subordination on the other which may be thus explained. It is significant that Riegl situates Michelangelo at the origins of the baroque, but is careful to note that his work is not the ultimate point of arrival – which occurred in the North. A more baroque solution in Riegl's view is a longitudinal plan, so Michelangelo's solution (and this holds for Italian art as a whole) was only baroque in part.

The only limited extent to which Riegl allows a key Roman monument at the centre of Catholicism to be representative of the baroque, points to the shadowy presence of confessional politics in Riegl's lectures.[38] While justifying the study of the baroque on the grounds that it was the instrument of the Catholic Church's *Weltmission* in the second half of the seventeenth and early-eighteenth centuries, he interjects a negative note: "We can define almost the exact day on which one Catholic nation – France – emancipated itself from Italian influence."[39] Although Riegl follows with a strong statement about the originality of Italian over French art, the idea that a nation's art needed to be "emancipated" from Italian art lines up with his polemical essay "Salzburgs Stellung in der Geschichte der Kunst."[40] A city based on an ancient Roman plan, lacking understanding of a Germanic *Kunstwollen* (witness the lack of Romanesque churches, hall churches, or a gothic cathedral), re-Italianized in the Renaissance by Bishop Wolf Dietrich, Salzburg was eventually "emancipated" from Italy. This occurred around 1700 with the Archbishop Johann Ernst Grafen, whose patronage helped to bring about a rejection of Italianate representation ("äusserlichen rappräsentativen Ruhe") for a Northern "inner movement." In the Salzburg churches of Fischer von Erlach Riegl charts the eventual emancipation of Austrian architecture from Italy with forms that are less subordinate, showing movement in depth, and drawing the beholder in closer to see its details. Although to my knowledge Riegl's Catholicism has never been questioned, his interest in emancipation from Italy suggests some sympathy with the Austrian "Los von Rom" movement which emerged in Salzburg in 1900, the same year he delivered in Salzburg itself the lecture on which the published essay was based. This could help to explain why Riegl follows Wölfflin as closely as he does in his passage on subordination at St. Peter's. For if the longitudinal plan is the baroque trend, then Michelangelo's overpowering centralized dome is not a progressive form. Rome, and Catholicism, even driven by Michelangelo's individual *Kunstwollen*, will not be able to overcome the inherent subordination of the South.

But if Riegl cannot see in St. Peter's how the objective and subordinating order of the South will be reconciled with the modern trend towards subjectivity characteristic of the North, he does see such a prospect in the baroque palace. For Wölfflin, secular and religious architecture alike exhibited the tendency toward massification. In baroque palaces the subordination of parts to the whole was visible at every level: bricks lost their individual contours under stucco, columns their individuality in a sequence or a wall, the courtyard its autonomy, its "recht für Sich" in the palace complex.[41] Riegl also saw tensions manifest not just in battling vertical and horizontal elements but also in the third dimension of depth. It is the façade of the private domestic building in particular that Riegl seizes upon as signalling the rise of subjectivity. He adopts the anthropomorphism of the façade – perhaps from Wölfflin's dissertation. ("Even though a house has little in common with a human form, we see the windows as organs that are similar to our eyes. We say they 'spiritualize' the building."[42]) Riegl writes:

> The façade is a wall that simultaneously declares the presence behind it of a space that recedes in depth. 1. "Behind it is a room:" the classical monumental façade did not imply this fact, but principally concealed it as it did not have windows. The door was a necessary evil, and thus given an unassuming treatment. Only more recent art, façade architecture, recognizes the "portal." The word façade derives from *faςe*, which means face, or mirror of the soul, and as no face is without eyes, so no façade is without windows.[43]

Wölfflin and Riegl saw that the gradual diminishment in importance of the courtyard and the concomitant rise of the façade were significant, if for different reasons. For Wölfflin the courtyard was losing "its rights," and the façade, increasingly massive, was marked by conflict between dominating and dominated elements, the individual locked in battle with an unnamed larger force. And whereas Wölfflin stressed the impenetrability of the exterior, Riegl argued that the history of the façade only begins with the window, when a relation is established between exterior and interior. The Farnese Palace is decisive; its windows achieve sufficient depth on the façade and declare space receding behind it. Riegl maps the history of the façade in such detail because the fenestrated baroque façade (in contrast to the unfenestrated ancient house) shows depth, and therefore interiority.

That Wölfflin wrote an uncharacteristically long note in the *Grundbegriffe* citing several works by Riegl suggests just how important it is for us to contend with Riegl's influence on his most widely read work on the baroque.[44] In 1908 Wölfflin reviewed Riegl's *Die Entstehung der Barockkunst in Rom*, complimenting Riegl for his contribution to an art history poor in concepts, amidst complaints about the final published form. It was, he writes, "a painstaking thing to experience his explanation of the baroque as a 'Gesamtphenomen'."[45] Though he assessed the work as nothing substantially new (returning the insult), most of all he noted how instructive the undertaking was for putting all the arts on the same ground. This latter point had a significant impact on the *Grundbegriffe*, Wölfflin's first book to consider all of the media together. Even more influential though, was Riegl's *Das holländische Gruppenporträt*; Wölfflin's rethinking of specific passages by Riegl about Rembrandt (around whom there had been a significant revival in Germany) helps to explain the key place now accorded to the Dutch artist in Wölfflin's baroque in general. Likely with Riegl's help, Wölfflin now saw the baroque as the epoch in the history of art that revealed the feeling for form of the Germanic North – even though the book revolves around period rather than regional or national styles.[46]

Joan Hart has noted that around the time of his review in 1908 Wölfflin had had a burst of ideas for the *Grundbegriffe* along the lines of the baroque as a unified phenomenon. On October 17 of that year he wrote in his notebook: "The seventeenth century to be erected from its components. Not a sequence of artists. The whole phenomenon to be seen in its entirety."[47] On December 5 he added:

> The unified perception of the [seventeenth century]. The focus of attention on *one* point. Architecture has *one* determined movement, no longer the equal harmony of independent parts. Painting is concentrated in *one* dominant light area on one contrast of colours indeed, one can state, the tense narration, the really unified comprehension of one fixed moment in the process, would be first an achievement of the seventeenth century. All in all, the North of more consequence than the South. The Italians have no story-teller = [equal to] Rembrandt.[48]

Wölfflin's new attention to depth, but now also to "attentiveness," to narrative concerns over spatial organization, responds specifically to *Das holländische Gruppenporträt*.

If Riegl had taken a page from Wölfflin's empathic readings of architecture, by the time Wölfflin came to write the *Grundbegriffe* he himself had already distanced himself from empathy theory. Under the influence of Fiedler, Wölfflin had turned in his *Die klassische Kunst* to an optically oriented history of the traces of seeing in works of art. Although he first defined the eminently optical concept of the painterly in *Renaissance und Barock* with reference to the medium of painting he did not dwell on it, focusing instead on architecture. In the *Grundbegriffe* his sense of the media in which the baroque expressed itself most forcefully shifted from architecture to painting. The baroque is no longer solid, forceful, massive, but an atmosphere that covers everything. There is a place for architecture, but painting is the medium that best models its unity.

"Unity" is to Wölfflin's *Grundbegriffe* what "subjectivity" is to Riegl's baroque. As the notebook passage cited above suggests, "unity" became central to Wölfflin's baroque, though he distinguished its effects from the causes posited by Riegl. If for Riegl the relations *between things* are important, for Wölfflin that which *is* between has taken on a life of its own. In the late Rembrandt, for example, "the individual bodies in the picture no longer carry the painterly movement; it is merely intimated on the stilled surface of the picture."[49] In another passage he points to the role of Riegl's spectator, bearer of subjectivity, in this effect of unity:

> What essentially distinguishes Rembrandt from Dürer is the vibration of the picture as a whole, and this still asserts itself even when the eye can no longer make out the individual marks that constitute the form. The effectiveness of the illusion certainly receives potent support from the fact that the viewer is given work to do in constructing the image and that to a certain extent the individual brushstrokes are only melded together in the act of viewing.[50]

In spite of the nod to Riegl's spectator the two would never agree on the terms of unity. Consider Wölfflin's response to Riegl's interpretation of Rembrandt's *Night Watch* as an anomalous work, the signal of imminent decline (of the uniquely democratic Dutch group portrait) with the introduction for the first time of subordination (to the captain) alongside the superior democratizing element of attention. Riegl is only able to rescue Rembrandt by arguing that subordination is acceptable in this work because it is not the captain but the spectator to whom all are subordinate.[51] Riegl's argument must have been compelling because in the *Grundbegriffe* Wölfflin rehearsed Riegl's point that there was an increasing tendency towards subordinate relations in Rembrandt's group portraits. Since Wölfflin had himself argued in *Renaissance und Barock* that the two periods differed precisely around the succession from coordinated elements in the sixteenth century to subordinate forms in the seventeenth we might imagine Wölfflin in agreement. But he had revised his view first in *Die klassische Kunst*, where *quattrocento* coordination became an inadequate form of "mere aggregation" and the Italian *cinquecento* a positive form of subordination; there, baroque subordination remained rather negative. In the *Grundbegriffe* he sees it yet less negatively, extolling Rembrandt's *Night Watch*, with "single figures, even groups of figures reduced almost to unrecognizability" so the "few intelligible motives leap to the eye as dominants with all the more force." He sees the same in the *Syndics of the Cloth Guild* and with the radical *Anatomy Lesson of Dr. Tulp* Rembrandt "demolishes the old scheme of co-ordination and subjects the whole company to one light and one movement," an "unforgettable impression" that is "characteristic of the new style."[52]

For Riegl, Rembrandt's *Syndics* had represented the solution to the Dutch group portrait after the problematical introduction of subordinated relations in the *Night Watch*:

> all the figures in the painting enjoy a convincing internal coherence because of their subordination to the spokesman, while at the same time the figures' subordination to the viewer ensures a satisfying external coherence. In a way typical of Holland, this subordination is compensated in that, although the speaker's colleagues are listening to their spokesman, they also assert their independence from his dominant position by sharing their attention with the other party at the same time.[53]

In Riegl's analysis coherence is achieved in the attentiveness of all figures (including, importantly, the servant who is pure attentiveness, which means without subordination), subordinate *only* to a beholder. Wölfflin's baroque is unified not by a form of community or understanding of relations akin to governance, but rather by an ineffable binding substance that surrounds them ("unity can only be apprehended in the sum of colour and light and form"); the spectator has no social-political relation to the figures represented but acts as a disembodied eye. Wölfflin will not entirely discount psychological relations amongst the figures. On the contrary, he returns to acknowledge the contribution of the spiritual accents to the unification of the picture, though he does not acknowledge the part of the spectator. Wölfflin thus rejects Riegl's constitution of a democratic pictorial ethos based on the psychological relations between figures and viewer.[54] Unity is thus key for both authors, but on entirely different terms.

Riegl's terms for the baroque in *Das holländische Gruppenporträt* had everything to do with political systems (Dutch democracy, Italian theocracy). By 1899 Wölfflin had turned from his earlier preoccupation with the form of the state to social questions: the implications of the new social order emerging in the seventeenth century, with the incipient breakdown in class structure and massification, as the roots of modern society. While Riegl's seventeenth-century spectator held the subjects of group portraits accountable, Wölfflin – who did not adopt Riegl's scheme of attentiveness, will and emotion – would not accord the spectator such a central role. Rather, he arrived in the *Grundbegriffe* at a more positive view of subordination to a nebulous aristocratic order perceptible to Wölfflin's own sovereign aristocratic eye. When he introduced painterly unity as the related key to the baroque in the *Grundbegriffe*, it did not point to the chaos and formlessness he feared in 1888 (unity at a cost). Now, in 1915, he saw in the baroque, alongside the beginning of the breakdown of class hierarchies, also a release, a sense of the living and spiritual, of subjective sensations that proffered a cure for the mechanization of modernity. But this was only possible for Wölfflin to think because painterly unity was an effect alone: baroque pictures only create the appearance of unity. Wölfflin's notion of the painterly was a conservative expression of romantic anti-capitalism.[55]

In the end the conservative Wölfflin remained sceptical, apart and distant, whereas the more liberal Riegl connected and saw hope. Wölfflin's conservatism did not, however, prevent his baroque from serving as a template for modernism for Sigfried Gidieon, Clement Greenberg or Alfred Barr, to name just a few of the most influential interpreters of the *Kunstgeschichtliche Grundbegriffe* whose accounts of modernism would shape their generation.

Endnotes

1 See Hopkins, "Riegl Renaissances." Some discussion is to be found in Hart, "Heinrich Wölfflin," with previous bibliography and Lurz, *Heinrich Wölfflin*. Important early analyses of Riegl and Wölfflin, though without specific regard to their writings on the baroque, include Panofsky, "The Concept of Artistic Volition;" and Wind, "On the Systematics of Artistic Problems."

2 Hans Aurenhammer, who studied Riegl's lecture manuscripts at the Kunsthistorisches Institut at the University of Vienna, informed me that when Riegl gave the first version of the lectures of 1894–95, he had not yet read Wölfflin's book. For the manuscripts see Witte, "Reconstruction of Riegl's 'Entstehung der Barockkunst in Rom'." All references will be to the English editions of these works: Wölfflin, *Renaissance and Baroque* and *Classic Art*; and Riegl, *The Origins of Baroque Art in Rome*.

3 Wölfflin, review of Alois Riegl, *Die Entstehung der Barockkunst in Rom*. References to Riegl, *Das holländische Gruppenporträt* will follow the English edition, *Group Portraiture of Holland*.

4 On the impact of *Lebensphilosophie* see Adler, "Painterly Politics."

5 See Gossman, "Imperial Icon" and Payne, "Portable Ruins."

6 Rampley compared Riegl's baroque only to Wölfflin's *Renaissance und Barock* as his primary object was Riegl's text. See Rampley, "Subjectivity and Modernism," 266. For a view of Riegl troubled by the excesses of modern subjectivity see Olin, "Forms of Respect," 291, 293–4.

7 As noted in Riegl, *Origins of Baroque Art*, 102; Hans Rose's lengthy commentary in the 4th edition of Wölfflin, *Renaissance und Barock* (1926), 182–3.

8 Schmarsow, *Barock und Rokoko*.

9 To an extent, Riegl's account is a corrective to Wölfflin and Gurlitt (see note 14 below), who, he notes, thought the question of the nature and origin of the baroque "could only be solved through the study of architecture." Riegl, *Origins of Baroque Art*, 12.

10 Riegl, *Origins of Baroque Art*, 122.

11 Riegl, *Origins of Baroque Art*, 122.

12 Riegl, *Origins of Baroque Art*, 122.

13 Riegl, *Origins of Baroque Art*, 100–101.

14 Gurlitt, *Geschichte des Barockstiles in Italien*; *Geschichte des Barockstiles des Rococo und des Klassicismus in Belgien, Holland, Frankreich, England*; and *Geschichte des Barockstiles und des Rococo in Deutschland*. Riegl notes that Gurlitt is a practising architect by way of a putdown, not an explanation of his audience. Riegl, *Origins of Baroque Art*, 100.

15 On the political implications of Wölfflin's *Renaissance und Barock* at a time Wölfflin was preoccupied with the question of the German state, see Levy, "The Political Project of Wölfflin's Early Formalism."

16 "Wölfflin's definition of the baroque style as 'massiveness and movement' is not profound enough, and we do not learn why these criteria became decisive. Wölfflin's baroque also appears to be an aberration and a decline, but it is never made clear to the reader why this was required for the purposes of a further progression." Riegl, *Origins of Baroque Art*, 101.

17 Wölfflin, *Renaissance and Baroque*, 30.

18 In terms of the relation between the interior and exteriors of buildings in the baroque Wölfflin is struck by the contrast between the calm peaceful interior of baroque churches behind agitated forceful façades. Secular palaces "followed a different law:" cold forbidding exteriors opened onto "sumptuous and intoxicating interiors." Wölfflin, *Renaissance and Baroque*, 131. All in all, he found the baroque palace to be Spanish and aristocratic in outlook – except the more sumptuous papal palaces that were bound to no "societal rules." Wölfflin, *Renaissance and Baroque*, 132.

19 For Riegl the Dutch figure is understood in relation to unifying space whereas the Italian figure remains isolated, the basis of the composition.

20 Hildebrand, *The Problem of Form*, 62.

21 See the excellent study of Riegl's attentiveness as an ethical position in Olin, "Forms of Respect."

22 Riegl, *Origins of Baroque Art*, 172.

23 Wölfflin, *Classic Art*, 188. Emphasis mine.

24 Wölfflin, *Classic Art*, 186.

25 Wölfflin, *Classic Art*, 191.

26 Riegl, *Origins of Baroque Art*, 113.

27 Riegl, *Origins of Baroque Art*, 113.

28 Riegl, *Origins of Baroque Art*, 116.

29 The [allegorical] figures "are immensely stimulating because of the variety of planes and the major contrasts of axial direction, yet they remain at rest in spite of all this enrichment." They "are contained within quite simple spatial boundaries: they are framed in space and arranged in strata, so that they can be apprehended as pure reliefs. … Dawn for all her movement, can be read as a single plane in this sense." Riegl, *Origins of Baroque Art*, 116. "Later artists learned movement by looking at Michelanglo and then attempted to outdo him, but they never understood his repose – least of all Bernini." Riegl, *Origins of Baroque Art*, 192.

30 Wölfflin, *Classic Art*, 192.

31 Riegl, *Origins of Baroque Art*, 118. Riegl distinguishes the Italian from the northern baroque as the difference between emotions tied to sensory perception (which is accompanied by a certain amount of isolating movement) conquering the will versus the northern artist who reaches psychological agreement and therefore has no obstacles to connection. Riegl, *Origins of Baroque Art*, 125.

32 Riegl, *Origins of Baroque Art*, 116.

33 Wölfflin, *Renaissance and Baroque*, 93. For this and other passages see further Levy, "The Political Unconscious of Wölfflin's Early Formalism."

34 An idea also expressed in Wölfflin, *Classic Art*, 94. Figure in the *Disputá* (94–5): "If the Northern spectator is inclined to think this an artificial reason for so emphatic and elaborate a motive he must be warned not to make over-hasty judgments, for the Italian is so much more given to gesticulation than we are, that for him the limits of the natural are quite different. Here Raphael is obviously following in Michelangelo's footsteps and under the influence of the more powerful personality he has, for the moment, lost his natural sensibility."

35 Riegl, *Origins of Baroque Art*, 153–4.

36 Riegl, *Origins of Baroque Art*, 155.

37 Riegl, *Origins of Baroque Art*, 155.

38 Symptomatically, Riegl isolates Rome as the focus of the baroque "for political reasons," the "presence of the papacy," its "universal supremacy in the wake of the Counter-Reformation is a guiding principle." Riegl, *Origins of Baroque Art*, 97. Wölfflin did not justify his choice of Rome but rather asserted it.

39 Riegl, *Origins of Baroque Art*, 95.

40 Riegl, "Salzburgs Stellung in der Kunstgeschichte."

41 Wölfflin, *Renaissance and Baroque*, 34, 40–41, 114.

42 Wölfflin, *Prolegomena*, 176.

43 Riegl, *Origins of Baroque Art*, 137.

44 Wölfflin, *Kunstgeschichtliche Grundbegriffe* (1915), vii. The note, left out of the 1932 English translation, is restored in *Principles of Art History* (2015), 73–4, note 2.

45 Wölfflin, review of Riegl, *Die Entstehung der Barockkunst in Rom*, 356.

46 Wölfflin, *Principles* (2015), 316. He would take up national styles in a concentrated way in his *Italien und das deutsche Formgefühl* of 1931. On the anti-nationalism of the *Principles* see Warnke, "On Heinrich Wölfflin."

47 Hart, "Heinrich Wölfflin," 415.

48 Hart, "Heinrich Wölfflin," 414–15.

49 Wölfflin, *Principles*, 109.

50 Wölfflin, *Principles*, 110.

51 Rampley, "Subjectivity and Modernism," 244.

52 Wölfflin, *Principles*, 170–72.

53 Riegl, *Group Portraiture of Holland*, 285.

54 If we follow Riegl's own distinction, recorded in his notes, between aesthetics (relations between parts and whole) and the relation of beholder to represented (art history) then Wölfflin could fall into the former category. The ethics of Wölfflin's formalism have yet to be decoded. Olin, "'Forms of Respect'," 286; Levy, "The Political Project of Wölfflin's Early Formalism."

55 For Wölfflin's investigation of style as resistance to the fast-paced changes of modern fashion, see Schwartz, *Blind Spots*, 1–25. The socio-political undergirding of Wölfflin's concept of the baroque is taken up fully in my *Baroque and the Political Language of Formalism (1845–1945)*.

Chapter 8
Beyond the Vienna School:
Sedlmayr and Borromini

Marco Pogacnik

Translated by Maarten Delbeke and Andrew Leach, with Andrea Bosio

"A work that expresses something terrible is understood better by those whose limbs are pervaded by terror ... he who is struck with terror does not speak of a *frisson nouveau*, does not cry out *bravo!*, and does not congratulate the artist for his originality."[1] Only terror is capable of recognizing the terrible, to the extent that, as Goethe observed, only the connection of like-to-like engenders knowledge. Sedlmayr quoted these words in his introduction to *Die Revolution der modernen Kunst* (1955, The Revolution of Modern Art) to warn once more – and even more dramatically than in *Verlust der Mitte* (1948; *Art in Crisis*, 1958) – of a great danger, a threat of which he had slowly become aware between 1930 and 1939, and hence between the first and the second editions of his book *Die Architektur Borrominis* (The Architecture of Borromini). In this tormented decade Sedlmayr defined the object that would occupy his research in the following years and specified those tools most adequate to its pursuit, all while examining in depth the cultural inheritance of the great historiographical school in Vienna to which he belonged.

The crisis of the Viennese historiographical tradition would emerge fully at the end of the 1930s.[2] At that time Sedlmayr's hope that the Nazi *Anschluß* would heal the harms spawned by the revolution of modernity had collapsed. By the end of that same decade, Sedlmayr's essays "Oesterreichs bildende Kunst" (1937) and "Die politische Bedeutung des deutschen Barock. Der 'Reichsstil'" (1938) would confer a completely new historical significance to his studies of both the Roman and Austrian baroque.[3] He identified therein the same "historiographical problem" – the same *Fragestellung* – which had for some years preoccupied that other great historian to have emerged from the "Young Vienna School" (Jüngere Wiener Schule), Emil Kaufmann: the origins of modernity.[4] For Kaufmann the architecture of Claude-Nicolas Ledoux represented the dawn of a new era, but for Sedlmayr it announced the end of the Ancient-Christian world and its notion of man-as-creature.[5] In contrast to Kaufmann's enthusiasms, Sedlmayr painfully acknowledged that the revolutions in Austria under Joseph II and in France in 1789 had dissolved, in Europe, the ancient *Reich* into the new *Staat*.[6] From that moment onwards, architecture had become a business for "craftsmen," furniture-makers and interior designers, and had forfeited its capacity to attend to man's destiny. Architecture as style took the place of architecture as tectonic. So it is hardly a coincidence that the decade of 1930, so significant for Sedlmayr's research, effectively commenced in 1929 with a journal article that discussed Le Corbusier's project for a "city for three million inhabitants" and ended in 1939 with a long essay on the spherical constructions of Etienne-Louis Boullée, Ledoux and Ivan Leonidov. Sedlmayr thus followed Kaufmann's trajectory, but trod it in reverse: he discovered Ledoux by starting from Le Corbusier and arrived at Joseph Kornhäusel by means of Adolf Loos – yet another indication of the urgency with which he experienced the danger of the present. If authorship of an idea rests not on the basis of its invention so much as when one selects it in the trajectory of one's own reflections, Sedlmayr may be credited with being the first to have tried to uncover the historical path that led from the age of the revolutions at the end of the eighteenth century to those of the first decades of the twentieth.[7] Kaufmann's work, in contrast, never extends far beyond the confines of "revolutionary architecture," and the idea suggested by the formula *Von Ledoux bis Le Corbusier* (1933) remains restricted to a few lines of his oeuvre, and to the felicitous title of the book – being the sole instance in which Le Corbusier is mentioned there at all.[8]

Sedlmayr's most complete appropriation of the historiographical tradition of the "Vienna School" coincides with its crises and its denouement, to which he contributed in no small measure. An extremely complex intellectual trajectory would allow him to combine Alois Riegl with Max Dvořák, Heinrich Wölfflin with Julius von Schlosser, Benedetto Croce with the *Gestalttheorie*, *Stilgeschichte* with *Strukturanalyse*, at the very moment when the "torchlight" that his master, Schlosser, had only a few years earlier proudly displayed as a symbol of a stable and long lasting tradition, was starting to fade. The Young Vienna School describes a generation of art historians who, rather than questioning the authority of their fathers, unmercifully laid bare their anachronisms.

In the obituary of his master, published in 1938, Sedlmayr remembers how in the early 1920s Schlosser was confined to "his" museum, working in complete isolation from the rest of the world, impervious to such revolutions as expressionism. His commemoration of Schlosser presented Sedlmayer with the opportunity to recall his years of apprenticeship and to assess the results achieved by the Young Vienna School. Sedlmayr confirms that during the first decades of the twentieth century the historical studies conducted therein had expanded the history of art enormously, both its scope and the methods it had accommodated and advanced. Art history now spanned from Paleolithic to popular art, from late Roman art to the applied arts of the present. "The price for this indisputable advantage is a progressive confusion of the proper methods of the history of art and a dangerous extension of the very notion of art. … The sense of artistic values is progressively lost. Consequently, a feeling of eradication, of crisis dominates the field of research."[9]

Still, Sedlmayr has the situation of art history corresponding closely to the phenomenon of expressionism in the arts, wherein he discerned the same dangerous mix of genius and destructive inclinations. And from the expressionist 1920s, when he first enrolled in the university, he dates his most distant memory of Schlosser, an image that will characterize the latter's intellectual figure in the eyes of his young pupils until the end of Schlosser's professorship.

> Since Schlosser neither fought nor refused expressionism, but simply did not acknowledge its existence, he did not even notice the emergence of many innovations in his own discipline. It was the time when he used to work in his museum, which he loved as a "museum" in the old sense of the word; it was the time when he could no longer be in tune "with his own time" and therefore seemed to be looking solely towards the past.[10]

Sedlmayr thus expresses very clearly that which separated his own group of young historians from the disciplinary tradition to which Schlosser belonged: he called it their intellectual duty not only to exercise scientific rigour, but also to be aware of their own contemporaneity.

In those restless years this group of younger scholars looked for a more solid ground for their historiography and they found it in the centrality of the artwork. Sedlmayr confirms, after Goethe, that "in every single artwork reposes all that is art." In scientific terms, this new direction was articulated as a rediscovery of the fundamental value of aesthetic judgement, that is, the need to establish criteria capable of determining incontrovertibly the "value" and the "rank" of the singular artwork. Sedlmayr unfailingly stressed that in "'Stilgeschichte' und 'Sprachgeschichte'" Schlosser himself had begun to trace the path that the Young Vienna School would follow between the end of the 1920s and the beginning of the 1930s. Yet with a crucial difference: Schlosser had assigned art or, more precisely, the work of art in its irreducible singularity, a central place as a result of his own personal intellectual relationship with such personalities as Karl Vossler and Benedetto Croce. For the Young Vienna School the same choice was the result of an autonomous effort that took up the challenge and the risky adventures into which they had been drawn by the expressionist "storms," and which Schlosser had tried to avoid.

The 1930s

As the preface to the first edition of *Die Architektur Borrominis* states, Sedlmayer started writing the book on New Year's Day of 1925 and finished it in May 1929. Published the following year by Frankenfurter Verlags-Anstalt of Berlin, the text incorporated two articles Sedlmayr published in 1925 and 1926 in the Viennese journal *Belvedere*.[11] The theoretical introductions to each chapter comprised of fragments from an essay that attempted to define the criteria for a rigorous and sure analysis of the artwork, part of which work would be included in the essay that Sedlmayr contributed to the *Kunstwissenschaftliche Forschungen* in 1931.[12] Sedlmayr did not revise the text for the book's second edition, which was published in 1939 by Piper in Munich, instead limiting himself to a reworking of the preface and introduction and adding a stand-alone essay as a new chapter, this entitled "Neuer Versuch über Borromini" (New Attempt on Borromini). This additional chapter reworked an essay that was written in 1937 but only published (as "Fünf römische Fassaden," Five Roman Façades) in 1959, in the second volume of *Epochen und Werke*. In his new introduction to *Die Architektur Borrominis*, Sedlmayer reiterated the themes of the earlier edition. But three changes testify to the development of his research over the course of the intervening decade: his engagement with the cultural inheritance of the Vienna School; his escape from the influence of Benedetto Croce, to whom he was introduced by Schlosser; and the self-critical revision of his personal views as part of the debate initiated by the publication of the book itself along with an article in the *Kunstwissenschaftliche Forschungen*.

In his introduction in 1930, Sedlmayr presented the history of the Vienna School as the sequence of four principal ages, each dominated by a "driving question": the historic–stylistic question, the psychological question, the question of the history of the spirit, and finally the historical–artistic question, which was, in turn, taken up as the core research question of the Young Vienna School. Max Dvořák, Eberhard Hempel, Dagobert Frey, Ernst Cassirer, and Erwin Panofsky are cast as the various protagonists of these ages. Sedlmayr reiterates these "driving questions" and reformulates them on the basis of his research on the architecture of Borromini to conclude that "there is no *single* 'correct' question amongst these different options, but together they objectively compose an indissoluble entity. The centre of this entity, we believe, is the fourth and most recent question."[13] Sedlmayr thus attempts to formulate a methodological syncretism of sorts, which rescues the heritage of ideas brought forth by the "Vienna School" in its entirety, even to the point of including the opposition between what Sedlmayr terms "stylistic analysis" and "structural analysis."

By the late 1930s, in his introduction to the second edition, Sedlmayr reduces these considerations to a far more concise point: "The current work privileges genetic and structural analysis, together with the stylistic analysis, today well-established if certainly open to improvement."[14] This statement reveals that, on the one hand, Sedlmayr now considered the programme of the "Young Vienna School" as completed and that, on the other, the notion of stylistic analysis had come to occupy an ever more central role in his research. In sum, starting from Riegl and following Schlosser's mediation, Dvořák's *Geistesgeschichte* had also become one of the fundamental references of Sedlmayr's culture. Without this complex of ideas, it would be impossible to understand his research of the post-war period, where in such works as *Verlust der Mitte* or *Die Revolution der modernen Kunst* the work of art, conceived as the "symptom and symbol of an era," became the object of his stylistic and iconological research.

The second shift between the introductions to the first and the second editions of *Borromini* pertains to Sedlmayr's uptake of Croce.[15] There is a direct relationship between the thinking of Croce and Sedlmayr: both attribute central importance to the artistic valuation of the artwork; and both deem the academic article and the monograph the privileged forms of historical research. In his new notion of the artwork, Sedlmayr also develops Croce's idea that in the figure of the artist, the empirical personality and the aesthetic personality need not necessarily coincide. The introduction to the first edition states:

> The present attempt at a monograph on Borromini … does not aim to offer a 'frame of the art and the personality' of an artist, but rather to face the object or, better, the objects that are very imprecisely connected to Borromini's name, on the basis of a set of precise questions to which we will try to provide verifiable answers (this is not the place to criticize the myth of a historiography "in full relief" that does not claim to illuminate the structure of an object, but rather the correspondence between surfaces).

According to Sedlmayr, therefore, Borromini's work is an object that cannot be described "in full relief." Ever since his early articles (like "Zum gestalteten Sehen," 1926) Sedlmayr set forth *zer-sehen* as the mode of vision proper to structural analysis, a type of perception that breaks the artwork down into its constitutive elements, each of which corresponds with different levels of reading – psychological, structural, geometric, social, iconological, etc. Just as in the figure of Borromini, the artist (the empirical, biographical persona) does not necessarily coincide with his aesthetic persona (as an architect), so the apparent homogeneity and coherence of each one of his individual works is shattered in the plurality of levels of which it is composed, and which no notion of style can unite. According to Sedlmayr, only a structural analysis, an analysis that takes as its starting point the original idea pursued by the artist, is able to preserve the work's intangible unity. Critical work is always monographic in nature, he argues, not in the sense that it provides a totalizing description of the artist's work as a coherent oeuvre with regard to all the aspects that condition the circumstances of the creative act (social, political, iconographical, etc.), but rather in that it can only attend to single works or isolated groups of works. The first should be termed a structural monograph, the second a genetic monograph.[16]

The introduction of the 1939 edition no longer invokes Croce at all. Once completed, the methodological syncretism Sedlmayr announced in the introduction to the first edition implied that all of the various methodological approaches would prove relative. The diminishing weight of Croce's views shifts first to Riegl and then to Dvořák, but this change of direction does not mean that Sedlmayer abandons his earlier ideas. This much transpires from the peremptory statement that opens an important article from 1956, wherein Croce's influence clearly shows through: "in every age art is *one*."[17] For Sedlmayr art history has never been the application of historical research to the study of artworks, but rather art criticism performed in an historical space.

First and Second Historiography

The third significant element that moves between the two introductions is constituted by the author's self-critical stance towards the structure he had chosen to espouse his theoretical theses. As he himself admits in the introduction to the second edition, the epistemological introductions to every chapter carry the imprint of that "constructivism" typical of the 1920s, eager to "[simplify] reality by abstraction."[18] This self-criticism, however, does not challenge the programme of the Young Vienna School so much as the modality of its expression.

With this self-criticism, Sedlmayr accepts to a large extent the accusations that Eberhard Hempel and Rudolf Wittkower had levelled at him.[19] Sedlmayer's confrontation with Wittkower was occasioned by a review of Coudenhove-Erthal's monograph on Domenico Fontana. In Sedlmayr's opinion the book was biased and incomplete to the extent that it formed part of the "first historiography," which was contrasted to a "second historiography" aimed at analysing the structural conception of the artwork. In the article "Zu einer strengen Kunstwissenschaft" (1931) Sedlmayr confirmed that the first historiography answers questions pertaining to what can still be known once it is accepted that the primary object of inquiry, the artwork, can no longer be understood. The second historiography, in contrast, examines what can be understood of the artwork if only the work itself is taken into consideration. The first historiography has the duty to date and attribute works, operations that require no direct understanding of the artwork. The second phase then seizes the structure and construction of artworks and links works one to another on the basis of genetic connections. The first historiography disregards the artwork's artistic significance since it is geared towards stylistic features; in the second historiography, on the other hand, judgement of artistic quality is fundamental, subtended by the ability to distinguish the major or minor artistic value of different works, or even between different parts of the same work. An *ideal* historiography results from cooperation between these two levels, between the auxiliary historiographical sciences and the true history of art.

Sedlmayr considered Coudenhove-Erthal's monograph as a reliable collection of material, and hence a good example of a "first historiography," a starting point from which the "second historiography" could establish the basis for a real understanding of Fontana's work. Wittkower questioned this evaluation of Coudenhove-Erthal's book on the basis of two major qualms that had escaped Sedlmayr: its choice of a theme that could not properly be dealt with in the absence of preliminary research on such architects of the first baroque as Carlo Maderno, Martino Longhi the Younger and Pietro da Cortona; and its failure to take into consideration the enormous amount of original material on the subject as kept in the Windsor Library in 27 heavy volumes.

To answer Wittkower's observations and to press his own views, Sedlmayr presents an exercise in structural analysis in which he compares the façades of San Marcello al Corso (1682–83, Carlo Fontana) and Santi Vincenzo e Anastasio a Trevi (Martino Longhi the Younger, 1646–50). His focus is on the meaning of how, at San Marcello, Fontana deforms the syntagma of the triad of columns (used also by Longhi) to articulate the older façade. In so doing, he illustrates the principal task the structural analysis sets itself: to reveal the concrete form of the artwork starting from a concept that can be seen, and is then pursued in all its morphological developments through to the finest details. Sedlmayr argues that neither Coudenhove-Erthal nor Wittkower could understand the structural principle that the triad of columns represents, implying their lack of comprehension of any element from the façade of San Marcello or of the architecture of Fontana, so that "not even the Windsor's twenty-seven volumes aid in furnishing any knowledge of his art."[20] Sedlmayr's disapproval of Wittkower assumes its fullest form in the final chapter of the second edition of *Borromini*, entitled "Stilanalyse und Strukturanalyse." Therein the "first historiography" is clearly identified with stylistic analysis and the "second historiography" with structural analysis. Sedlmayr criticizes stylistic analysis because it abandoned the field covered by the history of art and its adoption of a *Geistesgeschichte*, a history of the spirit, where the spirit in question could be, quite indistinctively, the *Zeitgeist*, the *Volksgeist*, or the *Geist* of either a generation or a single artistic personality.

Sedlmayr's evaluation of Hempel's book on Borromini sets it on a par with that of Coudenhove-Ehrtal: a decent example of that "first historiography" still incapable of understanding the inner meaning of the artwork. Hempel reacts pointedly to Sedlmayer's critical judgement, and Sedlmayr answers with an article that reiterates many of the themes already put forward against Wittkower. But Hempel's criticism of Sedlmayer went further than questioning the abstract character of Sedlmayr's historiographical hypotheses. It also accused him of moving away from the principles and lessons of the Vienna School. This accusation lent an "official" character to Sedlmayr's answer, and it was published in the periodical of the Osterreichische Institut für Geschichtsforschung (Austrian Institute for Historical Studies), the organ of the Vienna School produced under the responsibility of Schlosser, amongst others. Sedlmayr's response is passionate, as becomes immediately apparent from the very first lines of the essay, which cite the article that Schlosser wrote on the occasion of the Institute's 80th birthday. It concludes with a chapter titled "Die Wiener Schule der Kunstgeschichte," where Sedlmayr draws the balance of the heritage of the Vienna School from the perspective of the Young Vienna School. Hempel is again criticized for being "an historian borrowed to art," and Sedlmayr affirms his participation in the double tradition of the Vienna School: the first represented by the historical studies founded by Theodor von Sickel; the second in the history of art, rooted in the figure of Alois Riegl. The research of the Young Vienna School is cast as the point where these two traditions meet but do not merge, advancing their mutual autonomy and specific identity; investigating the origin and evolution of an artwork is a completely different matter from analysing an historical event or a social or political formation.

Following Croce, Sedlmayr confirms that art cannot be grasped by means of concepts but instead exists and reveals itself only in single artworks. The art historian's first task is therefore to recognize that the artwork should not be understood by means of collecting and cataloguing relevant "historical data" within the conceptual framework of "style," but rather by preserving the presence and completeness of its unique and singular character. Sedlmayr's understanding of historical inquiry thus follows Croce and Schlosser along with Franz Wickhoff and Konrad Fiedler, whereas at the opposite pole sits the *Stilgeschichte* practiced by Riegl and Wölfflin. Contrary to Riegl, however, Wölfflin examines the artwork from the observer's point of view and his *Sehformen* (visual forms), while the former approaches the artwork in relation to the *Kunstwollen* of a specific time or a particular "stylistic industry." Sedlmayer follows Riegl over Wölfflin because of his view that "style" has its own internal structure, and adopts the structural analysis that Riegl applied to "style" in the investigation of a single artwork. The notion of the structure of an artwork renders its supposed unity highly problematic and complex. Structural analysis separates the single layers that constitute the artwork, supposing a kind of understanding that Sedlmayr defines as an *anschauliches Begreifen* (visual understanding), a *gestaltetes Sehen* (formed sight). In many respects, these definitions trace back to the ideas of Croce, Fiedler and *Gestalttheorie*. Structural analysis identifies the essence of the artwork with the artist's creative act. Its own activity consists of tracing the elements and parts of which the artwork is comprised back to their original wholeness by means of a process of "visual comprehension."

Sight, Sedlmayr argues, has nothing to do with the sole act of sensory perception. The notion of *Sehen* acquires its meaning as part of such expressions as *gestaltendes Sehen*, *zer-sehen* and *verwandelndes Sehen* to suggest that the artwork can only be understood at the level of its vision, and that such vision must be supported by a structure that is as complex as that of the artwork under analysis. It is no coincidence that these reflections emerged as part of Sedlmayr's work of the mid-1920s on Roman and Austrian baroque architecture. The preface to *Österreichische Barockarchitektur* is entitled "Zum Sehen barocker Architekturen" (On Seeing Baroque Architecture) and it analyses the conditions that regulate and order the vision of baroque architecture.[21]

Sedlmayr's response to Hempel thus addresses two questions that define the different roles played by the multiple traditions at the heart of the Vienna School. With regard to the question of whether the "uniqueness" of the artwork should be privileged over stylistic analysis, Sedlmayr hews closely to Wickhoff and Schlosser. Concerning the matter of whether the vision of the artwork should be construed of as a perceptive or a reproductive act, the method of structural analysis appears closer to Riegl. That part of the Vienna School heritage still missing from Sedlmayr's critical approach in 1936 is the work of Dvořák, which would be rehabilitated once Sedlmayr came to privilege a genetic and structural analysis in analysing the artwork.[22] Only then could the "history of the spirit" have redeemed itself by passing from "history of styles as history of *Weltanschauung* … to history of the absolute essence's epiphany within the apertures of the human spirit influenced by time."[23]

At the end of the article all these reflections converge around the problem of the current intellectual condition, a situation that Sedlmayr described with Karl Jaspers's words from *Die geistige Situation der Zeit* (1933, The Spiritual Situation of the Age): "the time in which man can act is of short duration. He receives a task, but without guarantee of the continuation of his existence." Deprivation of the idea of the fatherland, and the ensuing existentialist pessimism, are opposed by Sedlmayer to belonging to a tradition of thought that he still deems effective: "In the Vienna School, in which we grew and to which we feel we belong, we had the experience of that which Jaspers claims to be lost. This experience has become fundamental for our spiritual existence in its entirety." These words still seem to be a far cry from Sedlmayr's dramatic description of the abyss of the modern; the feeling of belonging to an established school of thought still offers the illusion of a collective path, protected by a community of scientists who believe in common rules and principles. The contrast is striking, then, between this firm affirmation of the cultural solidity of the Old Vienna School in 1936 and the article on Ledoux's spherical buildings published barely three years later, in which Sedlmayr delineated the core claims of his *Verlust der Mitte*. In this very short period of time Sedlmayr's adherence to Nazism was also incubated. In his intellectual trajectory of the 1930s it represents the decisive moment when even the final illusion is ultimately shattered: the conciliatory reconstruction of the Vienna School that he inherited from Schlosser.

A preliminary conclusion: in the 1930s Sedlmayr's research confronted the inheritance of the Vienna School, and in particular the work of Alois Riegl – a trajectory shaped by Sedlmayr's reconsideration of his studies of the baroque.[24] Influenced by his encounter with Otto Brunner, his emerging insights on the baroque were formulated in the two articles mentioned above, "*Österreichs* bildende Kunst" (1937) and "Die politische Bedeutung des deutschen Barock. 'Der Reichsstil'" (1938). What still remains to be treated here is Sedlmayr's debt to Fiedler and his lively interest in contemporaneous studies on *Gestalttheorie* and *Typenpsychologie*. While Sedlmayr's interest in Fiedler can be attributed to his indebtedness to Croce's ideas about the centrality of the artwork and the difference between artistic object and aesthetic object,[25] his attention to *Gestalttheorie* and *Typenpsychologie* (the psychology of types) supported his own attempts to demonstrate the structural complexity of the artistic object by multiplying the artwork's points of view and, consequently, the different methodological approaches available to the art historian.

Creation and Interpretation

The book on Borromini was a provocation in that it applied the theoretical hypotheses that Sedlmayr would publish only the following year, in the *Kunstwissenschaftliche Forschungen*.[26] Borromini's architecture served as an object lesson illustrating the scope, methods and principles of the "second historiography," which he opposed to the "first historiography" represented by Hempel's monograph of 1924. As Sedlmayr admits in the Afterword, his book on Borromini was not concerned with any of the issues he assigned to Hempel's "first historiography," such as the dating, attribution or chronology of artworks, or the verification of sources and the archival record. All these data are simply accepted on the authority of those historians who had already worked successfully on the Roman baroque: Oskar Pollak, Dagobert Frey, Eberhard Hempel, Albert Brinckmann and Gerhart Egger. Sedlmayr's true provocation consisted, rather, in taking the framework of the available information for granted, while judging the authors he cited as incapable of understanding the real issue of Borromini's architecture: its artistic meaning. This problem is the sole province of the "second historiography," with its aims to define the conditions under which an understanding of the artwork itself is possible, a visual comprehension, regardless of iconographic, social, political or psychological factors.

The analytical tool proper to the "second historiography" is structural analysis, predicated on the existence of a plurality of methodological approaches (described above as a methodological syncretism) with each capable of emphasizing and highlighting a particular level of meaning of the artwork. Only by multiplying the points of view from which to develop an analysis could Sedlmayr calibrate the complexity of the artwork's structure. This ambition further explains Sedlmayr's curiosity with the new analytical tools borrowed from disciplines at an apparent remove from art history.[27]

The way that Gestalt theory conceptualized the perception of an object in relation to its background seemed to find a clear echo in the double structure that Sedlmayr attributes to the interiors of San Carlino and Sant'Ivo,[28] while his thoughts on psychological types have been interpreted as an historical application of clinical cases. On closer inspection, however, it appears that these analytical tools were already part of the art historical episteme, if in different forms. Paul Frankl's formalist analyses of Borromini are the direct antecedent of Sedlmayr's "Gestalt" readings; and Ernst Kretschmer's theories on psychological types had already been applied to the history of art by Wilhelm Pinder. For Sedlmayr, however, they formed part of a greater project to apply physiognomic analysis to the history of art. As such, his approach shows important affinities with a vast and sustained interaction between art history and physiognomy that originated in the eighteenth-century debate between Johann Kaspar Lavater and Georg Christoph Lichtenberg, and which was still very much present in the twentieth-century work of such scholars as Friedrich Nietzsche, Georg Simmel, Walter Benjamin, Siegfried Kracauer and Ernst Bloch. Giovanni Giurisatti's study of this theme highlights the affinity of physiognomy with this aspect of Sedlmayr's theoretical thesis:

> Physiognomy is highly regarded because it privileges the expressive, representative, material, concrete, synthetic and individual aspects of phenomena, because it stakes out the role of intuition, of vision and experience, because it is unsystematic, because it trusts micrological, monadological, analytical and phenomenological methods; it is highly regarded for its capacity for penetrating interpretation which, at the same time, values the surface. The hypothesis that "everything has a face, everything is a face," and therefore everything, as it is visible, is legible in physiognomic terms, provides a hermeneutic key of enormous practical efficiency.[29]

Indeed, as we have seen, Sedlmayr situated the primary experience of the artwork in precisely the relationship between the visible and the invisible this approach would claim to unlock.[30]

In *Die Architektur Borrominis* the readings based on Gestalt principles and physiognomic analysis nonetheless contain obvious weaknesses. Despite the undeniable brilliance and acumen of the author's formal eye, *Gestalttheorie* tended to flatten out the complexity of the works at hand as it forced an understanding of the whole from but a few formal elements. Physiognomic analysis is limited to indicating expressive elements identified on a merely stylistic basis, such as oppositions between organic and inorganic, hot and cold shapes, abstract and naturalistic characteristics.[31] Sedlmayr attempted to address these difficulties in one of his finest articles of the 1930s, in which he conducted a thorough study of Bruegel. Commencing from suggestions made by Croce,[32] "Die 'macchia' Bruegels" is written "in opposition to an interpretation of Bruegel's art that … considers his works as if they were ideograms of philosophical reflections."[33] Against this hermeneutic hypothesis Sedlmayr sought to prove that one could only understand Bruegel by starting from the shape itself or, better, the "pure visible shape." After the obscure nineteenth-century scholar Vittorio Imbriani, Croce had called this form the "spot," the image of the first and vague impression of an object or a scene that is captured by the artist's eye. Reiterating an observation he had earlier made about the principles governing the vision of baroque architecture,[34] Sedlmayr wrote that

> without doing anything, in a condition of passive visual reception, the human figures of the typical paintings by Bruegel start, after prolonged vision, to break down, to shatter into pieces. … When this process reaches its climax, a multitude of colorful flat spots with a well-delineated border and an homogeneous coloring, seeming to lay on the forefront without any relation and any order between each other, appear in place of the figures. They represent the *atoms* of the image.[35]

Sedlmayr's second brilliant article on Bruegel, published in 1956, would analyse the degree of autonomy attributable to different levels of meaning in the artwork: "the physiognomic understanding of the artwork," "the formal understanding," "the noetical understanding," "the integral understanding."[36] One year earlier Sedlmayr had conducted a similar exercise with architecture as its object, in "Die Schauseite der Karlskirche in Wien."[37] Taking the "double structure" as his starting point, he combed through the myriad obscurities and the meanings locked in Fischer von Erlach's masterpiece, the symbolic programme of which is built up from overlapping references to Augustus and Trajan, to the era of Solomon, to Saints Peter and Sophia, and finally to Charles V and Carlo Borromeo.

In this latter article on Bruegel Sedlmayr further developed the idea of the type of vision that subtends his structural analysis, for which he had invented in *Die Architektur Borrominis* a neologism intended to distinguish it from Heinrich Wölfflin's *Sehformen*: the latter's *sehen* of perception (in a stylistic sense) contrasts with the *zer-sehen* of the structural perception. The prefix *zer-* signals that sight implies the fragmenting, deconstructing and decomposing of the object in the multiplicity of layers constituting its structure. Sedlmayr had adopted this procedure as early as his "Zum gestalteten Sehen," wherein his analysis of San Carlino had consisted of identifying, one by one, the different and distinct layers of its structure: the overall architectural composition as defined by spatial bodies; the double articulation that reinterprets this spatial solution from the perimeter of the plot; the geometrical composition of the emerging figure; and the various technical and structural data. The object *zer-sehen* perceives is neither *Form* nor *Gestalt*, but *Gebilde*. The term *Gebilde*, as Sedlmayr uses it, is the product of a formative activity that can be either creative or perceptual: we see the world according to the same modalities with which we produce an artistic object. But *Gebilde* is also the collective term (prefix *GE-*) for images that can only be restituted by drawing from a plurality of *Bilder*, or images.[38] The constellation of images crystallizing within an object therefore constitutes its *Gebilde*. In "Die 'Macchia' Bruegels" the term *Zer-sehen* still signifies the decomposition of the figure in its constitutive elements (in this case the "spots") but also, at the same time, the interpretation of the artwork that retraces the artist's creative path. The "spot" that emerges from the art historian's process of decomposition represents at once the "atoms" that structure the figure and the primordial idea that gave rise to the creative act. *Zer-sehen* points to the connection between those two moments of creation and interpretation.

Riegl

Sedlmayr's references can be divided approximately into two groups, which correspond to the levels of the "first" and the "second" historiography. While certain authors were mined only for the necessary documents (Pollak, Frey, Egger, Franks, Hempel, Brinckmann), others provided him with an opportunity for interpretative and theoretical confrontation. In this division the figure of Alois Riegl stands alone, since Sedlmayr's interpretation of Borromini's architecture was shaped and developed by following, step-by-step, the theses of Riegl's *Entstehung der Barockkunst in Rom*.

Sedlmayer's intense involvement with the inheritance of Riegl's work commenced in the second half of the 1920s, and more in particularly in 1929, when Sedlmayr wrote an introduction to a collection of Riegl's essays and when Guido Kaschnitz-Weinberg published a review of the second edition of Riegl's *Spätrömische Kunstindustrie*. Sedlmayr considered this article a Copernican revolution in the interpretation of Riegl's work. Kaschnitz-Weinberg distinguished stylistic analysis from structural analysis: the first a synthetic and teleological kind of thought where the history of art dissolves into the field of broader historical enquiries, the other a methodological approach establishing the history of art as an autonomous discipline distinct from any other form of historical knowledge. In being severely critical of the positivist remnants in Riegl's historical categories, Kaschnitz-Weinberg delineated a new historical space for the investigation of the nature of the artwork where the essential, unique structure of the art object could finally be understood without contradicting the outcomes of a stylistic critique. Kaschnitz-Weinberg cast Riegl as the leader of both the stylistic and structural school of thought, and traced his work back both to the stylistic analysis that merged into the Dvořák's *Geistesgeschichte* and to the structural analysis of the Young Vienna School. As such, his article lays out the programme that Sedlmayr would expound in 1931 in his own contribution to the *Kunstwissenschaftliche Forschungen*.

With his own article on Riegl, Sedlmayr drew on the results of the intense debate that had surrounded the figure of the great Viennese historian since the publication of Wölfflin's *Grundbegriffe*, further developing his project for a *strenge Kunstwissenschaft*. The notion of "style" at which Sedlmayr arrived transpires from the following definition: "'style' is the variable that depends on internal structural principles ... the single 'stylistic marks' are comprehensible thanks to a higher structural principle." This structural principle, the definition of which Sedlmayr traces back to Riegl, is the key to explaining "those unseen procedures that lead to numerous points of views" that would otherwise be excluded from the possibilities for rigorous verification. In the chapter entitled "The Epistemological Value of New Theories," Sedlmayr illustrates the advantages of considering the notion of style as a structural principle by means of three examples. First: "I contend that someone who correctly observes a marble bust of Marcus Aurelius can imagine on his own account how portraits would have appeared at that time without having ever seen one encaustic painting" (Riegl). Second: "One could – in principle – reconstruct from a particular cultural region other aspects of that same culture; for example, if the art is given, one could specify, at least in a few strictly delineated areas, the religion that naturally forms part of it, or the philosophy or the science" (Sedlmayr). And third: "One could *a priori* construct the character of Constantine's or Teodosius' period simply by observing the origins of the imperial era" (Riegl). Each of these statements highlights a key problem with a long pedigree in the tradition of stylistic criticism, the only solution of which, according to Riegl, was the structural principle, based on three precepts: (1) stylistic characters that can be discerned in the different arts are mutually coherent and homogeneous; (2) the arts, religion, science share a vision of the world, a common *Weltanschauung*; and (3) historical evolution is characterized by an "internal destiny," a teleology, that leads all arts and knowledge in a precise and common direction.[39] Sedlmayr, like Kaschnitz-Weinberg, was critical of Riegl because he believed in causality and the teleology of history and founded his conceptual categories in physiology and nature, while considering certain methods implicit to the structural principle as acquired: that it is possible to determine the whole from a fragment (the meaning of the artwork from a syntagmatic element); to make layers that do not correspond with one another interact (a philosophical concept with a formal resolution); and to explain a succession of events as an historical process, the meaning of which is reiterated in the historiographical issue that lies at its basis.

After his contributions to *Belvedere*, *Die Architektur Borrominis* is Sedlmayr's first publication in the format of a "structural monograph" rather than an article. Having identified a group of genetically similar works on the basis of genetic similarities, Sedlmayr conducts their analysis on the basis of structural principles that Riegl had applied to the investigation of style. From these premises he endeavours to find the structural principle at the very core of Borromini's architecture, which he identifies as *Reliefeinheiten*, the "unit" articulating the surface of the spatial perimeter. If Riegl had argued that a marble bust allowed him to reconstruct the *Weltanschauung* of the social and cultural environment that had produced it, then the *Reliefeinheiten* enabled Sedlmayr to analyse a particular layer of Borromini's work. In explaining Borromini's peculiar way of articulating the perimeter wall, this analysis does not involve an identification of the type of geometrical construction adopted in the plan, determining the technical-constructive data, interpreting the symbolic programme that subtends the architectural choices, an individuation of the type of syntax, the composition of the volumes, etc. The structural principle is unable to explain the "three-dimensional" artwork in its entirety. It is instead able to individuate the element that characterizes its physiognomy, the face. Just as the peculiar quality of Bruegel's "spots" unequivocally defines his painting without communicating anything of its religious or philosophical content, the *Reliefeinheiten*, the peculiar articulation of the perimeter wall, constitutes the distinctive, expressive mark of Borromini's architecture.

Sedlmayr's insistence on the theme of "relief" reveals his most important debt to Riegl's interpretation of the baroque. In his volume on the Roman baroque Riegl had proposed a periodization that extended from the early 1500s, with the figure of Michelangelo, to the 1630s, and the death of Carlo Maderno. Riegl's characterization of the baroque evinces a new structural principle that had come to dominate architecture since the time of Michelangelo:

> reliefs in architecture being decorative fillings – something Michelangelo was not acquainted with, as everything he designed was structural. ... The change in Michelangelo's oeuvre can be dated between 1521 and 1524, when the designs for the Medici tombs and for the Laurenziana were made. ... [After] Michelangelo's "Baroque" period, the relief diminished in importance and he only worked with three-dimensional figures that he combined, when needed, into architectonic groups. What does this mean? A relief tends to remain on one plane, and the figures are not affected by or impaired by perception of them in strong foreshortening. When Michelangelo abandoned the relief ... he indicates his wish to no longer limit his compositions to a single plane.[40]

Besides the notion of "absolute plane," a concept that Sedlmayr would use only later, in the article he incorporated into the second edition of *Die Archiktur Borrominis*, Riegl's definition of the term *Relief* perfectly matches that used by Sedlmayr: (1) *Relief* concerns the decorative filling (or tamponade), and not the structural elements of a figure; (2) the tamponade is *einflächig*, a surface unity; and (3) the tamponade, as *Relief*, has a tactile character. To this definition Sedlmayr adds a corollary allowing him to switch from the structural analysis of single works to their arrangement in a genetic series: (4) the tamponade, as it does not involve any structural function, allows for infinite changes in the position of an agreement between its single constitutive elements. In the combination of individual elements to compose the "unit of the relief" in ever new ways it becomes possible to explain how figures go from one to another, a method that would allow Sedlmayr to simulate the design of figures in the "Borrominian style."[41]

Any acknowledgement of Sedlmayr's debt to Riegl should, however, stress that in Sedlmayr's thought the relief unit, as a structural principle, assumes a different meaning than in Riegl's "system." The latter opposes the *Reliefeinheit* to the "three-dimensional" figure, just as the tactile is opposed to the optical, proximity to distance (*nahsichtig-fernsichtig*), and the absolute plane to spatial depth (*Tiefraum*). According to Sedlmayr the *Reliefeinheit* is an original phenomenon (*Ur-phänomen*), the primordial element from which the genesis of a form can be explained. While in Riegl this element forms part of his positivist project so that the *Reliefeinheit* is, in the end, a conceptual category, for Sedlmayr it represents the concrete visible manifestation of the deeply hidden core of a form. To circumvent Riegl's system of positive categories, Sedlmayr calls forth the German critical and philosophical traditions of the first decades of the nineteenth century. More particularly, he takes recourse to Goethe's studies of nature, which examined the primordial formative principles of living organisms: the *Ur-pflanz* and the *Ur-tier*, the primordial plant and the primordial animal. It is in Goethe that Sedlmayr finds the first articulation of the notion that could be identified as the "original principle" from which his own reflection on form would develop: the idea that the structural principle is not a concept or a category, but rather a concrete element that our senses may perceive and recognize. Just as Goethe traces back the whole formative principle of the plant (its *Bildung*) to the *leaf*, so too does Sedlmayr locate the origin of the Borromini's structural principle in the *Reliefeinheit*.

Historical Consciousness

In this approach Sedlmayr lays bare a method of composition that simultaneously unveils the geometrical rigor at the basis of Borromini's formal solutions *and* lays bare the way through which his experimental attitude allowed him to re-think the problem of the relationship with tradition, by connecting it to historical experience in an entirely new way. The classicism that Frey had already discovered in some of Borromini's buildings, the Michelangelesque citations, the references to Bramante and Vignola, the memories of Lombardy, linked to Tibaldi and Montano, the reinterpretation of the monuments of late antiquity, all come to acquire, in this context, a meaning that no longer pertains to the continuity of an architectural tradition, but rather reveals the emergence of a new historical consciousness. The structural hypothesis at the heart of Sedlmayr's interpretation has the merit of signalling the crucial importance of the connection between Borromini's particular compositional approach as the syntactical decomposition–re-composition of the "relief unity;" the strategy of *bricolage* as the extreme outcome of such an approach to design; the anti-naturalistic character of the expressive form; the lack of any "organic" relationship between the building and the urban tissue where the building is located; the importance of the architectural type; and, finally, a horizon of historical references so vast as to condemn to irrelevance any notion of an architectural tradition embedded in historical continuity.

The ambit in which studies of Borromini studies presently operate, a cycle initiated with the conferences and research that formed part of the anniversary commemorations of 1967, could be identified with what Sedlmayr, with far too much arrogance, called "the first historiography." Manfredo Tafuri suggested as much in one of the first articles he dedicated to Borromini: "After the books of Frey, Hempel, Sedlmayr ... new verifiable critical perspectives can emerge only from the philological work that sought to fill existing documentary gaps and from in-depth research into the semantic structure of Borromini's production."[42] This new critical perspective to have been developed from the mid-1960s goes some way towards explaining why Sedlmayr's work on Borromini has been largely ignored by Borromini's historians. As this essay set out to show, however, Sedlmayr's approach of the architect belongs to a specific moment in the study of Borromini as well as to a specific moment in the history of historical scholarship. The implicit ban placed upon the figure of Sedlmayr and the relegation of his work to the outer limits of the historical discipline cannot be attributed solely to his adhesion to Nazism, or to his intransigent anti-modernism, but must also be understood in relation to the ambiguity of his research. Sedlmayr contributed decisively to the criticism and demolition of the positivist and romantic *Philosophiegeschichte*. His work signals the definitive emancipation of historical studies from their own nineteenth-century origins. After Sedlmayr, if not because of him alone, the notion of an historical space can no longer be reduced to conditions of meaning imposed by a rigorous and rigid system of conceptual categories and binary oppositions – it is the result of an always more autonomous and self-conscious project. Sedlmayr is perhaps the last representative figure of a tradition that he himself helped to destroy, subsumed into the ruins of the building that he himself demolished, while at the same time the Vienna School celebrates in his work one of the most eminent outcomes of its long historiographical tradition and one of the most emblematic moments of its dissolution.

Acknowledgement

This essay was first published as the critical introduction to the Italian edition of *Die Architektur Borrominis*.

Endnotes

1 Sedlmayr, *La rivoluzione dell'arte moderna*, 6.
2 On the Vienna School, see Sickel, "Das k.k. Institut für österreichische Geschichtsforschung"; Hirsch, "Das österreichische Institut für Geschichtsforschung 1854–1934"; and Schlosser, "Die Wiener Schule der Kunstgeschichte." A series of obituaries, largely published in the Institute's official organ, bear witness to the image of itself that the Vienna School produced and promulgated: Wickhoff, "Alois Riegl"; Ottenthal, "Theodor von Sickel"; Schlosser, "Franz Wickhoff"; Köhler, "Max Dvorak"; Hanhloser, "Zum Gedächtnis von Julius von Schlosser"; and Sedlmayr, "Julius Ritter von Schlosser. 1866–1938."
3 Sedlmayr, "Österreichs bildende Kunst" in *Epochen und Werke*, vol. 2, 278; and "Die politische Bedeutung des deutschen Barocks" in *Epochen und Werke*, vol. 2, 140–57.
4 On the "Young Vienna School," see Neumeyer's review of *Kunstwissenschaftliche Forschungen*; and Schapiro, "The New Viennese School."
5 See also Sedlmayr, "Bild und Raum," 2649–54.
6 Sedlmayr, "Österreichs bildende Kunst" in *Epochen und Werke*, vol. 2, 278. As the citations make clear, Sedlmayr undoubtedly developed the ideas behind these two essays in close contact with the contemporaneous historical research of Otto Brunner.
7 In *Architecture in the Age of Reason* Kaufmann recalls that it was his reading of Durand's *Architecture* that directed him toward the work of Ledoux. See Kaufmann, *Architecture in the Age of Reason*, 117, footnote: "Incidentally, it was from this copy [of Durand's *Architecture*, 1804] that my studies of Ledoux started more than thirty years ago."
8 This has already been observed by Teyssot in "Neoclassic and 'Autonomous' Architecture," 28. Kaufmann's relative disinterest in the historical trajectory from the eighteenth century to the early twentieth century is also illustrated by the fact that he barely acknowledges Sedlmayer's numerous observations and developments on his own work. See Kaufmann, *Architecture in the Age of Reason*, 166, where he reproached Sedlmayr for having forgotten that "the vast majority of Ledoux's projects were structures of stressed static character, solidly resting upon the ground," and that "out of the vagueness and weirdness of the revolutionary ideals emerged not only the *civil code* and a new social order, but also a new, consolidated architecture."
9 Sedlmayr, "Julius Ritter von Schlosser," 516.
10 Sedlmayr, "Julius Ritter von Schlosser," 516.
11 Sedlmayr, "Gestaltetes Sehen" (1925) and "Zum gestalteten Sehen" (1926).
12 Sedlmayr, "Zu einer strengen Kunstwissenschaft," 7–32.
13 Sedlmayr returns to this point in the 2nd edition of *Die Architektur Borrominis*, xxiii.
14 Sedlmayr, *Die Architektur Borrominis*, xxiv.

15 Croce's work is the subject of profound reflection within the German-language cultural debate. Consider, for instance, the pages dedicated by Walter Benjamin to the theses espoused by Croce in his *Breviario di estetica* in the "Epistemo-Critical Prologue" to *The Origin of German Tragic Drama*, 22–4.

16 See Sedlmayr, "Eine 'genetische Monographie'," 187–92.

17 See Sedlmayr, "Bild und Raum," 2649–54.

18 Sedlmayr, *Die Architektur Borrominis*, xxvi.

19 See Wittkower, "Zu Hans Sedlmayrs Besprechung von E. Coudenhove-Erthal," 142–5; and Hempel, "Ist eine strenge Kunstwissenschaft möglich?" 155–63. Sedlmayr responded to his critics in "Eduard Coudenhove-Erthal, Carlo Fontana und die Architektur des römischen Spätbarocks," 93–5; and in "Geschichte und Kunstgeschichte," 185–99. In an article for the *Art Bulletin* ("The New Viennese School") Meyer Schapiro had articulated a third position, highly critical of the theses advanced by the "Young Vienna School" in the *Kunstwissenschaftliche Forschungen*, yet his challenge remained unanswered.

20 Sedlmayr, "Eduard Coudenhove-Erthal, Carlo Fontana und die Architektur des römischen Spätbarocks," 93–5.

21 Sedlmayr, *Österreichische Barockarchitektur*, 5–21.

22 Dvořák's importance to Sedlmayr's research is apprehended by Fiore in "Hans Sedlmayr," 5–20.

23 Sedlmayr, "Storia dell'arte come storia dello spirito," 134.

24 Studies on the baroque and neo-classicism were integral to the first modern phases of the historiography of art. On this point, consider that the emblematic formative studies of Pevsner and Giedion were dedicated to baroque architecture. One dissonant voice stands out from these years, being Croce and his *Storia dell'età barocca in Italia* (1929).

25 Sedlmayr elaborates on the importance of Fielder's thought in "Geschichte und Kunstgeschichte," 191.

26 Sedlmayr, "Zu einer strengen Kunstwissenschaft."

27 Sedlmayr's sources on *Gestalttheorie* include Allesch, "Psychologische Bemerkungen zu zwei Werken der neueren Kunstgeschichte" (1922); and "Die ästhetische Erscheinungsweise der Farben" (1925); Koffka, "Zur Theorie der Erlebnis-Wahrnemung" (1923); Wertheimer, "Untersuchungen zur Lehre von der Gestalt" (1922); Wulf, "Beiträge zur Psychologie der Gestalt" (1922). Kretschmer presented complementary methodological sources in *Körperbau und Charakter*; and in *Geniale Menschen*, esp. from 56 onwards.

28 Fiore, "Hans Sedlmayr," 8.

29 Lavater and Lichtenberg, *Lo specchio dell'anima*, 59.

30 Sedlmayr, "Il legame fra visibile e invisibile nell'opera d'arte," 243–8. One of the themes discussed in this brief text is the link between physiognomy and *Stimmung* in the work of Adalbert Stifter, themes Sedlmayr had already treated in "Pieter Bruegel" (1957). See also Sedlmayr, "Über das Interpretieren von Werken der bildenden Künste" (1965).

31 In this sense the limits of this mode of analysis touch upon the dangers inherent in any structural analysis that would empty artistic language of its semantic content. Compare Tafuri, *Teorie e storia dell'architettura*, 202–3.

32 Croce, "Una teoria della 'macchia'," 236–46.

33 Sedlmayr, "Die 'Macchia' Bruegels," 138.

34 See also Sedlmayr, "Vom Sehen barocker Architekturen," 5–21.

35 Sedlmayr, "Die 'Macchia' Bruegels," 138.

36 Sedlmayr, "Pieter Bruegel" (1957).

37 Sedlmayr, "Die Schauseite der Karlskirche in Wien," 262–71.

38 Compare Perniola, *Dopo Heidegger*, 81.

39 Certainly aware that some phenomena continue to evade the historical process if it is interpreted in terms of continuity alone, Riegl has reduced these moments "waste" to the problem of "advances" and "anachronisms" within the alternation of epochs dominated at one moment by a tactile principle and in another by the optical. In this regard, it should be noted Sedlmayr welcomes *in toto* the criticisms of Kaschnitz-Weinberg, whose comments were directed at this point: the abstract character of its historical categories based on *a priori* conceptual oppositions.

40 Riegl, *The Origins of Baroque Art in Rome*, 112.

41 Sedlmayr, *Die Architektur Borrominis*, 144–9.

42 Tafuri, "Borromini e l'esperienza della storia," 42.

Chapter 9
Pevsner's *Kunstgeographie*: From Liepzig's Baroque to the Englishness of Modern English Architecture

Nikolaus Pevsner (1902–83) is widely recognized as one of the twentieth century's most prolific and influential historians of architecture. In Britain, Pevsner was for many years a household name largely due to his monumental architectural survey series, *The Buildings of Britain*, and his numerous BBC radio broadcasts.[1] Internationally he is remembered for such seminal books as the *Pioneers of the Modern Movement* (1936) and *An Outline of European Architecture* (1942), and as series editor of the "Pelican History of Art," all of the titles of which remain in print.[2] During his lifetime, and since his passing, Pevsner has also been the subject of a great deal of criticism, which arrived in three broad waves. The first emerged from his treatment as an émigré scholar in Britain. As a German he was criticized for his apparent lack of understanding of British cultural tradition, though more often than not, this reflected a nationalist chauvinism.[3] Secondly, towards the end of his career Pevsner attracted much criticism for his promotion of a teleological view of the development of architectural style, which privileged ideas of historical progress and *Zeitgeist* and the belief that history writing could also be boldly operative – an approach found most notably in his study and promotion of architectural modernism.[4] More recently, several studies have highlighted Pevsner's attitudes towards the geographical basis of art and architecture, some of which have conspired to bring his oeuvre into further disrepute for its own seemingly nationalist undertones.[5]

Elsewhere I, and others, have argued that much of this criticism has tended to overshadow not only the variety of Pevsner's output, but its extent.[6] A prime example of this phenomenon is the posthumous publication of *Visual Planning and the Picturesque* (2010). This book revealed Pevsner's little-researched contribution to urban design discourses through his involvement with the mid-twentieth-century British townscape movement, a movement which, like Pevsner's hitherto unpublished treatise, had largely evaded scholarly scrutiny for half a century.[7]

This chapter takes its lead from Pevsner's more recent critical reception around ideas of art and its relationship to nation, and discusses these within the wider context of twentieth-century architectural historiography and its reliance on developments in German language art historical discourses in the late nineteenth and early twentieth centuries and, in particular, those developed in parallel to the emergence of scholarship on the baroque. A key feature of Pevsner's work from the 1920s to the 1970s was a geographically and nationally specific conception of art and architecture, but few studies have focused on the origins of this thought and its outcomes.[8] This chapter proposes that Pevsner's formative context within the discipline of *Kunstwissenschaft* (the science of art) and the parallel development of *Kunstgeographie* (the geography of art), greatly impacted his historiography of modern architecture, and, furthermore, found its historical corollary in his nationally specific studies of the baroque.

This chapter proposes that the baroque provided Pevsner with a template for understanding national and regional episodes of art and architecture. For Pevsner, the baroque was a testing ground on which he refined his historical practice before turning his sights on the significant developments of his own day – the rise of modernism in architecture. The discussion of this trajectory from the baroque to modernism promises a closer view of Pevsner's method and its origins, illustrates the centrality of these ideas in Pevsner's historiography and, thereby, offers a large cross-section of twentieth-century architectural history. It also illustrates how Pevsner's geographically inflected art history was part of a broader tradition which was made to stretch back to the baroque as it continued through mid-century modernism to re-emerge at the end of the twentieth century within postmodern discourses generally and that of critical regionalism specifically.

Kunstwissenschaft and *Kunstgeographie*

The study of art in the German-speaking world was, from the end of the nineteenth century and beginning of the twentieth, dominated by the new field of *Kunstwissenschaft*, now associated with such influential figures as August Schmarsow (1853–1936), Alois Riegl (1858–1905) and Heinrich Wölfflin (1864–1945). Building on a tradition established by earlier pioneers in the history of art, from Franz Kugler (1808–58) to Jacob Burckhardt (1818–97), this generation made it their central task to develop more rigorous "scientific" methods for the study of art. These studies led to a more systematic classification of artworks and their relationships intended to divorce art history from connoisseurship and to determine art's essence and principles irrespective of period or locale. In this respect, *Kunstwissenschaft* stood in contrast with *Kunstgeschichte* (the history of art) and the various traditional approaches maintained elsewhere, which continued as exercises in connoisseurship – concentrating on artists, schools and epochs.[9] The first generation of *Kunstwissenschaftler* fostered new and diverse themes to the study of art and, within it, architecture: Schmarsow concentrated on space as architecture's essential quality; Riegl introduced the concept of *Kunstwollen* or artistic volition as the changeable notion of artistic production in different ages; and Wölfflin's analyses focused almost exclusively on the visual and formal aspects of art and their psychological effects.

As these spatial, visual or formal modes of analysis promised new findings, the study of art and architecture in connection with its regional or national location added another layer of detail to *Kunstwissenschaft*'s ever more sophisticated readings and categorizations. Sketching this problem in 1915, Wölfflin writes at the end of his seminal *Kunstgeschichtliche Grundbegriffe*: "The time will soon come when the historical record of European architecture will no longer be merely subdivided into gothic, Renaissance, and so on, but will trace out the national physiognomies which cannot quite be effaced even by imported styles."[10]

In fact, this time had already arrived, though Wölfflin was right to think that the most substantial development of *Kunstgeographie* would be left to a later generation who, it turned out, would include art historians and architects like Paul Schultze-Naumburg (1869–1949), Wilhelm Pinder (1878–1947), Albert Erich Brinckmann (1881–1958), and Dagobert Frey (1883–1962). Interest in the relationship of art with its location, or national setting, was already present in German-language art history, where it was most commonly discussed in connection with the impact of climate and ethnicity, extending the premises of earlier topological studies of art and architecture. Art historians before Wölfflin had been explicit in mapping national differences in architectural style, as demonstrated in the three nationally-ordered volumes on baroque art published by Cornelius Gurlitt (1850–1938) from 1886 to 1889.[11]

Thomas DaCosta Kaufmann's *Toward a Geography of Art* (2004) shows how ideas similar to those embodied in *Kunstgeographie* have not only been embedded in western culture since antiquity, but have remained central to the study of art until the term's introduction early in twentieth-century Germany. Kaufmann illustrates how earlier studies of art thought it a matter of fact to distinguish works of art and architecture based on location and national generalizations.[12] He shows how these were more than just categorizing tools, encompassing the issues of identity invoked and embedded in works of art and architecture. Describing this logic, Kaufmann writes:

> Linking an object with a country, region, city or an artist who worked in a particular place is based on a conscious or unconscious assumption that this object possesses certain features that may be found in other objects produced in that location. Classification according to place emphasizes the local rather than, or in addition to, the temporal aspects of identification.[13]

This was the particularly the case toward the end of the nineteenth century with the nascent study of the baroque. It appears more than an historical coincidence that *Kunstwissenschaft* emerged parallel to interest in the baroque as a new periodization and area of specialist scholarship, which further heralded the emergence of *Kunstgeographie*. The baroque was often used – though as neither the first nor only example – to illustrate a mobile European style, which had its origins in Roman architecture, but spread throughout the Continent, taking on different forms in different countries. Presumably Wölfflin has the baroque in mind when he refers to such "imported styles" and the resistance posed by a national imagination of art and architecture.

Wilhelm Pinder (1878–1947) is chiefly remembered for his work on precisely this question. Pinder's *Deutsche Barock*, first published in 1912, lays out the history of the German baroque in bold and emotive terms, describing the qualities of an architecture that had begun in Italy, but had undergone a substantial modification in Germany. The qualities of the *Barock* Pinder chose to identify as German seem forced and random in isolation, but fall into sharper focus when compared with the baroque of other nations – and for Pinder this clearly meant France. Pinder describes how each European country in which the baroque had traction developed the style in different ways, mainly resulting from its intersection with national traditions, but also from other such factors as the timing of its arrival or certain sculptural or painterly dispositions in each of those countries. A prime example of this national difference was Versailles, regarding which Pinder observes: "France was introduced to the baroque at an earlier stage, and, corresponding with to this country's intellectual clarity, it created its own note with a strong dose of classicism. It was exactly this note, which we [Germans] wished to have the least."[14] In Versailles the stairs were hidden, whereas the German baroque masters, such as Balthasar Neumann (1687–1753) tended to celebrate these elements. The love of stairs Pinder thought "totally un-French," and he further exclaims: "No people in the world have ever exceeded the stairways of the German baroque."[15] Elsewhere he writes:

> Whenever the timidity of German patrons called for the judgment of the French, they would criticize the lack of interior connections; the little concern for society; the waste of the stair houses, and they are right from their own point of view. The German master of the baroque is freer, is more fastidious, clumsy, and impetuous, he has many mistakes; but where a great architect succeeds, there we find a work that radiates the warmth of humanity.[16]

Pinder's writing reveals the difficulties inherent in *Kunstgeographie*, because the qualities of art and architecture identified by *Kunstgeographie* cannot exist in isolation, but rather within a system of relations and comparison. The identifications it allows must inevitably invoke ideas of nation, nationalist thought and identity, which is to say that an absolute *Kunstgeographie* is a logical impossibility. Retrospectively, the dangers of *Kunstgeographie* seem clear, especially when married with a nationalist political agenda as it would later come to be under the Nazi regime. Not surprisingly, Pinder's work went on to be explicitly nationalist and racist, and he was, indeed, among those German art historians who lent strong support to National Socialism.[17]

Pevsner

The experiences of Pinder and others demonstrate *Kunstgeographie*'s ideological extremes. Nevertheless, who would deny that there are national differences in the character of art and architecture? Today, few scholars would risk an explicitly nationalist history of art or architecture for fear of being libelled. This, however, was Pevsner's interest and he was highly cognizant of its dangers. The outer edges of this fascination can be traced from Pevsner's own education in Germany and his doctoral study of Leipzig's baroque architecture, through to studies of the art and architecture of his adopted country and perhaps his best known work of this kind, *The Englishness of English Art* (1956).

From the time of his education, a key tenet of Pevsner's work had been the geographical and national specificity of art and architecture. The research towards his dissertation was carried out from 1922–23, submitted in Leipzig in 1924, and published four years later as *Leipziger Barock: Die Baukunst der Barockzeit in Leipzig* (1928, Leipzig's Baroque: The Building Art of the Baroque Period in Leipzig). It was supervised by Pinder and followed very much the path of his mentor, whom Pevsner also saw as his role model.

Pevsner's study begins where earlier survey works by Gurlitt and others had finished.[18] He sets out the cultural, religious, social and industrial history of Leipzig, contrasting the city's formidable reputation in literature, music and the arts against that of its lesser-known architecture and town planning. With reference to a long list of the city's prominent admirers, Pevsner writes: "Whoever is of the opinion they will be disappointed by the city's architecture should check the series of accounts of Leipzig's *Stadtbild* (townscape) and its buildings from the eighteenth century."[19] To counteract the implication that Leipzig's architecture was disappointing appears to be one of Pevsner's chief objectives, an implication he attributes to Gustav Wustmann and his various architectural surveys of the city from the end of the nineteenth century.[20] Pevsner believed such opinions to be more a reflection of the distaste for the baroque *circa* 1880 than any inherent value of Leipzig's buildings or their makers.

Within the context of this chapter, Pevsner's dissertation is perhaps more significant for the ideas it assumes from his education than for its contribution to scholarship *per se*. Pinder's influence becomes clear by the third chapter, which is titled "The Turning Point around 1700." The date was significant in Pevsner's analysis as the emergence of a baroque architectural style that departed from "foreign artistic thoughts, from Italy or the Netherlands" and which "first became truly German."[21] The shifts around this moment allowed Leipzig's baroque architecture to achieve a level of "architectonic conviction, without a contemporary rival in the world who could keep step." The "true" German character and the passionate hyperbole are clearly reminiscent of Pinder, but Pevsner goes on to explain the mechanics of this change at the turn of the eighteenth century: "An external symptom is often the reduction in the number of foreign master-builders and their replacement by Germans, which resulted in the desired victory of Germanness, and corresponded to the exact same efforts in literature by Leibniz."[22]

Pevsner thought these developments heralded new architectural creations and developments in style, an observation that also reveals Pevsner's debts to Schmarsow and Wölfflin: "In terms of architectural history, the transition reveals itself … in a new synthesis (*Zusammenfassung*) of the building form toward the plastic-organic and unified … and a diffusion of the strict, heavy and restive majesty of the second half of the seventeenth century, towards increased movement [*Beweglichkeit*]."[23]

The tenth and final chapter of Pevsner's dissertation is yet more telling of the methods he absorbed from his teachers: "Art Historical and Art Geographical Conclusions." After several chapters of detailed discussion of specific buildings, motifs and architects, this final chapter returns to a general art historical discussion of Leipzig's history that nonetheless focuses on the wider geographical significance of the city's location within Saxony. As Pevsner wrote, this chapter was chiefly concerned with finding the "constant factor" of Leipzig's baroque architecture against the changing modes of architectural style.[24] He thought such a study to be useful for understanding puzzling aspects of particular building works, which he wrote "must have their causes in local particularities."[25] Pevsner describes this interaction between style and place in a manner that illustrates a clear continuity with later works in which he understood geography and national culture to impact upon architecture: "While the style of the times [*Zeitstil*] always develops anew and, even if it is related, though never identical, the style of the place is to a certain degree constant."[26]

In 1969, when reminiscing over his debts to Schmarsow, Wölfflin, and Pinder, Pevsner wrote off the value of his dissertation, stating, "in spite of this illustrious pedigree, my thesis on the baroque architecture of Leipzig was purely a matter of the history of forms, even of motifs."[27] Even if Pevsner regarded his doctoral thesis with the distaste traditionally accorded doctorates by their authors as mature scholars, its mode of analysis continued to feature in his most famous books, *Pioneers of the Modern Movement* (1936, later called *Pioneers of Modern Design*) and *An Outline of European Architecture* (1942), which both place a heavy emphasis on geographical context in the development of architecture. Indeed, shortly after his emigration from Germany, Pevsner published a lecture he had delivered in 1934 at University College London in the German newspaper *Deutsche Zukunft* under the title "Das Englische in der Englischen Kunst" (The Englishness in English Art).[28] In this article, he outlined a question that would go on to preoccupy him for the rest of his professional life. After briefly criticizing such predecessors as Wölfflin for what he understood to be their exclusive concentration on questions of form, Pevsner went on to praise Pinder and others for their work on *Kunstgeographie*, which he described as "art in its relationship with the nation." He asked "Which lessons can an open German learn of English art, if he tries to recognize the English character of English art?"[29]

Pevsner focused exactly on this question in his Reith Lectures, first broadcast on BBC Radio in 1955, and republished as *The Englishness of English Art* in 1956. Pevsner opens the book with an outline of his approach, entitled "The Geography of Art:"

> The following pages are an essay in the geography of art. Whereas the history of art is concerned with what all works of art and architecture have in common because they belong to one period, in whatever country within the same civilization they may have been made, the question asked by a geography of art is what all works of art and architecture of one people have in common, at whatever time that may have been made. That means that the subject of a geography of art is national character as it expressed itself in art.[30]

Since then, many of these national characteristics of "Englishness" have become famous: values such as the English love of contradiction, idiosyncrasy and compromise, or the contentment with hybrid and imperfect systems such as constitutional monarchy; or the disdain of pure reason in favour of empirical, imperfect realities, best seen in the comparison of case law and continental code law.[31] Pevsner thought many of these values had exerted a strong influence on English architecture and town planning, and he explores this point in *Visual Planning and the Picturesque* by pointing out recurring appearances of variety, contrast, irregularity, incongruity and admixture inherent in many historical examples of English architecture and planning. But Pevsner was also patently aware of the risks assumed by reading English architecture and planning against a notion of "Englishness," as he wrote:

> As soon as the question is posed in this way, two objections are bound to arise. First: is it desirable to stress a national point of view so much in appreciating works of art and architecture? Second: Is there such a thing at all as a fixed or almost fixed national character? Neither of these questions is confined to art.[32]

This mode of inquiry was not new. In *Englishness* Pevsner acknowledged a similar attempt by the disgraced Dagobert Frey and his 1942 work *Englisches Wesen in der bildenden Kunst* (The English Character of English Art), which Pevsner found to have reached many conclusions similar to his own.[33] The nationalism of German art historical discourses in this period has received a great deal of scrutiny in the post-war period and, as Pevsner's objections indicate, with good reason. Such thinking was not, however, limited to Germany alone, and was indeed a common mode of analysis in Britain, even if this work did not form part of the broader project of *Kunstwissenschaft*.[34]

In Britain, nation and ethnicity had long been part of the mainstream tradition in the study of art. John Ruskin's early writings, first published as a series of pseudonymous articles in John Claudius Loudon's *Architectural Magazine* in 1837 and 1838, demonstrate the widespread acceptance of such attitudes. The full title of his first contribution to the *Architectural Magazine* reads "The Poetry of Architecture; or the Architecture of the Nations of Europe considered in its Association with natural Scenery and national Character."[35] *The National Character of English Architecture*, published by Geoffrey Scott (1885–1929) in 1908, likewise predicates in a remarkably close way Pevsner's later attempts to locate the essence of English art and architecture. Scott devoted some effort to the discussion of Vanbrugh's architecture and its role in developing English character, writing:

> [Vanbrugh's] work, in spite of its relative inferiority, is far more suggestive of national distinction than that of Inigo Jones himself. It shows us northern instincts come to an artistic self-consciousness that belongs to the South, and borrowing its formulas for a foreign purpose. … But an art's limitation is also its opportunity; if English architecture is usually, unlike Vanbrugh's, reticent and reserved, it has perhaps found the language most fitted to the genius of the nation and the conventions of the art.[36]

Continuing this tradition into the second half of the twentieth century, Kenneth Clark, in a lecture to the English Association in 1962, promoted "provincialism" as a means of explaining variation between local and international styles in art and architecture.[37]

Returning to a pivotal moment in discussions of the relationship between architecture and location, Martin Shaw Briggs's *Baroque Architecture* was published in 1913 – one year after Pinder's *Deutsche Barock* appeared – and is remarkably close to its German counterpart. Briggs opens his commentary on baroque architecture in Germany and Austria with the lines, "It is so generally recognized that geography may influence architecture that one would naturally expect to find a striking difference between the buildings of Italy and those of the Teutonic lands." In a candid display of nationalism, presumably espousing the type of "foreign" perception of the German baroque that both Pinder and Pevsner sought to challenge, Briggs continues:

we find between Italy and Germany – neighbours as they are – a wide and distinct divergence. In no way is this more apparent than in their art; in no branch of art more than in their architecture. To the Italian the German was in ancient days simply a barbarian. It is perhaps the very fact of his barbarianism which has made his architecture so difficult to understand, for he has borrowed first from France, then from Italy, and has seldom created a whole series of normal development for himself.

With the exception of the age of the Lombard kings, and their export of brick churches to northern Italy, Briggs concludes, "we must admit that German architecture has only at times been really national."[38]

In his *Outline of European Architecture* of 1942, Pevsner's discussion of the baroque is reminiscent of Pinder's account of the wanderings of the baroque throughout Europe – a lineage practically acknowledged in Pevsner's lengthy discussion of Germany's baroque innovations to the stairway. Vanbrugh's Blenheim is likewise central to Pevsner's understanding of the impact of the baroque in England. Of the palace he writes that

the term Baroque could be used only with careful qualifications, these towers would be called Baroque by anyone familiar with the work of Bernini, Borromini and the others in Italy. ... Yet in spite of that Vanbrugh, seen side by side with Michelangelo or Bernini is also a classicist. It seems a contradiction but it is not. It simply is, just as in the case of Wren, the special English twist given to the Baroque. ... Vanbrugh's drama lies in the visible forcing of this English aloofness into the service of an overmighty plan. English Baroque is Baroque asserting itself against an inborn leaning towards the static and the sober.[39]

Pre-empting such later works as *Englishness*, in 1945 Pevsner again returned to the baroque and the variance and character of its national uptakes, incorporating cultural and religious causes. The occasion was provided by his review of Sacheverall Sitwell's book *English Architects and Craftsmen*, in which Pevsner wrote:

It is in fact this element of extravaganza that distinguishes British from Continental Baroque. In Italy, especially in the south, in Spain and Portugal, in Germany and Austria, Baroque is spontaneous and unashamed. By the eighteenth century the English upper classes were unable to adventure freely. Puritan self-discipline had left too deep a mark on them. So what there was of fancy had to find a less natural outlet; the crank came into being, and with him the folly, with all its picturesque incongruity, a perverse and delightful form of self-assertion.[40]

From the Baroque to Modernism

Following his doctoral dissertation on Leipzig's baroque and his first book on Italian painting (1928),[41] Pevsner's commitment to study the baroque was not sustained and his research appears to have been limited to the sporadic papers and the historical studies surveyed above. Of greater interest for the present discussion is the role played by the baroque in Pevsner's thinking and his approach to history writing. *Kunstgeographie* served him as a useful tool in understanding national deviations of the baroque, but it became a live issue when applied to the emergence of modern architecture in the early decades of the twentieth century. Read in this light, the baroque provided Pevsner another way of understanding modernism in his own day and, moreover, the uptake of international modernism in Britain.

Pevsner's portrayal of the developmental phase of modern architecture in *Pioneers of the Modern Movement* is now generally well-known: proto-modernist thought reached a crucial juncture in England under the aegis of William Morris and Arts and Crafts designers; but it had to go to Germany and the Deutscher Werkbund to be industrialized, and there it reached its fullest achievement at the hands of Walter Gropius.[42] Of course this schema goes a long way to explaining the subtitle of the book, *From William Morris to Walter Gropius*, which can also be seen as a partial attempt at flattering his new compatriots. This movement of ideas and styles around Europe and their tempering by various national dispositions is analogous to the treatment of the baroque by Pinder and his contemporaries. Although he does not directly cite the baroque in this connection in *Pioneers*, Pevsner's attitude is clear when he writes of the development of modern architecture: "Today, the new style – international, though as clearly divided into national modes as was Romanesque or gothic art – flourishes in all artistically creative countries of European Civilisation."[43] Of his particular art historical method in *Pioneers*, which would serve as the basis of much of his later writing on modernism, Pevsner observes: "The art historian has to watch national as well as personal qualities. Only the interaction of these with the spirit of the age produces the complete picture of the art of any epoch, as we see it."[44]

As noted at the outset of this chapter, Pevsner's approach was fundamentally criticized towards the end of his career and in his posthumous reception for its insistence on the teleological development of architecture and modernism's place as the *only* style appropriate to the spirit of the age.[45] Only recently have Pevsner's views on *Kunstgeographie* attracted more substantial scholarly scrutiny, aspects of which have tended to focus on Pevsner's nationalism.[46] For better or worse, Pevsner's insistence on the centrality of *Kunstgeographie*, the generous references to his mentor Pinder, and the existence of several early articles in which Pevsner looked favorably on early National Socialist art policy have paved the way over the last decade for a view of Pevsner as a Nazi sympathizer and an obsessively nationalistic historian of art and architecture. With reference to Pevsner's selection of exemplary architects and buildings for his 1936 *Pioneers*, Stephen Games cites Pevsner's 1931 review of Le Corbusier and Pierre Jeanneret's complete works as an example of this attitude.[47] Here Games interprets Pevsner's selection of architects and buildings as a simple preference for Gropius over Le Corbusier, based on Pevsner's supposed belief in German superiority in matters of art and culture. Games's reading is skewed. Rather than uncovering a pathological nationalist, Pevsner's article on Le Corbusier can also be seen as a youthful attempt to argue for a greater role of German-speaking architects and central European architecture (alongside that of the Netherlands and the Unites States) in early modernist scholarship, while placing more emphasis on the social issues around architecture and industry (Gropius) and less on artistic production and fantasy (Le Corbusier). Guilty by association, it would appear that Pevsner's *Kunstgeographie* has brought disrepute to his work and reception.[48]

Rarely have Pevsner's opinions on the national development of modernism and the international style been taken into account in this schema. Partly owing to *Pioneers* and his work with the *Architectural Review* (*AR*) from the 1930s onwards, Pevsner established a reputation as a supporter of modern architecture, which his critics often mistakenly thought to mean a support of the dominance of modernist over historic architecture. Pevsner's critics often portray his support of modernism as dogmatic and unswerving, whereas a closer reading shows his thoughts on the matter to be much more nuanced. In an article entitled "Modern Architecture and Tradition" (1947)[49] and in his *Visual Planning*, Pevsner made his stance on these issues explicit and operative by stating that modern architecture and planning had not yet arrived at their destination, but were at their origins, and needed to be adapted over time to local and national traditions, materials and needs. Pevsner noted that the most substantial problem in international modernism was its application in town planning and not its buildings, which he and others at the *AR* thought laudable. The key example to which this group referred time and again was the modern architecture of Scandinavia, which Pevsner and the *AR* circle thought to be a prime example of a polite, moderate and locally adapted modernism, which they named "The New Empiricism."[50]

Pevsner's essay "Modern Architecture and Tradition" is essential reading for those who still think of Pevsner as a dogmatic modernist. It is also a demonstration of the seamless synthesis of *Kunstgeographie* within his broader scheme of *Kunstwissenschaft*, evidenced in his particular mode of history writing. It is a remarkably concise outline of the role Pevsner saw for modern architecture and planning in his own day. He begins with a broad overview of the development of past styles from French gothic to Florentine Renaissance, before moving to his own day, asking "When we turn to modern architecture – whence comes the style which we may label the style of our own age as we can label gothic or Renaissance? And how has the style spread?"[51] Of examples by Le Corbusier, Oud and Gropius he noted, "The style they evolved ... appears essentially homogeneous and shows few national variations. How does this happen? and should we welcome it?"[52] Pevsner found the major causes of this homogeneity to lie in the changed circumstances of modern communications and internationalized materials:

modern inventions pass from land to land, from continent to continent with amazing speed, individual, provincial, national personality may easily be crushed and overwhelmed in the process.

Many people welcome this. Their argument is that architecture today has become scientific and that science is international. Look, they say, at building materials. In other ages there were districts known for their slate, their timber, their limestone or their marble. Today we can transport building materials anywhere. We can cut the hardest stone, as if it were cheese. We employ an increasing amount of synthetic materials whose use is not tied to any locality. And this is a blessing (they hasten to add), for nationalism is to blame for all wars of the twentieth century, and wars destroy culture. Hence nationalism in architecture is to be annihilated.[53]

While Pevsner maintained climate as a significant factor in the selection of appropriate materials for various countries, he thought that to exclude the possibility of a differentiation based on national character to gravely impoverish architecture. His explanation deserves a longer quotation:

it is not the climate alone, which determines the differences in national architecture, still less it is the terrifying twentieth-century myth of race. … Cities, provinces, nations, they all have their individualities recognizable in their architecture. Alas so much of it is now is lost forever.

If neither climate nor race be the cause behind the individuality of Rome, Paris or Vienna, whence does it come? The answer is from its history and tradition. Climate and race are only single threads in the fabric woven by these great forces; it is from a common heritage of experience, vision and knowledge, that the final garment of a city, its architecture, is composed. …

The problem of our own time is to find an accepted language variable according to areas and countries, a style of our own clearly embodying our own demands, and yet rooted in the civilization and aesthetic feeling of each province and each people. Just as both the gothic period and the Renaissance began with an international phase, so in our day we much pass through an international phase. Its task will be accomplished when all possibilities of mere imitations of past styles have finally vanished. When that point is reached – and no sooner – when the modern style has become the mother tongue generally understood, then, and only then, will it be strong enough to branch out into the wealth of different idioms so ardently hoped for.[54]

In "Modern Architecture and Tradition" Pevsner marks an issue that has continued to persist to the present day – perhaps only escalated by the recent interest in the effects of globalization on cities and architecture. Before "Modern Architecture and Tradition" and since its appearance, Pevsner had approached this subject more narrowly, arguing for a particularly English and sometimes British version of modernism.[55] With his involvement in the *AR*'s townscape campaign, Pevsner and others attempted to marry modern architecture with the British tradition of "visual" or "picturesque" planning to make buildings and cities that would be visually attractive, functional and, moreover, wedded to their locations and traditions. In this regard, Pevsner's work on townscape can be seen as an early reform of modernism; one that sought to subjugate the harder edges of modernism's ideal forms and functions through moderation and compromise with local tradition.

Of course, the idea that architecture (if not art) should be welded to its "place" and "context" is now familiar to all reaches of architectural culture, mainly owing to the resurfacing of this view in the postmodernism of the late 1970s and early 1980s. In architecture, the most articulate version of this appeared under the polite catchphrase of Critical Regionalism.[56] In the histories of the late twentieth century, and in contrast to Pevsner's recent reception, Critical Regionalism appears to have avoided the pitfalls of a *Kunstgeographie* instrumentalized for nationalist political agendas, posturing itself instead as a combatant to the seeming sameness of global architecture. It is in this light that I prefer to read Pevsner's interests in *Kunstgeographie* spanning from the baroque to modernism, rather than as a lens through which to view a more sinister nationalism.

Endnotes

1   For a comprehensive list of Pevsner's Radio Talks, see Games (ed.), *Pevsner on Art and Architecture*.

2   The series originally focused on England, and was published by Penguin from 1947 to 1974. It was eventually expanded to include Scotland, Wales and Ireland. Originally published by Penguin, the series continues to be published by Yale University Press, as the Pevsner Architectural Guides.

3   For example of this treatment, note Betjeman's reactions to Pevsner in Mowl, *Stylistic Cold Wars*.

4   Most notably in Watkin, *Morality and Architecture*.

5   Notably by Games. See *Pevsner on Art and Architecture*; "The Germanness of the English Historian;" and *Pevsner: The Early Life*.

6   Pevsner's most recent biography has also gone a long way to correcting the limited views of Pevsner achievements. See Harries, *Nikolaus Pevsner*. For other authors writings on this subject, see Aitchison, "Visual Planning and Exterior Furnishing;" "Townscape in Context;" "Visual Planning and the Picturesque;" and "Pevsner's Townscape." See also Macarthur and Aitchison, "Oxford vs. The Bath Road."

7   See also Macarthur and Aitchison. "Pevsner's Townscape."

8   Ute Engel's research has been instrumental in drawing attention to these aspects of Pevsner's works. See Engel, "Nikolaus Pevsner und der Leipziger Barock" and "The Formation of Pevsner's Art History."

9   See, for example, the recent collection of essays in Frank and Adler (eds), *German Art History and Scientific Thought*.

10   Wölfflin, *Principles of Art History*, 235.

11   Gurlitt published his survey of baroque art as part of the *Geschichte der Baukunst* series (The History of Architecture) begun by Franz Kugler. The first volume on the Low Countries, France and England was published in 1886, Italy in 1887, and Germany in 1889.

12   See Kaufmann's history of the development of the geography of art in *Toward a Geography of Art*, 17–104

13   Kaufmann, *Toward a Geography of Art*, 107–8.

14   Pinder, *Deutscher Barock*, 14. All translations from German sources are by the author.

15   Pinder, *Deutscher Barock*, 16.

16   Pinder, *Deutscher Barock*, 5.

17   A more extreme example of this leaning toward art history based on nationalism and ethnic discrimination is found in the works of Dagobert Frey and Paul Schulze-Naumburg, both of whom actively supported National Socialism and its racial views on art and architecture.

18   Pevsner, *Leipziger Barock*, 184, note 1.

19   All translations here and below by the author. Pevsner, *Leipziger Barock*, 4.

20   Pevsner, *Leipziger Barock*, 6.

21   Pevsner, *Leipziger Barock*, 34.

22   Pevsner, *Leipziger Barock*, 34–5.

23   Pevsner, *Leipziger Barock*, 35.

24   Pevsner, *Leipziger Barock*, 160.

25   Pevsner, *Leipziger Barock*, 148.

26   Pevsner, *Leipziger Barock*, 148.

27   Barr (comp.), *Sir Nikolaus Pevsner*, ix.

28   Pevsner, "Das Englische in Der Englischen Kunst," 15.

29   Pevsner, "Das Englische in Der Englischen Kunst," 15.

30   Pevsner, *The Englishness of English Art*, 11.

31   See Causey, "Pevsner and Englishness."

32   Pevsner, *The Englishness of English Art*, 11.

33   Pevsner, *The Englishness of English Art*, 9. Pevsner translates the title of Frey's book as "The English Character as reflected in English Art," and goes on to say that despite the wartime publication, the book was free from "hostile remarks, let alone any Nazi bias." The case of Frey is a good example of the extremities of art history instrumentalized for Nazi ideology.

34   For interrelations of *Kunstwissenschaft*'s methods and Anglophone art history in the first decades of the twentieth century, see Macarthur's essay in the present collection.

35   Ruskin published these articles from November 1837 to December 1938, using the nom de plume of "Kata Phusin."

36   Scott, *The National Character*, 41.

37   Cited in Kaufmann, *Toward a Geography of Art*, 94.

38   Briggs, *Baroque Architecture*, 134.

39   Pevsner, *An Outline of European Architecture*, 184.

40   Pevsner, "The English Eccentrics," 326; and "Baroque and Rococo." See also Leach, "The Future of the Baroque, c. 1945," in this volume.

41   Pevsner, *Die Italienische Malerei*.

42   "Gropius regards himself as a follower of Ruskin and Morris, of van de Velde and of the Werkbund. So our circle is complete. The history of artistic theory between 1890 and the war proves the assertion on which the present work is based, namely that the phase between Morris and Gropius is a historical unit understandable as such. Morris laid the foundations of the modern style; with Gropius its character was ultimately determined." Pevsner, *Pioneers of Modern Architecture*, 42.

43   Pevsner, *Pioneers of Modern Architecture*, 41.

44   Pevsner, *Pioneers of Modern Architecture*, 188.

45   Compare Watkin, "Sir Nikolaus Pevsner," 169–72.

46   See essays by Engel, Muthesius and Causey in Draper (ed.), *Reassessing Nikolaus Pevsner*.

47   See Games, *Pevsner*, 169–73. Compare, Pevsner, review of *Le Corbusier und Pierre Jeanneret*, 303–12.

48   Susie Harries's biography offers a much more sensitive interpretation of the same data which Games uses to indict Pevsner. Harries points to both Pevsner views on the social role of art and architecture and his insistence on the national character of art as two features of Pevsner's methodology, which have mistakenly been held as support of Pevsner's supposed sympathy with National Socialism.

49   Pevsner, "Modern Architecture and Tradition," 228–32.

50   In Pevsner's work, see "C20 Picturesque" and "Roehampton." On the *Architectural Review*'s New Empiricism see Pevsner (as The Editor), "The New Empiricism;" and Pevsner (as de Maré), "The New Empiricism."

51   Pevsner, "Modern Architecture and Tradition," 228.

52   Pevsner, "Modern Architecture and Tradition," 228.

53   Pevsner, "Modern Architecture and Tradition," 228.

54   Pevsner, "Modern Architecture and Tradition," 231–2.

55   Pevsner, "The Modern Movement in Britain," 8, 11–38; and later, Pevsner, "Zehn Jahre Bauen in Grossbritannien," 461–3.

56   The banner "Critical Regionalism" was originally coined by Alexander Tzonis and Liane Lefaivre in 1981 in their article, "The Grid and the Pathway" and subsequently taken up by Kenneth Frampton in "Towards a Critical Regionalism." See also Tzonis and Lefaivre, "Why Critical Regionalism Today?;" and Frampton, "Prospects for a Critical Regionalism" and "Place-Form and Cultural Identity."

Chapter 10
The Future of the Baroque, c. 1945

Andrew Leach

In a letter dated 22 June 1946, Erwin Panofsky wrote to his former student and fellow art historian William S. Heckscher. A fellow alumnus of the Kulturwissenschaftliche Bibliothek Warburg, Heckscher was then teaching courses in German language and English literature at the University of Manitoba as the tail end of a wartime interlude between academic appointments in the history of art. Panofsky's letter reads thus:

> Concerning Baroque as a style, I can only refer your friend to a forthcoming article by [Wolfgang] Stechow (Oberlin College) but I do not know whether he already has proof prints and would be willing to give them *avant la lettre*. Another impending article by [Ulrich] Middeldorf (Chicago University) is concerned with the vicissitudes of the term and will certainly be of interest but has not appeared either so far as I know. In the meantime, I am sending along an unpretentious lecture of my own fabrication which you may pass on to Mr. Daniells if *you are sure that he will return it*. I may want to use it again if occasion offers. It is not very good and full of typographical and other errors but he may get some ideas, if only by way of opposition.[1]

The "unpretentious lecture" to which Panofsky drew Heckscher's attention was his now famous piece "What is Baroque?" This was first prepared in the mid-1930s, substantially revised over several years and published posthumously in 1994 in an essay collection edited by Irving Lavin. The article of Stechow's was published in 1946 with the title "Definitions of the Baroque in the Visual Arts," appearing in "A Special Issue on Baroque Style in the Various Arts" of the *Journal of Aesthetics and Art Criticism*.[2] The essay of Middeldorf's to which Panofsky refers is recalled only to be set aside. Middeldorf's own writings and papers include no such piece, suggesting a name misremembered or, if our correspondent indeed accurately recalled writing by Middeldorf on this theme, it would seem that his reflections are, for the moment, beyond our reach.[3]

These reflections, including his own, to which Panofsky points Heckscher and his correspondent Daniells, each attend to the "vicissitudes of the term," as Panofsky put it, and to the expanded scope the idea of the baroque enjoyed after a period of inter-war reassessment within and beyond its earliest domain, namely the history of art. From the end of the nineteenth century onwards, historians of painting and sculpture, literature and music made their own claims upon the baroque, in some cases accommodating it where it had not previously appeared in the critical lexicon, and in others recalibrating the meaning most popularly ascribed to it by Heinrich Wölfflin and his generation to understand the post-Renaissance developments of the classical tradition, or by his predecessors to understand the stylistic consequences of the Counter-Reformation. In the light of a sustained attempt to consider the critico-historical value of baroque variously as an historical or platonic category for the history of letters, the visual arts, or music, the legacy of this 1930s expansion was an apparently more neutral image of the baroque than that which had entered the twentieth century – a term Panofsky already considered neutral in relation to the use made of it by writers of the eighteenth century and the early decades of the nineteenth.[4] As we will see, this neutrality was itself quietly contentious when seen in light of the relationship made explicit between art history and political ideology in the interwar years. Comparing Panofsky's critical ambitions with those of Stechow reveals two radically different attitudes towards the term's potency in the post-war era.

Among the reasons we might claim that the end of the Second World War prompted a moment of intellectual stocktaking, two stand out as distinctly pertinent to historians of art and architecture. On one hand, the War and Nazi anti-Semitism had provoked the relocation of a vast number of scholars from Germany, Austria and other nations of central Europe to, principally, Great Britain and North America. Alongside Panofsky, Nikolaus Pevsner, Aby Warburg, Richard Krautheimer, Rudolf Wittkower, and many others besides, enacted a translation of the field of German-language art historical debates into numerous Anglophone academic settings, altering their makeup and tone from that point onwards. Where students of the interwar period who had engaged with the German-language historiography of art largely did so at a geographical remove, or through the synthesizing studies of Geoffrey Scott or Martin Briggs (in the case of the baroque), increasingly from the start of the 1930s, students could actually follow the courses of Panofsky or Krautheimer at New York University, or Wittkower at the Warburg Institute in London and, later, at Columbia. Personal traumas notwithstanding, the War had served to catalyse the transmission of an historical discourse from one linguistic and cultural realm to another, thereby ensuring its perpetuity and, in the process, dramatically expanding the terms by which an Anglophone historiography of art engaged its subjects.

Parallel to the traffic of individuals, on the other hand, is evidence of a widespread reflection within the humanities and social sciences prompted by the circumstances and experience of the War itself – and confronting, necessarily, the horrific deformations of human reason embodied in the Holocaust. The most famous of these works include the *Philosophische Fragmente* written by Max Horkheimer and Theodor Adorno on the *Dialektik der Aufklärung* (1944, 1947), and Marc Bloch's meditations, written in 1944 on the historian's tools and tasks and posthumously offered as an *Apologie pour l'histoire* at the end of that decade. The ethics of instrumentalization is a fundamental theme of these studies, implicating the means by which knowledge is produced, organized and disseminated and the ideological consequences of the historian's choices. Bloch had the problem succinctly in the introduction to his *Apologie*, written from within the experience of an occupied France: "And, indeed, whenever our exacting Western society, in the continuing crisis of growth, begins to doubt itself, it asks itself whether it has done well in trying to learn from the past, and whether it has learned rightly."[5] It would be foolhardy to argue a direct causal relation between an atmosphere of cultural restitution read back into these post-war years and the reflections of art historians upon their tools and tasks. It is nonetheless difficult to regard the efforts of scholars to consider the premises of their work through an examination of methods, frames and nomenclature as entirely divorced from the intellectual inventory that Horkheimer, Adorno and Bloch are regularly asked to represent.

In the instances that Panofsky's letter to Heckscher prompts us to consider, we encounter evidence of one of the recalibrations of the baroque as a term of historiography and criticism to which the term has been periodically subject. On this occasion it indeed owes something to the migration of vocabularies and ideas between disciplines and linguistic communities. The essays considered below document a revised standard against which we can now measure the uptake of a critico-historical and platonic baroque by the historical discourse on architecture among the visual arts in the 1940s and 1950s. But where the parameters sketched out for the baroque in the essays of Panofsky and Stechow might now seem obvious and granted, even dated to our eyes, they were once making sense of a field that was rife with ambiguities and contradictions as a result of inconsistencies within and between historical disciplines. And in doing so, they document two reflections on the obligations of historical research and criticism – and by extension of intellectual work in general – to history itself, registered in light of the art historian's perspective on culture's civilizing force and on his or her capacity to undermine the same.

Stechow's "Definitions of the Baroque in the Visual Arts"

A German historian of seventeenth-century Dutch painting who migrated to the United States shortly before the outbreak of war, Stechow first presented his contribution to the baroque issue of the *Journal of Aesthetics and Art Criticism* to the annual conference of the Modern Language Association in 1945 before which audience he could claim art history's seniority on matters baroque and apologize for its abuses. He writes, "We were the first to use the term, but we were also the first to make a mess of it."[6] Stechow's ambition is, on the surface, relatively modest: to account for how art historians use and have used "baroque" in order to understand what is at stake in the way it appears in the critical lexicons of other fields. In just a few pages he ably charts out the broad strokes of the treatment of the baroque within the history of art and the problems raised by its adaptation, as a category and as a concept, to other disciplines and their problems. He sidesteps the seemingly formulaic obligation to attend to the term's origins,[7] noting merely that its stylistic meaning absorbs and, to an extent, neutralizes something that was originally derisive both in the contemporaneous reception of the buildings, paintings and sculptures to which it refers and in the first phases of modern art historiography.

Stechow suggests three basic tasks the concept of the baroque had hitherto been called upon to perform: to describe a coherent body of art (or, more specifically, and in its earlier moments, architecture alone); to explain that coherent body of work in relation to that work it follows (which, in turn, coheres around another critical term); and to diagnose the deeper conditions giving rise to, principally, an architecture demonstrating such coherence and which (in turn) is shared by similarly coherent bodies of work and thought in painting, sculpture, music, literature, politics, philosophy and so forth. The conceptual problem, then, is the relationship between that which is described as baroque and the complex of conditions that gives rise to that body of works that can be asked to cohere as such.

As a negotiation between appearance and content, Stechow identifies the three distinct meanings that had accrued to the term since the end of the nineteenth century. In stylistic terms, Stechow holds that the baroque is that which is "diametrically opposed to that classical composure and restraint which were considered indispensable by those using the baroque as synonymous with bad taste."[8] It spans from outward displays of "exuberance, dynamic stress, emotional grandeur" through to "a predilection for unrestrained emphasis on outward emotion or even inward expression provided they are apt to sacrifice composure and formal equilibrium to those 'baroque' qualities."[9]

Chronologically, the baroque is taken to span from between 1580 and 1600 to between 1725 and 1750, initially (after Jacob Burckhardt) describing a period of architecture's history before expanding to a broader complex of a "baroque music, baroque literature, baroque philosophy, baroque science," each with its own chronological characteristics. The relationship between chronology and style is, therefore, crucial to Burckhardt's approach, and to that of his student, Heinrich Wölfflin, who in *Renaissance und Barock* (1888) had followed Burckhardt's lead in preserving baroque for architecture alone, reflecting the formal unity in Italian architecture that was not shared by painting and sculpture, nor, initially, by architecture north of the Alps. Consolidating Wölfflin's conceptual advances, later art historians reassessed the classical painting and sculpture of the long seventeenth century as baroque on the basis of the relatively greater internal coherence found in works of that period than with works of other historiographically established periodizations.[10] A generation after *Renaissance und Barock* first appeared, Wölfflin formalized this point in his *Kunstgeschichtliche Grundbegriffe* (1915), and on its fulcrum the expanded, super-artistic baroque turned. Writes Stechow,

> if there is such a thing as an artistic *Zeitgeist*, it must be possible to see some essential unifying elements in all significance art works of a certain epoch. … [The] baroque in art is a unified style; but by the same token, it is also a partial expression of the *general Zeitgeist* of the seventeenth century.[11]

Hence, the relationship of baroque architecture to the baroque arts, and their reflection, in turn, of the baroque age.

The third meaning given to the baroque by interwar critics and historians, Stechow continues, is of a cyclic progression of the arts from a classical to baroque state, in which baroque occurs as a recurrent late phase. This idea, as we know well, was hardly Wölfflin's invention. It occurs, after all, in the way Burckhardt treats "rococo" in the history of the classical tradition.[12] But it was Wölfflin, and especially his *Kunstgeschichtliche Grundbegriffe*, whose work suggested scope for translating an historically specific term of historiography and criticism to such epochal developments as the medieval age and classical antiquity.[13]

Armed with the three usages of "baroque" that he calls to mind, Stechow presents his readers with two questions: "First, is there any conceivable justification for retaining a term which has taken on so many different meanings? Second, if there is, which meaning shall we recommend for adoption?"[14] In brief, his answer to the first problem is "yes" on the proviso that there can be some normalized definition of the term within and between each of the arts and cultural fields in which it appears. His call for linguistic precision is made alongside an admission of the impossibility of a baroque regularized on the basis of the term's alignment with "grandeur, heroic sweep, or the like," which holds it fast to "the original derogatory sense of the word."[15] Chronology offers no less ambiguous a basis for a critical definition. Recalling the various time-spans invoked for the term he asks, "What can we gain by calling this period – all of it – baroque?"[16] The use of a critical language to delineate and describe the territory of a discipline demands a degree of care. One danger of a term that can made to mean anything is that it will ultimately mean nothing when the audience expands beyond those who agree upon its use and encounters another that uses it elsewhere. Another is that it becomes prone to *mis*use.

Stechow's *"working hypothesis"* is that the content of those cultural manifestations that have been called baroque by their historians has a basic unity that is not merely stylistic. "A more comprehensive, all-embracing definition of the Baroque in art history will have to stand the acid test of our increasing factual knowledge which tends to dissolve that unity, but it may come, I believe, in the wake of a more penetrating analysis of the *content* of the art of that epoch."[17]

On the grounds of content, a body of literature, painting, architecture and music will show itself to have a greater degree of internal coherence than it might have in relation to the Renaissance or the Empire, to borrow Stechow's coordinates. His theory, to which he returns in his 1955 reflections on this theme, is that "one mainstay of this undertaking will have to be the interpretation of this baroque epoch as one revealing a basically new and optimistic equilibrium of religious and secular forces."[18] Stechow's key to a unified historical and trans-disciplinary definition of the baroque is the trading of form for content. It is not the unified appearance of the arts that holds together an age, but the culture those arts variously express. On this basis he remains sceptical of the value of the idea of a recurrent baroque as being something more than an historical reading of late style that registers an occasional verisimilitude with the formal or stylistic characteristics of seventeenth-century art. A truly recurrent baroque will be cultural rather than compositional or morphological, drawing in all forms of artistic expression. While he leaves this matter open, this observation does serve to flag another issue, to which we will return in conclusion, concerning the identification with the baroque in his own time as read through specific criteria. This is not his central conclusion, however, which is rather that for so many disciplines to identify with the art historical term used to address the work of the period the job remains to negotiate between the various historical fields that would describe their content as baroque and the basic nominalism at stake in seeing it as baroque in particular.

Panofsky's "What is Baroque?"

Where Stechow's essay offers us a snapshot of his views on the baroque and its critical fortunes, Panofsky's lecture "What is Baroque?" documents a position refined over quite some time. The posthumously published version of this general public lecture presents a somewhat, if not dramatically, palimpsestic document reworked at least three times for various audiences over the course of nearly 30 years, with two annotated versions of the lecture dating to around 1935, and a third annotated version, which Lavin (who treats this as the definitive version) puts after 1960.

It was neither his first nor his most important contribution to the scholarship or teaching of baroque art. His lengthy 1919 article on the Scala Regia of Bernini is a cornerstone of baroque historiography and served for nearly eight decades as the authoritative account of this work.[19] "Italian Baroque Art" was likewise among the first subjects Panofsky taught during his first visits to the United States as a guest of New York University's Institute for Fine Arts, and "What is Baroque?" was a question to which his American lectures turned on numerous occasions from 1934 or 1935 onwards.[20] Even earlier, he had lectured on "Barock" in 1931 at the University of Hamburg, where his subject expanded beyond the decidedly art historical subject matter of his teaching at NYU and roamed into literature and other forms of cultural expression.[21]

As a document principally of the 1930s, then, and primarily prepared for an audience largely unfamiliar with the German-language historiographical development of his subject, "What is Baroque?" still offered something to the question put to Panofsky by Heckscher on behalf of Daniells. Among the several extant lecture typescripts, the most widely distributed version derives from a lecture delivered in 1935 at Vassar College, recorded, typed and mimeographed by one of its students.[22] Excepting the lecture's introduction, which in the latest (and thus published) version took on a certainty regarding the term's origins that is wholly absent from its earlier layers, the Vassar version was not subject to large-scale amendments in subsequent revisions. It is likely this typescript that Panofsky dispatched in 1946.

Evidence suggests that Panofsky did not think highly of his own work on this theme. Lavin advises readers not to read too much of his characteristic, often rhetorical self-deprecation into this warning of both its overly general nature and the obsolescence of its project to neutralize the baroque as a corrective to its characterization, above all, by Wölfflin.[23] As Panofsky wrote in 1967, "what made sense and even may have been necessary in 1938 would be entirely superfluous today."[24] This self-conscious observation arguably speaks as much to the scope and content of the lecture as an introduction to baroque art as to the more general points concerning contemporary society that Panofsky scores in his treatment of this subject – among these, and perhaps surprisingly, his subtle negotiation of the cultural legacy of the Second World War and the Holocaust, as well as of the post-war threat posed by the nuclear age.

Panofsky reinforces many of the general points we have considered above in relation to Stechow's contribution on this theme. Extending it much further, however, he homes in on one operative failing of Wölfflin's dichotomies of classic and baroque art. Its rectification is, from Panofsky's perspective, crucial to understanding the inherent character of the baroque and its relationship to those other phases together comprising the long history of the Renaissance. He chastises Wölfflin's failure to "mention [in his *Grundbegriffe*] a single work of art executed between, roughly speaking, the death of Raphael in 1520 and the full-fledged seventeenth century," noting that, indeed, when one compares the artistic production on either side of a century-long void one naturally observes tendencies that can be systematically opposed, but that this opposition becomes artificial. These absent decades correspond almost exactly to the chronological scope of the earlier *Renaissance und Barock*, in which Wölfflin's subject is not the baroque, but its origins in what would soon be commonly known as "mannerism." Panofsky argued that when one accounts for the relation of those opposing periods *with* the work of the intervening decades then one must admit that "a much more complex development had taken place."[25]

This mannerist interlude holds the key to understanding the role of the baroque in the development of Italian art and culture, not as a period of license and decline but as a period of rectification. His subject, therefore, might be better put as "What is Baroque, after Mannerism?" for it is the recuperative quality of the art of Bernini and Cortona he values above all. Panofsky regards the baroque as a properly Italian phenomenon, echoed elsewhere in Europe "in partibus infidelium" in a way that reinforces "the customary categories of wildness, obscurity, etc., much better and more consistently than does the original, Italian version of the style."[26] Only in Italy do the visual arts fully explore the limits of the "classical principles" to the extent that the baroque can be construed as their "deliberate reinstatement" and, "at the same time, a reversion to nature, both stylistically and emotionally."[27] Although expressed elsewhere, Rome feels acutely the crisis of the Reformation; and the interior logic that binds the city's confrontation with this moment to its response lends, there, the baroque a specific poignancy.

Importantly, Panofsky does not undermine Wölfflin's general project to periodize the historical development of the visual arts, even if their criteria differ markedly. His counter-scheme is predicated on the idea that the Renaissance constitutes a much longer epoch – extending to the death of Goethe and the Industrial Revolution – within which a series of internal developments take place. The dichotomies do not exist for Panofsky between classic and baroque periods, but rather consistently *within* those developments as competing forces in search of an equilibrium, together constituting a four-phase Renaissance – not structurally dissimilar to the historiological scheme advanced by Wölfflin's student Paul Frankl.[28] Panofsky's phases are, put simply, the classic Renaissance of the fifteenth and early sixteenth centuries, a mannerist period extending to the end of the sixteenth century, the baroque, as conventionally defined for a long seventeenth century, and the neo-classical developments of the eighteenth and early nineteenth centuries, opening out onto a modern era. Two peaks, two troughs; and all bound together by a rolling reassessment of the techniques and limitations of the classical tradition and the irreconcilable values of "a classical revival and a quite nonclassical naturalism."[29] This, in turn, is informed by the complex interplay between the arts, society, economics, mentality, and so forth. If the baroque age is marked by melancholy and humour, then these traits fulfil the promise of the fifteenth-century rise of the individual in Italian society and overcome his suppression through the first band of reactions to the Reformation. If the baroque age advances a sense of self-consciousness and criticality, then this is predicated upon the historical consciousness of the Renaissance and surpasses the elementary (linguistic) games of the mannerist decades.

He casts the evolution of art's "psychological" dimension as "a fundamental aspect of Baroque art. A conflict of antagonistic forces merging into a subjective unity [elsewhere, 'intensification'], and thus resolved."[30] He points to a drawing by Jacopo Pontormo, a study for the *Deposition of Christ* (completed 1528, Uffizi, Florence), to demonstrate the artist's expression of the "problems of the outer world and the problems of his or her own self." It conveys the disruptions of a world-view that failed to reconcile "beauty and virtue, morality and freedom, humanism and Christianity, faith and science." Panofsky argues that the formal characteristics of "open, but disharmonious" also describe the psychological content of the work, an index of the cultural climate, not yet explicit, of the Reformation, as well as an account of how one might experience the painting.[31] His observations of Agnolo Bronzino's *Descent of Christ into Limbo* (1552, Santa Croce, Florence) make a similar point: "it is a consolidation, but a consolidation even more obstructive to classic harmony;" his movements are "overgraceful and at the same time constrained and bashful;" the "whole of the composition becomes a battlefield of contradictory forces, entangled in an everlasting tension."[32] The successive waves of mannerist artists working in the decades spanning from the Sack of Rome to the end of the sixteenth century – his chronology and theory of mannerism rests on Friedländer's work – found the various means to express the anxiety of their age and the dissolution of certainties it heralded.[33]

The baroque, in contrast, documents the capacity of seventeenth century artists to absorb those same anxieties and to live with them through a new self-awareness of the artificiality of exactly that reconciliation. "A baroque portrait," he writes, "is free and open to the world again." He continues:

> A modus vivendi had been found in every field; scientists were no longer burnt like Giordano Bruno …; Roman sculptures were no longer hidden in cellars; the system of the church was now so powerful and undisputed that it could afford to be tolerant towards any vital effort, and more than that: it would gradually assimilate and absorb those vital forces, and finally allow the very churches to be filled with that visual symphony of gay putti, glimmering gold and theatrical sceneries as seen in the *Cathedra Petri*.[34]

This self-awareness is akin, he goes on to observe, to the loss of innocence that gave Adam and Eve "the possibility of being 'like God', that is to say, superior to one's own reactions and sensations."[35] He sets aside the negative consequences of this to be found in sentimentality and theatricality, pointing instead to a new-found critical consciousness alongside a new capacity for humour, "the sense of humour in the true sense of the term."[36] All these qualities rely on a sense of self-detachment and self-awareness, but importantly all pertain to a now conscious complicity in the world one constructs and inhabits. As he observes of one of these in particular:

> For the sense of humour, as it appears in Shakespeare and Cervantes – not to be confounded with wit or mere comicality – is based on the fact that a man realizes that the world is not quite what it should be, but does not get angry about it, nor think that he is free from ugliness and from the major and minor vices and stupidities that he observes.[37]

The baroque knows its own internal conflicts. It celebrates them as it lays them bare in its art. But in doing so it sets aside the hamstrung self-awareness of the mannerist decades and sets its crises and insecurities aside, not by offering resolution, but by exercising the critical capacity "to [knowingly] build up a system of thought entirely independent of both brute matter of fact and dogmatic belief."[38] These capacities and the artistic production they allow render the baroque, in this sense, "the second great climax of this period and, at the same time, the beginning of a fourth era [following Antiquity, the Middle Ages and the Renaissance], which may be called 'Modern' with a capital M."[39]

Panofsky's concluding sentence always observed that this new epoch ("our own") was "still struggling for an expression both in life and art" and that it would "be named and judged by the generations to come." Amended in Panofsky's own script on the typed version of the lecture dating to some time after 1960 is a final caveat: "provided that it does not put an end to all generations to come."[40]

Shaping a Future for the Baroque

Reading these essays one alongside the other sheds light on two issues of broader importance to the post-war historiography of art and architecture. The first of these concerns the enduring identification among Anglophone scholars and students of the multi-faceted and complex terrain of German-language scholarship on the baroque with the two books by Heinrich Wölfflin that were translated into English and directly addressed this theme.

The *Grundbegriffe* had appeared early in the 1930s in Great Britain, with an American edition published by Dover in 1950. Wölfflin's views had a widespread appeal and his readership was broad. Among students and amateur historians his views dominated the reception of the baroque and continued to hold sway irrespective of the criticisms that were from the 1920s mounted against them in academic literature and the lecture hall, and irrespective of the refinements made to them by commentators within the art history discipline. The various attempts of Panofsky, Krautheimer, Wittkower and many others to introduce and negotiate the complexity of the inter-bellum scholarship of the baroque within the rather more caricatured historical image cultivated for the baroque in the English-speaking world sought to convey the depth of that discourse for an academic culture that had paid the period scant attention up to this time.[41] The displacement to North America, Great Britain, and the British Commonwealth of many European-trained historians of art prompted something of a rectification of the influence of Wölfflin over the Anglophone appreciation of the baroque. Wölfflin's formalistic analysis and cultural prejudice had served to advance art history methodologically while confirming a negative attitude towards the cultural and religious forces of the Counter-Reformation that was only partially counteracted by the contributions of synthesizing British writers like Martin Briggs and Geoffrey Scott towards a more balanced assessment of its art and architecture.

A corrective, then, but to what ends? In light of the much finer-grained readings of the baroque available to us now through an historical recovery of the intellectual developments within the historiography of art and architecture, these positions of Stechow's and Panofsky's will seem simple, even naïve. The writing by Stechow and Panofsky, however, speaks to a broader yet fractured effort to establish a new ground plane for a new public for the knowledge of artistic development after the Renaissance. It treats Wölfflin as a key, while moving past his work to lay the substrate for the intelligent reception of those many other writers whose American and British audiences had previously been restricted to specialists alone. The surge of interest in teaching in the history of baroque art and architecture in the 1930s, in which Panofsky was one of several scholars actively shifting attention to the hitherto underrepresented early modern era, owes something to what we can imagine to be an active effort to balance Wölfflin's dominance of the field as the authoritative voices of Krautheimer and Friedländer secured a toehold for the competing legacies of Wölfflin's disciplinary advances. Overall, this constituted a debate between the formal unity of the baroque as a style and its internal coherence, bound to content and context and expressed in composition and plastic form.

Stechow weighs up the factors that underwrite the baroque's endurance as a term of criticism and history; as does Panofsky, but with vastly different ends in mind.

If the promotion of a nuanced understanding of the development of thinking on the baroque is one shared historiographical consequence of this work, the second lies in the attitude towards this intellectual history as a predicate for positioning the scholarship of historians of art and architecture in the post-war era – and for positioning the baroque as a model therein, recognizing the intimate connection between the development of art history, its neutralization of the negativity associated with the baroque from the end of the nineteenth century, and its activation of the consequences of observing parallels between the baroque age and the modern era.[42] On these latter considerations the two authors significantly digress.

Stechow's project articulates with the broader ambitions of *Journal of Aesthetics and Art Criticism* to recalibrate aesthetic and art historical knowledge for the post-war world, introducing to art history such regularization of terms and values as would allow for a form of benign but overt control over the field – a reaction to the abuses made of so-called scientific knowledge in earlier decades.[43] Securing a working definition for the baroque forms part of that much larger project, shaping the deployment of critical vocabulary and concepts both in the books and articles of art historians as well as in those fields that read the history of art and translated art history's terms and concepts to their own ends. Illustrating this tendency well was the contribution of another writer in the baroque issue of the *Journal of Aesthetics and Art Criticism*, the literary historian René Wellek, whose essay in these pages has become a classic critical treatment of its theme. With reference to the history of letters, but also to the "general" concept of the baroque, Wellek reinforces and extends Stechow's position in claiming that the baroque functions to define a cohesive body of work within a given timeframe and art form, just as that work *called* baroque can explain, by means of illustration, shifts in the histories of art, culture or ideas to which art gives expression. He writes that "it would be an extreme and false nominalism to deny that such concepts as the baroque are *organs* of real historical knowledge. ... in reality there are pervasive styles, or turning-points in history which we are able to discern and which such terms help us in distinguishing."[44]

The historian's nomenclature is not natural in any sense, nor regarded as such here, even if it can be made to appear so. The question is one of appreciating the relationship between the history of art and the civilization it serves, of appreciating how disciplinary vocabulary shapes that relationship, and therefore of how to manage these terms to specific (neutral) ends. The answer appears acutely mindful of the service to which baroque art and its historiography was put towards the ideological goals of Nazism – a spectre unvoiced, but bound-up in the entire editorial ambitions of the *Journal* at the moment in which Wellek's and Stechow's work appears. Thus a largely tacit and occasionally open programme to rectify what were understood to be the inter-disciplinary confusions between one historical image of the baroque and another, between baroque in one discipline or media and another, was underpinned by a deeper problem involving the instrumentalization of baroque art for reactionary political ends. In addressing the complexity of German-language scholarship with which many of the authors in this issue are intimately familiar – but in returning to Wölfflin as the discursive Aunt Sally – one can have the largely false security of being able to negate the impact of such scholars as Wilhelm Pinder, Hans Sedlmayr and Albert Brinckmann, whose work has been shown to serve a deeply conservative ideological agenda, and whose politics were patently unsupportable after the Second World War.[45]

What follows, therefore, is a definition of baroque that is less austere than without ideological or conceptual content, a tool of a dry historiography that cannot be turned to evil ends:

> The term baroque is most acceptable, it seems to me, if we have in mind a general European movement whose conventions and literary style can be described fairly concretely and whose chronological limits can be fixed fairly narrowly, from the last decades of the sixteenth century to the middle decades of the eighteenth century in a few countries.[46]

Stechow takes this neutralization to a new level by suggesting that a committee formed of representatives of all the disciplines claiming some purchase on the baroque could meet and figure out the whys and wherefores of the term: its historical and conceptual scope as well as the terms under which it can be understood to have some validity in describing recurrent stylistic tendencies or recurrent relationships between the bases of culture and their manifestation in the arts. Indeed, this notion of agreement *in camera* by an interdisciplinary committee seems to be played out in the "Second Special Issue on Baroque Style in Various Arts," published by the *Journal of Aesthetics and Art Criticism* in 1955, when the *Journal* was at that stage edited by Thomas Munro.[47] Therein Stechow attempted a more systematic synthesis of the term's usage alongside (and, for some, within) a consideration of stylistic analysis for the histories of the various arts, in which representative scholars of literature, music, and art, voice their stake in the term.

In what sense, however, do these discussions comprise a democratization of the term? And what is at stake in the very idea of the baroque at this moment? The essays of Wellek, Stechow, Munro and their colleagues respond to the usefulness of the term baroque for historians and critics of the arts and for those branches of history in which it had gained traction at various moments since the end of the nineteenth century. They agree with Stechow that while baroque may not be all things, the term has sufficient scope to accommodate a broad range of historical events and artefacts within its historically and conceptually constituted limits. They agree, too, that this diffusion across a broad spectrum of cultural expression is not only acceptable, but desirable – within limits, informed by responsible scholarship. A baroque that spans culture and the arts with no natural hierarchy operating therein offered scholars of the immediate post-war moment one touchstone among the many it required to check whether "it has done well in learning from the past, and whether it has learned rightly." But this exposes us to a banal sense of democratization, a form of consensus building that flies in the face of a dramatically heterogeneous inter-war historiographical landscape.

It is a very different document than we find in Panofsky's lecture on this topic, which likewise does much to flatten out the richness of the pre-war discussion on baroque architecture, painting and sculpture, while *maintaining* the role of the baroque as an historical value against which cultural forms of that moment might hold themselves accountable. He posits the baroque as a period of profound invention and restitution following a moment of profound crisis that was acutely felt across Western culture and expressed in its arts – a diagnosis of historical conditions in the sixteenth and seventeenth centuries as much as a projection for his present. His work arises from a new perspective on the function of art historical knowledge, neither as the reflection of a modernist programme nor as a reactionary view of the relationship between past and present, but as the means by which to overcome the cultural and artistic crises provoked by the war. Panofsky's baroque models a way forward not because it offers formal or cultural solutions, but because it demonstrates that modern culture is obliged to reconcile itself with its crises. The lesson Panofsky would seem to find in the baroque is that society need not negate crises in order to surpass them. It can move forward by learning to accommodate the self-consciousness of a modern age – an age shaped by reason – that had introduced new crises in the realm of culture and new threats to civilization. Panofsky's emendations to the conclusion of his lecture strongly suggest that the nascent Atomic Age cast a heavy shadow over the prospects of both.

The concept of the baroque we find in the pages of the *Journal of Aesthetics and Art Criticism* is, however, not this. It is, rather, an acceptable baroque rather than a necessary baroque. It would be a baroque stripped of its cultural and political content and, therefore, neutralized *as* it was made available for the post-war generation of historians and architects who would find new ways to activate and attend to the baroque in their scholarship and architecture.[48] Both forms of the baroque would find expression in the decades to follow.

Endnotes

1   Cited in Lavin, "Introduction," *Three Essays on Style*, 201f. Judging from subsequent letters from Panofsky to various correspondents and cited by Lavin, Mr. Daniells did not return the lecture. He is likely Roy Daniells, later of the University of British Columbia, who in 1945 published "Baroque Form in English Literature" and, many years later, *Milton, Mannerism and the Baroque*.

2   Daniells also contributed to the issue of the *Journal of Aesthetics and Art Criticism* in which Stechow wrote with "English Baroque and Deliberate Obscurity," responding to a debate sparked off by Pevsner's review of Sitwell's *British Architects and Craftsmen* in the *Times Literary Supplement* (14 July 1945). Responses to Pevsner followed on 4 August (O.H. Leeney, with Pevsner exercising right of reply), 18 August (Ralph Edwards), 1 September (W.B. Honey), 8 September (W.B. Hartley), 22 September (Sir Herbert Baker) and 3 November (Robert Eisler).

3   See Leach, "The Future of the Baroque, ca. 1945," 11–12.

4   Panofsky, "What is Baroque?" 19–20.

5   Bloch, *The Historian's Craft*, 5.

6   Stechow, "Definitions of the Baroque in the Visual Arts," 110.

7   After Sarduy, Lambert suggests that the insecurity of the term's origins is "a proverbial bone in the throat of traditional baroque criticism." *The Return of the Baroque in Modern Culture*, 1.

8   Stechow, "Definitions of the Baroque in the Visual Arts," 110.

9   Stechow, "Definitions of the Baroque in the Visual Arts," 110–11. His example in the latter case is Georg Dehio's identification (in *Geschichte der deutschen Kunst*) of "the Baroque with the 'basic innate mood' of German art through the ages."

10 For example, Schmarsow, *Barock und Rokoko* and Strzygowski, *Das Werden des Barock bei Raphael und Correggio*.

11 Stechow, "Definitions of the Baroque in the Visual Arts," 111.

12 Stechow, "Definitions of the Baroque in the Visual Arts," 112. Stechow draws upon Waetzolt's study on Burckhardt in *Deutscher Kunsthistoriker*, 172–209.

13 Wölfflin, *Kunstgeschichtliche Grundbegriffe*, 249–51. Compare Lyttelton, *Baroque Architecture in Classical Antiquity* and Frankl, *The Gothic*.

14 Stechow, "Definitions of the Baroque in the Visual Arts," 112.

15 Stechow, "Definitions of the Baroque in the Visual Arts," 112–13.

16 Stechow, "Definitions of the Baroque in the Visual Arts," 113.

17 Stechow, "Definitions of the Baroque in the Visual Arts," 114.

18 Stechow, "Definitions of the Baroque in the Visual Arts," 114.

19 Compare Marder, *Bernini's Scala Regia at the Vatican Palace*.

20 Panofsky, "Italian Baroque Art," Heckscher-Archiv.

21 Heckscher, typed lecture notes from Panofsky, "Baroque, S. S. [June–July] 1931," Heckscher-Archiv.

22 Box 18 of the Heckscher-Archiv contains a mimeographed copy of "What is Baroque?" (12pp), with the name and address of one Janice Loeb of New York marked on the rear cardboard cover. This may have been the same Janice Loeb

as the painter and documentary filmmaker who, having written for the *Vassar Review* and presumably studied at that College, may have been responsible for the "Vassar version."

23   Lavin documents several letters pertaining to the latter lecture in his "Introduction," 200–203ff.

24   Corr. Panofsky to Peter Chobanian, 14 November 1967. In Lavin, "Introduction," 201f.

25   Panofsky, "What is Baroque?" 20. To be more specific, Panofsky writes in this same passage, "Wölfflin himself did not commit the sin of commission to call Tintoretto or El Greco 'Baroque', but he committed the sin of omission not to include them – and what they stood for – in his considerations at all." Panofsky's reading of mannerism in "What is Baroque?" is informed by his former teacher Walter Friedländer, whose *Mannerism and Anti-Mannerism in Italian Painting* existed in various forms since the 1920s.

26   Panofsky, "What is Baroque?" 36.

27   Panofsky, "What is Baroque?" 36.

28   Frankl, *Die Entwicklungsphasen der neueren Baukunst.*

29   Panofsky, "What is Baroque?" 25.

30   Panofsky, "What is Baroque?" 59, also 51.

31   Panofsky, "What is Baroque?" 59.

32   Panofsky, "What is Baroque?" 36.

33   For development of this observation, see Leach, "The Mannerist Imperative."

34   Panofsky, "What is Baroque?" 67.

35   Panofsky, "What is Baroque?" 75.

36   Panofsky, "What is Baroque?" 80.

37   Panofsky, "What is Baroque?" 80.

38   Panofsky, "What is Baroque?" 80.

39   Panofsky, "What is Baroque?" 88. Lavin elsewhere notes Panofsky's (passing) familiarity in draft with the *Habilitationsschrift* of Walter Benjamin, later published as *Ursprung des deutschen Trauerspiels* (1928). Lavin, "Going for Baroque," 429–30. Panofsky wrote disapprovingly of Benjamin's writing on the theme of Melancholy in a now lost letter to Hugo von Hofmansthal dated 1927. Lavin cites Broderson, "Wenn Ihnen die Arbeit des Interesses Wert erscheint," 87–91; and Kemp, "Walter Benjamin und die Kunstwissenschaft," 5–24. Lavin suggests that Panofsky's lecture have constituted a long response to Benjamin's views on the period and its relation to the modern age. Although this line, "'Modern' with a capital M," appears in the published version, the latest typescript version includes this line only as a handwritten amendment.

40   Panofsky, "What is Baroque?" 88.

41   Compare Marder, "Renaissance and Baroque Architectural History in the United States," 161–74.

42   Compare this thought from Millon's "Introduction" to *The Triumph of the Baroque*, 31: "The search for a theoretical base for the history of art and architecture, the growth of the history of art and architecture as a separate discipline, and the developing rehabilitation and appreciation of Baroque architecture evolved concurrently between 1880 and 1920."

43   Munro, "Knowledge and Control in the Field of Aesthetics," 1–12. Compare the titles of those essays that accompany Stechow's in the 1946 issue: Rene Wellek, "The Concept of Baroque in Literary Scholarship," 77–109; William Fleming, "The Element of Motion in Baroque Art and Music," 121–8; and Thomas Munro, "Style in the Arts: A Method of Stylistic Analysis," 128–58.

44   Wellek, "The Concept of Baroque in Literary Scholarship," 86.

45   Levy, *Baroque and the Political Language of Formalism (1845–1945).*

46   Wellek, "The Concept of Baroque in Literary Scholarship," 87.

47   Articles on this theme occupy the first part of the issue, pp. 143–74, and include contributions by Carl J. Friedrich ("Style as the Principle of Historical Interpretation"), Manfred F. Bukofzer (music), Helmut Hatzfeld (literature) and John Rupert Martin (art history). See, esp., Stechow, "The Baroque," 171–4.

48   I wish to acknowledge the advice and assistance of Irving Lavin, Evonne Levy, Hans Aurenhammer, Charlotte Schoell-Glass and the staff at the Warburg Haus, Hamburg, Elizabeth Sears and the Special Collections staff of the Getty Research Institute, Los Angeles.

Chapter 11
Giedion as Guide:
Space, Time and Architecture and the
Modernist Reception of Baroque Rome

Denise R. Costanzo

> I looked into the Gesù for a few minutes, but was again put off by the totalitarian atmosphere which had repelled me in St. Peter's: I cannot see what a whole altar made of lapis lazuli has to do with a religion that enjoins the virtues of poverty and humility. But altogether I am out of sympathy with the Baroque: we know altogether too much these days about the ways of absolutism here on earth to look with complacency upon its encroachments on the life of the spirit.
>
> Roger Hinks, 1945

That the "totalitarianism" of baroque Rome was viscerally repellent to the newly appointed head of the British Institute in October of 1945 seems entirely understandable in the immediate wake of Fascism. Yet over a decade later, in 1956, US journalist Sylvia Wright found that the Roman baroque remained profoundly disquieting for another foreign audience, American architects:

> What is more pointless than a curling Baroque façade, half of which backs empty air? Why paint impeccable *trompe-l'oeil* columns around a room? If you want columns, why not real ones? and they had better hold up the roof. … the endless angels, golden clouds, gilt, and garlands of Rome are more than purposeless; they are belligerently so.[1]

Wright surmised that such "violent extravagance" conflicted with her nation's innate pragmatism, but this reaction was also consistent with contemporary architectural ideology. America's professional establishment had widely embraced modernism by the mid-1950s. Its essential ideals of aesthetic abstraction, functionalist expression, and technological currency defined an ascetic ethos whose "profound hostility to decoration" contrasted starkly with the sensuous exuberance of seventeenth-century Italy, among the "horrors of Rome" vilified by Le Corbusier in 1923,[2] Moreover, the general irrelevance of historic architecture to practice had been propagated in the US by Harvard's Graduate School of Design (GSD) since 1936, when Dean Joseph Hudnut theatrically expelled all pre-1932 books from its architecture library,[3] After the 1937 appointment of Bauhaus founder Walter Gropius as Chair of the GSD's Department of Architecture, history would be drastically demoted in the school's curriculum, eventually reduced to a strictly elective subject from 1946–53.[4]

The general tenor of the mid-century profession made Rome a peripheral, even irrelevant, destination for American architects. Yet those observed by Wright had elected to spend at least a year there as fellows of the American Academy, an institution founded in 1894 to provide extended residency in the Eternal City to US architects, artists and (after 1913) scholars. By the 1950s, the cultural mission of this former bastion of the American Beaux-Arts had been drastically redefined to avert the looming threat of artistic obsolescence. Although these changes inaugurated a less doctrinaire, more intellectually and aesthetically open Academy, key questions remained unresolved. Wright noted that, while budding classicists and art historians had no difficulty making good use of their fellowships, Rome Prize Fellows in fine arts fields like architecture betrayed some uncertainty over the Academy's benefit to their careers. Apart from the recently completed Termini train station, Rome had few recent buildings with which "to inspire young architects directly."[5]

Taking direct inspiration from other eras – and particularly, perhaps, Rome's abundant baroque patrimony – could be professionally dangerous for an American designer. In 1952, the *Architectural Forum* described the newly completed United Nations General Assembly in New York as "something like a popular baroque, aiming at dramatic effect without too strong a regard for purity." While the article suggests this might be a positive creative liberation, most readers objected to this characterization. Unlike the Secretariat's glazed slab tower, the General Assembly's contoured, blister-domed exterior was condemned as "arbitrary," marking a perilous departure into gratuitously sculptural form.[6] Pietro Belluschi, Dean of Architecture and Planning at the Massachusetts Institute of Technology (MIT), spoke for many colleagues when he saw "deceit" and a "lack of integrity" in this design's theatricality.[7]

Another prominent figure of this moment was George Howe, then Chair of Yale's Department of Architecture. He agreed with many objections to the General Assembly design, while nonetheless refuting the usefulness of the term "baroque" in its contemporary criticism. He amplified the polarizing effects of this term among his fellow architects:

> So [the U.N.] has been called the Baroque phase of modern architecture? What does Baroque mean? Grotesque, gigantesque, involved, as some might use the word, or, as others might use it, comparable to the works of that brief moment in the history of architecture when "measure yielded to melody, the static to the dynamic?" ... I should prefer a more analytical and less emotional adjective.[8]

That Howe does not support one reading over the other may reflect his characteristic diplomacy, or his ambivalence about baroque design values. Either way, his opinions were likely influenced by his own recent stay in Rome, Howe having resided at the American Academy from March of 1948 through the end of 1949.[9] He had been appointed the American Academy's first Architect in Residence, a newly invented role designed to provide Rome Prize Fellows in the Fine Arts with short-term mentorship by leaders in representative fields. As one of America's most prominent International Style practitioners, Howe's residency publicly demonstrated the reoriented Academy's post-war embrace of modernism.[10]

The same is true of the architecture fellows with whom Howe and Wright interacted. Between 1947 and 1966, Rome Prize winners came from America's top modernist design programmes. Nearly one-third had graduated from Harvard, and two-thirds were alumni of only three programmes: the GSD, MIT and Yale.[11] With New York enthroned as the global capital of modern art, Jackson Pollock expressing no need to go to Europe in 1944, and Gropius and Mies readily accessible in Boston and Chicago, the Academy was obliged to sell the idea of the Rome Prize to a generation of architects trained to revere the artistic avant-gardes.[12] Soon after re-opening in 1947, its leaders turned their efforts to arguing for the institution's relevance to contemporary American architecture, as when President James Kellum Smith, head of the New York architecture firm McKim, Mead and White (another beaux-arts relic), wrote in 1948 that Rome Fellows will "return to America, not with the thought of imitating the great art of the past, but with a power that will enable them to interpret freely and naturally the life of their own times in their own country."[13] While they averred, however, that the days of archaeological studies and ink wash *envois* were over, Academy officials neglected to declare what architects might or should do instead.

The revised post-war application process, which required a written project proposal, effectively asked Rome Prize applicants to solve this conundrum for themselves. Preserved statements from architecture fellows – 38 in number from 1947–66 – document these young American architects' notions of how they might profit from spending a year in Rome.[14] Most invoke a set of common themes, like the cultural enrichment of overseas travel, or the architects' need for haptic knowledge of influential works. Very few discuss the architecture of post-war Italy and only one mentions Italy's interwar rationalist modernism. A far more frequent theme is one of supposedly little interest to this generation: architectural history. Over half of the proposals (22 of 38) make some mention of Italy's pre-modern architectural patrimony. What is even more unexpected is that eight fellows express a specific interest in the baroque era.[15] In some cases, it is only mentioned in passing, as when Ronald Dirsmith wrote in 1958 that "the Academy's situation in Rome provides an ideal centre in which to study and absorb the finest manifestations of the Roman, Renaissance and Baroque civilizations."[16] In contrast, a 1951 statement by Yale graduate Thomas Dawson is particularly explicit and emphatic:

> what is perhaps most particularly absent in the "modern movement" is an understanding (or worse, the absence of even the desire for an understanding) of the rich and meaningful forms developed during the Baroque period in Italy. I should like ... to incorporate their essence into my own design in such a manner as to contribute toward the recognition of their virtues by the contemporary architectural design world.[17]

Dawson's conviction that the baroque offers a crucial corrective to modernist practice seems rather precocious for 1951, a year before the iconic Lever House in New York City was completed by Skidmore Owings and Merrill (SOM). And yet a ninth fellow who professed interest in Italian rationalism in his statement has since confessed that he mentioned Terragni only to please the jury; a 1947 GSD graduate, James Lamantia's real, if tacit, motivation for going from Harvard to Rome in 1948 was that "I wanted to see the Baroque."[18]

Bauhaus Baroque

This enthusiasm for the baroque would make far more sense after 1966, when two new books inspired more widespread appreciation of the baroque among architects: Paolo Portoghesi's *Roma barocca*, with its seductively compelling photographic reading, and Robert Venturi's *Complexity and Contradiction in Architecture*, with its overt celebration of the baroque, mannerism and rococo. But how did ostensibly history-averse modernists become Borromini and Bernini fans as early as two decades before this moment? America's disciplinary epicentre of interest in the baroque during the 1940s and early 1950s was in art history, a nascent academic field dominated by Germanic émigré scholars.[19] By the late 1950s two major studies by transplanted authors were available in English: a posthumously published 1955 study by Emil Kaufmann (*Architecture in the Age of Reason*), and Rudolf Wittkower's 1958 volume for the Pelican History of Art, which cemented the baroque in the Anglophone canon.[20] However, five of the eight references to the baroque by Academy Fellows occur before 1955, raising the matter of what Panayotis Tournikiotis calls the "reading context."[21] We must clarify which works on the baroque enjoyed a wide readership among modern architects in America at a time when most design programmes held academic art history at arm's length.[22]

One clue is the lyric phrase Howe cites in 1952 in praise of the baroque era (when "measure yielded to melody, the static to the dynamic"). This is a direct quotation from Oswald Spengler's account of Michelangelo as "creator" of the Roman baroque in his 1918 book *Decline of the West*.[23] Spengler's popular, interdisciplinary history was read by architecture students at Yale through the mid-1950s, the same period when Howe was department chair.[24] But discussion of the baroque is only a brief episode in Spengler's larger treatment of the visual arts, itself embedded in a two-volume study of vast cultural, chronological and geographic scope. However inspiring, his passages on Michelangelo do not argue for the baroque's relevance to contemporary design, making Spengler, at best, a partial explanation for this interest among aspiring architects.

In fact, the earliest Rome Prize application to mention the baroque comes from a graduate of the GSD, not Yale. Its author, Charles Wiley, graduated from Harvard in 1941 and applied for the Rome Prize in 1947 while employed by SOM in Chicago. In response to the Academy's request that he explain his interest "in securing a Rome Fellowship," Wiley replied:

> A Rome Fellowship will permit me to travel in Europe, possibly work in offices, live in a foreign country so the contemporary work of that country will have meaning for me. I want to experience the space concepts of the Classic, Renaissance and Baroque planners. I do not know what program of study is required of a Rome Fellowship recipient, but I want to use Rome as a base for travel, work, and study in all parts of Europe.[25]

Wiley, who would work on SOM's Lever House after his return from Rome, sounds more interested in visiting modernist works throughout Europe than exploring Italy's historic sites. The only vaguely "Roman" purpose is his expressed desire "to experience the space concepts of the Classic, Renaissance, and Baroque planners."

Wiley does not use a direct citation, but his only possible inspiration is Swiss architectural historian Sigfried Giedion (1888–1968). They share a connection to Harvard, where Giedion was appointed as Charles Eliot Norton Professor of Poetry for 1938–39.[26] However, since Wiley came to the GSD in 1940, he most likely absorbed Giedion's ideas after the Norton lectures were published in 1941 as the magisterial *Space, Time, and Architecture: The Growth of a New Tradition*, a work whose impact on mid-century architecture is difficult to overstate. It remains the single best-selling book published by Harvard University Press, was often the only history text assigned to architecture students for decades, and still topped a list of books considered "indispensable for every architect" in the 1970s.[27] Kenneth Frampton wrote in 1981 that "*Space, Time and Architecture* has been continuously read by almost every architecture student for the past 40 years and, reviled or revered, it has exercised an important influence on every account of the Modern movement which has appeared since."[28] The saturation and influence of *Space, Time and Architecture* during the post-war years is only comparable to such indispensable gospels as Le Corbusier's *Vers une architecture*.

This book has been categorized as one of the "founding genealogies" of modern architecture that defined the movement's essence and teleology by tracing its origins ideologically, artistically and historically.[29] Like these, *Space, Time and Architecture* presents the nineteenth century as a period of crisis, defined by Giedion as a rift between intellectual and physical culture, aesthetics and material technology, resolved by the machine-age architecture of heroic modernists like Gropius and Le Corbusier.[30] Wiley's phrase "space concepts" echoes Giedion's frequent mention of "space conceptions," which constitute "the enveloping force of all architecture."[31] This is one of the book's central themes, occurring frequently in the text and twice in the section headings.[32] *Space, Time and Architecture* argues that a unified "space conception" defines the aesthetic and scientific nexus of any age: linear perspective for the Renaissance, movement and infinity for the baroque, and relativistic space-time for modernity.[33] An authentic space conception distils the essence of its age into spatial terms. Thus, the architect's highest aspiration is to be attuned to this intellectual and cultural essence and express it through design – to literally build the *Zeitgeist*.

Giedion's influence best explains the overt Hegelianism of many Rome Prize proposals. In 1950, Princeton graduate David Leavitt aspired to comprehend "the relation between man's philosophical growth and his growing artistic and architectural concept of space."[34] While in Rome, Leavitt intended to prepare materials

> for the future publication of a book entitled *The Concept of Space*. This will include an analysis of the development of the concept of space, a discussion of the current ideas, and projection of what may be expected in the future. It will be related not only to architecture, but also to fine art, sculpture, landscape design, music and literature. It will of course, involve social, political, scientific, religious and philosophic references.[35]

The breadth of his subjects mirrors the ambition of Giedion's "space conception," and Leavitt even adapts the operative phrase for his title. His project also includes deep historic dimensions, which would include

> the linear efforts of the caveman, to the static art of Egypt and Greece, up through the Oriental preoccupation with planes – Medieval with structure – Renaissance with volume, on to Baroque which begins to break through the volume, to Cezanne [sic] who uses planes to create three-dimensional space, and finally arrives at the current experiments with a new demension [sic] which, for want of a better name, is called time. This growth progresses and retrogresses, but in general follows a sweeping spiral.[36]

Space, Time and Architecture begins with a meditation on how and why architects should look at history and the architectural historian's disciplinary role.[37] Historic awareness is crucial to Giedion's vision of architecture as both cultural symptom and palliative solution to the crisis of modernity: "we must understand the architectural inheritance of our period, the knowledge which had been continuously evolved in the preceding periods."[38] The nearly infinite scope of fields in Leavitt's ambitious (and, unsurprisingly, unrealized) project reflects the thesis of *Space, Time and Architecture*, ideal cultural integration. However, Giedion takes a deliberately non-encyclopaedic, highly selective approach to historic analysis:

> it is more helpful to examine rather carefully cross sections of decisive stages in the history of architecture. We prefer to deal with fewer events more penetratingly, in close-up view. A few facts seen clearly enough may lead to a knowledge of something more important than the isolated facts themselves: the inner structure of architecture at the stage of growth which it has reached in our time.[39]

In the section entitled "Our Architectural Inheritance," Giedion provides just such a penetrating, "cross-sectional" analysis of two "decisive stages" that prefigure themes he considers salient to the development of modernism: the Renaissance and the baroque. Of the two, the baroque receives greatest prominence. This imbalance is most pronounced in the book's first edition, in which discussion of the Renaissance is 11 pages long, while the baroque occupies 54 pages. In the third edition of 1954 Giedion doubled the section's total length, resulting in 85 pages on the baroque and 45 on the Renaissance.[40] Thus, for *Space, Time and*

Architecture's first 13 years of publication (and hence influence), its section on the baroque was five times longer than that treating the Renaissance, and roughly twice as long after 1954.

Even the expanded, post-1954 version of the "Inheritance" chapter still occupies a relatively slender portion of an increasingly lengthy tome, which devotes most of its space to the nineteenth and early twentieth centuries.[41] However, Baroque references recur throughout the book, and Giedion often presents the period's intellectual, cultural and artistic synthesis as a datum against which modernity is evaluated. Before launching into discussions of Cubism and relativity in "The New Space Conception: Space-Time," the author reminds the reader that "a thoroughly integrated culture produces a marked unity of feeling among its representatives. For example, a recognizable common spirit runs through the whole baroque period. It makes itself felt in activities as distinct from each other as painting and philosophy or architecture and mathematics."[42] Giedion does not present the baroque as one of multiple equivalent examples of the cultural integration he celebrates in modern architecture. It provides a rare and instructive success story that demonstrates how an architectural movement can transcend the limits of style to express the "unity of feeling" of an age. The baroque is treated as the historic period *par excellence*, the one era a modern architect must understand to do meaningful work in the present.[43]

In addition to arguing for the period's immediate creative relevance, Giedion's ekphrases of baroque works in *Space, Time and Architecture* filter established historic interpretations through modernist aesthetics and priorities. His description of how the "abstract spirals" and "animation and movement" of Borromini "gave flexibility to stone, changed the stone wall to an elastic material" suggests recent concrete structures by Maillart or Nervi. Borromini also illustrates Giedion's view of the proper creative relationship with history: "he was not an imitator of shapes or facades and did not use history as a substitute for imagination." He was an architect who "did not imitate the shapes of bygone epochs: he made them part of his own creations. Much as we try to do today, he found in his relations with history a source of power for further development."[44] While Borromini embodies the boldly inventive figure of the modern artist, Guarini's multifaceted persona (Theatine abbot, philosophy professor, mathematician, engineer and architect) exemplifies Giedion's ideal of intellectual and creative integration. Guarini's highly-educated, well-travelled and up-to-date mind allows him to transform the binding arches of the tenth-century mihrab dome of Cordova into an "architectural vision [that] pushes to the limit of constructional resources in striving to produce the impression of infinity," to "satisfy by architectonic means the baroque feeling for mystery and infinity" at San Lorenzo in Turin.[45] This image of the architect as a cosmopolitan, multidisciplinary intellectual who synthesizes technological and humanistic knowledge into an expression of contemporary culture perhaps reflects no one as well as Giedion himself, who was educated as an engineer before his doctoral study in art history, wrote plays and even designed.[46]

These discussions are instrumental to Giedion's argument that great architecture emerges from a broad cultural education and innovative but historically informed creativity. *Space, Time and Architecture* also gives the baroque rare prominence compared to the profile sustained in other modernist texts. Although both Kaufmann and Hitchcock extend their histories of the modern movement to the middle- to late-eighteenth century, those authors present the baroque as emphatically "pre-modern," the last gasp of a cultural era being supplanted.[47] The baroque chapter in Pevsner's 1942 *Outline of European Architecture* is simply another episode from late antiquity through to the First World War, receiving no greater prominence than the gothic, Renaissance, or romantic eras.[48] In contrast, the way Giedion extracted the baroque from the broader historic continuum, planted it firmly in the foreground, and insisted on its relevance to modernist architects gave it a new, vastly amplified importance. His unforgettable visual pairings of Borromini's domes with works by Tatlin and Picasso make the baroque modernism's spiritual ancestor, mentor, and twin.

Baroque in Translation

Powerful imagery is instrumental to *Space, Time and Architecture*'s argument for the baroque's contemporary validity. The book's most dynamic images are Giedion's own photographs, products of an eye fully attuned to a modernist appreciation of form and space. Carefully composed shots and anachronistic juxtapositions complement a layout designed to facilitate apprehension by a "hurried reader" – techniques Giedion had learned directly from Le Corbusier.[49] The book's abundant, heavily-captioned images approach parity with the main text, which is divided into bite-size portions by frequent topical headings and marginal indices to key points. The result is a readily navigable, eminently user-friendly reference for visually acute (and occasionally text-averse) architectural readers who wish to quickly locate a subject, skim the relevant paragraph or caption, and return to the drawing board.

Although *Space, Time and Architecture* deliberately addresses an audience of professional designers, this could not guarantee their acceptance of Giedion's linkage of modernism to the baroque. His doctoral research on the eighteenth century, which contrasted late baroque and "romantic classicism," presented the latter as a confused and fragmented language, inadequate for expressing a rapidly changing culture. Although his advisor Wölfflin's stylistic dichotomies generally favoured the Renaissance over the Baroque, for Giedion the baroque era embodied the cultural synthesis which modernity needed to recapture.[50] While this made it natural, even inevitable, for him to consider modern architecture through a baroque lens, and vice versa, such an approach seems unlikely to appeal to the neo-Bauhaus GSD where Giedion first presented this argument. Gropius believed that history "ruins" design students because exposure to past figures and monuments blocks authentic creative expression.[51] He expressed particular opposition to "symmetrical" and "façade" architecture, which certainly included the Renaissance and the baroque.[52] Gropius openly discouraged his students from taking any history courses, and the relationship between the art history department and the GSD was described as one of "I mind my business, you mind yours and we'll get along fine."[53]

Yet when 1947 Harvard graduate Paul Rudolph wrote his scathing critique of the UN General Assembly for the *Architectural Forum* in 1952 he contrasted its tepid attempts at movement and drama (likened to a Hollywood "B" movie set) with "true baroque architecture," marked by "a delicate balance of movements."[54] Rudolph thus appreciated the baroque as a positive standard against which to measure contemporary efforts. This might suggest that reading Giedion had tempered his GSD education. However, the programme's anti-historicism has also seen some exaggeration.[55] Officially, history was only elective if students had taken three courses prior to enrolment, and many students took art history classes despite Gropius's discouragement.[56] This disapproval also faded gradually over the course of Gropius's tenure as he himself gained appreciation for the exceptional teaching of faculty like Kenneth Conant.[57]

Furthermore, whatever distance Gropius maintained with architectural history in general, his relationship with Giedion was cooperative and longstanding.[58] Gropius helped orchestrate Giedion's appointment as Norton Professor in 1938, and the two had been close allies for a decade. Besides Giedion's ample published support of the modern movement (which by then already included the first of his two laudatory monographs on Gropius), they had worked closely in the Congrès internationaux d'architecture moderne (CIAM) since 1928.[59] As CIAM's Secretary General, Giedion was a leading author of the modernist agenda rather than a detached commentator. In the introduction, he tells readers that his ideas are shaped as much by his CIAM activities and modern art as they are by his art history training.[60] For an audience of modern architects, Giedion's close connections to the modern movement's chief protagonists, along with his visibility, activism, intellectual credentials, and even his engineering background, all conferred unique legitimacy on the presentation of the baroque in *Space, Time and Architecture*. This imprimatur made the book's advocacy of an otherwise questionable era far more likely to be absorbed.

Gropius's support of Giedion's project went beyond mere professional courtesy towards a supportive colleague and fellow-traveller. While Gropius did not share Giedion's enthusiasm for the Renaissance and baroque, most of *Space, Time and Architecture* reflects their considerable ideological confluence. This is evident in their use of common terminology like "space conceptions," "tradition" (which, unlike "history," Gropius supported) and "planners" over "architects." When Giedion christened Pope Sixtus V "the first of the modern town planners" because "it was in Rome that the lines of the traffic web of a modern city were first formulated, and were carried out with absolute assurance," he tied the baroque to another pressing modernist concern: urbanism.[61] The CIAM conferences consistently treated architecture and urbanism as fully integrated disciplines.[62] Giedion's account of Sistine Rome, including his now-ubiquitous diagram of its network of avenues and nodes, was among the 1954 additions that increased *Space, Time and Architecture*'s emphasis on the Italian city. But all editions of the book discuss the urban and landscape design of the French baroque along with Rome's famous squares, Piazza San Pietro and Piazza del Popolo.

Mid-century Rome Prize proposals echo the intensity of this interest; urbanism is mentioned in nearly half of the post-war proposals.[63] In 1964, GSD graduate Theodore Liebman asserted that first-hand knowledge of one iconic baroque piazza is the *sine qua non* for his own practice:

> Since completing my formal education, I have been a designer for the new Government Center in Boston, and I
> have had to make design decisions affecting urban public spaces, building relationships, and architectural scale
> and character. Without having even seen the square of St. Peter's, can I fully discharge this responsibility? No,
> I must see it and more before I can produce my own work with conviction.[64]

Of course, the Piazza San Pietro was found in dozens of readily available sources by 1964, from the venerable Banister Fletcher to Lewis Mumford's extensive 1961 discussion in *The City in History*. But Liebman's certainty that it was practically reckless for him to design public urban space in Boston without experiencing Rome's most paradigmatic baroque piazza first-hand undoubtedly echoes the gospel of Giedion.

Ten years earlier, in 1954, prospective Academy Fellow Robert Venturi also described baroque *piazze* as central to his interest in Rome: "Its Baroque piazzas reveal a sensibility in the relationship of buildings which we have a chance of paralleling, perhaps for the first time since the sixteenth century, now that our architecture of the individual buildings is beginning to develop a consistent vocabulary."[65] While Venturi's approach diverges from Giedion's CIAM-influenced view of urban planning, he has explicitly described this book as having been "all the rage" during his youth, and it was one of his chief handbooks to the architectural meaning of Rome.[66] Venturi's letters home document his fascination with the baroque. His fellowship coincided with the residency of Richard Krautheimer, who Venturi describes as "a wonderful art historian here whose great enthusiasm is Roman baroque architecture."[67] He took special pains to return from his travels in time to attend one of Krautheimer's informal lecture tours of Borromini's work around Rome, and followed an itinerary of baroque monuments in Bavaria provided by Krautheimer.[68] Venturi was enthusiastic about other baroque sites in southern Italy, like Noto in Sicily, where he marvelled at seeing "an entirely baroque town designed & executed all at once – in one stroke – with beautiful detail & golden masonry – consisting of a series of terraces with great ramps & stairs tumbling down a hill." At the "fabulous" Carthusian monastery at Padula, the "most interesting thing about it to an architect, besides its amazing vistas & lengthy arcades, is a great staircase, very daring & dynamic structurally & spatially – the quintessence of Baroque."[69]

Venturi's extended stay in Rome also provided rare opportunities to see its baroque churches in action during major liturgies, such as the beatification he attended at St. Peter's:

> The basilica was crowded with people & the ceremony involved in a great way the art of display – Baroque
> display with the most theatric lighting and musical fanfare etc. And it makes you realize that Baroque
> interiors were made to be seen in connection with ceremony – music – lighting which is certainly second
> not even to Barnum & Bailey or probably Ziegfeld. The pope's entrance was the great climax heralded by a
> magnificent fanfare (not disimilar [sic] to the entrance of the elephants at the circus) – (but then the circus is a
> Baroque development).[70]

He also participated in a lengthy sequence of Easter Vigil liturgies across the entire city in 1956:

> We visited St. Peters, Santa Maria Maggiore, S. Giovanni in Laterano, S. Maria in Aracoeli, Il Gesu, and
> St. Peters again. … In St. Giovanni for instance in the beautiful basilica nave by Borromini for this evening,
> you enter and find almost complete darkness. Then a long procession appears with the cardinal at the end in
> complete silence without music. They walk to the western front of the church where there is a brazure [sic] with
> a fire burning. The cardinal blesses the fire and from that fire every one receives light for his candle (you have
> in the meantime been handed a candle) so that the bottom of the church is ablaze with all of these twinkling
> lights. The procession then moves to the alter [sic.] front of the church where water is blessed and gradually
> all the lights of the church are lit (Broadway lighting experts could not do it more theatrically) and then music
> is added to the chanting. All this time you are being overcome by incense also. … At midnight bells ring and
> horns blow like New Year's Eve. This occurred on St. Peter's piazza.[71]

A Quaker-raised Italian-American from Philadelphia, Venturi's perspective on these spectacles is both riveted and ironic, simultaneously detached and deeply engaged.

Sylvia Wright must have just missed Venturi when she visited the Academy, because otherwise her article would surely have been infected by his still-undiminished enthusiasm for Rome. While Venturi's evocations of Broadway, the circus, and even television preaching are prophetic of the cross-readings of high and popular culture found in his later work with Denise Scott Brown, his determination to see Rome's baroque churches activated through light, incense, and liturgy, can be considered part of the legacy of *Space, Time and Architecture*.[72] Through its pages, Giedion's often historically underexposed readership of modern architects absorbed the counter-intuitive idea that the baroque was fully relevant to their immediate priorities. His rejection of any pretence of detached objectivity and deployment of a persuasive visual language drawn from theoretical polemics resulted in an unorthodox history that ultimately sold history.[73] Manfredo Tafuri would rightly hold Giedion up as a paradigm of operative criticism, incisively critiquing the ideological perils of his "actualization" of baroque urbanism while also giving full credit for his pioneering role in "re-linking modern architecture to the past."[74] Of course, the former explains the latter, as when Le Corbusier redefined the Periclean Acropolis in terms of machine-age abstraction. So too, had Giedion's most influential book made the baroque appear modern to "eyes that can see."

Endnotes

1 Wright, "America's Most Favored Tourists," 42.

2 Harbison, *Reflections on the Baroque*, x. Le Corbusier illustrates three "Renaissance" frescoes from the mid-sixteenth and seventeenth centuries, and the Mannerist-Baroque revival Palazzo di Giustizia in *Vers une architecture*, 139.

3 On Hudnut's pivotal role in modernizing the GSD, see Pearlman, "Joseph Hudnut's Other Modernism at the 'Harvard Bauhaus'," 452–77; *Inventing American Modernism*, 56–7, 120–21; and Anthony Alofsin, *Struggle for Modernism*, 252–3.

4 The requirement was reduced from three history courses to one in 1939. See Sekler, "Sigfried Giedion at Harvard University," 269–71; Pearlman, "Hudnut's Other Modernism," 472. For the GSD's 1946 curriculum, see Herdeg, *The Decorated Diagram*, 83, Figure 105. For a synthesis of this period, see Alofsin, "1920–1945."

5 Wright, "Most Favored Tourists," 40–42. Fifteen years later, Russell Lynes reported that fine arts fellows remained unsure whether the Rome Prize would burnish or tarnish their reputations: "After Hours – The Academy That Overlooks Rome."

6 "UN General Assembly" (October 1952), 140–49.

7 "UN Assembly" (December 1952), 114–15. Belluschi, a native of Italy, studied engineering in Rome before moving to the United States in 1923.

8 George Howe to *Forum* editor Douglas Haskell, 19 September 1952, cited by Stern in *Howe*, 207–8. An excerpt from Howe's letter was reprinted in "UN Assembly," 114–15.

9 Costanzo, "Architectural Amnesia," 353–89.

10 David Brownlee refers to Howe as "senior statesman among American modernists" in *Out of the Ordinary*, 10.

11 Of 39 new fellowships awarded between 1947–66, 12 went to GSD graduates, eight to Yale, and six to MIT. MIT formalized its modernist orientation with the appointment of William Wurster as Dean in 1945 (Belluschi would replace him in 1950). Yale would do the same by appointing Howe as its Department Chair in 1950 (all Yale's Rome Prize architecture Fellows won after this date). See Costanzo, "The Lessons of Rome," 69–73.

12 Harold Rosenberg, "The Fall of Paris" (*Partisan Review*, 1940) and Jackson Pollock, "Answers to a Questionnaire" (*Arts and Architecture* 61, February 1944), reprinted in Harrison and Wood (eds), *Art in Theory 1900–1990*, 541–4, 560. See, too, the essential discussion by Guilbaut, *How New York Stole the Idea of Modern Art*.

13 "Available Traveling Fellowships: The Rome Prize Fellowships," 36–7.

14 The Statements of Purpose for each Rome Prize Fellow are held with their application documents, filed by name in the Fellows Files, Archives of the American Academy in Rome (AAR Archives). Of the 40 Fellows in Architecture during this period, two did not submit statements (one had originally won in 1940, the other won in 1947).

15 See statements by Wiley (1947), Leavitt (1950), Dawson (1951), Venturi (1954), Dirsmith (1958), Larson (1962) and Liebman (1964).

16 Fellows Files: Dirsmith, Ronald L., 1958–1960, AAR Archives.

17 Fellows Files: Dawson, Thomas L. Jr, 1951–1952, AAR Archives. Dawson graduated from Yale in 1949, the year before Howe's arrival as Department Chair.

18 Lamantia also equated the city and the style ("Rome *is* Baroque") in an interview with the author, 24 May 2006.

19   Marder, "Renaissance and Baroque History in the United States," 161–74.

20   Kaufmann, *Architecture in the Age of Reason*; Wittkower, *Art and Architecture in Italy, 1600–1750*.

21   Tournikiotis, *The Historiography of Modern Architecture*, 6.

22   Marder, "Renaissance and Baroque History," 164–5.

23   Spengler, *Decline of the West*, 277.

24   James Polshek (Yale 1955) recalls Spengler was assigned by Eugene Nalle, Yale's First-Year Director since the late 1940s. Weisman, *Louis I. Kahn*, 61. Howe was at Yale from 1950–54.

25   Charles D. Wiley to Mary T. Williams on 25 April 1947; Fellows Files: Wiley, Charles D., 1947–1948, AAR Archives.

26   The Norton Professorship, begun in 1926, defined "poetry" loosely enough to include art and music in its purview. Giedion was the first scholar of architecture so honoured; the only subsequent ones involved with architecture have been Pier Luigi Nervi (1961–62) and Charles Eames (1970–71).

27   Georgiadis, *Sigfried Giedion*, 97. According to Sekler, 65,000 copies were sold between 1941–62 – "Giedion at Harvard," 270. Polshek recalls both Giedion and Spengler were assigned at Yale – Weisman, *Louis I. Kahn*, 61. Lamantia (FAAR 1948) received the book as an award at Tulane University, prior to attending the GSD. Lamantia, interview with author, 25 May 2006.

28   Frampton, "Giedion in America: Reflections in a Mirror," 45.

29   Tournikiotis groups *Space, Time and Architecture* with Nikolaus Pevsner's *Pioneers of Modern Architecture from William Morris to Walter Gropius* of 1936, Emil Kaufmann's *Von Ledoux bis Le Corbusier* of 1933, and Henry-Russell Hitchcock's *Modern Architecture* of 1929, although he discusses the latter work separately because it is "operative" instead of "objective." *The Historiography of Modern Architecture*, 21–49. See also Anthony Vidler, *Histories of the Immediate Present*, 1–15.

30   See Georgiadis's discussion of Giedion's thesis in "The First Great Synthesis," in *Sigfried Giedion*, 97–150, and Frampton's critical analysis in "Giedion in America," 45–8.

31   Giedion, *Space, Time and Architecture*, 23.

32   "The New Space Conception: Perspective," in Part II and "The New Space Conception: Space-Time," in Part VI of the 1st edition.

33   For example: "in the Renaissance the dominant space conceptions found their proper frame in perspective;" and "integral calculus, taking definite shape at the end of the seventeenth century, found its architectural equivalent in the complicated treatments of space that appeared at the same time." – Giedion, *Space, Time and Architecture*, 16, 56.

34   The lists of "suggested reference books" for Princeton students first include *Space, Time and Architecture* in the 1942–43 academic year, just after its publication. See Jean Labatut Papers, Box 50, Folder 3, RBSC, Princeton University.

35   Fellows Files: Leavitt, David, 1950–1951, AAR Archives.

36   Fellows Files: Leavitt, David, 1950–1951, AAR Archives.

37   "History as Part of Life," *Space, Time and Architecture*.

38   *Space, Time and Architecture*, 23.

39   *Space, Time and Architecture*, 27.

40   The sections added to Part II in 1954 were "Perspective and Urbanism," "Perspective and the Constituent Elements of the City," "Leonardo da Vinci and the Dawn of Regional Planning," and "Sixtus V and the Planning of Baroque Rome." Part II would remain unchanged in subsequent editions. Much of this new material had been published by Giedion in 1952; see his "Space and the Elements of the Renaissance City" "Sixtus V and the Planning of Baroque Rome."

41   The book grew from 588 pages in 1941 to 881 pages in the 5th edition. Some discussions of *Space, Time and Architecture* make no mention of the baroque, such as Heynen, *Architecture and Modernity*, 29–43.

42   Giedion, *Space, Time and Architecture*, 350.

43   Leach has observed that for Giedion "the baroque is at once a disciplinary mirror, a methodological touchstone, an historical material and a path for the reassessment of contemporary architecture's intellectual and artistic limits." "*Francesco Borromini and the Crisis of the Humanist Universe*," 301–35.

44   Giedion, *Space, Time and Architecture*, 55.

45   Giedion, *Space, Time and Architecture*, 58–9.

46   Georgiadis, *Sigfried Giedion*, 1–13.

47   While Kaufmann's *Von Ledoux bis Le Corbusier* of 1933 has been translated into French, Italian, Spanish, and Japanese, no English edition exists.

48   The chapter on architecture after 1914 was added for the 5th edition of 1957.

49   Harry Mallgrave and David Goodman note Giedion uses this phrase when addressing his readers in *Bauen in Frankreich, Bauen in Eisen, Bauen in Eisenbeton* of 1928. See *An Introduction to Architectural Theory*, 55, 241, note 12. They describe Giedion's appropriation of avant-garde visual techniques in *Modern Architectural Theory*, 260.

50   Giorgiadis, *Sigfried Giedion*, 15–32.

51   Walter Gropius, "Blueprint of an Architect's Education," in *Scope of Total Architecture*, 53. See also Pearlman, "Hudnut's Other Modernism," 471–2.

52   Harvard colleague Jean-Paul Carlhian described Gropius' response to the threat that the GSD's accreditation would be revoked because of the lack of history courses. See Alofsin, *The Struggle for Modernism*, 242. See also Gropius, "Blueprint of an Architect's Education" in *Scope of Total Architecture*, 53 and Pearlman, "Hudnut's Other Modernism," 471–2.

53   The quote comes from John Coolidge, an architectural historian in Harvard's Art History department from the 1940s – Alofsin, *The Struggle for Modernism*, 246. This supports Marder's observations in "Renaissance and Baroque Art History," 164–5.

54   Rudolph's comments were quoted at length in "UN General Assembly," 144–6.

55   Under Gropius' successor, J.L. Sert (GSD Dean from 1953–69), four history courses would again be required. Sert also hired Giedion onto the Harvard faculty in 1953 to teach history. See Sekler, "Giedion at Harvard," 269–71.

56   See Appendix B in Herdeg, *The Decorated Diagram*, 108–21, which reproduces excerpts from the *Bulletin, Graduate School of Design, Harvard University*, 1946–47. Page 14 of the *Bulletin* details the programme's history requirements. Dean Hudnut's position differed from Gropius's. See Alofsin, *The Struggle for Modernism*, 141–2, 158–9 and Joseph Hudnut, "What a Young Planner Ought to Know," 60.

57   When Gropius arrived at Harvard, architectural history was taught by Hudnut and Conant, a distinguished Carolingian and Romanesque scholar. Conant was unusually open to modernism, and had long been a rare, recognized practitioner of "high quality" architectural history instruction. – Bosworth and Jones, *A Study of Architecture Schools*, 35.

58   See Geiser, "Giedion In-Between."

59   They likely met in 1923, when Giedion attended and reviewed the first Bauhaus exhibition in Weimar. Georgiadis, *Giedion*, 35–6. Siegfried [sic.] Giedion, *Walter Gropius* (1931) and *Walter Gropius* (1954).

60   *Space, Time and Architecture*, 4.

61   *Space, Time and Architecture*, 5th edition, 100, 76.

62   On city planning as an academic discipline, first established at Harvard in 1929, see Bernard Cohen, "Harvard and MIT," 23–6, and Alofsin, *The Struggle for Modernism*, 42–6, 64–6. The modernist integration of building and urban design is evident in Tafuri and Dal Co's *Modern Architecture*, which devotes eight of its 21 chapters to urbanism. See esp. 246 and Mumford, *The CIAM Discourse on Urbanism*.

63   It occurs in 16 of 38 preserved statements. Costanzo, "The Lessons of Rome," 115–30.

64   Fellows Files: Liebman, Theodore, 1964–66, AAR Archives. For another GSD graduate's 1961 mention of the Piazza San Pietro, see Fellows Files: Larson, Thomas N., 1962–64, AAR Archives.

65   Fellows Files: Venturi, Robert; 1954–56, AAR Archives.

66   The others were Le Corbusier's "The Lessons of Rome" from *Towards a New Architecture* and the venerable Baedecker guide. See Stierli, "In the Academy's Garden," 45; and "Interview with Venturi and Scott Brown," 3 January 2002, AAR Archives. See also Venturi's "Centennial Lecture," *Iconography and Electronics*, 50.

67   Letter, R. Venturi to R. and V. Venturi, 3 April 1956, "Rome: notes: letters," VSB Collection, AAUP. In 1956, Krautheimer had just completed his *Lorenzo Ghiberti* and would publish his *Early Christian and Byzantine Architecture* in 1965. However, the interest in baroque Rome that Venturi records would crystallize decades later into his *Roma Alessandrina*.

68   Letters, R. Venturi to R. and V. Venturi, 6, 9, and 15 May 1956, "Rome: notes: letters."

69   Letter, R. Venturi to R. and V. Venturi, 12 June 1955, "Rome: notes: letters."

70   Letter, R. Venturi to R. and V. Venturi, 12 June 1955, "Rome: notes: letters."

71   Letter, R. Venturi to R. and V. Venturi, 3 April 1956, "Rome: notes: letters."

72   It is fitting that Giedion wrote his introduction to its fifth, final edition during his own residency at the American Academy in Rome in 1966.

73   Mumford's annotated bibliography describes *Space, Time and Architecture* as "Brilliant: but often cavalier in presenting facts and judgments" (597).

74   Tafuri, *Theories and History of Architecture*, 151–3. See also Jameson, "Architecture and the Critique of Ideology," 65.

Chapter 12
Reading Aalto through the Baroque:
Constituent Facts, Dynamic Pluralities, and Formal Latencies

Eeva-Liisa Pelkonen

Alvar Aalto's international reputation was cemented with his inclusion in the second edition of Sigfried Giedion's *Space, Time and Architecture: Towards a New Tradition*, published in 1949. Not only does Giedion invite Aalto to join the company of Gropius, Le Corbusier, Frank Lloyd Wright and Mies van der Rohe as one of the modern masters celebrated in this book, but makes the chapter devoted to him the longest of them all: 39 pages, compared to Gropius's 35, Le Corbusier's 31, Frank Lloyd Wright's 27, and Mies van der Rohe's meagre 23 pages.

In a letter written to Aalto in January 1949, Giedion addresses the reason behind the outcome as follows:

> Recently, I have been working on the chapter on you for [the second edition of] *Space, Time and Architecture*, as I just now have gained some clear new insight. It has become somewhat long in comparison to the other chapters – Gropius, etc., which might cause anger [*Unwillen*] among some of my friends. Yet, as far as I am concerned, the chapter has made the book much clearer.[1]

The last sentence implies Aalto's importance for Giedion's intellectual construct: the chapter culminates the book's thesis.

One could well ask why Aalto had not been included in the first edition of *Space, Time and Architecture*. Giedion had first written on Aalto in an article published as early as 1931 and his interest in the architect intensified after Aalto launched his bent wood Paimio Chair at the Milan Triennale in 1933. On this occasion Giedion even writes him a postcard, exclaiming "Sie werden zu noch zum 'Magus des Nordens'!"[2] (You will one day become the Magician of the North!). He significantly refers to Aalto with the *nom de plum* of the famous nineteenth-century counter-Enlightenment philosopher Johann Georg Hamann, credited for introducing historicity and certain earthiness to intellectual affairs. Furthermore, by the time Giedion began the lectures he delivered at Harvard as Charles Eliot Norton Professor of Poetry in 1938–39 that formed the basis of his book, Aalto's international fame had been cemented with a retrospective exhibition at New York's Museum of Modern Art in 1938. The show and its catalogue highlighted the curvilinear form as Aalto's signature motif, just as Giedion did in the pages of *Space, Time and Architecture*.

In what follows, I speculate that Aalto's reception in general and Giedion's reading of him in particular were greatly affected by the events surrounding the Second World War and that Aalto offered a perfect case study of an age-old methodological problem: how to make sense of the historicity of architectural form, both in terms of a particular moment of time and place, as well as in terms of the *longue durée*. Significantly, as far as the particular historical moment was concerned, Giedion published the first version of what became his chapter on Aalto as an article entitled "Irrationalität und Standard" (Irrationality and Standard) in the Swiss magazine *Die Weltwoche* in May 1941, shortly after Aalto himself gave a lecture on Finnish reconstruction in Zurich after the Finno-Russian Winter War (1939–40) and just a month before the outbreak of the Continuation War (1941–44). It is in this article that Giedion establishes the link between Aalto the person and Finland, his country of origin, by stating that "Finland is with Aalto wherever he goes."[3] He repeats this verbatim in *Space, Time and Architecture*.

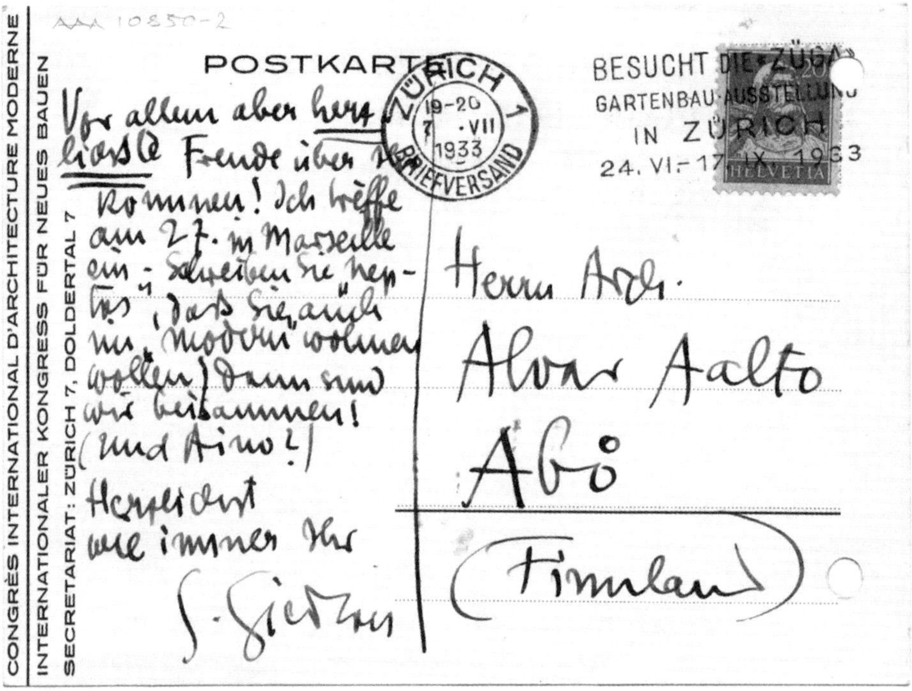

Figures 12.1 and 12.2   Sigfried Giedion, postcard to Alvar Aalto, sent 7 July 1933

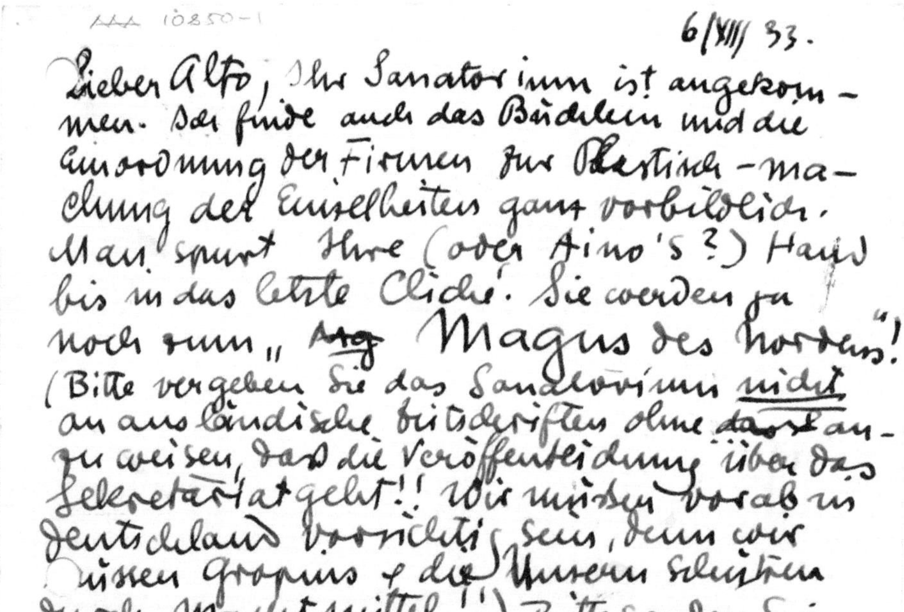

Source: Alvar Aalto Archives, Helsinki.

The chapter on Aalto in *Space, Time and Architecture* adds the curvilinear form into this equation. This essay will demonstrate how this formal motif, when read through the baroque, provided a conceptual model allowing Giedion to merge Aalto's persona, biographical encounters, historical events, and visual references, both historical and contemporary, all into one continuous topology. A close reading of the chapter reveals that Giedion employed the curvilinear form as a model for a "textual process,"[4] whereas themes and associations weave in and out of focus, while triggering the reader to add their own.

Baroque Sense of *Time*

We are all familiar with the basic contents of Giedion's book: retelling the history of modern architecture since the Renaissance as an alternation between disintegration and integration, between reason and feeling, tending towards a synthesis. In his chapter on Aalto, Giedion suggests that the protagonist represented an ultimate example in this regard: "By 1930 the new means of expression had been attained. Now it was possible to strive for further development and to dare to leap from the rational-functional to the irrational-organic,"[5] suggesting that the latter position represented for him the ultimate realm of the synthesis. Aalto's historical role was nothing less than to "to re-establish a union between life and architecture."[6]

The undulating wall, which occupies a significant role in Giedion's book on the whole, plays a crucial role in this synthesis. He traces the motif to the baroque era, and more specifically to Francesco Borromini's Church of San Carlo alle Quattro Fontane, wherein Borromini is credited for his ability to merge different building elements into one synthetic whole. "Baroque manifests itself as a new power to mold space, and to produce an astonishing and unified whole from the most various parts," writes Giedion.[7] Importantly, he treats undulating walls in the building both as products of their time, defined by social, economic conditions, and technical means, as well as elements that anticipate new uses and technologies beyond the present time.

Giedion's treatment of Borromini makes it clear that he was not interested in reviving baroque as a historical style, nor does he associate its characteristic formal motif exclusively with the period "baroque" tends to define. Instead, he treats the baroque as a state of mind tending towards a synthesis between inside and outside, not only in architectural terms – something that Giedion discusses through the case of Borromini – but also in human terms, marking a moment when the world is shaped by inner desires and vice versa. The resurfacing of its key formal trope is read, above all, as a sign of the reappearance of this synthetic mindset.

Giedion inherited his interest in baroque from his teacher Heinrich Wölfflin, who in his seminal book *Renaissance und Barock* (1888; *Renaissance and Baroque*, 1964) established the style that had until then been regarded as too pathological to be considered by many as a serious field of study. Giedion's dissertation *Spätbarocker und Romantischer Klassizismus* (1922, *Late Baroque and Romantic Classicism*) contributed to what was then the vibrant discussion on the baroque by interpreting it as a distinct historical style through which the past resonated with the present. He refers to baroque "universalism" marked by the "unconscious" "recall" of earlier primitive and "volkisch" forms.[8] It goes without saying that his idea that art and architecture could "recall" and recycle past forms and evoke past eras countered the Hegelian notion of *Zeitgeist* or a spirit of the age that served as a foundation of a modern movement that was still in a nascent state at the time Giedion published his first book.

Space, Time and Architecture continues to challenge the inevitability of the historical progress by charging individuals and civilizations to question their relationship to their own time. Giedion introduces this new historical paradigm through Wölfflin's teacher, Jacob Burckhardt, writing in the opening chapter of the book as follows: "Jakob Burckhardt had no love for his own time: he saw during the [eighteen] forties an artificially constituted Europe which was on the verge of being overwhelmed by a flood of brutal forces."[9] He continues to argue that Burckhardt did not simply study history for the sake of history, but used the Renaissance as a model for the "regeneration" of his own age. "Burckhardt was a man of great vitality, and a man of vitality cannot entirely desert his own time," Giedion exclaimed.[10] The true representatives of "present-day art" were, like Burckhardt, able to see the problems of their time in the light of larger historical and geographical trajectories. Their mindset was universal and pantheistic:

> Part of the essence of present-day art is its true representatives originate in a definite human environment and their work is not created in a vacuum. But it is also part of its essence that barriers between space and time, barriers between countries, and barriers between future and past are torn down, and with a bold sweep our own period, the whole world, and the whole of history are embraced.[11]

Aalto is placed in the same category as Picasso and James Joyce – the former's *Guernica* is cited as an example of the highest artistic achievement – as artists able to embrace whole histories and human destines in their art. The ultimate measure of great art and architecture was the ability to fold together past and present, local and universal. Giedion calls this ability to think and feel beyond one's temporal and geographic confines a "universal outlook upon the world."[12] A parallel can be drawn between Giedion's treatment of the best of "present day art" and the baroque: both embodied this universal and pantheistic worldview.

It is likely that Giedion was aware of the resurgence of interest in the baroque during the 1930s. He might well have read the work of the work of the famous Catalan philosopher Eugenio d'Ors, in whose book *Lo Barroco* (1930; French trans. *Du Baroque*, 1935) the baroque is treated as an attitude rather than style. If Giedion indeed read d'Ors he would have been drawn to the idea of time and place that was marked by infinite folding of different temporalities and geographies into what could be called a baroque sense of time and place. D'Ors's introductory chapter recalls a visit to Vienna's baroque museum by Johann Lukas von Hildebrandt, which in his words shows "the virulence of the baroque and its identical rhythm in the most remote regions of the world, and even beyond the world."[13] D'Ors treats the baroque as an historical constant that spans into infinite modalities through time and discovers it, for instance, in the work of Milton, Wagner, Rousseau and El Greco.

The most important chapter in this regard is entitled "The Eon," which refers to a trans-temporal notion of history that treats time as a continuous process, a transformation, and a mutation. In d'Ors' words the "eon" refers to "an eternity that knows the vicissitudes."[14] It is in this chapter that d'Ors introduces the idea of a "constant" that represents stability amidst change. Baroque figures as a "style of dispersion, archetype of the polymorphous, and yet, which at the same time manifests the presence of a common denominator, revelling the secret of a certain human constancy."[15] Had Giedion read the book he would doubtless also have been sympathetic to the chapter entitled "The Lost Paradise," which plays a central role in d'Ors's definition of the baroque: "The baroque is secretly animated by the nostalgia for Paradise."[16] Giedion's idea of synthesis comes to mind. Like the idea of paradise it represents both the "beginning and end of history;" we recognize it in the past and yearn for it to return in the future.[17]

Only a few years after d'Ors first published his book the French art historian Henri Focillon builds upon the notion of recurrent baroque superseding place and time. In his 1934 book *Vie des formes* (*The Life of Forms in Art*, 1942) he writes: "the Baroque State reveals identical traits existing as constants within the most diverse environments and period of time."[18] As with d'Ors, the baroque exemplified for Focillon a different historical model, one that highlights continuities and associations over time, thereby resisting periodization.

The fact that d'Ors's book was published in French translation in 1935 suggests that the book was known in France soon after its original publication in Catalan, and the parallels between the readings of the baroque tabled by both Focillon and d'Ors are as obvious as they are explicable. Consider this statement in the beginning of Focillon's book: "A work of art results from an altogether independent activity; it is the translation of a free and exalted dream. But flowing together within it the energies of many civilizations may be plainly discerned."[19] Focillon, like d'Ors, treats the baroque both as something real – an actual work of art – as well as something virtual – a potentiality of something yet to be realized, if only for a passing moment. He observes how baroque forms "live with passionate intensity a life that is entirely their own; they proliferate like some vegetable monstrosity. They break apart even as they grown; they tend to invade space in every direction, to perforate it, to become as one with all its possibilities."[20]

Although it is difficult to verify his bibliographical references in this regard,[21] Giedion's conceptualization of the relation of artistic form to time certainly bears strong resemblance to the ideas of d'Ors and Focillon. The idea of an "eon" is echoed in the Giedion's quotation of Georges Braque in his chapter on Aalto: "L'avenir est la projection du passé, conditionee part le par le present" (The future is the projection of the past, conditioned by the present).[22] It is also hard to overlook the similarity of d'Ors's idea of "constancy" to Giedion's treatment of the undulating wall as a "constituent fact," that is, one of "those tendencies which, when they are suppressed, inevitably reappear."[23] The ability of the curvilinear form to migrate into different historical contexts and locations is made apparent in the parallel drawn between two aerial photographs, one of Aalto's Baker House and the other of Landsdowne Crescent in Bath. Paraphrasing Focillon's idea of a "life of forms," almost verbatim, Giedion argues that architecture is not bound by time, not simply a response to historical conditions, but "has a life of its own, it grows or dwindles, finds new potentialities and forgets them again."[24] A further parallel can be drawn between what Focillon calls the "confusion between form and sign"[25] that, according to him, characterizes baroque art and architecture, and Giedion's treatment of the undulating wall as a kind of floating signifier, acquiring materiality and functionality in different ways at different times.

However much indebted to d'Ors and Focillon Giedion might actually have been, *Space, Time and Architecture* nonetheless expands in terms neither writer would not have found entirely disagreeable to the discussion of the modern movement beyond the limited geographic and temporal domain normally assigned to it. In Giedion's words: "the historian nowadays seems more concerned with the links between periods, the lines of force that persists and develop through several periods, than with those especial aspects which separate each period from every other."[26] Since he was writing the history of the modern movement one must appreciate how he managed to balance progress – the movement's key historical construct – with nostalgia, a concept outside that progressive discourse. The undulating wall was important in this regard for the way it challenged the idea of architecture as solely a product of its time, proposing a model where forms (and formal motifs) could have a past as well as a projective role.

Baroque as *Latency*

To be sure, it is hard to pinpoint the determinants of baroque form when these are neither functional nor material; they seem to serve no other purpose rather than the production of visual and experiential pleasure. In Focillon's words, "the confusion between form and sign never becomes more complete [as in the baroque, where ...] form is tortured to fit a 'meaning'."[27]

Similarly, in Giedion's analysis Aalto's curvilinear form seems to linger in a state of complete vagueness – it can be anything and mean anything – while settling upon very concrete meanings and functions at any given moment in time. An aerial view of the Finnish lake landscape juxtaposed with the Savoy Vase, the plan of the Finnish Pavilion at the New York World's Fair, and an oblique bird's-eye view of Baker House visualizes the multitude of references and associations suggesting that the form has the power to metamorphose into anything at any scale. Not only can it migrate from landscape to architecture and objects but also into different functions and materials (Figure 12.3). The curvilinear form can morph into a vase, an acoustic ceiling, a projection wall, and even into the shape of a complete building, as is the case with the Forest Pavilion (1938).

Importantly, as if to counter the dogma of form follows function, Giedion seems to suggest that the curvilinear form has the ability to generate multiple meanings. It is not only the *outcome* of a creative process, but its *trigger*. For example, in the acoustic ceiling at the Viipuri Library it represents "freedom of opportunity to excite the plastic imagination of an artist."[28] In other words, curvilinear form has powers that allow it to become a productive force with the capacity to unleash imagination and creativity to the fullest extent, allowing unpredictable new solutions to perennial architectural problems to emerge.

By calling the curvilinear form a "constituent fact," one of the "things [that] are constant but only occasionally reappear," Giedion emphasizes that the curvilinear form is not simply a personal idiosyncratic gesture, but part of a longer historical trajectory.[29] This definition suggests a kind of latency; the most important things are not always visible, and some ideas remain hidden yet ready to percolate to the surface. Giedion actually uses the term to imply how certain architectural ideas – like the interpenetration of space and volume – were latent until the right technology – glass and steel – made them possible. At other times latency manifests itself as a sense of nostalgia and longing. Giedion writes of how "out of forgotten strata of consciousness the elements of primitive man which are dormant in us are again brought to light, and at the same time unity is sought with the present day."[30]

Figure 12.3   Alvar Aalto, material study with laminated wood, dated 1929–35
Source: Museum of Finnish Architecture Collection.

Figure 12.4   Alvar Aalto, Vuoksenniska Church, 1955–57, detail of the windows and of the sliding partition wall
Source: Museum of Finnish Architecture Collection. Photograph by Heikki Havas.

Figure 12.5   Cover of a special issue on Finland, Architectural Forum (1940)
Source: Architectural Forum (June 1940).

A key concept behind Giedion's phenomenological epistemology, latency is based on the notion that in our daily experiences we are surrounded by things that we cannot quite apprehend or see, that is, things that are unconscious. As Maurice Merleau-Ponty stated: "Perception is unconscious."[31] In psychoanalysis it refers to a preconscious state, that which surrounds us in conscious life. Giedion, in fact, uses several psychoanalytical terms, like "subconscious" or "unconscious," throughout his book. Freud's notion of *Latenzzeit* is also relevant to his analysis, the idea that human life is dominated by a period during which blockades are built to hinder natural drives, like the free sexual life that characterizes early childhood. Yet, as we have learned from Freud, rather than remaining buried and hidden, these latencies translate into virulent figures, guiding out deepest thoughts and impulses.[32] Giedion's reference to the "irrational" in his writing on Aalto can be linked to these psychoanalytical ideas, signifying that, at best, most synthetic architecture is not just a product of the conscious, rational mind, but also an outcome of deeper, irrational levels of human psyche. Giedion's idea of history is organized along similar lines: he calls the period in which he himself is writing a "period of transition,"[33] implying a yet-to-be-fulfilled latency about to burst through the surface.

In Giedion's eyes the historian's task was to detect such latent forces. Reading Aalto through the baroque allowed him to see hidden meanings, impulses, and associations behind a single architectural element – irrespective of whether it was a vase or an acoustic ceiling. Giedion suggests that history writing is a hermeneutic project. A "contemporary historian," even when looking backwards, "transforms its object: every spectator at every period – at every moment, indeed – inevitably transforms the past according to his own nature."[34] And as he further explains: "History is not simply the repository of unchanging facts, but a process, a pattern of living and changing attitudes and interpretations."[35] We can gain access to that which fuels history through the act of interpretation, which in turn demands that we insert into the equation our present desires and motivations.

Giedion's book is organized along the lines of this argument: themes appear, disappear and reappear endlessly without being reduced to a simple linear narrative; his tone and style allow ideas to come to the fore as others recede. This is certainly not a standard piece of scholarly writing according to today's standards. The fact that his chapter on Aalto makes for a rather puzzling piece of architectural history writing, with its minute recordings of Aalto's actions, can further be credited to this psychologizing take on the baroque. To discuss the baroque meant, for Giedion, as for many of his contemporaries, going beyond the historiographical standards of their teachers and those of their contemporaries who were content with a merely descriptive, empirical analysis in order to make and take a position about the world in which they were living.

Baroque *Space*

Throughout their respective books, d'Ors, Focillon and also Giedion place emphasis on the human being, be it an artist, an historian, or an experiencing subject. The appeal of their prose lies in writing that mimics the movements of the minds of artist and beholder alike. This stylistic technique implies that the subject is inseparable from the world in which he or she lives, the objects he or she encounters, and the buildings he or she occupies – a quality of continuity that they all assign to the baroque. Focillon puts it succinctly: art is integral to life, or in his words, "a work of art is situated in space."[36]

"Space" appears in the title of Giedion's book and is likewise a key concept for Focillon. In the opening chapter of *La vie des formes*, "Forms in the Realm of Space," Focillon writes how the "space of life" and "space of art" converge through art's ability to change space according to its own needs. Space itself is a "plastic and changing material."[37] The ultimate ecstasy is to merge with space and to mould it, as it were, with one's moving body. In this equation art expresses the vitality of the world and, subsequently, the subject is fulfilled when it allows the world to pour in. Giedion was looking for something similar when referring to Leibniz's – the key mathematician of the baroque period – notion of the "monad" with its "internal relationships to the entire universe"[38] wherein everybody and everything is conceived as both a distinct entity and as part of a greater whole. The historical baroque provided a model because it did not obey a clear frame, bursting out of its seams, as it were, moulding space and investing it with a dynamism that can only be experienced through the moving body.

All in all, the baroque provided a new epistemological paradigm, marking a shift from the emphasis upon abstract knowledge and seeing to a multi-sensorial experience and response to the world around, or in the words of great baroque philosopher Spinoza, a moment when *homo cogitat* (man thinks) supplants Descartes' notion of *cogito ergo sum* (I think therefore I am). Here all thinking and being is directed to the world and there is no foundational prior self.[39] Tellingly, Focillon's book culminates in a chapter named "In Praise of Hands," which treats hands not simply as executioners of an idea or a concept but as multisensory living things – "receptive organs" that have a life of their own together and beyond the mind.[40]

Hence, it comes as no surprise that, more than any other chapter in *Space, Time and Architecture*, the one devoted to Aalto pays particular attention to the personality of the man. "One cannot speak about Aalto the architect without speaking about Aalto the man," exclaims Giedion, as he continues: "people are at least as important to him as architecture."[41] He refers to Aalto's restlessness, his ability to connect with people, to absorb and appropriate ideas and formal motifs from his contemporaries into his own work in a fluid and organic manner. Giedion even goes to far as to record how Aalto talks to old ladies in train – this being the ultimate sign of his humanity and engagement with the world around. True to the baroque legacy, Aalto's imagination is truly synthetic. The curvilinear form acts as a notation of his actions and experiences unfolding in real space and time. Aalto himself is treated as a sponge: a sum of the events, encounters, and influences. Yet, somehow he still manages to come across as a distinct persona.

In the way he links Aalto's persona and his signature formal motif, Giedion comes close to the way that his wife, the famous art historian Carola Giedion-Welcker, treats Jean Arp and his biomorphic art. It is worth noting that Aalto probably saw Arp's work for the first time during a 1931 visit to the Giedions in

Zurich.[42] Importantly, Giedion-Welcker did not see biomorphic abstraction simply as a formal counterpoint to geometric abstraction – a reading promoted by Alfred Barr in the 1936 exhibition *Cubism and Abstract Art* at the Museum of Modern Art – but rather in a manner similar to how d'Ors, Focillon and Giedion as an outcome of a synthetic mindset able to merge different temporalities as well as different impulses into a whole. As Giedion-Welcker put it, Arp's work was "pure poetry, which allows everything anecdotal and specific, as well as psychological and individual, to flow into one large reservoir."[43]

Giedion similarly interprets Aalto's Finnish origins in a highly embodied manner. He imports into *Space, Time and Architecture* the lead sentence of his 1941 article, "Finland is wherever Aalto goes."[44] In the same context he writes of Aalto's "restlessness" and "how he does not always remain in the pine and birch forests of Finland" as if wanting to register in minute detail the movements of his minds in addition to his actions, while suggesting that, even when he is travelling, Aalto could forget his origins or his country's war-time troubles. It is important to note that never in that chapter does Giedion claim that Aalto's architecture is the outcome of some kind of mystical genius loci of the country. His emphasis is instead on a more open-ended process. Echoing his reading of Arp's native Alsass, Giedion considers Finland a *Randstaat*, a border-state, which is in a constant state of cultural and geographical becoming. The aerial view of Finnish lake landscape – an image Aalto himself began to use in both his buildings and articles from around 1937 – captures the argument. The image depicts Finland as half water and half land – an ultimate liminal zone – evolving without a clear ideological script. The depiction therein of logs floating on the water further underlines the procedural and temporal aspect of that country. Giedion's message is, of course, not at all without ideological and political subtext: Finland appears a pure geographic narrative without political motivations during the most difficult time of its modern existence, finding itself at war with Russia.[45]

The curvilinear line certainly has many roles in Giedion's narrative. First, it acts as a conceptual diagram of the malleable and porous relationships between "monads" and the world around, whether that "world" is an individual or a country. He also treats the form as a kind of seismographic notion of mental activity. And thirdly, Giedion uses the form as an ideogram that allows different strata – formal, personal, geographical, and historical – to fold into one topological continuum to the point that it is difficult to separate life from architecture, a person from his or her country, form from its creator, one historical moment from another, or, for that matter, the critic from his or her subject.

(Neo-)Baroque *Architecture*

The search for a baroque sensibility in Aalto's architecture culminates in the work of the Italian critic Gillo Dorfles, for many years a professor of aesthetics at Milan University as well as an active member of both the Italian Movimento Arte Concreta and the France-based Gruppe Espace, both founded in the late 1940s, the latter by the architect Andre Bloc. In Dorfles's modestly illustrated book *Barocco nell'architettura moderna* (1951) Aalto is represented by the Savoy vase and an interior perspective of the Finnish Pavilion at the New York World's Fair, examples that, again following Giedion, identify the curvilinear form as the leitmotif of Aalto's oeuvre.

Dorfles based his book upon a review he had written of d'Ors book *Lo barroco* for *Domus*, published in 1946 as "Attualità del barocco," or the "timeliness of the baroque." Building upon d'Ors, he maintained that the baroque had remained a constant since the beginning of art and was conterminous with modernity. Baroque is read by Dorfles as the new *Kunstwollen*, as it were, in which the dynamic overcomes the static, the tactile the optical, the organic or plastic over the geometric – whether it be in architecture, design, painting, music, or any other medium of art.

While to a certain extent continuing d'Ors's project of the permanent baroque, Dorfles departs from his argument in one significant point. What he defines as "neo-baroque" refers to a specific historical period, namely the twentieth century. Aalto is therefore placed into the company of such figures as Carlo Mollino and Oscar Niemeyer, continuing the tradition laid out by the cubism and expressionism in the early part of the twentieth century. Different, too, is Dorfles's willingness to assign to those forms he casts as characteristic of the neo-baroque a very explicit ethical and moral dimension: free form meaning softer, more humane values.

Figure 12.6   Alvar Aalto drawing
Source: Zodiac 3 (1957). Photographs by Göran Schildt.

Therefore, while d'Ors and Focillon, and subsequently Giedion, spread the idea of pantheistic baroque mindset, Dorfles instrumentalized the baroque towards a vision of post-war architecture that enters the social realm by becoming more concrete, real and palpable. Here Aalto's architecture represented for him a kind of saturated reality effect, much needed to revive the post-war aporia. Dorfles's goal is best captured in the manifesto of the Groupe Espace he helped to craft in 1951, which calls for "art that is inscribed in real space, responding to all functional requirements and all human needs – both simple and most elevated."[46]

All in all, Aalto was particularly beloved in war-torn Italy, not least because of the revival of interest in the historical baroque that country had witnessed during the 1950s.[47] In the post-war Italian context Aalto's architecture represented, like the baroque itself, the ultimate "open work," to foreshadow the term coined some 10 years later by Umberto Eco to refer to work that is completed only in its reception. Understandably, architecture liberated from explicit meaning represented freedom in a country that had fallen under totalitarianism during the war. A special issue of the journal *Zodiac* devoted to Aalto in 1958 bore witness to the intensity of sensations that architects, artists and critics felt when they experienced one of Aalto's sculpted, baroque-like spaces – such as the interior of Vuoksenniska Church. The painter and critic Pier Carlo Santini writes, as if in a trance: "With what does it rhyme this strange architecture that escapes any classification in its ultimate greatness? With what indeed, if not with beauty nowadays so oft wronged, so oft denied in man's life?"[48] Aalto, like the best architects of the historical baroque, had perfected his craft to the point that one could simply sit back in awe. Instead of meaning, the spaces simply delivered a sensation.

The opening images in this issue of *Zodiac* depict Aalto drawing, capturing, perhaps better than any words, what post-war critics found so compelling in him (Figure 12.5): embodied engagement and feeling. The chapter of Focillon's book "In Praise of Hands" comes to mind. In it, he calls the hand the window to the human soul and celebrates the creative act conducted by hands as an unmediated registering of the movements of the mind. He writes: "Through his hands man establishes contact with the austerity of thought. They quarry its rough mass. Upon it they impose form, outline and, in the very act of writing, style."[49]

Indeed, Aalto's reception during the immediate post-war years was never limited to formal questions. The baroque offered a model for architecture that was motivated by something deeper, embodying the presence of the soul and a way of looking at the world, and a model for architecture that would reside in the realm of feelings and senses. D'Ors, Focillon and Giedion were all interested in the question of how style conveys mentality, or sensibility. The latter found an ideal link between the curvilinear form and Aalto's endlessly curious mind and restless feet. If the now greatly forgotten early twentieth-century German architectural historian Karl Scheffler once defined Hans Poelzig with words "There is gothic in him,"[50] Giedion and Dorfles could have well have stated: "There is baroque in Aalto." Their contemporaries would have known right away what it meant: an author of architecture that embodies whole worlds and destines.

Endnotes

1   Letter from Siegfried Giedion to Alvar Aalto, 10 January 1949, Alvar Aalto Museum, Helsinki.

2   Siegfried Giedion, postcard to Alvar Aalto, 7 July 1933, Alvar Aalto Museum, Helsinki.

3   Giedion, postcard to Aalto, 7 July 1933.

4   I have been inspired to draw the parallel between visual and textual process by Spyros Papapetros, who uses it to comment on writings by Detlef Mertins. See his review "Transparencies that passed and plenty more to come."

5   Giedion, *Space, Time and Architecture* (2nd edn), 566. Unless otherwise indicated, subsequent references are to the 2nd edition of this work.

6   Giedion, *Space, Time and Architecture*, 565.

7   Giedion, *Space, Time and Architecture*, 109.

8   Giedion, *Space, Time and Architecture*, 14.

9   Giedion, *Space, Time and Architecture*, 3.

10 Giedion, *Space, Time and Architecture*, 4.

11 Giedion, *Space, Time and Architecture*, 567.

12 Giedion, *Space, Time and Architecture*, 7.

13 D'Ors, *Du Baroque*, 15.

14 D'Ors, *Du Baroque*, 94.

15 D'Ors, *Du Baroque*, 96.

16 D'Ors, *Du Baroque*, 37.

17 D'Ors, *Du Baroque*, 37.

18 Focillon, *The Life of Forms in Art*, 15, quoted in Hills, "The Baroque," 22.

19 Focillon, *The Life of Forms in Art*, 31.

20 Focillon, *The Life of Forms in Art* (1992), 58.

21 Consultation with the Giedion Archive in the gta/ETH, Zurich, did not reveal books by either author in his collection.

22 Giedion, *Space, Time and Architecture*, 567.

23 Giedion, *Space, Time and Architecture*, 18.

24 Focillon, *The Life of Forms in Art* (1992), 23.

25 Focillon, *The Life of Forms in Art* (1992), 23.

26 Focillon, *The Life of Forms in Art* (1992), 21.

27 Focillon, *The Life of Forms in Art* (1992), 21.

28 Focillon, *The Life of Forms in Art* (1992), 579.

29 Focillon, *The Life of Forms in Art* (1992), 529.

30 Focillon, *The Life of Forms in Art* (1992), 621.

31 Merleau-Ponty, *Visible and Invisible*, 189.

32 See Diekmanna and Khurana (eds), *Latenz* for further discussion on the topic.

33 Giedion, *Space, Time and Architecture*, 11.

34 Giedion, *Space, Time and Architecture*, 5.

35 Giedion, *Space, Time and Architecture*, 5.

36 Giedion, *Space, Time and Architecture*, 63.

37 Giedion, *Space, Time and Architecture*, 65.

38 Giedion, *Space, Time and Architecture*, 22.

39 Wolfe, "From Spinoza to the Socialist Cortex," 190.

40 Focillon, *The Life of Forms in Art* (1992), 158.

41 Giedion, *Space, Time and Architecture*, 603.

42 For more information about Aalto's relationship with the Giedions, see Jokinen and Maurer, *Magus des Nordens*.

43 Giedion-Welcker, "Hans Arp," 246.

44 Giedion, *Space, Time and Architecture*, 567.

45 See my book *Alvar Aalto* for more discussion about the link between architectural ideas and geopolitical narratives and events.

46 *Gruppe Espace Manifesto* (October 1951), 27.

47 Argan, *Borromini*.

48 Santini, "Alvar Aalto from Sunila to Imatra," 27–8.

49 Focillon, *The Life of Forms in Art* (1992), 157.

50 Karl Scheffler, "Das große Schauspielhaus," quoted in Georgiadis, *Sigfried Giedion*, 11.

Chapter 13
Taking the Sting out of the Baroque: Wittkower, 1958

Andrew Hopkins

Unlike the notable impact on modernist architects of Rudolf Wittkower's *Architectural Principles in the Age of Humanism* (1949), there is very little recognition of the importance and influence on architects and other readers of *Art and Architecture in Italy 1600–1750*, his book on the Italian baroque commissioned by Nikolaus Pevsner for the hugely influential Pelican History of Art and published in 1958.[1] Yet within its field of academic art history, Wittkower's work quickly became the "Bible of the Baroque" and because, by the time of its publication, he had moved from London to New York, this extraordinary scholar was able to set as the subject of numerous doctoral dissertations all the unanswered questions about the plethora of secondary figures he had listed in his footnotes but was unable himself to research further. This alone ensured the work's decisive influence over succeeding generations.[2]

Towering over His Precedessors?

Because of its importance and its success, critics tend mainly to praise the author for his formidable energy in imposing a unified vision on the field, without analysing what obstacles Wittkower faced when confronting his task.[3] Apart from its obvious merits, the book's success was primarily based on the fact that it was the first work of its kind to be written and published in English and most critics tend to overlook how indebted Wittkower actually was to his German-language predecessors in the field. Just as many of the elements that constitute the foundations for the innovations of Andrea Palladio – one of Wittkower's favourite architects – can be traced back to earlier work in the Veneto, including that by Giovanni Falconetto, Michele Sanmicheli and Jacopo Sansovino, so too, if one decides to look closely at *Art and Architecture in Italy* one can see how deeply indebted Wittkower was to such studies as Cornelius Gurlitt's *Geschichte des Barockstiles in Italien* (1887), Albert Erich Brinckmann's *Die Baukunst des 17. und 18. Jahrhunderts in den Romanischen Ländern* (1919), Hermann Voss's *Die Malerei des Barock in Rom* (1925) and Nikolaus Pevsner's own *Barock Malerei in den romanischen Ländern* (1928), to name just four of the most important texts.[4] In the same way, just as Palladio might be said to have stolen his predecessor's and contemporaries' ideas but then used his extraordinary capacity to create striking new architectural images out of these existing and well-known elements, so too Wittkower's remarkably strong and coherent vision could be considered to be solidly based on the building blocks put in place by Gurlitt, Brinckmann, Voss and Pevsner. Alina Payne has noted that Gurlitt's book, which was never translated into English, was so "completely absorbed" within Wittkower's that there was no longer any need to read it.[5] Something similar might be said for Pevsner's work of 1928 as well as that of Voss from 1925, although the latter remains rewarding as its recent translation into Italian and English testifies. Wittkower's attention to Turin and Piedmont must be acknowledged to be directly indebted to Brinckmann's pioneering examination of this region.

Wittkower's decisions regarding content, periodization and the overall structure of his volume need therefore to be examined in the light of his predecessors' contributions to the field to explain and assess some of the choices he made in the period from receiving the commission to write the book in post-war Britain to its publication a decade later, including how he apparently managed to take the sting out of what had been an especially poisonous debate about the baroque as exemplified by Benedetto Croce's broadside of 1929, in which the art of this era was described as a "Brutto Artistico" and, as such, "not art at all" – a tyrannical tirade that ironically came hard on the heels of the writing of the first of several exemplary monographs on such architects as Borromini and the Fischer von Erlachs by such noted authors as Eberhard Hempel, Dagobert Frey and Hans Sedlmayr.[6]

Before cross-examining Wittkower, as it were, to answer the charge of purloining from his predecessors, one should first let him speak in his own defence even if his explanation is *ex post facto*. He recorded his intentions regarding the writing of his volume of the Pelican History of Art in a Roman conference paper delivered in 1960, "Il Barocco in Italia." This is the only place where he clearly sets out criteria, of which there are three, for structuring an account of the baroque, as well as setting his own work in an historiographical context. Here he says: "the value of the generic term baroque, applied to the entire historical period from 1600 to 1750, lies in its capacity for differentiation of (1) topography (Roman, Neapolitan, Venetian), (2) chronology (early, full and late [baroque]), (3) artistic tendencies (dynamic and emotive, Baroque classicism, populist realism)."[7] These categories can then be combined, as Wittkower goes on to say, rather like German word combinations. He offers the example "classicismo tardo barocco Bolognese" (late baroque Bolognese classicism), which he says immediately evokes a specific regional artistic style in a specific historical moment – a highly formalist formulation, to say the least, that served him as a pigeonholing positivism that avoided polemic by being based on form, style and region.

Wittkower also gives a fair indication of which art historians were important to him when thinking about his book. He describes three phases in the modern historiography of the baroque: the first, pioneering phase of Cornelius Gurlitt, Heinrich Wölfflin, August Schmarsow and Alois Riegl, that went from 1887 to 1914. He criticized Wölfflin for being attracted to the idea that baroque visual forms could be equally found in other periods and declared himself against this concept. Wittkower particularly praised Gurlitt for being the first to attempt a differentiation of styles, "a revolutionary work," and the same methodology underpins Wittkower's own text: those accomplished stylistic descriptions that one can still set for students as primers of this approach.[8] Where Gurlitt went wrong was also useful for prompting efforts at resolution. Alois Riegl had flagged up some of the issues in his posthumously published work of 1908, which Wittkower knew well:

> Gurlitt – who attempted to write the first monograph on baroque architecture, primarily on the Italian baroque: this … was a continuation of Burckhardt's history of the Renaissance …; he lacks a real urge to condense or to highlight common characteristics, being more interested in particulars rather than general aspects. He describes the architecture, but he does not explain.[9]

Hence the introductory section in Wittkower's book of 1958 presents both a concept of the baroque and an account of the most important historical events preceding 1600. Riegl's other specific criticism of Gurlitt was that "anyone seeking a clear definition of the character of baroque style, or the continuous line of its development, will be disappointed."[10]

Wittkower's very clear delineation of baroque style and periodization in 1958 is outlined in his conference paper of 1960. Distancing himself from Wölfflin's compare-and-contrast approach with its carefully chosen – almost skewed – series of examples, Wittkower's work was also the polar opposite of August Schmarsow's highly theoretical, philosophical approach. As for Riegl's posthumously published book of 1908, its account concluded with Caravaggio, thus terminating (unintentionally) its examination at more or less the point where Wittkower begins. It might well be argued, however, that Wittkower was influenced by Riegl's work in a much more profound way than periodization alone. Just as Riegl had focused on Correggio and Michelangelo – at the expense of a range of other artists – so, too, Wittkower focused on such key figures as Bernini and such themes as the unity of the visual arts to pinpoint significant change. The construction of a tightly focused and cogently argued narrative thesis is surely one of the keys to the success of Wittkower's work. It is also what makes Riegl's work so fascinating even today. As Joseph Connors and Jennifer Montagu, the editors to the last revised edition of Wittkower, put it in 1999: "unlike most survey books, which maintain an even pace of narration, Wittkower deliberately alternated between fast-forward chapters, which cover dozens or hundreds of artists, and chapters which focus closely, almost luxuriantly, on a single figure," this perhaps being the most brilliant part of his strategy.[11]

Wittkower considered the second phase of baroque studies, between the two world wars, as its real Renaissance. He lists Roberto Longhi, Guido Marangoni, Giuseppe Fiocco, Antonio Munoz, Giuseppe De Logu, Werner Weisbach, Heinrich Bodmer, Hans Posse and Dagobert Frey along with Brinckmann, Voss and Pevsner.[12] He considered this group of scholars particularly important as they counterbalanced the anti-baroque stance of Croce and the militant opposition to the art of this period by recognized authorities such as Bernhard Berenson.[13] He perceived these scholars as following two tendencies: the first developing Wölfflin's visual categories. Hans Rose – his student – exemplified this approach in his *Habilitationsschrift* of 1920, written under Wölfflin's direction and published in 1922 as *Spätbarock*.[14] There Rose addressed the question of the late baroque through a history of secular architecture from 1660 to 1760. In the preface he explains his pursuit of his *Doktorvater*'s systematically developed set of contrasting concepts for distinguishing Renaissance and baroque, here transposed to define the successive contrast between high and late baroque. To counterbalance Wittkower's assessment I think one could argue that shortly after this time both Rose and Wölfflin clearly saw the limits of this approach as Rose's updated and expanded edition of Wölfflin's *Renaissance and Baroque* of 1926, undertaken with his supervisor's express approval, moved deliberately away from these visual categories.[15]

The second tendency Wittkower identified in these scholars' work was their move towards art history as cultural and intellectual history (*Kultur-* and *Geistesgeschichte*). Baroque art as conditioned by such external factors as religion and politics was exemplified by Werner Weisbach's *Der Barock als Kunst der Gegenreformation* (1921), which Wittkower discounts as not historically convincing.[16] He also laments that, in this period, insufficient attention was paid to documents along the lines that Oskar Pollak had established. This was, however, caused by Pollak dying young in the war in 1915 and exacerbated by Dagobert Frey's decision to sit on the documents in the Vatican archives that Pollak had transcribed. Frey used these to publish a long essay of his own on the architecture of the Roman baroque in 1924 – despite being heavily based on his privileged access to Pollak's unpublished *Nachlass* – and he only published Pollak's work four years later in 1928.[17]

Wittkower also believed both that not enough attention had been paid to printed sources and that too few monographs had been written.[18] Of note is his observation that there was little study of architecture or sculpture, and that drawings were hardly studied at all (besides his and Heinrich Brauer's own volume on Bernini drawings, published in 1931 as *Die Zeichnungen des Gianlorenzo Bernini*). Wittkower maintains that the principal focus of art historians was on seventeenth-century painting, with little attention to the eighteenth century except for Venetian painting (something later exacerbated by Francis Haskell's focus in *Patrons and Painters* of 1963). This last affirmation is only partially true, however, as Voss intended his excellent account of 1925 as the first of two volumes to comprise the *Geschichte der italienischen Barockmalerei*. The second tome was to have been dedicated to "Italian Painting 'Outside Rome' 1600–1800," but sadly was never written.[19] His volume of 1925 brilliantly and thoroughly treats painting in the Eternal City over the full two centuries and the structure adopted in *Baroque Painting in Rome* offers both a theoretical and an historical account in its Introduction:

I History and Historiography. II. The Individual and the Nation. III. The Organic Character of Culture and its Functions. IV. Particular Developments and International Currents. V. Art History and Art Historiography. VI. Survey of the Italian Renaissance Movement. VII. The Artistic Development of Italy from the 14th to the 16th Century. VIII. The Universal Significance of the Italian Renaissance.[20]

A series of plates follows this text and these in turn are followed by biographies with descriptive lists of individual artists and their works divided into two parts: "I. Caravaggio and the School of Naturalism. II. Annibale Carracci and the Reform of Monumental Painting."

Voss's watershed of 1600, published in 1920 as *Painters of the Late Renaissance in Rome and Florence* and *Baroque Painting in Rome*, published in 1925, did for painting what Brinckmann had accomplished for architecture in his *Die Baukunst des 17. und 18. Jahrhunderts* of 1919. The shift from examining the sixteenth and seventeenth centuries together to instead treat as a block the seventeenth and eighteenth centuries was accepted and deliberately deployed by Pevsner in his assignment of the various volumes of the Pelican History of Art, indicating a serious shift from his own earlier periodization of the baroque as will be discussed below. Even if publication of his own book was to be years away, because Wittkower knew that other adjacent volumes with their century-long slots were planned he was able to offer the barest of sketches of the art history preceding 1600. This suited his purpose of moving decisively away and distancing his work from important earlier literature such as Gurlitt (1887), Riegl (1908), and also Paul Frankl's *Die Entwicklungsphasen der neueren Baukunst* of 1914, which emphasised the so-called "second period" of 1550–1700, with respect to which Wittkower shifted his start and end dates by half a century.[21] Indeed already by page 21 of a text of over 400 pages, Wittkower was treating Caravaggio rather than Correggio. He also ended up lopping off – in theory if not entirely in practice – the last 50 years between 1750 and 1800, which would not, therefore, be covered at all, either in his volume or elsewhere in the series. Yet this hardly seems a crime since he had already packed the pages of his book full to bursting and, moreover, got it into print – unlike a number of Pelicans that never saw the light of day.[22]

The first part of Wittkower's book is dedicated to Caravaggio and the Carracci in that order (as well as Caravaggio's followers and the Carracci School in Rome), following Voss's decision of 1925 to begin with Caravaggio and Naturalism (Part 1) – followed by Annibale Carracci and the reform of painting (Part 2) – rather than Jacob Burckhardt's arrangement in his *Cicerone* whereby the Carracci were examined before Caravaggio (a structural arrangement repeated by Riegl in his *Origins of Baroque Art in Rome* of 1908, and by Ellis Waterhouse in his volume on seventeenth-century painting in Rome), a choice that is seemingly insignificant but actually important for beginning with naturalism rather than classicism in order to emphasize change over continuity. "Painting outside Rome" is followed by "Architecture and Sculpture to 1625" to complete part one, thus preparing the ground for Wittkower's "Age of the High Baroque" and his incontestable triumvirate.

Indeed, in his paper of 1960 Wittkower came out clearly for chronology by saying that limits needed to be set and that the baroque really begins in Rome in 1630 with Gianlorenzo Bernini, Francesco Borromini and Pietro da Cortona. Cynically one might say that "The Age of the High Baroque," his chapters 8, 9 and 10, were largely prompted by Wittkower's need to find a structure that differentiated his own presentation of the period from earlier attempts to do so, and that the way forward was offered by his hero Bernini, as well as by Cortona, who worked in more than one medium. He could thus take up the methodological approach developed by Riegl to analyse the arts of the baroque together rather than separately.[23]

Brinckmann's part stylistic and part typological account was perhaps less influential on Wittkower than the earlier but more useful Gurlitt, but it had the merit of dealing judiciously with pan-Italian examples – a distinct advantage as the typological approach enabled the author to slot in a wide range of buildings, and it was Brinckmann who had pioneered examination of Piedmontese architecture and urbanism in his volume of 1919. Although the first 56 pages mainly concentrate on the sixteenth-century legacy as a preamble to the seventeenth century, the majority of his account is focused clearly on the period of the seventeenth and eighteenth centuries. While this may seem obvious, when Pevsner wrote his own volume for the same *Handbuch der Kunstwissenschaft* series in 1928 he reverted to a much more outdated conception of the period.[24]

Indeed, Pevsner's *Die Italienische Malerei vom ende der Renaissance bis zum ausgehenden Rokoko* of 1928 is a throwback to the debates of the first half of the 1920s.[25] He begins this survey account in 1520 with the crisis in style in the first chapter dedicated to "Mannerism and Proto-Baroque" followed by a second part, "Early and Full Baroque." Yet, after the Second World War, when he came to divide up and apportion the volumes in his series, he made a significant shift to adopt Voss's watershed and have century-long slots that separated out the sixteenth and seventeenth centuries. Wittkower in 1958 thus presents a compressed preamble of key earlier events and focuses instead on history, rhetoric and the role of the *concetto*. Pevsner's account was useful for Wittkower, but most likely as a model of careful pigeonholing and breaking a monumental subject up into smaller, digestible pieces.

In 1960 Wittkower also identified a third phase in the historiography of the baroque, following the Second World War, characterized by such scholars as Giulio Briganti, Luigi Grassi, Giulio Carlo Argan, Roberto Longhi, Cesare Gnudi, Denis Mahon, Emile Mâle, Mario Praz, Roberto Battaglia, Hans Kauffmann and Herbert von Einem.[26]

Of all these scholars, it was Argan who had the most impact on Wittkower's theoretical approach to the subject of the baroque. Indeed, the latter took up and fully endorsed Argan's "unitary interpretation" in his important contribution of 1954 "La rettorica e l'arte barocco" (published in 1955) that posited Aristotelian rhetoric as the basis for baroque artistic process.[27] Argan's argument was both genial and convincing in identifying rhetoric and the art of persuasion as the technique that characterized the baroque, the medium rather than the message, the technique of rhetoric and the condition of rhetoricity, which in the seventeenth century had an autonomous development and was configured as both method: more precisely it was a method that became a system and shaped a worldview. Just how important Wittkower's immediate support for this piece, which revolutionized the understanding and interpretation of the baroque, needs to be emphasized, given that his own text was being written in those same years. His introductory section specifically nominates Argan: "the technique of these artists is that of persuasion at any price. Persuasion is the central axiom of classical rhetoric. In an illuminating paper G.C. Argan has therefore rightly stressed the strong influence of Aristotle's Rhetoric on Baroque procedure."[28] Wittkower went on in the relevant footnote: "The ideas of this concise paper have influenced my argumentation."[29] Thus in one fell swoop, like a bolt of lightning striking first in Italy and then in Britain and America, Argan, through Wittkower, definitively brushed aside once and for all Croce's dismissal of the baroque, replacing it with a concept – one that continues to be convincing today – that provided the baroque with an intellectual foundation in ancient thought. The echo of Argan's idea can be heard in Wittkower's chapters on the "Age of the High Baroque," in such sub-titles as "Rhetoric and Baroque Procedure."

European Geography and Pelican Periodization

Both at the outset, and subsequently as further volumes appeared, there was considerable debate about the way that World and European Art History had been divided up and space apportioned by Pevsner for each volume of his Pelican series.[30] His task was to break up into constituent periods and parts the geographical areas assigned to his various authors. How those authors then divided up their own subjects up into manageable portions in terms of period region is worth examining. Does the overall arrangement of other Pelican volumes shed some light on the choices Pevsner made? Many of them, including that of Wittkower, mainly played variations on the regional tour, enjoyed at national level (Italy, France, Britain, Belgium) or at supra-national level when their Pelican covered several nation states as in Eberhard Hempel's 1965 *Baroque Art and Architecture in Central Europe*, with its coverage of Germany, Austria, Switzerland, Hungary, Czechoslovakia and Poland.[31] The disarming preface to the 1959 volume by George Kubler and Martin Soria dedicated to *Art and Architecture in Spain and Portugal and their American Dominions* bluntly states that the commissioning editor sought a work that would "treat the art and architecture of the Iberian Empires from the Renaissance to the Napoleonic Wars." The authors apologize that after 10 years' work they had to omit "Asia, Oceania, Africa and the rest of Europe" because "the literature on the Spanish and Portuguese works of these continents is not ready for use." The authors go on to explain their guiding principles: "We have kept two aims always in mind: to respect regional groupings, even at the expense of nationalist sentiment; and to treat style as our most important concern."[32] Because Kubler wrote on architecture and Soria on sculpture and painting, the media are recounted separately, more or less along the same geographical lines of "Spain," "Spanish America," and "Portugal and Brazil," with each of these macro areas divided into smaller chronological sections.

Quite different is Hempel's 1965 account of the vast subject of the baroque of Central Europe.[33] Following Part One, which offers an historical introduction, the following four parts are arranged chronologically into periods – 1600–1639, 1640–82, 1683–1739 and 1740–80 – and in each of these is examined systematically architecture, sculpture and painting in various matrices, sometimes adopting architecture by region and then all of sculpture and then all of painting, or by nation state, giving accounts of the three arts all at once. This more or less follows Wittkower's volume of 1958, with Early, Late and High Baroque in Architecture, Sculpture and Painting here played out on a supra-national scale.

Rome and the Rest: Primacy and Periphery

The various arts may have been united by Wittkower but one of the most forceful decisions he made in structuring *Art and Architecture in Italy* was to impose a "Rome-Outside Rome" division on his material. Was he influenced by Wölfflin's early volume, *Renaissance and Baroque* of 1888, that focused primarily on Rome for its series of strongly contrasting comparisons? Or was the impetus provided by Voss's published work and its unpublished companion? Certainly this structure enabled Wittkower to give Rome its due while also permitting him to single out for examination prominent examples from elsewhere in Italy without the obligation to systematically discuss all the other regions of Italy, one after the other, in which there might have been but a single important work. The literature also reflected and may have encouraged the adoption of this framework: in bibliographic terms there was a plethora of studies on Rome, which Wittkower knew intimately from his research at the Hertziana, while the study of other Italian regions made for a much patchier library. It is worth pointing out, however, that Giuseppe De Logu had strikingly divided his account of Italian architecture of the seventeenth and eighteenth centuries into two volumes – not divided according to century, but rather into Rome and elsewhere.

It is in the first part of his book that Wittkower initiates its organization according to "Rome" and "Outside Rome" divisions, cunningly passing from the "Bolognese in Rome" to "Painting Outside Rome" to begin with painting in Bologna as the first port of call before passing to other cities, from Florence and Siena to the north (but not to the south of Rome, a rejection or revulsion shared by almost all the other volumes dedicated to Italy in this series). This structure is later repeated for his chapters on Architecture and Sculpture. Among other reasons, the impetus for this arrangement was probably to break up the discussion of painting into smaller parts to ameliorate the appearance of Wittkower's reliance on Voss, and yet to continue to make great use of that reliable and perceptive work for his section on Rome while himself gathering together what he might on those other cities that were, to a certain degree, under-researched. The irony of this division of material is that while it comes across to the reader as Romanocentric, Wittkower actually went out of his way, and dedicated much of his energy, to researching and writing exemplary case studies of non-Roman architecture in regions like Venice and Turin.

Wittkower then astutely deals with "High Baroque Classicism in Painting and its Aftermath," sandwiching between these two chapters two others, both exemplary and innovative, dedicated to "Architectural Currents of the High Baroque" and "Trends of High Baroque Sculpture," both likewise divided into Roman and non-Roman parts. But with all the sympathy in the world for Wittkower's heroic efforts, placing Longhena, Silvani and Fanzago after Carlo Rainaldi, Martino Longhi the Younger, Vincenzo della Greca, Antonio del Grande and Giovan Antonio de' Rossi is bewildering, to say the least. If ever there was a case for simply reversing the order of habit and for once putting architecture *outside* Rome before that *of* Rome, to which a triumphal return could have been staged, then this would have been the ideal moment.

The consequences of this rigid division are played out in Part Three: "Late Baroque and Rococo" (c. 1675 to c. 1750), where two chapters on architecture deal with Carlo Fontana and the eighteenth century in Rome, Northern Italy, Florence, Naples and Sicily, only *then* turn to the architecture of Piedmont and Guarino Guarini, Filippo Juvarra and Bernardo Vittone, a positioning of Guarini that on the one hand makes it impossible to understand him in the context of his real contemporaries, while instead setting him up as an individual pioneer responsible for the flowering of baroque architecture in Piedmonte.

Wittkower's concluding chapters are on sculpture and painting, which meant that he could finish on the high note of Venetian painting, including the work of Sebastiano Ricci and, of course, Giambattista Tiepolo, although as John Pope-Hennessy rightly (but slightly spitefully) noted in his review of the first edition of *Art and Architecture in Italy*: "the chapters on painting are consistently less interesting" and that

> Professor Wittkower has as a whole tended to concentrate on those parts of the history in which he has some individual contribution to put forward, at the expense of those parts where he has not, so that, to take an extreme instance, the Piedmontese architect Vittone, a figure of considerable interest but not of world importance, is accorded more space than Giambattista Tiepolo.[34]

Postscript

How might Wittkower's account been different? It must be remembered that, although published in 1958, his preface reveals that he "dictated a rough draft of large parts of the manuscript in the summer of 1950." He continues: "Most of my spare time in the following seven years was given to elaborating, revising, and completing the work. The manuscript reached the editor in batches from the beginning of 1956 onwards; by the summer of 1957 almost the entire text had been dispatched."

The book was, then, largely conceived and written in 1950, five years after the Second World War had finished and hard on the heels of his enormously successful *Architectural Principles in the Age of Humanism*. Anyone who has written a long book will know just how hard it is to keep everything to length and with just proportions. Wittkower built up his overall account over years in various libraries: "The book was prepared and written mainly with the resources of the Warburg Library and the Witt Library (Courtauld Institute), London; the Bibliotheca Hertziana, Rome; the German Art Historical Institute, Florence; and the Avery Library, Columbia University, New York." The brilliant collections of the Avery library were presumably used to update his bibliography rather than for substantive research, since the book was mostly finished before his move to the United States.

Wittkower was also working in relative isolation on baroque architecture, since in post-war London most studies were focused on the Renaissance, as was the Warburg itself. In the year before publication, in 1957, Desmond Zwemmer appointed Rudolf Wittkower and Anthony Blunt founding editors of what would come to be regarded as Zwemmer's finest publishing achievement: the series *Studies in Architecture*, the prospectus of which was launched in 1957. The two leading scholars of baroque studies in the United States (since Wittkower's move to Columbia in 1956–57) and in Britain, as Director of the Courtauld Institute of Art in London (1949–74), thus led the charge for one of the most serious series in which baroque and later European architecture was presented on equal terms with the Renaissance. So too, with the appearance of Wittkower's magisterial survey in 1958, architecture was accorded equal status with the other arts and, perhaps because of his particular penchant for it, one might consider that in his contribution to the Pelican History of Art, architecture occupies a special place.

In the first edition of what would become the series' best-selling volume, the author thanked his commissioning editor for his "infinite patience." But, in fact, because this enormous, and soon to be enormously influential, volume had been consigned to the editor so far behind schedule, Pevsner was furious with Wittkower, even recounting to Reyner Banham "that on meeting Wittkower in the Warburg Library he found himself unable to exchange a civil word with him because the promised volume in the Italian Baroque was eighteen months late."[35] Certainly it had been a long gestation and one that was also, in the end, a late delivery. Yet this overdue and over-length account of one of the richest periods of Italian art also managed to squeeze inside its covers a brilliant account of a century and a half of artistic creation in painting, sculpture and architecture that inspired many Anglo-American academics to heed the call and themselves become scholars of the Italian baroque. But this was not, or not necessarily, its greatest achievement. For the first time, the sting had finally been taken out of the baroque, and for this Wittkower was much more indebted to his German-language predecessors than has been previously recognized or admitted. This is not to underestimate his achievement, but merely to locate it in the historical context to which this great émigré scholar belonged.

Author's Note

My thanks to Francesco Benelli, Joseph Connors, Ute Engel, Susie Harries and Douglas Lewis for helpfully answering questions during the course of this research.

Endnotes

1　Payne, "Rudolf Wittkower and Architectural Principles in the Age of Modernism," 322–42. Reviews of Wittkower's *Art and Architecture in Italy* included those by Pope-Hennessy, Coffin and Salerno. For Wittkower's influence on his Warburg doctoral student Colin Rowe see Benelli, "Rudolf Wittkower e Colin Rowe," 97–111. For the American period see Martin, *Utopia's Ghost*, xix–xx; and Vidler, *Histories of the Immediate Present*.

2　In the 2nd edition, published in 1965, he says: "In the five and a half years since the appearance of the first edition of this book Italian Baroque Studies have taken immense strides forward."

3　In the "Introduction to the New Edition" (ix–xv) of the 6th revised edition (1999), the editors Joseph Connors and Jennifer Montagu write: "Wittkower began to interest himself in the undervalued fields of Baroque architecture and sculpture" (ix), an assessment that is only relatively true if one intends an English-language context. They also noted

(x) his immense "organizational powers" and that, for each task, he adapted his method and approach to that most suited to the material, or the audience. They also noted (xi) his ability to be "able to reduce this vast mass of material to a coherent and readable history."

4   There was no comparable work on sculpture, as Wittkower noted in his bibliography (391), adjudicating Brinckmann's *Barockskulptur* as "[a] spirited enterprise, now largely antiquated," whereas he much appreciated "Voss, 1924. The basic study without which no work in the field can be undertaken."

5   Payne, "Beyond 'Kunstwollen'," 23. She notes: "posterity has not taken him at his word and noticed just how much of Gurlitt appears on his every page, from periodization to the treatment of individual buildings and architects."

6   Croce, *Storia della età barocca in Italia*, 24. He writes: "dunque, il Barocco è una sorta di brutto artistico, e, come tale, non è niente di artistico, ma anzi, al contrario, qualcosa di diverso dall'arte, di cui ha mentito l'aspetto e il nome." Compare Gigliucci, *Croce e il Barocco* and see also Hopkins "Not Enough Baroque," 118–21.

7   Wittkower, "Il Barocco in Italia," 323.

8   Wittkower, "Il Barocco in Italia," 319. *Baroque Architecture*, by Martin Briggs, is lapidarily liquidated in Wittkower's bibliography as "antiquated" (392). Wittkower's reference to 1914 implies the beginning of the First World War and perhaps also the publication of Frankl, *Die Entwicklungsphasen der neueren Baukunst*; and Ricci, *Architettura barocca in Italia*.

9   Riegl, *The Origins of Baroque Art in Rome*, 100.

10 Riegl, *The Origins of Baroque Art in Rome*, 100.

11 Connors and Montagu, "Introduction to the New Edition," xi.

12 Observation of the period is taken up in Hopkins, "Riegl Renaissances," 60–87.

13 Wittkower, "Il Barocco in Italia," 321.

14 Brinckmann observes: "Er will hierbei die von Wölfflin formulierten kunstgeschichtlichen Grundbegriffe systematisch weiterbilden (was allerdings keineswegs deutlich wird)," 242.

15 On Rose see Fuhrmeister, "Hans Rose," 434–55.

16 Wittkower, "Il Barocco in Italia," 324: "chi cercava una fonte primaria: Contrariforma, Gesuita … non funzione."

17 Frey, "Beiträge zur Geschichte der römischen Barockarchitektur," 5–113. This essay, which helped establish Frey's reputation, appeared four years before his edition of Pollak's own research (*Die Kunsttätigkeit unter Urban VIII*) as Frey was somewhat of a *Nachlass* profiteer as part of his ambitious strategy to dominate the field. The other documentary study of the period was Orbaan, *Documenti sul barocco in Roma*.

18 Both Hempel (*Borromini*) and, to a certain extent, Sedlmayr (*Die Architektur Borrominis*) were notable exceptions, but Sedlmayr had also published *Fischer von Erlach* in 1925, so Wittkower is not quite right. He deliberately avoids Hempel's Bellorian mode of history, organizing his account into three chapters that divide Borromini's work by papal reign (Urban VIII, Innocent X, Alexander VII).

19 Voss thus began his account in 1600, then unchartered territory, since Adolfo Venturi's magisterial survey had only reached the fifteenth-century volumes. On Venturi see D'Onofrio (ed.), *Adolfo Venturi e la storia dell'arte oggi*.

20 Voss, *Die Malerei des Barock in Rom*, Introduction.

21 Wittkower also carefully avoided another difficult debate by entitling his last part "Late Baroque and Rococo," thus putting them together rather than trying too hard to separate them out and concluding his account in 1750 rather than in 1800. Pevsner envisaged a separate volume for Italian architecture of the fifteenth and sixteenth centuries (Heydenreich and Lotz), another for Italian painting of the sixteenth century (Freedburg) and a third (which never saw the light) dedicated to Italian sculpture of the sixteenth century. Possibly one of Pevsner's reasons for this change in thinking was prompted by his reading and review of Hoffmann's unsatisfactory volume of 1938, *Hochrenaissance-Manierismus-Frühbarock*.

22 Harries, *Nikolaus Pevsner*, 563, notes that by December 1946 Pevsner had signed contracts with John Summerson, Anthony Blunt, Rudolf Wittkower and Ellis Waterhouse. In the prospectus of 1955 Wittkower's volume is given as "Art and Architecture of the 17th and 18th Centuries." See Slive, "Nikolaus Pevsner's Contribution as Editor of the Pelican History of Art Series," 73–86, in particular the prospectus reproduced on 82–3.

23 Wittkower, "Il Barocco in Italia," 322.

24 Pevsner, in *Barock Malerei in den romanischen Ländern*, on "Italien" opens with "Manierismus und Protobarock" and "Die Stilkrise um 1520." In the second volume by Grautoff, *Die Malerei im Barockzeitalter in Frankreich und Spanien*, El Greco is unsurprisingly the opening figure as his Italian sojourn and classification as a key exponent of Mannerism provides a perfectly convenient point of departure. In the same year Pevsner published "Beiträge zur Stilgeschichte des Früh- und Hochbarock."

25 Presumably Pevsner fell into this trap because of his preceding involvement in the then current Mannerism debate with his articles "Gegenreformation und Manierismus" and "Beiträge zur Stilgeschichte des Früh- und Hochbarock." Compare Engel, "Barockforschung," 584–5; and Bredekamp, "Der Manierismus," 109–29. Werner Weisbach "replied" in that same year (1928) with "Gegenreformation – Manierismus – Barock." See also Engel, "The Formation of Pevsner's Art History," 29–55.

26 Argan's *L'architettura barocca in italia* had no impact on Wittkower's study. Venturi's *Caravaggio* contains Croce's apologia: "La medesimezza del giudizio non è possibile in modo assoluto, perché il corso della storia non ammette giudizii definitivi e concordi; ma ha bene un senso relativo e accetabile." See also Hopkins "Riegl Renaissances," 68, 84–5.

27 Argan, "La 'Rettorica' e l'arte barocca" was cited in Wittkower, "Il Barocco in Italia," 324, but first in *Art and Architetecture in Italy 1600–1750* where, in the bibliography, along with Argan he also praises another paper in the same volume by Tagliabue, "Aristotelismo e Barocco." Discussed in Levy, "Rhetoric or Propaganda?" 91.

28 Wittkower, *Art and Architetecture*, 92.

29 Wittkower, *Art and Architetecture*, 352.

30 See the reviews by Banham, "The Pelican History of Art," and the editorials of the *Burlington Magazine* of issues 95 (1953) and 109 (1967). In the latter the Editor writes: "Wittkower, Summerson, Waterhouse and Blunt, who seemed to be set impossible tasks but who by lucidity and erudition managed to tame their wild beasts." Gilbert's review in the *Journal of the Society of Architectural Historians* (*JSAH*) reads: "The finest Pelicans – those most often mentioned are Wittkower's Italian Baroque and Krautheimer's Early Christian and Byzantine Architecture, both from the great immigrant scholar generation – resolve the problem in a heroic way. Both successfully imposed on the material a firm interpretive viewpoint all their own … Wittkower, dealing with a huge but little studied mass of objects, worked it by suppressing the middle distance, emphasizing a few great heroes and then offering long quick lists of small figures, less bothersome here than usual because they had been defined by the adjacent great," 150–51.

31 Compare Gerson and Ter Kuile, *Art and Architecture in Belgium 1600 to 1800*, reviewed by Damm in the *Journal of the Society of Architectural Historians*, 202–3. Bialostocki, in the *Art Bulletin*, asks: "How reasonable is it to discuss the sixteenth century architecture of the Southern Netherlands separately from that of the Northern provinces?," 70. Such issues were forlornly flagged by Pevsner in a disarming "Editor's Note:" "It must be admitted that the title of the volume is faulty in two ways," one being the abovementioned issue, the other being that strictly speaking Belgium "did not come into being until 1830," xix.

32 Kubler and Soria, *Art and Architecture in Spain and Portugal*, xxv.

33 Here architecture covered was from the sixteenth to the eighteenth centuries but in painting and sculpture only the seventeenth and eighteenth centuries, in theory.

34 Pope-Hennessy, review, *Times Literary Supplement*, 341, 343.

35 Harries, *Nikolaus Pevsner*, 2011, 564 citing Banham, "Out of the Air."

Chapter 14

Pierre Charpentrat and Baroque Functionalism

Maarten Delbeke

For Lucia

A Pennant Marked Baroque

"This is what slipshod, complacent language, and what the superficial mind (the shrug of the shoulders in club and salon with its 'Well, why not?') types as, 'Baroque' or, should you prefer it, 'Baroquism'." Thus Le Corbusier opened the preface, dated "Christmas 1956" and ominously titled "Voilà," of the American publication celebrating, in 1957, the inauguration of the chapel of Notre Dame du Haut in Ronchamp. Further on in the same preface:

> This little chapel of pilgrimage, here at Ronchamp, is not a pennant marked "baroque." Reader, you do understand. I hate this term just as, in the same way I have never liked, nor looked at, nor been able to admit baroque art. An ambiguous epithet, an accusation. Modern criticism silenced by the violence of the contemporary plastic arts and aesthetics waves this garment unhooked from its cloakroom of epithets; the bigwigs chat – to each other.[1]

The recent discovery that "Corbu is baroque," as he mockingly puts it, fits not at all with what he stands for. "Baroque" is "an accusation," a dismissal of the sincerity of a life's work hastily produced by frenzied journalism rather than thoughtful criticism, proof of a superficial interest in the psyche of the star architect to the detriment of his work. Le Corbusier scorns the speculation about his personal beliefs that the architecture of the chapel invites and he ends his preface by accusing certain journalists of "[breaking] the rules" and entering the site of the chapel before its inauguration, "[gunning] me with their flash-cameras." One of them, an American of course, pursued him with the question of whether it required a Catholic to build such a chapel. Le Corbusier replied with "foutez-moi le camp."[2]

By bristling at the label "baroque" Le Corbusier implicitly reacted to two strains in the critical reception of his work: the first issuing from French Catholic circles, the second from the milieu of architecture. The baroque was a pawn in the French debate about the reform of religious art. In 1951 *La Maison-Dieu*, the main French journal on Catholic liturgy, published two opposing interpretations of the baroque. Paul Roque deemed it an essentially Roman art form that could serve as a model for contemporary religious art for being the last style able to bridge the gap between the secular intellectualism of classicism and popular, medieval piety. Pie-Raymond Regamey, then editor-in-chief and principal author of *L'Art sacré*, a progressive journal on religious art run by the French Dominicans, responded with a well-informed essay on baroque and rococo architecture. He questioned Roque's Roman genealogy of the style and doubted whether the baroque could be squared with true religiosity and sacrality. The baroque was, after all, an art of effect, illusion, theatricality and easy emotions.[3] This position would be reiterated in the first issue of *L'Art sacré* under Regamey's successor, Augustin Maurice Cocagnac, a staunch supporter of Le Corbusier.[4] The theme of the issue was "Silence," and Cocagnac's lead essay opened with the section "Le baroque face au silence," in which he condemned the baroque's pomp and "clamor." True sacrality, Cocagnac contended, required the silence evocative of the apocalyptic visions of St. John: "le baroque devient mirage lorsqu'il ne respecte pas ce silence."[5] The essay's illustrations juxtaposed the interior of the Swabian baroque church of St. Martin with austere views of Romanesque country churches and details of the *Unité d'habitation* in Marseille. Le Corbusier was hailed for creating havens of silence from the very forms and artifacts of the machine age.[6] One year later, the chapel at Ronchamp would consecrate the exemplary role assigned to Le Corbusier in the progressive reform of religious art. Indeed, *L'art sacré* devoted an issue to the

Notre Dame du Haut immediately following its inauguration on 25 June 1955.[7] Cocagnac therein attacked those who mistook the forms of the Notre Dame for baroque, recalling his earlier condemnation of the baroque's "noisiness" in terms that would be echoed by Le Corbusier two years later in the preface quoted at the outset.[8]

Among progressive Catholics the apparently widespread labelling of Ronchamp as "baroque" landed on well-prepared soil. In their view it amounted to incorporating the chapel into the dark side, defending the pompous "style de St. Sulpice" for Catholic art against their propagation of Le Corbusier as a valid model for a new religious architecture.[9] The Catholic discussion will have fed into Le Corbusier's rage at the label baroque but another discussion must have played its role as well. "Baroque" also resonated with suspicions held by Le Corbusier's fellow architects as they reassessed the legacy of the master in the light of his later work, which seemed to deviate from the principles he had espoused in the 1920s. It is no accident that further in the same preface quoted above Le Corbusier recalls his six weeks spent studying the Parthenon as further proof of his being definitely not for the baroque. But the label evidently stuck, to the extent that in his valued overview *New French Architecture*, published in 1967, Maurice Besset devoted considerable energy to refuting Corbu's baroqueness. Le Corbusier's "Architecture of light," Besset argued, "has neither drama nor illusion, but simply the music of serenity," whereas "[b]aroque made light the principal actor in a wonderful theatrical performance, employing it to conceal the reality of forms, dimensions and materials, in order to give to space the dramatic tension to which the spectator was invited to respond."[10] Besset's apology is reminiscent of Cocagnac's musings on the same theme, all the more for referencing Le Corbusier's predilection for Cistercian architecture. But it is also entirely divorced from a religious agenda. Besset simply sought to straighten the record over the architect's formal repertory.

Whether labelling Le Corbusier "baroque" in the 1950s is indeed anything other than easy criticism inspired, for instance, by the omnipresent association of Oscar Niemeyer's work with Brazilian baroque, remains to be seen. But the vocal reactions of Le Corbusier, Cocagnac and Besset to the label suggest that such classification accrued different meanings according to the context in which it was received. Ten years after Le Corbusier's lash-out against the baroque, the critic and art historian Pierre Charpentrat (1922–77) published a short book that aimed to describe exactly these contexts, *Le mirage baroque* (1967). Probably without intending to the title recalls Cocagnac's invective against baroque illusionism ("le baroque devient mirage") and, indeed, one chapter addresses the issue that informed Cocagnac's apology of Ronchamp, namely the role of the baroque in contemporary debates about the reform of religious art and liturgy that would culminate with the Second Vatican Council (1962–65). On this topic, Charpentrat quoted from *Paris-Match* the musings of a French prelate: "My God, that a bomb or two fall on the Vatican so that some of that gilt is knocked to the ground."[11] With undisguised glee he remarks that the same baroque once deemed un-French had now become a stalwart of French conservatives, who eagerly assumed the mantle of the preservationist protecting the seventeenth- and eighteenth-century church interiors of which reformers sought to divest the Church.[12] At the same time he identified the deadlock that would ultimately condemn *L'Art sacré*. The emerging "aesthetics of nudity" of the 1960s, as Charpentrat termed them, would outflank the reformers of Christian art and eventually consign them to irrelevance.

In *Le mirage baroque* the debate on religious art is but one aspect of an expansive, at times ironic, but ultimately sympathetic analysis of what Charpentrat called the French infatuation with the baroque. Built on an array of uses of "baroque" culled from newspapers, magazine articles and novels, Charpentrat sought to understand what it meant for French post-war society to embrace with such gusto a notion that was no less slippery for its relatively recent coinage. As such *Le mirage baroque* reflected Charpentrat's own lifelong preoccupation with the theme. The first article in an issue of the journal *Critique* dedicated to Charpentrat's work, published a year after his death, was titled "In the Heart of the Baroque Adventure,"[13] an accolade that Charpentrat deserved not only on the strength of *Le mirage baroque*, parts of which had been road-tested in *Critique*, but also for his three books on the historical baroque: *Baroque. Italie et Europe central*, published in French in 1964 in the *Architecture Universelle* series of the Swiss publisher Office du Livre, and translated into English, German, Dutch, Italian and a number of other languages between 1964 and 1967; *L'art baroque*, a wide-ranging survey published by the Presses Universitaires de France in 1967; and *Du maître d'ouvrage au maître d'oeuvre*, a study of the seventeenth- and eighteenth-century religious architecture of southern Germany, published in 1974 in Pierre Francastel's series *Le Signe de l'art*. Between 1959 and 1976 Charpentrat wrote many articles for *Critique* as well as for the *Annales*, *La mercure de France*, the *Nouvelle revue française* and, indeed, the serial *Baroque*, published by the Centre international de synthèse du baroque in Montauban.

Despite the many translations made of his first book, Charpentrat's reception seems to have been confined largely to France, where his oeuvre is given a central place in the historiography of the seventeenth and eighteenth centuries. Still, an essay on the French reception of Wölfflin in which Jacques Thuillier discussed the work of the Swiss literary historian Jean Rousset and the historian Victor Tapié, whose work will be examined in some more detail below, while omitting to mention either Charpentrat or his teacher, Pierre Francastel, speaks clearly to their marginal position in French institutional art history.[14] But even in their warmest tributes historians of the baroque rarely take Charpentrat's sizeable corpus of architectural criticism into consideration, a division of minds well exemplified in the very title of the issue of *Critique* that commemorates his contribution to the field, which juxtaposes baroque and architecture.[15] That Charpentrat himself did not discuss contemporary architecture in *Le mirage baroque*, his best-known book, may well have contributed to this division.[16] Charpentrat's criticism also seems to have circulated at some distance from the architectural culture of the moment, while in *Critique* and other journals it rubbed shoulders with essays of Michel Foucault, Gilles Deleuze and Jacques Derrida, whose writings would nonetheless inform the architectural discourse of the 1980s in France and beyond.[17]

What has largely disappeared from view in the reception of Charpentrat's work is how academic art history and architectural criticism, an involvement with the present and an interest in the past, once worked together. Key to this endeavour was the baroque, both as an object of study and as a point of departure for historical and critical explorations. Charpentrat's work illuminates the possible meanings and uses of the baroque as an historical and a critical notion in post-war France and illustrates the intensity of the discussion on the baroque in that particular period. At the same time, Charpentrat's baroque affords us an oblique glance into French architectural culture of the 1960s, a time when, as Jean-Louis Cohen has argued, the chasm between architectural and intellectual culture was at its widest.[18] With a number of other contributors to *Critique* Charpentrat seems to have been one of the rare French intellectuals who seriously and consistently engaged with contemporary architecture in the decades before Gilles Deleuze's *Le pli* (1988) became required reading in schools of architecture. In so doing, Charpentrat made the "baroque" operative in the discussion about the course of post-war modernism. He, too, thought that Le Corbusier was baroque, but in a manner perhaps more sympathetic to the old master.

The French Baroque Adventure, An Introduction

On 30 March 1965 Pierre Charpentrat wrote to Jean Piel, the editor-in-chief of *Critique*, about his doubts concerning *Le mirage baroque*:

> I have the impression that the "fureur baroquisante" is diminishing. Is there a baroque? Am I the victim of an illusion of specialists, where everybody starts by agreeing on the fact that we can only answer this question in the negative? … I very much feel like making a small book that, without being a thesis, will not risk of being treated like an art book, as was the case with my *Baroque* of Freiburg, a perfect coffee table book.[19]

The starting point of his "small book" was an article published in *Critique* in 1964, "De quelques acceptations du mot 'baroque'." But between writing the article and the letter to Piel the situation seemed to have changed, and the "ère furieusement baroquisante" identified in the article was on the wane.[20] *Le mirage baroque* would offer a snapshot of a moment when "baroque" first acquired new – if still uncertain – meaning in the circles of specialists, only to become a buzzword applicable to every aspect of French culture, including such emblematic achievements as the *nouveau roman*.

Le mirage baroque characterizes this period as a break with earlier conceptions of the baroque. Even if most French readers could only acquaint themselves directly with the work of Heinrich Wölfflin in 1952, when his *Kunstgeschichtliche Grundbegriffe* first appeared in translation (*Renaissance und Barock* would follow in 1967), scholars in France had engaged with his work from early in the twentieth century onwards.[21] In pre-war France the baroque was mainly shaped by two highly critical readers of Wölfflin: Eugenio d'Ors and Henri Focillon.[22] In *La vie des formes* of 1934 Focillon had identified a baroque stage in the cycle of development of the living forms of art, the moment of degeneration after classicism.[23] Eugenio d'Ors's essay *Du baroque* of 1935 postulated a baroque entity, the eon, a "constant of culture" manifesting itself across time and space as the very principle of change and variation. As such, he opposed it to the eternal eon of the classical.[24] In Focillon and d'Ors "baroque" was a quality of forms neither confined to nor produced by a particular moment in history. D'Ors especially was vocally dismissive of the notion of an historical baroque. In 1931, at one of the *Décades* in Pontigny, he famously challenged those art historians wedded to an historical baroque – like Rudolf Wittkower – to argue how a window of the twelfth-century cloister of Tomar could *not* be termed baroque.[25]

The "new," post-Second World War baroque was initiated by a series of studies that Charpentrat reviewed and referenced in the essay "Les français devant le Baroque." He discussed, amongst others, Victor Tapié's *Baroque et classicisme* of 1957, the acts of the Congrès archéologique de France held in 1947 on the Swabian baroque and Pierre Moisy's book on French Jesuit churches predating the order's suppression. Together with these books Charpentrat's references – which also include the issue on the baroque that Tapié authored for the series *Que sais-je?* – testify to the lively interest in the baroque that Pierre Francastel, too, would signal in his own review of *Baroque et classicisme* for the *Annales*.[26] Likewise, Jean Rousset, in an essay written at the end of his life, would reminisce how he was

> involved, in the 1950s and 60s, in what was a collective discovery, perhaps one should say invention of a literary baroque in France; and this was the work of a post-war generation, prepared since the beginning of the century in the limited circles of art historians, mainly outside of France.[27]

Rousset's landmark study *La littérature de l'âge baroque en France. Circé et le paon* of 1953 indeed contributed much to this "invention," and it was successful to the extent that in his *Estétique du rococo* of 1959, the Belgian art historian Philippe Minguet could provide a detailed and critical account of the concept of the baroque, acknowledging its general acceptance as well as its protean guise.[28]

Taken together these publications convey the suggestion that the "settling" of the baroque in the French-speaking world implied a firm reassessment of the pre-war notion combined with an expansion in its field of action, from the visual arts to literature and back to the arts. The process that "baroque" underwent in France was similar to, and fed by, German and Anglophone discussions that emerged in, for instance, the important thematic issues of the *Journal of Aesthetics and Art Criticism*.[29] Still, it was Tapié's *Baroque et classicisme* that Charpentrat and others saw as a new departure.[30] Tapié approached the baroque as the product of a particular configuration of society and its economics. In his view, the baroque was the style that originated in Rome and became adopted in feudal societies where a small elite spent the wealth of the land on triumphant expressions of communal religion. Classicism emerged as its urban, sophisticated counterpart that reached its full development when Louis XIV institutionalized the teaching and production of art. Rather than considering classicism as the style succeeding and correcting the baroque, Tapié saw them as largely synchronous and competing trends within European culture.[31]

In his review Francastel welcomed Tapié's study as a valid alternative to Focillon and d'Ors because it addressed the most problematic aspect of their baroque, being its dissociation from a particular moment in history. His reading of the pre-war historiography of the baroque inflected his skepticism of a-historicist notions of style with a sense of urgency. In *L'histoire de l'art instrument de la propagande germanique* of 1945 Francastel had argued that the baroque underpinned the claim that Germany rather than France or Italy was the birthplace of civilization. Francastel saw "a menacing construction: idealist art, the art of movement, Protestant art, living art; all this becoming attached to a kind of entity, the baroque, and to a nebulous species, German genius."[32] Discussing in detail the exchange about the "life of forms" between Henri Focillon and Josef Strzygowski, in Francastel's view the most despicable exponent of the Germanic position, Francastel argued that Focillon's conception of the baroque was unable to undo the German claims that the baroque manifests "the constant push of their genius, the Nordic genius, in history" because it was itself based on similar premises. Those who postulated the primacy of the Germans simply reversed Focillon's valuation of the baroque and "decided that the baroque, the art of movement, art of life, was their genius, their art."[33] This usurpation of the baroque moved Francastel to dismiss an "eternal baroque," an idea he traced back to the seventeenth century in the writings of Giulio Mancini, through Giambattista Vico and Jules Michelet up to d'Ors and Focillon.

A second objection against the eternal baroque that Francastel shared with Tapié and which would feed directly into Charpentrat's work is that it casts the baroque as the negation of that stable and coherent system generally identified with classicism. In this view, baroque is that which escapes rules and exists by dint of the organic, the frivolous and the irrational. If art is a particular and to a certain extent self-sufficient form of knowledge articulated in a coherent system of concrete forms, as Francastel believed, then the category of the baroque, too, is valid only insofar as it describes a form of art with its proper rationality.

Conversely, Francastel was inimical to essentialist definitions of the baroque or classicism. This was his main qualm with Tapié's book, which he accused of ignoring the variegated *emergence* of the baroque across the world and over the course of three centuries in favour of a baroque produced in Rome in the first decades of the seventeenth century and then exported across the globe: "we do not accept them [baroque or classicism], we do not choose them as though choosing a piece of clothing or a horse."[34] "Baroque" is not a given that is embraced or rejected but a constellation of agencies pertaining to specific art works and their various settings. In Francastel's view art, as a particular form of knowledge, entered into a complicated yet by no means predetermined relation with its historical circumstances. The art historian endeavours to identify the dynamic between historical agents at work in the production of art and the agency of art itself upon its historical and geographical circumstances. This is well illustrated by Francastel's monumental *Les architectes célèbres* (1958), comprising two volumes in a series of very fine coffee table books on famous people. Since architecture, perhaps more than any other art, results from the intricate interplay between individual creativity, formal inventiveness and a wide range of societal factors, Francastel took as his starting point the problem of attaching authorship to buildings. As a result, much of his first volume was dedicated to architecture without architects. Along similar lines Francastel found baroque art inconceivable as the *product* of the Counter-Reformation Church. He argued the converse; that the institution had been obliged to accept artistic developments occurring beyond its control that drove toward forms of art that went far beyond the changes necessary for religious reform.[35]

Le mirage baroque

As indicated in Charpentrat's letter to Piel, by 1964 the baroque was no longer a matter of mere academic debate but had percolated into everyday discourse. Charpentrat endeavored to understand both why that had happened and what could be salvaged from the avalanche of baroque across contemporary French culture. *Le mirage baroque* accordingly proceeds in three stages. First, Charpentrat examined five myths through which the baroque entered French culture (one is the aforementioned baroque despised by progressive Catholics, another, the baroque as "art nègre"). The second part, which developed the article "De quelques acceptations du mot 'baroque'," took issue with what Charpentrat considered to be the predominantly literary approach to the baroque in France. Rousset's milestone *La littérature de l'âge baroque en France* sought assistance in the visual arts to define the literary baroque and in so doing encoded the art and architecture of the seventeenth century with the apparatus of literature. Charpentrat argued that this had instigated a formalist and idealist notion of the baroque.[36] Finally, Charpentrat once again examined the historical baroque and entered into an implicit dialogue with such contemporary art historians as Yves Bonnefoy, Georges Cattaui and Hervé Bazin who, like Wittkower in his contemporaneous *Art and Architecture in Italy 1600–1750*, presented an increasingly stable and unproblematic corpus of work of baroque art.[37] Charpentrat used the irreconcilable differences between Bernini and Borromini to argue against the baroque as a unified and coherent phenomenon. In so doing he criticized Bonnefoy who, in his review of Charpentrat's first book, had treated those same two artists as composing a Janus-faced yet coherent baroque that would collapse with the emergence of rococo.[38]

Charpentrat opposed the increasing establishment of the baroque as a fixed corpus of art works not only on the basis of historical knowledge but also because, in his view, the baroque is never entirely historical. In the first section of the book Charpentrat assigned special importance to two related post-war phenomena. First, he describes the discovery of Southern Germany by the French troops stationed there after the 1945 armistice and the emergence of modern tourism. He conjures up an image of disciplined groups of wide-eyed French officers wandering around the churches of Swabia and Bavaria, trying to make sense of what they saw there. The acquaintance of the French with a hitherto barely known Germany was not simply an artistic, nor even an historical matter. Right after the war the venerable Société archéologique de France organized two annual conferences on the baroque of Southern Germany under the auspices of the supreme French commander of the region, with the explicit aim of demonstrating the renewed cultural and political relations between France and Southern Germany.[39] Baroque Germany promoted this rapprochement, Charpentrat argued, because it conveyed the image of a prelapsarian past, recalling a Europe that predated the recent trauma of the war.[40]

Charpentrat is careful to emphasize that this appraisal of the Southern German baroque is rooted in lived experience.[41] Baroque churches trigger irenic fantasies about Germany when this particular past is encountered in the present, but not when it is read as the historical representation of a mentality or a culture. "Baroque" no longer reorganizes history in the service of ideology, as Francastel bemoaned, but is a discovery enabled by the new conditions of the post-war era wherein traditional prejudices spawned by nationalism and cultural elitism had evaporated. The intrusion of the baroque into French culture is not due to idealist or academic conceptions of an historical era but rather to the tourist experience of a French middle class that had forgotten about Montaigne or Montesquieu when walking the streets of Rome but which in fact relishes the guilty pleasure of an art that is vaguely familiar yet fundamentally strange.

Le mirage baroque illustrates this process with Michel Butor's novel *La modification*, first published in 1957. This *nouveau roman* relates the ruminations of Léon Delmont over the course of a surreptitious journey by night train from his hometown of Paris to Rome, where he intends to surprise his mistress – Cécile, a French woman working for the embassy – with his decision to leave his wife and family. Charpentrat seizes upon the role that Butor assigned to baroque Rome in the narrative.[42] When Léon, a regular visitor to Rome, met Cécile, their first walk together was devoted to Francesco Borromini. The baroque continues to provide the backdrop of their romance, a tempting alternative to the well-known sights and histories of the Urbs. The novel emphasizes that Léon had been unable to conjure up the well-established historical narratives for his Catholic wife when they were together in Rome, based on the humanist myth of the Eternal City; Léon's affair allowed him to construct another Rome with a different historical and ideological relation to Paris. The transformation of the protagonist thus exemplifies the French attitude towards the baroque that Charpentrat seeks to examine, and his reflections in *Le mirage baroque* resonate closely with the intentions of Butor, who was himself another *Critique* stalwart.[43] In notes to the Chinese edition of *La Modification* Butor marks the baroque as a central feature of his novel. As he explained to his future non-Western readership, the baroque bears witness to revolutionary transformations in society on a par with those traversing their own world in that moment. Baroque Rome embodies the ability of the Catholic Church and its Papal See to convey order in the face of instability.[44]

Like Charpentrat, Butor thus advances the propensity of the baroque to combine a sense of history and order with the acknowledgment of its disruption. In so doing it creates a new historical experience wherein the tourist becomes a manifestation of the historian and the historian is always to some extent a marvelling visitor. Historiography is thus tinged with a lived nostalgia that carries the baroque from the realm of art history deep into that of popular culture.[45] It comes as no surprise, then, that the meaning of the notion remains elusive; Duke Ellington, too, can be baroque.[46] But its wide dissemination suggests that a culture like that of post-war France *required* the baroque both as an historical phenomenon and as a descriptor of its experiences in order to reposition itself both historically and intellectually – just as at other moments it would avail itself of "romanticism" or "mannerism." Far from being a-historical the baroque signifies the irruption of one particular moment of history into another, a process that generates myths detached from history itself as well as historical concepts and insights that can operate in contemporary criticism and historiography. As Charpentrat writes: "The baroque: attribute, as it has been sometimes said, of culture in eras of transition? No – but of the slightly terrified look that an era of transition may cast on culture."[47]

As a consequence, whether objects or ideas are baroque is as much a matter of how they are perceived as of what they are.[48] Throughout his oeuvre Charpentrat emphasized that the devices conditioning how we see history are intrinsic to the formation and meaning of the critical categories we use to organize it. In his review of Claude Roy's *Arts baroques* (1963) Charpentrat criticizes how the photographs emphasize the voluptuous and capricious fragment, privileging a decorative and frivolous baroque in much the same way as other modes of photography fostered the image of a pure and disembodied modernism.[49] Conversely, an influential article on the *trompe-l'oeil* argues against the idea that baroque illusionism should be understood as a form of trickery.[50] Charpentrat quite rightly states that no one ever believed that what an illusionistic painting shows is real. The device of illusionism aims, instead, to signal a Presence, something that is other than images or ideas that are not subjected to the same regime of representation; it is a technique to differentiate certain representations from others. Similarly, in an essay for the journal *Traverses* on "Maquillage" – on the heels of Paul Virilio's essay on camouflage and a French translation of Adolf Loos's "Ornament and Crime" – Charpentrat reads the application of colour and stucco statues of female saints in baroque church interiors not as naive attempts at a seductive naturalism but rather as a register of representation directing the viewer to mark them as, literally, other-worldly.[51] Like the *trompe-l'oeil*, this interior decoration is not an all too transparent lie but a truth of its own making.

Charpentrat thus carefully and persistently recalibrates the baroque as an ambiguous image that is neither a lie nor an illusion but instead a persistent challenge. (The conclusion of *Le mirage baroque* likens "baroque" to the Far West.) He rejects the suspicions of progressive Catholics and champions of the Enlightenment concerning the sincerity and rationality of the baroque, while walking the tightrope between the all too general and purely formal baroque instigated by Eugenio d'Ors and the flattened stylistic label upon which art history had come to settle – two extremes each divorcing the baroque from its religious and political content. Strange as it may appear to be, Charpentrat argues, the baroque is a rational system tied to specific convictions and agendas. It is neither a delusion nor an aberration; and while historical and geographical delineations allow for an acceptable working definition of the baroque, it may always be found where it is least expected.

Baroque Functionalism

The irreducible strangeness of an enticing presence that is never entirely desirable or understandable turns the baroque into a perfect foil for modern architecture in post-war France. Charpentrat suggests as much in his letter to Piel as he assured his editor that he was working on his essay "De l'abus de la méthode en architecture," a criticism of the taboo-ridden attitude towards contemporary architecture in France on the part of both architects and the public.[52] This article would parallel an essay about the ambivalent position of the French towards the baroque, "Les français face au baroque," which contained the remark that the public was equally eager to associate the forms of the baroque and of contemporary architecture with meanings that were not necessarily flattering.[53] The dysfunctional attitude of French society towards modern architecture tracks the French appreciation of the baroque and rests on similar hidden preoccupations.

By drawing this parallel Charpentrat proposed an intellectual approach of contemporary architecture in what was otherwise a rather desolate critical landscape. As noted above, Cohen identified the 1960s as the moment in which architectural culture was at the greatest remove from other discourses. After the Second World War modernism had become accommodated in a state-led building enterprise that called less for intellectual reflection on the architect's part than an increasing assimilation of engineering and construction practices into architectural design.[54] Architects consequently disengaged from intellectual culture, which in turn reciprocated its lack of comprehension. Cohen admittedly pays limited attention to the lively discussion on sacred architecture evoked at the outset or the regular contributions on architecture in the journals in which Charpentrat published by such authors as Françoise Choay, Paul Virilio or Hubert Damisch. But the fact remains that together with Pierre Francastel they were among the few intellectuals who addressed contemporary architecture.[55] Cohen sees this mutual inability for exchange reflected in the thematic issues on architecture and urbanism published by *Esprit* (1969) and *Critique* (1973) in the wake of May 1968, where sociological, political and economic considerations engulfed any claim on architecture's disciplinarity or artistic identity.[56] In his own review of the same issue of *Esprit*, published in *Critique* in 1970 under the title "Architecture et politique," Charpentrat saw matters differently.[57] The problem was not that commissioners – the state and its functionaries – do not understand the architect and his art; patrons have never collaborated with their designers. Rather, the contemporary processes involved in designing and realizing buildings no longer instigates the necessarily conflictual exchange between the various parties involved in a project that has always characterized architecture. Creating these opportunities is the real political mission of architecture, not reforming the building administration or adopting sociological models when designing housing. Francastel's influence on this argument is as obvious as the theme that emerges from all Charpentrat's writings on architecture: architecture is an autonomous art form existing within the complex interplay of forces that produce buildings.

Charpentrat develops this point in many of his writings, where he forges a powerful tool from the historical coincidence of the French "fureur baroquisante" and the crisis of contemporary architecture.[58] The baroque not only shares its peculiar place in French culture with post-war modernism – it is also modernism's foremost example. Writing in "Remarques sur la structure de l'espace baroque" (1961), Charpentrat attempted to seize the essential features of baroque architectural space and concluded: "the assassins of the baroque have killed architecture for 150 years, and it is only today that space, barely contained by glass and concrete, will live again in the harmony of mankind and the world."[59] The periodization is important, as it connects modernism with neo-classicism. Well aware that Emil Kaufmann rooted modernism in the neo-classicist purging of baroque and rococo ornamentation, Charpentrat constructed a counter-history wherein neo-classicism is not a corrective to the baroque but rather its monumental and urban fulfilment.[60] As a consequence, baroque, neo-classicism and modernism are all opposites of classicism, a design system that exists by dint of the pure application of formal principles. Elsewhere Charpentrat noted that those countries with the strongest classicist traditions (like France) had been most reluctant to embrace modernism, precisely because of their entrenched academism. Baroque and modernism alike engage with the novelty required by the demands of societies undergoing change.[61]

This parentage does not call for formal emulation – quite the contrary. In a passage from the "De quelques acceptations du mot 'baroque'" that did not survive into *Le mirage baroque*, Charpentrat berated those who cast the baroque as the antithesis of functionalism, as in their invocation of it in the criticism (or admiration) for the late work of Le Corbusier. According to such a simplistic view, "baroque" is mere style, that which escapes necessity. As Charpentrat ironically has it:

> Let us not attempt to isolate, among other "styles" in contemporary architecture, a *baroque style*: there is, actually, no style but baroque. It is not a matter of curves or tangles, nor even of treatment of space: building is a science, and a building should make sociological laws concrete; all the rest, whether one revels in it or bans it, is baroque.[62]

In his view, the real and valuable "baroqueness" of architecture resides in the exact opposite of superfluous excess: functionalism. In an essay devoted to the analogy between the baroque and modernism Charpentrat writes that "the baroque invented, or resuscitated, functionalism."[63] Functionalism is the ability of buildings to address what Charpentrat calls programme, the set of not necessarily coherent demands made of them by a patron or society. In the opening pages of *Du maître d'ouvrage au maître d'oeuvre* Charpentrat develops this view in detail, stressing how the religious architecture of Southern Germany can only be understood by means of a meticulously close reading of its buildings that would seek to reveal how their every aspect interacts with the demands and requirements of sophisticated patrons.[64] He writes, for instance, of the programme of a pilgrimage church as being to mediate the contradictory requirements of housing and protecting a small miraculous object while broadcasting its presence and accommodating ever-increasing throngs of worshippers eager to enter into contact with that very object. Architectural form is as much the instrument as the agent of this mediation. In the footsteps of Francastel Charpentrat refuses to see architecture – be it historical or contemporary – as the three-dimensional translation of a series of demands, but rather considers it as a practice concerned with concrete form shaped by knowledge and creativity. In the encounter between architecture and society surfaces the programme and, along with it, true functionalism.[65]

As functionalism shapes, in this sense, both the baroque and the modern, in both the baroque and the modern era it is architecture that imposes an order onto the city, not urbanism: "architecture itself creates its own order. Each building, because of its destination and structure, implies a situation."[66] Charpentrat attaches great importance to this form of architectural agency; in fact, his appraisal of the baroque as the model of a functionalist architectural order gives Charpentrat the leverage to criticize recent developments in architecture that seem to forego modernism's prerogatives. Reviewing the exhibition *Structures mathématiques – architecture contemporaine* at the Palais de la découverte – which showed the work of, amongst others, Frei Otto, Zygmunt Makoswki and Giò Ponti, and opened with an image of Guarini's dome of San Lorenzo in Turin – Charpentrat lamented that contemporary architects were reluctant to embrace the new possibilities of "giving form:" "while [contemporary architecture] wants to introduce an order into the world, it is paralysed by the idea that this order can be *invented*."[67] In a review of the proceedings of the CIAM meeting at Otterlo in 1959 Charpentrat discovers a new generation of architects paralysed by the ambivalent success of modernism, omnipresent as an architectural idiom yet utterly incapable of achieving its main goal of building a better world. He shares their disappointment but believes that their criticism misses its mark, sensing a creeping conservatism and a reluctance to employ architecture to its full capacity. In a rather scathing description of Aldo Van Eyck's Burgerweeshuis in Amsterdam Charpentrat conveys its overall lack of form. While still rooted in the modernist paradigm, the building dissolves into a series of accidents that have nothing to do with architecture, but everything to do with psychology.[68] What Charpentrat found particularly hard to stomach, though, is the persistent criticism of Le Corbusier:

> one of these "forty year old architects" who took part in the discussions at Otterlo recently accused [Le Corbusier] of languishing in formalism. And, so as to make his case impervious to appeal, he added: "a baroque formalism." He was thinking of La Tourette, but in fact condemned the entire oeuvre.[69]

In Charpentrat's view this attitude towards Le Corbusier is yet another instance of a younger generation's anxiety in the face of formal invention rooted in an individual's artistic practice. This young architect may have been right to call Le Corbusier baroque, but he did not understand what it means to be so.

Author's Note

I am indebted to Véronique Patteeuw for directing me to literature on the French architectural debate of the 1960s. All translations are mine.

Endnotes

1   Le Corbusier, *The Chapel at Ronchamp*, n.p.
2   Le Corbusier, *The Chapel at Ronchamp*, n.p.
3   Roque, "La signification du baroque"; Regamey, "Notes sur le baroque." The two essays constitute a section on the baroque, introduced as follows: "Les Français se méfient du baroque. Le mot est souvent pris en mauvais part. Il semble au moins évoquer quelque chose de peu sérieux qui ne s'accorde pas aux exigences du culte. *La Maison-Dieu* voudrait, non pas réhabiliter un style qui a ses lettres de noblesse, mais mettre en lumière les problèmes de spiritualité, de théologie, d'esthétique religieuse éveillés par cette manifestation, un peu surprenante pour des gens trop raisonnables, d'un christianisme exubérant et ingénu. On verra vite, en lisant ces études, qu'il s'agit de bien autre chose que d'histoire d'art."
4   See Caussé, *La revue* l'Art Sacré, 197.
5   Cocagnac, "Le baroque face au silence," 11, compare with Regamey, "Notes sur le baroque," 156–9 and esp. 163, where true religious silence is opposed to the "étourdissement" of baroque works such as the vault of the St. Ignatius in Rome.
6   Cocagnac, "Le baroque face au silence," 18.
7   Cocagnac thus respected the embargo that Le Corbusier referred to when he wrote that certain journalists "broke the rules." See Caussé, *La revue* l'Art Sacré, 404–5.
8   Cocagnac, "Editorial," 8–9: "Notre-Dame du Haut a un secret: elle le révèle à ceux qui acceptent de faire un effort pour s'en emparer. C'est pourquoi, malgré ce qu'on a pu en dire, Ronchamp n'est pas une oeuvre baroque. On a pu se laisser prendre à des ressemblances superficielles et confondre l'inspiration des Autrichiens ou des Espagnols avec celle de Ronchamp; en fait, profondément, Le Corbusier et Le Borromini divergent. Au génie du décor, au goût des Apocalypses bruyantes et des gloires, aux réussites trop habiles, Le Corbusier oppose la simplicité de son regard. Son architecture n'a pas de façade et d'enfilades perspectives: elle n'est pas faite pour l'oeil d'un homme assis mais pour l'enveloppement d'une foule qu'elle attire ou contient pour l'enlever d'un coup d'aile. Le lyrisme est pur de toute effervescence baroque, c'est l'expression calme d'un fécondité inépuisable. Une trouvaille plastique répond à une autre. Le regard est affranchi, ne considère que la fonction spirituelle. Le métier, parfaitement possédé, demeure à son service."

9   The group around *L'Art sacré* had limited yet decisive influence in securing the commission of Ronchamp for Le Corbusier. See Caussé, *La revue* l'Art Sacré, 404–407. Cocagnac would publish a book on Le Corbusier in 1967.

10   Besset, *New French Architecture*, 28, 32.

11   Charpentrat, *Le mirage baroque*, 50: "Mon Dieu, faites qu'une bombe ou deux tombent sur le Vatican, qu'on flanque un peu de cette dorure par terre." Charpentrat would use the same quote in "L'architecture du diable," 21.

12   See also Minguet, *Esthétique du rococo*, 96–7.

13   The issue was entitled *Pierre Charpentrat. Le baroque et l'architecture*, and contained a bibliography of Charpentrat's writings (568–71) as well as essays by Jean Rousset, Louis Marin, Georges Raillard, Marc Le Bot, Jacques Le Goff and André Miquel.

14   Thuillier, "Wölfflin et la France," 24–7. Francastel's "sociologie de l'art" was an attempt to frame the historical study of art in the humanities as well as the sciences in a way that differed markedly from the *Kunstwissenschaft*. See Francastel, "Spécificités de l'histoire de l'art." Charpentrat was a functionary of the French Ministery of Education and would become an assistent of Pierre Francastel at the Ecole Pratique des Hautes Etudes. See "Pierre Charpentrat n'est plus;" Raillard, "Charpentrat, Pierre."

15   For instance, le Bot, in "L'architecture: raisons et deraisons," reads Charpentrat's coupling of "baroque" and "functionalism" in a purely conceptual key and not as an intellectual engagement with two historical periods. Jean-Pierre Martinon's incisive analysis of Charpentrat's work on the historical baroque, "Pierre Charpentrat et la question du fonctionnalisme baroque," does not deal with Charpentrat's writings on contemporary architecture.

16   The article that formed the basis for the second part of *Le mirage baroque* did discuss the uses of baroque in contemporary architectural criticism, see note 62 below.

17   Charpentrat, "Résidez: nous ferons le reste," is dedicated to Roland Barthes.

18   Cohen, *La coupure entre architectes et intellectuels*.

19   Quoted from Patron, *Critique. Une encyclopédie*, 92.

20   Charpentrat, "Quelques acceptations du mot 'baroque'," 651.

21   Borissavlievitch, *Les théories de l'architecture*; Levy, *Henri Wölfflin*.

22   Minguet, *Esthétique du rococo*, 65, reads Wölfflin as the source of Focillon and d'Ors, as Francastel and Charpentrat would.

23   Focillon, *La vie des formes*, 16–17, 21–2; see also Hills, "The Baroque," 22–3. Thuillier, "Wölfflin et la France," 21–2. Thuillier, "La *Vie des formes*," 87 and note 31, quotes a letter from Focillon to Georges Opresco: "Il me faut la peau de Wölfflin pour décorer mon cabinet de travail."

24   For an efficient exposition of d'Ors's baroque, see Lambert, *The Return of the Baroque*, 41–8.

25   Thuillier, "Wölfflin et la France," 20–21.

26   Francastel, "Baroque et classicisme: histoire ou typologie des civilisations?" 142; Francastel, "Baroque et classique: une civilisation," 207.

27   Rousset, "Mon baroque," 49: "… mêlé, dans les années 50 et 60, à ce qui fut une découverte collective, faut-il dire même l'invention d'un baroque littéraire en France; ce fut le travail d'une génération d'après-guerre, preparé dès le début du siècle dans les cercles restreints d'historiens de l'art, surtout hors de France."

28   Minguet, *Esthétique du rococo*, 15–121.

29   See Minguet, *Esthétique du rococo*, 25, 66, 84, 91, 113–14.

30   Tapié returned the compliment to Charpentrat in the preface to the 2nd edition, see Tapié, *Baroque et classicisme*, 45.

31   Tapié, *Baroque et classicisme*, 171–92 and 254–79.

32   Francastel, *L'histoire de l'art instrument de la propagande germanique*, 238: "… une menaçante construction: art idéaliste, art du mouvement, art protestant, art vivant; tout cela allant se rattacher à une espèce d'entité, le baroque, et à une espèce de nébuleuse, le génie allemand."

33   Francastel, *L'histoire de l'art instrument de la propagande germanique*, 244.

34   Francastel, "Baroque et classicisme: histoire ou typologie des civilisations?" 150.

35   Dufrêne, "Lire Francastel aujourd'hui: un historien de l'expérience artistique," 8.

36   Charpentrat, *Le mirage baroque*, esp. 73–8.

37   See Bazin, *Baroque, classique et rococo*. The introduction of Cattaui, *Baroque et rococo*, 7–19, develops an eponymous essay first published in *Critique* (1957). In *Le mirage baroque*, Charpentrat mainly employs the captions of the illustrations to challenge Bazin or Wittkower.

38 Bonnefoy, "Pierre Charpentrat et l'architecture baroque," 1002–5; Charpentrat, *Le mirage baroque*, 145–57. See also Bonnefoy, *Rome, 1630*, 78–84.

39 Reviewed by Charpentrat in "Les français devant le Baroque."

40 Charpentrat, *Le mirage baroque*, 38–46.

41 Charpentrat first tested the hypothesis that the baroque comes to life in an individual experience enhanced by historical circumstances in his study of Baudelaire's reaction to the Belgian baroque, "Baudelaire et le baroque."

42 Charpentrat, *Le mirage baroque*, 32–7.

43 See also Charpentrat, *Le mirage baroque*, 105–6, and Charpentrat, "Quelques acceptations du mot 'baroque'," 663.

44 Butor, *Improvisations sur Michel Butor*, 97–9. See Raillard, "De quelques éléments baroques," 190–92; and Duffy, "Art, Architecture, and Catholicism," 46–60.

45 Jouhaud, *Sauver le Grand-Siècle*, 220–32 and esp. 229–31.

46 Charpentrat, "Quelques acceptations du mot 'baroque'," 652, 659; Charpentrat, *Le mirage baroque*, 98.

47 Charpentrat, *Le mirage baroque*, 128: "Le baroque, attribut, comme on l'a dit parfois, de la culture des époques de transition? Non – mais du regard un peu affolé qu'une époque de transition peut jeter sur la culture." Note the reference to mannerism on 126. See also 179.

48 See Charpentrat, "Relecture de Wölfflin," esp. 39–41.

49 Charpentrat, "Le baroque, ou l'art des autres"; see also Charpentrat's criticism of Hitchcock's *Rococo Architecture in Southern Germany* (1968) in "L'architecture baroque et ses usagers," 1000.

50 Charpentrat, "Le trompe l'oeil." See Marin, "Représentation et simulacra."

51 Charpentrat, "L'architecture du diable," 23: "Ces pseudo-personnages, si prestement résorbés dans un ciel imaginaire, matérialisent (si l'on peut dire) une fonction." And 26: "Le travail de maquillage ne garde son intérêt que si l'on en perçoit après coup le subtil cheminement et, du fait qu'il n'est jamais gratuit, la signification spécifique et la justification fonctionelle précise."

52 Patron, *Critique*, 92. Charpentrat, "De l'abus de la méthode en architecture."

53 Charpentrat, "Les français devant le Baroque," 1067.

54 Cohen, *La coupure entre architectes et intellectuels*, 38–44; see also Le Dantec, *Architecture en France*, 9–34.

55 Cohen, *La coupure entre architectes et intellectuels*, 62–8.

56 Cohen, *La coupure entre architectes et intellectuels*, 48–9. Charpentrat did not contribute to this issue of *Critique*.

57 Charpentrat, "Architecture et politique."

58 le Bot, "L'architecture: raisons et deraisons," 553. This essay is emblematic of the distance between the intellectual profile of a journal like *Critique* and the milieu of contemporary architecture. No mention is made of the current state of the discipline of architecture in France, a key issue in Charpentrat's criticism.

59 Charpentrat, "Remarques sur la structure de l'espace baroque," 230.

60 Charpentrat's "L'architecture au Siècle des Lumières" is a review of Kaufmann's eponymous book of 1963, with another reference to the contemporary criticism of Le Corbusier on 465. See also Charpentrat, "Fonction, fonctionnel et fonctionnalisme en architecture"; Charpentrat, "Relecture de Wölfflin," 38; and Charpentrat, *Le mirage baroque*, 140–44.

61 Charpentrat, "L'architecture contemporaine: au dela du baroque?" 459.

62 Charpentrat, "Quelques acceptations du mot 'baroque'," 652, 660–61: "Ne cherchons pas à isoler, parmi d'autres 'styles' de l'architecture contemporaine, un *style baroque*: Il n'y a, au fond, de style que baroque. Il n'est question ni de courbures ni d'enchevêtrements, ni même de traitement de l'espace: bâtir est une science, un édifice doit concrétiser des lois sociologiques; tout le reste, qu'on le savoure ou qu'on le proscrive, est baroque." Charpentrat, "Les français devant le Baroque," 1062 refers to Christ, *Projets et divagations de Claude-Nicolas Ledoux*, 14.

63 Charpentrat, "L'architecture contemporaine: au delà du baroque?" 458.

64 Charpentrat, *Du maître d'ouvrage au maître d'œuvre*, 1–18, esp. 14 ("le *programme* ne se confond pas avec une liste de fonctions"), 18. See Martinon, "Pierre Charpentrat et la question du fonctionnalisme baroque."

65 See Charpentrat's *in memoriam* of Francastel, "Pierre Francastel" (1135) for a comment on Francastel's treatment of the church building as a "programme." This essay illustrates the close corrolations between Charpentrat's and Francastel's thinking. On Charpentrat's notion of the programme, see also "L'architecture baroque et ses usagers," 1005; Charpentrat, "L'architecture et son public. Les églises de la Contre-Réforme," 93.

66 Charpentrat, "L'architecture contemporaine," 461; also Charpentrat, "À propos de l'architecture des années 60," 319.

67 Charpentrat, "À propos de l'architecture des années 60," 312.

68 Charpentrat, "Crise de l'architecture moderne?" 1087. See also Charpentrat, "L'urbanisme ou les reveries d'un arpenteur solitaire," 662: "Aimons la Ville sans introduire parmi nous, blottis au creaux d'effigies faussement propitiatoires, camouflés par des mythes comme le core."

69 Charpentrat, "Crise de l'architecture moderne?" 1087–8. Charpentrat perhaps refers to the backhanded elogy of Le Corbusier offered by Giancarlo de Carlo. See Newman (ed.), *Ciam '59 in Otterlo*, 83–6.

Chapter 15

From Spatial Feeling to Functionalist Design: Contrasting Representations of the Baroque in Steen Eiler Rasmussen's *Experiencing Architecture*

Anthony Raynsford

In the fall of 1953 a 55-year-old professor of architecture, named Steen Eiler Rasmussen, arrived as a visitor to MIT's School of Architecture and Planning, where he gave a series of public lectures under the title "Experiencing Architecture."[1] Drawing large crowds of architecture students intrigued by his vividly sensory, especially tactile, accounts of historical and modern architecture, these lectures formed the basic outline for his well-known book of 1959, *Experiencing Architecture*, first published in Danish in 1957 as *Om at Opleve Arkitektur*. While *Experiencing Architecture* has become an international classic in architectural pedagogy, few have considered its role in reorienting the architectural historiography of baroque "space." In fact, the book constructed an entire set of experiences around the baroque, both narrowly and broadly understood, that profoundly countered the dominant, largely de-materialized and spatial account of the baroque within modernist architectural discourse. *Experiencing Architecture*, in fact, drew on much of the same baroque pedigree as Sigfried Giedion's *Space, Time and Architecture* (1941), including Heinrich Wölfflin's historical hermeneutics and Albert Erich Brinckmann's empathetic accounts of "plasticity" and "space" (*Plastik und Raum*, 1922). It invoked these categories, however, not to construct a teleology from an imagined baroque synthesis to a modernist "space-time," but rather to relativize and de-mystify these categories, both within seventeenth-century European architecture and within an open-ended set of modernist "experiences." The buildings and piazzas of Roman baroque "space," in all their tactile and theatrical materiality, become for Rasmussen the subtle foil for the alternative aesthetic experience of such cities as Delft. By de-mystifying the perceptual psychology of "spatial feeling" that had surrounded the Roman baroque and by contrasting Rome with the very different cities of the northern baroque, Rasmussen's work opened up a pragmatic and empirical understanding of seventeenth-century European architecture that aimed, simultaneously, to de-mystify architectural modernism.

Symptomatic of this new orientation to the baroque was a passage from the introduction to *Experiencing Architecture* in which Rasmussen employed the example of Carlo Rainaldi's seventeenth-century façade and piazza for Santa Maria Maggiore in Rome. In a passage that seems outrageously naïve and ahistorical, Rasmussen explained the aesthetic experience of the piazza through the medium of children's games. Recalling an observation while on a 1952 study trip to that city, he described a group of school children playing a ball game against the massive, curving wall of the stone-clad apse, perched over a set of semi-circular travertine steps that led, in turn, down to the piazza below with its obelisk. The ball became a tactile prosthesis for discovering not only the shape but also the stoniness of the travertine mass. Through the instrument of the ball and the sensations of their own bodies, they extended themselves into the very material of the space, sensing the hardness of the wall, and "quite unconsciously they experienced certain basic elements of architecture: the horizontal planes and the vertical walls above the slopes. And they learned to play on these elements."[2] Merely watching the game, Rasmussen claimed, caused him to experience the entire urban space in a new way. This account was also a new way of describing the experience of Rome, not from the centres of its monumental piazzas, but from the intimate point-of-view of exploring some of its texture on the back side of one of its churches. Experiencing this piece of Rome meant grasping its thing-like quality through a synthesis of the different senses: visual, tactile, acoustic, and also kinaesthetic, without reducing any of these elements to "space."

The seemingly willful naïveté and a-historicism of Rasmussen's account emerged, in fact, out of a gradual re-reading and revision of early twentieth-century German art historical accounts of baroque space that still continued to dominate into the middle of the twentieth century. Rasmussen deliberately grounded this empathetic experience in the materiality of Roman construction methods by substituting in English the word "cavity" for the more commonly used word "space," which by the 1950s had taken on increasingly vague but also highly abstract and polemical significations. As Rasmussen explained, "cavity" came closer than "space" to the original German sense of *Raumgefühl*, or feeling of spatial enclosure. To contextualize Rasmussen's tactile, embodied account of the Roman piazza, it is important to recall the kinds of vague abstractions that dominated the discourses of space and "spatial feeling" in many post-war modernist accounts of baroque architecture and urbanism. It is also important to recall the degree to which historians in the German tradition had tried to draw a direct genealogy between an abstractly conceived baroque space and the European modernist architecture of the 1920s. Most famously, in his *Space, Time and Architecture* of 1941, Giedion placed the baroque city at the centre of his narrative of modernist space, which then became a continuation of the baroque on a higher plane:

> The distinguishing mark of the baroque age is the method of thinking and of feeling that prevails in it; its outstanding feature is the development of a specific kind of universality. In our field, this manifests itself as a new power to mold space, and to produce an astonishing and unified form from the most various parts.[3]

With this passage, Giedion explained one of his major historical theses: that modern architecture and city planning was approaching a new universal synthesis parallel to that of the European baroque. It was a synthesis, not only between art and science, but also among different parts of the city into a unified "space conception," which Giedion compared with that of modern artists.

Given this image of modernism, Giedion's claim that the baroque anticipated a certain kind of modern spatial experience depended to a large extent on the imprecision of what the term "space" actually signified in this context. Juxtaposing Giuseppe Valadier's late baroque design of the Piazza del Popolo in Rome with a neo-plasticist drawing of 1920 by the Dutch artist Theo Van Doesburg, Giedion described the spatial effects of the piazza in modernist terms: "In the Piazza del Popolo, Valadier embodies a hovering sensation in the total effect produced by his design by bringing into relation with each other two horizontal areas of different levels: the terrace on the Pincino and the *piazza* proper."[4] With this particular comparison, Giedion intended to demonstrate "the relation between horizontal and vertical surfaces as a basis for aesthetic responses of a special sort."[5] This formalizing abstraction, equating the aesthetic response within an urban space to that of viewing an axonometric line drawing of non-representational planes, was a further attempt to demonstrate how "spatial feeling" might traverse different modes of representation. Its believability also depended, however, on a certain vagueness of analogy, which was meant to prefigure an even more vague and abstract analogy with the Einsteinian physics of space-time.

For Rasmussen, by contrast, the baroque sense of spatial feeling was a specific material and artistic technique that could be uncovered and reproduced through observation. Thus, the stony niches, piazzas and interiors of the Italian baroque were, in no sense, to be conflated with the transparent, floating planes of the Dessau Bauhaus, and even less with a drawing by Theo van Doesburg. In *Experiencing Architecture*, baroque Rome would be assimilated to the needs of modern architecture, neither in terms of the grandiose totalization of Giedion's space-time, nor in terms of the spectacle of monumentality, but rather as elements in a palette for the everyday dwelling places, offices and stores of the post-war welfare state, whose social and symbolic formation seemed to Rasmussen to be completely opposed to the ceremonial and hierarchical formations of baroque Italy. No longer would a vague idea of baroque space be able to stand in for an almost infinite variety of visual and intellectual phenomena. It would be brought down to concrete techniques of architectural material, form and illusionism.

The modern children's ball game against the baroque apse of Santa Maria Maggiore, thus, was a kind of parable for the modernist appropriation of architectural history. To play on the surfaces of baroque Rome meant to learn to experience its "thingness," to feel its forms empathetically, and to mentally master its specific elements, not thereby to recapitulate the baroque but to understand how it worked, to unpack it experientially. To be useful for modern architects, however, such principles could not be understood through abstract historical knowledge alone. They had to be experienced directly. One had to learn to play on architecture as upon a musical instrument: "Architecture is not created by knowledge, but by experience, and only by making the tones of this instrument familiar, hearing them within oneself, can one learn to play it."[6] This idea that modern architects and architecture students were out of touch with experience and that they need to learn essential principles of architectural aesthetics by, for example, encountering the forms of baroque buildings, was not in itself a new idea. It was, in fact, a reinvention and expansion of a certain strain of German art historiography of the baroque in which the baroque had been seen to embody aesthetic principles that had become lost or debased over the course of the nineteenth century. This historiography, moreover, had been the common root of both Rasmussen's and Giedion's ultimately opposing interpretations of the baroque and its relevance to modernism.

Diverging Receptions of Baroque Historiography

For both Rasmussen and Giedion, the historiography of the baroque had been instrumental in shaping their interpretations of contemporary architecture in the 1920s but with very different results. For Rasmussen the discourses on baroque aesthetics did not imply any abstract parallel with twentieth-century modernism as a whole. Rather it had served as the concrete and self-conscious theory for a very specific moment in early twentieth-century architecture that had quickly again faded away. Even while still a student at the Royal Danish Academy during the First World War, Rasmussen had come under the influence of the German art historian Albert Erich Brinckmann, known for his teachings on baroque architecture and urbanism. Brinckmann's 1912 book, *Platz und Monument* (Square and Monument), exercised an enormous influence in Denmark in this period among a circle of younger architects to which Rasmussen belonged, who were actively searching for a more rigorous theory of design. By 1919, this group of architects had begun to turn away from the Arts and Crafts teachings of the Danish Academy, which they found to be eclectic and fussy in its details while lacking in any effective theory of overall composition, and they found in Brinckmann's accounts of baroque space suggestions for the emergence of a modernist architecture that would find its expressive basis in principles of spatial and plastic composition rather than in ornament or the details of craft.[7]

In 1921, Rasmussen attended three lectures by Brinckmann, delivered to the Royal Danish Academy under the title, "Die Baukunst in ihrer räumlichen und plastischen Gestaltung, ihre Beziehung zur Skulptur und Malerei" (Architecture as Spatial and Plastic Creation, Its Connection to Sculpture and Painting).[8] The three lectures constituted a condensed summary of the book *Plastik und Raum*, published one year later, in which Brinckmann expanded on the theme that he had begun to explore in *Platz und Monument*: namely the relationship between sculptural plasticity and the sensation of space, and, more especially the interaction between the two. Thus, Pietro da Cortona's Piazza of Santa Maria della Pace became a central example of this contrapuntal interpenetration: "Even this plastic mass is again penetrated by elements of space."[9] More than in his previous works, Brinckmann used the baroque, especially the Roman baroque, in order to elaborate a general theory of aesthetic experience that privileged a "synthesis" or "interpenetration" between plasticity and space as the highest aesthetic goal.[10]

Brinckmann's account of the baroque in *Plastik und Raum* (Plasticity and Space) concluded by addressing the emerging modernisms of the period around the First World War, which could now be judged according to parallel aesthetic criteria. According to Brinckmann, a unified expression of plasticity and space had reached its height in the High Italian Baroque and the South German Rococo and then fallen into a gradual decline. With the advent of neo-classicism in France, sculpture, painting and architecture had increasingly begun to fall into separate activities, less and less constructing a unified relation of plasticity and space. In the eclectic historicism of the nineteenth century, the situation had only become worse, with different kinds of ornament being applied to otherwise monotonous housing blocks, bearing little relation to their respective forms or spaces. As architects had begun to react against neo-classicism in the nineteenth century, even returning to a kind of neo-baroque historicism, they had lost the spatial-plastic essence of the baroque as well as the meaningful relationship of architecture to painting and sculpture. Modern architecture, hence, could not return directly to the high baroque. It had to go back through a kind of neo-classicism, which Brinckmann saw as a reductive, simplified baroque, in order thereby to re-assert principles of space and plasticity, especially in new building materials. At the same time, Brinckmann pointed towards the formal clarity of vast vaulting structures newly made possible by engineering advances in concrete construction. Showing an image from the unfinished interior of Heinrich Küster's 1908 ferroconcrete market hall in Breslau, Brinckmann claimed that out of the new forms of the engineers, long covered by decoration, the basis for a "new spatio-plastic and functional feeling" might emerge.[11] Whether architects turned towards neo-classicism or towards engineering mattered less than the idea that they return to basic formal principles of plasticity and space by eliminating the visual clutter of unrelated historicist, sculptural or ornamental motifs.

Brinckmann's rhetoric immediately struck a sympathetic chord among the Danish advocates of the so-called New Classicism (*Nyklassicisme*) of the 1910s and 1920s, a movement which could already be seen as performing the very kind of aesthetic purification that Brinckmann advocated. Such architects as Carl Petersen and Aage Rafn had begun explicitly to evoke the forms and theories of late eighteenth-century neo-classicism, particularly in its use of simple cubic masses, sparsely ornamented surfaces and dramatic contrasts in order to heighten sensations of the sublime. Through dramatic juxtapositions of scale, massing and lighting they had sought to amplify architecture's sensorial possibilities. Seemingly aware of these developments, Brinckmann noted in *Plastik und Raum* that architects had again turned to neo-classicism in order to purge architecture of the arbitrary and the eclectic: "This new interest in the art from around 1800" should not, however, be judged as a new form of historicism. Such a judgement would ignore the fact "that the will for clarity over fundamental principles, particularly of the shaping of space, is becoming ever stronger, and that this will can find few other resolutions, as in its own time neo-classicism found its resolutions in the reduction of the baroque artwork."[12] Thus ironically, neo-classicism, which had paved the way for the end of the baroque synthesis, might now point the way towards a new synthesis. The neo-classical reduction of the baroque to simpler forms of plasticity and space might reveal something of the aesthetic principles of plasticity and space as such.

As a participant in this movement in the early 1920s, Rasmussen began to apply Brinckmann's lessons on the baroque, not to ferroconcrete engineering or to the emerging expressionist architecture in Germany, but rather to the Danish New Classicism. Recalling this period in 1939, Rasmussen wrote: "In the years around 1920, the Danish architects studied all the means which the classicists knew to express spaces and masses. The instrument was determined from which a pure architectural music could be played."[13] In attempting visually to purify architectural language and thereby heighten the visual sensations and theatrical effects of space and mass, these architects turned away from the earlier concern with craft and detail.[14] This particularly Danish interpretation of Brinckmann's baroque as method of alternating solid masses with dramatic voids, rather than a more abstract idea of "spatial interpenetration," would remain a central component of Rasmussen's *Experiencing Architecture*, but with no attempt to connect such techniques with any "will" or *Geist* of modernism. On the contrary, Rasmussen would often characterize such baroque effects in the twentieth century as a kind of empty theatrics. The most explicit reference to Brinckmann's historiography of the baroque occurs in the third chapter of *Experiencing Architecture*, "Contrasting Effects of Solids and Cavities" – the chapter title itself a paraphrase of Brinckmann's *Plastik und Raum*. In a passage that deploys the animating motifs of German empathy theory that had also infused Brinckmann's discourse, Rasmussen describes the Piazza of Santa Maria della Pace in Rome (Figure 15.1):

> The interior seems to be pressing against the wall, pushing it out in a tremendous bulge. You can almost see how it bursts apart, forming an opening which is held together by the segmented pediment which fills the shadow of the large gable. And this whole huge tense body emerges from the deep niche of the concave façade, just as the loggia below juts out into the court.[15]

This dramatic reading of Roman baroque theatricality is, at the same time, accompanied by a deflation of its aesthetic content and a relativization of its historical and geographical significance. The very same chapter of *Experiencing Architecture* that explains the contrasting baroque effects of Santa Maria della Pace concludes with a passage on the Copenhagen Police Headquarters, a major monument of Danish New Classicism, completed by Aage Rafn in 1924. This building, Rasmussen claims, seems to have no other function than "the purely aesthetic one of creating effective contrasts" through monumental courts:

S. Maria della Pace, Rome. Pietro da Cortona's façade seen from point B on plan below

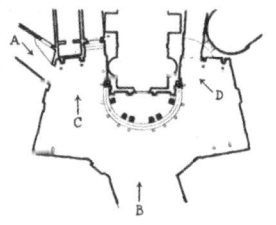

Figure 15.1   Piazza of Santa Maria della Pace, Rome

Source: Steen Eiler Rasmussen, *Experiencing Architecture*, 2nd edition, figure and photograph, page 69 © Massachusetts Institute of Technology, by permission of the MIT Press.

"The only impression one receives is of a temple dedicated to 'grand architecture', or rather to grand architectural effects."[16] The implication is that the New Classicist experiments culminate in a certain empty monumentality, with virtuoso architectural aesthetics being divorced from the social activities or functions they were meant to serve. This passage also signals the fundamental aesthetic break and functionalist ethos that Rasmussen perceived in the International Modernism of Central Europe at around the same time.

Up until about 1926, Brinckmann's work formed the single most decisive model for Rasmussen's own design and teaching. Soon after he had been appointed to a newly created position as lecturer in city planning at the Royal Academy in 1924, Rasmussen wrote to Brinckmann, asking for advice and wondering if he might visit him at the newly founded Art Historical Institute in Cologne: "From your books, I already know you as an outstanding scholar, and it would therefore be meaningful for me to see you as a teacher in action."[17] Upon receiving an invitation from Brinkmann to attend his lectures in Cologne, Rasmussen planned a trip to Germany and France in the summer 1926. This sojourn, by Rasmussen's own account, was a major turning point in his writing and teaching. It was then that Rasmussen began to doubt the universality of Brinckmann's accounts of plasticity and space, and this doubt was partly prompted by his encounter with the architecture of Le Corbusier. After spending most of June in Cologne, Rasmussen then travelled to Paris to meet Le Corbusier and then to his recently built town of Pessac. In gazing at Pessac, Rasmussen recalled experiencing neither any sense of spatial depth nor of any mass, but rather the impression of floating, depthless colour planes. It was an experience that Rasmussen would later call the "third perception" (*den tredje opfattelse*), fitting the categories of neither plasticity nor space.[18] Pessac thus constituted an absolute break, rather than a continuity, with the aesthetics of the baroque.

Sigfried Giedion had visited Pessac around the same time but had come to very different conclusions. Rather than viewing the relative flatness and lightness of the Pessac houses as demonstrating an aesthetic experience opposite or antithetical to that of the baroque, Giedion understood Pessac as embodying a new kind of spatio-plastic synthesis. In describing Pessac in his 1928 book *Bauen in Frankreich, Bauen in Eisen, Bauen in Eisenbeton* (*Building in France, Building in Iron, Building in Ferro-Concrete*, 1995), Giedion used language that very closely echoed Brinckmann's description of the high baroque with its spatial and plastic interpenetrations:

> How could one judge the space and plasticity of, for instance, the brown row houses of the smallest type without taking into account the oscillating relations between things? These houses that so rigorously respect the planar surface are themselves being penetrated with expansive, onrushing cubes of air which among themselves receive new stimulations and modulation – as by the swelling – visually hard to discern vaults (pantries). The row houses as a whole again reach into the space next to and behind them.[19]

In fact, Giedion's entire account of Pessac and of Le Corbusier more generally, with its language of interrelating units and spatial interpenetration (*Raumdurchdringung*), so closely mirrored the art historical descriptions of the baroque by Brinckmann and other German art historians that it would seem a very short step for Giedion to later claim such architecture as constituting a reformulation of the baroque within modernist "space-time." For Rasmussen, by contrast, the power of baroque plasticity was inseparable from its appearance of heavy massiveness, and "space" or *Raum* was the aesthetic complement of the mass, the hollows and openings that penetrated into the solid forms. This reading was reinforced by actual buildings of Danish New Classicism which dominated the 1920s and which Rasmussen saw as an application of baroque historiography to modern architectural practice.

Rasmussen, then, interpreted the subsequent International Modernism as something fundamentally different from and not at all explainable by Brinckmann's account of the baroque, and this break began Rasmussen's increasing relativization of baroque aesthetics as being just one among several poles of experience. In *Experiencing Architecture*, Rasmussen relativized and deflated the significance of such Roman baroque spaces as the Piazza of Santa Maria della Pace by claiming that its theatricality constituted, in fact, a marginal and somewhat extreme form of architectural expression, perhaps more appropriate to the seventeenth-century Counter-Reformation than to contemporary architecture: "The employment of masses and cavities together in effective contrasts leads to works which lie in one of the peripheries of architecture, close to the art of theatre and at times to that of sculpture."[20] Contemporary architects who resorted to such techniques, Rasmussen implied, were those who often sought the most theatrical and sculptural results. He thus compared the Roman Fontana di Trevi with what he called Frank Lloyd Wright's "fantasy over cavity, rock, architecture, and sculpture" at Fallingwater or the interpenetration of concave and convex forms at the Johnson Wax Headquarters in Racine, Wisconsin.[21]

Functionalist Design and the Case of Baroque London

To understand Rasmussen's materially and functionally grounded approach to the baroque, it is important to underscore the fact that he had never interpreted Brinckmann's discourse in purely spatial terms; spatial aesthetics always connected to the methods and materials of building – and by extension to the social and cultural conditions of that building. Recounting decades later the impression made by his reading of *Platz und Monument*, Rasmussen remembered having been impressed by one of Brinckmann's last sentences: "City building means: shaping space with the materials of housing!"[22] What Brinckmann meant by this was that, aesthetically, the forms and materials of individual buildings, especially ordinary dwellings, were inseparable from the spatial experience of the street. Thus, narrow, winding medieval streets had narrow, vertical houses while baroque avenues and squares were built of elongated apartment blocks and *palazzi*. The collective building types, their respective construction materials, and the spaces between buildings all contributed to the aesthetic experience of the city. Thus, Brinckmann had written that city building could not arise from abstract thinking, but only from "sensual thinking, thinking in the material" (*sinnliches Denken, Denken im Material*).[23] This phrase, which resonated with Rasmussen's own continuing interest in the Danish craft tradition, suggested a connection, not only between the construction of individual building facades and the aesthetic character of the larger city, but also between the innermost domestic interior and the most public, monumental urban square. Here, Rasmussen began to take up one of the central concerns of modernist architects in the late 1920s, namely the reform of tenement housing and the rejection of baroque-inspired "corridor" streets, with grandiose facades hiding cramped, dark apartments. This was the primary objective, in fact, of Rasmussen's major project on the architectural history of London, in which seventeenth-century London stood in for the resistance to the form of the continental baroque city. Thinking the materiality of seventeenth-century London, then, also meant presenting an alternative baroque that reversed many of the governing principles of baroque Rome and that coincided with a modernist ideal of domestic comfort.

Rasmussen's functionalist ideal of architectural and urban form was inseparable from his deeply Anglophile understanding of aesthetics and comfort in design. Following the *Werkbund* Exhibition in Copenhagen in 1918, one of Rasmussen's mentors, the Danish art historian Vilhelm Wanscher, published an article, entitled "The Thing is the Real!" in which he called for applied artists to be less concerned with making objects beautiful by applying ornament, than with making them "real," designed for their function.[24] Then in 1932, Rasmussen himself curated an exhibition entitled *Britisk Brugskunst* (British Applied Art), which explained these same functionalist virtues. The designs of English "things" not only had achieved a "classic" form in their unornamented functionalism, but they also fit the sensations and movements of the body. The various balls used in English sports, for example, were not simply mathematical spheres to be admired as pure forms; they were things to take and to touch: "From earliest childhood the Englishman is raised to handle different kinds of balls. This develops his sense for the physical qualities of things."[25] This discussion of English objects being made for touching and holding, extended wider notions that the English designed for personal comfort rather than for ostentatious display. Rasmussen's admiration of English functional design in the 1930s then extended to the scale of the city of London and also contributed to his relativistic understanding of baroque architecture and its lessons for the present.

Rasmussen's research on the history of London, undertaken in the 1930s, resulted in a project intended as an attack on the continental tradition of baroque city planning, whose visible effects were not only to be seen in Rome and Paris but also in his native Copenhagen. His 1934 Danish-language book, entitled *London, den Vidtudbredte Storby* (literally, "London, the widely-scattered metropolis"), was critical of the dense apartment blocks of central Copenhagen and attempted to induce Danish architects and planners to adopt the English models of row-houses and garden cities. Meanwhile, the 1937 English edition, *London: The Unique City*, was meant to convince Londoners of their own native genius and to resist the importation of continental European experiments, above all Corbusian apartment blocks.

For Rasmussen, the lesson of English functionalism in the present lay not in its monumental spectacle but in its informal elaboration of private life and private functions in a variety of different kinds of spaces. He readily admitted that London was less spectacular in its spatial and monumental effects than were many continental cities, but it would be a mistake, he clarified, to judge it in those terms.[26] In describing the London squares of the eighteenth century, Rasmussen emphasized their lack of monumental hierarchy. Where others saw megalopolitan sprawl and a lack of planning, Rasmussen saw the *ad hoc* growth of London as a type of bourgeois, populist functionalism that had produced an urban form as valid formally as the baroque cities of the continent, and superior to them in socio-political terms. Citing the failure to enact Christopher Wren's baroque plan of 1666 as a triumph for the "idea of London," Rasmussen noted: "That the king had to give up [Wren's] plan immediately is but one of the numerous expressions of the failure of Absolutism in England."[27] It was precisely the lack of centralized planning for monumental streets and squares, Rasmussen maintained, that had allowed London, especially in its residential districts, to become functionally superior to its continental counterparts, in which congested apartments hid behind monumental façades. In describing the London squares of the eighteenth century, Rasmussen emphasized their lack of monumental hierarchy:

> A French or a German Baroque square was intended to be a monument for Absolutism and consequently must have a climax in some monument or other, it had to lead the eye to some public building, a castle, a church or whatever the monument might be. The English square, on the contrary, was merely a place where many people of the same class had their houses and it was therefore perfectly in keeping that it should be like the courtyard of a convent.[28]

This contrast between the baroque monumentality of the continental city and the domestic simplicity of the English city would soon be echoed in Lewis Mumford's distinction between the "mechanical order" of baroque planning by a despot and the "organic order" of the New England village.[29] It was, likewise, Rasmussen's distaste for the political symbolism of Absolutism and what he saw as its twentieth-century equivalents that drove him in the 1930s to construct eighteenth-century London as an opposing model to the prevalent form of the baroque European city.

This polemic against the "absolutist" baroque cities of continental Europe did nothing, however, to diminish the pace or scale of Rasmussen's interest in seventeenth-century Rome. In fact, Rasmussen's curious fascination with baroque Rome, which continued all through the 1950s, seemed part of a determined effort to reveal the techniques of its design methods in order, both to demystify its aesthetic effects and to demonstrate its extreme artifice and distance from contemporary modes of life. It was almost as though he needed baroque Rome in order to clarify the kind of domestic functionalism that he admired in London. In his 1951 book, *Towns and Buildings*, Rasmussen emphasized the distance between the monumental spaces of baroque Rome and modern ideas of dwelling: "It is difficult to think of these palaces as homes, difficult to imagine an everyday existence in such monumental surroundings."[30] Similarly, after having his students make painstaking, measured drawings of the Spanish Steps in the summer of 1953, Rasmussen incorporated the following conclusion in *Experiencing Architecture*, alluding to the restrictive clothing, mannered gestures and elaborate courtly rituals of the early eighteenth century: "Thus in the Spanish Steps we can see the petrification of the dancing rhythm of a period of gallantry; it gives us an inkling of something that was, something our generation will never know."[31] This was a stark contrast to Rasmussen's account of the informal comforts of English design, and it fit with Rasmussen's larger conclusion that baroque Rome was, in its public theatricality, quite distant from the directions taken by modernist architecture in the twentieth century.

Vermeer, Delft and the Alternative Space of the Dutch Baroque

By the 1950s Rasmussen had added a third pole to this European geography, now focusing on the seventeenth-century Dutch cities of Delft and Amsterdam. In these Dutch cities Rasmussen found a modern, functionalist counterpoint to the aesthetic virtuosity of baroque Rome. Whereas his London project had begun with functionalism and housing reform, dealing with aesthetics only intermittently, this Dutch project consistently bore the lens of art history, especially the historiography of Johannes Vermeer. Dutch art historian P.T.A. Swillens, whom Rasmussen read carefully in the 1950s, was of the opinion that there was no dramatic or allegorical content whatsoever in Vermeer's art. Vermeer, according to Swillens, was almost completely lacking in fantasy or imagination.

Figure 15.2   Portion of 1732 engraving of Delft, by Leon Schenk
Source: Rasmussen, "The Dutch Contribution," pl. 35.

His skill, rather, lay in his ability to experience, precisely and empathetically, the objects and spaces of his world as a play of light and colour: "In feeling and viewing, he experiences in a special way the 'whole', that is to say a mutual, indivisible connection of things."[32] Vermeer, in short, was an expert experiencer of buildings and things, and subsequently able to represent his experience pictorially. When Rasmussen first began travelling regularly to Delft to research its urban form, he did so already with this painterly sense of experience in mind, trying to find the exact sites where Johannes Vermeer and his contemporary, Pieter de Hooch, had constructed their compositions, testing his own experiences of the city against the visual representations of the paintings.

Whereas Swillens was interested in the way that Vermeer's aesthetic consciousness organized everyday things and spaces into an experience of the whole, Rasmussen was mainly interested in how the material construction of the city itself made Vermeer's aesthetic experience possible in the first place. Thus Rasmussen's writings on Amsterdam and Delft began with the material construction of the cities rather than with the paintings. He described the process of building, beginning with the canals: "The long strait channel was dug out and fortified with bulwarks – later replaced by embankment walls. Then along the embankment streets rows of houses appeared, quite narrow and very deep – standing close together with gables fronting on the canal. The side walls are the supporting structures."[33] Showing a view of Delft from 1732, Rasmussen noted the way in which this method of building produced certain characteristic patterns of street frontage (Figure 15.2). Because the houses were long and narrow, with bearing walls only along the shared sides of the buildings, the fronts could be opened up by a relatively light, timber frame, filled on the ground floor by great expanses of windows, by which to light the deep interior rooms of the first floor.

This pattern of building produced a spatial and visual experience entirely different from that of the typical baroque city. Turning to the Dutch painters, Vermeer and De Hooch, Rasmussen examined their visual compositions in terms of what he took to be this characteristically Dutch way of seeing and building. Art historians had already pointed to the relationship between these painters' use of light and the large, curtained windows of the *voorhuis*, where light could be regulated in sophisticated ways. Rasmussen was also, however, interested in the way in which the painted scenes of Delft had been based on similarly careful observations of the city. Rasmussen spent time in Delft attempting to match existing buildings to de Hooch's painted views, but with little success. He concluded that de Hooch had, nevertheless, conveyed an accurate experience: "Though probably not one of de Hooch's canvases gives a correct picture of a particular spot in Delft, every one gives a true impression of the town."[34] The truth of the paintings was not of a topographic kind, but of a compositional one: the series of asymmetrically connecting interiors, the relationships between houses and gardens, and the way in which light passes from one space to the next. The consequence of the Dutch manner of building was not just a characteristic pattern of house and street, but a characteristic way of thinking about form. In his journal notes from August 1950 Rasmussen observed that, "While the Italians must have thought of their houses as massive blocks, through which one bored windows, for the Dutch it was a complete contrast, and windows were not holes in a mass; they themselves formed wall planes."[35] Dutch cities flouted all of the compositional rules of the Italian baroque, producing houses that appeared heavy above and light below and were composed not of sculpted masses forming deep shadows, but a series of flat wall planes, alternately transparent and opaque. Describing Vermeer's painting "A Street in Delft," which depicted a small house and two adjacent doorways leading to rear gardens, Rasmussen wrote:

> In the little street picture with a gabled house in Delft, one sees a day-clear representation of a building entirely without mysticism. … One guesses that the entire city is built up of houses in the same crystalline character without any ornament, sheer, simple volumes and regular spaces and clear planes.[36]

There were those architects, Rasmussen claimed, who found modernist functionalism too empty and sterile, who sought to introduce symbols and ornament. Vermeer's painting proved that functionalism did not have to imply sterility, that the bare things, in their very simplicity could produce an aesthetic experience.[37] The things were already the aesthetic content. Thus, Delft, alongside seventeenth-century London and Amsterdam, became for Rasmussen an inversion of baroque Rome, a city of bourgeois functionalism rather than a place of dramatic spatial sequences, in which theatricality was replaced by the subtle tones of light falling through windows and doorways, illuminating the objects of domestic life.[38]

Conclusion

At work in Rasmussen's relativization of baroque aesthetics was a strand of Scandinavian functionalist thinking closely tied to the empirical observations of everyday life and completely opposed to what seemed, from a functionalist point of view, various forms of mysticism and idealism surrounding baroque spatiality. Significantly, Rasmussen delivered his lectures on "Experiencing Architecture" shortly after the debates on the so-called "New Monumentality," then being promoted by Sigfried Giedion, Jose Luis Sert and others. In his 1944 essay "The Need for a New Monumentality," Giedion had advocated shaping the emotional life of the masses by creating public spectacles from the forms of the modernist artist, "who created these symbols out of the anonymous forces of our period."[39] In the subsequent debates it was, above all, the Swedish art historian Gregor Poulsson who attacked such idealist assumptions as well as the idea of a monumentality that would symbolically transcend everyday functions and patterns. Poulsson replied to Giedion by returning to the functionalist doctrines of democratic design:

> The modern architect has derived all his creative force, all his revolutionary ability through the very fact of his *denial* of this aesthetic difference in categories and his most decided defence of the thesis that the artistic value is principally the same – naturally not actually so – in the design of cutlery, a worker's home, an underground station, a town hall.[40]

Rasmussen's understanding of functionalist design was quite similar. The purpose of experiencing architecture in its "thingness" was to understand it as an extension of ordinary objects, such as balls and tennis racquets, whose aesthetics resulted from the patterns and rhythms of everyday life rather than from an unconscious symbolism that might be somehow created as a deliberate, public spectacle.

Thus, in a period when Giedion and others were urging a "new monumentality" that would recapitulate in modernist terms the spatial theatricality (and supposed cultural synthesis) of the Roman baroque, Rasmussen reformulated an earlier Scandinavian functionalism, but now in terms of an open ended set of baroque experiences that could be consciously applied to an architecture of everyday life. In a 1957 article, entitled "The Architect in Society," Rasmussen wrote that the idea that there existed some kind of *Zeitgeist*, with the architect acting out the social unconscious in the manner of automatic writing, was entirely erroneous and misguided: "There is no time-spirit, no single being that expresses itself but a number of human beings with a common pattern of behavior."[41] If the Danish New Classicism of the 1920s had successfully appropriated the aesthetic lessons of the baroque, it had failed to connect the everyday functions and rhythms of modern life and ended as an exercise in theatrical monumentality for its own sake. On the other hand, isolated baroque gestures of alternative concave and convex surfaces, liberated from their baroque axes and symmetries, could be made to synchronize with modern functions and the experience of the baroque translate into the modern. Thus, Rasmussen extolled the informal rhythms of Alvar Aalto's recently built Baker House, which, he claimed, corresponded with the modern, informal rhythms of the American dormitory. By breaking down experience into small pieces that could apply to numerous situations – be it the falling of sunlight or the texture of stone – Rasmussen released experience from historical contingencies, freeing it to be used as a tool for modern architects in new ways. In its pluralistic and relativizing account, *Experiencing Architecture* likewise released baroque aesthetics from the constricting teleology of modernist "space."

Endnotes

1   The lectures were not part of the regular course instruction in architecture but were designed as a series of public talks, intended to address not only architecture students, but also a general audience interested in architecture. Scheduled twice a week over the course of five weeks in October and November 1953, they were publicized in MIT's "Calendar of Events" and they apparently began to draw ever-larger crowds of students, both from inside and outside the school of architecture.

2   Rasmussen, *Experiencing Architecture*, 17.

3   Giedion, *Space, Time and Architecture*, 43.

4   Giedion, *Space, Time and Architecture*, 89. The periodization of this early nineteenth-century square was debatable. In *Town and Square*, 162–3, Paul Zucker categorized it as neo-classical.

5   Giedion, *Space, Time and Architecture*, 89.

6   Rasmussen, "Om at Opleve Arkitektur" (1950), 32. Unless otherwise indicated, translations from Danish and German are my own.

7   The flashpoint for this criticism was Martin Nyrop's Copenhagen City Hall, finished in 1905, which, despite its functional expressiveness, was found to be visually weak in its division according to multiple projecting elements and its somewhat arbitrary choice of ornament.

8   Rasmussen mentions the impact of these lectures in "Nogle pesonlige noter," *Om at Opleve Arkitektur*, 240.

9   Brinckmann, *Plastik und Raum*, 42.

10   In his summary of the high baroque in Italy, Brinckmann writes: "In architecture plastic and spatial elements interpenetrate one another. Sculpture becomes a plastic-spatial synthesis." *Plastik und Raum*, 42.

11   Brinckmann, *Plastik und Raum*, 87–8.

12   Brinckmann, *Plastik und Raum*, 76–7.

13   Rasmussen, *Nordische Baukunst*, 112.

14   Rasmussen recalls the following: "Already on October 10, 1921, I gave a lecture on solids and cavities, whose content is organized as chapter two of this book, to the young architects' association. … The plans of the Grundtvig Church and the Copenhagen Police Headquarters had just been published, so one clearly had two distinct examples of a solid-based and a cavity-based architecture respectively." Rasmussen, "Nogle pesonlige noter," *Om at Opleve Arkitektur*, 240. These bibliographical notes were only published in the Danish edition.

15   Giedion, *Building in France, Building in Iron, Building in Ferroconcrete*, 176.

16   Rasmussen, *Experiencing Architecture*, 82.

17   Steen Eiler Rasmussen to Albert Erich Brinckmann, 1926, copy, Steen Eiler Rasmussen Papers, 1991/41, VI, folder 45, Royal Danish Library, Copenhagen (hereafter Rasmussen Papers).

18   Rasmussen recalls: "*The Third Perception*, which is discussed in section IV and which deals with experiencing neither solids nor cavities but rather weightless planes, arose for me on a July day in 1926, when at that time I saw the completely new buildings of Le Corbusier near Pessac, explained on pages 96–8 in this book. In May 1956 I had a similar experience in Venice." Rasmussen, "Nogle Personlige Noter," *Om at Opleve Arkitektur*, 241

19   Giedion, *Building in France*, 176.

20   Rasmussen, *Experiencing Architecture*, 82.

21   Rasmussen, *Experiencing Architecture*, 75–8.

22   Brinckmann, *Platz und Monument*, 170. Rasmussen recalls having read of spatial effects through the work of Danish Art historian Vilhelm Wanscher and that he and his fellow students at the academy had then deepened their understanding of this theme through Brinckmann's *Platz und Monument*: "Wanscher had spoken and written of 'spatial' effects, and through A.E. Brinckmann's little book, *Platz und Monument* (1912), we had deepened our understanding of the subject. [The book's] motto lies on the last page: 'City-building means shaping space with the material of housing'." *Om at Opleve Arkitektur*, 240.

23   Brinckmann, *Platz und Monument*, 169.

24   "For the fewest of us sense, what things – or the harmony of things – are; therefore we seek blindly after a new art instead of arriving at the single task *that shall be done*, and that as much from within as from without." Wanscher, "Tingen er det Egentlige!" 399.

25   Rasmussen, *Britisk Brugskunst*, 8.

26   Rasmussen, *London*, 202.

27   Rasmussen, *London*, 113.

28   Rasmussen, *London*, 199.

29   See Mumford (1939), 133–42. In the annotated bibliography to *The Culture of Cities* Mumford cites Rasmussen's *London*, published two years earlier. Unlike Mumford, however, Rasmussen did not idealize the small community with its visible boundaries. Quite the contrary, he focused on what he considered the essential character of London as a decentralized and "scattered" city that had quite early sprung from its walls and freed itself from royal authority.

30   Rasmussen, *Towns and Buildings*, 53.

31   Rasmussen, *Experiencing Architecture*, 136.

32   Swillens, *Johannes Vermeer*, 146.

33   Rasmussen, "The Dutch Contribution," 163.

34   Rasmussen, *Towns and Buildings*, 86.

35   Journal notes (handwriting on graph paper), 29 August 1950, Rasmussen Papers, 1991/41, appendix 104, III, folder 36.

36   Rasmussen, "Om at Opleve Arkitektur" (1950), 30.

37   There is an interesting parallel between Rasmussen's observations on the empirical realism of Dutch baroque painting and Svetlana Alpers's much later argument in *The Art of Describing* (1993) that Dutch baroque art, in contrast to the narrative, theatrical qualities of Italian baroque painting, involved an "art of describing" the surfaces of the visual world.

38   Nevertheless, baroque Rome could still also be domesticated in functionalist terms. In 1965, in criticizing a parking lot that now stretched beneath Le Corbusier's *Unité d'Habitation*, Rasmussen remarked: "I think that we can very well live among stones provided they are as civilized as the many little squares in Rome, where every stone was formed with care to serve man." Rasmussen, "Lessons for Modern Urban Design," 76.

39   Giedion, "The Need for a New Monumentality," 564.

40   Poulsson, "In Search of a New Monumentality," 123.

41   Rasmussen, "The Architect and Society," 382.

Chapter 16
From Michelangelo to Borromini: Bruno Zevi and Operative Criticism

Roberto Dulio

Translated by Maarten Delbeke and Andrew Leach

The cultural action of Bruno Zevi from the middle of the 1950s brought to maturity the premises of his trilogy of *Verso un'architettura organica* (1945), *Saper vedere l'architettura* (1948) and *Storia dell'architettura moderna* (1950), which Manfredo Tafuri in 1994 defined as being of immense historiographical significance.[1] A fundamental contribution to modern architectural historiography, this action also points in a properly disciplinary sense to Zevi's declarative vocation: the operative role. In order to affect the work of architects, as operativity implies, the complex threads of history need to be ordered according to a construction that is intelligible in terms of the architectural project. The so-called operative criticism constitutes, in this light, an element mediating between history and architectural design.

The legitimation of architectural design through examples drawn from the architecture of the past is a practice that can lay claim to a long tradition. Before the birth of a true and properly autonomous discipline of architectural history it is, in fact, impossible to distinguish between the treatment of the past by architectural treatise writers and architectural historians. On one hand, within this tradition, history is examined through the questions raised by the practice of architecture. On the other, the forms and typologies derived from historical study have evident formal consequences for architectural design.

History offers the linguistics roots of the new architecture of modernism, in its substantial novelty, both syntactic and expressive, a formal and typological legitimation. Among the many strata of the practice of validating the present through history, the Italian architecture of the 1930s comprises one of the most recent layers. In its expressions one can locate – more or less directly, and albeit subject to different tensions and degrees – an effort to conjugate the new forms of this moment according to the study of the past.[2] The most rhetorical tendency of this culture in whose shadow Zevi was educated was the desire to ameliorate the image of fascism by invoking the most emphatic elements of the architecture of Imperial Rome.

Well aware of this immediate and embarrassing precedent, Zevi attempted to recuperate the heritage of history according to a more refined mechanism. The difference between Zevi's efforts and those of earlier generations acquired substance as his operativity surpassed the immediate echo and formal recognizability that characterized the instrumentalizaion typical of the 1930s. By means of a system of analysing the work, its internal space (*Saper vedere l'architettura*) and its novel character (*Storia dell'architettura moderna*), Zevi arrived at the definition of interpretative instruments, both graphic and three-dimensional, that allowed for the abstraction of those same elements. The theoretical formulation of an apparatus adequate to the task of reinstating the relationship between history and the project is, then, defined by Zevi from 1950 onwards, in parallel to the *Storia*, with the publication of his book *Architettura e storiografia*.[3]

Missing from this apparatus, however, and consistent with problems inherent in the chimera of "organic architecture," was an example of how to study the past according to this model.[4] The theoretical treatment of historical exemplars in *Architettura e storiografia* pushed him toward formal abstraction without clearly specifying the concrete modalities of this new incarnation of operative history. The work of Zevi's Venetian students (to whom he dedicated *Architettura e storiografia*) pursued precisely this objective. The exhibition of 1956 and the subsequent volume on Biagio Rossetti, published in 1960, as well as the book and exhibition on Michelangelo in 1964, through to Zevi's polemical interventions on Borromini in 1967, would come to constitute the concrete examples of history's operative role that remained absent from the earlier book in which its principles were espoused. These examples were truly and properly operative in terms both of research and in the formal ends of the architectural project.

In his book of 1960 – *Biagio Rossetti architetto ferrarese* – Zevi emphasized Rossetti's role to the extent of transforming him into the maker of Ferrara, which, as later studies would show, Rossetti was not. It was Tafuri who sharply seized upon the paradox that Zevi's text "is a great history book," but that "Biagio Rossetti does not exist." And also how

> through Biagio Rossetti, in 1960 Zevi was indicating what the urban planning policy for the first Italian center-left [government] might be. Only that he was saying it indirectly: he was speaking of Biagio Rossetti and was in fact indicating Luigi Piccinato as the possible urban planner for own beloved city's moment of opening to the left.[5]

There can be no doubt that Zevi cultivated this obfuscation, also in light of the rather enlarged political horizon of this moment. It is significant that the meeting in Zevi's house between socialist luminary Pietro Nenni and American intellectual Arthur Schlesinger, which bestowed an informal American blessing on the first Centre-Left government, occurred in 1962. But already in 1960 his volume on Rossetti begins to describe the recourse to a series of graphic solutions abstracted from a Rossettian architecture that, in a certain way, could serve as models of formal interpretation, rendering the lessons of Rossetti's architecture available to his present.

Instead of gathering the documentary and bibliographical apparatus at the end of each of the chapters – work which was undertaken by students of the Istituto Universario di Architettura di Venezia (IUAV, where Zevi taught from 1948 to 1963)[6] under the guidance of Giusseppe Mazzariol and Marino Berengo – or the photographic campaign of Gianni Berengo Gardin realized together with the architect Luigi Pellegrin, depictions of Rossetti's buildings (which also occasioned a parallel project for an "inventory of monuments") conferred upon this the substantial volume an image both authoritative and normalizing. The critical sketches, however, revealed a character of immediate novelty. The volumetric values of Palazzo Schifanoia, the distribution of the openings on its façade, or on that of the Casa Rossetti, the planimetric perception of the crossroads on to which the Palazzo dei Diamanti faces – rather than studies of the penetration of light in San Francesco – not only came to comprise interpretative schemes of the works Zevi attributed to Rossetti, but also elements independent of Rossetti's pedigree. Thanks to a sparse and rigorous graphic language, geometrically symbolic, these schemes could aspire to properly serving as abstract models in the operative sense.[7]

The exhibition mounted to mark the fourth centenary of the death of Michelangelo – and above all the volume edited by Zevi together with Paolo Portoghesi – constitutes a crucial manifesto for operative criticism: both in the sense of historical research and its effect in architectural design. Indeed, Zevi explicitly declared his intentions in this respect in the volume's introduction, which was significantly entitled "Attualità di Michelangiolo architetto" – "The Contemporaneity of Michelangiolo, Architect." He wrote: "Over the course of fifteen years of teaching in Venice, course themes have been debated with students in light of the peculiar eagerness of the modern architect for history, that is, for a research into the old polarized on the consciousness of contemporary art." To this declaration of principle he adds a precise reference to Michelangelo, who "against all appearances is the figure from whom today's architects have the most to learn insofar as he acted in a sociological, linguistic and professional situation that presents extraordinary analogies with that situation in which we ourselves live."[8]

Zevi seems more precise – and more daring – in defining these analogies between the present and the past: "the delusion enacted through the treason against the popular character of the Reformation, which frustrated the final hope of the cultured man of the Renaissance, could be compared, without forcing the analogies, with that of progressive intellectuals faced with the totalitarian involution of communist society." A fatal conclusion: "We pass through an historical phase very similar to that of Michelangelo, in which coincide corrupt rationalist persistencies, recuperated pre-organic or organic phenomena, and in the midst of it all, the ebb of evasions and exasperations at once intellectualistic, pseudo-structuralist and exotic."[9]

After Zevi's programmatic declarations follow a series of essays by other authors (amongst whom number Giulio Carlo Argan, Roberto Pane, Renato Bonelli and Sergio Bettini, not to mention Portoghesi) to which Zevi himself adds essays on the fortifications of Florence and on Santa Maria degli Angeli. If the recourse to "critical sketches" appears more moderate in these contributions in comparison to those of his earlier book on Rossetti (likely due also to the ameliorating effect of the presence of the other authors), a number of original drawings that form part of Zevi's two contributions are revealing. A reworking of a number of planimetric drawings of the Florentine fortifications belies an extraordinary similarity to the contemporary calligraphic themes of some noted painters – Carla Accardi rather than Giuseppe Capogrossi – who are at that moment involved in research on abstract art. Michelangelo's interventions in the Diocletian baths become, for the Roman historian, through recourse to his principle of the *non-finito*, the occasion for a final actualization of Michelangelo's work as directed toward contemporary critical categories.[10]

In parallel to the impressive volume edited by Zevi and Portoghesi, Zevi published a monographic issue of his journal *L'Architettura cronache e storia*, which was dedicated not only to the publication of "critical sketches" but also to the presentation of "creative photographs" and "interpretative sculptures" of Michelangelo's works as executed by his students at Venice. The analysis of façades, plans, and architectural volumes had, to a large extent, informed the character of the critical sketches included in the larger volume. On this occasion, though, and with an obvious rehearsal of the theoretical baggage of *Sapere vedere l'architettura*, Zevi concentrated his treatment above all on the spatial incursions, interior and exterior, of Michelangelo's architectural works. The photographs and models – but the models above all – are instrumental in the introduction of the larger volume on Michelangelo, wherein Zevi maintains that "the most laudable works built in the world today begin from rational models and in adulterating the syntaxes, proportions and the objective weaving."[11]

If the starting model, in this case, is that of Michelangelo, the "interpretative sculptures" of the Venetian students do nothing if not distorting "the syntaxes, proportions and objective weaving," taking it to such a degree of abstraction as to allow for its immediate recuperation in the design phase. The models of the Cappella Medicea, the Biblioteca Laurenziana, the fortifications of Florence, the Campidoglio, San Pietro, the Cappella Sforza in Santa Maria Maggiore, right through to Santa Maria degli Angeli, translate the works of Michelangelo into signs, lines of force, undulating walls, dynamic suggestions, spatial reticulations, volumetric agglomerations and informal concretions. Above all, the profiles of the walls containing and defining Michelangelo's spatial invasions are rendered sufficiently abstract as to accommodate new planimetric solutions, which, obviously, alters the recognizability of the model.[12]

In fact, it is according to this procedure that Portoghesi proceeded to design the exhibition of 1964 – a project undertaken in collaboration with Vittorio Gigliotti, Luciano Rubino and Mauro Boudet. In the exhibition halls of the ground floor of the Palazzo delle Esposizioni on the via Nazionale the heart of the exhibition is entirely hidden. The intentions explicitly theorized and declared in the pages of the catalogue, to

> withdraw the documentation of Michelangelo's work from an overwhelming confrontation with the academically styled environments of the palazzo that serves the exhibition as its host. The halls, rectangular and covered in box vaults more than ten meters high, would have annihilated every possibility of visual collegiality within the exposition material. For this reason, cut into the interior of this old environment are a sequence of spaces closely connected in their ideation to the materials that need to be laid bare, lending continuity to the itinerary along a succession of bands of homogenous material that acts as an invitation to new surroundings.

The dialectical relationship between the exhibition design and Michelangelo's project is explained thus:

> In the case of those architectural works we sought to underscore, some of their aspects, critically analyzed, were invoking through allusive form and in an unprejudicially modern language in the exhibition environment. In particular, in the room of the Florentine fortifications we reproduced in their basic outline some of the interior spaces of the projects designed by Michelangelo to defend the Florentine public.

Finally, attention is drawn to the material used for the exhibition design, white panels of expanded polystyrene, by recalling its artificial character and original purpose "for the thermal isolation of walls and tubes."[13]

The citation in the project of elements derived from the history of architecture and the processes of their abstraction to which the use of materials proper to new modes of production further attested represents the fulfilment of an operative criticism. The reliance, also operative, on the study of history is specular.

The title of the opening speech made by Zevi in the Aula Magna of the rectorate of the University of Rome, "in the heart of Piacentini's project for the Città Universitaria," on 18 December 1963, the day following his call to the capital, is significant: "La storia come metodologia di fare architettonica." The assertion could, obviously, be inverted, rendering it into architectural design as a method of history. Zevi is lucidly aware of this:

> The history-design traffic is not unidirectional. If history finds a purpose as methodological component of design, design, in its turn, extends into history its criteria and instruments; which is to say, it proposes an historical-critical operation of a new type, a history of architecture written with the expressive instruments of the architect and no solely with those of the art historian.[14]

In this way Zevi thus sanctions, even if *a posteriori*, the projective character of his *Storia dell'architettura moderna*, published 13 years earlier. It confirms, moreover, the necessity of a new type of graphic toolbox from which to attain lessons materially while avoiding the explicit formal reprisal of historical models. Zevi specifies that "the history of architecture as taught by architects is only valid insofar as it manages to extricate itself [from the past] other than with verbal instruments and the writings of the history of art through a graphic and three-dimensional operative criticism that induces one to think architectonically."[15]

Significantly, an analogous engagement in these themes that can be credited to the milieu of operative criticism – developed along lines quite independent of Zevi's thought, even if it shares something of their origins – and demonstrates extraordinary parallels with regard to methods and taste (Michelangelo, Borromini, up to Capogrossi) is realized by Luigi Moretti.[16]

At the start of the 1930s, Moretti was engaged as an assistant of Vincenzo Fasolo in the history course on the "Storia e stili dell'architettura," which Zevi, as a student, followed in 1938.[17] An early and recently recovered text by Moretti, entitled "Canovaccio per un saggio sull'architettura di Michelangelo e del Borromino" (1927), testifies without doubt to the affiliation of his thinking on these figures with the frame maintained by the course of Fasolo. Moretti often uses axonometric views with the view from below, perspectival sections and exploded views that show the distributive and tectonic conception of the building. But the essay also reveals knowledge of other critical approaches to his subject that may have pushed Moretti to search out a fuller and more refined integration of architectural knowledge. These approaches likely include those conveyed in the reflections of August Schmarsow on architecture as an art of spatial configuration in relation to movement, which shaped the theoretical underpinnings of the work of the young Roman architect. Likewise evident is the influence of the models for the spatial reading of buildings Albert Erich Brinckmann.[18]

The practice of re-drawing imposed by Fasolo in his lessons likely constitutes – even beyond Zevi's caustic affirmations – a common ground between Moretti's experience and that of Zevi himself. Indeed, this was probably catalysed by the complexity of the spatial reading that Moretti may have imprinted on Fasolo's course. Drawing, in fact, stood as an instrument allowing for a direct experience of architecture that focused the attention of his pupils less towards stylistic and decorative apparatus but rather towards planimetric organization, towards the sequencing of interior spaces within a building and its tectonic logic. From the experience shared by Moretti and Zevi emerged two quite independent research trajectories, which beyond their respective points of reference and in the complementary particularity of their modes and moments, abut significantly in their indubitably consonant approaches to history's instrumentality.

It perhaps seems surprising to discover that two of the central themes of Zevi's historiographical project – space as the protagonist of architecture and the rapport between history and design – coincide with the scope of cultural and projective initiatives that Moretti begins in the post-war period, enriched as they are by the logico-mathematical interests that the architect cultivates in parallel with his engagement with history. The subtitle of *Saper vedere l'architettura* is *Saggio sull'interpretazione spaziale dell'architettura*. *Spazio* is the name Moretti chooses for his own journal. The models of the spatial interpretation of buildings, recalling the drawings demanded by Fasolo of the students in the course taught by Moretti and followed by Zevi became, for both, not only a basic critical instrument, but also an affirmation that is significant in and of itself as a rounded critical interpretation. And so in the pages of *Spazio* one finds the models of Moretti, while the "interpretative sculptures" of the students of Zevi's course in Venice appear in the aforementioned monographic issue of *L'Architettura cronache e storia* dedicated to Michelangelo.[19]

A profound conviction of the necessity of an historical culture as the premise and stimulus for architectural design, and vice versa, brings together the different personalities of these two architect-historians. Their respective attention to interior space induces both Moretti and Zevi to re-elaborate, each along their own lines of inquiry, the analytical models suggested by the architectonic plans of Fasolo. The refusal of explicit formal citations and of the reprisal of a simplified volumetry of historical architecture likewise brings them together in their shared opposition to the institutional and pedagogical legacy of Gustavo Giovannoni.

It is revealing that the attention Moretti bestows on such artists as Michelangelo and Borromini, and even the object of his early, youthful study on Canovaccio, come to constitute the nucleus of Zevi's own studies. Likewise both Moretti, with his reflection on the relationship between ideal and real structures, and Zevi, with his interpretative sculptures and the baggage of operative criticism, quickly and precociously distance themselves from the passive deployment of historical forms. And, all the while, both recur constantly to history, filtering and idealizing its effects upon the architectural project and rendering operative its constitutive processes.

If the recourse to history, however, has an important role in architecture, it nonetheless remains difficult to discern – with a superficial glance – the precise references to the past and to architectural models in the architectures that are conceived by Moretti and valued by Zevi. Indeed, the idea of the recourse to history and of the conceptual and informal recuperation of its models is clearly fundamental to the design activity of the one and to the criticism of the other. Over the course of the 1950s and 1960s, Moretti's work was a perfect substantiation in architecture of the critical activity of Zevi, who in turn, and significantly, dedicated to it only few observations, and who did not regard it exempt from his reservations, as documented in the pages of *L'Espresso*. Under different circumstances, their roles might well have become integrated along strictly complementary lines, one the historian and critic, the other the architect and theoretician, although neither figure was immune to such revealing disciplinary transgressions as embodied in the limited corpus of Zevi's architecture and the truly historical writings of Moretti.

The idea, furthermore, of a close connection between the world of building and that of architectural culture, which Zevi energetically promotes at the end of the 1950s and which would take shape in his Istituto Nazionale di Architettura (InArch) potentially offers the common ground for their collaboration. And yet, as prefigured in the limited but revealing surviving correspondence between Zevi and Moretti, the dramatic heritage of the events of 1938 weighed heavily on their respective destinies and on the fate of their relationship: Zevi, Jewish and forced into exile; and Moretti, a fascist who did not renege on his political creed, not even after the War. This dramatic heritage kept open the fracture that would undermine any rapport these two figures might possibly have sustained.[20]

Another of Zevi's elective affinities who, furthermore, we might (at least initially) regard as his true disciple would in fact come to wreck himself on the vicissitudes of operative criticism. This, obviously, is Portoghesi. The Casa Baldi, which the Roman architect designed between 1959 and 1961, had represented the ideal model of the design theories to which Zevi could lend support. But subsequent works of Portoghesi – who was also an historian – tended to render his historical references less than abstract, even to the point of adopting an evident citationism. The contrasts between Portoghesi and Zevi's respective approaches to history were furthermore accentuated in the field of historical research, and especially in their treatments of one of Zevi's favourite themes: Borromini.

By 1967 and the *Convegno di Studi Borrominiani*, held at the Accademia di San Luca in Rome to mark the third centenary of Borromini's death, the division between the two figures is sharp and unbridgeable. Zevi's contribution to the event is significantly titled "Attualità di Borromini." The historian and critic indeed begins his talk by substantiating the central premise of that actuality:

> In the blazing and melancholy setting of baroque theatricality, Borromini personified the task of a systematic and desperate contestation that, with regards to the seventeenth century cultural frame, assumes the value of a heresy. Hence, on ethical grounds, his pregnant actuality: the entire history of modern architecture is made of contestations and heresies – battles against an ever resurgent academic classicism, and against that more subtle and insidious classicism seeking to crystallize the linguistic conquests of the last century, to render them static, to close off their problems. That Borromini constitutes a font of inspiration for contemporary architects more inclined to research appears natural and, now, almost self-evident.[21]

The second element that recurs in Zevi's intervention regards a direct relationship between Borromini and a number of the protagonists of twentieth-century architecture, principally Antonio Gaudí and Frank Lloyd Wright. In naming the figures with whom Borromini's case specifically resonates, Zevi welded his theorization of operative criticism to that of the organic architecture, for which Wright represented a crucial vector. Continues Zevi:

> The analogies between Borromini and Wright are stupefying: consider their spatial inventions, their studies into compressed and dilated cavities, their monitoring and qualification of light, their use of triangles, hexagons, and coils, their treatment of the shell as a diaphragm between interior and exterior and, most importantly, a common design methodology that extends from simple initial schemes to ever more complex conceptions, and a system of recesses that can unite as well as juxtapose in order to concentrate energy only to disperse it over the city and landscape.[22]

On this point Zevi's discourse moves toward a precarious equilibrium within which he seeks a direct relationship between contemporary architecture and that of the past without having to refer to an indirect modality, sophisticated or subtle, as Rudolf Wittkower had done, for example, with the architecture of the Renaissance,[23] but also without falling back upon easy formalisms derived from history. In fact, according to Zevi, connecting experiences of the past to those of the present – either from the perspective of the project or of the study – seems

> positive insofar as it continues and accentuates the tension of modern research. In his process of unearthing, of self-individuating, this research feeds itself with the past while actualizing that past, rejuvenating the readings, rediscovering the past with new eyes and in the key of the modern movement: the past is truly very modern, revolutionary for he who succeeds in tearing himself from academic decrees and who deciphers it for what it is; perhaps a Greek temple, read according to its truth, that lies beyond the imbroglios of neo-classical interpretation to reveals elements that burn effervescently. But this operation is difficult, dense with risks. A loss of modern architecture's tension is enough for the recuperation of the past in an active function and key to transform itself into a reactionary recuperation of the past. It takes but a moment, one lapse: one ends up deceiving oneself and corrupting others.[24]

To conclude with a pairing of images that often appears in Zevi's publications: the lantern of Borromini's Sant'Ivo alla Sapienza and the Guggenheim of Wright. At the Borromini congress he announced:

> Tomorrow evening we will meet at the Guggenheim: not at the lantern of Sant'Ivo, folded onto itself, as it is, enjoyable only by the few fools who climb the stairs along the drum, which is, in fact, not that enjoyable; we meet at the Guggenheim, at Wright's open coil, projected upon the city, a continuation of the urban itinerary. We will find ourselves there because it is necessary to begin with Wright in order to discuss concretely how to vindicate Borromini at a distance of three centuries.[25]

And also:

> Be careful not to adopt history in the service of equivocal conservators, which would be a system allowing us to avoid discussing and verifying once more the heritage of the modern movement, but instead allowing us to negate it in honor of poorly directed academic recuperations hiding behind an intellectual apparatus that is nonetheless sophisticated, charming, ambivalent and equivocal, obedient to the code of common dominion. Such as has happened after Borromini, and yet again today, the reemerging of the classicist code, and this has been while the best among us are hesitating, rethinking, verifying, remedying, distinguishing between various tendencies, re-discussing, demystifying, de-dramatizing, formulating hypotheses, trying new ways without being aware of how they contribute to the dilapidation of the patrimony of modern architecture by indulging in the "dialectical rapport between new and old," in the "stringent dialogue with the setting," in the "deep comprehension" of each phenomenon and its opposite, in the tragedy that is enjoyed for its own sake and consumption, in the rebellious attitude that is so intimate that no one could manage to discover it. Borromini

refused such an attitude, even though he lived in the closed climate of the Counter-Reformation. After the time of Wright and Le Corbusier, we act in a difficult context, but a context that is undoubtedly rather less oppressing and paralyzing. We have the right and the duty to go forward with a joyous perspective that is revealed by the revolutionary heritage of modern architecture.[26]

The accusation of taking recourse to "an intellectual apparatus that is ... sophisticated, charming, ambivalent and equivocal, obedient to the code of common dominion" rather than to "the 'deep comprehension' of each phenomenon and its opposite" are directed against Portoghesi and the balance of his arguments against the militant interpretations of Zevi. Zevi recognizes Portoghesi as being amongst "the best" at "hesitating, rethinking, verifying, remedying, distinguishing between various tendencies, re-discussing, demystifying, de-dramatizing, formulating hypotheses, trying new ways without being aware of how they contribute to the dilapidation of the patrimony of modern architecture." But beyond Zevi's disagreement with the historical reading of Portoghesi that is quite easy to identify in his words, it is his concern over architectonic tendencies that are well exemplified by that same Portoghesi and are moreover shared by international architectural debate.

Portoghesi recalls that:

> during the *Convegno di Studi* for the third centenary of the birth [sic.] of Borromini, the film I had made with Stefano Roncoroni was shown and Zevi seized the occasion to contrast his interpretation of Borromini against my own, accusing me of having "Berninized" Borromini. Since then the distance between us has become ever greater and our two ways have parted, up to the point of becoming openly divergent and, as regards the fate of architecture, openly antithetical.[27]

From the 1970s onwards, the modernist orthodoxy was in crisis, both in Italy and internationally. In various settings can be found architects taking recourse to history in a manner far removed from the refined filter of operative criticism. The historical citation becomes direct, and if it finds mediation, it becomes further mediated by other such contexts as Pop Art – as with *Learning from Las Vegas* in 1972 – than the abstract model of Zevi. In 1977 Charles Jencks published *The Language of Postmodern Architecture*. Between 1979 and 1984 Philip Johnson and Grant Burgee realized the AT&T Building in New York City. In Italy, it was Portoghesi himself, with the exhibition *La Presenza del Passato* at the 1980 Biennale di Venezia, who would consecrate in a tangibly stylistic sense the common ground between American and European historicist tendencies.

It is the very words of Zevi, as he updates his *Storia dell'architettura moderna*, that renders explicit the contingency of this moment and its effect on Zevi's critical project:

> The necessity to contrast the dissipating processes of contemporary architectural culture induced me to fix basic principles in the text *Il linguaggio moderno dell'architettura. Guida al codice anticlassico*, of 1973. That operation served to limit the academic regurgitations sustained by agnostic and arrogant critics who, having been blindly faithful to the international style and deaf to any instance of the organic movement, from one day to the next convert themselves into ferocious and indiscriminate accusers of that for which they themselves had fought for decades.[28]

The volume of 1973 comprises the most militant and perhaps the least convincing stance of operative criticism. The title is obviously drawn from that of John Summerson's book, *The Classical Language of Architecture*, translated in 1970 by the publisher Einaudi and published in the same series, "La piccola Biblioteca Einaudi," where Zevi's own book would shortly appear. The citation is instrumentally polemical. Where Summerson sought to define the continuity of the category of the classical in architecture, Zevi took it upon himself to define seven invariables that "confuse the classicist preconceptions to which we have succumbed and that offer the key to understanding contemporary messages."[29]

In *Linguaggio moderno dell'architettura* coagulates a series of instances that had, over the years, become central to Zevi's reflections, such as the fear that the language of modern architecture might transmogrify into yet one more style, as already expressed in 1941 in *An Opinion on Architecture*, or the necessity to equip the architect and the historian with defined instruments with which to direct both historical research and architectural design. This volume, moreover, once more brings together within a single treatment the recourse to old, modern, and contemporary architecture that had characterized Zevi's critical trajectory: *Dal Paleocristiano al Gotico*, the idealized Middle Ages, Michelangelo, Borromini, Wright and the myth of organic architecture. Zevi's writing also reflects the long wave of semiological inquiry, in those years at the center of both Italian and international cultural debate. Zevi seems to want to indulge it on its own terms, indeed more than an autonomous discourse might allow: "The semiological inquiry is fundamental, but we cannot pretend that it resolves architectural problems outside of architecture."[30]

But defining the rules in such biblical terms, the seven invariants, to decry those other rules of the classical language seems a contradiction. Zevi's invariables are precise: listing as design methodology; asymmetry and dissonance; antiperspectival three-dimensionality; the syntax of four-dimensional decomposition; cantilever, shell and membrane structures; space in time; reintegration of building, city and landscape. The apodictic charge with which it is argued bestows on his case an authoritative and assertive tone that transforms the volume into a sort of lay breviary to be used as a manifest profession of Zevian faith.

One should not forget that the book inserts itself in a specific historical juncture in which Zevi's effort to codify a counter-language sought to neutralize other more doctrinaire architectural theories. Besides the experience at the Facoltà di Architettura at Rome, where Zevi taught from 1963, and his relationship with the overcrowding of the university after 1968, which pushed the Roman historian towards the study of a didactic methodology that became ever more adherent to the instructive dimension of his work and to the fine-tuning of a kind of critical vade-mecum, the uses of which exceeded strictly disciplinary limits. Such was the case with *Saper vedere l'architettura*, with which *Il linguaggio moderno dell'architettura* shares, without equal, its critical and editorial fortunes.

Endnotes

1   Tafuri, "Il testamento di Manfredo Tafuri," 483. On Zevi's historical and cultural project, see Dulio, *Introduzione a Bruno Zevi*.

2   On Italian architectural culture between the wars, see Ciucci, *Gli architetti e il Fascismo*.

3   Zevi's *Architettura e storiografia* was revised in 1974 with the subtitle *Le matrici antiche del linguaggio moderno*.

4   See Dulio, *Introduzione a Bruno Zevi*, 23–42, 52–9.

5   Tafuri, "Il testament di Manfredo Tafuri," 483.

6   See Dulio, *Introduzione a Bruno Zevi*, 78–82. On Zevi's teaching at IUAV see also Dulio, "Samonà, Zevi e le 'chiamate' eccellenti," 91–8.

7   These "critical sketches" appear in Zevi, *Biagio Rossetti architetto ferrarese*, 31, 34, 42, 166, 303–4. All the graphic interpretations originally used in this volume are held in the Archivio Bruno Zevi, Fondazione Bruno Zevi in Rome (hereafter AZ).

8   Zevi, "Attualità di Michelangiolo architetto," 9–27, esp. 11, 17. The exhibition was accompanied by the catalogue *Mostra critica delle Opere Michelangiolesche*.

9   Zevi, "Attualità di Michelangiolo architetto," 21.

10   Zevi, "Le fortificazioni fiorentine," 377–424; and "Santa Maria degli Angeli," 761–812, both in *Michelangiolo architetto*. The sketches cited above appear on page 388.

11   Zevi, "Attualità di Michelangiolo architetto," 21.

12   Zevi, *Michelangiolo in prosa*, resp. 657–9, 662–5, 670–71, 676–7, 686–91, 700–701, 706–9.

13   Zevi and Portoghesi (eds), *Mostra critica delle Opere Michelangiolesche*, 10–11.

14   Zevi, "La storia come metodologia del fare architettonico," 13.

15   Zevi, "La storia come metodologia del fare architettonico," 13.

16   On this point see Dulio, "Le affinità elettive," 437–41; and "'Il mio miglior nemico'," 69–73.

17   See Rostagni, "Biografia," 210–12; and Rostagni, *Luigi Moretti*, esp. 8–19.

18   On the reprise of interior spatial models in Brinckmann, see Bucci, "Le parole dipinte," 136–55. See also Rostagni, *Luigi Moretti*, 8–19.

19   Bucci, *"Le parole dipinte,"* 148–9.

20 Compare Zevi, "Luigi Moretti double-face."
21 Zevi, "Attualità del Borromini," 509.
22 Zevi, "Attualità del Borromini," 510.
23 On this point see Payne, *Rudolf Wittkower*.
24 Zevi, "Attualità del Borromini," 525.
25 Zevi, "Attualità del Borromini," 530.
26 See Zevi's risposte with Portoghesi in *Studi sul Borromini*, 537–42.
27 Portoghesi, "Postfazione," 280–83.
28 Zevi, *Storia dell'architettura moderna*, vol. 2, 673.
29 Zevi, *Il linguaggio moderno dell'architettura*, back cover.
30 Zevi, *Il linguaggio moderno dell'architettura*, 10.

Chapter 17

Between History and Design:
The Baroque Legacy in the Work of Paolo Portoghesi

Silvia Micheli

Architecture can fix the old rules and invent new ones.

Guarino Guarini

Paolo Portoghesi (born in Rome, 1931) is an architect and one of Italy's most respected architectural historians of the twentieth century. His studies have ranged from the Renaissance, including the investigation of Leonardo's technical drawings and an edition of Leon Battista Alberti's *De re aedificatoria*, through to the architecture of Michelangelo, nineteenth-century Art Nouveau and contemporary architecture.[1] Nevertheless, Portoghesi's historical research has predominantly focused on the architecture of the Italian baroque. Portoghesi began writing articles on the baroque while still a student in Rome. In 1956 he published his first book on Guarino Guarini and at the same time his attention became increasingly devoted to the work of Francesco Borromini. Portoghesi's intuition was that aspects of modern architecture could be read and understood through the investigation of baroque architectural experience, a study that could provide useful design tools for developing contemporary architectural composition. Driven by an anticlassicist passion inherited from Bruno Zevi, Portoghesi's attention was caught by Borromini's skills in breaking the theoretical and projective rules seemingly fixed by Renaissance architecture. Setting itself free of conventions, Borromini's work became a symbol of liberation and innovation. From Portoghesi's Casa Baldi (1959–61), through to his design of the Mosque and Islamic Cultural Centre (1974–95), both in Rome, to the Via Novissima at the first Biennale di Architettura in Venice (1980), the historical lessons of baroque architecture had meaningful reverberations in Portoghesi's design work.

Paolo Portoghesi: The Architect, the Historian

The path towards baroque culture was, for Portoghesi, an experience rooted in his childhood in Rome. He recalls how the buildings of Borromini had caught his attention in daily life:

> Of all the character-architectures that populate my memories of childhood, there are two that captivated and intrigued me more: the dome of Sant'Ivo alla Sapienza I saw every day going to school, at first three-quarters hidden by the Palazzo Maccarani, then, turning back – and how many times I did it instinctively, even if it was late and I had to rush – as the bright background of the Piazza de' Caprettari; and the façade of the Casa dei Filippini, next to the Chiesa Nuova.[2]

And he remembers with how much patience he had to wait to visit the dome of Sant'Ivo alla Sapienza:

> When I was twenty, I received permission and managed to climb over the metal cage that crowns [the church] at the top. For me it was the kingdom of the swallows and the north wind, a fairy-tale country in which I wanted to live looking for I know not what treasures. So different from all the other things I knew, it had been for years, in childhood, the physical representation of architecture, the personification of this activity, this craft of building.[3]

When Portoghesi enrolled at the Faculty of Architecture in Rome, he was aware of two arguments that could guide his training. The first was that baroque architecture anticipated the theme of freedom from tradition and, secondly, that modern architecture had its origins in classicism. Portoghesi, who was formed in the wake of Zevi's anticlassicism, opted to recover the inheritance of the baroque.[4]

In the 1950s, at the beginning of Portoghesi's career, a broader disciplinary discussion devoted to the critical revision and recovery of the architectural heritage of the seventeenth century was initiated by the "third generation of historians."[5] As a result, Portoghesi had access to such influential books as Giedion's *Space, Time and Architecture* (1941), Wittkower's *Art and Architecture in Italy 1600 to 1750* (1958); Dorfles's *Barocco nell'architettura moderna* (1951), and *Borromini* (1952), *L'architettura barocca in Italia* (1957) and *L'Europa delle capitali 1600–1700* (1964) – both by Argan.[6] Expressly, Portoghesi recalls the particular importance of Argan's essay on Santa Maria in Campitelli, which argued for the conscious abandonment of the desire to represent absolute values through architecture. From these international high-scientific debates, Portoghesi was able to confirm his own intuitions, in so doing producing a mature line of research.

Portoghesi published his first book, *Guarino Guarini 1624–1683*, in 1956. His analysis of Guarini's buildings commenced with analogies and contrasts with the work of Borromini. At the time of writing *Guarini*, Portoghesi was also preparing significant articles on Borromini, whose work he claimed was his "favourite issue."[7] Although Portoghesi is recognized as being among the most prominent scholars of Borromini, the importance of his studies on Guarini, along with his 1972 essay on Bernardo Vittone and the eighteenth-century baroque tradition cannot be overstated.[8] In fact, his book on Guarini was highly regarded by both Wittkower and Argan, who quickly came to consider the young Portoghesi as one of the leading experts on baroque architecture in the Italian post-war context.

When, in 1964, Portoghesi published *Borromini nella cultura europea* (Borromini in European Culture) (Figure 17.1), he documented more than a decade's research into baroque architecture – an achievement quickly followed by *Roma barocca* (1966). In the foreword to his book of 1964, Portoghesi significantly presented himself as an "architect," rather than as an "historian," as one might expect: "This book written by an architect has been, in its time and in its chapters, a tool of methodological research, of clarifying issues, not only in respect to critical and historical operations but also in respect to the active intervention in the field of modern architectural culture."[9]

Portoghesi soon positioned himself as one of the principal heirs of the architectural tradition of the baroque in the twentieth century. "Heir," and not "custodian," for one who guards aspires to maintain without changing the object which has come into his or her possession, whereas Portoghesi instrumentally turned the principles of baroque architecture upon contemporary architecture as a "live matter." Unique among his generation of historians, Portoghesi showed that the foundations of baroque architecture, subject to a process of critical review, had a surprising utility in the contemporary context. His research activity thus played out on two fronts: the theoretical stances obtained from historical investigations methodically poured into the project. If the project becomes a site for checking the validity of theoretical assumptions recovered by the legacy of tradition and the moment of its being surpassed, it is therefore necessary to consider the project as a tool of architectural analysis and criticism as well as a historical text.

Argan observed that "Portoghesi, as an architect, puts in his critical vision an operative interest that gives to his prose a unique character in our criticism of architecture, unique because Portoghesi has the architect's sensibility for architectural form."[10] In respect of a method that crosses historical epochs, Portoghesi insists that his greater ambition was to create a bridge between writing history indirectly, by designing, and writing history directly, by investigating the legacy of the past. In *Le inibizioni dell'architettura moderna* (1974, The Inhibitions of Modern Architecture), his first theoretical book, he explains:

> In architecture you can build history, "write it" in a metaphorical sense, by designing and building works of architecture: it is by designing, for example, that architects of the early Renaissance reorganized their knowledge of the classical heritage into a unified *corpus*; it is by designing that Borromini has brought to light such methods as gothic diagonality, anticipating an analytical re-reading of medieval heritage. Each generation of architects, even without the direct and specific contribution of criticism, wrote history, interpreting it in a different way according to the problems of their time.[11]

Figure 17.1   Paolo Portoghesi, *Borromini nella cultura europea* (1964)

Portoghesi had initially participated in architectural debate as an historian of architecture, but in a seemingly ambiguous position. His academic career, split between Rome and Milan, saw him profiled as an historian rather than as a designer. It was not, in fact, until 1995 that he was appointed as a professor of architectural design at the Faculty of Architecture "Valle Giulia" of La Sapienza in Rome.[12] Yet Portoghesi was constantly engaged in the architecture profession even prior to his graduation in 1957 – an engagement that he did not at any time place on hold.

Consider that his first project for the Town Hall of Civitacastellana (Viterbo) dates back to 1954, only a year after the publication of his first essay on Borromini[13] and coinciding with the appearance of his second essay, "L'opera di Borromini per l'altare della chiesa di S. Paolo a Bologna." This project was, then, followed by a residential area at Valchetta, near Rome (1955), and the construction of buildings for ENPAS – the Ente Nazionale Previdenza e Assistenza ai dipendenti Statali – in Pistoia, Lucca, Florence and Cesenatica between 1957 and 1964.[14] The Casa Baldi (1959–61) and the design for the Opera House in Cagliari (1965) served as experimental laboratories for his historical explorations. And yet it was not until the 1970s that Portoghesi's design work was recognized as a consistent corpus of projects. In 1975 the Norwegian architect and architectural historian Christian Norberg-Schulz – who himself had written two books on the baroque – published *Alla ricerca dell'architettura perduta*, which positioned Portoghesi's architectural work within the theoretical framework of the "genius loci." Four years later, Francesco Moschini edited the book *Paolo Portoghesi. Progetti e disegni 1949–1979*, an excursus through Portoghesi's work that is proceeded by analogical combinations of drawings and photographs presenting Portoghesi's projects in light of his precedents to disclose the sources to which the architect turned for inspiration.

Portoghesi's duality as a "scholar" (architect/historian) becomes clearer if framed in the broader context of Italian architectural culture of the 1950s and 1960s. In this moment, the support of Ernesto N. Rogers for greater dialogue with the history of architecture in order to achieve compositional "freedom" exerted significant influence. "History" and "project" were considered synergic factors and architects accordingly undertook rigorous historical studies during their training. At that time a new generation of architects sought a critical review of the modern movement, the themes of which were considered germane for a renewal of design. This educational approach was typical in the working group of the Milan-based office of *Casabella-continuità*, the most influential architectural journal in Italy and directed between 1953 and 1964 by Rogers himself, whose work was well-known to Portoghesi. At the same time in Rome, Zevi was likewise, in the pages of *Metron* and *L'Architettura cronache e storia*, insisting on the need for the critical-operative recovery of the organic dimensions of modern architecture and a "direct confrontation" with its architectural problems. These experiences, based on the synergy of design and history, in turn informed the editorial line of the architectural magazine *Controspazio*, which was founded in 1969 and directed by Portoghesi.[15]

History as a Ritual of Contamination

In a moment of intense debate concerning the role that history of architecture should take in relation to design, it was of primary importance to find a way for orientating oneself, a valid method to which to refer. Disappointed by academic teaching, Portoghesi took an autonomous path based on the concept of "contamination." He was sure that each form of architecture was generated by other architectures "by a not so fortuitous convergence among precedents combined together by the imagination."[16]

Baroque culture formulated a new method of design that broadened the formal historical repertoire. In order to recover that lesson, Portoghesi figured Borromini as the "ideal master." He chose Borromini particularly for his relationship with the Renaissance tradition. Portoghesi observes that "while claiming responsibility for the right to invent new things,"[17] Borromini sought always for a dialectic between the new and the ancient. This was a goal pursued with the same determination by Borromini's follower Guarini, who was conscious of the need to adhere to the spirit of the age.[18] Portoghesi's goal, in turn, was to find the logic in which the architecture of antiquity was revealed to the modern consciousness as a problem of contemporary culture.

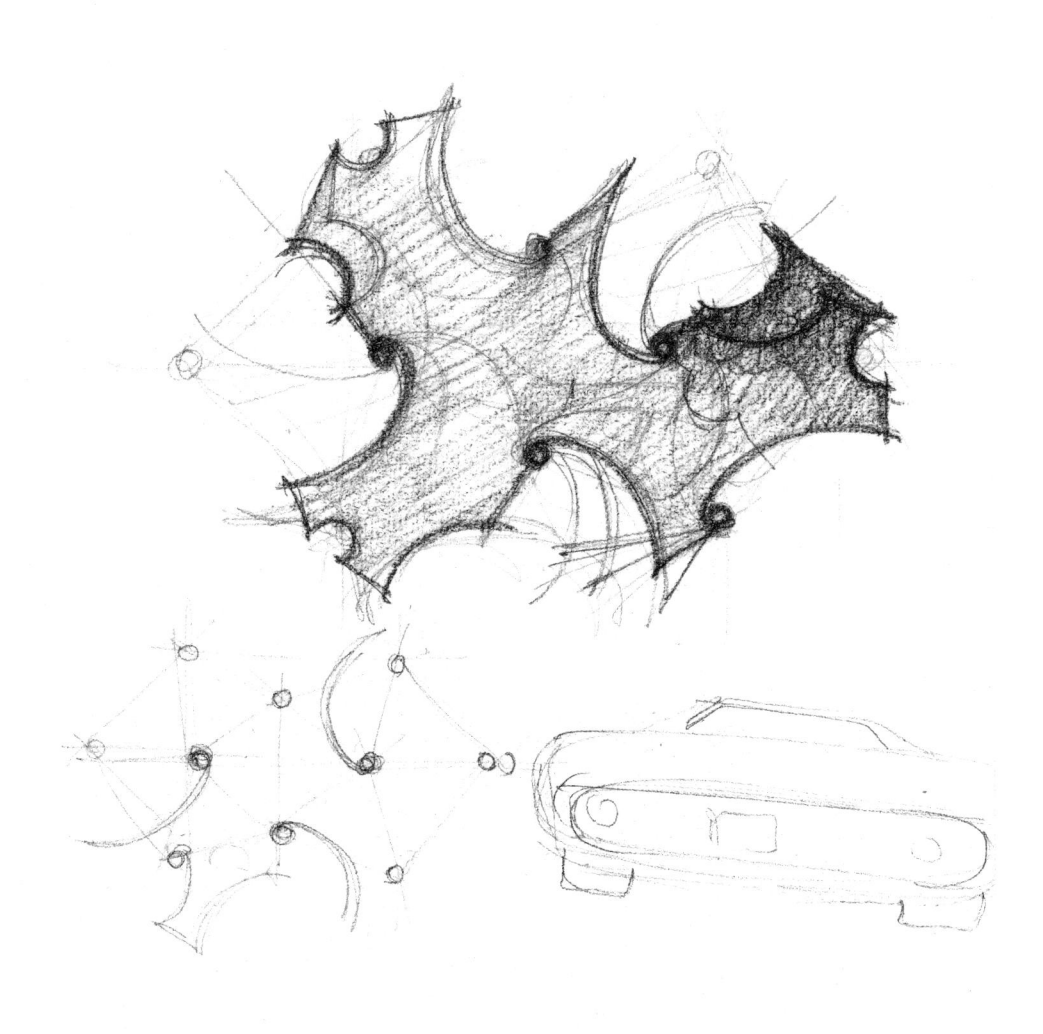

Figure 17.2   Paolo Portoghesi, Casa Baldi (Rome, 1959–61), sketch of the plan
Source: Centre Pompidou.

> Before being an occasion of historical and philological analysis, the knowledge of the work of Borromini is a tool for the self-criticism of modern culture. Against its own intentions for the expansion of classical orthodoxy, Borromini's controversy ultimately undermines the very foundations of the linguistic conventions restored by the Renaissance, overcoming, in its most intense moments, hesitations and inhibitions that still weigh, like mortgages, on modern architecture itself.[19]

Borromini and Guarini's shared interest in the dialogue between "revolution and tradition, rule and freedom"[20] indicated a way to avoid a contemplative or revival-like approach to history, then considered an impractical turn for architectural design. Portoghesi was fascinated by the critical attitude – neither burlesque nor subversive – that his *maestro* Borromini revealed when using the classical tradition in a new way.

1-2. Architettura e memoria. Particolare della lanterna di S. Ivo alla Sapienza a Roma, di F. Borromini, e particolare della casa Baldi (1959-62).

Figure 17.3 **"Architettura e Memoria," photographic comparison between Sant'Ivo alla Sapienza and Casa Baldi**

Source: Portoghesi, *Le inibizioni dell'architettura moderna* (1974): 41.

For Borromini it is no longer only to rebuild and restore a legacy, but to widen it from the inside and to deny the dogmatic and authoritarian character claimed for it by its contemporary interpreters. … [He] bravely faces, without compromise, the problem of redeeming the culture of his time from dogmatism, shallowness, and the passive celebration of the present.[21]

He recognizes Borromini's innovative spirit in Sant'Agnese in Rome's Piazza Navona, the façade of which reproduces the structure of the circus in a minor scale. Again, in the façade of Propaganda Fide, the relationship between interior and external space is mediated by a diminutive doric temple.

Portoghesi was keen to use the history of architecture as a "repertoire" of solutions, using neither direct "quotations" nor formal "mechanical transpositions."[22] Hence Portoghesi's buildings do not suffer from *borromonismo* but comprise, rather, of considered returns to those matters in the baroque that proved useful for the renewal of the modern language of architecture. The control of "space," the drawing of the "curve," the definition of the "corner," and the problem of the "opening," questions often darkened by modernist orthodoxy, are liberated and seen by Portoghesi as design instruments of direct pertinence to his own architectural production. As Argan observed, history is not soaked in politics for Portoghesi, as it is for Zevi; rather, it is dedicated to the investigation of form and its meanings.[23]

The Casa Baldi (Rome 1959–61) was Portoghesi's first opportunity to rebel against the modernist orthodoxy. He explained that the design process of the building had neoplastic origins and came from "the transformation of the joint experimented with by Rietveld in the Schröder house. … But while Rietveld's space is geometric, the goal of my research is to create an organic, pulsating space."[24] The stiffness of Rietveld's orthogonal scheme is overtaken by way of Borromini's example, his boldness in breaking the rules while at the same time being aware of the limits of action, because "his rebellion, his protest is 'put into verse', in a controlled and subtle form."[25] The space of the Casa Baldi is defined by the combination of inflected walls that absorb light (Figure 17.2). The dialectic relationship of its concave-convex forms renders the space continuous but not monotonous. The iconographic analogy between the lantern of Sant'Ivo alla Sapienza and the soffit edge of the Casa Baldi[26] suggests that the cornice obtained by the alternation of concave and convex lines in Sant'Ivo has been elaborated by Portoghesi as an element to join together the inflected walls and to amplify their expressive power (Figure 17.3). By using the curve, Portoghesi reconsidered the lesson of De Stijl in order to broaden its thematic horizon. In the section "Dissolvenze incrociate" in the book edited by Francesco Moschini, the neoplastic model serving as a precedent for the Casa Baldi is presented through photographic combinations that show the desire of "contamination:" the Schröder house has been placed in proximity to Ronchamp Chapel by Le Corbusier and to the house for the Berlin exhibition by Ludwig Mies van der Rohe.[27] As Portoghesi emphasizes: "From then up to now, the game has turned into a ritual."[28]

The Critical Drawing

In 1967, during the celebrations of the third centenary of Borromini's death, an international congress was organized at the Accademia nazionale di San Luca in Rome. Portoghesi was invited to moderate the third roundtable, entitled "L'eredità di Borromini in Italia" (The Legacy of Borromini in Italy). While this discussion afforded an opportunity for Portoghesi to explore Borromini's importance for his present moment, his views were, in fact, pulled sharply into focus during a polemic debate with Bruno Zevi, following Zevi's lecture on the "Attualità del Borromini" (The Contemporaneity of Borromini).[29] Distancing himself from the assumptions of Zevi, "who needs to hide some emergent aspects of Borromini's work in order to present him as 'subversive',"[30] Portoghesi insisted on the recovery of those aspects of Borromini's design process that were "useful" instruments for the present. His declared aim was to formulate a historical interpretation of Borromini's architecture based on objective values. Avoiding "reading Borromini as Bernini-like" (*berninizzare il Borromini*), as Zevi would appear to intend, Portoghesi argued that philological analysis and critical observations are insufficient for the task at hand: it is necessary to enact the "verification of the drafting table" in order to continue that interrupted research so full of premises.[31] The "critical drawing" is a means of this verification, the middle passage between word and project.[32]

This conviction permeates the exhibition *Disegni di Francesco Borromini* (The Drawings of Francesco Borromini), curated by Portoghesi at the Accadamia di San Luca in that same *anno borrominiano*. In the preface to its catalogue, Portoghesi confesses his fascination with the analytical technique of representation that unites the drawings on display, but also with the obsessive geometrical construction of the forms. Borromini's drawings not only reveal an exceptional "drawing ability" but also "a rigorous design logic."[33] In order to understand what Portoghesi means by "drawing ability," it is useful to examine the analytical boards included in the catalogue. He regards the drawing of board number 50, representing the section and the front of the lantern of Sant'Ivo alla Sapienza (Albertina 510), "as one of the most fascinating accounts to date of the art of construction." Borromini's boldness relies, for Portoghesi, on the simultaneous representation of structural development and form: "The drawing, with its transparencies, its veilings, is a true X-ray that shows, where it is needed, the internal structure, qualifying itself as a section or describing the surfaces as an elevation, or both together."[34]

Beyond Borromini's capacity to synthesize the idea of space, structure and the technologies of building in architectural drawing, Portoghesi observes, too, his "rigorous design logic," which he understands as the ultimate instrument to face the problems posed by historical tradition.[35] Indeed, the design phase occurs in two different moments: the "design genesis" and its "geometric verification."[36] The "design genesis" precedes the "geometric verification" and is based on a method of typological and linguistic synthesis. In order to demonstrate this thesis, Portoghesi turns to San Carlo alle Quattro Fontane. Its crooked curve is the result of the contamination of the classical language by gothic infiltrations, a tradition inherited by Carlo Maderno in Lombardia and absorbed in the first stage of Borromini's working life. The "design genesis" (ideational phase) is followed by the "geometric verification" (a control phase), based on the scientific construction of plans and façades.[37]

Portoghesi notes the extent to which Borromini's projects are both verified and verifiable, since architecture embraces geometry as "a means of extending to wider and wider fields the process of rationalizing visual knowledge."[38] This practice allows for the removal of every approximation of form and whim of invention, tracing each structure back to a universally legible scheme. Having recovered the geometrical bases of San Carlo, for instance, Portoghesi can observe that Borromini faces "the problem of carrying out the scheme through a rigorous method capable of reducing empirical choices."[39]

Portoghesi pursues the theme of the geometrical principle as a moment for the project's verification in the first section of *Borromini nella cultura europea*, entitled "La geometria borrominiana. Saggio di analisi sintattica" (Borrominian Geometry: An Essay on Syntactic Analysis).[40] Its position at the beginning of the book indicates its importance. Through a series of analytical panels Portoghesi points to the potential origins of the architectural ideas underpinning San Carlo alle Quattro Fontane, Sant'Ivo alla Sapienza, Sant'Andrea delle Fratte and the Collegio di Propaganda Fide. Portoghesi schematically redraws their plans or details, following step-by-step the geometrical traces. His interpretative schemes serve to empirically demonstrate Borromini's design principles, which in turn rely upon the combination of regular forms. The consequences of Borromini's method, case after case, are a series of complex schemes dominated by a curved line determined by choices that are far from arbitrary. In their own research, Wittkower and Argan were likewise engaged in the discovery of the genesis of Borromini's work; but Portoghesi's studies reveal an originality of method that sets his own work apart from the scholarship of this earlier generation.

He reconstructs, for instance, the development of San Carlo by starting with the original drawing kept at Albertina Museum in Vienna and published in the very first pages of *Borromini nella cultura europea*. In contrast to Wittkower and Argan, who suggest the hall of the Piazza d'Oro in Villa di Adriano at Tivoli as a precedent for this project,[41] Portoghesi suggests an origin for the church in Michelangelo's scheme for San Pietro. He concurs with Wittkower's assessment that the geometrical foundation of the plan is a pair of equilateral triangles with a common base.[42] Yet Portoghesi takes his explanation further:

> Plate B – San Carlino 2. … The first phase of the layout concerns the design of the oval of the dome, constructed with the rule of equilateral triangles; the vertices of two raised triangles determine the centres of the four segments of the circle that form the oval, while their bisectors mark the horizontal axis and the intersection of curves of different radii. Thus, the equilateral triangle, a symbol of the Trinity, occurs as a latent form, at the origin of the compositional process.[43]

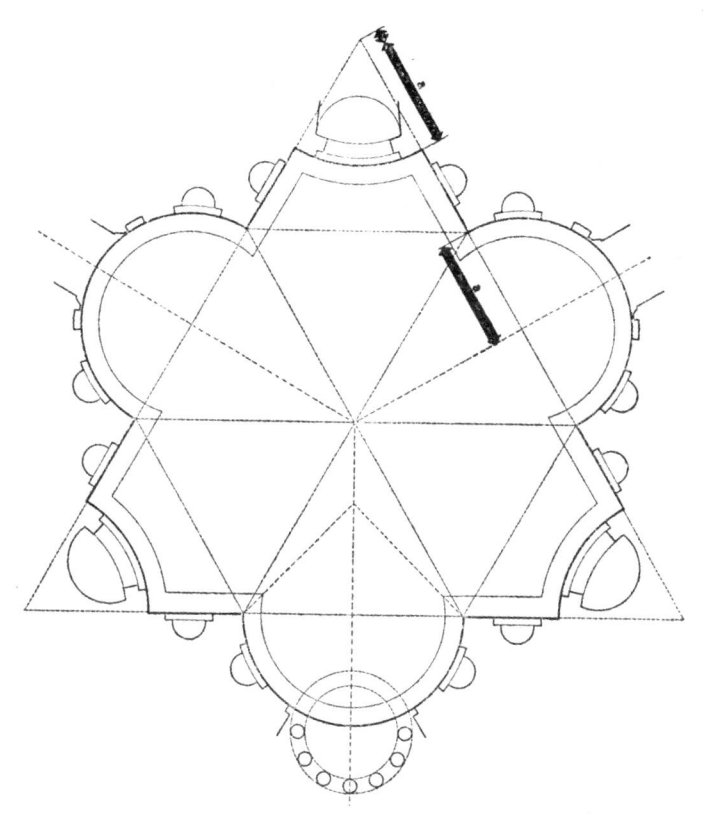

TAV. H - S. Ivo 2.

Tracciate le tre absidi semicircolari, sugli altri lati dell'esa-
gono, inscritto nel triangolo generatore, si appoggiano altri nuclei
spaziali dal contorno mistilineo; in parte essi si avvalgono dei lati
del triangolo che in tal modo determina direttamente parte del
perimetro fondamentale. Le terminazioni convesse sono realizzate
con archi di cerchio che hanno il loro centro sui vertici dello stesso
triangolo. Il raggio di questi archi è però diverso da quello delle
absidi semicircolari. L'abside colonnata presente nel primo pro-
getto fu soppressa nella realizzazione.

Figure 17.4   Plan of Sant'Ivo alla Sapienza, critical drawing by Paolo Portoghesi
Source: Borromini nella cultura europea.

The same analytical furor distinguishes the verification of Sant'Ivo alla Sapienza. Portoghesi focuses his attention on the scheme of the church, wherein an equilateral triangle contains a hexagon. Wittkower provided an overall picture of the religious complex and a plan of the church showing the rhythmic construction of the alternating convex and concave niches, yet Portoghesi focuses on redesigning the layout of the church, starting with an equilateral triangle in which is inscribed a hexagon, generating its overall shape. To this extent Portoghesi agrees with both Wittkower and Argan. While a comparative reading of their three respective interpretations could well result in a sharp exchange among peers, Portoghesi's analysis ameliorates this to a degree through the development of his critical drawings, which take on a key role in his interpretation of these plates (Figure 17.4).

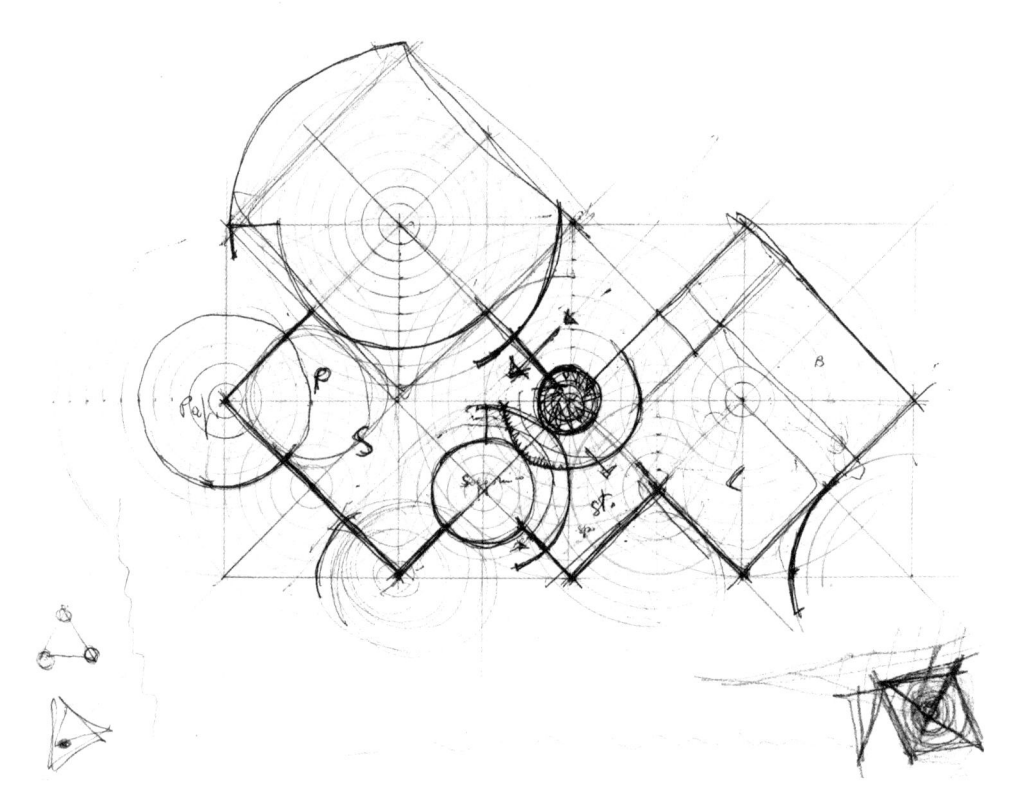

Figure 17.5   Paolo Portoghesi, Casa Andreis (Scandriglia, 1964–69), plan
Source: Centre Pompidou.

> Plate G – S. Ivo 1. The geometric matrix of the interiors of S. Ivo is the equilateral triangle. The illustrations in this plate show the different steps of its geometric genesis. (1) The triangle is divided into sub-triangles. (2) On the intermediate triangles of each of the sides is set a semicircle of corresponding diameter.[44]

In drawing up these schemes, Portoghesi sets himself in the role of the humble scholar executing a task of self-discipline through which he might acquire a logical and rational method of design able to secure him that "freedom" for which he seeks. Indeed, Zevi recognized in Portoghesi's totalizing research on Borromini a "relationship of affinity and almost of identification" with his subject.[45]

Considering *that Borromini nella cultura europea* was in preparation for a period of more than 12 years, it is plausible that some of the issues it documents were already under observation when Portoghesi began his activity as an architect. Three house projects bear this out. The Casa Baldi, first of all, offers a moment that speaks to Portoghesi's experimental adaptation of Borromini's method. In this sense the sketches of the house are revealing. One of these shows the emergence of its geometric construction through the placement of generative dots of curve segments – "force fields," as Christian Norberg-Schulz described them. They are fixed within the perimeter of a hexagon, the hypothesis of the pentagon having been soon abandoned.[46] The "force fields" generate "grammatical chords" obtained by the juxtaposition of inflected walls that determine the various openings in the plan.[47] The drawings for the Casa Andreis (Scandriglia, Rieti, 1964–69) are likewise exemplary for the understanding they demonstrate of a geometrically constructed "regulating layout" and of its volumetric development (Figure 17.5). A first sketch shows that Portoghesi had been working on a grid of modular squares, the vertices of which generated concentric circles. The drawing evolves into a second layout wherein three adjacent scalene triangles led him to fix the "centres of curvature."[48] Only the geometric organization of the plan can bring a rhythm to the surface, the disposition of which is ruled by a principle of "order in movement." That geometric order characterizing the houses of Portoghesi's exordium is stressed emphatically in the Casa Papanice (Rome, 1966–70), in which the geometry of its layout is more complicated, the spatial rhythm becomes psychedelic and the overall volume of the building, generated through the exhausting repetition of cylinders, deliberately assumes a playful, even ironic character.[49]

These methodological premises – explored above in designs for family houses located beyond the city centre – are verified in two urban projects, which present a real test of this approach for Portoghesi and his collaborator Vittorio Gigliotti: the competition for the Opera House in Cagliari (1965) and for the extension of the Chamber of Deputies in Rome (1967). In Rome, to control the process of rooting the building in its context in order to obtain a dialogue with its surrounds, the architects proposed a plan system generated by a central core that coincides with the axis of vertical paths, and around which develops an aggregation of triangular modules that grows, in turn, into a broken spiral. In his study of the Chamber of Deputies competition, Manfredo Tafuri wrote that Portoghesi had

> been theorizing for a long time the need for a rigorous, programmed structure of geometric types, in which it is possible to recover the irrational and a sensitivity to the morphology of the place. In his competition project, the modular grid and the spiral that generates the contraction of the vitreous volume sloping upwards serves to confirm and criticize one another, as if to prove that unique and true freedom lies in the rigor with which the limits are set.[50]

The Arts Academy in L'Aquila (1978–82) is the synthesis of three models of star-shape plan: Santuary of Žďár by J. Santini Aichl, Haus des Himmels by Bruno Taut and Lina House by Mario Ridolfi. The strong centrality of the layout is controlled by the form of a regular pentagon. Its sides, with respect to the five prismatic bodies that compose the building, are rotated by one degree to soften the rigidity of geometric pattern.

If in Portoghesi's poetic, the contamination of historical forms becomes "ritual," then the geometric verification of drawings becomes systematic. The historical-design method thus obtained on the back of the legacy he recovers from the architecture of Borromini and Guarini is not a personal invention: he has never claimed its paternity.

Artificial Universe

In 1975 Paolo Portoghesi became involved in a project that proved to be decisive for its complexity and its visibility in relation to his historical research: the Islamic Cultural Centre in Rome, designed together with Vittorio Gigliotti and Sami Mousawi and completed in 1995. The programme of the building was problematic in both political and religious terms: in the late 1970s the international economy was placed under threat through a global oil crisis; and the building, moreover, was the first Islamic edifice to be built in the heart of the Catholic capital. Portoghesi focused his efforts on the question of how to put into dialogue the Islamic and Christian tradition – a problem for which the "ritual of contamination," developed over two decades and inherited from Borromini and Guarini, would prove decisive in his location of the means to secure a perfect formal balance and to reach an advanced degree of structural complexity.

As in the case of Borromini's projects for the Convento dei Trinitari and San Carlo alle Quattro Fontane, the organism centre-mosque was likewise generated by a "psychological programme" played out in the gap between the simplicity of facilities spaces and the complexity of the linguistico-spatial setting of worship. The mosque's plan was derived from the regular repetition of a square matrix (Figure 17.6). The architectural idea of the building, which renders the building's interior an impressive "artificial universe," is based on a crossed-arch system. Portoghesi himself recalled that the cross-arch system is a recurring motif in both the eastern and western histories of architecture, from the Armenian example of Acphat[51] to the interwoven ribs of gothic edifices, from Leonardo da Vinci's explorations for the structural system of the lantern of the Duomo in Milan to the Florentine project by Pier Luigi Nervi for the Berta Stadium.[52] It offers a high degree of "cultural synthesis:" "While posing interwoven ribs once more for the mosque in Rome, I wanted to offer the minds of observers a commuter route from East to West, recalling meetings that had already taken place between Islamic and Italian cultures, resuming a dialogue that had on several occasions been interrupted."[53]

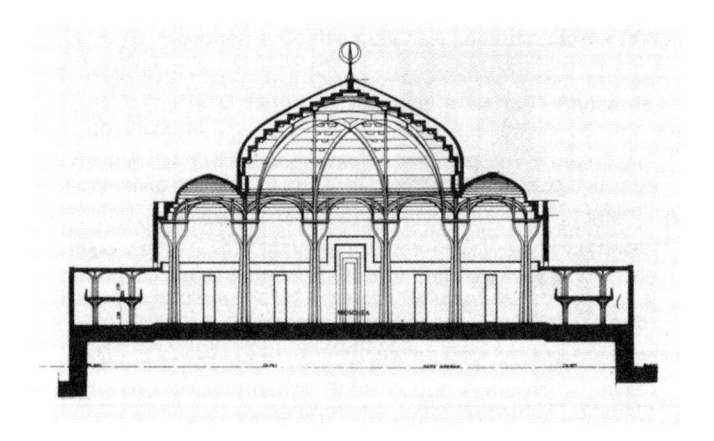

**Figure 17.6   Paolo Portoghesi (with Vittorio Gigliotti and Sami Mousawi), Mosque and Islamic
Centre (Rome 1974–95), section of the mosque**
Source: Massobrio, Ercadi and Tuzi, *Paolo Portoghesi architetto* (2001).

The approach to the solution of the cross-arch system as an architectural motif bridging between eastern and western cultures likewise invokes the study of the baroque. As Norberg-Schulz observed: "It is already possible to glimpse a synthesis of these two cultures in the work of Guarini."[54] Portoghesi regards this "Borrominian recruit" in great esteem, admiring his "highly receptive approach, that exceptional openness to listening,"[55] but also his structural boldness, both factors that likewise characterize the work of Borromini. Portoghesi had also taken the opportunity to appreciate Guarini's extraordinary formal rigor, elaborated in its geometry and rendered, therefore, available as a fruitful compositional tool. Among Guarini's buildings, the church of San Lorenzo in Turin caught Portoghesi's attention. Its structure, he recalled, is animated by a "calculated" movement of which "the famous plot of the dome, … a wonderful petrified flower" obliged Portoghesi to pursue its precedents. Beyond the dome of Mir'hab of the al Hakem Mosque in Cordova, already named by Giedion in the pages he dedicated to the baroque in *Space, Time and Architecture*, Portoghesi suggests the narthex of the Romanesque church of Sant'Evasio in Casale Monferrato.[56] Nevertheless, the most direct inspiration is once more from Borromini and, in particular, crossed arches of the chapel dedicated to the Magi in the Collegio di Propaganda Fide.[57] The whole arched structure of the Roman mosque is independent from the intrados of the dome, increasing spatial tension and imbuing the building with a high degree of architectural expressiveness. The stellar plot of the arches even serves to propagate the lateral spaces, covered by 16 smaller domes, thereby providing an effect of spatial unity despite the difference in their heights. The arches of the central space soar from the tops of eight columns, which together recall, too, an Art Nouveau influence in their distinctive form.

In conceiving of this conceptual solution for the mosque, Portoghesi faced the problem of light control – and again the solutions offered by the baroque proved extremely "useful." The stepped central dome is rhythmically pierced by narrow openings, with the effect that the natural light is at once homogeneous and lends the structure a surprisingly anti-gravitational effect – a device borrowed from the spatial solution developed by Guarini for the Cappella della Santa Sindone in Turin. Here, although characterized by a delirious upward pace, the weight of the dome structure of the chapel seems to dematerialize due to the effect of suspension procured from the light filtering into the space through these small openings.

In 1995, at the opening of the Islamic Centre in Rome, Argan confessed to Portoghesi: "Until a few days ago I admired you more as an historian of architecture than as an architect. Maybe I was not entirely wrong, then: but now, yes. Only a great historian could make a great architectural work, as you have done."[58]

After Modern Architecture

In 1980 Portoghesi was appointed director of the first Biennale di Architettura di Venezia, significantly entitled "La Presenza del Passato" ("The Presence of the Past").[59] As a decisive moment in the process of marking and overcoming modern architecture, the exhibition can be considered the culmination of the historical inquiry Portoghesi had commenced as early as the 1950s. With the three solo shows on Philip Johnson, Ignazio Gardella and Mario Ridolfi, Portoghesi honoured those architects who had distinguished themselves for their efforts in recovering history within their designs in the post-war years. It was, however, the staging of the Via Novissima at the Corderie building in the Arsenale that properly became the "show" of the event. As an urban backstage realized at full scale, Via Novissima was a real "street" comprising of 20 façades (10 on each side of the street), each one commissioned from the offices of architects both within Italy and abroad. The main criterion used by Portoghesi for the selection of his guests was their ability to abandon the modernist orthodoxy in order to offer solutions in tune with their own time.[60] The research he had commenced in Italy in a state of relative autonomy was thus enriched by new international contributions.

The theme of the composition of the "frontage" is exquisitely baroque. In its conception, architects were given leave to tackle purely linguistic-formal design issues, since each façade was a temporary structure made of timber, behind which the work of individuals was exhibited. This compositional exercise led directly to another theme central to Portoghesi's fascination with the baroque: "popular persuasion," or form as a vehicle of communication. As he observed as early as 1964: "The rhetorical and persuasive essence of the baroque, its search for a direct communication beyond the conventions of a restricted category, its substantial popularity."[61]

More than in any other project in Portoghesi's oeuvre, the design of his façade for the Strada Novissima (with Francesco Cellini and Claudio D'Amato) made explicit homage to Borromini, borrowing distinctive elements from the formal façade of the Oratorio dei Filippini (Figure 17.7). Portoghesi conveys the same idea of motion that innervates the façade of that Roman building featured in his drawing, which, however, gives greater prominence to vertical lines of force rather than to the horizontal. Ideas regarded as typical of baroque architecture – tying together all the elements of the façade, alternating between concavity and convexity – still survive, although the tension generated by the compression of the façade of the Oratorio is not, in Venice, fully reached. Nevertheless, the most surprising compositional moment occurred in the termination of the façade, which literally becomes a quotation: such explicit formal provocations were never before found in the buildings of Portoghesi. An intentional, single act of *borrominismo* within a 20-year period of research demonstrated that the process of appropriating the architectural heritage of the architectural baroque had reached its full maturity.

In the same year of the exhibition, Portoghesi's second "theoretical" book on architecture appeared: *Dopo l'architettura moderna* (After Modern Architecture). It presents the evolution of his historical and design research as developed in the wake of the baroque tradition. A close examination of its topics – "The Post-modern," "Architecture and the Energy Crisis," "The Primitives of a New Sensibility," "The American Affair" together announce a new phase in Portoghesi's scholarly trajectory.

The characteristics of this post-modern architecture are captured mainly in its difference compared to the modern movement, but also in its analogy with the cultural production of historical periods similar to ours, such as mannerism and the baroque. First, the post-modern is more evolutionary than revolutionary, does not deny the modern tradition, but freely interprets and integrates, critically recounting the glories and the mistakes. Against the dogmas of uniqueness, of personal stylistic consistency, static or dynamic balance, against the purity and the absence of any "vulgar" element, post-modern architecture re-evaluates ambiguity and irony, the plurality of styles, the dual code that allows one to turn, on one hand, to popular taste by means of historical or vernacular quotations and, on the other, back to the insiders.[62]

With the publication of his 1982 book *Postmodern: L'architettura nella società post-industriale* (Postmodern: Architecture in Post-industrial Society), written after the construction of Strada Novissima, Portoghesi sealed his place among the founding fathers of architectural postmodernism. Even in this intense period of theoretical and design evolution, enhanced by new architectural themes and dialectical relationships with new partners, Portoghesi continued his investigations into history, so synergic were they with the postmodern project. From his studies on the work of Borromini and the culture of the baroque, Portoghesi finally turned his attention to the "Liberty" style, focusing in particular on the work of Victor Horta – considered, by him, the most Borrominian figure in the world of Art Nouveau.[63]

Figure 17.7   Strata Novissima (Venice, 1980), façade designed by Paolo Portoghesi, Francesco Cellini and Claudio D'Amato

Source: "La presenza del Passato," *Controspazio*, nos 1–6, 1980.

Endnotes

1   For Portoghesi's complete bibliography see Massobrio, Ercadi and Tuzi, *Paolo Portoghesi architetto*. See, specifically, Portoghesi, "I disegni tecnici di Leonardo," 6–24; Alberti, *L'architettura*, edited by Portoghesi; Portoghesi and Zevi, *Michelangiolo architetto*; Borsi and Portoghesi, *Victor Horta*; Massobrio and Portoghesi, *Album del Liberty*; and Portoghesi, Quattrocchi and Quilici, *Barocco e Liberty*.

2   Portoghesi, *Le inibizioni dell'architettura moderna*, 35.

3   Portoghesi, *Le inibizioni dell'architettura moderna*, 40.

4   Portoghesi interviewed by Micheli, Calcata, Rome, 25 February 2011.

5   Barroero, "Wittkower ven'anni dopo," xxx.

6   Portoghesi stated his interest in Argan's interpretative thesis on baroque architecture and Borrimini in "Intervento di P. Portoghesi sulla relazione di B. Zevi," 536. The proximity of Portoghesi's position to Argan's thesis is confirmed on the back cover Portoghesi, *Le inibizioni dell'architettura moderna*.

7   Portoghesi, *Le inibizioni dell'architettura moderna*, 85.

8   Portoghesi, "Vittone nella cultura europea," 38–52.

9   Portoghesi, *Borromini nella cultura europea*, vii.

10 Argan's endorsement of Portoghesi, *Roma Barocca*, back cover.

11 Portoghesi, *Le inibizioni dell'architettura moderna*, 74–5.

12 Portoghesi began teaching in 1958 at the Scuola di Perfezionamento per lo Studio e il Restauro dei monumenti in Rome, and from 1961 he taught history of criticism at the Faculty of Architecture at La Sapienza. He became Professor of the History of Architecture at the Faculty of Architecture of the Politecnico di Milano from 1966 to 1979, where he furthermore he served as Dean between 1968 and 1976. From 1976 to 1980 he taught design at the Politecnico di Milano and, from 1982, he has been Professor of Architectural History at Rome.

13 Portoghesi, "Borromini in ferro," 50–53.

14 For a survey of the early-career design work of Portoghesi see Priori, *Paolo Portoghesi*.

15 For a deeper analysis of the period, see Micheli, "Italian Architecture," 80–89.

16 Priori, *Paolo Portoghesi*, 15.

17 Portoghesi, "Intervento di P. Portoghesi sulla relazione di B. Zevi," vol. 1, 534.

18 Portoghesi, *Borromini nella cultura europea*, 13.

19 Portoghesi, *Borromini nella cultura europea*, introductory note.

20 Portoghesi, *Borromini nella cultura europea*, introductory note.

21 Portoghesi, "Intervento di P. Portoghesi sulla relazione di B. Zevi," 532–3.

22 Zevi, "Attualità del Borromini," vol. 1, 509.

23 Argan, "Nella crisi del mondo moderno," 13.

24 Portoghesi, "Casa Baldi sull'ansa della Flaminia, a Roma," 512.

25 Portoghesi, "Intervento di P. Portoghesi sulla relazione di B. Zevi," 532–3.

26 Portoghesi, *Le inibizioni dell'architettura moderna*, 41.

27 Priori, *Paolo Portoghesi*, 79–152.

28 Priori, *Paolo Portoghesi*, 16.

29 See the discussion between Zevi and Portoghesi in *Studi sul Borromini*, vol. 1, 507–42. See also Massobrio, Ercadi, Tuzi, *Paolo Portoghesi architetto*, 37–9.

30 Portoghesi, "Intervento di P. Portoghesi sulla relazione di B. Zevi," 531.

31 Portoghesi, *Le inibizioni dell'architettura moderna*, 76–80.

32 Portoghesi, *Le inibizioni dell'architettura moderna*, 85.

33 Portoghesi, *Disegni di Francesco Borromini*, 3.

34 Portoghesi, *Disegni di Francesco Borromini*, 19.

35 Manfredo Tafuri in "Il metodo di progettazione del Borromini," by Roberti et al., vol. 2, 16.

36 Portoghesi, "Intervento di P. Portoghesi sulla relazione di B. Zevi," 533–4.

37 This moment of the project has already been suggested by Wittkower in *Arte e architettura in Italia*, 170–71.

38 Portoghesi, *Borromini nella cultura europea*, 15.

39 Portoghesi, *Borromini nella cultura europea*, xi.

40 Portoghesi, *Borromini nella cultura europea*, ix–xxiv.

41   Argan, *Borromini*, 71–2; Wittkower, *Arte e architettura in Italia*, 173.

42   Wittkower, *Arte e architettura in Italia*, 170.

43   Portoghesi, *Borromini nella cultura europea*, xi.

44   Portoghesi, *Borromini nella cultura europea*, xvi–xvii.

45   Zevi, "Borromini Today. In the 400th anniversary of his birth, 1599," 55.

46   Centre Pompidou Drawings Archive/AM 2009-2-856. The drawing has been only partially published in Ercadi (ed.), *Paolo Portoghesi*, 44.

47   Portoghesi, "Casa Baldi sull'ansa della Flaminia, a Roma," 512.

48   Portoghesi, "Casa Andreis a Scandriglia, Rieti," 713.

49   Priori, *Paolo Portoghesi*, 54.

50   Tafuri, *Il concorso per i nuovi uffici della Camera dei Deputati*, 42.

51   See Massobrio, Ercadi and Tuzi, *Paolo Portoghesi architetto*, 190.

52   On the list of precedents, see Portoghesi, "Roma, Moschea e Centro Islamico Culturale d'Italia, 1974–1995" in Massobrio, Ercadi and Tuzi (eds), *Paolo Portoghesi architetto*, 190; Priori, *Paolo Portoghesi*, 124–33.

53   Portoghesi, "Roma, Moschea e Centro Islamico Culturale d'Italia, 1974–1995," 194.

54   Norberg-Schulz, "Paolo Portoghesi, un architetto romano" in Massobrio, Ercadi and Tuzi (eds), *Paolo Portoghesi architetto*, 8.

55   Portoghesi, *Guarino Guarini 1624–1683*, cit. (pages not indicated).

56   Portoghesi, *Guarino Guarini*, unpaginated. See also Giedion, *Space, Time and Architecture* (2nd edn), 59–60.

57   For the repertoire of precedents for this project see Priori, *Paolo Portoghesi*, 124–33.

58   Letter published in Argan, "Nella crisi del mondo moderno," 18.

59   See Szacka, "The Presence of the Past," 132–5.

60   The invited architects were Ricardo Bofill, Costantino Dardi, Frank O. Gehry, Thomas Gordon Smith, GRAU, Michael Graves, Allan Greenberg, Hans Hollein, Arata Isozaki, Joseph-Paul Kleihues, Leon Krier, OMA, Charles Moore, Franco Purini e Laura Thermes, Massimo Scolari, Robert Stern, Stanley Tigerman, Oswald M. Ungers and Venturi, Rauch and Scott-Brown. See Portoghesi (ed.), *La Presenza del Passato*.

61   Portoghesi, *Borromini nella cultura europea*, 5–6.

62   Portoghesi, *Dopo l'architettura moderna*, 59.

63   Zevi, "Attualità del Borromini," 514.

Chapter 18
Steinberg's Complexity

Michael Hill

Figure 18.1   Leo Steinberg, c. 1957

Source: Sheila Schwartz.

Leo Steinberg was nearing 40 and a late starter to graduate studies, but he hit the ground running with a dissertation submitted at the end of 1959 to New York University's Institute of Fine Arts, *Borromini's San Carlo alle Quattro Fontane: A Study in Multiple Form and Architectural Symbolism.*[1] Steinberg showed little of the normal doctoral caution: methods were challenged and the image of Borromini's architecture overturned. One attitude in particular that he rejected was an understanding of the church in terms of Borromini's supposedly conflicted, even disturbed genius. Steinberg was wary of psycho-biography and insisted that if personality must be discussed, then it should be derived from San Carlo rather than imposed upon it. Instead, the church is in the foreground on almost every page and contexts as they arise are woven into the visual analysis. Steinberg argued, here implicitly but more overtly later in his career, that art historians should prioritize images, reversing their normal evidentiary value compared to written sources. This was more than formalism, because another feature of the dissertation is its conviction that in a work like San Carlo form is always symbolic, meaning and its expression being dissolved one into the other.[2] Open-ended as well, for Steinberg implied that San Carlo generated interpretation rather than was contained by it. Steinberg wrote as a student, in part discovering what he believed along the way, and once finished latent features would crystallize into a method that looked forward to aspects of the new art history and post-modernist architectural theory. Yet on another level, Borromini was the figure Steinberg had been looking for, having already developed an interpretive approach when he wrote as a critic throughout the 1950s.

After leaving London's Slade School with a fine arts diploma in 1940, Steinberg spent the next decade working out what to do, having realized that he lacked that indefinable something that could have made him an artist. Along the way he honed his literary skills (he had only begun to learn English in 1933) with translations from the Yiddish of Jacob Pat's *Ashes and Fire* (1947) and Sholem Asch's *Mary* (1949). Entering his 30s, he committed to writing about art and studying its history, beginning with two statements of intent: "The Twin Prongs of Art Criticism" in 1952, and "The Eye is a Part of the Mind" in 1953. Although Steinberg disowned the first essay a decade later, its incipient approach is telling. It argues that a work of art will outlive any specific interpretation and that no system of aesthetics can adapt to its persistent vitality. The critical criterion of what Clive Bell called "significant form" is too fragile to be of long-term aid, resting as it does on the mistaken idea that the modern pundit speaks from a prospect at the end of humanism, art having liberated itself from content.[3] The proposition of the second essay is simple but far reaching: "natural fact can be purely apprehended only where the human mind has first endowed it with the status of reality."[4] Perception cannot stand unviolated by thought and no threshold separates representation and abstraction, because thinking eyes automatically situate perceived data, whether from the world beyond or the pictorial surface near at hand, into the metaphorical fabric of the mind; contrawise, naturalism is not transparent that it is innocent of subjectivity.[5] Steinberg's attention to the cultural sediment beneath modernist imagery would be a feature of his short career as reviewer for *Arts Magazine*, commenced in November 1955 at the behest of Hilton Kramer and completed July 1956 at the exhaustion of the author.[6]

A piece on Willem De Kooning's *Woman*, for example, observes not her semi-abstraction but the depth of her meaning, "unsteeped from a tangle of desire and fear, with some millennia of civilizing evolution still ahead of her."[7] In short, when Steinberg set himself to writing on Borromini he was in the midst of an argument with those who esteem art for its shapes and patterns alone, pleading the historian's case for symbolic context.

Steinberg's initial topic was the afterlife of the Romanesque, but when he went to his advisor Richard Krautheimer with a change of mind he was spurned for a method founded more in the experience of architecture than in texts. Without identifying the speaker, it was undoubtedly Krautheimer who said to Steinberg, "But it's only an interpretation; two years from now someone will come up with another interpretation, and then what have you got?" Steinberg's *l'esprit d'escalier* 20 years later was that such "rhetorical warning … simply failed to foresee the rigor and the controls attainable by hermeneutics," by which he meant that interpreter was tethered to the internal mechanism of the work.[8] So he switched to Wolfgang Lotz, whose walking seminar in 1957 had first sparked his interest in Borromini.

Steinberg grounded his interpretation of San Carlo in a reconstruction of the plan's geometry, as suggested by Borromini's autograph drawings held in the Albertina, Vienna; drawings long known to the curator, Erwin Hainisch and his slow-to-publish friend Heinrich Thelen, but unknown to scholars at large. The authentic drawings allowed him to discard the oval-based plans that Eberhard Hempel and Rudolf Wittkower had treated as early ideas for the church. In their place he identified six sheets (Az. Rome, 170–73 and 175–6) – only one of which had been published – that demonstrate the evolution of Borromini's scheme and which are now listed among the more significant plans in the history of architectural draughtsmanship.[9]

Steinberg itemized 12 separate scholarly interpretations of the primary geometrical construction of the plan. He proposed that it was not a matter of choosing which one was correct, because almost all of them held some water. In fact, the plan did not repel diverse readings, but accommodated them; multivaliant, he was convinced that it embodied three forms in one – oval, octagon, and cross. Once discovered, Steinberg would find Trinitarian triformity everywhere, and not just in the plan: a vital force animating the decorative surfaces and dwelling within the spatial zones from bottom to top. Steinberg recalled that the revelation of the Trinitarian scheme arrived after constant replaying of the visual evidence in his mind, before suddenly seeing that the plan was like music, with figures layered one over the other.[10]

Two-thirds of the dissertation is spent confirming the formal proposition via close visual analysis. Behind this were many hours of on-site looking, the student absorbing everything he could in an effort to reconstruct Borromini's architectural character. Not all the evidence made it to court: for example, reams of material were accrued on the sunken column (Figure 18.2), yet the outcome is a mere half-sentence, an example of "the inner necessity for Borromini to make walls and orders work in interdependence."[11] For Steinberg, trained as an artist and immersed in contemporary New York art, it was crucial that the argument was rock solid in its formal basis. Here is a passage on the curvature of San Carlo's lateral chapels:

> Once the underlying continuity of the four aedicular bays is established – established as the condition of an intermittent exterior oval – it becomes clear why no simple, one-centred curve can comprehend the sum of the bays that comprise the lateral chapels. The curves of the aedicular bays at the sides of the church respond to the aedicular bays in the long axis – they obey a remote affinity as compelling as the adjacency of the bays by which they are flanked. These latter, meanwhile, double-function even more strenuously. They belong triadically to the lateral chapels, but they belong no less to the grouping of triple bays in the diagonals. And each of these functions – the function of pertaining to the chapels and that of pertaining to the triple travées in the diagonals – demands its appropriate curvature.

> This surely explains why the path of these bays is traced freehand in the autograph plans. The curvatures here are not geometric but organic and ever-changing, determined by a dual necessity. On the one hand, they must attend the pendentive piers in symmetry with the corresponding bays borrowed from the semi-circular axial chapels. … At the same time, they must participate in the formation of chapels of totally different radius. Hence their change of curvature from swerve to bend. They are pivots in a mechanism of ambiguity.[12]

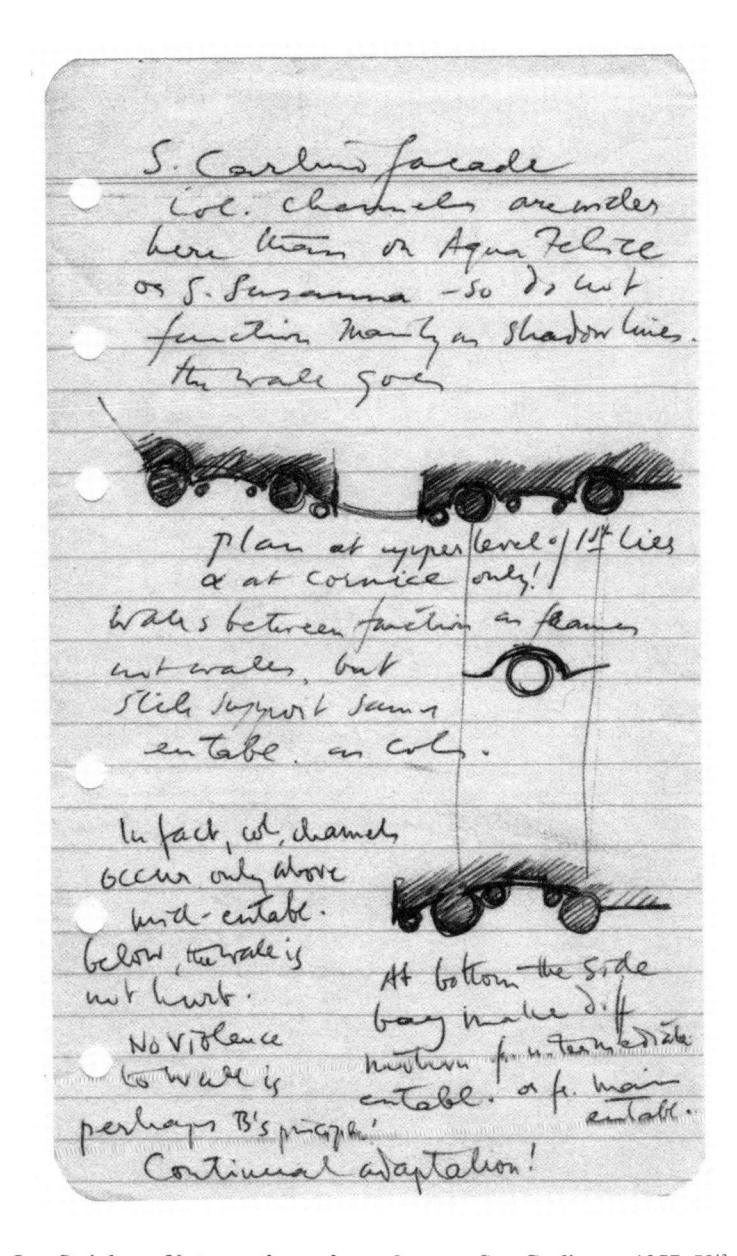

Figure 18.2   Leo Steinberg, Notes on the sunken column at San Carlino, c. 1957–58[13]
Source: Sheila Schwartz.

Steinberg viewed San Carlo as a self-controlling organism, multi-layered in complexity and with parts that speak to each other in expressions of mutual dependency.[14] The key concept of "double function" (that is, doing two things at once) derived from Rudolf Wittkower's analysis of Michelangelo's Laurentian Library, used to describe a "law" of the unstable architecture of mannerism, compared to the "static of the Renaissance [and] the directed movement of the Baroque."[15] But Steinberg refigured the term, leading not to Wittkower's troublesome "unstable movement," but the more positive "pivots in a mechanism of ambiguity," a phrase that echoes throughout the dissertation as well as Steinberg's career at large.

The quoted passage gives a sense of constantly shifting inflections, and Steinberg's general rule is this: details perform in variant ways depending on their circumstance. In "The Eye is a Part of the Mind" he referred to a hand in Picasso's *Three Musicians*, which the eye connects not only to what the hand looks like, but to an endless range of other things bespeaking manual activity: in other words, the concept of something is not limited by its outward shape.[16] "Perform" is also a critical term for Steinberg, expressing a communicative ideal of the work, which at moments might break into dance. Discussing the three-bay diagonal piers flanking the lateral chapels, Steinberg had a vision of the entire structure in a step:

> The agitation conveyed by the alternately curved and straight planes is steadied by the sameness of niches and panels. While we see the bay triad in motion, perceiving the pendentive pier in the process of emerging out of the wall, the constant featuring of the bays implies an anterior condition of the same group at rest. … [The pier's] uniform horizontal articulation maintains an apparent smooth flow of wall, even as – in the vertical sense – the central pendentive bay constitutes a disruptive step into the center. It is – to adapt a simile from Procopius – as if certain participants in a circle dance were taking a step inward while still holding hands with their neighbours; though the circle has been disturbed, it remains implied by the joining of hands. And it is in this sense that the oval perimeter of S. Carlino remains implied by the walls and grouped columns in the diagonals. They have the dual appearance of emerging and holding back – moving inward to form the octagonal crossing, but not far enough to efface a sense of an outer ellipse. … There is a strange double-play here, a tension between irreconcilables to which no visitor fails to respond.[17]

The closing remark about irreconcilables was one of Steinberg's favourite images, namely, that San Carlo holds opposites together, a condition he noted was called in the Middle Ages *coincidentia oppositorum*. Later in the dissertation there is an extended encomium to Borromini's habit of reversing things: "forms grow simultaneously convex and concave … inside and out become mutually convertible states … high and low, large and small, void and plenum become interchangeable … hardness and softness forget themselves."[18] The emphasis is important: Borromini's doubleness is duplex rather than duplicitous, open-ended rather than conflicted. And this was also Steinberg, for doubleness – in the shape of the imaginative occupation of more than one critical platform at a time, along with the habit of perceiving in multiple layers – was a desideratum of his critical approach from the early 1950s.[19] Steinberg observed doubleness in Borromini and, 10 years later, it has transformed into a general quality of artistic intelligence, used to explain, for example, Picasso's aversion to unity, so that stylistic disharmony within one of his paintings – such as *Les Demoiselles d'Avignon*, where the young women on one side are less savagely stylized than those on the other – offends not the artist but the singular-loving critic.[20] Such a model of complex art being ill-served by reductive criticism would then guide Steinberg's reappraisal of Guercino's Saint Petronilla altarpiece of 1623, whose bifurcated stylistic registers of chiaroscuro naturalism down below and ideal classicism up top are seen not as a symptom of Guercino's supposed feebleness (that is, the provincial incapable of absorbing the imperatives of Rome) but an intellectual suppleness, an ability to use diverse modes for different expressive purposes.[21] Steinberg attributed his own sensitivity to multiple meanings to James Joyce, the formative writer of his youth, which in turn ratified his conviction that the past could be reanimated by critical perspectives derived from contemporary experience.[22]

At the end of the section on oppositions, Steinberg declared that Borromini created fully functioning and interdependent organisms.[23] San Carlo is a little world, which is to say the larger one in perfected miniature. This is how the thesis ends:

> Our study has attempted to lay a heavy symbolic burden on S. Carlino – heavier perhaps than any building will bear. What we imply is that Borromini, being called on to build his first church, had asked himself – what is a church; what does it stand for? His answer … is that the church building is a microcosm of the Church universal; therefore it stands for the See of St. Peter and the mystic Body of Christ, for the world's circuit suffused by the Cross, and – in the singleness of its substance and its manifold forms – for the nature of God.[24]

In "The Twin Prongs of Art Criticism" of 1952 Steinberg had stated his belief in the microcosmic quality of art, "a counter Creation into which we enter to transcend the human condition, in which life is not undergone, but overcome."[25] A microcosm offers scope for hermeneutics; insofar as San Carlo is a little world, the principle standard for interpretation is that of internal consistency, assessing the meaning of its parts by reference to its entire creative logic, while divining that logic from prolonged formal analysis.[26] Such a poetical approach is an alternative to the social history of art, in which art is seen as an end product of material and cultural factors.[27] And it suits masterpieces more than the humdrum. As he later wrote in an essay on the relative merits of art and science, great art is exceptional precisely because of its animistic charge, midway between "the inanimate and the ensouled, intrusive life."[28] Indeed, throughout his career Steinberg focussed on works proverbial for their centrality to the tradition of art history – Leonardo's *Last Supper*, Michelangelo's *Last Judgement*, Velázquez's *Las Meninas*, Picasso's *Les Demoiselles d'Avignon*, and so on.[29]

Steinberg's immersion in San Carlo as a created world also went to his general critical advocacy of subjectivity. He often wrote in the first person and in such distinctive prose that his personality was rarely invisible. For Steinberg, interpretation was a process of the work coming alive in the imagination, which could only happen if it is internalized and set in conversation with the interpreter. This is apparent in his attention to gestures – although frozen in space, they embody duration and movement, and thus the viewer's inhabitation of the world. In a 1956 review of the sculptor Julio Gonzalez, Steinberg had written of another sort of bodily beauty, resulting from the gestured arcs of experience:

> [This] has nothing to do with the surfaced physique; it is the beauty which our body borrows from the bend of a baroque staircase as it moulds the path of our climb; in which a driver participates as he rounds a well-banked curve in the road. It is the beauty of a gesture which even a misshapen limb might describe, or which a skater unfolds in the duration of motion. It is the beauty of the diagonal you make striding into the wind; of the lean upright you draw when you stretch your full height; of all those felt lines of force which traverse the felt interiors of the body ... the kingdom of Gonzalez is within you, and his types are the internal aspirations of your body and mine.[30]

Physical gestures suggest duration, but there is also the mental gesture of understanding. In his reading of San Carlo, Steinberg often recounted an unfolding of understanding, as if that too were temporal, the church revealing itself in synchrony with the spectator's dawning recognition. Discussing plans for the façade, he recreates Borromini's intention from the multiple viewpoints of the beholder moving along the sidewalk, first adjacent, then from an angle, and then head-on.[31] Steinberg locked himself into the appraisal; later he confessed that he had the feeling that the church (or Borromini) was addressing him directly, trying to tell him something.[32]

All this points to phenomenology, which others have associated with Steinberg's method as it developed through the 1970s and 1980s.[33] However, on this subject we are groping in the dark, for there is no reference to the topic anywhere in Steinberg's work; nor is phenomenology mentioned in the extensive interview conducted with him in 1998. His argumentation is so transparent that he appears to write from first principles, and source hunting can be beside the point. As noted, he disavowed the 1952 article "Twin Prongs of Art Criticism" because he thought it pretentious. His literary ideal was to show and not tell, and he thus retrospected the start of his résumé with an article that had duly achieved the required level of maturity – "The Eye is a Part of the Mind," published in 1953. In his later writing he rarely supported his method by reference to philosophy, other than to supply an anecdote or observation, reported as if overheard.[34] He disliked philosophical aesthetics and had actually begun his art history lecturing with a course at New York's 92nd Street YMHA entitled "An Introduction to Art and Practical Esthetics," where art works passed judgment on art theories (which were found wanting), rather than the other way round.[35] Steinberg wished neither to theorize through examples nor to dress up observation with theory, but rather to conjoin perception and ratiocination. The point is that his interpretative persona was such that it coincidentally evoked a position akin to the emerging phenomenology of architectural theory and historiography. What annoyed Steinberg most in the 1950s was what he took to be the aridity of formalist aesthetics, and what he strived to advance was how it needed to be tempered by self-awareness – which brackets him with a range of mid-century writers, not only the Continental phenomenologists.[36] In fact the passage on Gonzalez cited above has something of the rhythm and reason of a passage by John Dewey in *Art as Experience*:

> The sources of art in human beings will be learned by him who sees how the tense grace of the ball-player infects the on-looking crowd; who notes the delight of the housewife in tending her plants [and] the zest of the spectator in poking the wood burning on the hearth and in watching the darting flames and crumbling coals.[37]

Dewey argued that all the criteria for the perception of art – aesthetics, in other words – are available to anyone attuned to the way one lives in the world; he also held to the view, much as Steinberg would do, that theory was art's poor cousin, forever belated in coming to grips with the complexity of expressive picturing. This comprised a plea to look more closely at art for its capacity to observe the un-noted and explain the un-theorized.[38]

It was mentioned earlier that the central idea of the dissertation on San Carlo was the founding of the plan in tri-formity, a multi-valency that enabled Steinberg to absorb diverse readings of what was taken to be the shape of the plan. In his later book on Leonardo, he trod a similar route, developing a layered interpretation that incorporates earlier contradictory views. He consistently argued that critics are smaller than the art they interpret and judge; that their views are fragmentary and are not rendered false by the existence of alternatives; that purity of meaning depends on critical authoritarianism, whereas other criteria of interpretation must always be at hand to avoid getting stuck. In other words, he argued for ambiguity. Moreover, ambiguity was no mere interpreter's gambit, because artists and architects of the past conceived forms ambiguously as well. Although the word ambiguity itself appears only twice in the dissertation, the analysis throughout refers to motifs in transition, betwixt and between, particles of a mutability that cannot be categorized in singular terms.[39] As Steinberg acknowledged in the preface, Borromini taught him method. After finishing with San Carlo, he worked on Michelangelo's *Doni Madonna* and apropos the uncertainty of whether the child is being handed up or down began gathering notes on how ambiguity had been understood over time, while also parsing the literature of art to find the extent to which the concept had been straightened by singular interpretative modes, eventually lecturing explicitly on the topic in 1965.[40] Here Steinberg ventured the idea that ambiguity usually turns on motion, since forward or back is often unclear because a pose is frozen in time. His thoughts on the matter were frequently lit by dance, which was for him a common standard on points of method: life stylized is dance, as is art plus movement.[41] Thereafter the ambiguity of art would become a major category in his writing, the class under which recurrent motifs such as simultaneity and duplexity became sub-headings.[42] Ambiguity pervades the Michelangelo essays, testament to an allegorical frame of mind that encompassed the entire experience of Christianity; it threads its way through the many studies of Picasso, expressing the Spaniard's reluctance to accept the brittleness of being only one thing at a time and explaining why he has so often been only partially diagnosed by critics; and it looms in the study of the *Last Supper*, culminating in the final chapter in which the work becomes an emblem and embodiment of the doubleness of rendered vision. Ultimately, Steinberg's critical home was that shape-shifting place where everything is on the verge of becoming something else.[43]

Complexity is also tantalizing, and in this light it is worthwhile restating Steinberg's commitment to the canon: by making a masterpiece ambiguous, he was displacing it from the still centre to the dynamic edge. Reintegrating old work into a living tradition is an act of creative revival, and in this sense the literary verve was appropriate to his critical approach.[44]

Joseph Koerner linked Steinberg's appetite for ambiguity to William Empson's *Seven Types of Ambiguity* (1930), one of the precursor texts for the New Criticism that emerged in literature studies in the 1950s.[45] Empson had argued that the practice of sifting through the range of possible meanings of a poetic phrase or word in search of the correct one was too often mistaken. Ambiguity was not the result of sloppy writing but inherent to language – and older poets knew it. As Steinberg would do in almost everything he wrote, Empson was apt to reel off plausible interpretations, insisting that the text did not compel definition. Empson likewise argued for the admission of subjectivism, which is a consequence of the simple fact that when someone is moved by art, "what are moving in him are the traces of a great part of his past experience and of the structure of his past judgments."[46] Although Koerner is unable to demonstrate that Steinberg read Empson (although he did own a 1966 edition of the book), his point is that Steinberg was a one-man version of the New Criticism that art history never had, having gone straight from iconology to post-structuralism.[47] The characterization might be formulated thus: Steinberg's dissertation on San Carlo was the beginning of what would be clarified into an interpretive strategy of ambiguity; sub-strata of thinking were laid down for treating images in terms of open-endedness, as was the corollary of subjectivism. Put this way, Steinberg sounds indeed like he anticipates approaches that flourish in art history over the following decades, even if his un-theoretical prose expresses a literary standard from another time.[48]

Shortly after completing the PhD, Steinberg published a three-page synopsis in *Marsyas*. Then, nothing happened. He sought grant money to allow him a year in Rome so that he could turn it into a book, but with no luck: eight applications were rejected, and he later heard that Richard Krautheimer, whom Steinberg had listed as a referee, wrote negative reports.[49] So he worked on other subjects – Michelangelo and Picasso especially. The thesis lay dormant, and at the 1967 conference to mark the tercentenary of Borromini's death Eugenio Battisti chided Steinberg for denying scholars a published version of the research.[50] When the text eventually appeared in the Garland Series of Outstanding Dissertations in the Fine Arts in 1977, the emerging Borromini scholar Joseph Connors opened his review with a sentence that suggested its semi-legendary status, "Here at last is Steinberg's thesis."[51] Yet by now Steinberg had gained a reputation as a brilliant but dangerous high wire act.[52] Accordingly, Connors was there to set the record straight: Steinberg's exalted image of Borromini was barking up the wrong tree; in reality the church was based upon a more straightforward set of references to well-known prototypes; Steinberg should have paid more attention to patronage and other issues of social history; patient research (of the sort Connors would provide in his forthcoming study on Borromini's Oratory of St. Philip Neri) would reveal Borromini as a man of his time, concerned with status and career advancement. For Steinberg's part, the review was the revenge of the professional art historian, incapable of generating interpretation except via precedent and text. Materialist as well: after the review appeared Steinberg commented to a friend, "I took a Borromini who had been the preserve of the formalists, and I turned him into a Christian, and now Joseph Connors is turning him into an American."[53]

In fact Steinberg gave up writing on architecture after Borromini. He later admitted that his lack of architectural knowledge made him feel like a fake: he could understand what a wall looked like, but not what kept a dome from falling down.[54] Architects, however, liked his thesis. Paolo Portoghesi, a fellow traveller on the Borromini trail since the 1950s, described it as "without doubt the richest and most illuminating account on San Carlo in the literature of art."[55] Another architect, Peter Carl, encountered the thesis at the American Academy in 1973 and was impressed by its concern with symbolism, which at the time seemed a welcome change. He later told his Cambridge students "[that] this is the best thing on Borromini ... actually, it's one of the best things ever written on architecture."[56] Steinberg himself remembered finding (likely in the 1980s) a copy of his book in the collection of Richard Meier, who told him "we [architects] all read it."[57] What seemed strange to the reader in 1960, namely the concept that architecture might spring from symbolism, was no longer so in 1977, architectural theory having come around to the viewpoint expressed in his doctoral dissertation.

A similar herald of changing attitudes was Robert Venturi's *Complexity and Contradiction in Architecture*, published in 1966 after a decade of study that had begun in Rome.[58] Just as Steinberg insisted on the symbolic foundation of San Carlo, so too Venturi addressed symbolism as the currency of the past, provocatively targeting the critical symbolophobia of 1950s architectural modernism. Echoing Steinberg's demand that art criticism should couple both ends, Venturi wrote that, "Architecture is form *and* substance – abstract *and* concrete – and its meaning derives from interior characteristics and its particular context."[59] A glance at the aesthetic and interpretative categories that Venturi wanted to revive suggests a remarkable affinity with the principles Steinberg has discovered in Borromini. Venturi refers to "the difficult whole," "both/and," "ambiguity" (of which, Venturi observed, San Carlo is a signal case), "double-functioning" – the last phrase, also used by Steinberg, derived from Wittkower via the Renaissance literary history of Wylie Sypher.[60] Among other justifications for this embrace of multi-layered complexity, Venturi cited Cleanth Brooks's *The Well Wrought Urn*, another classic text of New Criticism, along with Empson's *Seven Types of Ambiguity*. Of course Steinberg and Venturi are very different in style, but the difference is balanced by a kinship of intention: when Venturi says he preached a manifesto, he meant it ironically, for his empirical and historicist orientation is in contrast with the axiomatic grandeur of modernism. And both responded to artists and architects who respond complexly to tradition, who absorb its motifs to reset them in different contexts. Michelangelo was one such architect, Borromini another, "an artist," said Steinberg, "with the largest awareness of the total vocabulary of possible forms. The mastery of wide ranging vocabulary is the reward for bringing to an idiom the keenest sense of its meaning. And Borromini's profound sense of meaning of forms seems to me grounded in his architect's conscience."[61]

The relationship of Steinberg and Venturi is not causal, but is significant nevertheless, indicating perspectives yet to become commonplace, and with a chiastic structure: two students studying in Rome in the 1950s, both restless with the state of play; one reassessing Borromini via a critique of modern formalism, the other rethinking modern architecture through the tradition of which Borromini was a master.

Author's Note

Thanks to Fabio Barry, Peter Carl, and Georgina Cole. Above all, I am deeply indebted to Sheila Schwartz, Leo Steinberg's long-time assistant.

Endnotes

1   Steinberg was born in Moscow in 1920. Three years later, his family escaped to Berlin, then to London in 1933. Steinberg studied at the Slade School of Art 1936–40. He moved to New York with his family in 1945. From 1949 to 1960 he taught life drawing and art history at the Parsons School of Design, New York. Following submission of his PhD he secured an academic post at Hunter College of the City University in New York, remaining there until 1975, when he was appointed Benjamin Franklin Professor at the University of Pennsylvania, from which he retired in 1991. Steinberg died in 2011. Biographical details in the text are provided in an interview conducted by the Getty Research Institute: Steinberg, "The Gestural Trace." See also, "False Starts, Loose Ends," *The Brooklyn Rail*; and Steinberg, *Encounters with Rauschenberg*. For general sketch of Steinberg's ideas, see Hill, "Steinberg, Leo (1920–2011)," in Kelly (ed.), *Encyclopedia of Aesthetics*, 2nd edn, vol. 6, 44–8.

2   Steinberg declared his impatience with critics who separate form and content in one of his earliest publications: "Undying Antiquity," 74.

3   In the 1971 preamble to his study of Rodin (1963), Steinberg recalled how at the age of 17, Fry was his "revered mentor:" *Other Criteria*, 323.

4   Steinberg, "The Eye Is a Part of the Mind," 297.

5   Greenberg was not mentioned in either essay but he was in view: Steinberg, "The Gestural Trace," 55; Steinberg, *Encounters with Rauschenberg*, 23 and passim, in which his resistance to Greenberg is something of a leitmotif. I have explored this at greater length in, "Leo Steinberg vs Clement Greenberg, 1952–1972."

6   Seven of the nine reviews were collected in *Other Criteria*. They earned Steinberg the College Art Association's Frank Jewett Mather Award for criticism.

7   Steinberg, "De Kooning's Woman" (1955), in *Other Criteria*, 259.

8   Steinberg, *Borromini's San Carlo*, xviii–xix. The warning about interpretation continued to rankle. In the preface to *Michelangelo's Last Paintings*, Steinberg wrote, "A word needs to be said about the limits and license of interpretation. I am aware of the position that frowns on excessively free speculation at the expense of the Masters. But there are, after all, two ways to inflict injustice on a great work of art; by over-interpreting it, or by under-estimating its meaning … the probity of resisting interpretation is not the virtue to which I aspired. Michelangelo's idiom is so highly charged and so impregnated with thought, that nothing would seem to me more foolhardy than to project upon his symbolic structures a personal preference for simplicity."

9   The discarded sheets were Az. Rom., 165–7. Since then, however, Joseph Connors (introduction to Borromini, *Opus architectonicum*, lvii) has argued that only two of the drawings (Az. Rom. 171 and 172) are from the preparatory stage in the 1630s, with the others dating from 1660s and intended for engraved publication. Federico Bellini goes further to suggest that the geometry that appears in Az. Rom. 173 and other drawings is a post facto iconographic rationalization and has little significance to the actual space of the church: *Le cupole di Borromini*, 139–47. I have critiqued this revisionist view of the drawings in a recent article, "Symbolic and Practical Geometry in Borromini's San Carlo alle Quattro Fontane."

10   Steinberg, "The Gestural Trace," 37.

11   Steinberg, *Borromini's San Carlo*, 361.

12   Steinberg, *Borromini's San Carlo*, 151–2.

13   Text reads [additions in brackets]: San Carlino façade. Col. channels are wider here than on Aqua Felice or Santa Susanna, so do not function mainly as shadow lines. The wall goes … plan at upper level of 1st lies [thus,] and at

cornice only! Walls between function as frames not walls, but still support same entab[lature] as cols. In fact, col. channels occur only above mid-entab[lature]; below, the wall is not hurt. No violence to wall is perhaps B.'s principle! [that is, because only the lower level was completed under Borromini's supervision; the upper level was executed and revised by Bernardo Castelli after 1669]. At bottom the side bay make diff[erent] motion fr[om] intermediate entab[lature] and for main entab[lature]. Continual adaptation!

14 Which of course is how the interior had been described by Fra Juan de San Buenaventura, *Relatione del Convento di San Carlo alle Quattro Fontane* (c. 1650), 72–4; a passage that Steinberg quoted in full, *San Carlo*, 338–9.

15 Wittkower, "Michelangelo's Biblioteca Laurenziana," 123–218, esp. 209. Thanks to Maarten Delbeke for pointing out to me that the term "double function" derives from Wittkower: see Delbeke, "Mannerism and meaning in Complexity and Contradiction in Architecture," 271.

16 Steinberg, "The Eye is a Part of the Mind," 302.

17 Steinberg, *Borromini's San Carlo*, 190–91.

18 Steinberg, *Borromini's San Carlo*, 363–9. Wittkower had observed a similar "theme of insoluble conflict in every detail," in the Laurentian vestibule: "Michelangelo's Biblioteca Laurenziana," 207.

19 See Shiff, review of *Leonardo's Incessant Last Supper*, 23.

20 See Steinberg, "The Polemical Part," 123.

21 Steinberg, "Guercino's *Saint Petronilla*," 211.

22 "Joyce's remark – 'some of the means I use are trivial, and some are quadrivial' – fits Borromini very well." Steinberg, *San Carlo*, 348. In "Objectivity and the Shrinking Self" (1968), *Other Criteria*, 307, Steinberg urged his academic colleagues to let the reader in on whatever private circumstance might have cultivated a view on an art historical topic. Another example: Steinberg noted that Michelangelo's Paolina frescoes, long-ignored because they did not fit the pattern of High Renaissance and Mannerism, were reabsorbed into criticism when the emergence of modern formalism prepared historians to see the peculiar energy animating the designs: *Michelangelo's Last Paintings*, 20.

23 Steinberg, *Borromini's San Carlo*, 373.

24 Steinberg, *Borromini's San Carlo*, 443–4.

25 Steinberg, "Twin Prongs of Art Criticism," 425.

26 Paraphrasing Steinberg, *Borromini's San Carlo*, xviii–xx.

27 Steinberg was largely indifferent to economics: see, Steinberg, "The Gestural Trace," 28. Also, see his response to Joseph Connors's review, below note 53.

28 Steinberg, "Art and Science," 14.

29 Refer to the bibliography for Steinberg's major monographic studies. The exception is his most famous work, *The Sexuality of Christ in Renaissance Art and in Modern Oblivion*.

30 Steinberg, "Julio Gonzalez" (1956), reprinted in *Other Criteria*, 241–2.

31 Steinberg, *Borromini's San Carlo*, 101.

32 Steinberg, *Borromini's San Carlo*, 424.

33 David Rosand bracketed Merleau-Ponty and Steinberg together in a footnote, apropos the bodily perception of art: "Art History and Criticism," 445. Rosalind Krauss associated Steinberg's method at large to phenomenology: editor's introduction to the revised publication of The Philosophical Brothel." See also Carrier, "Postmodernism is Dead! (Long Live Leo Steinberg)," *The Aesthete in the City*, 165–78; Harrison, "Leo Steinberg: Pop, "Post-Modernist" Painting and the Flatbed Picture Plane," in *Pop Art and the Origins of Post-Modernism*, 96–117.

34 For example, a reference to Sartre (*Essays in Aesthetics*) in *Michelangelo's Last Paintings*, 37, does no more than furnish a query about the decorum of foreshortening. Three references to Nietzsche's *Birth of Tragedy* are made in "The Philosophical Brothel," 43, 46, and 53–4 (Lisa Florman, however, argues that the Nietzschean perspective informs Steinberg's position at large: "The Difference Experience Makes in the 'The Philosophical Brothel'," 769–83). Steinberg made the dissimulating confession that, "I think the failure of my life is perhaps due to the fact that I have not wanted to go into these larger theoretical formulations. My illusion was that theoretical conclusions may fall automatically from test cases. In a work of art like Borromini's San Carlo ... I thought first you have to show what the work is." "The Gestural Trace," 106. In 1954 Steinberg had taken a summer course on Kant and toyed with the idea of graduate studies in philosophy.

35 Sheila Schwartz, personal communication, 2011.

36 Steinberg cited Susanne Langer, *Feeling and Form* in "Objectivity and the Shrinking Self," 319 (and would continue to do so in lectures, as attested by Peter Kohane, who recalls Steinberg's approving discussion of Langer in a 1987

lecture at the University of Pennsylvania). Steinberg would have known Langer's work as early as the mid-1950s, as she anthologized his 1953 essay, "The Eye is a Part of the Mind" in her *Reflections on Art*, 243–61. It is significant that Greenberg did not admire Langer's work: de Duve, *Clement Greenberg Between the Lines*, 127.

37 John Dewey, *Art as Experience* (1934), New York: Penguin, 1980, 3.

38 On theory versus art, see John Dewey, "A Comment on the Foregoing Criticisms," 208, note 8. Steinberg quoted Dewey (*Art as Experience*, 30) in "The Eye is a Part of the Mind" to the effect that artists condense abstract ideas into the realm of sense. Steinberg himself antedates the development of phenomenology in American schools of architecture in the 1970s, which partly resulted from the need to "rescue" architecture from art historical taxonomy: see Jorge Otero-Pailos, *Architecture's Historical Turn*.

39 On page 125, "double-functioning ambiguity;" then on page 152, "pivots in a mechanism of ambiguity." A third reference, on page 185, is negative.

40 Steinberg's hand-written copy of an unpublished lecture on the *Doni Madonna*, c. 1965, along with diverse study notes of the 1970s and 1980s, were sent to me by Sheila Schwartz.

41 In the 1965 lecture Steinberg referred approvingly to a statement on open-endedness by the dancer, Merce Cunningham: "what I don't like about working with Martha Graham is the idea that a particular movement meant something specific … the ambiguity of a dance movement is always the interesting part for me" (*New Yorker*, 4 May 1968, 53). He quoted Cunningham again in 1998, on the danger of the impromptu: Steinberg, "The Gestural Trace," 1. Later in the interview, he says, "I can tell instantly [what scholars] have never danced and have never drawn. I could tell Panofsky had never danced or drawn. They have no real understanding." Steinberg, "The Gestural Trace," 89.

42 In "False Starts, Loose Ends," Steinberg voiced a complaint on his critics' behalf: "Steinberg likes to complicate what we know to be simple. The ambiguities he goes on about are his personal hang-up; pay no attention."

43 Steinberg would refer to such instability with a phrase that derives from the first sentence of the Proteus chapter of James Joyce's *Ulysses*: "Ineluctable modality of the visible." In Part II of "Resisting Cezanne: The Polemical Part" of 1978, Steinberg paraphrased, "Faced with a run of African figures, Picasso discovered the ineluctable mutability of the makeable … A head, a torso, or bottle … is still a rethinking and a re-imaging of its total ever fluctuant stereometry." (125). Then, in the final chapter of *Leonardo's Incessant Last Supper*, an unacknowledged quotation is wrapped in a pun: "the trapezoid is, daedally speaking, the ineluctable modality of the visible." (Shiff, review of *Leonardo's Incessant Last Supper*, noted the reference to Stephen Dedalus, hero of *Ulysses*.) In "Objectivity and the Shrinking Self," 320, Steinberg called *Ulysses* and *Finnegan's Wake* the pabulum of his youth.

44 On reintegration as revival, see Steinberg, "Undying Antiquity," 74.

45 Koerner, Review of *Leonardo's Incessant Last Supper*, 781. Koerner's extensive review is perhaps the outstanding evaluation of Steinberg's art historical writing.

46 Empson, Preface to 2nd edition, *Seven Types of Ambiguity*, 2nd edn, xv.

47 Purchased in 1979. Sheila Schwartz told me the following: "The only chapter in the book with annotations at all is Chapter 7, the seventh type of ambiguity – which strongly suggests to me that Leo, a habitual glosser, never read any other part of the book; the glosses here concern Empson's misunderstanding of Christianity."

48 In this respect Arthur Danto said Steinberg possessed one of the "transfiguring subjectivities of our time:" Review of *Other Criteria*, 569. See also the memoriam by Rosalind Krauss, "The Slung Leg Hypothesis."

49 Steinberg, "The Gestural Trace," 40.

50 Eugenio Battisti, "Il simbolismo in Borromini."

51 Connors, "Review of *Borromini's San Carlo*, 283–5.

52 For example, Paul Johannides described Steinberg as a "dangerous model … His method could be described as associational formalism … At moments one suspects that what is produced is a more Steinbergesque, than a Michelangelesque, Michelangelo," review of *Michelangelo's Last Paintings*; Gombrich repeated the charge, Review of *Michelangelo's Last Paintings*.

53 Steinberg, "The Gestural Trace," 133. Steinberg added, "That's not entirely fair to Connors, who is a very good scholar, but that is how I felt about it."

54 Steinberg, "The Gestural Trace," 145.

55 Portoghesi, *Storia di San Carlino alle Quattro Fontane*, 160. In the 1977 acknowledgements, Steinberg wrote, "I have saved to last the name of Paolo Portoghesi, the architect and Borromini scholar, whose friendship since 1958 has been my special pride." *Borromini's San Carlo*, xxii. Further details on their relationship are given in the 1998 interview.

56 Email correspondence with Peter Carl, 2011. The Cambridge student was Fabio Barry, who recalled Professor Carl's exact words.

57 1998 Getty oral history interview, transcript, 133.

58 Venturi won the Rome prize in 1954, living there for two years, and returning periodically thereafter; Steinberg studied in Rome off and on from 1956, and was a guest of the American Academy in 1958 and 1959.

59 Venturi, *Complexity and Contradiction in Architecture*, 20.

60 Venturi, *Complexity and Contradiction*, 26–8; Sypher, *The Four Stages of Renaissance Style*, 123–7; Maarten Delbeke, "Mannerism and meaning in Complexity and Contradiction in Architecture," 272–5. In the preface to the 2nd edition in 1977, Venturi thanked Richard Krautheimer, Steinberg's initial advisor, for sharing his insights on the Roman Baroque. Charles Brickbauer further attested to Krautheimer's impact: "He [Krautheimer] was responsible for stimulating my interest in the baroque and I am sure he had the same influence on Bob [Venturi]." Martino Stierli, "In the Academy's Garden," 55. However, what Venturi says about Borromini does not sound much like Krautheimer, unless Krautheimer was repeating observations that had been made by his former doctoral student.

61 Steinberg, *Borromini's San Carlo*, 215.

Chapter 19

The "Recurrence" of the Baroque in Architecture: Giedion and Norberg-Schulz's Approaches to Constancy and Change

Gro Lauvland

In *Space, Time and Architecture* (1941), one of the central texts of the modern movement in architecture, Sigfried Giedion dealt with what he called "constituent facts:" a basic architectural language. "Constituent facts," he wrote, "are those tendencies which, when they are suppressed, inevitably reappear. Their recurrence makes us aware that these are elements which, all together, are producing a *new tradition.*"[1] Later, in his First Gropius Lecture at Harvard University in 1961, Giedion developed his understanding of the emergence of tradition in history by introducing the concepts of "constancy and change."[2]

In his book *Stedskunst* (The Art of Place), published in Norwegian in 1996, Christian Norberg-Schulz (1926–2000) drew attention to these notions, and to how Giedion related them to time and place by means of his discussion of "monumentality" and "regionalism."[3] Giedion had been Norberg-Schulz's tutor at the Eidgenössische Technische Hochschule (ETH) in Zurich, and may well have imparted his interest in the Germanic art historical tradition to the Norwegian. Certainly, Norberg-Schulz's view of modern art and architecture is indebted to Giedion.

Stedskunst encapsulates nearly 20 years of work on the phenomenology of place: a "place theory" aimed at providing a comprehensive understanding of the work of architecture. The first significant turn towards phenomenology in Norberg-Schulz's work occurred in *Genius Loci: Towards a Phenomenology of Architecture* (1980). Until then he had adopted the methods of the human sciences of the 1950s and 1960s; in art history, language theories related to structuralism, to Gestalt therapy. In the 1970s his work shifted from a theory-oriented approach to an experience-based understanding of the architectural work, rooted in philosophical phenomenology and deeply influenced by Edmund Husserl, Martin Heidegger as well as by Maurice Merleau-Ponty.

Norberg-Schulz's phenomenological understanding of architecture sheds light on Giedion's discussion of "constancy and change." The criticism of modernity implied in Giedion's putting forward of these notions is given new epistemological grounds, now by means of the phenomenological critique of modernity, and is rooted in a different understanding of Man as an historical being. As is well known, Giedion saw the origins of the modernist understanding of architectural space in the baroque architecture of Francesco Borromini, Guarino Guarini and Balthasar Neumann, even though he recognized the different social and political conditions of his own time. Norberg-Schulz's study of the baroque, in turn, informed his phenomenological understanding of architecture. Both Giedion and Norberg-Schulz believe that the historical manifestation of change and constancy in the baroque opened the way to a modernist conception of space, just as it predicated modernism's problems in dealing with those same phenomena.

Heidegger and Arendt on the Environmental Crisis of Modernity

Norberg-Schulz and Giedion share an awareness of an environmental crisis, which they attribute to the influence of the scientific world on society and on humanity's consciousness of itself. The same point of view had been held within the phenomenological project since its very inception. Edmund Husserl, the founder of modern phenomenology, sought to study the different phenomena to which humanity relates, the way they appear for the human consciousness. His objects of study are phenomena in their *givenness*. This approach was founded in a critique of the rationality of the modern sciences. Husserl, like his philosophical heirs, studied the conditions under which what may be known of the concrete world by means of intuition might be perceived.

In *Stedskunst* Norberg-Schulz writes that Merleau-Ponty developed a new understanding of perception based on Husserl's phenomenology and on Gestalt therapy, where "the separation between thinking and feeling" was solved, the same separation that early functionalism was intended to heal.[4] Then, Norberg-Schulz contends, Heidegger took a step forward when he defined Man as *Dasein*, or "Being-in-the-World," presenting a radical – in the true sense of the word – understanding of the totality, an understanding "that destroyed the traditional relationship between the subject and the object that had been important for our understanding of the world, the reason for the separation between thinking and feeling since Descartes."[5] He writes:

> When the subject is seen as *cogito*, the object turns out to be something to which one stands *opposite*, perceived in a visual-perspective way. In other words, Man becomes a *viewer*, rather than a *participator*, and the community dissolves into a "sum" of singular individuals. For Heidegger, on the contrary, Man is no longer standing "opposite," but *understands* [*verstehen*] in the sense that he stands *amidst*. Thus, existence becomes a multiplicity of relations, and life becomes an open "mirroring" of *manners of being*.[6]

Here, Norberg-Schulz argues, Man is transformed from being a viewer to being a participant, and the world becomes a totality, "the totality that modern art tried to express, but was only partly able to realize."[7]

On the basis of Heidegger's writings – and especially "Bauen Wohnen Denken" (1951) – Norberg-Schulz connects a modern sense of homelessness to a failure to understand the relationship between living and building.[8] By investigating the etymology of the world "living" (*wohnen*), Heidegger revealed the relation between being and living. He also demonstrated how the old German world *buan* is intimately related to the German world *bin*, or "is." To be and to live has the same meaning, just as living means that we build both houses and landscapes, according to Norberg-Schulz.[9] This means, he contends, that humanity is to look after and to care for its environment, an attitude that implies an attentive approach to that which is already given us through nature.

Although the German-American political thinker Hannah Arendt's critique of modernity stands a tradition other than Heidegger's, and aspires to other ends, her differentiation between thought and cognition can be related to Heidegger's philosophical thinking, and – through Heidegger's work – to the writings of Norberg-Schulz. They hold in common a philosophy running counter to the dominant lines of contemporary thinking by identifying reality not with humanity's own production of meaning but with something that *is given*, that precedes humanity itself. Indeed, humanity is conditioned by the earth and risks its own destruction should it oppose the conditions the earth bestows upon it.

In her major work, *The Human Condition* (1958), Arendt argues that the distinction between thought and cognition can be interpreted in the light of a critique of *hubris*, of our boundless action within modernity. "Thought, the source of art works, is manifest without transformation or transfiguration in all great philosophy, whereas the chief manifestation of the cognitive processes, by which we acquire and store up knowledge, is the sciences."[10] Arendt makes it clear that cognition always pursues a definite aim. When this aim is reached the cognition process has come to an end. She continues:

> Thought, on the contrary, has neither an end nor an aim outside itself, and it does not even produce results; not only the utilitarian philosophy of *homo faber* but also the men of action and the lovers of results in the sciences have never tired of pointing out how entirely "useless" thought is – as useless, indeed, as the works of art it inspires.[11]

The "Theory of Place" and the Art of Architecture

The fundamental distinction between, on one hand, Heidegger's theory of "building and living" and Arendt's distinction between thought and knowledge and, on the other, the ideas of Norberg-Schulz is that the former do not deal with architecture as an academic field or discipline and its own set of problems, but rather as the source of a philosophical question. Norberg-Schulz incorporates these questions into a theory that attempts to solve the problem raised by his experience of an environmental crisis in the modern world and its manifestation in "the loss of place." He agrees with Heidegger and Arendt's assessment of the consequences of the environmental crisis promoted by technical-scientific rationality and its influence on modern society, on human lives and self-consciousness.[12] These consequences are manifest in what mankind produces and builds today. Norberg-Schulz's "place theory" sought to establish a new academic grounding; a qualitative understanding of what he regards as the purpose of the modern movement in architecture: the re-definition of architecture as an art form. Understanding should be based on experience, and living and building rooted in *attentiveness*. This is a philosophical point of view: architectural production, first of all, becomes a question of choosing among *qualities* rather than resulting from procedures leading to predictable consequences.

His theory is an attempt to bring forward a systematic presentation of "the concrete qualities of place," and includes what Norberg-Schulz called a phenomenological method for the understanding of place. Thus, Norberg-Schulz's "place theory" is meant to make visible a formal language of architecture, conditioned by place and time, which simultaneously reveals a universal architectural language: "The present work [*Stedskunst*] intends to account for this dynamic process, with the purpose of preparing meaningful relations in a world that, in a new way, seem to dissolve into incompatible fragments."[13] As it positions architecture as an art form, this understanding that *Stedskunst* sought out initiates a unification of different academic fields and their own respective approaches to place and architecture.[14] Architecture thereby becomes the art of place in the fullest sense of the term, underpinned by a "place theory" that furthermore incorporates a normative specification of the work of architecture, which might be understood as taking up the Aristotelian idea that "art follows and prolongs nature."[15]

Norberg-Schulz thus argues for the importance of a *qualitative understanding* as a basis for the development of cities and our built environments. In so doing, the Norwegian theoretician emphasizes the importance of the relation between language and reality, and between art form and the form of life. The qualitative, he claims, is what we all have in common, and architecture, seen as the *art of place*, is the means by which the qualitative is made present. The art of place is the result of a qualitative understanding that is both general and particular. "Place theory" first of all relates to a general understanding of place, but Norberg-Schulz argues that every single place needs also to be analysed according to its own specific qualities. Architecture should be attentive to the nature of any given place, just as the analysis of architecture should be open to the qualities to be found in the place itself.

The Problem of Modernism

With the "place theory" of *Stedskunst*, Norberg-Schulz sought to "open out onto the qualitative modernism that was the true motive of the pioneers – a motive that in the 1930s and in the post-war period was lost under the pressure of totalitarian ideologies, commercial interest and conservative 'taste.'"[16] He continues: "The new place includes many historical traces; it expresses a continuous interaction between qualitatively diverse phenomena that appear and hide again, that are maintained and changed."[17] When Norberg-Schulz set out to explore how the human environment might retain vestiges of the past despite its exposure to all manner of changes, he identified Giedion's 1961 lecture "Constancy and Change" as a key to the problem.[18] Although Norberg-Schulz's understanding of the inherited natural conditions for the production of architecture arises from his reading of Heidegger, it is also a response to the problem of how architectural production persists as an art form in an industrialized world, the very issue Giedion raised by connecting constancy and change in his own thought. The pioneers of the modern movement were searching for an architecture that corresponded to a world in flux.[19] Before 1945 – and alongside Nikolaus Pevsner (1902–83) and Emil Kaufmann (1891–1953) – Giedion fashioned himself as a spokesman for the idea that the spirit of the age (*Die Zeitgeist*) was manifest in particular formal expressions. This notion allowed him to develop different genealogies for a "new," truly modern architecture.[20] According to Giedion, this modern architecture should set out to "recapture the most obvious things, as if nothing had taken place before" – to recapture, and not to start from the very beginning, this in spite of his claim in *Space, Time and Architecture* that new architecture should abolish the "alienating" historicism of the nineteenth century that had caused a schism "between science and its techniques on the one hand and the arts on the other, and hence between architecture and construction."[21] Norberg-Schulz extends this observation to argue that modern architecture was "intended as *art*, and that the aim was to heal the separation between thinking and feeling that was rooted in the *cogito* of Descartes."[22] His phenomenological understanding of architecture attempts to integrate the field of architecture in the life-world, and to re-establish the (broken) connection between architecture and the everyday-life, not as a singular and functional response in building, but as a comprehensive frame that allows life to take place "in its complexity, full of contradictions."[23]

In line with Heidegger's philosophical phenomenology, Norberg-Schulz argues that early modernism was correct to focus on the new home "for the daily life of everyone," on the necessity of understanding the environment in qualitative terms, and on what he calls a search for origins.[24] He emphasizes that the early modernist interest in origins concerned the question of how the practical and the expressive might have initially coexisted. In *Stedskunst* he points out that the founding principles of modernism actually encompassed this unity, as in, for instance, Le Corbusier's "Les cinq points d'une architecture nouvelle." In *Principles of Modern Architecture* (2000) Norberg-Schulz quotes approvingly from Ludwig Mies van der Rohe to underscore the importance of respecting the anonymous masters of the past: "Where can we find greater structural clarity than in the wooden buildings of old? Where else can we find such unity of material, construction and form? What warmth and beauty they have! They seem to be echoes of old songs. What better examples could there be for young architects?"[25]

Norberg-Schulz also sees Giedion's proposal of "constituent facts" as an expansion on the pioneers' interest in origins. These "facts" are eternal "truths," what Giedion describes as "those tendencies which, when they are suppressed, inevitably reappear."[26] Giedion contrasts "constituent facts" to those "phenomena of transition" that last for but a short while because they lack the necessarily inherent ability to endure. The historical moment in which the modern configuration of the relation between constituent facts and phenomena of transition first emerged is, for both Giedion and Norberg-Schulz, in the baroque.

The Baroque and the Constituent Facts of Architecture

In Norberg-Schulz's reading of *Space, Time and Architecture*, Giedion demonstrated that the modernist perception of space (*Raum*) was formed in the baroque period. The Norwegian's debt to Giedion's view of the baroque is immediately apparent in such statements as this: "In fact, there is hardly any historical epoch which more evidently manifests a correspondence between the form of life and the architectural environment."[27] Like Norberg-Schulz after him, Giedion focused on how the baroque masters transmuted the forms developed in the Renaissance. The interiors they produced are marked by a "union of two kinds of interests usually encountered separately: they are at once the products of purely mathematical speculations of a high order of complexity, and completely visionary or mystical imaginative creations." The baroque is the development of a specific form of universality, and "this manifest itself as a new power to mould space, and to produce an astonishing and unified whole from the most various parts."[28]

Giedion also argued that "baroque methods and ways of feeling survive until the disintegration produced by the industrial age sets in and brings with it a temporary destruction of the universal point of view."[29] Although on terms other than those tabled by Giedion, Norberg-Schulz positions this understanding of the relation between "thinking and feeling" in the baroque as being relevant for modern architecture and for the architecture of his own present day. During the 1960s Norberg-Schulz worked on two extensive volumes on the baroque period, *Baroque Architecture* and *Late Baroque and Rococo Architecture*, both initially published in Italian in 1971, in the series *Storia dell'architettura* directed by Pier Luigi Nervi. Therein Norberg-Schulz posits that the architecture of the baroque can be understood as a manifestation of the combination of style and tradition. The baroque conception of place gives buildings a particular presence. As he reads it, this synthesis of "the common and the local" was lost during the eighteenth century. The Enlightenment replaced experience by means of "reason and taste" and the subsequent separation of thinking and feeling reshaped the field of the arts. *Late Baroque and Rococo Architecture*, the English edition of which appeared in 1974, articulates this with reference to the philosophy of science and its persistence in the present. The author emphasizes that today we "begin to understand that the Enlightenment and the scientific development that followed it did not account for the whole relationship between man and his environment. … Still, the Age of Reason pointed out the dangers of *a priori* thinking, a lesson that should never be forgotten."[30] And he continues: "The world, in fact, is still dominated by those who put the conclusion at the beginning."[31]

If such observations expose Norberg-Schulz, as an architectural historian, to the same accusations as were levelled at Giedion – mixing descriptive and normative approaches to historical architecture – his empirical studies of the baroque period should to some extent be considered in relation to his attempt to understand and criticize the contemporary work of architecture and to define its new academic grounds. This attempt was first described in his work *Intentions in Architecture* (1963) and the thinking of this book framed his entire career, including his work on the historical baroque. In fact, the preface to *Baroque Architecture* recalls that *Intentions in Architecture* sought to "establish a comprehensive theory of architecture." This project called for "concentrated attention on the analysis of spatial structures [and] understanding space as one of man's basic existential dimensions" – the precise approach he applied in his studies of the baroque.[32] Later, Norberg-Schulz finds confirmation for his phenomenological understanding of architecture by revisiting his earlier studies of the baroque, wherein he had described the baroque as the historical period in which the single building within the city "loses its plastic individuality and becomes part of a superior system."[33] As a result, in both Giedion's work and that of Norberg-Schulz, it is the baroque that establishes the modernity of the interaction between constancy and change, while showing how modernity itself forfeits the benefits of that same interaction.

In *Stedskunst* Norberg-Schulz writes that already in the 1940s and 1950s, at the same moment as he identified modernism's negligence towards constancy and change, Giedion had defined their mutual relation as the interplay between "monumentality" and "regionalism":

> According to Giedion "monumentality" did not signify magnificence and splendor, but rather the memories and symbols that provide Man with a foothold in *time*. Likewise "regionalism" did not refer to provincialism and nationalism but instead to the need for a foothold in *space*, implying that space is understood as "place." Taken together, monumentality and regionalism should lead the way to humanization – which, according to Giedion, was, the goal of modernism's second phase – following its initial focus on the practical aspects of dwelling. However, when I deploy the word "constancy" to monumentality and regionalism, I do not argue that monumentality and regionalism depend on eternal, ideal *forms*. They rather point towards unchanging *relations* between humanity and its surroundings, which require continuous reinterpretation. For this reason, "constancy and change" are not at all contradictory.[34]

Norberg-Schulz's Phenomenological Interpretation of Giedion's Constancy and Change

The constituent and transitory facts of Giedion helped to articulate the relation between "Gestalt" and "figure" in Norberg-Schulz's own theory of place. The single work of architecture interprets the durable basic form in its local and historical relation and becomes a "figure." This operation is central in Norberg-Schulz's theory. He transfers Heidegger's ontological distinction between "what there is" (*Sein*) and the "being of what there is" (*Seiendes*) on to the notions "Gestalt" and "figure," stating that together Gestalt and figure define the typical. He asks: "So, what *is* the typical that remains in time and space? The typical is simply what comes through, when we regard 'something as something'," [35] Norberg-Schulz emphasizes that our ability to perceive distinctions and therefore also similarities is *given to us* and that it therefore forms the basis of our intuitive understanding of forms.[36]

This emphasis introduces a historical dimension in the analysis that underpins the art of architecture as based in "place theory." In order to retrieve what is given, analysis of architecture should also include its history as a place. Taken together with a general understanding of place, analysis should contribute to an "identity" of a place that surpasses all the different changes to which it had, over time, been subject, so that the place "in other words *remains the same, although it never is the way it was*."[37] As such, "place theory" may be regarded as an effort to delve deeper into and to solve problems that Giedion had merely identified when he proposed the relationship between constancy and change as constitutive of the built environment. Indeed, as a central notion in "place theory," "the identity of place" is a crucial aspect of this effort to better understand the relation between constancy and change. Understood as Norberg-Schulz's answer to the crisis of modernity that took root in the baroque, his "place theory" might, therefore, be construed as a sustained critique of Giedion.

In his work on "place theory" after the 1980s, Norberg-Schulz takes a marked distance from Giedion's sociological approach to the task of understanding the outside world that characterized the modern movement.

When Man is seen as "being-in-place," the "functional" acquires new depth. Functions are no longer related to measurable "needs" that can be satisfied. They consist of a use where every single action is to be seen as part of a context. As "being-in-place" this context implies a changing interaction between qualitatively distinct parts. Its totality is, though, at the same time characterized by stability – a stability concerning the place itself, and which Norberg-Schulz describes as *stabilitas loci*. In *Stedskunst* he writes: "This is the apparent paradox to which Giedion referred to as 'constancy and change'. Husserl solved the paradox through a phenomenology that revealed the inter-subjective basis for all changes."[38] But Heidegger, according to Norberg-Schulz, went so far as to posit the possibility of expressing a qualitative presence. This happens in the work of art or, more precisely, in the *image*. The image represents something new and exceptional. It does not mean something that could be found anywhere else, but it refers to that which *gathers a world*, thereby including more than the sum of the components of which it consists.

According to Norberg-Schulz, the modern movement never really recovered from its demise in the 1960s because it was unable to transcend its internal shortcomings as exemplified in the unsolved problem of "*the contradiction between constancy and change*."[39] Consciously or otherwise, the pioneers of the modern movement embraced European idealism. They understood "origin" as an idea or *Ding an Sich* ("the Thing itself"). The principle of constancy then became expressed through the repetition of absolute forms, a corollary to the dream of total harmony. Giedion's constituent fact, too, was ultimately read as an ideal entity. This misunderstanding provoked the crisis in architectural modernism. The illusion that this problem could be solved from below – parallel to the way that the Bauhaus, "by their pseudo-scientific attitude whereby everything was perceived as a composition of atomistic elements," tried to unite thoughts and feeling – was embraced with equal enthusiasm by new rationalists and deconstructivists.[40] That constancy continues to be misunderstood as the recurrence of particular forms is also apparent, as evidenced in the criticism Norberg-Schulz offered in his essay "Den nye tradisjon" (1997, The New Tradition) of the "figural elements" of Michael Graves.[41]

Conclusion: The Academic Grounds for Architecture as an Art of Place

In order to describe and to legitimize the meaning of architecture as art, Norberg-Schulz proposed "place theory" as a construction – a bridge – between two central themes. The first, based on experience and reading, dealt with the historicity of architecture, and changes in architectural praxis over time. The second theme draws on philosophical phenomenology that concerns that which characterizes our presence as human beings and that which is constant in the relation between man and the environment. It considers the conditions of our earthly lives and the relation between what is given us through nature and our own production – humanity being both part of nature and a carrier of a *common* world. These two themes become manifest in the experience of crises and loss that Norberg-Schulz and Giedion share. In Norberg-Schulz's "place theory" the experience of crisis and loss acts both as a critique of modernity and as an architectural critique of what he describes as the formal changes to have occurred after the baroque era, when scientific rationality reshaped society in general and, consequently, humanity's relationship with itself. The experience of crisis and loss, rooted in the cultural fortunes of the baroque age, constitutes both the horizon and the premise of "place theory" as a theoretical construction.

Author's Note

I am grateful to Edward Robbins for comments on this text.

Endnotes

1   See Giedion, *Space, Time and Architecture* (1967), 18. Constituent facts are opposed to transitory facts, which do not enjoy the same durability. See 18–19.
2   "Constancy and Change" was the title of the lecture given by Giedion in the First Gropius lecture series at Harvard University in 1961. It is also a theme in *Space, Time and Architecture* (1961). See 859–69.

3 See Norberg-Schulz, *Stedskunst*, 5. Norberg-Schulz's book *Architecture: Presence, Language, Place*, published after his death, is a translation of Stedskunst into English, and in addition this book includes a section called "Language" divided into chapters "Typology," "Morphology" and "Topology." But as Anthony Shugaar says in his translator's note: "This translation … is an odd hybrid. It is based in fact on an Italian-language version of the original Norwegian, a version that was however approved as a basis for the English version by the author before his death. This sequence of versions inevitably gives rise to a sort of Chinese Telephone effect. Chinese Telephone, of course, is a children's game where a message is whispered by one child to another; in the end the impossibly garbled version is compared to the original message, to comic effect. It is to be hoped that such is not the case with the present translation." Shugaar also states that Norberg-Schulz's intial message "is in any case not the easiest sort of reading," and that Norberg-Schulz is "making words mean what he chooses." All translations are mine.

4 Norberg-Schulz, *Stedskunst*, 7.

5 Norberg-Schulz, *Stedskunst*, 7.

6 Norberg-Schulz, *Stedskunst*, 7–8.

7 Norberg-Schulz, *Stedskunst*, 8.

8 See Heidegger, *Vorträge und Aufsätze*, vol. 2.

9 Norberg-Schulz, *Mellom jord og himmel*, 22.

10 Arendt, *The Human Condition*, 170.

11 Arendt, though, albeit in terms that differ from both Heidegger and Norberg-Schulz, stresses the double conditions of our lives: we are conditioned both by the earth and the world. In *The Human Condition* she is concerned with the predicaments from which politics must start. Where Heidegger and also Norberg-Schulz focus on the connections of our conditions to what is given us through nature, Arendt focuses on human plurality as a condition for our lives on earth. She is interested in what characterizes human beings and makes us *different from nature.* In other words, it is the human *condition*, not human *nature* with which Arendt's book is concerned.

12 This is an assessment which has been part of the phenomenological thinking from its very inception.

13 Norberg-Schulz, *Stedskunst*, 10.

14 In other words, here architecture is seen as an art form, in contrast to a plain erection of buildings.

15 Gro Lauvland, "Verk og vilkår," 67–8.

16 Norberg-Schulz, *Stedskunst*, 10. The quotation from the Foreword dates to 1 September 1996. The Foreword to *Genius Loci* is dated June 1976.

17 Norberg-Schulz, *Stedskunst*, 10.

18 Norberg-Schulz, *Stedskunst*, 10.

19 Here, modern architecture and the modern movement are indications for the new architecture that shot up in Europe during the 1920s and 1930s, and also for the determination of this phenomenon both as physical form and ideology over the subsequent three decades.

20 Tournikiotis makes a differentiation between "genealogies" and "stories" in *The Historiography of Modern Architecture*. By genealogies he means an explanation of origins, a narrow developmental logic, often technological and normative, while stories implies a broader descriptive presentation, a field of possibilities.

21 Giedion, *Space, Time and Architecture*, 211.

22 Norberg-Schulz, *Stedskunst*, 6.

23 Norberg-Schulz, *Stedskunst*, 18; Lauvland, "Verk og vilkår," 72.

24 See Heidegger, *Der Ursprung des Kunstwerkes*.

25 Norberg-Schulz, *Principles of Modern Architecture*, 38; Mies van der Rohe, "Inaugural Address as Director of Architecture at Armour Institute of Technology, 1938," 192.

26 Giedion, *Space, Time and Architecture*, 18.

27 Norberg-Schulz, *Baroque Architecture*, 10.

28 Giedion, *Space, Time and Architecture*, 109.

29 Giedion, *Space, Time and Architecture*, 109.

30 Norberg-Schulz, *Late Baroque and Rococo Architecture*, 13.

31 Norberg-Schulz, *Late Baroque and Rococo Architecture*, 13.

32 See the preface to *Baroque Architecture*, 6.

33 Norberg-Schulz, *Baroque Architecture*, 12.

34 Norberg-Schulz, *Stedskunst*, 6–7.

35   My translation is based on the unpublished Norwegian manuscript *Architecture: Presence, Language and Place.* In the published book Norberg-Schulz writes: "At this time I wonder: what is the typical that lasts over time and space? And I am obliged to answer that it is simply that which is emanated when something is recognized as such." *Architecture*, 134.

36   Lauvland, "Verk og vilkår," 71.

37   Norberg-Schulz, *Stedskunst*, 182.

38   Norberg-Schulz, *Stedskunst*, 8.

39   Norberg-Schulz, *Øye og hånd*, 142. Norberg-Schulz's italics.

40   Norberg-Schulz, *Øye og hand*, 142. Neither Peter Eisenmann nor Bernard Tschumi on the one hand, nor Aldo Rossi and his disciples on the other, were able to make a synthesis of constancy and change – a synthesis that could overcome the "split between thought and feelings," according to Norberg-Schulz.

41   Norberg-Schulz, *Øye og hand*, 143.

Chapter 20
The Future of the Baroque, c. 1980

Maarten Delbeke and Andrew Leach

The tercentenary commemorations in 1967 of Borromini's death had demonstrated how an historical subject like the oeuvre of this key figure of the Roman baroque could sustain the attentions of many varied modes of historical analysis. Lectures, exhibits, books, films and many other interventions treated Borromini's buildings (realized and otherwise), his drawings and inventories (as sources and documents alike), the *Opus Architectonicum*, secondary historical and biographical accounts and so forth as legitimate historical subjects. They had visited upon them the disciplinary tools of art historians from Rudolf Wittkower to Giulio Carlo Argan alongside new scholarship by those invested in Borromini's archives, in the restoration of his buildings, in his manner of design, in his reception and in the lessons offered by his work to the present. Borromini emerged from this event as a complex and interdisciplinary historical and biographical subject that could exist in an architectural culture experiencing a watershed moment of disciplinary maturity – a form of détente between conflicting historiographical investments, with the academic and public program of the *anno borrominiano* demonstrating a format within which these interests could occupy the same corpus. The investment of the architect-historian in such a figure as Borromini was, at this time, as legitimate as that of the art historian specializing in architecture (or, even generally, in the art of the seventeenth century), as was that of the architect practicing (and thinking) in a manner demonstrating his or her cognizance of the present's historicity.

The Borromini commemorations of 1967 were hardly free of disciplinary tensions – these are well documented in the two-volume acts, *Studi sul Borromini* – but as an event they nonetheless described how architectural history could operate as an interdisciplinary field in which the grasp of specialists – and the hegemony, in particular, of German-language art historiography – had been tempered by the maturity of competing modes of historical analysis and the tools attendant to their aims, and all this within relatively new academic geographies that had absorbed and advanced the model of *Kunstwissenschaft*. The event aimed at an authority, an openness of debate (all discussions, supportive and dissenting were faithfully documented) and an academic acuity to overcome the criticisms that had been leveled at the "instrumentalization" to which *Michelangiolo Architetto* (curated by Bruno Zevi and Paolo Portoghesi) had been subject three years earlier.[1] And indeed it did not rule this view on history as out of place among a range of rigorously argued methods for which the balance of opposing views would always prove necessary. It was a conference on the figure of Borromini, on his relationships with others and his impact on European architecture over three centuries; it considered his place in the history of architecture, of architectural ideas and their intersections with philosophy, philology and geometry; it reflected on his compositional technique and its implications for the work and Borromini's legacy alike; it considered meaning, form, functionality; it treated buildings as objects of study and lenses through which to direct a view intent on landing elsewhere. Importantly, it was an event in which architects concerned with history and historians concerned with architecture could meet on an even field.

Within a generation, all this had changed. In a review of the activities marking the tercentenary of Gianlorenzo Bernini's death Alessandro Rinaldi explicitly juxtaposed Paolo Portoghesi's work on Borromini in the years leading up to the 1967 celebrations – which in his eyes qualified as "operations at once historical-critical and militant" that pertained to "a design practice attentive to the values of the *locus* and memory" – to the range of "individual" studies of Bernini's work presented at three conferences organized on the artist in Rome in 1980 and 1981, which to a large extent aimed at "a full historical contextualization of the work of Bernini."[2] The net result of these latter contributions to Bernini scholarship, Rinaldi contends, was both a further, and beneficial, demolition of the clichés that persistently clung to the baroque in favour of an historical understanding of the production, forms and meanings of Bernini's art, and a fragmentation of this field of specialist research into an array of ever more refined historical cases.

This new work internalized Argan's notion of the baroque's rhetoricality and applied it to individual fragments of an oeuvre in lieu of an explicit historiographical stance on the baroque as a whole. It is no coincidence that Rinaldi felt compelled to organize the mass of historical research presented in 1980 around two of Bernini's signature achievements: the colonnade of St. Peter's square and the Cornaro chapel. Interpreted as theatres of Catholic religiosity, ecclesiastical splendour and seventeenth-century mysticism, these two cases demonstrated how the relation between the art form of the baroque, its visual repertory and the religious and political programs to which it pertains is no longer problematic *per se*, but rather a given – its modalities and articulations now forming the object of the art historian's inquiry. Rinaldi further argued that the exhibition *Bernini in Vaticano* demonstrated how Bernini and his workshop were able to forge an unmistakable artistic identity from extremely variegated commissions issued by an ever-changing cast of patrons.[3] In other words, the now generally accepted programs of baroque art as bound to circumstances and imperatives beyond art were shown to have in no way impeded the flourishing of artistic genius. The situation was, indeed, quite to the contrary.

When it was again Borromini's turn to be celebrated – 1999 marked the quatercentenary of his birth – the interventions were not noticeably different from those marking his rival's demise and birth (commemorated a year earlier): art historical conferences, restoration campaigns, and heritage trails drawing attention to his major contributions to the history of architecture, but also to the lesser known works of the master's oeuvre.[4] The institutionalization of this commemorative formula, which was also clearly apparent in the attention paid to Pietro da Cortona in 1997 (on the quatercentenary of *his* birth), at once demonstrated art history's ability to generate and sustain a public involvement in historical architecture, assert and maintain its legitimacy as the main party interested in this work (in close conjunction with preservationists) and, finally, its ever-growing distance from the historically inflected discourse of architects increasingly cast as architectural theory or a form of architectural history (architect-history) distinct from what happened in the history of art. Except in the guise of the professional art historian, now absent was the mode of historical inquiry that three decades earlier had seemed to reach a maturity and a legitimate claim to a seat at the table of the historiography of architecture as an important agent in the contemporary apprehension and analysis of Francesco Borromini. In sum, art history had become the disciplinary hegemon governing serious knowledge of the baroque.[5]

By 1970 the seventeenth century was firmly established as an art historical specialization in its own right, and in the wake of major contributions to the subject by such authorities as Richard Krautheimer, Rudolf Wittkower and Henry Millon a series of monographs on key figures of the Roman baroque had appeared. Howard Hibbard's *Carlo Maderno and Roman Architecture 1580–1630* (1971), for instance, filled the historiographical void that Wittkower had identified in Coudenhove-Erthal's monograph on Domenico Fontana.[6] The definition of a neutralized canon, in no small part due to Wittkower's *Art and Architecture in Italy 1600–1750*, stimulated monographic research that progressively covered the baroque's historical and geographical terrain. The new methods and frameworks to emerge as part of this research were not driven by the historian's (or architect's) preoccupations with the present, but rather by the vicissitudes of historical inquiry *per se*, within the broader tendency towards a greater professionalization on the part of the art history discipline. Patricia Waddy's interpretation of the architecture of Roman *palazzi* in terms of their ceremonial use, or Joseph Connors's analysis of the complicated processes that governed the shaping of public space in seventeenth-century Rome have unquestionably opened up new paths in the history of art and architecture.[7] They have, however, found little resonance in architectural culture beyond the confines of the history of art, and this despite their clear relevance to such architectural issues as user-driven design or bottom-up decision making in urban planning, which their work throws into historical relief. Architecture was, instead, preoccupied in these years with coming to grips with the historical trajectories sketched out by Peter Collins, Colin Rowe, and Manfredo Tafuri, for whom the increasingly distant tomes of Sigfried Giedion and Nikolaus Pevsner, rather than the contemporary disciplinary ascendency of the history of art over the history of architecture, offered the most apparently relevant points of contention for historical and critical debate.[8]

In short, by 1980 architectural culture had come to assume a new relationship to history, embracing the historical and formal eclecticism, ironies, and rejection of the normalizing tendencies of the modern that Charles Jencks had documented in *The Language of Postmodern Architecture* (1977), and by trading the modern "metanarrative" for complexity, embracing the mentality captured by Jean-François Lyotard in 1979 as *la condition postmoderne*. Two events in particular stand out as markers of architecture's relationship with its history at this moment: the exhibition *Roma Interrotta* (1978) – inscribing contemporary architectural gestures over Giambattista Nolli's eighteenth-century map of Rome – and the first Biennale di Architettura in Venice (1980), curated by Paolo Portoghesi under the title "La presenza del passato" ("The Presence of the Past").

The history traced in the present volume suggests that the baroque would loom large in these two contexts. This might have been through the themes that its architects and their historians had mined over the course of the twentieth century: the baroque as the moment when architecture becomes aware of its historicity; or as a monumental architecture giving shape to the city. Or, indeed, by addressing the absences that those same architects (and their modern historians) had clearly left behind, like the ornamentality of baroque architecture, or its affinity with visual and verbal language. Yet in *Roma Interrotta*, for instance, many of the proposals showed a hypersensitivity to architecture's historical and semantic dimensions while remaining blithely impervious to those aspects of baroque Rome which had already been, by 1978, the object of intense historical scrutiny.[9] Rather than suggesting a tentative bridge between the realms of history and architecture, historical research and the architectural project, *Roma Interrotta* illustrated the increasing distance separating one from the other.

Yet new kinds of relationships between contemporary architecture and the baroque had begun to emerge. Returning to the celebrations of Bernini that followed *Roma Interrotta* two years later, Rinaldi's overview of the *anno berniniano* suggests that the actuality of the baroque, now divested from its role in the architectural debate, rested in its theatricality: its capacity for spectacle in those instances wherein the boundaries blurred between what were now read as distinct artistic disciplines. September 1980 saw Cesare Berlingeri's multimedia work *Aria, acqua, terra, fuoco: i quattro elementi del Barocco* (Air, Water, Earth, Fire: The Four Elements of the Baroque) installed on the Spanish Steps. On 1 May 1981, a *Concerto grosso di primavera per macchinerie barocche* (Large Spring Concert for Baroque Machines) was staged by Carlo Montesi and Fabrizia Magnini at the Piazza del Popolo, a contemporary "festa barocca" that, besides the inevitable pyrotechnics and hot air balloons, involved the active participation of the public.[10] Resonating closely with those ideas about seventeenth-century Roman festival culture argued by Maurizio and Marcello Fagiolo dell'Arco in their first monograph on Bernini (and since), these events also called to mind Irving Lavin's characterization of Bernini's *bel composto* (the unification of the three visual arts in one whole, as Lavin had it) as an all-encompassing "existential happening."[11] Theatre and theatricality came here to assume centre stage in these baroque events, no longer only as the slightly suspect characteristics of an instrumentalized art but as the modalities of an experimental artistic practice bridging the gap between past and present. With regards to architecture, though, the common ground between the historical baroque, as presented with ever finer shades of detail, and present-day architectural practice, which relied on their abstraction to activate baroque as a model, shifted away from concepts or operations deemed essential to architecture (the manipulation of space, the dialogue with history) and towards architecture's capacity to transcend its disciplinary boundaries in quest of a new spectacular and immersive aesthetic. It is no coincidence that recent attempts to establish an art historical dialogue between the historical and contemporary "baroque" took either "aesthetics" or the conceptualization of the baroque itself (in history, criticism and philosophy) as starting points, eschewing the insights to be gained from close attention to a specific artistic discipline or historical figure.[12]

As a consequence, the discursive context of the baroque also shifted in these decades. Spurred on to no small extent by the immense popularity of Gilles Deleuze's *Le pli* (1988, translated as *The Fold* in 1992), the baroque was seen to signify an epistemology constituted, as Jon Snyder wrote, of "passion and pathos ..., an extremely elaborate style, the power of the imagination, the metaphoricity of language, the disintegration of cultural truths and the quest for an ephemeral beauty."[13] Filtering several decades' worth of research on the linguistic artifice theorized in seventeenth-century Europe and on the philosophical precursors of (and alternatives to) German idealism, *Le pli* managed to furnish the imagination of researchers and artists across disciplines with a baroque that held out the promise of a radical critique of existing hegemonic paradigms. As a consequence, the baroque played its role in the dissolution of those strong disciplinary boundaries that had hitherto been understood to define architecture (Architecture), and in helping to open it up to such emerging fields as cultural studies and media studies on the basis of the transdisciplinary and interdisciplinary gains of critical theory. Indeed, if the baroque is identified first and foremost as a system of signifiers operating in an analogous way across all forms and expressions of culture, this notion was set to assist architecture's theoreticians and critics to return architecture and the discourses it sustained to the larger field of culture rather than rendering this production accountable to architectural debate or the traditional disciplinary work of art history – which was at the same time undergoing its own institutional upheavals.

The shift between the modern and postmodern regard for the baroque might be illustrated by comparing the reception of writing on this theme by Deleuze with that of Pierre Charpentrat – two thinkers whose articles shared the pages of the very same journals, but whose impact on the contemporary image of the baroque could not be more disparate.[14] Regardless of what the contingency of their respective receptions might signify in terms of an intellectual exchange, it signals a simultaneity in the same field of reception that quickly became read against the dominance of Deleuze. Therein, Charpentrat concludes for the history of ideas a process, initiated at the outset of the twentieth century, of coming to terms with the architecture of the historical baroque by placing it into a sustained and multifarious dialogue with the present. Deleuze initiated another process whereby a philosophical baroque – albeit informed by the historiographical "classics" – became factored into the fields of architecture, theatre and art and the discursive environment of "theory" in which they were then immersed.[15] As such, the baroque was integral to the theoretical turn within and beyond architecture, and an index of the trajectory of the place of historical knowledge and the scholarship in architectural discourse and theory.

The values that maintained a specific association with the baroque throughout the twentieth century and which have been identified in this volume as conductive to the traffic between architecture and its history bear witness to this trajectory. Space and its experience maintained a pivotal role in architectural discourse, yet became inflected by the critique of phenomenology offered by Deleuze and his compatriot Jacques Derrida.[16] Postmodern responses to this critique fall into a schematic (admittedly rather neat) of three responses: embracing a turn towards the darker side of our experiential involvement with architecture under the sign of decay, revulsion and discomfort (as in the rather different studies of Bernard Tschumi and Jennifer Bloomer); towards data as an objectifiable means of access to the world (predicated in the experimental publication formats of Rem Koolhaas and his colleagues at the Office for Metropolitan Architecture and, thereafter, in the work of his "children," MVRDV and BIG); and, finally, towards the promise of total immersion, resulting in a symbiosis between the human subject and his or her environment (as pursued by writers as different as Manuel De Landa and Juhani Pallasmaa).[17] That this all adds up to a snapshot of architectural theory in the wake of the postmodern turn is hardly surprising, given the central role of history and historiography in defining the subjects and tactics of this discursive moment. As Jorge Otero-Pailos has argued, the ambiguous role assigned to history in the wake of the bifurcation of architectural discourse into intellectual and anti-intellectual camps – a crude characterization, but not indefensibly so – set up precisely the kind of problem that this book has sought to unpack, namely how to account for the production, uptake and maintenance of historical knowledge in architectural culture in terms that sustain anachronisms within a history of ideas that aims at acuity in the construction of this history and its effects.[18]

And so in taking recourse to historical authority without submitting to the rigours of history and the tools it uses to conscientiously position the present in relation to the past (and vice versa), the decades after 1980 witnessed a broadening gulf between, on one hand, an increasingly specialized and professional domain of art historical research into the baroque and, on the other, historical models for architectural theory and design for which the history's preoccupation with the fine-grain and the historical mission to account for "what happened" proved decidedly unwelcome.[19] Indeed, the state of the disciplinary distance between architecture and the history of art doubtless meant that it became as difficult to convincingly translate knowledge from the latter to the former as from the history of religion or literary criticism – none of which were impossible, as many examples demonstrate, but nonetheless requiring a competence across two or more fields rather than authority in one alone. As a subject caught in these circumstances, the baroque is a good story for which facts can get in the way – and its facts do indeed tend to undermine its availability as a narrative that either leads to the twentieth century or that allows present-day theoreticians to defend a mode of autochthonous thought within architecture. One reads Patricia Waddy rather than George Hersey for the facts of the matter, Elisabeth Kieven rather than Mieke Bal.[20] Contemporary architectural writing on the baroque simply undertakes a different role, and for a different constituency, than the tasks and responsibilities assumed by historians of art (and those who work like them) as they write the history of architecture. It has drifted towards the kind of projective, speculative, broad strokes thinking to which architectural theory and criticism (and a kind of history) seems to naturally gravitate, but over which it hardly holds a monopoly.

In the wake of a postmodern moment that disrupted architectural history's disciplinary trajectories while opening all manner of once-inconceivable critical and discursive possibilities, the work done by history for architecture has in recent decades shifted decisively away from the tasks it performed across much of the twentieth century.[21] It is neither accidental nor helpful to observe that much of the writing that seems proper to the intellectual genealogy of a contemporary historiography of architecture still anchored to architecture is also the patrimony of the history of art. It is likewise important to recognize the disciplinary abstractions being made in these observations that are undone precisely by the work undertaken in the present moment by books like this. What, therefore, is at stake in trying to untangle the various strains of today's historiographical attention to architecture without demanding unproductive disciplinary distinctions? If the history of art can claim a strong sense of disciplinarity (even in relation to the idea and practice of interdisciplinarity), then architectural history can merely imitate any confidence it sees among its disciplinary cousins. And in this, too, the baroque can serve helpfully as a lens for apprehending the broader issues in play.

There is a crucial conceptual distinction, for instance, between a neo-baroque, a baroque recurrence, and the baroque as an historical source for contemporary architecture that, in their various uses, suggest quite different views on the nature of historical knowledge and its place in present day architectural culture. All point to an historical consciousness, albeit split into forms of historicism framed on rather different terms from one another, each one susceptible to historicization as ideas that govern the relationships between past and present informing the very idea of history. The idea of a neo-baroque shifts markedly from its invocation at the intersection of style and a mode of modern perception in the world of *fin-de-siècle* Vienna to its presentation by Omar Calabrese as *A Sign of the Times* in his *Neo-Baroque* (first published in 1987) or to its use by Angela Ndalianis (2004) to explain *Jurassic Park* as a question of aesthetics and spectacle.[22] Calabrese's suggestion, for instance, that neo-baroque had come to serve in a positive sense to describe the taste and mentality of the culture in which he wrote in the mid-1980s articulates the principles of a baroque mentality divorced from any historical specificity – transhistorical relationships mediated by taste rather than by historical acts or artefacts.

Three decades earlier Gillo Dorfles had observed the same mentality across the spectrum of the arts (from fine art to kitsch) and called what Zevi named the anti-classical another form of neo-baroque. To the extent that it is a neo-baroque, its source is not drawn from history, but from a present made to resonate with a moment of the past on those terms, after Calabrese, that defined the postmodern era – irony, historical quotation, complexity and contradiction – but that recognized a verisimilitude based upon a correspondence of mentalities. That this term, too, described the style and culture of the first modern department stores and of the developer's rounded corner site in the Viennese 1890s, or the art of German expressionism in the 1920s, or the sinuous forms of Alvar Aalto's vases speaks not to an invisible line drawn through the history of western culture but to the recollection of tactics, forms and ideas that resonate most profoundly with the art of a highly visible moment in the Roman seventeenth century – in which certainties were dramatically removed and new forms served to lend this moment its expression. As Walter Benjamin made clear in his *Ursprung des deutschen Trauerspiels*, the baroque is an origin for the modern world, but only in a certain sense.[23]

What Gregg Lambert terms "the (New) Baroque" and Moser and Goyer a "baroque resurgence" – a baroque, that is, in recurrence – is something more obviously resting upon a cyclical notion of history: of the eon as a device of temporal organization championed by Eugenio D'Ors; or of the kinds of formal recurrences observed by Henri Focillon; or of the interaction of classical and baroque phases in art and culture that allowed Margaret Lyttelton to read a baroque stage in the late arts of antiquity. A neo-baroque might draw a kind of authority from the resonances it invokes, but recurrence is a return, a history rendered present, a reprise not as postmodern pastiche or irony but of the kernel – the essence – finding again some new basis for expression.

The extent, for example, to which contemporary parametric design practices respond to the kind of thinking underpinning Luigi Moretti's identification in the 1950s and 1960s of "spatial algorithms" and "parametric architectures" with the compositional and iterative logics of the baroque will determine it either as a conscious return and revision of an historical model or a mode of thinking explored through the process of determining and testing the limits of architectural design.[24] Is it a resonance (accidental or forced), or a conscious return to what is presented as an origin for contemporary problems? One could well argue Frank Gehry's Guggenheim Bilbao or Zaha Hadid's MAXXI as neo-baroque buildings, but to treat them as a baroque in recurrence takes us much further into the relationships between the work and its historiographical field: the form is less the answer than the clue. History is not a scaffolding for this "recurrence," even if it gives shape to the claim it makes upon a kind of indigenous architectural knowledge to which history has long offered authority. The baroque is not the source for this, but rather another moment, alongside others, in which has been identified the capacity to think on architectural terms without, rhetorically speaking, the need to record in writing what was embedded in the work of art.[25] Where the notion of a neo-baroque speaks to a revival of the model from one moment in history by another (a present already conceived in historical terms), the idea of recurrence dissolves historicity as a way of understanding relationships across time, in which abstractions and essentials find their way back into focus as circumstances conspire with artists and architects and writers and scientists to revel in their combined complexity and multiplicity. This is history understood on one hand as criticism – a past perpetually open to the present – and on the other as a repository of referents – loaded referents maintained in a structure that is itself rendered neutral.

While reading the history of architecture through the intellectual history of architectural culture offers us the pretence of some critical distance from the subject at hand, it also demands that we admit to the historicity of the frames with which we ourselves work. If there is a recurrence at work in this volume, it perhaps lies with the insistence, again, of taking distance from those instances of historical consciousness that would each be untenable in the present in order to treat as artificial and constructed that which can too readily be construed as the product of reflex. The architecture of Bernini, Borromini, Pietro da Cortona, Guarini and their contemporaries points to the necessity of revisiting the bases of architectural practice and thought, of relationships between architecture's conceptual interior and its exterior, to extend tradition through architectural practice rather than to adopt it as a set of constraints, to ensure that architectural thought could remain in step with the world beyond the workshop. Guarini reaped the fruits of setting aside narrow cultural and religious referents, just as Borromini demonstrated the value of returning to the ancient and medieval past unhindered by the sense that it was necessary to reconcile it with the classical tradition.[26] They suggest a moment in which the fruits of verifying the authority of history are, for us, reading them as history, plain to see.

The essays in this book have likewise described a section through the history of modern architecture – a period with extremely porous boundaries – in order to articulate the ongoing role of history in shaping architectural practice and thought and the enduring demands that architecture makes of history. The risk is to define as normal and natural that which turns out to be anything but, and in this the role of historiography and historical research remains vital for the realm of contemporary architecture – even as it contributes to fields of knowledge well beyond its reach. The claims made here for history itself as the paradigm best equipped for understanding the relationship of the present to the past can sustain our close attention, mindful that historiography itself only ever remains pertinent and incisive in a state of self-awareness. Much like that architecture we hold to be baroque.

Endnotes

1   See Dulio's essay in this volume, as well as Leach, "Modern Architecture and the Actualisation of History," 501–16.

2   Rinaldi, "Il centenario di Bernini e il rilancio del barocco," 374–6. Consider Micheli's essay on Portoghesi's work from this period above, as well as Dulio's insights into the criticism it offered to Zevi's approach.

3   *Bernini in Vaticano* (staged in the Braccio di Carlo Magno, Vatican City, in 1981). This argument would be pushed to its limit by Damian Dombrowksi in *Dal trionfo all'amore*.

4   See, for instance, Bösel and Frommel (eds), *Borromini e l'univero barocco*; and Millon (ed.), *The Triumph of the Baroque*. See also Spagnesi and Fagiolo dell'Arco (eds), *Gian Lorenzo Bernini architetto e l'architettura europea del Sei- Settecento*.

5   Tod Marder elaborates the consequences of the American rise of studies in the art history of the baroque, described herein by Hopkins as one result of Wittkower's move from London to New York in the wake of publishing *Art and Architecture in Italy*. See Marder, "Renaissance and Baroque Architectural History in the United States," 161–74. Compare James Ackerman's reservations regarding this increased professionalization, already registered in 1958, in "On American Scholarship on the Arts," 357–62.

6   See Pogacnik's essay in this volume.

7   Waddy, *Seventeenth-Century Roman Palaces*; Connors, "Alliance and Emnity in Roman Baroque Urbanism," 205–94.

8   We refer to such books as Collins, *Changing Ideals in Modern Architecture* (1965); Rowe, *The Mathematics of the Ideal Villa* (1982); Tafuri, *Teorie e storia dell'architettura* (1968, Engl. 1980) and *Progetto e utopia* (1973, Engl. 1976); Giedion, *Space, Time and Architecture* (1941); and Pevsner, *Outline of European Architecture* (1943).

9   See Delbeke, "Roma Interrotta," 37–49.

10 Rinaldi, "Il centenario," 382.

11 Fagiolo dell'Arco, *Bernini*; compare Lavin, *Bernini e l'unità delle arti visive*, 151.

12 Schütze (ed.), *Estetica barocca*; and Hills, *Rethinking the Baroque*, which resulted from the eponymous conference held in York, 5–7 July 2006. Compare Hopkins's review of the latter, "Not Enough Baroque."

13 Snyder, *L'estetica del Barocco*, 26.

14 Charpentrat, "Architecture et politique" was published in the same issue of *Critique* as Gilles Deleuze's essay "Un nouvel archiviste," a review of Michel Foucault's *L'archéologie du savoir* which would be included in Deleuze's *Foucault* (1986). Similarly, Charpentrat, "L'architecture du diable" sits in the same issue of *Traverses* as Jean Baudrillard, "Crash," which uses J.G. Ballard's novel of the same name to oppose a "classical" perspective on technology to its "baroque and apocalyptic version" (see Baudrillard, "Crash," 24).

15 Holden, "Finding the Architecture in Deleuze." See also Cache, *Earth Moves*; and Ballantyne, *Deleuze and Guattari for Architects*, esp. 102–3.

16 Otero-Pailos, "Architectural Intellectuality at the Dawn of Postmodernism" in *Architecture's Historical Turn*, ix–xxxiv.

17 Consider Tschumi, *Architecture and Disjunction*; Bloomer, *Architecture and the Text*; OMA, Koolhaas and Mau, *S, M, L, XL*; OMA/AMO and Koolhaas, *Content*; MVRDV, *Metacity/Datatown*; Ingels, *Yes is More*; and Pallasmaa, *Eyes of the Skin*. On De Landa, see Tawa, "Emergence in Architecture."

18 Otero-Pailos, *Architecture's Historical Turn*, xiv.

19 We borrow the clarity of this "mission" from Reinhold Martin's paper "Modern Housing."

20 For Hersey, see *Architecture and Geometry in the Age of the Baroque*. For Bal, see "Pour une histoire perverties," 61–87 (and the collection in which it appears in support of the general point – Moser and Goyer (eds), *Résurgences baroques*). Consider, too, Ostwald's study *The Architecture of the New Baroque*.

21 Consider Simon Sadler's position paper, "Autonomy's Ghost and General Education."

22 Calabrese, *Neo-Baroque*, 12–17. Compare Ndalianis, *Neo-Baroque Aesthetics and Contemporary Entertainment*.

23 As Irving Lavin notes: "Allegory, in the sense that the work of art refers to concepts and values beyond, or beneath, what is actually represented, was the defining nature of the style and ultimately the key to its relevance for the present, both of which, that is, the Baroque and the Modern, Benjamin saw essentially as periods of decadence." Lavin, "Going for Baroque," 429. Later in this essay (437–44), Lavin even shows step-by-step how Gehry Associates (like Bernini) "deep down … went for baroque."

24 See Tedeschi, "Algorithmie spaziali," 137–77 and Navone, "'Un nuovo linguaggio per il pensiero architettonico'," 409–18.

25 On this point see Delbeke, *The Art of Religion*.

26 Tafuri, "Borromini e Piranesi," 89–101.

Bibliography

Ackermann, James. "On American Scholarship in the Arts." *College Art Journal* 17(4) (1958): 357–62.

Adler, Daniel and Mitchell Benjamin Frank (eds). *German Art History and Scientific Thought: Beyond Formalism.* Farnham: Ashgate, 2012.

Adler, Daniel. "Painterly Politics: Wölfflin, Formalism and German Academic Culture, 1885–1915." *Art History* 27(3) (June 2004): 431–56.

Adorno, Theodor W. "Der mißbrauchte Barock." In *Ohne Leitbild. Parva Aesthetica*, by Theodor W. Adorno, 133–57. Frankfurt am Main: Suhrkamp, 1967.

Aitchison, Mathew. "Pevsner's Townscape." *AA Files* 61 (2010): 130–31.

Aitchison, Mathew. "Townscape in Context: The Picturesque, Nikolaus Pevsner, 'Visual Planning' and the Concept of Context in Post-War British Architecture and Urban Planning." Paper presented at *Recovering Post-War Europe: Art and Architecture 1945–1970.* University of Pennsylvania, October 2004.

Aitchison, Mathew. "Visual Planning and Exterior Furnishing: A Critical History of the Early Townscape Movement, 1930 to 1949." PhD dissertation, University of Queensland, 2009.

Aitchison, Mathew. "Visual Planning and the Picturesque: Sir Nikolaus Pevsner and Townscape Revisited." In Andrew Leach and Gill Matthewson (eds), *Celebration: Proceedings of the 22nd Annual Conference of the Society of Architectural Historians, Australia and New Zealand*, 17–24. Napier, NZ: SAHANZ, 2005.

Alberti, Leon Battista. *L'architettura.* Edited by Paolo Portoghesi. Milan: Il Polifilo, 1966.

Allesch, Gustav Johann von. "Psychologische Bemerkungen zu zwei Werken der neueren Kunstgeschichte." *Psychologische Forschung* 4(2) (1922): 368–81.

Allesch, Gustav Johann von. "Die ästhetische Erscheinungsweise der Farben." *Psychologische Forschung* 6(1) (1925): 1–80, 215–81.

Alofsin, Anthony. "1920–1945: Challenges to Beaux-Arts Dominance." In Joan Ockman with Rebecca Williamson (eds), *Architecture School: Three Centuries of Educating Architects in North America*, 90–119. Cambridge, MA: MIT Press, 2012.

Alofsin, Anthony. *Struggle for Modernism: Architecture, Landscape Architecture and City Planning at Harvard.* New York, NY: W.W. Norton & Co., 2002.

Alpers, Svetlana. *The Art of Describing: Dutch Art in the Seventeenth Century.* Chicago, IL: University of Chicago Press, 1983.

AMO/OMA [Office for Metropolitan Architecture] and Rem Koolhaas. *Content.* Cologne: Taschen, 2004.

Anon. "A Second Look at the Pelican History." *Burlington Magazine* 109(774) (1967): 491–2.

Anon. "Available Traveling Fellowships: The Rome Prize Fellowships." *Journal of the American Institute of Architects* (January 1948): 36–7.

Anon. "Pierre Charpentrat n'est plus." *Critique* 367 (December 1977): 1148.

Anon. "Prof. Panofsky Lectures Here about Baroque. Comparison with Mannerism Made. Explains Parallel in Drama and Literature. Baroque Period is the Second Great Climax of the High Renaissance." *Vassar Miscellany News*, 8 May 1935.

Anon. "The Pelican History of Art." *Burlington Magazine* 95(607) (1953): 319.

Anon. "UN Assembly: How Do Architects Like It? First Reaction: Most of Them Don't." *Architectural Forum* 97 (December 1952): 114–15.

Anon. "UN General Assembly: Does it Mean a Turning Point of Modern Architecture? Or is it the 'Bankruptcy' of the International Style?" *Architectural Forum* 97 (October 1952): 140–49.

Arend, Sabine. "Albert Erich Brinckmann (1881–1958)." In Jutta Held and Martin Papenbrock (eds), *Kunstgeschichte an den Universitäten im Nationalsozialismus.* Special issue, *Kunst und Politik: Jahrbuch der Guernica-Gesellschaft* 5 (2003): 123–43.

Arend, Sabine. "'Einen neuen Geist einführen?' Das Fach Kunstgeschichte unter den Ordinarien Albert Erich Brinckmann (1931–1935) und Wilhelm Pinder (1935–1945)." In Rüdiger vom Bruch (ed.), *Die Berliner Universität in der NS-Zeit*. Vol. 2, *Fachbereiche und Fakultäten*, 179–98. Stuttgart: Steiner, 2005.

Arendt, Hannah. *The Human Condition*. Chicago, IL: University of Chicago Press, 1958.

Argan, Giulio Carlo. *Borromini*. Milan: Bruno Mondadori, 1952.

Argan, Giulio Carlo. *L'architettura barocca in italia*. Milan: Garzanti, 1957.

Argan, Giulio Carlo. "La 'Rettorica' e l'arte barocca." In Enrico Castelli (ed.), *Atti del III Congresso internazionale di studi umanistici* (1954), 9–14. Rome: F. Bocca, 1955.

Argan, Giulio Carlo. *L'Europa dei capitali 1600–1700*. Translated by Anthony Rhodes as *The Europe of the Capitals 1600–1700*. Geneva: Skira, 1964.

Argan, Giulio Carlo. "Nella crisi del mondo moderno." In Paolo Portoghesi, Giulio Carlo Argan and Mario Pisani (eds), *Paolo Portoghesi*, 13–18. Rome: Gangemi, 1993.

Argan, Giulio Carlo. "S. Maria in Campitelli." *Commentari* 10 (1960): f. 1

Arangio-Ruiz, Vicenzo (ed.). "Manierismo, barocco, rococo. Concetti e termini." Special issue, *Problemi attuali di scienza e di cultura* 52 (1962).

Aurenhammer, Hans. "Max Dvorák (1874–1921)." In Ulrich Pfisterer (ed.), *Klassiker der Kunstgeschichte*. Vol. 1, *Von Winckelmann bis Warburg*, 214–27. Munich: Beck, 2007.

Baberowski, Jörg. *Der Sinn der Geschichte. Geschichtstheorien von Hegel bis Foucault*. Munich: Beck, 2005.

Bal, Mieke. "Pour une histoire pervertie." In Walter Moser and Nicolas Goyer (eds), *Résurgences baroques. Les trajectoires d'un processus transcultural*, 61–87. Brussels: La lettre volée, 2001.

Ballantyne, Andrew. *Deleuze and Guattari for Architects*. London: Routledge, 2007.

Banham, Reyner. "Out of the Air." *Listener*, 25 August 1983.

Banham, Reyner. "Pelican History in 48 Volumes." *Architectural Review* 114 (November 1953): 285–8.

Banham, Reyner. *Theory and Design in the First Machine Age*. London: Architectural Press, 1960.

Barroero, Liliana. "Wittkower vent'anni dopo." In Rudolf Wittkower (ed.), *Arte e architettura in Italia 1600–1750*, xxix–xxxvi. Turin: Einaudi, 2002.

Battaglia, Roberto. *La cattedra berniniana di S. Pietro*. Rome: Reale istituto di studi romani, 1943.

Battisti, Eugenio. "Il simbolismo in Borromini." In *Studi sul Borromini. Atti del convegno promosso dall'Accademia Nazionale di San Luca*, vol. 1, 229–84. Rome: De Luca editore, 1967.

Baudrillard, Jean. "Crash." In "Fonctionnalismes en dérive Traverses." Special issue, *Traverses* 4 (1976): 24–9.

Bayer, Josef. "Stilkrisen unser Zeit." 1886. In Josef Bayer and Robert Stiassny (eds), *Baustudien und Baubilder, Schriften zur Kunst*, 289–95. Jena: Diederichs, 1919.

Bazin, Germain. *Classique, baroque et rococo*. Paris: Larousse, 1965. Translated by Jonathan Griffin as *Baroque and Rococo*. London: Thames and Hudson, 1964.

Beavan, Clare, dir. "Bernini." *Simon Schama's Power of Art*. BBC, 2006.

Beil, Ralf and Claudia Dillmann (eds). *Gesamtkunstwerk Expressionismus. Kunst, Film, Literatur, Theater, Tanz und Architektur, 1905–1925*. Exhibition catalogue. Darmstadt: Hatje Cantz, 2010.

Belcher, John. *Essentials in Architecture: An Analysis of the Principles and Qualities to Be Looked for in Buildings*. London: Batsford, 1907.

Belcher, John and Mervin E. Macartney (eds). *Later Renaissance Architecture in England: A Series of Examples of the Domestic Buildings Erected Subsequent to the Elizabethan Period, Ed., with Introductory and Descriptive Text*. 6 vols. London: BT Batsford, 1897–1901.

Bellini, Federico. *Le cupole di Borromini: la scientia costrutiva in età barocca*. Milan: Electa, 2004.

Benelli, Francesco. "Rudolf Wittkower e Colin Rowe: continuità e frattura." In Mauro Marzo (ed.), *L'architettura come testo e la figura di Colin Rowe*, 97–111. Venice: Marsilio, 2010.

Benjamin, Walter. *Ursprung des deutschen Trauerspiels*. Berlin, Rowohlt, 1928. Translated by John Osborne as *The Origin of German Tragic Drama*. London: NLB, 1977. Translated into Italian by Enrico Filippini as *Dramma barocco Tedesco*. Turin: Einaudi, 1971.

Berger, Stefan, Mark Donovan and Kevin Passmore (eds). *Writing National Histories: Western Europe since 1800*. London and New York, NY: Routledge, 1999.

Bergson, Henri. *Creative Evolution*. Translated by Arthur Mitchell. London: Macmillan, 1911.

Berman, Marshall. *All that is Solid Melts into Air: The Experience of Modernity*. New York, NY: Verso, 1982.

Besset, Maurice. *New French Architecture*. London: The Architectural Press, 1967.

Betthausen, Peter. *Georg Dehio. Ein deutscher Kunsthistoriker*. Berlin and Munich: Deutscher Kunstverlag, 2004.

Bialostocki, Jan. Review of *Art and Architecture in Belgium 1600 to 1800*, by Horst Gerson and E.H. Ter Kuile. *Art Bulletin* 45(1) (1963): 68–70.

Bie, Oskar. "Das Waarenhaus." *Neue Deutsche Rundschau* 12 (1901): 96.

Bloch, Marc. *Apologie pour l'histoire ou métier d'historien*. Paris: A Colin, 1949. Translated by Peter Putnam as *The Historian's Craft*. Manchester: Manchester University Press, 1992.

Blomfeld, Reginald. *The Mistress Art*. London: Edward Arnold, 1908.

Bloomer, Jennifer. *Architecture and the Text: The (S)crypts of Joyce and Piranesi*. New Haven, CT: Yale University Press, 1995.

Blunt, Anthony. *Some Uses and Misuses of the Terms Baroque and Rococo as Applied to Architecture: Lecture on Aspects of Art*. London: Oxford University Press for the British Academy, 1973.

Böhme, Margarete. *W.A.G.M.U.S.* Berlin: F. Fontane & Co., 1911. Translated as *The Department Store: A Novel of To-Day*. New York, NY and London: D. Appleton, 1912.

Bollenbeck, Georg. *Bildung und Kultur. Glanz und Elend eines deutschen Deutungsmusters*. Frankfurt am Main: Suhrkamp, 1996.

Bollenbeck, Georg and Clemens Knobloch (eds). *Semantischer Umbau der Geisteswissenschaften nach 1933 und 1945*. Heidelberg: Winter, 2001.

Bonnefoy, Yves. "Pierre Charpentrat et l'architecture baroque." *Critique* 223 (December (1965): 999–1015.

Bonnefoy, Yves. *Rome, 1630*. First published in 1970. Paris: Flammarion, 2000.

Borissavlievitch, Miloutine. *Les théories de l'architecture: essai critique sur les principales doctrines relatives à l'esthétique de l'architecture*. Paris: Payot, 1926.

Borromini, Francesco. *Opus architectonicum*. Edited by Joseph Connors. Milan: Polifilo, 1998.

Borsi, Franco and Paolo Portoghesi. *Victor Horta*. Rome: Edizioni del Tritone, 1969.

Bösel, Richard and Christoph L. Frommel (eds). *Borromini e l'universo barocco*. Milan: Electa, 2000.

Bosworth, F. and R.C. Jones. *A Study of Architecture Schools*. New York, NY: Charles Scribner's Sons, 1932.

Bowlt, John E. (ed. and trans.). *Russian Art of the Avant-garde: Theory and Criticism, 1902–1934*. New York, NY: Viking Press, 1976.

Brauer, Heinrich and Rudolf Wittkower. *Die Zeichnungen des Gianlorenzo Bernini*, 2 vols. Berlin: Heinrich Keller, 1931.

Bredekamp, Horst. "Der Manierismus: zur Problematik einer kunsthistorischen Erfindung." In Wolfgang Braungart (ed.), *Manier und Manierismus*, 109–29. Tübingen: Max Niemeyer, 2000.

Bredekamp, Horst. "Erwin Panofsky (1892–1968)." In Ulrich Pfisterer (ed.), *Klassiker der Kunstgeschichte*, vol. 2, *Von Panofsky bis Greenberg*, 61–75. Munich: Beck, 2008.

Breuer, Stefan. *Grundpositionen der deutschen Rechten (1871–1945)*. Tübingen: Diskord, 1999.

Briggs, Martin Shaw. *Baroque Architecture*. London: Adelphi Terrace, 1913. Translated into German as *Barock-Architektur*. Berlin: Baumgärtel, 1914.

Briggs, Martin Shaw. "The Genius of Bernini." *The Burlington Magazine for Connoisseurs* 26(143) (1915): 197–8.

Brinckmann, Albert Erich. *Barockskulptur. Entwicklungsgeschichte der Skulptur in den romanischen und germanischen Ländern seit Michelangelo bis zum 18. Jahrhundert*, 2 vols. Handbuch der Kunstwissenschaft. Berlin-Neubabelsberg: Athenaion, 1919.

Brinckmann, Albert Erich. *Die Baukunst des 17. und 18. Jahrhunderts in den Romanischen Ländern*. Wildpark-Potsdam: Akademische Verlagsgesellschaft Athenaion, 1919.

Brinckmann, Albert Erich. "Die Baukunst in ihrer räumlichen und plastischen Gestaltung, ihre Beziehung zur Skulptur und Malerei." Lecture announcement and synopsis from the Royal Danish Academy for the Fine Arts for a lecture series 13–15 April, 1921. Nachlass Albert Erich Brinckmann, Archive of the Kunsthistorisches Institut, Cologne.

Brinckmann, Albert Erich. *Plastik und Raum*. Munich: R. Piper & Co., 1922. Translated into Russian by E.A. Nekrasov as *Plastika i prostranstvo*, edited and introduced by M.V. Aplatov. Moscow: Izdatelstvo Akademii Arhitekturi, 1935.

Brinckmann, Albert Erich. *Platz und Monument*. Berlin: Ernst Wasmuth, 1912.

Brinckmann, Albert Erich. *Von Guarino Guarini bis Balthasar Neumann. Vortrag in der Mitgliederversammlung des Deutschen Vereins für Kunstwissenschaft am 11. Juni 1932 zu Berlin*. Berlin: Deutscher Verein für Kunstwissenschaft, 1932.

Brinckmann, Albert Erich. Review of *Spätbarock*, by Hans Rose. *Monatshefte für Kunstwissenschaft* 15 (1922): 241–4.

Brinitzer, Sabine. *Organische Architekturkonzepte zwischen 1900 und 1960 in Deutschland. Untersuchungen zur Definition des Begriffs organische Architektur*. Frankfurt am Main: Lang, 2006.

Broderson, Momme. "Wenn Ihnen die Arbeit des Interesses Wert erscheint … Walter Benjamin und das Warbug-Institut: einige Dokumente." In Horst Brederkamp, Michael Diers and Charlotte Schoell-Glass (eds), *Aby Warbug: Akten des internationalen Symposions*, 87–91. Hamburg: Warburg-Archivs, 1990.

Brownlee, David. *Out of the Ordinary: Robert Venturi, Denise Scott Brown and Associates. Architecture/Urbanism/Design*. New Haven, CT: Yale University Press, 2001.

Bucci, Federico. *"Le parole dipinte."* In Federico Bucci and Marco Mulazzani (eds), *Luigi Moretti. Opere e scritti*, 136–55. Milan: Electa, 2000.

Bungay, Stephen. *Beauty and Truth: A Study of Hegel's Aesthetics*. Oxford: Clarendon Press, 1987.

Burckhardt, Jacob. *Der Cicerone*. Basel, 1855. Translated by Blanche Clough as *The Cicerone: An Art Guide to Painting in Italy for the Use of Travellers and Students*. London: John Murray, 1879.

Burckhardt, Jacob. *Die Kultur der Renaissance in Italien*. 1860. Berlin: Deutsche Buch-Gemeinschaft, 1936. Translated by S.G.C. Middlemore as *The Civilization of the Renaissance in Italy*. Vienna: Phaidon; New York, NY: Oxford University Press, 1900.

Bushart, Magdalena. *Der Geist der Gotik und die expressionistische Kunst. Kunstgeschichte und Kunsttheorie 1911–1925*. Munich: Schreiber, 1990.

Bushart, Magdalena. "'Form' und 'Gestalt'. Zur Psychologisierung der Kunstgeschichte um 1900." In Otto Gerhard Oexle (ed.), *Krise des Historismus – Krise der Wirklichkeit. Wissenschaft, Kunst und Literatur 1880–1932*, 147–81. Göttingen: Vandenhoeck & Ruprecht, 2007.

Butor, Michel. *Improvisations sur Michel Butor. L'écriture en transformation*. Paris: La Différence, 1993.

Cache, Bernard. *Terre meuble*. Written 1983, published Orléans: HYX, 1997. Translated by Anne Boyman as *Earth Moves: Furnishing Territories*. Cambridge, MA: MIT Press, 1995.

Calabrese, Omar. *L'età neobarocca*. Rome: Laterza, 1987. Translated by Charles Lambert as *Neo-Baroque: A Sign of the Times*. Princeton, NJ: Princeton University Press, 1992.

Campbell, Mark. "Aspects Not Things: Geoffrey Scott's View of History." *AA Files* 59 (2009): 42–9.

Campbell, Mark. "Geoffrey Scott and the Dream-Life of Architecture." *Grey Room* 15 (2004): 61–78.

Carrier, David. *The Aesthete in the City: The Philosophy and Practice of American Abstract Painting in the 1980s*. University Park, PA: Penn State University Press, 1994.

Castedo, Leopoldo. *The Baroque Prevalence in Brazilian Art*. New York, NY: Charles Frank, 1964.

Cattaui, Georges. "Baroque et rococo." *Critique* 122 (July 1957): 613–43.

Cattaui, Georges. *Baroque et rococo*. Paris: Arthaud, 1973.

Causey, Andrew. "Pevsner and Englishness." In Peter Draper (ed.), *Reassessing Nikolaus Pevsner*, 161–74. Aldershot: Ashgate, 2004.

Caussé, Françoise. *La revue "l'Art Sacré." Le débat en France sur l'art et la réligion (1945–1954)*. Paris: Éditions du Cerf, 2010.

Celik, Zeynep. "Kinaesthetic Impulses: Aesthetic Experience, Bodily Knowledge, and Pedagogical Practices in Germany, 1871–1918." PhD dissertation, Massachusetts Institute of Technology, 2007.

Charpentrat, Pierre. "À propos de l'architecture des années 60." *Mercure de France* (February 1964): 311–19.

Charpentrat, Pierre. "Architecture et politique." *Critique* 274 (March 1970): 257–64.

Charpentrat, Pierre. *Baroque, Italie et Europe centrale*. Fribourg: Office du livre, 1964.

Charpentrat, Pierre. "Baudelaire et le baroque." *Nouvelle revue française* 7(82) (October 1959): 697–706; 7(83) (November 1959): 880–85.

Charpentrat, Pierre. "Crise de l'architecture moderne?" *Critique* 187 (December 1962): 1079–89.

Charpentrat, Pierre. "De l'abus de la méthode en architecture." *Critique* 221 (October 1965): 864–74.

Charpentrat, Pierre. *Du maître d'ouvrage au maître d'œuvre, l'architecture religieuse en Allemagne du Sud, de la guerre de Trente Ans à l'Aufklärung*. Paris: Klincksieck, 1974.

Charpentrat, Pierre. "Fonction, fonctionnel et fonctionnalisme en architecture." In "Fonctionnalismes en dérive Traverses." Special issue, *Traverses* 4 (1976): 88–97.

Charpentrat, Pierre. "L'architecture au Siècle des Lumières." *Mercure de France* (October 1963): 461–66.

Charpentrat, Pierre. "L'architecture baroque et ses usagers." *Critique* 306 (November 1972): 997–1015.

Charpentrat, Pierre. "L'architecture contemporaine: au delà du baroque?" *Annales. Economies, Sociétés, Civilisations* 16(3) (1961): 457–68.

Charpentrat, Pierre. "L'architecture du diable." In "Le maquillage." Special issue, *Traverses* 7 (1977): 21–8.

Charpentrat, Pierre. "L'architecture et son public. Les églises de la Contre-Réforme." *Annales. Economies, Sociétés, Civilisations* 28(1) (1973): 91–108.

Charpentrat, Pierre. *L'Art baroque*. Paris: Presses universitaires de France, 1967. Translated as *Baroque: Italy and Central Europe*. Lausanne: Taschen, 1995.

Charpentrat, Pierre. "Le baroque, ou l'art des autres." *Critique* 210 (November 1964): 1002–4.

Charpentrat, Pierre. *Le mirage baroque*. Paris: Minuit, 1967.

Charpentrat, Pierre. "Le trompe l'oeil." In "Effets et formes de l'illusion." Special issue, *Nouvelle revue de psychanalyse* 4 (1971): 161–8.

Charpentrat, Pierre. "Les français devant le Baroque: de la légende à l'Histoire." *Critique* 175 (December 1961): 1059–69.

Charpentrat, Pierre. "L'urbanisme ou les reveries d'un arpenteur solitaire." *Critique* 242 (July 1967): 649–62.

Charpentrat, Pierre. "Pierre Francastel." *Annales. Economies, Sociétés, Civilisations* 26(5) (1971): 1132–9.

Charpentrat, Pierre. "Quelques acceptations du mot 'baroque'." *Critique* 206 (July 1964): 651–66.

Charpentrat, Pierre. "Relecture de Wölfflin." *Baroque. Revue internationale. Journées internationales d'étude du baroque* 4 (December 1969): 37–41.

Charpentrat, Pierre. "Remarques sur la structure de l'espace baroque." *Nouvelle Revue Française* 104 (August 1961): 216–30.

Charpentrat, Pierre. "Résidez: nous ferons le reste." *Critique* 252 (May 1968): 522–32.

Christ, Yvan. *Projets et divagations de Claude-Nicolas Ledoux, architecte du roi*. Paris: Minotaur, 1961.

Ciucci, Giorgio. *Gli architetti e il Fascismo. Architettura e città 1922–1944*. Turin: Einaudi, 1989.

Cocagnac, Augustin Maurice. "Le baroque face au silence." *L'Art sacré* 1–2 (September–October 1954): 10–27.

Cocagnac, Augustin Maurice. "Editorial." *L'Art sacré* 1–2 (October–November 1955): 3–11.

Coffin, David. "Review of *Art and Architecture in Italy 1600 to 1750*, by Rudolf Wittkower." *Journal of the Society of Architectural Historians* 18(4) (1959): 164–5.

Cohen, Bernard. "Harvard and MIT: Where It All Began." *Planning* 47(3) (March 1981): 23–6.

Cohen, Jean-Louis. "La coupure entre architectes et intellectuels, ou les enseignements de l'italophilie." *In Extenso. Recherches à l'Ecole d'Architecture Paris-Villemin* 1 (1984): 182–223.

Colby, Veneta. *Vernon Lee: A Literary Biography*. Charlottesville, VA: University of Virginia Press, 2003.

Collins, Peter. *Changing Ideals in Modern Architecture, 1750–1950*. Montreal: McGill University Press, 1965.

Colze, Leo. *Berliner Warenhäuser*. Leipzig and Berlin: H. Seemann, 1908.

Congrès archéologique de France, 105e session, tenue en Souabe en 1947 par la Société Française d'Archéologie. Baden: Art et Sciences, 1949.

Connors, Joseph. "Alliance and Emnity in Roman Baroque Urbanism." *Römisches Jahrbuch der Biblioteca Hertziana* 25 (1989): 205–94.

Connors, Joseph. *Borromini and the Roman Oratory: Style and Society*. New York, NY: Architectural History Foundation; Cambridge, MA: MIT Press, 1980.

Connors, Joseph. Review of *Borromini's San Carlo alle Quatro Fontane*, by Leo Steinberg. *Journal of the Society of Architectural Historians* 38(3) (1979): 283–5.

Connors, Joseph and Jennifer Montagu. "Introduction to the New Edition." In Joseph Connors and Jennifer Montagu (eds), *Art and Architecture in Italy 1600 to 1750*, by Rudolf Wittkower, 6th revised edition. New Haven, CT: Yale University Press, 1999.

Costanzo, Denise R. "Architectural Amnesia: George Howe, Mario De Renzi, and the U.S. Consulate in Naples." *Memoirs of the American Academy in Rome* 55–6 (2011–12): 353–89.

Costanzo, Denise R. "The Lessons of Rome: Architects at the American Academy, 1947–1966." PhD dissertation, Penn State University, 2009.

Costanzo, Denise R. "'A Truly Liberal Orientation': Laurence Robert, Modern Architecture, and the Postwar American Academy in Rome." *Journal of the Society of Architectural Historians* 74(2) (June 2015): 223–47.

Costelloe, Karin. "An Answer to Mr Bertrand Russell's Article on the Philosophy of Bergson." *The Monist* 24(1) (1914): 145–55.

Costelloe, Karin. "What Bergson Means by 'Interpenetration'." *Proceedings of the Aristotelian Society* (New Series) 13 (1912–13): 131–55.

Coudenhove-Erthal, Eduard. *Carlo Fontana*. Vienna: Anton Schroll, 1930.

Crary, Jonathan. "Attention and Modernity in the Nineteenth Century." In Caroline Jones and Peter Gallison (eds), *Picturing Science, Producing Art*, 475–99. New York, NY: Routledge, 1998.

Crary, Jonathan. "Attention, Spectacle, Counter-Memory." *October* 50 (Fall 1989): 97–107.

Crary, Jonathan. *Suspensions of Perception*. Cambridge, MA: MIT Press, 2000.

Crary, Jonathan. "Unbinding Vision." *October* 68 (Spring 1994): 21–44.

Crary, Jonathan. "Unbinding Vision: Manet and the Attentive Observer in the Late Nineteenth Century." In Leo Charney and Vanessa R. Schwartz (eds), *Cinema and the Invention of Modern Life*, 46–71. Berkeley and Los Angeles, CA: University of California Press, 1995.

Croce, Benedetto. *Storia della età barocca in Italia. Pensiero-poesia e letteratura vita morale*. Bari: Laterza, 1929.

Croce, Benedetto. "Una teoria della 'macchia'." In Benedetto Croce (ed.), *Problemi di estetica e contributi alla storia dell'estetica Italiana*, 236–46. Bari: Laterza, 1910.

Cunningham, Colin. "A Case of Cultural Schizophrenia: Ruling Tastes and Architectural Training in the Edwardian Period." *Architectural History* 44 (2001): 64–81.

Czeike, Felix. *Historisches Lexikon Wien*, 6 vols. Vienna: Kremayr und Scheriau, 1992–97.

Damm, Margaret. "Review of *Art and Architecture in Belgium 1600 to 1800*, by Horst Gerson and E.H. Ter Kuile." *Journal of the Society of Architectural Historians* 20 (1961): 202–3.

Daniells, Roy. "Baroque Form in English Literature." *University of Toronto Quarterly* 14(4) (July 1945): 393–408.

Daniells, Roy. "English Baroque and Deliberate Obscurity." In "Special Issue on Baroque Style in the Various Arts." *Journal of Aesthetics and Art Criticism* 5(2) (1946): 115–21.

Daniells, Roy. *Milton, Mannerism and the Baroque*. Toronto: University of Toronto Press, 1963.

Danto, Arthur. "Review of *Other Criteria*, by Leo Steinberg." *Journal of Aesthetics and Art Criticism* 32(4) (Summer 1974): 569.

de Angelis d'Ossat, Guglielmo. *Studi sul Borromini. Atti del Convegno promosso dall'Accademia nazionale di San Luca*, 2 vols. Rome: De Luca, 1967.

de Bruijn, David, Maarten Delbeke, Job Floris, Christiph Grafe, Ruben Molendijk and Tom Vandeputte (eds). "Barok" = "Baroque." Special issue, *Oase: Tijdschrift voor Architectuur* 86 (2011).

de Duve, Thierry. *Clement Greenberg between the Lines, Including a Previously Unpublished Debate with Clement Greenberg*. Translated by B. Holmes. Paris: Éditions dis Voir, 2010.

de San Buenaventura, Fra Juan. *Relatione del Convento di San Carlo alle Quattro Fontane*, c. 1650. Edited by J.M.M. Garcia. Rome: Polifilo, 1999.

Dehio, Georg. *Geschichte der deutschen Kunst*. Vol. 3, *Die Neuzeit von der Reformation bis zur Auflösung des Alten Reichs. Renaissance und Barock*. Berlin and Leipzig: de Gruyter, 1926.

Dehio, Georg. *Geschichte der deutscher Kunst*, 2nd edition, vol. 3. Berlin, Leipzig: Walter de Gruyter, 1931.

Delbeke, Maarten. "Mannerism and Meaning in *Complexity and Contradiction in Architecture*." *Journal of Architecture* 15(3) (2010): 267–82.

Delbeke, Maarten. "Roma Interrotta: The Urbs that is Not a Capital." *Incontri. Rivista europea di studi italiani* 26(2) (2011): 37–49.

Delbeke, Maarten. *The Art of Religion: Sforza Pallavicino and Art Theory in Bernini's Rome*. Farnham: Ashgate, 2012.

Deleuze, Gille. *Foucault*. Paris: Minuit, 1986. Translated by Seán Hand. Minneapolis: University of Minnesota Press, 1988.

Deleuze, Gille. *Le Pli. Liebniz e le baroque*. Paris: Minuit, 1988. Translated by Tom Conley as *The Fold: Liebniz and the Baroque*. Minneapolis, MN: University of Minnesota Press, 1992.

Deleuze, Gille. "Un nouvel archiviste." *Critique* 274 (1970): 195–209.

Delogu, Giuseppe. *L'architettura italiana del Seicento e del Settecento*, 2 vols. Florence: Novissima enciclopedia monografica illustrata, 1935.

Dewey, John. *Art as Experience*. 1934. New York, NY: Penguin, 1980.

Dewey, John. "A Comment on the Foregoing Criticisms." Response to Benedetto Croce. *Journal of Aesthetics and Art Criticism* 6(3) (March 1948): 207–9.

Diekmanna, Stefanie and Thomas Khurana (eds). *Latenz: 40 Annaherungen an einen Begriff*. Berlin: Kulturverlag Kadmos, 2007.

Dokuchaev, Nikolaj. *Arhitektura Vchutemasa*. Moscow: Izdanie Vchutemasa, 1927.

D'Onofrio, Mario (ed.). *Adolfo Venturi e la storia dell'arte oggi*. Modena: Franco Cosimo Panini, 2008.

D'Ors, Eugenio. *Lo barroco*. Madrid: Espasa Calpe, 1932. Translated into French by Agathe Rouardt-Valéry as *Du Baroque*. Paris: Gallimard, 1935.

Dombrowksi, Damian. *Dal trionfo all'amore. Il mutevole pensiero artistico di Gianlorenzo Bernini nella decorazione del nuovo San Pietro*. Rome: Argos, 2003.

Draper, Peter (ed.) *Reassessing Nikolaus Pevsner*. Aldershot: Ashgate, 2004.

Duffy, Jean. "Art, Architecture, and Catholicism in Michel Butor's 'La Modification'." *Modern Language Review* 94(1) (1999): 46–60.

Dufrêne, Thierry. "Lire Francastel aujourd'hui: un historien de l'expérience artistique." In Thierry Dufrêne (ed.), *Pierre Francastel. L'hypothèse même de l'art*, 5–21. Paris: INHA, 2010.

Dulio, Roberto. "'Il mio miglior nemico'. Moretti e Zevi." In Corrado Bozzoni, Daniela Fonti and Alessandra Muntoni (eds), *Luigi Moretti. Architetto del Novecento*, 69–73. Rome: Gangemi, 2011.

Dulio, Roberto. *Introduzione a Bruno Zevi*. Rome: Laterza, 2008.

Dulio, Roberto. "*Le affinità elettive. Moretti e Zevi*." In Bruno Reichlin and Letezia Tedeschi (eds), *Luigi Moretti. Razionalismo e trasgressività tra barocco e informale*, 437–41. Milan: Electa, 2010.

Dulio, Roberto. "Samonà, Zevi e le 'chiamate' eccellenti." In Guido Zucconi and Martina Carraro (eds), *Officina Iuav, 1925–1980. Saggi sulla scuola di architettura di Venezia*, 91–8. Venice: Marsilio, 2011.

Dunn, Richard M. *Geoffrey Scott: A Life*. Privately published, 2011.

Dunn, Richard M. *Geoffrey Scott and the Berenson Circle: Literary and Aesthetic Life in the Early 20th Century*. Lewiston, NY: The Edwin Mellen Press, 1998.

Dunn, Richard M. *The Letters of Geoffrey Scott*. Privately published, 2011.

Durth, Werner. "Die Neuerfindung der Welt als gute Wohnung im All. Bruno Taut und die Gläserne Kette." In Ralf Beil and Claudia Dillmann (eds), *Gesamtkunstwerk Expressionismus. Kunst, Film, Literatur, Theater, Tanz und Architektur, 1905–1925*, 336–46. Darmstadt: Hatje Cantz, 2010.

Dvořák, Max. "Uber Greco und den Manierismus." In Karl Maria Swoboda and Johannes Wilde (eds), *Kunstgeschichte als Geistesgeschichte. Studien zur abendländischen Kunstentwicklung*, 259–76. Munich: Piper, 1924.

Ebe, Gustav. *Die Spät-Renaissance: Kunstgeschichte der europäischen Länder von der Mitte des 16. bis zum Ende des 18. Jahrhunderts*, 2 vols. Berlin: Julius Springer, 1886.

Eckel, Jan. *Geist der Zeit. Deutsche Geisteswissenschaften seit 1870*. Göttingen: Vandenhoeck & Ruprecht, 2008.

Ejchenbaum, Boris. "Teorija 'formal'nogo metoda'." In *Literatura, kritika, polemika*, 116–48. Leningrad, 1927. Translated into Italian as "La teoria del 'metodo formale'." In Tzvetan Todorov (ed.), *I formalisti russi. Teoria della letteratura e metodo critic*, 30–72. Turin: Einaudi, 2003.

Empson, William. *Seven Types of Ambiguity*, 2nd edition. London: Chatto and Windus, 1949.

Engel, Ute. "Barockforschung. Barock und Rokoko, die deutsche Kunstgeschichte und die Frage der nationalen Identität, ca. 1855 bis 1933." Habilitationsschrift, University of Mainz, 2010.

Engel, Ute. "Nikolaus Pevsner und der Leipziger Barock." *Sächsische Heimat Blätter* 49(2) (2003): 164–74.

Engel, Ute. "Riegl on the Baroque." *Journal of Art Historiography* 7 (December 2012): 1–6. Online at http://arthistoriography.files.wordpress.com/2012/12/engel-riegl-review.pdf (accessed 12 September 2013).

Engel, Ute. *Stil und Nation. Barockforschung und deutsche Kunstgeschichte, ca. 1830 bis 1933*. Paderborn: Wilhelm Fink Verlag, 2014.

Engel, Ute. "The Formation of Pevsner's Art History: Nikolaus Pevsner in Germany, 1902–1935." In Peter Draper (ed.), *Reassessing Nikolaus Pevsner*, 29–55. Aldershot: Ashgate, 2004.

Ercadi, Maria and Fabrizio Da Col (eds). *Paolo Portoghesi. Disegni 1949–2003*. Milan: Federico Motta, 2003.

Fagiolo dell'Arco, Maurizio and Marcello. *Bernini. Una introduzione al gran teatro del barocco*. Rome: Mario Bulzoni, 1967.

Favorskij, Vladimir A. *Literarno-Teoretičeskoe nasledje*. Moscow: Sovetski Hudozhnik, 1988.

Feigenbaum, "Die Reklame: Ihre Entwickelung und Bedeutung." *Deutschland: Monatschrift für die Gesamte Kultur* 7 (1905–6): 427–36, 589–602.

Fellows, Richard A. *Sir Reginald Blomfield: An Edwardian Architect*. London: A. Zwemmer, 1985.

Fernie, Eric (ed.). *Art History and its Methods: A Critical Anthology*. London: Phaidon, 1995.

Feulner, Adolf. *Bayerisches Rokoko*. Munich: Wolff, 1923.

Fiore, Francesco Paolo. "Hans Sedlmayr: Verità o metodo?" *Op. Cit.* 62 (1985): 5–20.

Fleming, William. "The Element of Motion in Baroque Art and Music." In "Special Issue on Baroque Style in the Various Arts." *Journal of Aesthetics and Art Criticism* 5(2) (1946): 121–8.

Florenskij, Pavel. *Lekcii vo Vchutemase 1923–24 gg*. Translated into Italian and edited by Nicoletta Misler as *Lo spazio e il tempo nell'arte*. Milan: Adelphi, 1995.

Florman, Lisa. "The Difference Experience Makes in the 'The Philosophical Brothel'." *Art Bulletin* 85(4) (2003): 769–83.

Focillon, Henri. *Vie des formes*. 1934. Paris: Quadrige & Presses Universitaires de France, 1967. Translated by Charles Beecher Hogan and George Kubler as *The Life of Forms in Art*. New Haven, CT: Yale University Press, 1942; New York, NY: Zone, 1992.

Foucault, Michel. *Archéologie du savoir*. Paris: Gallimard, 1969. Translated by Rupert Swyer as *The Archaeology of Knowledge & The Discourse on Language*. New York, NY: Pantheon, 1972.

Frampton, Kenneth. "Giedion in America: Reflections in a Mirror." *Architectural Design* 51(6–7) (1981): 44–51.

Frampton, Kenneth. "Place-Form and Cultural Identity." In John Thackara (ed.), *Design after Modernism: Beyond the Object*, 51–66. New York, NY: Thames and Hudson, 1988.

Frampton, Kenneth. "Prospects for a Critical Regionalism." *Perspecta* 20 (1983): 147–62.

Frampton, Kenneth. "Towards a Critical Regionalism: Six Points for an Architecture of Resistance." In Hal Foster (ed.), *The Anti-Aesthetic: Essays on Postmodern Culture*, 16–30. Seattle, WA: Bay Press, 1983.

Francastel, Pierre. "Baroque et classicisme: histoire ou typologie des civilisations?" *Annales. Economies, Sociétés, Civilisations* 14(1) (1959): 142–51.

Francastel, Pierre. "Baroque et classique: une civilisation." *Annales. Economies, Sociétés, Civilisations* 12(2) (1957): 207–22.

Francastel, Pierre (ed.). *Les architectes célèbres*, 2 vols. Paris: Lucien Mazenod, 1958.

Francastel, Pierre. *L'histoire de l'art instrument de la propagande germanique*. Paris: Libr. de Médicis, 1945.

Francastel, Pierre. "Spécificités de l'histoire de l'art." In Thierry Dufrêne (ed.), *Pierre Francastel. L'hypothèse même de l'art*, 30–33. Paris: INHA, 2010.

Frank, Mitchell B. and Daniel Adler (eds). *German Art History and Scientific Thought: Beyond Formalism*. Aldershot: Ashgate, 2012.

Frankl, Paul. *Die Entwicklungsphasen der neueren Baukunst*. Berlin and Leipzig: Teubner, 1914. Translated by James F. O'Gorman as *Principles of Architectural History: The Four Phases of Architectural Style, 1420–1900*. Cambridge, MA: MIT Press, 1968.

Frankl, Paul. *The Gothic: Literary Sources and Interpretations through Eight Centuries*. Princeton, NJ: Princeton University Press, 1960.

Franz, Rainald and Andreas Nierhaus (eds). *Gottfried Semper und Wien. Die Wirkung des Architekten auf "Wissenschaft, Industrie und Kunst."* Vienna: Böhlau, 2007.

Freedberg, Sidney. *Painting in Italy 1500 to 1600*. Pelican History of Art 34. Harmondsworth: Penguin, 1971.

Frey, Dagobert. "Beiträge zur Geschichte der römischen Barockarchitektur." *Wiener Jahrbuch für Kunstgeschichte* 17 (1924): 5–113.

Frey, Dagobert. *Johann Bernhard Fischer von Erlach: eine Studie über seine Stellung in der Entwicklung der Wiener Palastfassade*. Augsburg: B. Filser, 1922.

Friedlaender, Walter. "Die Entstehung des antiklassischen Stiles in der italienischen Malerei um 1520." In *Repertorium für Kunstwissenschaft* 46 (1925): 49–86.

Friedlaender, Walter. *Mannerism and Anti-Mannerism in Italian Painting*. New York, NY: Columbia University Press, 1957.

Friedrich, Carl J. "Style as the Principle of Historical Interpretation." In "Second Special Issue on Baroque Style in the Various Arts," *Journal of Aesthetics and Art Criticism* 14(2) (December 1955): 143–51.

Fritzsche, Peter. *Reading Berlin 1900*. Cambridge, MA: Harvard University Press, 2009.

Fry, Roger. "A Possible Domestic Architecture: A Challenge to Self-Conscious Picturesqueness." In *Vision and Design*, by Roger Fry, 272–8. London: Chatto and Windus, 1920.

Fry, Roger. *Architectural Heresies of a Painter: A Lecture Delivered at the Royal Institute of British Architects, May 20th 1921*. London: Chatto & Windus, 1921.

Fry, Roger. "The Baroque: *Kunstgeschichtliche Grundbegriffe*, by Heinrich Wölfflin, 4th edition, München (Bruckman), 1920." *Burlington Magazine for Connoisseurs* 39(222) (1921): 145–8.

Fry, Roger. *Giovanni Bellini*. London: At the Sign of the Unicorn, 1899.

Fry, Roger. "The Regent Street Quadrant." *Times*. London, October 3, 1912.

Fuhrmeister, Christian. "Hans Rose: eine biographische Skizze." In Pablo Schneider and Philipp Zitzlsperger (eds), *Bernini in Paris: das Tagebuch des Paul Fréart de Chantelou über den Aufenthalt Gianlorenzo Berninis am Hof Ludwigs XIV*, 434–55. Berlin: Oldenbourg Akademieverlag, 2006.

Gabričevskij, Aleksandr G. *Morfologija iskusstva*. Moscow, 2002.

Gabričevskij, Aleksandr G. *Sbornik Materialov*. Moscow, 1992.

Gabričevskij, Aleksandr G. *Teorija i istorija arhitekturi. Izbranie sočinenija*. Kiev, 1993.

Gagel, Mandy. "1897, A Discussion of Plagiarism: Letters between Vernon Lee, Bernard Berenson, and Mary Costelloe." *Literary Imagination* 12(1) (2010): 154–79.

Gale, Harlow. "On the Psychology of Advertising." *Psychological Studies*, 39–69. Minneapolis, 1900.

Games, Stephen. "The Germanness of the English Historian." *Architecture Today* 136 (March 2003): 26–8, 30.

Games, Stephen (ed.). *Pevsner on Art and Architecture: The Radio Talks*. London: Methuen, 2002.

Games, Stephen. *Pevsner: The Early Life: Germany and Art*. London: Continuum, 2010.

Garberson, Eric. "Baroque Architecture and German National Identity in Art Historical Texts, ca. 1900." In Andreas Kreul (ed.), *Barock als Aufgabe*, 165–79. Wiesbaden: Harrassowitz, 2005.

Garberson, Eric. "Historiography of the *Gesamtkunstwerk*." In *Struggle for Synthesis 1999: The Total Work of Art in the 17th and 18th Centuries*. Conference proceedings, vol. 1, 53–72. Lisbon: Ed. do Instituto Portugues do Patrimonio Arquitectonico, 1999.

Geiser, Reto. "Giedion In-Between: A Study of Cultural Transfer and Transatlantic Exchange, 1938–1968." PhD dissertation, ETH Zurich, 2010.

Georgiadis, Sokratis. *Sigfried Giedion: An Intellectual Biography*. Translated by Colin Hall. Edinburgh: Edinburgh University Press, 1993.

Gerson, Horst and E.H. Ter Kuile. *Art and Architecture in Belgium 1600 to 1800*. Pelican History of Art 18. Harmondsworth: Penguin, 1960.

Gilbert, Creighton. "The Pelican History of Art." *Journal of the Society of Architectural Historians* 39(2) (1980): 150–51.

Gigliucci, Roberto. *Croce e il Barocco*. Rome: Lithos, 2011.

Ginzburg, Moisej. *Ritm v arhitekture*. Moscow: Sredi kollekcionerov, 1923. Translated into Italian by C. Di Paola as *Saggi sull'architettura costruttivista. Il ritmo in architettura, Lo stile e l'epoca, L'abitazione*. Milan: Feltrinelli, 1977.

Ginzburg, Moisej. *Stil' i epoha*. Moscow: Gosudarstvenno izdatelstvo, 1924.

Giedion, Sigfried. *Bauen in Frankreich, Bauen in Eisen, Bauen in Eisenbeton*. Leipzig: Klinkhardt & Biermann, 1928. Translated by Sokratis Georgiadis as *Building in France, Building in Iron, Building in Ferroconcrete*. Santa Monica, CA: Getty Center for the History of Art and the Humanities, 1995.

Giedion, Siegfried. "Sixtus V and the Planning of Baroque Rome." *Architectural Review* 3 (April 1952): 217–26.

Giedion, Siegfried. "Space and the Elements of the Renaissance City." *Magazine of Art* 45 (January 1952): 3–10.

Giedion, Siegfreid. *Space, Time and Architecture: The Growth of a New Tradition*. Cambridge, MA.: Harvard University Press, 1941. 2nd revised edition, 1949. 5th revised edition, 1967.

Giedion, Siegfried. "The Need for a New Monumentality." In Paul Zucker (ed.), *Modern Architecture and City Planning*, 549–68. New York, NY: Philosophical Library, 1944.

Giedion, Siegfreid. *Walter Gropius*. Paris: Editions Crès, 1931.

Giedion, Siegfried. *Walter Gropius: Work and Teamwork*. New York, NY: Reinhold, 1954.

Giedion-Welcker, Carola. "Hans Arp: Dichter und Maler." Reprinted in *Carola Giedion-Welcker: Schriften, 1926–1971*. Cologne: M. Dumont Schenbert, 1973.

Gladbach, M. and Dr. Engel. "Beitrag zur Warenhausfrage." *Soziale Revue: Zeitschrift für die sozialen Fragen der Gegewart* 6 (1906): 274.

Göller, Adolf. *Das ästhetische Gefühl. Eine Erklärung der Schönheit und Zergliederung ihres Erfassens auf psychologischer Grundlage.* Stuttgart: Zeller & Schmidt vorm. E. Rupfer, 1905.

Göller, Adolf. *Die Entstehung der architektonischen Stilformen: Eine Geschichte der Baukunst nach dem Werden und Wandern der Formgedanken.* Stuttgart: Konrad Wittwer, 1888.

Göller, Adolf. "What is the Cause of Perpetual Style Change in Architecture?" In Harry Francis Mallgrave and Eleftherios (eds), *Empathy, Form, and Space: Problems in German Aesthetics 1873–1893*, 193–226. Los Angeles, CA: Getty Center for the History of Art and the Humanities, 1994.

Göller, Adolf. *Zur Aesthetik der Architektur. Vorträge und Studien.* Stuttgart: Konrad Wittwer, 1887.

Gombrich, Ernst. "Talking of Michelangelo." Review of *Michelangelo's Last Paintings*, by Leo Steinberg. *New York Review of Books*, January 20, 1977.

Gossman, Lionel. "Imperial Icon: The Pergamon Altar in Wilhelminian Germany." *Journal of Modern History* 78 (2006): 551–87.

Gramiccia, Anna and Comitato vaticano per l'anno berniniano (eds). *Bernini in Vaticano*. Exhibition catalogue. Rome: De Luca, 1981.

Grebing, Helga. *Die Worringers. Bildungsbürgerlichkeit als Lebenssinn – Wilhelm und Martha Worringer (1881–1965).* Berlin: Parthas, 2004.

Greenberg, Clement. *The Collected Essays and Criticism. Vol. 3, Affirmations and Refusals, 1950–1956.* Edited by John O'Brian. Chicago, IL: University of Chicago Press, 1993.

Gropius, Walter. *Scope of Total Architecture*. New York, NY: Harper and Row, 1955.

Gross, Karl. *Die Spiele Der Menschen*. Jenna: G Fischer, 1899.

Gruppe Espace, "Manifesto." October 1951. Reprinted in Luciano Berni Canani and Giorgio Di Genova (eds), *MAC/ESPACE: Arte concreta in Italia e in Francia, 1948–1958*. Bologna: Edizioni Bora, 1999.

Guilbaut, Serge. *How New York Stole the Idea of Modern Art: Abstract Expressionism, Freedom, and the Cold War*. Translated by A. Goldhammer. Chicago, IL: University of Chicago Press, 1983.

Gunn, Peter. *Vernon Lee: Violet Paget 1856–1935*. London: Oxford University Press, 1964.

Gurlitt, Cornelius. "Berliner Architektur." *Die Gegenwart* 2 (1892): 30.

Gurlitt, Cornelius. *Geschichte des Barockstiles, des Rococo in Deutschland*. Stuttgart: Ebner & Seubart, 1889.

Gurlitt, Cornelius. *Geschichte des Barockstiles, des Rococo, und des Klassicismus in Belgien, Holland, Frankreich, England.* Stuttgart: Ebner & Seubert, 1886.

Gurlitt, Cornelius. *Geschichte des Barockstiles in Italien*. Stuttgart: Ebner & Seubert, 1887.

Hagen, Oskar. *Deutsches Sehen*. Munich: Piper, 1920.

Halbertsma, Marlite. *Wilhelm Pinder und die deutsche Kunstgeschichte*. Worms: Werner, 1992.

Halliday, Nigel Vaux. *More than a Bookshop: Zwemmer's and Art in the 20th Century*. London: Wilson, 1991.

Hanhloser, Hans R. "Zum Gedächtnis von Julius von Schlosser." *Belvedere* 13(5–8) (1938–43): 137–41.

Harbison, Robert. *Reflections on the Baroque*. Chicago, IL: University of Chicago Press, 2000.

Häring, Hugo. "Wege zur form." *Die Form* 1 (1925): 3–5.

Harries, Karsten. *The Bavarian Rococo Church: Between Faith and Aestheticism.* New Haven, CT: Yale University Press, 1983.

Harries, Karsten. *The Ethical Function of Architecture*. Cambridge, MA: MIT Press, 1997.

Harries, Susie. *Nikolaus Pevsner: The Life*. London: Chatto and Windus, 2011.

Harrison, Charles and Paul J. Wood (eds). *Art in Theory 1900–1990: An Anthology of Changing Ideas*. Oxford: Blackwell Publishing, 1992.

Harrison, Sylvia. *Pop Art and the Origins of Post-Modernism*. Cambridge: Cambridge University Press, 2001.

Hart, Joan Goldhammer. "Heinrich Wölfflin: An Intellectual Biography." PhD dissertation, University of California, Berkeley, 1981.

Haskell, Francis. *Patrons and Painters: A Study in the Relations between Italian Art and Society in the Age of the Baroque*. New York, NY: Knopf, 1963.

Hassold, Ernest C. "The Baroque as a Basic Concept of Art." *College Art Journal* 6(1) (1946): 3–28.

Hausenstein, Wilhelm. *Vom Geist des Barock*. Munich: Piper, 1920.

Hausmann, Frank-Rutger. *Die Geisteswissenschaften im "Dritten Reich."* Frankfurt am Main: Klostermann, 2011.

Hauttmann, Max. *Geschichte der kirchlichen Baukunst in Bayern, Schwaben und Franken 1550–1780*, 2nd edition. First published 1921. Munich: Weizinger, 1923.

Hegel, G.W.F. *Aesthetics: Lectures on Fine Art*. Translated by T.M. Knox. 2 vols. Oxford: Clarendon Press, 1975.

Hegel, G.W.F. *Werke in zwanzig Bänden*. Edited by E. Moldenhauer and K.M. Michel. 20 vols. Frankfurt am Main: Suhrkamp Verlag, 1969–86.

Heidegger, Martin. *Der Ursprung des Kunstwerkes*. Stuttgart: Reclam 1960.

Heidegger, Martin. *Vorträge und Aufsätze*, vol. 2. Pfullingen: Neske, 1967.

Held, Jutta. "Kunstgeschichte im 'Dritten Reich'. Wilhelm Pinder und Hans Jantzen an der Münchner Universität." In Jutta Held and Martin Papenbrock (eds), *Kunstgeschichte an den Universitäten im Nationalsozialismus*. Special issue, *Kunst und Politik: Jahrbuch der Guernica-Gesellschaft* 5 (2003): 17–60.

Hempel, Ebehard. *Baroque Art and Architecture in Central Europe. Germany, Austria, Switzerland, Hungary, Czechoslovakia, Poland*. Pelican History of Art 22. Harmondsworth: Penguin, 1965.

Hempel, Ebehard. *Francesco Borromini*. Vienna: Anton Schroll, 1924.

Hempel, Ebehard. "Ist eine strenge Kunstwissenschaft möglich?" *Zeitschrift für Kunstgeschichte* 3 (1934): 155–63.

Herdeg, Klaus. *The Decorated Diagram: Harvard Architecture and the Failure of the Bauhaus Legacy*. Cambridge, MA: MIT Press, 1985.

Hersey, George L. *Architecture and Geometry in the Age of the Baroque*. Chicago, IL: University of Chicago Press, 2000.

Hevesi, Ludwig. "Kunst auf der Strasse." *Fremdenblatt*. Vienna, May 30, 1899.

Heydenreich, Ludwig and Wolfgang Lotz. *Architecture in Italy 1400 to 1600*. Translated by Marie D. Hottinger. Pelican History of Art 38. Harmondsworth: Penguin, 1974.

Heynen, Hilde. *Architecture and Modernity: A Critique*. Cambridge, MA: MIT Press, 1999.

Hildebrand, Adolf. "Beitrag zum Verständnis des künstlerischen Zusammenhangs architektonischer Situationen." *Die Raumkunst* 19 (1908): 289–96.

Hildebrand, Adolf. *Das Problem der Form der Bildenden Kunst*. Revised and translated into English by Max Meyer and Robert Morris Ogden as *The Problem of Form in Painting and Sculpture*. New York, NY: G.E. Stechert & Co., 1907. Translated into Russian as *Problema formy v izobrazitel'nom iskusstve i sobranie statej*. Moscow: Musagaet, 1914.

Hildebrand, Adolf. "Visual and Kinesthetic Ideas." In Harry Francis Mallgrave and Eleftherios Ikonomou (eds), *Empathy, Form and Space: Problems in German Aesthetics, 1873–1893*, 229–32. Santa Monica, CA: Getty Center for the History of Art and the Humanities, 1994.

Hill, Michael. "Leo Steinberg vs Clement Greenberg, 1952–1972." *Australian and New Zealand Journal of Art* 14(1) (2014): 21–9.

Hill, Michael. "Steinberg, Leo (1920–2011)." In Michael Kelly (ed.), *Encyclopedia of Aesthetics*, 2nd edition, vol. 6, 44–8. New York, NY: Oxford University Press, 2014.

Hill, Michael. "Symbolic and Practical Geometry in Borromini's San Carlo alle Quattro Fontane." *Journal of the Society of Architectural Historians* 72(4) (December 2013): 554–83.

Hills, Helen. "The Baroque: The Grit in the Oyster of Art History." In Helen Hills (ed.), *Rethinking the Baroque*, 11–36. Farnham: Ashgate, 2011.

Hills, Helen (ed.). *Rethinking the Baroque*. Farnham: Ashgate, 2011.

Hinks, Roger. *The Gymnasium of the Mind: The Journals of Roger Hinks, 1933–1963*. Edited by John Goldsmith. Salisbury: Michael Russell, 1984.

Hirsch, Hans. "Das österreichische Institut für Geschichtsforschung 1854–1934." *Mittheilungen des Instituts für österreichische Geschichtsforschung* 49 (1935): 1–14.

Hitchcock, Henry-Russell. *Modern Architecture: Romanticism and Reintegration*. New York, NY: Payson & Clarke, 1929.

Hitchcock, Henry-Russell. *Rococo Architecture in Southern Germany*. London: Phaidon, 1968.

Hoffmann, Hans. *Hochrenaissance-Manierismus-Frühbarock*. Zurich and Leipzig: Leeman & Co., 1938.

Hofstädter, Hans. "Hugo Karl Maria Schnell 1904–1981." *Das Münster* 35 (1981): i–ii.

Holden, Susan. "Finding the Architecture in Deleuze." In Stephen Loo and Katherine Bartsch (eds), *Panorama to Paradise: Scopic Regimes in Architectural and Urban History and Theory. XXIVth International Conference of the Society of Architectural Historians, Australia and New Zealand, Adelaide, 21–24 September 2007*. Adelaide, SA: SAHANZ, 2007. CD-ROM.

Holly, Michael Ann. "Wölfflin and the Imagining of the Baroque." In Klaus Garber (ed.), *Europäische Barockrezeption*, vol. 2, 1255–64. Wiesbaden: Harrasowitz, 1991.

Hopkins, Andrew. "Not Enough Baroque." Review of *Rethinking the Baroque*, edited by Helen Hills. *Kunstchronik* 66(3) (2013): 118–21.

Hopkins, Andrew. "Riegl Renaissances." In Andrew Hopkins and Arnold Witte (eds and trans), *The Origins of Baroque Art in Rome*, by Alois Riegl, 60–89. Los Angeles, CA: Getty Research Institute, 2010.

Horkheimer, Max and Theodor W. Adorno. *Dialektik der Aufklärung* (1944). Amsterdam: Querido, 1947.

Hoyer, Egbert Ritter von. "Köstlin, August." *Allgemeine Deutsche Biographie* 51 (1906): 342–3.

Hudnut, Joseph. "What a Young Planner Ought to Know." *Journal of the American Institute of Architects* 7 (February 1947): 59–66.

Ilg, Albert. *Alt-Wien in Wort und Bild*. Wiener Illustrirten Extrablattes. Vienna: Verlag des Wiener Alterthumsvereines, Gerold, 1893.

Ilg, Albert. "Das neue Hofburgtheater." *Die Presse*. Vienna, 9 October 1888.

Ilg, Albert. *Die Zukunft des Barockstils, eine Kunstepistel von Bernini dem Jüngern*. Vienna: Manzsche, 1880.

Imorde, Joseph. "Barock und Moderne. Zum Problem zeitgebundener Geschichtsschreibung." In Andreas Kreul (ed.), *Barock als Aufgabe*, 179–212. Wiesbaden: Harrasowitz, 2005.

Imorde, Joseph. "Selbstberauschung. Zur expressiven Barockrezeption in der Moderne." In Federico Celestine, Moritz Csáky and Ulrich Tragatschnig (eds), *Barock als ein Ort des Gedächtnisses. Interpretament der Moderne/Postmoderne*, 299–350. Cologne, Weimar & Vienna: Böhlau, 2007.

Ingels, Bjarke. *Yes is More: An Archicomic on Architectural Evolution*. Cologne: Taschen, 2009.

Jäger-Sunstenau, Hanns. "Lind, Karl (1831–1901)." In *Österreichisches Biographisches Lexikon*, vol. 5, 1815–1950, 217–18. Vienna: Verlag der Österreichischen Akademie der Wissenschaften, 1993.

Jameson, Fredric. "Architecture and the Critique of Ideology." In Joan Ockman (ed.), *Architecture, Criticism, Ideology*, 51–87. New York, NY: Princeton Architectural Press, 1985.

Janatková, Alena. *Barockrezeption zwischen Historismus und Moderne. Die Architekturdiskussion in Prag, 1890–1914*. Berlin: Mann; Zurich: gta, 2000.

Jaretzki, Hans. "Reklame und Architektur." In Paul Ruben (ed.), *Die Reklame: Ihre Kunst und Wissenschaft*. Berlin: Hermann Paetel, 1915.

Jarzombek, Mark. *The Psychologizing of Modernity: Art, Architecture, and History*. Cambridge: Cambridge University Press, 2000.

Jaspers, Karl. *Die geistige Situation der Zeit*. Leipzig: Walter de Gruyter, 1933.

Jencks, Charles. *The Language of Post-Modern Architecture*. New York, NY: Rizzoli, 1977.

Johnson, Philip C. *Ludwig Mies van der Rohe*. New York, NY: Museum of Modern Art, 1947.

Johnston, William M. *The Austrian Mind: An Intellectual and Social History 1848–1938*. Berkeley, CA: University of California Press, 1972.

Johannides, Paul. Review of *Michelangelo's Last Paintings*, by Leo Steinberg. *Burlington Magazine* 118 (October 1976): 112.

Jokinen, Teppo and Bruno Maurer. *"Magus des Nordens": Alvar Aalto und der Schweiz*. Zurich: gta-Verlag, 1998.

Jouhaud, Christian. *Sauver le Grand-Siècle: présence et transmission du passé*. Paris: Seuil, 2007.

Junod, Philippe. "Gesamtkunstwerk." *Kritische Berichte* 35(3) (2007): 72–6.

Kanz, Roland. "Kunstgeschichte als 'geisteswissenschaftliche Biologie'. Wilhelm Pinders Pathologisierung des Manierismus und Ernst Kretschmers Typenlehre." In Tobias Kunz (ed.), *Nicht die Bibliothek, sondern das Auge. Westeuropäische Skulptur und Malerei an der Wende zur Neuzeit, Festschrift Hartmut Krohm*, 325–34. Petersberg: Imhof, 2008.

Kaschnitz-Weinberg, Guido von. "Review of *Die spätrömische Kunstindustrie*, by Alois Riegl, 2nd edition. (1927)." *Gnomen* 5 (1929): 195–213.

Kassal-Mikula, Renata. "Alt-Wien unter die demolierungskrampen." In Wolfgang Kos and Christian Rapp (eds), *Alt Wien, die Stadt die niemals war*. Exhibition catalogue, 46–61. Vienna: Wien Museum-Czernin Verlag, 2004.

Kauffmann, Hans. "Romgedanken in der Kunst Berninis." *Jahresbericht der Max-Planck-Gesellschaft* (1953/54): 55–80.

Kaufmann, Emil. *Architecture in the Age of Reason: Baroque and Post-Baroque in England, Italy, and France*. Cambridge, MA: Harvard University Press, 1955.

Kaufmann, Emil. *Von Ledoux bis Le Corbusier: Ursprung und Entwicklung der Autonomen Architektur*. Vienna: Passer, 1933.

Kaufmann, Thomas DaCosta. *Toward a Geography of Art*. Chicago, IL: University of Chicago Press, 2004.

Kemp, Wolfgang. "Walter Benjamin und die Kunstwissenschaft. Tiel 2: Walter Benjamin und Aby Warburg." *Kritische Berichte* 3 (1975): 5–24.

Klonk, Charlotte. "Patterns of Attention: From Shop Windows to Gallery Rooms in Early Twentieth-Century Berlin." *Art History* 28(4) (September 2005): 468–96.

Koepnick, Lutz. *Framing Attention: Windows on Modern German Culture*. Baltimore, MD: Johns Hopkins University Press, 2007.

Koeppen, Alfred. "Bernhard Sehring. Gedenkblatt zu seinem 60. Geburtstag." *Berliner Architekturwelt* 18 (1916): 83–6.

Koerner, Joseph. "Review of *Leonardo's Incessant Last Supper*, by Leo Steinberg." *Art Bulletin* 86(4) (2004): 77–81.

Koffka, Kurt. "Zur Theorie der Erlebnis-Wahrnemung." *Annalen der Philosophie* 3 (1923): 375–99.

Köhler, Wilhelm. "Max Dvorak" (obituary). *Mittheilungen des Instituts für österreichische Geschichtsforschung* 39 (1923): 314–20.

König, Christoph and Eberhard Lämmert (eds). *Literaturwissenschaft und Geistesgeschichte, 1910–1925*. Frankfurt am Main: Fischer, 1993.

Köss, Juliet. *Modernism after Wagner*. Minneapolis, MN: University of Minnesota Press, 2010.

Köstlin, August. "Das Neue Wien." *Allgemeine Bauzeitung* (1885): 1–4.

Krauss, Rosalind. "Editor's introduction to 'The Philosophical Brothel', by Leo Steinberg." *October* 44 (Spring 1988): 3–6.

Krauss, Rosalind. "The Slung Leg Hypothesis." *October* 136 (Spring 2011): 218–21.

Krautheimer, Richard. *Early Christian and Byzantine Architecture*. Harmondsworth: Penguin, 1965.

Krautheimer, Richard. *Lorenzo Ghiberti*. Princeton, NJ: Princeton University Press, 1956.

Krautheimer, Richard. *Roma Alessandrina: The Remapping of Rome under Alexander VII, 1655–67*. Poughkeepsie, NY: Vassar College, 1982.

Krautheimer, Richard. *The Rome of Alexander VII 1655–1667*. Translated by Giuseppe Scattone. Rome: Edizione dell'Elefante, 1987.

Kretschmer, Ernst. *Geniale Menschen*. Berlin: Springer, 1929.

Kretschmer, Ernst. *Körperbau und Charakter. Untersuchungen zum Konstitutionsproblem und zur Lehre von den Temperamenten*. Berlin: Springer, 1921, 1926, 1929, 1931.

Kruft, Hanno-Walter. *A History of Architectural Theory from Vitruvius to the Present.* New York, NY: Princeton Architectural Press; London: Zwemmer, 1994.

Kubler, George and Martin Soria. *Art and Architecture in Spain and Portugal and their American Dominions 1500 to 1800.* Pelican History of Art 17. Harmondsworth: Penguin, 1959.

Ladd, Brian *Urban Planning and Civic Order in Germany, 1860–1914.* Cambridge, MA: Harvard University Press, 1990.

Ladovskij, Nikolaj. "Iz protokolov zasedanija komissii zhivopisno-skulpturno-arhitekturnogo sinteza." 1919. In *Mastera arhitekturi ob arhitekture,* vol. 2, 343–4. Moscow: Iskusstvo, 1972–75.

Ladovskij, Nikolaj. "O roli prostrannstva v arhitekture i o haraktere sinteza arhitekturi, skulpturi i zhivopisi." 1920. *Mastera arhitekturi ob arhitekture,* vol. 2, 344. Moscow: Iskusstvo, 1972–75.

Ladovskij, Nikolaj. "Psiho-tehnicheskaja laboratorija arhitekturi." *Izvestija Asnova* (1926): 7.

Lambert, Gregg. *The Return of the Baroque in Modern Culture.* London: Continuum, 2004. Revised as *On the (New) Baroque.* Aurora, CO: Davies Group, 2008.

Lange, Konrad. "Der japanische Farbenholzschnitt." *Die Grenzboten. Zeitschrift für Politik, Literatur und Kunst* 57 (1898): 83–94, 121–33.

Langer, Susanne. *Feeling and Form, A Theory of Art Developed Philosophy in a New Key.* London: Routledge, 1953.

Langer, Susanne. *Reflections on Art: A Source Book of Writings by Artists, Critics, and Philosophers.* Baltimore, MD: Johns Hopkins University Press, 1958.

Larsson, Lars Olof. "Nationalstil und Nationalismus in der Kunstgeschichte der zwanziger und dreissiger Jahre." In Lorenz Dittmann (ed.), *Kategorien und Methoden der deutschen Kunstgeschichte 1900–1930,* 169–84. Stuttgart: Steiner, 1985.

Lauvland, Gro. "Verk og vilkår: Christian Norberg-Schulz' stedsteori i et arkitekturfilosofisk perspektiv." PhD dissertation, Oslo School of Architecture and Design, 2007.

Lavater, Johann Caspar and Georg Christoph Lichtenberg. *Lo specchio dell'anima, pro e contro la fisiognomica. Un dibattito settecentesco.* Edited by Giovanni Gurisatti. Padua: Il Poligrafo, 1991.

Lavin, Irving. *Bernini e l'unità delle arti visive.* Rome: Edizione dell'elefante, 1980.

Lavin, Irving. "Going for Baroque: Observations on the Post-Modern Fold." In Sebastian Schütze (ed.), *Estetica barocca. Atti del convegno internazionale tenutosi a Roma dal 6 al 9 marzo 2002,* 423–52. Rome: Campisano, 2004.

Lavin, Irving. "Introduction." In *Three Essays on Style,* by Erwin Panofsky, 1–14. Cambridge, MA: MIT Press, 1994.

Le Bot, Marc. "L'architecture: raisons et deraisons." In "Pierre Charpentrat. Le baroque et l'architecture." Special issue, *Critique* 373–4 (June–July 1978): 549–53.

Le Corbusier. *The Chapel at Ronchamp.* New York, NY: Frederick A. Praeger Publishers, 1957.

Le Corbusier. *Vers une architecture.* Paris: G. Crès, 1924.

Le Dantec, Jean-Pierre. *Architecture en France.* Paris: Ministère des affaires étrangères, ADPF, 1999.

Leach, Andrew. "*Francesco Borromini and the Crisis of the Humanist Universe,* or Manfredo Tafuri on the Baroque Origins of Modern Architecture." *Journal of Architecture* 15(3) (2010): 301–35.

Leach, Andrew. "The Future of the Baroque, ca. 1945: Panofsky, Stechow (and Middeldorf)." In Antony Moulis and Deborah van der Plaat (eds), *Audience: Proceedings of the XXVIIIth International Conference of the Society of Architectural Historians, Australian and New Zealand.* Brisbane: SAHANZ, 2011, CD-ROM.

Leach, Andrew. "The Mannerist Imperative." *Project* 4 (2015): 44–9.

Leach, Andrew. "Modern Architecture and the Actualisation of History: Bruno Zevi and *Michelangiolo Architetto.*" In Grazia Dolores Folliero-Metz and Susanne Gramatkzki (eds), *Michelangelo Buonarroti: Leben, Werk und Wirkung. Positionen und Perspektiven der Forschung = Michelangelo Buonarroti: Vita, Opera, Ricezione. Approdi e prospettive della ricerca contemporanea,* 510–16. Frankfurt am Main: Peter Lang, 2013.

Leach, Andrew. *What is Architectural History?* Cambridge: Polity, 2010.

Lee, Stephen J. *The Weimar Republic,* 2nd edition. London: Routledge, 2010.

Lee, Vernon. *The Beautiful: An Introduction to Pscyhological Aesthetics.* Cambridge: The University Press, 1913.

Lee, Vernon and Clementina Anstruther-Thomson. *Beauty and Ugliness and Other Studies in Psychological Aesthetics*. London: John Lane, The Bodley Head, 1911.

Lepper, Marcel. "Typologie, Stilpsychologie, Kunstwollen. Zur Erfindung des 'Barock' (1900–1933)." *Arcadia. Zeitschrift für allgemeine und vergleichende Literaturwissenschaft* 41 (2006): 14–29.

Levy, Evonne. *Baroque and the Political Language of Formalism (1845–1945): Burckhardt, Wölfflin, Gurlitt, Brinckmann, Sedlmayr*. Basel: Schwabe, 2015.

Levy, Evonne. "The Political Project of Wölfflin's Early Formalism." *October* 139 (2012): 39–58.

Levy, Evonne. *Propaganda and the Jesuit Baroque*. Berkeley, CA: University of California Press, 2004.

Levy, Evonne. "Rhetoric or Propaganda? On the Instrumentality of Baroque Art." In Sebastian Schütze (ed.), *Estetica barocca. Atti del convegno internazionale tunutosi a Roma dal 6 al 9 marzo 2002*, 89–98. Rome: Campisano, 2004.

Levy, Evonne. "The German Art Historians of World War I: Grautoff, Wichert, Weisbach and Brinckmann and the Activities of the Zentralstelle für Auslandsdienst." *Zeitschrift für Kunstgeschichte* 74 (2011): 373–400.

Levy, Hanna. *Henri Wölfflin. Sa théorie. Ses prédécesseurs*. Rottweil: Rothschild, 1936.

Lind, Karl. "Das k.und k. Schloss Belvedere, als Bauwerk besprochen." *Allgemeine Bauzeitung* (1880): 103–4.

Lind, Karl. "Das Zeughaus der Stadt Wien." *Allgemeine Bauzeitung* (1879): 79.

Lind, Karl. "Der Brunnen auf dem Hoher Markte zu Wien." *Allgemeine Bauzeitung* (1879): 63–4.

Lind, Karl. "Der fürstlich Schwarzenberg'sche Sommer-Palast in Wien." *Allgemeine Bauzeitung* (1880): 104–5.

Lind, Karl. "Die Alte Aula in Wien (Gebäude der k. Akademie des Wissenschaften)." *Allgemeine Bauzeitung* (1880): 72–3.

Lind, Karl. "Die Johannes-Kapelle nächst dem Karlssteg in Wien." *Allgemeine Bauzeitung* (1879): 47.

Lind, Karl. "Die Karlskirche in Wien." *Allgemeine Bauzeitung* (1880): 9–11.

Lind, Karl. "Erinnerungen eines alten Wieners an Wiener Stadtbilder." *Berichte und Mittheilungen des Alterthums-Vereines zu Wien* 35 (1900): 105–11.

Lind, Karl. "Portal des fürstlich Liechtenstein'schen Palais am Minoritenplatz in Wien." *Allgemeine Bauzeitung* (1879): 79–80.

Lipps, Theodor. "Dritter ästhetischer Literaturbericht." *Archiv für systematische Philosophie* 6(3) (1900): 377–409.

Locher, Hubert. *Kunstgeschichte als historische Theorie der Kunst 1750–1950*. Munich: Fink, 2001.

Loeb, Janice. "Surrealism." *Vassar Review* (February 1935): 5.

Long, Christopher. "An Alternative Path to Modernism: Carl König and Architectural Education at the Vienna Technische Hochschule, 1890–1913." *Journal of Architectural Education* 55(1) (September 2001): 21–30.

Loos, Adolf. "Ornament and Crime." 1908. In Ulrich Conrads (ed.), *Programs and Manifestoes on 20th-Century Architecture*, 19–24. Cambridge, MA: MIT Press, 1970. Translated into French as "Ornement et crime." In "Le maquillage." Special issue, *Traverses* 7 (1977): 15–20.

Lurz, Meinhold. *Heinrich Wölfflin. Biographie einer Kunsttheorie*. Worms: Wernor, 1981.

Lützeler, Heinrich. "Zur Religionssoziologie deutscher Barockarchitektur (im Zusammenhang des methodischen Problems)." *Archiv für Sozialwissenschaft und Sozialpolitik* 66 (1931): 557–84.

Lynes, Russell. "After Hours – The Academy That Overlooks Rome." *Harper's Magazine* 228 (May 1969): 28–32.

Lyotard, Jean-Francois. *La condition postmoderne. Rapport sur le savoir*. Paris: Minuit, 1979. Translated by Geoff Bennington and Brian Massumi as *The Postmodern Condition: A Report on Knowledge*. Minneapolis, MN: University of Minnesota Press, 1984.

Lyttelton, Margaret. *Baroque Architecture in Classical Antiquity*. London: Thames & Hudson, 1974.

Macarthur, John. *The Picturesque: Architecture, Disgust and Other Irregularities*. London: Routledge, 2007.

Macarthur, John and Mathew Aitchison. "Oxford vs. The Bath Road: Empiricism and Romanticism in the *Architectural Review*'s Picturesque Revival." *Journal of Architecture* 17(1) (2012): 51–68.

Macarthur, John and Mathew Aitchison. "Pevsner's Townscape." In Mathew Aitchison (ed.), *Visual Planning and the Picturesque*, by Nikolaus Pevsner, 1–43. Los Angeles, CA: Getty Research Institute, 2010.

Macleod, Robert. *Style and Society: Architectural Ideology in Britain 1835–1914*. London: RIBA Publications, 1971.

Maertens, Hermann. *Das optische Maßstab oder die Theorie und Praxis des ästhetischen Sehens in den bildenden Künsten*. Bonn, 1877.

Mâle, Emile. *Studien über die deutsche Kunst*. Edited by Otto Grautoff. Leipzig: Klinkhardt & Biermann, 1917.

Mallgrave, Harry Francis. *Modern Architectural Theory: A Historical Survey, 1673–1968*. Cambridge: Cambridge University Press, 2005.

Mallgrave, Harry Francis and David Goodman. *An Introduction to Architectural Theory: 1968 to the Present*. Malden, MA: Wiley-Blackwell, 2011.

Mallgrave, Harry Francis and Eleftherios Ikonomou (eds). *Empathy, Form and Space: Problems in German Aesthetics 1873–1893*. Santa Monica, CA: Getty Center for the Arts and Humanities, 1994.

Marder, Tod A. *Bernini's Scala Regia at the Vatican Palace: Architecture, Sculpture, and Ritual*. Cambridge: Cambridge University Press, 1997.

Marder, Tod A. "Renaissance and Baroque Architectural History in the United States." In Elisabeth Blair MacDougall (ed.), *The Architectural Historian in America: A Symposium in Celebration of the Fiftieth Anniversary of the Founding of the Society of Architectural Historians*. Studies in the History of Art 35, 161–74. Washington, DC: National Gallery of Art; Hannover and London: University Press of New England, 1990.

Marin, Louis. "Représentation et simulacre." In "Pierre Charpentrat. Le baroque et l'architecture." Special issue, *Critique* 373–4 (June–July 1978): 534–43.

Markuzon, Viktor. "Aleksandr G. Gabričevskij (1981–1968)." *Sovetskoe iskusstvoznanie* 1 (1976): 346–7.

Martin, Reinhold. "Modern Housing, An Afterword." Paper presented to the 2nd International Conference of the European Architectural History Network, Brussels, 2012.

Martin, Reinhold. *Utopia's Ghost: Architecture and Postmodernism, Again*. Minneapolis, MN: University of Minnesota Press, 2010.

Marx, Karl. *Karl-Marx-Ausgabe: Werke, Schriften, Briefe*. Edited by Hans-Joachim Lieber. 7 vols. Darmstadt: Wissenschaftliche Buchgesellschaft, 1962–75.

Martinon, Jean-Pierre. "Pierre Charpentrat et la question du fonctionnalisme baroque." *Baroque. Revue internationale. Journées internationales d'étude du baroque* 9–10 (1980): 112–15.

Masheck, Joseph. *Adolf Loos: The Art of Architecture*. London: I.B. Taurus, 2013.

Massobrio, Giovanna and Paolo Portoghesi. *Album del Liberty*. Rome: Laterza, 1975.

Massobrio, Giovanna, Maria Ercadi and Stefiania Tuzi. *Paolo Portoghesi architetto*. Milan: Skira, 2001.

Merleau-Ponty, Maurice. *Visible et l'invisible*. Paris: Gallimard, 1964. Translated by Alphonso Lingis as *Visible and Invisible*. Evanston, IL: Northwestern University Press, 1968.

Micheli, Silvia. "Italian Architecture: The 1960s and 1970s." In Frédéric Mygairou (ed.), *La Tendenza: Italian Architectures 1965–85*, 80–89. Paris: Centre Pompidou, 2012.

Mies van der Rohe, Ludwig. "Inaugural Address as Director of Architecture at Armour Institute of Technology, 1938." In Philip Johnson (ed.), *Mies van der Rohe*, 192. New York, NY: The Museum of Modern Art, 1947.

Milizia, Francesco. *Memorie degli Architetti antichi e moderni*, 2 vols. Bassano, 1785. Reprint. Bologna: Sala Bolognese, 1978.

Miller Lane, Barbara. *Architecture and Politics in Germany, 1918–1945*. Cambridge, MA: Harvard University Press, 1968.

Millon, Henry A. *Carlo Maderno and Roman Architecture, 1580–1630*. University Park, PA: Penn State University Press, 1971.

Millon, Henry A. (ed.). *The Triumph of the Baroque: Architecture in Europe, 1600–1750*. London: Thames & Hudson, 1999.

Minguet, L. Philippe. *Esthétique du rococo*. Paris: Vrin, 1966.

Mitrović, Branko. "Apollo's Own: Geoffrey Scott and the Lost Pleasures of Architectural History." *Journal of Architectural Education* 54(2) (2000): 95–103.

Mommsen, Wolfgang J. *Bürgerliche Kultur und politische Ordnung. Künstler, Schriftsteller und Intellektuelle in der deutschen Geschichte, 1830–1933*. Frankfurt am Main: Fischer, 2000.

Moretti, Luigi. "Canovaccio per un saggio sull'architettura di Michelangelo e del Borromino e su quella barocca in genere; e intorno alla natura dell'architettura e alle possibilità di una nuova critica architettonica" (1927). *Casabella* 745 (June 2006): 70–80.

Moretti, Luigi. "The Series of Generalized Structures in Borromini's Work." "Barok" = "Baroque." Edited by David de Bruijn, Maarten Delbeke, Job Floris, Christiph Grafe, Ruben Molendijk and Tom Vandeputte. Special issue, *Oase: Tijdschrift voor Architectuur* 86 (2011): 48–55.

Moschini, Francesco (ed.). *Paolo Portoghesi. Progetti e disegni 1949–1979*. Florence: Centro Di, 1979.

Moser, Walter. "Barock." In Karlheinz Barck (ed.), *Ästhetische Grundbegriffe. Historisches Wörterbuch in sieben Bänden*, vol. 1, 578–618. Stuttgart and Weimar: Metzler, 2000.

Moser, Walter and Nicolas Goyer (eds). *Résurgences baroques. Les trajectoires d'un processus transcultural*. Brussels: La lettre volée, 2001.

Mowl, Timothy. *Stylistic Cold Wars: Betjeman Versus Pevsner*. London: John Murray, 2000.

Müller, Hans-Harald. *Barockforschung. Ideologie und Methode. Ein Kapitel deutscher Wissenschaftsgeschichte 1870–1930*. Darmstadt: Thesen, 1973.

Müller, Hans-Harald. "Die Übertragung des Barockbegriffs von der Kunstwissenschaft auf die Literaturwissenschaft und ihre Konsequenzen bei Fritz Strich und Oskar Walzel." In Klaus Garber (ed.), *Europäische Barockrezeption*, vol. 1, 95–112. Wiesbaden: Harrasowitz, 1991.

Mumford, Eric. *The CIAM Discourse on Urbanism, 1929–1960*. Cambridge, MA: MIT Press, 2000.

Mumford, Lewis. *The City in History: Its Origins, its Transformations, and its Prospects*. New York, NY: Harcourt, Brace and World, 1961.

Munro, Thomas. "Knowledge and Control in the Field of Aesthetics." *Journal of Aesthetics and Art Criticism* 1(1) (1941): 1–12.

Munro, Thomas. "Style in the Arts: A Method of Stylistic Analysis." In "A Special Issue on Baroque Style in the Various Arts," *Journal of Aesthetics and Art Criticism* 5(2) (1946): 128–58.

Muthesius, Hermann. "Die künstlerische Zeitungsreklame." In *Festschrift zur Feier des fünfzigjährigen Bestehens der Annoncen-Expedition Rudolf Mosse*. Berlin, January 1, 1917.

MVRDV. *Metacity Datatown*. Rotterdam: 010, 1999.

Navone, Annalisa Viata, "'Un nuovo linguaggio per il pensiero architettonico'. Ricerca operativa e architetura parametrica." In Bruno Reichlin and Letezia Tedeschi (eds), *Luigi Moretti. Razionalismo e trasgressività tra barocco e informale*, 409–19. Milan: Electa, 2010.

Ndalianis, Angela. *Neo-Baroque Aesthetics and Contemporary Entertainment*. Cambridge, MA: MIT Press, 2004.

Neumann, Carl. "Ist wirklich Barock und Deutsch das Nämliche?" Review of *Geschichte der deutschen Kunst* by Georg Dehio, vol. 3. *Historische Zeitschrift* 138 (1928): 545–9.

Newman, Oscar (ed.). *Ciam '59 in Otterlo. Arbeitsgruppe für die Gestaltung soziologischer und visueller Zusammenhänge. Dokumente der Modernen Architektur* 1. Stuttgart: Karl Krämer Verlag, 1961.

Neumeyer, Alfred. Review of *Kunstwissenschaftliche Forschungen* 2 (1933). *Zeitschrift für Aesthetik und allgemeine Kunstwissenschaft* 28 (1934): 285–93.

Nierhaus, Andreas. "*Höfisch und Österreichisch. Zur Architektur des Neobarock in Wien.*" In Moritz Czaky, Federico Celestini and Ulrich Tragatschnig (eds), *Barock — Ein Ort des Gedächtnisses Interpretament der Moderne – Postmoderne*, 79–100. Vienna: Böhlau, 2007.

Nierhaus, Andreas. "Schauplatz und Handlungsraum. Zur visuellen und räumlichen Inzenierung des Wiener Kaiserforums." In "Politische Raumtypen. Zur Wirkungsmacht öffentlicher Bau- und Raumstrukturen im 20. Jahrhundert." Special issue, *Jahrbuch der Guernica Gesellschaft* 11 (2009): 46–60.

Nipperdey, Thomas. *Deutsche Geschichte 1866–1918*, 2 vols. Munich: Beck, 1998.

Norberg-Schulz, Christian. *Alla ricerca dell'architettura perduta. Le opere di Paolo Portoghesi, Vittorio Gigliotti 1959–1975*. Rome: Officina, 1975.

Norberg-Schulz, Christian. *Architettura barocca*. Milan: Electa, 1971. Translated as *Baroque Architecture*, History of World Architecture. New York, NY: Harry N. Abrams, 1974.

Norberg-Schulz, Christian. *Architettura tardobarocca*. Milan: Electa, 1971. Translated as *Late Baroque and Rococo Architecture*, History of World Architecture. New York, NY: Harry N. Abrams, 1974.

Norberg-Schulz, Christian. "Den nye tradisjon." In *Kunst og Kultur* 1 (1991). Reprinted in *Øye og hånd: Essays og artikler: ny rekke*, by Christian Norberg-Schulz, 136–47. Oslo: Gyldendal, 1997.

Norberg-Schulz, Christian. *Genius loci: paesaggio, ambiente, architettura*. Milan: Electa, 1979. Translated as *Genius loci: Towards a Phenomenology of Architecture*. London: Academy Editions, 1980.

Norberg-Schulz, Christian. *Intentions in Architecture.* Oslo: Universitetsforlaget, 1963.

Norberg-Schulz, Christian. *Øye og hånd: Essays og artikler: ny rekke.* Oslo: Gyldendal, 1997.

Norberg-Schulz, Christian. *Principles of Modern Architecture.* London: Andreas Papadakis, 2000.

Norberg-Schulz, Christian. *Stedskunst.* Oslo: Gyldendal, 1996.

Oechslin, Werner. "'Barok'. Zu den negativen Kriterien der Begriffsbestimmung in klassizistischer und späterer Zeit." In Klaus Garber (ed.), *Europäische Barockrezeption,* vol. 2, 1225–54. Wiesbaden: Harrasowitz, 1991.

Oechslin, Werner. "The Evolutionary Way to Modern Architecture: The Paradigm of *Stilhülse und Kern.*" In Harry Francis Mallgrave (ed.), *Otto Wagner: Reflections on the Raiment of Modernity,* 363–410. Los Angeles, CA: The Getty Center for the History of Art, 1993.

Oechslin, Werner. *Otto Wagner, Adolf Loos and the Road to Modern Architecture.* Translated by Lynnette Widder. 1994. Cambridge: Cambridge University Press, 2002.

Oexle, Otto Gerhard. "'Zusammenarbeit mit Baal'. Über die Mentalität deutscher Geisteswissenschaftler 1933 – und nach 1945." *Historische Anthropologie* 8 (2000): 1–27.

Office for Metropolitam Architecture, Rem Koolhaas and Bruce Mau. *S, M, L, XL.* Edited by Jennifer Sigler. Rotterdam: 010, 1995.

Öhlschläger, Claudia. *Abstraktionsdrang. Wilhelm Worringer und der Geist der Moderne.* Munich: Fink, 2005.

Ol'ga Severzeva, Fedor Stukalov-Pogodin, *"Breve profilo di un intellettuale negli anni di Stalin. A. G. Gabricevskij."* In Alessandro De Magistris (ed.), *URSS anni '30–'50: Paesaggi dell'utopia staliniana.* Milan: Mazzotta, 1997.

Olin, Margaret. "Alois Riegl: The Late Roman Empire in the Late Habsburg Empire." In Ritchie Robertson and Edward Timms (eds), *The Habsburg Legacy: National Identity in Historical Perspective,* 107–20. Edinburgh: Edinburgh University Press, 1994.

Olin, Margaret. "The Cult of Monuments as a State Religion in Late 19th Century Austria." *Wiener Jahrbuch für Kunstgeschichte* 38 (1985): 177–218.

Olin, Margaret. "Forms of Respect: Alois Riegl's Concept of Attentiveness." *Art Bulletin* 71 (1989): 285–99.

Orbaan, Johannes. *Documenti sul barocco in Roma,* 2 vols. Rome: Società Romana di Storia Patria, 1920.

Österreichische Akademie der Wissenschaften. *Österreichisches Biographisches Lexikon 1815–1950,* 15 vols. Vienna: Verlag VÖAW, 1993.

Ostwald, Michael. *The Architecture of the New Baroque: A Comparative Study of the Historic and New Baroque Movements in Architecture.* Singapore: Global Arts, 2006.

Otero-Pailos, Jorge. *Architecture's Historical Turn: Phenomenology and the Rise of the Postmodern.* Minneapolis, MN: University of Minnesota Press, 2010.

Ottenthal, E. Von. "Theodor von Sickel" (obituary). *Mitheilungen des Instituts für österreichische Geschichtsforschung* 29 (1908): 545–59.

Ottlinger, Eva B. *"Von Blondel'schen Styl zum Maria Theresien Stil.* Albert Ilg und die Rokoko-Rezeption in der Wiener Wohnkultur des 19. Jahrhunderts." In Friedrich Polleroß (ed.), *Fischer von Erlach und die Wiener Barocktradition,* 345–69. Vienna: Böhlau, 1995.

Pallasmaa, Junahi. *The Eyes of the Skin: Architecture and the Senses.* London: Wiley, 2005.

Panofsky, Irwin. "Baroque, S. S. [June–July] 1931." Syllabus (34pp) Universität Hamburg, box 9, Hechscher-Archiv, Warburg Haus, Hamburg.

Panofsky, Irwin. "Die Scala Regia im Vatikan und die Kunstanschauungen Berninis." *Jahrbuch der Preuszischen Kunstsammlungen* 40 (1919): 241–78.

Panofsky, Irwin. "Italian Baroque Art." Syllabus (57pp), New York University, box 18, Hechscher-Archiv, Warburg Haus, Hamburg.

Panofsky, Irwin. *Meaning in the Visual Arts: Papers in and on Art History.* Garden City, NY: Doubleday Anchor Books, 1955.

Panofsky, Irwin. "The Concept of Artistic Volition." Translated by Kenneth J. Northcott and Joel Snyder. *Critical Inquiry* 8(1) (1981): 17–33.

Panofsky, Irwin. *Three Essays on Style.* Edited by Irving Lavin. Cambridge, MA: MIT Press, 1994.

Panofsky, Irwin. "What is Baroque?" In Irving Lavin (ed.), *Three Essays on Style,* by Erwin Panofsky, 17–88. Cambridge, MA: MIT Press, 1994.

Papapetros, Spyros. "Transparencies that passed and plenty more to come." Review of *Modernity Unbound: Other Histories of Architectural Modernity*, by Detlef Mertins. *Journal of Architecture* 17(5) (2012): 813–17.

Patron, Sylvie. *Critique. Une encyclopédie pour l'esprit moderne*. Paris: IMEC, 1999.

Payne, Alina. "Architecture, Ornament and Pictorialism: Notes on the Relationship between the Arts from Wölfflin to Le Corbusier." In Karen Koehler (ed.), *The Built Surface: Architecture and the Pictorial Arts from Romanticism to the Twenty-First Century*, 54–72. Aldershot: Ashgate, 2002.

Payne, Alina. "Beyond 'Kunstwollen': Alois Riegl and the Baroque." In Andrew Hopkins and Arnold Witte (eds), *The Origins of Baroque Art in Rome*, by Alois Riegl, 1–33. Los Angeles, CA: Getty Research Institute, 2010.

Payne, Alina. "Portable Ruins: The Pergamon Altar, Heinrich Wölfflin, and German Art History at the Fin De Siècle." *Res* 53–4 (2008): 168–89.

Payne, Alina. "Rudolf Wittkower and Architectural Principles in the Age of Modernism." *Journal of the Society of Architectural Historians* 53(3) (1994): 322–42.

Pearlman, Jill. *Inventing American Modernism: Joseph Hudnut, Walter Gropius and the Bauhaus Legacy at Harvard*. Charlottesville, VA: University of Virginia Press, 2007.

Pearlman, Jill. "Joseph Hudnut's Other Modernism at the 'Harvard Bauhaus'." *Journal of the Society of Architectural Historians* 56(4) (December 1997): 452–77.

Pehnt, Wolfgang. *Expressionistic Architecture*. London: Thames and Hudson, 1973.

Pehnt, Wolfgang. *Deutsche Architektur seit 1900*. Munich: Deutsche Verlags-Anstalt, 2005.

Pelkonen, Eeva-Liisa. *Alvar Aalto: Architecture, Modernity, and Geopolitics*. New Haven, CT: Yale University Press, 2009.

Perceva, T.M. "Poiski form vsaimosvjazi nauki i iskusstva (po materijalom Gahna)." *Trudy VNIITE* 21 (1979): 30–42.

Pérez-Gómez, Alberto. *Architecture and the Crisis of Modern Science*. Cambridge, MA: MIT Press, 1983.

Perniola, Mario. *Dopo Heidegger. Filosofia e organizzazione della cultura*. Milan: Feltrinelli, 1982.

Pevsner, Nikolaus. *An Outline of European Architecture*. Harmondsworth: Penguin, 1943.

Pevsner, Nikolaus. "Baroque and Rococo." Reponse to a Letter from O.H. Leeney. *Times Literary Supplement*, August 4, 1945.

Pevsner, Nikolaus. "Beiträge zur Stilgeschichte des Früh- und Hochbarock." *Repertorium für Kunstwissenschaft* 49 (1928): 225–46. Translated by David Britt as "Early and High Baroque." In *Studies in Art, Architecture and Design*, by Nikolaus Pevsner, vol. 2, 34–55. London: Thames and Hudson, 1968.

Pevsner, Nikolaus. "C20 Picturesque. An Answer to Basil Taylor's Broadcast." *Architectural Review* 115(688) (April 1954): 227–9.

Pevsner, Nikolaus. "Das Englische in Der Englischen Kunst. Die Retrospektive Austellung Britischer Kunst in Der Londoner Akademie." *Deutsche Zukunft: Wochenzeitung für Politik Wirtschaft und Kultur* 2(4) (February 1934): 15.

Pevsner, Nikolaus. "Foreword." In *Sir Nikolaus Pevsner: A Bibliography*, compiled by John Darr, n.p. Charlottesville, VA: University of Virginia for the American Association of Architectural Bibliographers, 1970.

Pevsner, Nikolaus. "Gegenreformation und Manierismus." *Repertorium für Kunstwissenschaft* 46 (1925): 243–62. Translated by David Britt as "The Counter-Reformation and Mannerism." In *Studies in Art, Architecture and Design*, by Nikolaus Pevsner, vol. 1, 10–33. London: Thames and Hudson, 1968.

Pevsner, Nikolaus. *Leipziger Barock: Die Baukunst Der Barockzeit in Leipzig*. Dresden: Wolfgang Jess, 1928.

Pevsner, Nikolaus. "Modern Architecture and Tradition." *The Highway: Workers' Educational Association* (August 1947): 228–32.

Pevsner, Nikolaus. *Pioneers of the Modern Movement from William Morris to Walter Gropius*. London: Faber and Faber, 1936.

Pevsner, Nikolaus. Review of *Hochrenaissance-Manierismus-Frühbarock*, by Hans Hoffmann. *Burlington Magazine for Connoisseurs* 75(438) (1939): 136.

Pevsner, Nikolaus. Review of *Le Corbusier und Pierre Jeanneret: Ihr gesamtes Werk von 1910 bis 1929*. *Göttingische gelehrte Anzeigen* 193(8) (August 1931): 303–12.

Pevsner, Nikolaus. "Roehampton. LCC Housing and the Picturesque Tradition." *Architectural Review* 126(750) (July 1959): 21–35.

Pevsner, Nikolaus. "The English Eccentrics: Land of Follies in Architecture." Review of *British Architects and Craftsmen*, by Sacheverall Sitwell. *Times Literary Supplement*, 14 July 1945.

Pevsner, Nikolaus. *The Englishness of English Art: An Expanded and Annotated Version of the Reith Lectures Broadcast in October and November 1955*. London: Architectural Press, 1956.

Pevsner, Nikolaus. "The Modern Movement in Britain." In Susannah Charlton, Elain Harwood and Alan Powers (eds), *British Modern: Architecture and Design in the 1930s*, 11–38. London: The Twentieth Century Society, 2007.

Pevsner, Nikolaus. *Visual Planning and the Picturesque*. Edited by Mathew Aitchison. Los Angeles, CA: Getty Research Institute, 2010.

Pevsner, Nikolaus. "Zehn Jahre Bauen in Grossbritannien." *Bauen +Wohnen* (1964): 461–3.

Pevsner, Nikolaus, as Eric de Maré. "The New Empiricism: The Antecedents and Origins of Sweden's Latest Style." *Architectural Review* 103(613) (January 1948): 9–10.

Pevsner, Nikolaus, as The Editor. "The New Empiricism: Sweden's Latest Style." *Architectural Review* 101(606) (June 1947): 199–200.

Pevsner, Nikolaus and Otto Grautoff. *Barockmalerei in den romanischen Ländern. Vol. 1, Die italienishce Malerei vom Ende der Renaissance bis zum ausgehenden Rokoko*. Wildpark-Potsdam: Akademische Verlagsgesellschaft Atenaion, 1928.

Pevsner, Nikolaus and Otto Grautoff. *Barockmalerei in den romanischen Ländern*. Vol. 2, *Die Malerei im Barockzeitalter in Frankreich und Spanien*. Wildpark-Potsdam: Akademische Verlagsgesellschaft Atenaion, 1928.

Pinder, Wilhelm. *Das Problem der Generation in der Kunstgeschichte Europas*. Berlin: Frankfurter Verlags-Anstalt, 1926.

Pinder, Wilhelm. *Deutscher Barock. Die grossen Baumeister des 18. Jahrhunderts*. Die Blauen Bücher. Düsseldorf and Leipzig: Langewiesche, 1912. Republished Munich: Karl Robert Langewiesche, 1961.

Pogodin, Fedor. *A. G. Gabričevskij. Biografia e cultura*. Special issue, *Slavia* 1 (2004).

Pollak, Oskar. *Die Kunsttätigkeit unter Urban VIII*. Edited by Dagobert Frey, 2 vols. Vienna: B. Filser, 1928.

Pope-Hennessy, John. "Review of *Art and Architecture in Italy 1600 to 1750*, by Rudolf Wittkower." *Times Literary Supplement*, January 30, 1959. Reprinted in Walter Kaiser and Michael Mallon (eds), *On Artists and Art Historian: Selected Book Reviews of John Pope-Hennessy*, 340–43. Florence: Leo S. Olschki, 1994.

Portoghesi, Paolo. "Borromini in ferro." *Civiltà delle macchine* 2 (1953): 50–53.

Portoghesi, Paolo. *Borromini nella cultura europea*. Città di Castello: Officina, 1964.

Portoghesi, Paolo. "Casa Andreis a Scandriglia, Rieti." *L'Architettura cronache e storia* 137 (1967): 706–19.

Portoghesi, Paolo. "Casa Baldi sull'ansa della Flaminia, a Roma." *L'architettura cronache e storia* 86 (1962): 510–21.

Portoghesi, Paolo (ed.). *Disegni di Francesco Borromini*. Exhibition catalogue. Rome: De Luca, 1967.

Portoghesi, Paolo. *Dopo l'architettura moderna*. Rome: Laterza, 1980.

Portoghesi, Paolo. *Guarino Guarini 1624–1683*. Milan: Electa, 1956.

Portoghesi, Paolo. "I disegni tecnici di Leonardo." *Civiltà delle Macchine* 1 (1955): 6–24.

Portoghesi, Paolo. "Intervento di P. Portoghesi sulla relazione di B. Zevi." In Guglielmo de Angelis d'Ossat (ed.), *Studi sul Borromini. Atti del Convegno promosso dall'Accademia nazionale di San Luca*, vol. 1, 531–6. Rome: De Luca, 1967.

Portoghesi, Paolo (ed.). *La presenza del passato*. Special issue dedicated to the I Mostra Internazionale di Architettura della Biennale di Venezia, *Controspazio* 1(6) (1980).

Portoghesi, Paolo (ed.). *La presenza del passato. Mostra internazionale di architettura*. Venice: La Biennale di Venezia; Milan: Electa, 1980.

Portoghesi, Paolo. *Le inibizioni dell'architettura moderna*. Rome: Laterza, 1974.

Portoghesi, Paolo. "L'opera di Borromini per l'altare della chiesa di S. Paolo a Bologna." *Palladio* 3 (1954): 3–11.

Portoghesi, Paolo. "Postfazione." In Franco Purini, Luigi Calcagnile, Dino Nencini and Francesco Menegatti (eds), "La formazione degli architetti romani negli anni Sessanta." Special issue, *Rassegna di architettura e urbanistica* 112–14 (2004): 280–83.

Portoghesi, Paolo. *Postmodern: l'architettura nella società post-industriale*. Milan: Electa, 1982.

Portoghesi, Paolo. *Roma Barocca. Storia di una civiltà architettonica.* Rome: C. Bestietti Edizioni d'Arte, 1966.

Portoghesi, Paolo. *Storia di San Carlino alle Quattro Fontane.* Rome: Newton and Compton, 2001.

Portoghesi, Paolo. "Vittone nella cultura europea." *Controspazio* 10 (1972): 38–52.

Portoghesi, Paolo, Luca Quattrocchi and Folco Quilici. *Barocco e Liberty. Lo specchio della metamorfosi.* Trento: Luigi Reverdito Editore, 1986.

Poulsson, Gregor. "In Search of a New Monumentality." *Architectural Review* (September 1948): 117–28.

Prange, Regine. *Die Geburt der Kunstgeschichte. Philosophische Ästhetik und empirische Wissenschaft.* Cologne: Deubner, 2004.

Priori, Giancarlo. *Paolo Portoghesi.* Bologna: Zanichelli, 1985.

Pudor, Heinrich. "Erziehung zur Eisenarchitektur." *Der Architekt* 9 (1903): 24–6.

Raillard, Georges. "Charpentrat, Pierre (1922–1977)." In *Encyclopédia Universalis.* Available at http://www.universalis.fr/encyclopedie/pierre-charpentrat/ (accessed 26 September 2013).

Rampley, Matthew, "Subjectivity and Modernism: Riegl and the Rediscovery of the Baroque." In Richard Woodfield (ed.), *Framing Formalism*, 265–86. Amsterdam: G+B Arts International, 2001.

Rampley, Matthew. "The Idea of a Scientific Discipline: Rudolf von Eitelberger and the Emergence of Art History in Vienna, 1847–1873." *Art History* 34 (2011): 54–79.

Rasmussen, Steen Eiler. "The Architect and Society." *RIBA Journal* (July 1957): 381–3.

Rasmussen, Steen Elier. *Britisk Brugskunst.* Copenhagen: Det Danske Kunstindustrimuseum, 1933.

Rasmussen, Steen Eiler. *London: The Unique City.* New York, NY: Macmillan, 1937.

Rasmussen, Steen Eiler. *Nordische Baukunst.* Berlin: Ernst Wasmuth Verlag, 1940.

Rasmussen, Steen Eiler. "Om at Opleve Arkitektur." *Prisma* 3 (1950): 15–32.

Rasmussen, Steen Eiler. *Om at Opleve Arkitektur.* Copenhagen: Gads Forlag, 1957. Translated as *Experiencing Architecture.* Cambridge, MA: MIT Press, 1959.

Rasmussen, Steen Eiler. "The Dutch Contribution." *Town Planning Review* 24 (October 1953): 161–76.

Rasmussen, Steen Eiler. *The Metropolitan Future.* Berkeley, CA: University of California Press, 1965.

Rasmussen, Steen Eiler. *Towns and Buildings.* Cambridge, MA: Harvard University Press, 1951.

Read, Herbert. *Classic Art: An Introduction to the Italian Renaissance.* London: Phaidon, 1952.

Redtenbacher, Rudolf. "Die Baubestrebungen der Gegenwart." *Allgemeine Bauzeitung* (1877): 61–3, 77–80.

Redtenbacher, Rudolf. "Die Baukunst der Vergangenheit und ihre Stellung zu derjenigen der gegenwart." *Allgemeine Bauzeitung* (1881): 1–4, 17–20.

Reed, Christopher. *Roger Fry's Durbins: A House and Its Meanings.* London: Cecil Woolf Publishers, 1999.

Regamey, Pie-Raymond. "Notes sur le baroque." *La Maison-Dieu* 26 (1951): 143–64.

Reichlin, Bruno and Letizia Tedeschi (eds). *Luigi Moretti. Razionalismo e trasgressività tra barocco e informale.* Milan: Electa, 2010.

Reijen, Willem van. "Adorno und das Barock." In Klaus Garber (ed.), *Europaische Barockrezeption* vol. 1, 155–68. Wiesbaden: Harrasowitz, 1991.

Reuveni, Gideon. *Reading Germany: Literature and Conumser Culture before 1933.* New York, NY: Berghahn Books, 2006.

Ricci, Corrado. *Architettura barocca in Italia.* Bergamo: Istituto Italiano d'Arti Grafiche, 1912.

Riegl, Alois. "Das holländische Gruppenporträt." *Jahrbuch der Kunsthistorischen Sammlungen des Allerhöchsten Kaiserhauses* 23 (1902): 71–278. Published in book form as *Das holländische Gruppenporträt*, 2 vols. Vienna: Österreichischen Staatsdruckerei, 1931. Translated by Evelyn M. Kain and David Britt as *The Group Portraiture of Holland.* Los Angeles, CA: Getty Publications, 1999.

Riegl, Alois. *Die Entstehung der Barockkunst in Rom.* Edited by Arthur Burda and Max Dvořák. Vienna: Anton Schroll, 1908. Edited and translated by Andrew Hopkins and Arnold Witte as *The Origins of Baroque Art in Rome.* Los Angeles, CA: Getty Research Institute, 2010.

Riegl, Alois. *Die spätrömische Kunstindustrie nach den Funden in Österreich-Ungarn.* Vienna: Österreichischen Staatsdruckerei, 1901. Translated by Rolf Winkes as *Late Roman Art Industry.* Rome: G. Bretschneider, 1985.

Riegl, Alois. "Salzburgs Stellung in der Kunstgeschichte." In Karl M. Swoboda and Hans Sedlmayr (eds), *Gesammelte Aufsätze*, 111–32. Augsburg: Filser, 1929.

Rinaldi, Alessandro. "Il centenario di Bernini e il rilancio del barocco." *Studi Romani* 30(3) (1982): 373–83.

Roberti, Salvatore Caronia, et al. "Il metodo di progettazione del Borromini." In Guglielmo de Angelis d'Ossat (ed.), *Studi sul Borromini. Atti del Convegno promosso dall'Accademia nazionale di San Luca*, vol. 2, 5–34. Rome: De Luca, 1967.

Roque, Paul. "La signification du baroque." *La Maison-Dieu* 26 (1951): 125–42.

Rosand, David. "Art History and Criticism: The Past as Present." *New Literary Theory* 5(3) (Spring, 1974): 435–45.

Rose, Hans. *Spätbarock. Studien zur Geschichte des Profanbaues in den Jahren 1660–1760*. Munich: Bruckmann, 1922.

Ross, Corey. *Media and the Making of Modern Germany: Mass Communications, Society, and Politics form the Empire to the Third Reich*. New York, NY: Oxford University Press, 2008.

Rostagni, Cecilia. "Biografia." In Federico Bucci and Marco Mulazzani (eds), *Luigi Moretti. Opere e scritti*, 210–12. Milan: Electa, 2000.

Rostagni, Cecilia. *Luigi Moretti 1907–1973*. Milan: Electa, 2008.

Rousset, Jean. *La littérature de l'âge baroque en France. Circé et le paon*. Paris: José Corti, 1953.

Rousset, Jean. "Mon baroque." In Michel Jeanneret (ed.), *L'aventure baroque*, 49–62. Carouge, Geneva: Zoé, 2006.

Rowe, Colin. *The Mathematics of the Ideal Villa and Other Essays*. Cambridge, MA: MIT Press, 1982.

Rowe, Colin and Fred Koetter. *Collage City*. Cambridge, MA: MIT Press, 1978.

Ruskin, John. *The Library Edition: The Works of John Ruskin*. Edited by E.T. Cook and Alexander Wedderburn. London: George Allen, 1903–12.

Sadler, Simon. "Autonomy's Ghost and General Education." *Architectural Histories* 1(1) (2013): 16. Available at http://dx.doi.org/10.5334/ah.au (accessed 3 February 2014).

Salerno, Luigi. "The Italian Baroque." *Burlington Magazine* 103(701) (1961): 361.

Santini, Pier Carlo. "Alvar Aalto from Sunila to Imatra: Ideas, Projects and Buildings." *Zodiac* 3 (1958): 27–8.

Sarduy, Severo. *Baroque*. Paris: Gallimard, 1972.

Schnell, Hugo. *Der baierische Barock. Die volklichen, die geschichtlichen und die religiösen Grundlagen. Sein Siegeszug durch das Reich*. Munich: Dreifaltigkeitsverlag, 1936.

Schnell, Hugo. "Zur Bewertung des baierischen Barock im 19. und 20. Jahrhundert." In Karl Bringmann (ed.), *Festschrift für Anton Betz*, 181–208. Düsseldorf: Rheinisch-Bergische Druck- und Verlags-Gesellschaft, 1963.

Schapiro, Meyer. "The New Viennese School." *Art Bulletin* 18(2) (1936): 258–66.

Schapiro, Meyer. *Theory and Philosophy of Art: Style, Artist, and Society*. New York, NY: George Braziller, 1994.

Scheffler, Karl. *Die Architektur der Großstadt*. Berlin: Gebr. Mann Verlag, 1998.

Scheidig, Walther. *Crafts of the Weimar Bauhaus: 1919–1924: An Early Experiment in Industrial Design*. London: Studio Vista, 1967.

Schliepmann, Hans. "Das Geschäftshaus als Architekturproblem." *Bauwelt* 3(12) (1912): 10–12.

Schliepmann, Hans. "Zur Unseren Bildern: Architektur." *Berliner Architekturwelt* 3 (1901): 318–28.

Schlosser, Julius von. "Die Wiener Schule der Kunstgeschichte. Rückblick auf ein Säkulum deutscher Gelehrtenarbeit in Oesterreich." *Mittheilungen des Instituts für österreichische Geschichtsforschung* 13 (1934): 145–210. Translated into Italian as "La scuola viennese dell'Arte. Sguardo ad un secolo di lavoro di eruditi tedeschi in Austria" in *La storia dell'arte nelle esperienze e nei ricordi di un suo cultore*, by Julius (Giulio) von Schlosser, 118–36. Bari: Laterza, 1936.

Schlosser, Julius von. "Franz Wickhoff" (obituary). *Mittheilungen des Instituts für österreichische Geschichtsforschung* 30 (1909): 554–60.

Schlosser, Julius von. "'Stilgeschichte' und 'Sprachgeschichte'." *Sitzungsberichte der Bayerischen Akademie der Wissenschaften: Philosophisch-historische Abteilung* 1 (1935): 3–39.

Schmarsow, August. *Barock und Rokoko. Eine kritische Auseinandersetzung über das Malerische in der Architektur*. Leipzig: S. Hirzel, 1897. Critical edition by Jasper Cepl. Berlin: Mann, 2001.

Schmarsow, August. *Das Wesen der architektonischen Schöpfung*. Leipzig: Hiersemann, 1894. Translated by Harry Francis Mallgrave and Eleftherios Ikonomou as "The Essence of Architectural Creation," in Harry Francis Mallgrave and Eleftherios Ikonomou (eds), *Empathy, Form, and Space: Problems in German Aesthetics, 1873–1893*, 281–98. Los Angeles, CA: Getty Center for the Arts and Humanities, 1994.

Schütze, Sebastian (ed.). *Estetica barocca. Atti del convegno internazionale tenutosi a Roma dal 6 al 9 marzo 2002*. Rome: Campisano, 2004.

Schwartz, Frederic. *Blind Spots: Critical Theory and the History of Art in Twentieth-Century Germany*. New Haven, CT: Yale University Press, 2005.

Schwartz, Frederic. "Cathedrals and Shoes: Concepts of Style in Wölfflin and Adorno." *New German Critique* 76 (Winter 1999): 3–48.

Schwartz, Frederic. *The Werkbund: Design Theory and Mass Culture before the First World War*. New Haven, CT and London: Yale University Press, 1996.

Scott, Geoffrey. *The Architecture of Humanism: A Study in the History of Taste*, 1914, 2nd edition. London: Constable, 1924. Reprinted London: W.W. Norton & Company, 1999.

Scott, Geoffrey. *The National Character of English Architecture*. Oxford: B.H. Blackwell, 1908.

Scripture, E.W. *Thinking, Feeling, Doing*. Meadville, PA: Flood and Vincent, 1895.

Sedlmayr, Hans. "Bild und Raum: Weltepochen der Kunst." In Alexander Randa (ed.), *Handbuch der Weltgeschichte*, 2649–54. Olten: Walter-Verlag, 1954.

Sedlmayr, Hans. *Die Architektur Borrominis*. Berlin: Frankfurter Verlags-Anstalt, 1930.

Sedlmayr, Hans. "Die Einheit von Sinnen und Geist im Kunstwerk." *Mitteilungsblatt der Gesellschaft für Ganzheitsforschung* 3 (1957): 1–7. Translated into Italian as "Il legame tra visible e invisibile nell'opera d'arte." In the Istituto Accademico di Roma (ed.), *Eternità e storia*, 243–8. Florence: Vallecchi, 1970.

Sedlmayr, Hans. "Die 'Macchia' Bruegels." *Jahrbuch der Wiener Kunsthistorischen Sammlungen* 8 (1934): 137–60.

Sedlmayr, Hans. "Die politische Bedeutung des deutschen Barocks." In *Gesamtdeutsche Vergangenheit: Festgabe für Heinrich Ritter von Srbik zum 60*, 126–40. Munich: Bruckmann, 1938. Reprinted in Hans Sedlmayr, *Epochen und Werke: Gesammelte Schriften zur Kunstgeschichte*, vol. 2, 140–57. Vienna: Herold, 1960.

Sedlmayr, Hans. *Die Revolution der modernen Kunst*. Hamburg: Rowohlt, 1955. Revised edition with Postscript by Friedrich Piel. Cologne: Dumont, 1985. Translated into Italian by Mariangela Donà as *La rivoluzione dell'arte moderna* (1958). Milan: Garzanti, 1961.

Sedlmayr, Hans. "Die Schauseite der Karlskirche in Wien." In Wolfgang Braunfels (ed.), *Kunstgeschichtliche Studien für Hans Kauffmann*, 262–71. Berlin: Gebr. Mann, 1956. Reprinted in *Epochen und Werke: Gesammelte Schriften zur Kunstgeschichte*, vol. 2, 174–87. Vienna: Herold, 1960.

Sedlmayr, Hans . "Eduard Coudenhove-Erthal, Carlo Fontana und die Architektur des römischen Spätbarocks." *Kritische Berichte* 3 (1930–31): 93–5.

Sedlmayr, Hans. "Eine 'genetische Monographie'." Review of *Die Medici-Kapelle Michelangelos*, by A.E. Popp. *Kritische Berichte* (1928–29): 187–92.

Sedlmayr, Hans. *Epochen und Werke. Gesammelte Schriften zur Kunstgeschichte*, 2 vols. Vienna: Herold, 1959–60.

Sedlmayr, Hans. *Fischer von Erlach der Ältere*. Munich: R. Piper & Co., 1925.

Sedlmayr, Hans. "Fünf römische Fassaden" (1937). In *Epochen und Werke: Gesammelte Schriften zur Kunstgeschichte*, by Hans Sedlmayr, vol. 2, 57–79. Vienna: Herold, 1960.

Sedlmayr, Hans. "Geschichte und Kunstgeschichte." *Mittheilungen des Instituts für österreichische Geschichtsforschung* 50 (1936): 185–99.

Sedlmayr, Hans. "Gestaltetes Sehen." *Belvedere* 8 (1925): 65–73.

Sedlmayr, Hans. "Julius Ritter von Schlosser. 1866–1938" (obituary). *Mittheilungen des Instituts für österreichische Geschichtsforschung* 52 (1938): 513–19.

Sedlmayr, Hans. "Kunstgeschichte als Geistesgeschichte: Das Vermächtnis Max Dvoraks." *Wort und Wahrheit* 4 (1949): 264–77. Translated into Italian as "Storia dell'arte come storia dello spirito," in *Arte e verità. Per una teoria e un metodo della storia dell'arte*, by Hans Sedlmayr, 115–35. Milan: Rusconi, 1984.

Sedlmayr, Hans. *Österreichische Barockarchitektur 1690–1760*. Vienna: Filser, 1930.

Sedlmayr, Hans. "Österreichs bildende Kunst." In Joseph Nadler and Heinrich von Srbik (eds), *Österreich: Erbe und Sendung im deutschen Raum*, 329–46. Leipzig: Pustet, 1936. Reprinted in Hans Sedlmayr, *Epochen und Werke: Gesammelte Schriften zur Kunstgeschichte*, vol. 2, 278. Vienna: Herold, 1960.

Sedlmayr, Hans. "Pieter Bruegel: Der Sturz der Blinden." *Hefte des Kunsthistorischen Seminars der Universität München* 2 (1957): 1–48. Reprinted in *Epochen und Werke: Gesammelte Schriften zur Kunstgeschichte*, vol. 1, 319–57. Vienna: Herold, 1959.

Sedlmayr, Hans. *"Über das Interpretieren von Werken der bildenden Künste."* In Helmut Kuhn et al. (ed.), *Interpretation der Welt. Festschrift für Romano Guardini zum Achtzigsten Geburtstag*, 349–65. Würzburg: Echter-Verlag, 1965.

Sedlmayr, Hans. *Verlust der Mitte: Die bildende Kunst des 19. und 20. Jahrhunderts als Symptom und Symbol der Zeit.* Salzburg: O. Müller, 1948. Translated as *Art in Crisis: The Lost Centre.* Chicago, IL: H. Regnery, 1958.

Sedlmayr, Hans. "Zu einer strengen Kunstwissenschaft." *Kunstwissenschaftliche Forschungen* 1 (1931): 7–32. Translated into Italian by Francesco Paolo Fiore as "Storia dell'arte come storia dell'arte," in *Arte e verità. Per una teoria e un metodo della storia dell'arte*, by Hans Sedlmayr, 67–112. Milan: Rusconi, 1984.

Sedlmayr, Hans. "Zum gestalteten Sehen." *Belvedere* 9–10 (1926): 57–62.

See, Klaus von. *Barbar, Germane, Arier. Die Suche nach der Identität der Deutschen.* Heidelberg: Winter, 1994.

See, Klaus von. *Freiheit und Gemeinschaft. Völkisch-nationales Denken in Deutschland zwischen Französischer Revolution und Erstem Weltkrieg.* Heidelberg: Winter, 2001.

Sekler, Eduard. "Sigfried Giedion at Harvard University." In Elisabeth Blair MacDougall (ed.), *The Architectural Historian in America*, Studies in the History of Art 35, 265–73. Washington, DC: The National Gallery of Art, 1990.

Senkevitch, Anatole Jr. "Aspects of Spatial Form and Perceptual Psychology in the Doctrine of the Rationalist Movement in Soviet Architecture in the 1920s." *VIA* 6 (1983): 78–115.

Senkevitch, Anatole Jr. "Introduction." In Moisei Ja, Ginzburg, *Style and Epoch*. Cambridge, MA: MIT Press; New York, NY: Opposition Books, 1982.

Senkevitch, Anatole Jr. "Trends in Soviet Architectural Thought, 1917–1932: The Growth and the Decline of the Constructivist and Rationalist Movements." PhD dissertation, Cornell University, 1974.

Shiff, Richard. "Flying Colors." Review of *Leonardo's Incessant Last Supper*, by Leo Steinberg. *Artforum* (May 2001): 23–4.

Sickel, Theodor. "Das k.k. Institut für österreichische Geschichtsforschung." *Mittheilungen des Instituts für österreichische Geschichtsforschung* 1 (1880): 3–18.

Sitte, Camillo. *Der Städtebau nach seinen künstlerischen Grundsätzen*. Vienna: Carl Graeser, 1889. Translated into English by Charles T. Stewart as *The Art of Building Cities: City Building According to its Artistic Fundamentals*. New York, NY: Reinhold, 1945.

Sitte, Camillo. "Offenes Schreiben an Dr. Ilg." *Salzburger gewerbeblatt*, 1879. Republished in Klaus Semsroth, Michael Mönninger and Christiane Collins (eds), *Schriften Zu Städtebau und Architektur*, vol. 2, 185–7. Vienna: Böhlau, 2010.

Sitte, Camillo. "Wiener Styl." *Neues Wiener Tagblatt*, 1881. Republished in Klaus Semsroth, Michael Mönninger and Christiane Collins (eds), *Schriften Zu Städtebau und Architektur*, vol. 2, 188–99. Vienna: Böhlau, 2010.

Sitwell, Sacheverell. *British Architects and Craftsmen: Taste, Design and Style 1600–1830*. London: B.T. Batsford, 1945.

Skansi, Luka. "Form, Style, History, Autonomy: Moisej Ginzburg and *Ritm v arhitekture*." In "Style." Special issue, *Fabrications: The Journal of the Society of Architectural Historians, Australia and New Zealand* 17(2) (2007): 26–49.

Skansi, Luka. "What is Artistic Form? Munich-Moscow 1900–1925." In Christoph Flamm, Henry Keazor and Roland Marti (eds), *Russian Émigré Culture: Conservatism or Evolution?* Cambridge: Cambridge Scholars Publisher, 2013.

Slive, Seymour. "Nikolaus Pevsner's Contribution as Editor of The Pelican History of Art Series." In Peter Draper (ed.), *Reassessing Nikolaus Pevsner*, 73–86. Aldershot: Ashgate, 2004.

Smyth, Ethel. *What Happened Next.* London: Longmans, Green & Co., 1940.

Snyder, Jon. *L'estetica del Barocco.* Bologna: Il Mulino, 2005.

Söntgen, Beate. "Wilhelm Worringer (1881–1965)." In Ulrich Pfisterer (ed.), *Klassiker der Kunstgeschichte. Vol. 2, Von Panofsky bis Greenberg*, 21–30. Munich: Beck, 2007.

Spagnesi, Gianfranco and Marcello Fagiolo dell'Arco (eds). *Gian Lorenzo Bernini architetto e l'architettura europea del Sei-Settecento*, 2 vols. Rome: Istituto della enciclopedia Italiana, 1983.

Spalding, Frances. *Roger Fry: Art and Life*. London: Granada, 1980.

Spengler, Oswald. *Decline of the West*. Vol. 1, *Form and Actuality*. Translated by Charles Francis Atkins. New York, NY: Knopf, 1926.

Springer, Elisabeth. "Biographische Skizze zu Albert Ilg (1847–1896)." In Friedrich Polleroß (ed.), *Fischer von Erlach und die Wiener Barocktradition*, 319–45. Vienna: Böhlau, 1995.

Stachel, Peter. "Albert Ilg und die 'Erfindung' des Barocks als Österreischischer 'Nationalstil'." In Moritz Czaky, Federico Celestini and Ulrich Tragatschnig (eds), *Barock – Ein Ort des Gedächtnisses – Interpretament der Moderne – Postmoderne*, 100–152. Vienna: Böhlau, 2007.

Stachel, Peter. *Mythos Heldenplatz*. Vienna: Pichler Verlag, 2002.

Stachel, Peter. "'Vollkommen passende Gefäße' und 'Gefäße fremder Form': Die Kritik des Kunsthistorikers Albert Ilg (1847–1896) an der Architektur der Wiener Ringstrasse, ihr identitätspolitischer Hintergrund und ihre kunstpolitischen Auswirkungen." *East Central Europe* 33(1–2) (2006): 269–92.

Stamm, Rudolf. *Die Kunstformen des Barockzeitalters*. Munich: Lehnen Verlag, 1956.

Stansky, Peter. *On or About December 1910: Early Bloomsbury and Its Intimate World*. Cambridge, MA: Harvard University Press, 1997.

Stechow, Wolfgang. "Definitions of the Baroque in the Visual Arts." In "A Special Issue on Baroque Style in the Various Arts," *Journal of Aesthetics and Art Criticism* 5(2) (1946): 109–15.

Stechow, Wolfgang. "The Baroque: A Critical Summary of the Essays by Bukofzer, Hatzfeld, and Martin." In "Second Special Issue on Baroque Style in Various Arts." *Journal of Aesthetics and Art Criticism* 14(2) (December 1955): 171–4.

Steinberg, Leo. "A Corner of the *Last Judgment*." *Daedalus* 109(2) (Spring 1980): 207–73.

Steinberg, Leo. "Art and Science: Do They Need to Be Yoked?" *Daedalus* 115(4) (Fall 1986): 1–16.

Steinberg, Leo. *Borromini's San Carlo alle Quattro Fontane: A Study in Multiple Form and Architectural Symbolism*. New York, NY and London: Garland Publishing Co., 1977.

Steinberg, Leo. *Encounters with Rauschenberg (A Lavishly Illustrated Lecture)*. Houston, TX: The Menil Foundation; and Chicago, IL: University of Chicago Press, 2000.

Steinberg, Leo. "False Starts, Loose Ends." Lecture to the College Art Association Annual Conference, Chicago, IL, February 21, 2001. Republished June 2006 in *The Brooklyn Rail*. Available at http://www.brooklynrail.org/2006/06/leo (accessed 2 December 2012).

Steinberg, Leo. "Guercino's *Saint Petronilla*" (1977). In Henry Millon (ed.), *Studies in Italian Art History*, vol. 1, 207–34. Cambridge, MA: The MIT Press, 1980.

Steinberg, Leo. "Leonardo's Last Supper." *Art Quarterly* 36 (1973): 297–410. Expanded as *Leonardo's Incessant Last Supper*. New York, NY: Zone Books, 2001.

Steinberg, Leo. "Michelangelo's Florentine *Pietà*: The Missing Leg." *Art Bulletin* 50(4) (December 1968): 343–53.

Steinberg, Leo. *Michelangelo's Last Paintings: The Conversion of St. Paul and the Crucifixion of St. Peter*. London: Phaidon, 1975.

Steinberg, Leo. *Other Criteria: Confrontations with Twentieth-Century Art*, by Leo Steinberg. Oxford: Oxford University Press, 1972.

Steinberg, Leo. "Resisting Cézanne: Picasso's *Three Women* of 1908" (Part 1). *Art in America* (November–December 1978): 114–33.

Steinberg, Leo. "The Algerian Women and Picasso at Large." In *Other Criteria: Confrontations with Twentieth-Century Art*, by Leo Steinberg, 125–35. Oxford: Oxford University Press, 1972.

Steinberg, Leo. "The Eye Is a Part of the Mind." *Partisan Review* (March–April 1953): 194–212. Republished in *Other Criteria: Confrontations with Twentieth-Century Art*, 289–306. Oxford: Oxford University Press, 1972.

Steinberg, Leo. "The Gestural Trace: Leo Steinberg." Interview (1998) with Richard Candida Smith for the series *Interviews with Art Historians*. Art History Oral Documentation Project. 2001. Special Collections, Getty Research Institute, Los Angeles.

Steinberg, Leo. "The Metaphors of Love and Birth in Michelangelo's *Pietàs*." In Theodore Bowie and Cornelia V. Christenson (eds), *Studies in Erotic Art*, 231–335. New York, NY: Basic Books, 1970.

Steinberg, Leo. "The Philosophical Brothel." First published in *Art News* (1972). Revised in *October* 44 (Spring 1988): 7–74, with an added "Retrospect."

Steinberg, Leo. "The Polemical Part" (Part 2 of "Resisting Cezanne"). *Art in America* (March–April 1979): 114–27.

Steinberg, Leo. *The Sexuality of Christ in Renaissance Art and in Modern Oblivion*, 2nd edition. First published in *October* 25 (Summer 1983). Chicago, IL: University of Chicago Press, 1996.

Steinberg, Leo. "Twin Prongs of Art Criticism." *Sewanee Review* 60(3) (1952): 418–44.

Steinberg, Leo. "'Undying Antiquity'. Review of *The Survival of Pagan Gods*, by Jean Seznec." *Art News* (January 1954): 53, 73–4.

Steinberg, Leo. "Velázquez's *Las Meninas*." *October* 19 (Winter 1981): 45–54.

Steinberg, Leo. "Who's Who in Michelangelo's *Creation of Adam*: A Chronology of the Picture's Reluctant Self-Revelation." *Art Bulletin* 74 (December 1992): 552–66.

Stephen, Karin. *The Misuse of Mind: A Study of Bergson's Attack on Intellectualism*. London: Kegan Paul, Trench, Trubner & Co. Ltd, 1922.

Stern, Robert A.M. *George Howe: Toward a Modern American Architecture*. New Haven, CT: Yale University Press, 1975.

Stierli, Martino. "In the Academy's Garden: Robert Venturi, the Grand Tour and the Revision of Modern Architecture." *AA Files* 56 (2007): 41–62.

Stöppel, Daniela. "Wilhelm Pinder (1878–1947)." In Ulrich Pfisterer (ed.), *Klassiker der Kunstgeschichte. Vol. 2, Von Panofsky bis Greenberg*, 7–20. Munich: Beck, 2007.

Strzygowski, Josef. *Das Werden des Barock bei Raphael und Correggio: Nebst Einem Anhang Uber Rembrandt*. First published in 1898. Whitefish, MT: Kessinger Publishing, 2010.

Summers, David. "Art History Reviewed. Heinrich Wölfflin's *Kunstgeschichtliche Grundbegriffe*, 1915." *Burlington Magazine* 151 (2009): 476–79.

Summerson, John. *Architecture in Britain: 1530 to 1830*. London: Penguin, 1953.

Summerson, John. *The Classical Language of Architecture*. Cambridge, MA: MIT Press, 1963. Translated into Italian as *Il linguaggio classico dell'architettura*. Turin: Einaudi, 1970.

Swillens, P.T.A. *Johannes Vermeer: Painter of Delft, 1632–1675*. Utrecht: Spectrum, 1950.

Sypher, Wylie. *The Four Stages of Renaissance Style: Transformations in Art and Literature, 1400–1700*. New York, NY: Doubleday, 1955.

Szacka, Léa-Catherine. "The Presence of the Past: Postmodernism Meets in Venice." In Glenn Adamson and Jane Pavitt (eds), *Postmodernism: Style and Subversion, 1970–1990*, 132–5. London: V&A Publishing, 2011.

Tafuri, Manfredo, "Architettura. Per una storia storica." *La Rivista dei Libri* 4(4) (April 1994): 10–12. Reprinted and translated into English as "Il testamento di Manfredo Tafuri" = "Manfredo Tafuri's Testament." *L'architetura* 40(482) (July–August 1994): 482–3.

Tafuri, Manfredo. "Borromini e l'esperienza della storia." *Comunità* 129 (1965): 42–63.

Tafuri, Manfredo. "Borromini e Piranesi. La città come 'ordine infranto'." In Alessandro Bettagno (ed.), *Piranesi tra Venezia e l'Europa. Atti del convegno internazionale di studio promosso dall'Istituto di storia dell'arte della fondazione Giorgio Cini per il secondo centenario della morte di Giovan Battista Piranesi, Venezia, 13–15 ottobre 1978*, 89–101. Florence: Leo S. Olschki, 1983.

Tafuri, Manfredo. *Il concorso per i nuovi uffici della Camera dei Deputati. Un bilancio dell'architettura Italiana*. Rome: Edizioni universitarie italiane, 1968.

Tafuri, Manfredo. *Progetto e utopia. Architettura e sviluppo capitalistico*. Bari: Laterza, 1973. Translated by Barbara Luigi La Penta as *Architecture and Utopia: Design and Capitalist Development*. Cambridge, MA: MIT Press, 1976.

Tafuri, Manfredo. *Teorie e storia dell'architettura* (1968), 4th edition. Rome: Laterza, 1976. Translated by Giorgio Verrecchia as *Theories and History of Architecture*. New York, NY: Harper and Row, 1980.

Tafuri, Manfredo and Francesco Dal Co. *Architettura contemporanea*. Milan: Electa, 1976. Translated by R.W. Wolf as *Modern Architecture*. New York, NY: Harry N. Abrams, 1979.

Tagliabue, Guido Morpurgo. "Aristotelismo e Barocco." In Enrico Castelli (ed.), *Atti del III Congresso internazionale di studi umanistici*, 119–95. Rome: F. Bocca, 1955.

Tapié, Victor L. *Baroque et classicisme*. Paris: Hachette, 1980.

Tawa, Michael (ed.). "Emergence and Architecture." Special issue. *Architectural Theory Review* 17(1) (2012).

Tedeschi, Letizia. "Algoritmie spaziali. Gli artisti, la rivista *Spazio* a Luigo Moretti, 1950–1953." In Bruno Reichlin and Letizia Tedeschi (eds), *Luigi Moretti. Razionalismo e trasgressività tra barocco e informale*, 137–77. Milan: Electa, 2010.

Teter-Schneider, Patricia and Nancy Yeide. "S. Lane Faison, Jr. and Art under the Shadow of the Swastika." *Archives of American Art Journal* 47(3–4) (2008): 24–37.

Teyssot, Georges. "Neoclassic and 'Autonomous' Architecture: The Formalism of Emil Kaufmann." *Architectural Design* 51(6–7) (1981): 28.

Thoenes, Christof. "'Die Formen sind in Bewegung geraten'. Zum Verständnis der Architektur Borrominis" = "'Form has been set in motion'. On Understanding the Architecture of Borromini." *Daidalos* 67 (March 1998): 63–73.

Thuillier, Jacques. "La *Vie des formes*: une théorie de l'histoire de l'art." In Mattais Waschek (ed.), *Relire Focillon*, 75–96. Paris: Musée du Louvre Éditions and École nationale supérieure des beaux-arts, 1998.

Thuillier, Jacques. "Wölfflin et la France." In Mathias Waschek (ed.), *Relire Wölfflin*, 13–29. Paris: Musée du Louvre Éditions and École nationale supérieure des beaux-arts, 1995.

Tietze, Hans. "Der Kampf um Alt-Wien." *Kunstgeschichtlichen Jahrbuch der k.k. Zentralcommission* 4 (1910): 33–62.

Tietze, Hans. "Neue Literatur über den deutschen Barock (1911–1914)." *Repertorium für Kunstwissenschaft* 37 (1915): 301–10.

Tintelnot, Hans. "Zur Gewinnung unserer Barockbegriffe." In Rudolf Stamm (ed.), *Die Kunstformen des Barockzeitalters. Vierzehn Vorträge*, 13–91. Munich: Lehnen, 1956.

Tournikiotis, Panayotis. *The Historiography of Modern Architecture*. Cambridge, MA: MIT Press, 1999.

Tschumi, Bernard. *Architecture and Disjunction*. Cambridge, MA: MIT Press, 1996.

Tzonis, Alexander and Liane Lefaivre. "The Grid and the Pathway: An Introduction to the Work of Dimitris and Susana Antonakakis." *Architecture in Greece* 15 (1981): 164–78.

Tzonis, Alexander and Liane Lefaivre. "Why Critical Regionalism Today?" *A+U: Architecture and Urbanism* 236 (May 1990): 22–33.

Venturi, Adolfo. *La pittura del Cinquecento*, 7 vols. Milan: Poepli, 1925–34.

Venturi, Adolfo. *La pittura del Quattrocento*, 4 vols. Milan: Hoepli, 1911–15.

Venturi, Adolfo. *L'architettura del Quattrocento*, 2 vols. Milan: Hoepli, 1923–24.

Venturi, Adolfo. *Storia dell'arte italiana*, 11 vols. Milan: Hoepli, 1901–40.

Venturi, Lionello. *Il Caravaggio. Con prefazione di Benedetto Croce*. Novara: Istituto geografico de Agostini, 1951.

Venturi, Robert. *Complexity and Contradiction in Architecture*, 2nd edition. First published in 1966. London: The Architectural Press, 1977.

Venturi, Robert. "Notes for a Lecture Celebrating the Centennial of the American Academy in Rome Delivered in Chicago." In *Iconography and Electronics upon a Generic Architecture: A View from the Drafting Room*, by Robert Venturi, 47–56. Cambridge, MA: MIT Press, 1996.

Venturi, Robert, Denise Scott Brown and Steven Izenour. *Learning from Las Vegas*. Cambridge, MA: MIT Press, 1972.

Veseley, Dalibor. *Architecture in the Age of Divided Representation*. Cambridge, MA: MIT Press, 2004.

Vidler, Anthony. *Histories of the Immediate Present: Inventing Architectural Modernism*. Cambridge, MA: MIT Press, 2008.

Virilio, Paul, "Esthétique de la disparition." In "Le maquillage." Special issue, *Traverses* 7 (1977): 6–14.

Voll, Karl. *Vergleichende Gemäldestudien*. Munich: G. Müller, 1908.

Voss, Hermann. *Die Malerei des Barock in Rom*. Berlin: Propyläen-Verlag, 1925. Revised and translated by Thomas Pelzel as *Baroque Painting in Rome*. San Francisco, CA: Alan Wofsy Fine Arts, 1997. Translated into Italian by Andrea G. De Marchi as *La pittura del barocco a Roma*. Vicenza: Niri Pozza, 1999.

Voßkamp, Wilhelm. "Deutsche Barockforschung in den zwanziger und dreißiger Jahren." In Klaus Garber (ed.), *Europäische Barockrezeption*, vol. 1, 683–703. Wiesbaden: Harrasowitz, 1991.

Waddy, Patricia. *Seventeenth-Century Roman Palaces: Use and the Art of the Plan*. Cambridge, MA: MIT Press, 1990.

Waetzolt, Wilhelm. *Deutscher Kunsthistoriker*, 2 vols. Leipzig: E.A. Seeman, 1924.

Waley, H.D. "The Swing of the Pendulum: Principles of Art History. The Problem of the Development of Style in Later Art by Heinrich Wölfflin." *Burlington Magazine* 62(362) (1933): 246–7.

Wanscher, Vilhelm. "Tingen er det Egentlige!" *Architekten* 20 (July 1918): 398–9.

Warnke, Martin. "Die Entstehung des Barockbegriffs in der Kunstgeschichte." In Klaus Garber (ed.), *Europäische Barockrezeption*, vol. 2, 1201–23. Wiesbaden: Harrasowitz, 1991.

Warnke, Martin. "On Heinrich Wölfflin." *Representations* 27 (1989): 172–87.

Waterhouse, Ellis. *Baroque Painting in Rome: The Seventeenth Century*. London: Macmillan, 1937.

Watkin, David. Foreword to *The Architecture of Humanism: A Study in the History of Taste*, by Geoffrey Scott, 2nd edition. London: Architectural Press, 1980.

Watkin, David. *Morality and Architecture: The Development of a Theme in Architectural History and Theory from the Gothic Revival to the Modern Movement*. Oxford: Clarendon Press, 1977.

Watkin, David. "Sir Nikolaus Pevsner: A Study in 'Historicism." *Apollo* 136(367) (September 1992): 169–72.

Wehle, J.H. *Die Zeitung: Ihre Organisation und Technik*. Vienna, Budapest, and Leipzig: A. Hartleben's Verlag, 1883.

Weisbach, Werner. *Der Barock als Kunst der Gegenreformation*. Berlin: Paul Cassirer, 1921.

Weisbach, Werner. "Gegenreformation – Manierismus – Barock." *Repertorium für Kunstwissenschaft* 49 (1928): 16–28.

Wellek, René. "The Concept of Baroque in Literary Scholarship." In "A Special Issue on Baroque Style in the Various Arts," *Journal of Aesthetics and Art Criticism* 5(2) (1946): 77–109.

Wertheimer, Max. "Untersuchungen zur Lehre von der Gestalt." *Psychologische Forschung* 4(1) (1922): 47–58.

Westheim, Paul. "Architektur." *Das Kunstblatt* 3(4) (1919): 100–101.

Westheim, Paul. "Festspielhaus in Salzburg." *Das Kunstblatt* 5(3) (1921): 245–7.

Wickhoff, Franz. "Alois Riegl" (obituary). *Mittheilungen des Instituts für österreichische Geschichtsforschung* 27 (1906): 203–4.

Wiener, Alfred. "Geschäftsbauten und Reklame." In Paul Ruben (ed.), *Die Reklame: Ihre Kunst und Wissenschaft*. Berlin: Hermann Paetel, 1915.

Wimböck, Gabriele. "Heinrich Wölfflin (1864–1945)." In Ulrich Pfisterer (ed.), *Klassiker der Kunstgeschichte. Vol. 1, Von Winckelmann bis Warburg*, 124–40. Munich: Beck, 2007.

Wind, Edgar. "On the Systematics of Artistic Problems." Translated by Fiona Elliott. *Art in Translation* 1(2) (2009): 211–57.

Wiseman, Carter. *Louis I. Kahn: Beyond Time and Style*. New York, NY: W.W. Norton, 2007.

Witte, Arnold. "Reconstructing Riegl's 'Entstehung der Barockkunst in Rom'." In Andrew Hopkins and Arnold Witte (eds), *The Origins of Baroque Art in Rome*, 34–59. Los Angeles, CA: Getty Research Institute, 2010.

Wittkower, Rudolf. *Art and Architecture in Italy 1600 to 1750*. Pelican History of Art 16. Harmondsworth: Penguin, 1958. 6th revised edition. Edited by Joseph Connors and Jennifer Montagu. New Haven, CT: Yale University Press, 1999.

Wittkower, Rudolf. "Il Barocco in Italia." 1960. In Vincenzo Arangio-Ruiz (ed.), "Manierismo, Barocco, Rococò: concetti e termini." Special issue, *Problemi attuali di scienza e di cultura* 52 (1962): 319–26.

Wittkower, Rudolf. "Michelangelo's Biblioteca Laurenziana." *Art Bulletin* 16(2) (June 1934): 123–218.

Wittkower, Rudolf. "Problems of the Theme." In Rudolf Wittkower and Irma B. Jaffe (eds), *Baroque Art: The Jesuit Contribution*, 1–14. New York, NY: Fordham University Press, 1972.

Wittkower, Rudolf. "Zu Hans Sedlmayrs Besprechung von E. Coudenhove-Erthal: Carlo Fontana." *Kritische Berichte* 3–4 (1930–31, 1931–32): 142–5.

Wolfe, Charles T. "From Spinoza to the Socialist Cortex: Steps Toward the Social Brain." In Deborah Hauptmann and Warren Niedich (eds), *Cognitive Architecture: From Biopolitics to Noopolitics. Architecture & Mind in the Age of Communication and Information*, 184–207. Rotterdam: 010, 2010.

Wölfflin, Heinrich. *Die Klassische Kunst. Eine Einführung in die italienische Renaissance*. Munich: F. Bruckmann, 1899. Translated by Peter and Linda Murray as *Classic Art: An Introduction to the Italian Renaissance*. Ithaca, NY: Cornell University Press, 1980. Translated into Russian as *Klassičeskoe iskusstvo. Vvedenije v izučenie ital'janskogo vozroždenija*. St. Petersburg: Brokgauz-Efron, 1912.

Wölfflin, Heinrich. *Italien und das deutsche Formgefühl. Die Kunst der Renaissance*. Munich: Bruckmann, 1931.

Wölfflin, Heinrich. *Kunstgeschichtliche Grundbegriffe. Das Problem der Stilentwicklung in der neueren Kunst*, 2nd edition. First published in 1915. Munich: Hugo Brückmann, 1917. Translated by Marie D. Hottinger as *Principles of Art History: The Problem of Style in Later Art*. 1932, New York, NY: Dover, 1950. Translated by Jonathan Blower as *Principles of Art History: The Problem of the Development of Style in Early Modern Art*. Edited by Evonne Levy and Tristan Weddigen. Los Angeles, CA: Getty Research Institute, 2015. Translated into Russian as *Osnovnye ponjatija istorii iskusstv. Problema evoljucii stilja v novom iskusstve*. Moscow: Del'fin, 1922.

Wölfflin, Heinrich. *Prolegomena zu einer Psychologie der Architektur*. 1886. Afterword by Jasper Cepl. Berlin: Gebrüder Mann Verlag, 1994. Translated by Harry Francis Mallgrave and Eleftherios Ikonomou as "Prolegomena to a Psychology of Architecture." In Mallgrave and Ikonomou (eds and trans), *Empathy, Form, Space: Problems in German Aesthetics 1873–1893*, 149–87. Los Angeles, CA: Getty Center for the History of Art, 1994.

Wölfflin, Heinrich. *Renaissance und Barock: eine Untersuchung über Wesen und Entstehung des Barockstils in Italien*. Munich: T. Ackermann, 4th revised edition. Edited by Hans Rose. First published in 1888. Munich: Bruckmann, 1926, reprinted Leipzig: Koehler & Amelang, 1986. Translated by Kathrin Simon as *Renaissance and Baroque*. London: Collins, 1964; Ithaca, NY: Cornell University Press, 1966. Translated into Russian as *Renessans i barokko*. St. Petersburg: Griaduščii den, 1913.

Wölfflin, Heinrich. "Review of Alois Riegl, *Die Entstehung der Barockkunst in Rom*." *Repertorium für Kunstwissenschaft* 31 (1908): 356–7.

Wölfflin, Heinrich. *The Sense of Form in Art*. Translated by Alice Muehsam and Norma A. Shatan. New York, NY: Chelsea Publishing Company, 1958.

Wölfflin, Heinrich. "Ueber den Begriff des Malerischen." *Logos* 4 (1913): 1–7.

Wölfflin, Heinrich. "Wie man Skulpturen Aufnehmen Soll." *Zeitschrift für bildende Kunst* 7 (1896): 224–8. Reprinted in *Zeitschrift für bildende Kunst* 26 (1915): 237–44.

Woolf, Virginia. *Roger Fry: A Biography*. New York, NY: Harcourt, Brace and Company, 1940.

Woolf, Virginia. *Mr Bennett and Mrs Brown*. London: Hogarth Press, 1924.

Worringer, Wilhelm. *Abstraktion und Einfühlung. Ein Beitrag zur Stilpsychologie*, 3rd edition 1908. Munich: Piper, 1911. Translated by Michael Bullock as *Abstraction and Empathy*. New York, NY: Routledge, 1953.

Worringer, Wilhelm. *Formprobleme der Gotik*. Munich: Piper, 1911. Translated by Herbert Read as *Form in Gothic*. London: Tiranti, 1957.

Wright, Frank Lloyd. "The Passing of the Cornice." In *Modern Architecture: Being the Kahn Lectures for 1930*. First published in 1931. Princeton, NJ: Princeton University Press, 2008.

Wright, Sylvia. "America's Most Favored Tourists." *Reporter* (12 July 1956): 40–42.

Wulf, Friedrich. "Beiträge zur Psychologie der Gestalt." *Psychologische Forschung* 4(2) (1922): 333–73.

Zevi, Bruno. *An Opinion on Architecture*. Boston, MA: The Century Press, 1941.

Zevi, Bruno. *Architettura e storiografia*. Milan: Libreria Editrice Politecnica Tamburini, 1950. Revised edition published as *Architettura e storiografia. Le matrici antiche del linguaggio moderno*. Turin: Einaudi, 1974.

Zevi, Bruno. "Attualità del Borromini." In Guglielmo de Angelis d'Ossat (ed.), *Studi sul Borromini. Atti del Convegno promosso dall'Accademia nazionale di San Luca*, vol. 1, 507–30. Rome: De Luca, 1967.

Zevi, Bruno. "Attualità di Michelangiolo architetto." In Paolo Portoghesi and Bruni Zevi (eds), *Michelangiolo architetto*, 9–27. Turin: Einaudi, 1964.

Zevi, Bruno. *Biagio Rossetti architetto ferrarese. Il primo urbanista moderno europeo*. Turin: Einaudi, 1960.

Zevi, Bruno. "Borromini Today: In the 400th Anniversary of His Birth, 1599." *L'Architettura cronache e storia* 519 (1999): 47–58.

Zevi, Bruno. *Il linguaggio moderno dell'architettura*. Turin: Einaudi, 1973. Translated as *The Modern Language of Architecture*. First published in 1978. New York, NY: Van Nostrand Reinhold, 1981.

Zevi, Bruno. "La storia come medotologia del fare architettonico." Inaugural lecture, University of Rome, December 18, 1963.

Zevi, Bruno. *Lezioni di storia dell'architettura italiana*, vol. 1, *Dal Paleocristiano al Gotico*. Rome: Ferri, 1947.

Zevi, Bruno. "Luigi Moretti double-face. Ambizione contro ingegno." *Cronache di Architettura* 9(982) (1978): 145.

Zevi, Bruno. *Michelangiolo in prosa. L'opera architettonica di Michelangiolo nel quarto cenetenario della morte*. Special issue, *L'Architettura cronache e storia* 99 (January 1964).

Zevi, Bruno. "Riposta di B. Zevi a P. Portoghesi." In Guglielmo de Angelis d'Ossat (ed.), *Studi sul Borromini. Atti del Convegno promosso dall'Accademia nazionale di San Luca*, vol. 1, 537–42. Rome: De Luca, 1967.

Zevi, Bruno. *Saper vedere l'architettura. Saggio sull'interpretazione spaziale dell'architettura*. Turin: Einaudi, 1948. Translated as *Architecture as Space: How to Look at Architecture*. New York, NY: Horizon Press, 1957.

Zevi, Bruno. *Storia dell'architettura moderna*. Turin: Einaudi, 1950.

Zevi, Bruno. *Storia dell'architettura moderna*. Vol. 2, *Da Frank Lloyd Wright a Frank O. Gehry: l'itinerario organico*. Milan: Edizioni di Comunità, 2001.

Zevi, Bruno. *Verso un'architettura organica. Saggio sullo sviluppo del pensiero architettonico negli ultimi cinquant'anni*. Turin: Einaudi, 1945. Translated as *Towards an Organic Architecture*. London: Faber & Faber, 1950.

Zevi, Bruno and Paolo Portoghesi (eds). *Michelangiolo architetto*. Turin: Einaudi, 1964.

Zevi, Bruno and Paolo Portoghesi. *Mostra critica delle Opere Michelangiolesche*. Exhibition Catalogue. Rome: Istituto Grafico Tiberino, 1964.

Zorn, Christa. *Vernon Lee: Aesthetics, History and the Victorian Female Intellectual*. Athens, OH: Ohio University Press, 2003.

Zucker, Paul. *Town and Square*. New York, NY: Columbia University Press, 1959.

Index